CONTENTS

PREFACE

I would like to say a few words here about the nature of this work. Its purpose is doctrinal in order, not historical. Yet the systematic examination of the fundamental problems of moral philosophy has been left to a second volume which I hope to undertake after the publication of the present one; a central fragment of this projected volume has already been offered in outline form—however incomplete—in a few lessons previously published.[1] The present work is devoted to the historical and critical examination of a certain number of great systems which are, in my opinion, the most significant ones with respect to the development and the adventures of moral philosophy, and those which it is most important to consider for the work of *prise de conscience* and intellectual renewal to which our age seems called, at least in the eyes of a few who still care for wisdom.

I don't claim to tackle my subject without making use of any previously acquired philosophical equipment, or any philosophical frame of reference. We always do have a philosophical frame of reference; what matters is to be aware of this very fact and to be able to judge our own philosophy freely. My frame of reference is that which one may expect to encounter in a philosopher who has been inspired throughout his life by the thought of Thomas Aquinas. This does not mean that in my opinion Saint Thomas has said everything, and that in particular one finds in him, in the form of an explicitly formulated body of doctrine, the moral philosophy which we recognize is needed today. Far from it!

The *Secunda Pars* of the *Summa theologiae* offers us a complete and perfectly articulated theological treatise on human conduct. But we have other things to do than to follow and comment on this treatise. For our task is philosophical, not theological.

Although so eminently classic a field as that of moral philosophy was extensively elucidated by Thomas Aquinas in his commentaries on Aristotle, and by his own disciples and commentators, we believe that a moral philosophy conceived in the light of his principles, and capable of illuminating our modern problems has yet to be developed, and we hope that the present investigation may prepare the way.

In our opinion moral philosophy has not yet been formally singled out in its own right, from moral theology in the traditional teaching of Thomist philosophy (which after all it might perhaps be better not to call by that name, (1) because doubtless it would have greatly displeased Saint Thomas himself,

[1] *Neuf leçons sur les notions premières de la philosophie morale*, Paris: Téqui, 1950.

(2) because it is inappropriate to attach the name of a theologian to a philosophical doctrine, (3) because it is inappropriate to attach the name of any man, be he the greatest of thinkers, to a philosophy which, identifying itself with the *philosophia perennis*, must renew itself from generation to generation and from century to century, and nourish itself with all the past in order to move constantly beyond the past. Yet must we have a name for it? Let us call it then, if you wish, philosophy of being and of the analogicity of being, or *ontosophy*.) Well then, what we find in the courses or text-books on ethics which are related to this philosophy is too often a simple traced copy of Saint Thomas' theological *exposé*, withdrawn from the light of theology proper and carried into the light of natural reason and of philosophy, retaining all the while the order and structure of the theological treatise which inspired it. The product thus obtained is neither philosophical nor theological, it is a sterilized theology offering itself as philosophy.

Our perspective will therefore be that of the method proper to moral philosophy as an authentically philosophic discipline. And our object will be to discover the general design and the proper procedure of this moral philosophy founded integrally on reason which, as we just remarked, has yet to be worked out. It is therefore primarily a task of research and of approximation which we will initiate. Our ambition is not to compose a complete treatise on moral philosophy, but rather to clear the ground and to open avenues, to mark the essential connections and to determine the normal order of the questions which an authentically philosophical ethics must examine. We don't intend to undertake more; it will already be a great deal for us to be able to carry out this exploratory work.

Since in the matter of ethics one may not, *pace* Spinoza, proceed *more geometrico*, but must on the contrary attach oneself to the moral experience of men in order to interpret this experience rationally, and since furthermore what interests us is the establishment of an authentic moral philosophy, it was fitting to begin our inquiry with an historical and critical analysis devoted to the great moral theories. Other approaches are conceivable. It is to be hoped, for example, that some day a philosopher well versed in ethnology will apply himself to the task of sifting out from the myths of primitive men—from the conceptions they had, within their regime of magic thought, of the destiny of man and of his relation with the universe, and finally, of course, from their social customs and tribal rules—the germinal ideas and fundamental data of humanity's moral experience. We, however, given our purpose, must turn to the philosophers themselves, and to the various systems of moral philosophy which have followed one upon the other since Socrates, in order that the various phases of philosophical reflection on the moral life of men, and the conflicting views which this reflection has given rise to, may instruct us on the subject of our research, may introduce us, thanks to the very current of the history of ideas, straight into the center of the debates, conflicts, and opposing points of view revealed by the moral experience of humanity, and may bring us step by step—not didactically but experientially—in sight of the basic notions and fundamental problems which we will have to distinguish explicitly in our second volume,—if it is given us to write it.[1]

We will make use in this way of the reflections of philosophers on human morality as a prospector's instrument, to seek out the ideas and questions of central importance for the establishment of a rational theory of human action. This is to say that we will be less concerned with the detail of the various systems, with their genesis in the minds of the philosophers who elaborated them, and with the interpretations (never definitive) which may be given to the thought of these philosophers, than with the general meaning and typical characteristics with which these systems entered the history of culture, and appeared there as *witnesses* to the fundamental moral realities confronting man in his spontaneous activity, and to the problematic offered to reflection by the nature of moral experience.

This approach is no other than the method used with such care by Aristotle when he related and discussed—to prepare for, and before presenting, his own solutions—the positions of the various schools of thought which had touched upon the problem he was treating. It was all the more imperative for us to use this method since we were concerned, truth to tell, less with any particular problem of moral philosophy than with a sort of rediscovery of the very discipline itself.

Such an approach is normally called for because it gives credit—and not simply lip-service—to the work done by human thought throughout the centuries. It is normally called for also because it obliges us to face the mistakes, the excesses, the false conceptualizations to which this work was exposed as it moved forward at man's pace. As far as ethics is concerned, it must be admitted that the proportion of errors thus mingled with certain discoveries or with certain intuitions, and with certain grandiose views, has in modern times been such that moral philosophy now finds itself in complete disarray. And this is true not only in the case of moral philosophy, but also of large segments of the common consciousness of contemporary humanity.

As a result we were obliged to make our critical study quite extensive, and to deepen it according to the exigencies of the subject. It is for this reason that a whole volume had to be devoted to an historical and critical analysis of the great systems which we chose as being particularly characteristic.

I will note here that the extent of the various chapters of this work is not in keeping with the importance *in itself* of the various systems examined, but rather with the importance of their impact on contemporary thought, either from the point of view of errors to be unmasked, or from the point of view of

[1] We would like to give this second volume the following sub-title: "Doctrinal Examination of the Great Problems."

doctrinal aspects which I wished to bring to light. Indeed I found it sufficient to treat in a conversational tone, in as condensed a manner as possible, and with quite few notes and references, systems which have had their place for many years in our programs of academic study, and which are familiar to everyone (chapters 1 to 6). From Hegel onwards (chapters 7 to 14), the subject of our analyses required a much more detailed treatment. I just mentioned Hegel. May I be permitted to note that having begun my philosophical endeavours by setting principles I hold to be true in confrontation with Bergsonian anti-intellectualism,[1] and by criticizing a master for whom my gratitude and affection have never ceased to grow, I was not sorry to have to undertake, as I reach the end of my researches, a similar confrontation and critique with respect to a thinker who carried the effort and ambition of modern rationalism to its peak,[2] and who found himself at the same time at the origin of an irrationalism—today in full flower—which is incomparably more pernicious for the mind than the irrationalism which preyed on the conceptualizations of Bergson.

Have I succeeded in making felt the intensity of the intellectual drama involved in the vicissitudes of the history which forms the matter of this book? It is a voluminous book, and one which doubtless will take as much care to be read closely as it took to be written. Our hope is that if it has the good fortune to find a few readers patient enough to become aware of its inner movement, as of a thematic unfolding, and of the twists and turns of the multiform thought whose development, progress and back-slidings it analyzes, it may help them to discern the nature of the ills which beset moral philosophy in our time, and above all to recognize, *in actu exercito*, the philosophical bases of ethics and the value of the primary concepts which it brings into play. All the subject matter and all the truths which we would like to discuss doctrinally and systematically in our second volume are present here, in an unsystematic state and in a form which is so to speak fluid, but, in a sense, or at least we believe so, perhaps more stimulating for the mind.

[1] *La philosophie Bergsonienne*, études critiques, Paris: Marcel Rivière, 1914; second edition, with preface, Paris: Téqui, 1930. The English translation (*Bergsonian Philosophy and Thomism*, New York: Philosophical Library, 1955), for which the French text was revised and trimmed, may be regarded as the definitive edition of this work.

[2] On the original outburst and first great formulation of this effort and this ambition, see our work *The Dream of Descartes*, New York: Philosophical Library, 1944. ("Rationalism dreams a great deal" could be read on the jacket of the original French edition, published in Paris by Corrêa in 1932.)

PART ONE

THE ADVENTURES OF REASON

1

THE DISCOVERY OF ETHICS

Socrates

Orient and Occident

1. It is fitting for everyone to try to put his own house in order. Thus it is the great moral systems elaborated in the course of the history of Western culture that a western philosopher will have to discuss if he intends to see clearly into his own tradition and to seek the materials for a doctrinal renewal of ethics through a critical study of the past. In examining the Occidental systems which seem to us—given our purpose—the most significant, we will however not forget the treasures of Oriental thought, nor the fact that Christianity, without which neither western civilization nor western thought would be what they are, was born in Israel, and transcends by its universality both Orient and Occident.

Moreover, if we had undertaken a history of moral philosophy, we would obviously have begun with the philosophical heritage of the Orient: notably Indian thought (although India does not seem to have succeeded in according to ethics a domain really distinct from that of metaphysics or of religion),[1] and above all Chinese thought, which, on the contrary—especially in the Confucian tradition—is turned chiefly toward matters relating to human conduct, and offers us the most ancient and venerable forms of moral systematization. It would be most profitable to study the ways by which China thus established a body of natural ethics. As Mr. John C. H. Wu[2] has noted, in particular: "Confucianism had attained to a vision of the natural law which comes even nearer to that of the Christian" than what is said on this subject by the Greek and Latin philosophers. "Let one quotation from the Confucian classic *The Golden Mean* suffice: 'What is ordained by Heaven is called essential nature. Conformity to the essential nature is called the natural law. The refinement of the natural law is called culture.' "

The fact remains that what we have undertaken is not at all a history of moral philosophy, but a critical examination of certain characteristic systems. It is enough for our purpose, as we have explained, to keep in mind the lessons offered by the development of moral ideas in Western culture. Though we regret the possibility of seeming—much against our will—to accept the overly

[1] Cf. *Du Régime Temporel et de la Liberté*, Paris: Desclée De Brouwer et Cie, 1933, p. 21; and chap. V below.

[2] In his excellent book *Fountain of Justice, A Study in the Natural Law*, New York: Sheed and Ward, 1955, p. 219; London: Sheed and Ward, 1959.

narrow perspective of traditional accounts, we will begin by examining the principal testimonies of Greek thought.

Greek Sophism

2. The Sophists were far from being all charlatans of wisdom. Their role in the history of culture was that of a potent revulsive. Many of them were men of superior intelligence, but intoxicated with the appearances and probabilities with which reason plays when it is disputing about common notions (not yet philosophically elaborated) and is not yet trained to the disciplines of scientific conceptualization. Taken as a whole, their enterprise displays the following traits.

They engaged in a critique of traditional morality, accepted ideas and sacred norms, of authentic principles grown into prejudices and taboos of the social group, a critique which invoked nature and reason against the conservatism of the Greek city, against the authority of custom and the apparently inviolable prestige of human laws and institutions. The appearance of Sophism in the 5th century before the Christian era, in that period of philosophical crisis and of scepticism which followed the effort of the great pre-Socratic "physicists", and the domination it exercised over general education, thus marked the advent of a free and daring rationalism, but a rationalism which made a primarily negative use of reason and whose perspective remained naïvely empirical. And who would be surprised at that? When reason is not drawn back into its own depths by the intuition of being or by experience of the interior world, it frolics with the senses, among phantasms, without even noticing that it is their prisoner.

Thus the Sophists were able to discourse, criticize and argue while making use of an authentically rational equipment (whose own exigencies however escaped them) and while giving value to the true as well as to the false (but without being in a position to tell the one from the other); they remained—it is at this spot that Socrates would aim, and thrust home his blade—ignorant men bearing the arms of knowledge. Thus they were able at times to put forward accurate and profound ideas, and even, like Hippias, to bring to light the notion of natural law and of a human community superior to the particularism of the city, in spite of the fact that these notions challenged the distinction between Greeks and barbarians, as well as an economic regime based on slavery. The unwritten laws, eternal and unalterable, said Hippias, derive from a higher source than the decrees of men; and all men are naturally fellow-citizens.[1] God made all men equally free, said Alcidamas;[2] nature made no man a slave. But these truths remained the chance discoveries of an

[1] Cf. Heinrich Rommen, *Die ewige Wiederkehr des Naturrechts*, Leipzig: Hegner, 1936. We have used the excellent English translation, *The Natural Law*, St. Louis: Herder, 1947, p. 9.

[2] Cf. George S. Sabine, *A History of Political Theory*, Revised Edition, New York: Henry Holt, 1950, p. 30; London: Harrap, 1951.

essentially arbitrary mental process. And Callicles also spoke of natural law, but only to see it as the law that force succeeds.

3. In short they did not possess an internal principle of wisdom. And what they believed to be wisdom (because they confused wisdom and power) was but an art of seducing and persuading minds. The intellectual life took for them the form of a competitive sport, it was a combat of eloquence in which the point was to triumph publicly over the thesis of the adversary (either by analyses and arguments that were truly convincing, or sometimes by foul blows), and in which the audience played the primary role. The verdict of the bystanders was the final judgment.

They were professors of conduct. They taught those virtues and accomplishments with which the individual must equip himself in order to operate in life. The "virtues" thus formed the principal subject of their oratorical tournaments. But these virtues were conceived as powers or talents enabling men to make known their value, to escape from their phobias and inferiority complexes, to succeed in public life and to take advantage of their opportunities—however negligent of itself and however ill-governed in its interior universe the soul that used them might be. The great thing for those who listened to these masters was to become virtuosos or experts in the technique of a brilliant and prosperous life and in the recipes of success, above all political success.

It was thus an art of making one's way in the world which in the end emerged from a conception of life dominated by a general relativism and by a universal scepticism concerning that which can relate human conduct to ends and values superior to the advantage of the individual.

With the Sophists we do not yet have moral philosophy. They concerned themselves with the whole subject-matter of human morality, scrutinizing it with an intelligence and a penetration that were sometimes superior—but they handled that subject-matter only with the instruments of empiricism.

But we owe them thanks. They made Socrates possible. Socrates, in the act of combating them, could even appear externally as one of them (witness that evil tongue of Aristophanes). It is not the only time in intellectual history that counterfeit money has preceded and prepared for the appearance of genuine money.

Socrates and the Sophists

4. How shall we characterize the effort of Socrates as distinguished from that of the Sophists?—The critical spirit (critical in the philosophical sense of the word) apprehends questions and tests ideas according to their intrinsic value, independently of the judgment of the crowd. If the intellect continues to exercise itself in controversy, what matters is no longer the blows exchanged in the arena, but the work accomplished in that workshop of trial and proof

which is within the mind. The passion for truth has taken the place of the passion for success.

In a sense Socrates presents himself as a conservative. He undertakes the defense of the traditional norms of the city, he holds human law in veneration and insists upon unconditional obedience to it—even when it unjustly causes him to die. But this is because in his case an extremely powerful spiritual intuition and the attention of a purified intellect plunge deeply enough into things human to see how the moral foundations of the city are justified by reason. Irrational respect for social taboos is shaken by the same blow (and more effectively than by the arguments of the Sophists). They lose the power on which political conservatism depends most heavily, the power of authority blindly accepted. If they are not founded on reason they are nothing. Nothing keeps things in their place but truth.

The work of critical laying bare undertaken by the Sophists was done in the name of a universal relativism. But relativism, with its negative and destructive apparatus, is quite ready in fact to turn itself into servile submission to rules the spirit does not believe in; by virtue of its absolute attachment to truth, the manner in which Socrates defended the tradition was in reality much more revolutionary than the manner in which the Sophists attacked it.

The notion of authentically intellectual knowledge—established on the level of the proper lights and proper exigencies of the intellect—the notion of science, thus clearly emerged. That is why Socrates took pains to render us conscious of our ignorance. That ignorance—at least I am aware of it. If the idea of science were not there, would I have the idea of my ignorance? Socratic ignorance is an artifice which one must not be taken in by. Aristotle assures us that Socrates "treats of the moral virtues and strives in this regard to discover universal definitions. He is in search of what things are: because he applied himself to doing syllogisms, and the principle of syllogisms is what things are. . . ."[1] This assertion of Aristotle has been contested by certain scholars who remark that instead of defining the virtues Socrates busied himself rather with emphasizing the failure of all our attempts to define them (so for courage in the *Laches*, piety in the *Euthyphro*, temperance in the *Charmides*). But is this failure definitive? Inevitable of itself? Or due to a wrong way of going about it? Aristotle does not say that Socrates put his finger on definitions of the virtues; he says that he sought for them. The whole Socratic enterprise bears witness to the fact that it must in the end be possible to define the virtues. And thus what matters above all is that the ideal of a knowledge which is firm and incontestable in itself, a *science* of moral matters, is now brought out.

At the same time an essential change in the direction of the attention is taking place. The attention is now turned inward, toward the discovery of that interior world which we carry within us and which answers to the

[1] *Metaphysics*, XIII, 4, 1078 b 18–25.

Socratic concept of the soul—the word "soul", which insofar as it expresses a common or pre-philosophical notion has a past as ancient as human thought, and whose contrasting meanings evoke at times life in the biological sense, at times life in the spiritual sense, and at times both at once,—this word has for Socrates and will keep for Plato a meaning which is above all, moral. It is a matter of making the interior world good, of so acting that the soul will be healthy, good and beautiful.

The Socratic Enigma

5. When all this is said, is it not possible to go a little further, and to try to get a more searching idea of this inward movement which Socrates forced upon Greek thought, and of this ignorance which he professed, and of his irony?

On the latter point let us say at once that Kierkegaard is no doubt right to make the irony of Socrates one of the major points of his condemnation. This irony questioned too many things for Socrates' fellow-citizens, and appeared to them a refusal to become involved which was dangerous for public order. The city and public opinion naturally detest irony. But for the rest, and as concerns what relates to the very nature of Socratic irony, Kierkegaard's systematization in his *Essay on the Concept of Irony*[1] gives a manifestly false picture of Socrates.

Socrates was by no means an ironist in the sense in which Kierkegaard understood the term, that is an ironist whose great triumph was to make all things problematical[2]—"like Samson, Socrates shakes the pillars which support the temple of knowledge and hurls the whole edifice into the nothingness of ignorance"[3]—and whose essential purpose is to enjoy his irony itself as an "absolute negativity",[4] and as "a naught which consumes all, a foundation on which one may not even set foot, which at once is and is not".[5] When Kierkegaard declares that although the enjoyment of the ironist is of all enjoyments "the most empty of content"[6] it is nevertheless this subjective enjoyment which counts above all,[7] one may wonder if the attitude thus defined ever really characterized Kierkegaard himself; at any rate it is certain that in

[1] Kierkegaard was twenty-eight at the time of this doctoral dissertation (1841), which is extensively analyzed by Pierre Mesnard in *Le Vrai Visage de Kierkegaard* (Paris: Beauchesne, 1948, pp. 117–179). The quotations given by the author refer to the German translation of Wilhelm Rutemeyer, *Der Begriff der Ironie mit ständiger Rücksicht auf Sokrates*, München: Kaiser Verlag, 1929.

[2] Cf. Pierre Mesnard, *op. cit.*, p. 125.

[3] *Ibid.* (*Der Begriff* . . ., p. 38).

[4] *Ibid.*, p. 139.

[5] *Ibid.*, p. 137 (*Der Begriff* . . ., p. 134).

[6] *Ibid.*, p. 140.

[7] *Ibid.*, pp. 140–141. Kierkegaard wrote in *Der Begriff* . . ., p. 159: "In his constant effort to transcend the phenomenon by passing into idea, that is to say into his dialectical activity, the individual is repulsed and must beat a retreat toward reality; but reality itself *has no other value* than to offer him ceaselessly the opportunity to escape from reality, without any possibility that this will occur; the individual is thus led to repress these efforts of subjectivity and to *bury them in his personal satisfaction*; but it is precisely this attitude which constitutes irony." (Italics ours.)

attributing it to Socrates he completely misrepresented him. Socrates did not shelter—by means of irony's disconcerting approach and perpetual denials—a joy of the subjectivity conscious of the vanity of the world of objective knowledge and freed of all hope of conquering rationally the being of things—in other words a victory chalked up against Hegel with the help of Hegelian negativity itself. His irony did indeed shelter something, but something totally different, the fruit of a profound and incommunicable spiritual experience.

6. We know that Socrates "*habitually* practised spiritual introversion, and achieved from time to time—whether spontaneously or methodically it is impossible to say—uncommon states of concentration".[1] The famous episode of the campaign of Potidaea, related by Plato, demonstrates this astonishing faculty of total self-absorption. "He stood in meditation on the spot where he had been since daybreak, pondering some question, and, when he made no headway with it, he did not give up, but stood and sought. It was already midday, and people noticed, and, wondering, were telling one another that, since early in the morning, Socrates had stood thinking about something. Finally, when evening came, some of the observers after dinner (and it was summer then) brought their pallets out, at once to sleep where it was cool and to watch and see if he would also stand all night. There he stood till daylight came and sunrise. Then, when he had prayed to the Sun, he went away."[2]

"From the beginning of the *Symposium*," Olivier Lacombe remarks,[3] "Plato had prepared us for such a scene, almost banal in India, extraordinary in Greece." "And another of the servants came with the announcement: 'Your Socrates has withdrawn into the neighbors' vestibule, is standing there, and won't come in when I call.' 'Incredible talk' said Agathon. 'Go straight and call him, and don't let him off.' And then (said Aristodemus) I spoke up: 'No, No! Just let him be. This is a habit he has. At times he turns aside, and takes his stand wherever he happens to be. He will be coming soon, I think. Don't disturb him; let him be.' "[4]

How can one not be struck by the analogy between this behavior and that of the Indian holy men known as the "living delivered ones"?[5] In the study quoted above, where the whole matter is thoroughly analyzed, with perfect rightness, Olivier Lacombe underlined this analogy and showed at the same time the irreducible differences which exist between Socrates and the Yogis. Without doubt, "this man who never feels the cold, and who never feels the heat; who is the only one who knows how to fast, and the only one who knows how to drink; the only one who knows how to love youth and the only

[1] Olivier Lacombe, *Chemins de l'Inde et Philosophie Chrétienne*, Paris: Alsatia, 1956 ("Socrate et la sagesse indienne," pp. 56–57).

[2] *Symposium*, 220, in *Plato*, trans. Lane Cooper, Oxford University Press, 1938.

[3] *Op. cit.*, p. 56.

[4] *Symposium*, 175, trans. Lane Cooper, *op. cit.*

[5] Cf. Roger Godd, *Socrate et le Sage Indien*, Paris: Les Belles Lettres, 1953.

one who knows how to remain chaste in this love . . . this man is no longer a man, and, if he is not a god either, he is at least . . . a truly exceptional being, a god among men, and a man who participates in the life of the gods";[1] yet, although "Indianity . . . tends toward a spiritual state of pure, absolute and simple self-transparency",[2] "contemplation (of the soul), in Socrates, is not accomplished, as far as we know, by a doctrine of the void";[3] whereas "the self of the Indian sage is placed beyond the opposition of self and other, beyond all dialogue and all relation—even spiritual"[4] "the Socratic Self is profoundly engaged in the network of social relations."[5] "Socrates is a townsman."[6] This man, who is capable of being immobilized for hours by inner concentration, spends his time gossiping, dawdling, asking questions, nettling and teasing people to convince them of their ignorance but also to try to learn something from them;[7] he is the master of conversation; and finds his joy in dialogue and dialectics.

7. It seems that we now might attempt—however hypothetically—to draw up an interpretation of the Socratic enigma along the following general lines (subject of course to all kinds of retouching).

More Greek than ever, though possessing a secret which the Greeks did not know, Socrates appears to have experienced states of natural mysticism analogous to those of the Indian sages,[8] but he put them to quite a different use than that assigned to them by Indian wisdom. As we noted above, he has no doctrine of the void; apropos of the scene which so impressed the soldiers during the siege of Potidaea, Plato tells us that Socrates applied himself all that day, from dawn onwards, to "pondering some question, and, when he made no headway with it, he did not give up, but stood and sought". What this description suggests is that, in reality, the idea which he sought did not come to him because, once engaged in intellectual concentration, he passed

[1] Léon Robin, in *Platon, Oeuvres complètes, Le Banquet*, Paris: Les Belles Lettres, p. cviii, n. 2. (With reference to the eulogy of Socrates pronounced by Alcibiades at the end of the *Symposium.*)

[2] Olivier Lacombe, *op. cit.*, p. 58. The author continues: "For it [Indianity], concepts and discourses, relations and oppositions are no more, to be exact, than mental constructs, super-structures added to the essential, and are deforming and enslaving. To liberate the spirit is to unencumber and 'empty' it of all that adventitious content, whether static or dynamic."

[3] *Ibid.*, p. 59.

[4] *Ibid.*, p. 60. The Self of the Indian sage "is absolute, and, for the most important of the Brahmin schools, total and unique".

[5] *Ibid.*, p. 59.

[6] *Ibid.*

[7] Cf. *Phaedrus*, 230, trans. Lane Cooper, *op. cit.*: "I am a lover of learning; the country-side and the trees will not instruct me; 'tis the people in the city are my teachers."

[8] Cf. our essay "L'expérience mystique naturelle et le vide", in *Quatre Essais sur l'esprit dans sa condition charnelle*, 2nd ed., Paris: Alsatia, 1956. English translation of this essay as it appears in the first edition, in *Ransoming the Time*, New York: Scribners, 1941, ch. X.; *Redeeming the Time*, London: Bles, 1943.

from that moment further on, and entered a night where without concepts or images or any specific representation he was seized by an experience of the profound being of the Self, in itself inexpressible. Yes, but in this experience, similar to that of the sages of India, it was neither isolation in the seizure nor the void which produced it which captivated above all Socrates' mind; it was rather the concrete certainty—unshakeable, though essentially negative—which he held there: certainty peculiar to a wisdom which transcended the fluctuating opinions of men.

And, unlike the sages of India, Socrates emerged from his states of concentration incomparably strengthened in his conviction of the essential value, and prime importance for human life, of discursive reason and conceptual knowledge. He ascended from the deep springs of spiritual unconsciousness toward the wisdom of reason, toward human discourse and toward the social and political life of men, possessing his own secret, the idea of full certainty which he had experienced—and which, in a different way assuredly, and according to the communicable pattern proper to rational discourse, was also to characterize *science* as a work of reason. It follows that, if our interpretation is correct, the idea which Greece elaborated—and which played such a fundamental role in the whole history of Western culture—of science, with its absolutely firm characteristic certitude, as the summit of knowledge depended in fact, to take with Socrates definite form in human reason, on the activating effect exerted on the rational sphere by a mystic plunge into the experience of self.

Now we can understand better the nature of Socratic irony. The incommunicable spiritual experience which we have spoken of, and the indisputable certainty it comprised (and which required as an after-effect a certitude on the level of discursive reason which though doubtless not identical was analogous, being founded unshakeably on reason)—here is the secret treasure which this irony carefully sheltered.

We can also understand better the nature of the ignorance which Socrates professed. This ignorance, we said above, was a feint; doubtless it was, but in a sense it was more than a feint. To tell the truth, was this not perhaps the only thing that Socrates was aware of really *knowing*: that which he attained by an ineffable mode in a spiritual concentration superior to distinct notions? On the other hand he possessed, with great firmness, the idea of rational science, rather than the science itself. He sought the definition of virtues, he chased essences—he did not yet possess them. However profound his intuitions in ethical matters, and however clearly stressed (though still open to many ambiguities) the main lines of his moral doctrine—this was not yet science. But he knew that this science which he did not possess had to be attained, and that he was clearing the way to it. If his search was without respite, it was also without anguish, because of that great hidden certainty which fed his strength and his strange power.

Finally, we can see better what the inward conversion he preached consisted of, and how it differed from the Indian effort toward deliverance. Even if the doctrine set forth in the *Phaedo* has something in common (though greatly transposed) with the experience of Socrates, it is still much more Platonic than Socratic: "And this separation and release of the soul from the body is termed death? To be sure. . . . And the true philosophers, and they only, are ever seeking to release the soul. Is not the separation and release of the soul from the body their especial study?"[1] Socrates himself actually never taught such a "death". He kept to himself his mystic experience of the self. When he told his listeners to turn toward self-knowledge, he was not directing them to a metaphysical grasp of the *esse* of the soul through the discipline of the void; he was directing them toward a rational knowledge of the realities of the moral world and the essences it comprises, achieved by the consciousness and by introspection, and requiring for its perfection the definitions and demonstrations of discursive science. The separation of the soul from the body, which, according to the *Phaedo*, is the task of philosophers, and the kind of supra-morality into which they are led by Platonic deliverance, did not exempt Plato from working to establish a morality rationally. As for Socrates, he is totally dedicated to morality. He preaches no mystic deliverance, but true virtue and true happiness—which are one. And he has not only the burden of calling upon reason to discover the practical science of human conduct; he has also the burden of acting upon others, of enlisting them in the quest which he himself pursues without respite, of awakening them to an authentic and upright moral life.

8. Thus it is true that the mission of Socrates was not a speculative or scientific mission, but a practical one. He was "attached to the Athenians by the will of the gods in order to needle them as a gad-fly stings a horse".[2] He had to put men to the test. Apollo had "assigned him a task, to live philosophizing, examining himself and examining others".[3] The only knowledge he claimed for himself was that of knowing that he knew nothing.[4] He forced people to become aware that they were ignorant of themselves, and that they did not know what they were saying. But at the same time he said to them: *know thyself*, and perhaps he believed that that knowledge, and the abyss of the "thyself", was too easily accessible to the glance of reason.

It is true that his great care is to develop uneasiness and anxiety in those who listen to him. But it is precisely in that way that the awakening of philosophy begins.

It is true that his distinctive art is the one which his mother, the mid-wife Phaenarete, practised—maieutics, the art of delivering minds. But it is

[1] *Phaedo*, 67, in *The Dialogues of Plato*, trans. B. Jowett, New York: Random House, 1937, vol. I.; London: O.U.P.
[2] *Apology*, 30. [3] *Ibid.*, 21, 28. [4] *Ibid.*, 21, 23.

obviously with a view to causing a fruit of knowledge to issue from them, not a simple admission of ignorance, that this obstetrics assists minds.

The commonplace to which Kierkegaard and Hegel subscribed, which makes of Socrates the founder of moral philosophy—at least for Occidental thought—is, then, justified. Certainly the intuitions of the great pre-Socratics had not excluded the ethical domain; one perceives a singularly rich moral experience in some of Heraclitus' fiery flashes; and Democritus appears to possess an already well-delineated moral vocabulary.[1] But there was no moral philosophy properly speaking before Socrates, and no philosophical wisdom with human conduct as its distinct object. He founded moral philosophy paradoxically, not by doctrinal teaching, but by dint of doubts, of questions and interrogations. And he even perceived so well the value of the practical reason that he seems sometimes too rationalist, sometimes too pragmatist. Like everything which bears within it an exceptional poetic grandeur, his personality involves a large measure of ambiguity: he is equivocal as genius is. His famous irony is the defense and the expression of his complexity, and above all, as we have seen, of the incommunicable spiritual experience which was his hidden treasure. He makes mysteries secular and he initiates us into humanism as a mystic and an inspired one; he is an enchanter, he has a mission which is in some sort religious, and he reveals reason to itself; he knows nothing and he discovers science; he dissembles ceaselessly for the love of truth; he invokes the most barefaced reasons of expediency and he is the master of the interior life, of asceticism and abnegation; he hurls discourse into the intoxication of distinctions, divisions, logic chopping and the manipulation of essences and he is the most "existential" of the Greek thinkers.

"Reason has never been set so high," as Bergson wrote in a remarkable passage.[2] "At least that is what strikes us at first. But let us look closer. Socrates teaches because the oracle of Delphi has spoken. He has received a mission. He is poor, and poor he must remain. He must mix with the common folk, he must become one of them, his speech must get back to their speech. He will write nothing, so that his thought shall be communicated, a living thing, to minds who shall convey it to other minds. He is indifferent to cold and hunger, though in no way an ascetic; he is merely delivered from material needs, and emancipated from his body. A 'daemon' accompanies him, which

[1] Cf. Kurt von Fritz, *Philosophie und sprachlicher Ausdruck bei Demokrit, Plato und Aristoteles*, New York: Stechert, undated, and Gregory Vlastos, "Ethics and Physics in Democritus", *Philosophical Review*, LIV, 6 (Nov. 1945), 578–592 and LV, 1 (Jan. 1946), 53–64.—The word ἀθαμβίη, remote ancestor of the Epicurean ataraxy, and which Prof. Vlastos translates as *undismay* (*loc. cit.*, LIV, 6, p. 582), designates for Democritus the state of mind proper to a sage, whom nothing can ruffle and nothing can depress (Fritz, p. 32). In his conclusion (LV, pp. 62–64), Prof. Vlastos very rightly characterizes the naturalism of Democritus as opposed to that of Anaximander and Heraclitus as well as that of Parmenides and Empedocles.

[2] *The Two Sources of Morality and Religion*, trans. R. Ashley Audra and Cloudesley Brereton, New York: Henry Holt, 1935, p. 53; London: Macmillan, 1935.

makes its voice heard when a warning is necessary. He so thoroughly believes in this 'daemonic voice' that he dies rather than not follow it; if he refuses to defend himself before the popular tribunal, if he goes to meet his condemnation, it is because the 'daemon' has said nothing to dissuade him. In a word, his mission is of a religious and mystic order, in the present-day meaning of the words; his teaching, so perfectly rational, hinges on something that seems to transcend pure reason."

There we have the founder of moral philosophy, which would do well not to forget its origins.

The Morality of Socrates

9. For him, as for all the Greeks, one supreme question dominated the whole field of ethics, that of the supreme good of human life, which is *eudaemonia*, happiness, but happiness is not simply being favored by the gods —good fortune, *eutukhia*, which depends on external conditions and the propitious accidents of chance or on an empirical research; happiness is at the same time acting well and perfect success in action, *eupraxis*, a term which envelops in its fecund equivocity the great drama of moral speculations which were at play in Hellenic and Hellenistic thought, for ought not acting well, or good conduct, being the perfect fulfilment of our nature, in fact be or involve by the same token the perfect satisfaction of the desires of our nature, which is what we call happiness?

As our previous analyses have shown, Socrates' moral doctrine could not present itself as a system in which philosophical reflection had attained the state of science; it could be but a rough sketch, with strongly marked features, but whose potentialities were to develop in very different directions in the course of the history of Hellenic thought.

It seems to me that in order to characterize the ethical thought of Socrates —insofar as we can know it through Plato and Xenophon, and Aristotle—we may construct the following picture:

The Good

10. First of all comes the idea of the Good. This idea, which is natural to the human intelligence, like that of being, was not disengaged without difficulty—a long history was necessary for this. At first it was just a hidden ferment, which was manifested to the consciousness and in notional language only through substitutes in which its intelligible value was concealed by the particularism of the senses and the imagination, and the prohibitions and myths of the social group. It took the intuitions of the first Sages and the reflection of the Tragedians on destiny, the passage from family law to the code of the city, then the action of the Mysteries and of Orphism stimulating in the conscience a hope of personal "salvation" which transcended the closed morality of the family and the city; and also the great effort, rational and mystical at

the same time, of the Pythagorean Order, its undertaking of moral reform, its practices of purification, its recommendation of daily examination of the conscience; and finally, the critique of the Sophists and the summons served on reason by the apparently logical nihilism of their analysis of cases of conscience and of moral ideas—all this was necessary in order that the idea of the Good should make its way in the depths of Hellenic thought and be disengaged for itself,—as distinct from the particular goods, objects of the gregarious instinct or irrational opinion, which it encompasses in its universality,—and finally, with Socrates, liberate and cause to surge up before the reason the intelligible value of an object proportioned to the amplitude and spirituality of the reason and to the freedom of the person—a universal term as vast as the spirit and at the same time problematical in relation to desire. At the very moment when it thus appeared in full evidence, moreover, the idea of the Good dazzled the human mind. It seems that for Socrates the notion of metaphysical good and that of moral good were confused—just as that of virtue and that of happiness. In the realm of human life, the good is to act well and not to miss out on one's life, it is to attain happiness.

The End

11. The second leading idea to be disengaged at the same time is that of the End.

It certainly seems that for Socrates that end—happiness, for the sake of which we have to act as we ought—is implied in our action itself, as a fruit which is immediately attached to it. In this respect the Epicureans and the Stoics will only be returning to a primitive Socratic position, outlining more sharply, transforming into formal theses, views which with Socrates remained as it were ethereal and undifferentiated. The art of morality is not the art of living morally *with a view to* attaining happiness; it is the art of *being happy* because one lives morally.

Happiness is one with Virtue

12. And so there is produced an interiorization of the idea of happiness. Happiness becomes internal, and it is determined rationally according to *what man is*; it is by the essence of the human being that his happiness is known. Know thyself—descend into the depths where your daemon lives and where you become conscious of the exigencies of your essence and of the value of your soul, which is a universe unto itself. To be happy is not to possess riches or good health, it is to have a good soul. Happiness is identical with good conduct. The more experience seems to give the lie to this axiom, the more heroically the sage affirms it—it is discredited by experience only in the eyes of the fool. Happiness and the Good are identified, but with insistence primarily on the Good; it is the Good which constitutes Happiness. Happiness does not consist in the perishable things of the exterior world, it consists

in the goods which are proper to the soul, and to the essence of man, the specific mark and distinctive force of which is the power of knowledge and rational discernment. Happiness consists in the lasting goods which are within us, it consists in having a mind free of agitation, dedicated to lofty knowledge and to truth, it consists in knowing how to think. It is within our grasp, we have only to look for it where it is.

Virtue is Knowledge

13. The history of the word virtue is itself full of significance. It meant first, in a very general way, the proper and characteristic power or excellence by which a certain nature exercised its fundamental activity: virtue of the magnet, virtues of herbs, virtue of music, virtue of the architect or of the artisan. But what is the virtue—the power or excellence—most characteristic of the human being if not the solidly established disposition which intrinsically perfects his rational activity in a given line, and above all in the line of the proper conduct of his life, and which, if we put it to work, causes us without fail to act well? It is thus that the notion of virtue which was current in the time of the Sophists and of Socrates was finally delineated, although the philosophical definition and the theory of moral virtues date only from Aristotle.

Socrates' idea, the thesis which was to become celebrated under his name throughout the history of moral philosophy, is that virtue consists in knowing and in thinking well. The virtues are all sure and true knowledges, sciences: "He thought that all the virtues were sciences," says Aristotle.[1] All sinners are ignorant. One is not wicked because one wills evil, but because one does not know the good.

These aphorisms were to be interpreted in all kinds of ways. But for Socrates they carried their full force and must be understood literally. It seems that he did not make a clear distinction (that was to be the work of Aristotle) between speculative knowledge and practical knowledge. He was probably thinking of a practical knowledge, of a moral knowledge, primarily, but conceiving of it as a theoretical knowledge of the object of the virtues, in such a way that he identified moral excellence with the knowledge of morality.

We find here a remarkable example of an intuition of central importance wrongly conceptualized. What Socrates saw in a decisive fashion, the truth, then quite new, that everything revealed and recalled to him, was the rational dignity of the human being, and the essential rationality inherent in the good act. And he had also that insight—which I express here in a thoroughly banal fashion but which in itself is capable of filling a heart and making a man give his life to a missionary task—that we all want to be happy, that we wish for true happiness, but that we do not know where it is. Stumbling against all the obstacles, we all seek the reality which delivers and the true meaning of our

[1] *Eudemian Ethics*, I, 5.

existence, and in our ignorance we grope blindly along, and in place of what we are seeking we grasp phantoms.

What he saw thus he saw for all time. But he conceptualized it too hastily. What is reason, if not the power of knowing in all its excellence? What is rationality inherent in the good act, if not the mastery of knowledge over the action it lights and conducts? *Therefore*—and it is here that Socrates makes a mistake, that he goes too fast—therefore the immediate principle of the good act, the stable excellence which causes us to act well each time it is brought into play, in other words the virtue, is knowledge. It suffices to know well in order to do well. Is it not true that the soul is good when it *knows how to make use of* riches, health, power or pleasure as it should? Yes, no doubt; but Socrates does not distinguish between this *knowing how to make use of* which is entirely practical and derives from the prudence of the virtuous man, not from science, and *knowing* (through the science of the moralist) *how one ought to make use of.*

Therein lies the paradox of Socratic thought: a general inspiration, a fundamental impulse, which is above all practical—even pragmatist—issues in systematic conclusions which reduce morality to knowledge, to knowing, to the vision of what is. Every moral fault comes from ignorance, is involuntary.

But the practical had to have its revenge. It is a question of knowing. But of knowing *what*? What is the content of this knowledge? In order to make us discern what our comportment ought or ought not to be in the concrete, what principle of determination does it grasp, what criterion of the good and proper and virtuous? At this stage of philosophical reflection, no other criterion than utility. Socrates aimed too high—the world of essences. Coming back to earth he has nothing in his hands, as implement of his theoretical knowledge and his speculative judgment concerning the occurrences of conduct, but the calculation of utility. In the end it is utilitarianism which gets the upper hand. Socrates himself and the essential inspiration of his thought are nowise utilitarian. There was nothing of Bentham in him; he did not die like a utilitarian. The idea that happiness consists in having a good soul is as little utilitarian as possible. But in its application, or rather in its philosophical explication, he was caught in the trap of the "science" he was searching for. The only instrument of "science" at his disposal is the notion of that which serves expediently, of the means proportioned to its end. A transcendent utilitarianism no doubt, since that end is to have a good soul and goes beyond our moral existence. But how are we to know how or why this or that is conducive to making the soul good? When Socrates comes down to explications and reasons, to talking about various particular examples of virtue, he descends to the commonplaces of the immediate utilitarianism of popular morality.

No doubt Socrates himself had an experiential knowledge of the virtues he spoke of prior to any conceptualization or explanation—a knowledge "by inclination" or "by connaturality", which had nothing to do with these commonplaces. From another point of view, his recourse to the platitudes of popular morality must have been in large part a sort of outer camouflage well designed to afford him secret amusement. I am well aware that Xenophon (whom I have no desire to defend against the sarcasms of Kierkegaard) was unable to discern the ironical intent hidden therein. The fact remains, however, that his report probably gives us the most exact image of the letter of the Socratic teachings. We must endure privations because the hardened man is more vigorously healthy; we must be modest because in provoking jealousies the arrogant man soon makes trouble for himself; we must be obliging because it is always useful to make friends; and so on. The Socratic insistence on science, intelligence and speculative truth in moral matters, the very theory of knowledge-virtue ends up in utilitarian criteria.

Popular Mores and Philosophical Morality

14. A fifth remark must be made, which has to do rather with a disparity, an internal weakness. This weakness, which is very noticeable in Socrates, is also to be found in the majority of those who were to come after him. In fact, it poses a critical problem prejudicial to the whole of moral philosophy. We have just observed that there exists a void, a discontinuity, a fault, between the general principles of Socratic morality and the justification it gives of the particular values and norms of the moral life. Socrates is not the only one in this situation. Let us add now that the norms and values in question are those of an already established morality, a morality already in existence which reigns and prevails in the common opinion of the historical and social milieu. For men did not await the coming of the moralists in order to have moral rules, and the moralists justify a given which ante-dates them and which has more practical consistency and more existential density than the theories by means of which they attempt to account for it. They are educators and reformers of customs, and they depend on customs. Fine reformers, who in the end justify what the baker and the candlestick-maker already firmly believed in (even if they did not act accordingly).

The fact is that here, as elsewhere (but in an entirely different way than in speculative philosophy), it is a question of discerning the necessary beneath the accidental and the contingent. The specifically Hellenic notion of "beauty-goodness" (*kalo-kagathia*) refers to a complex of qualities—beauty of body and of character, nobility of stock, culture of mind, magnanimity, liberality, courage—a complex which formed the ideal of the popular conscience in a given period and in a given society; it is not however impossible to draw from it a universal content which is useful in reflection on the idea of value in moral philosophy.

Socrates founded moral philosophy in the Occident. His inspiration awakened the intelligence to the supreme principles of human conduct, the subjects he dwelt on were to nourish the thought of moralists for centuries, and the contrasting virtualities of his doctrine were to be actualized in the opposing systems of the great schools of Greece. In the application to particular cases he simply defends against the Sophists the morality of common sense prevalent in his age; the particular rules of conduct, the ethical values that he justifies, were those which guided the moral judgments of the good citizen of Athens in the second half of the fifth century.

2

THE DISCOVERY OF ETHICS

Plato

The Idea of the Good

1. Let us try to characterize, by indicating in rough outline the traits which seem most significant to us, the contributions which moral philosophy has received from Plato, or at least has incorporated into its heritage as bearing the mark of Platonism.

The ethics of Plato, like that of Socrates, is an ethics of happiness. But the happiness of man is only a participation in a transcendent Absolute, whose reality is independent of us and of human life: the Good, which is identical with the One, and "beyond essence"; subsistent Good, the Idea of the Good, which, despite this term "Ideal" which we are indeed obliged to apply to it by reason of Platonic dialectic, is superior to all intelligibility and to being itself, since in the last analysis, for Plato, being cannot be freed from the multiplicity inherent in mutual relations among intelligible types or essences. In the perspective of Platonism carried to its logical extreme,[1] God—who, like the Sun, illumines and vivifies all that is below him and who is cause of the order and harmony of the cosmos and of the soul—is beyond Intellect just as he is beyond Essence, and is finally attained in some degree only by a kind of mystical death of the intellect, swallowed up in the Good under the impulse of the supreme Eros. The end which the initiate aims at above all in his moral activity (and which only the philosopher, or the sage, can attain) is therefore to free himself from the prison of the body and to purify himself by asceticism and love, turning toward the interior in order to bring out the divine resemblance which is instinct in the soul, a divine thing, and to contemplate the divine, to "escape from here to the beyond", to achieve "assimilation to God" by means of a death that wisdom brings about and that is incomparably more perfect and more liberating than physical death, and that alone enables physical death to *succeed*, by triumphing over transmigration.

Here again, analysis of the moral thought of the philosopher reveals five themes or typical characteristics. The first theme is that of the Good. The Good is now disengaged, in the fullness of its meaning, more decisively and

[1] In this perspective the thought of Plotinus—though it had other sources also and developed in an entirely different intellectual climate—does indeed seem like a supreme consummation of the thought of Plato. But to achieve this it had to drop many things (in particular the major interest in politics) which in fact were of vital importance to Plato.

more forcefully than with Socrates. At the summit of beings and of eternal archetypes, beyond the shadows of becoming, it is the light which nourishes the eternal contemplation of the Gods, whom Plato in the *Laws*[1] regards as the souls which control the revolution of the Firmament. All that which we call good is so only by participation in this subsistent Good, which is at the same time the sovereign metaphysical Good of the universe, and the ideal moral good of human life, for the most fundamental tendency of Platonic ethics seems to be not, doubtless, to suspend the moral from the supra-moral as Christianity was to do—that is, as a matter of principle and universally—but to do so at least *for the sage* (and for him alone). It is from a supra-morality concerned with the conditions and laws of ascetic and mystical progress toward the Transcendent (and from which are derived the moral virtues in him whom wisdom puts in harmony with divine measures) that the sage descends to the world of men to teach them morality and to make them practise it (if they were not so mad) in governing their political life. The good does not belong to the empirical world, or belongs to it only as a reflection. And our knowledge of the subsistent Good is rather divination than knowledge, because it is beyond everything, even, as we remarked above, beyond being.

In relation to this transcendent Good, happiness in this conception appears as a never-ending ascent, a progress in participation which never arrives at its ultimate limit. And this very fact, this transcendence of the Good in relation to Happiness—carrying Plato, or the internal logic of Platonism, beyond Hellenic thought—marks a distinction between the Good and Happiness which in general the moral philosophy of the Greeks never made explicit. It is as if the trans-natural or trans-philosophical desire which lies within us were awakened in philosophy itself in order to make it aspire, not, surely enough, to the intuitive vision of the separate Good (which would be to superimpose on Platonism a Christian interpretation, which is not at all appropriate to it), but to an endless ascent toward such a unity—regarded as unattainable—with that separate Good. But this is only a virtuality of Platonic thought. In fact Plato, in the *Phaedrus*, makes happiness consist in fixation in an end and a state of achieved perfection—but far from the supreme unity, in direct contemplation of the Ideas or separate Forms, a happiness like that of the gods, souls unencumbered by the body.

The Transcendence of the End

2. The second theme is that of the End. The End of human life is now absolutely transcendent. This transcendence of the Good and of the End was doubtless already suggested in certain virtualities of Socratic thought; nevertheless the opposition between Socrates and Plato on this point seems to me quite clear. Whereas for Socrates, in the last analysis, the end of human activity, though implicitly superhuman, is inherent in human activity, which

[1] *Laws*, Book X, 898–899.

if it is good makes us happy by the same token, whereas for him morality is the art of being happy through right living, for Plato, on the contrary, morality is the art of preparing oneself for a felicity which transcends human life, since, beginning with earthly existence, and continuing afterward, the true life is beyond life, the true happiness is beyond happiness.

Supra-empirical Happiness

3. The third theme is that of Happiness. Happiness is not only internal, but it loses all empirical character. Happy is the just man who is being tortured—this extreme consequence of Socratic logic shatters the unstable structure of Socratic happiness. In reality it is above all a paradoxical challenge and refers to a hoped-for felicity, to a supreme *élan* of separation and passing beyond. But Plato cherished this assertion and put all his fervor into it, because in the ethical order as in the metaphysical order his thought is entirely dominated by the idea of participation. For him it is not a matter of obtaining a beatitude to be purchased here below through suffering. It is a matter of participating here below in a beatitude which transcends all earthly conditions; it is quite necessary, then, that the just man who is tortured *be* really happy, but that itself is only possible because the immortal in us constitutes our only reality, and because the true happiness is not happiness—whence the sarcasms of Aristotle directed against the sublimity of Plato.

Let us look again at a few of the celebrated passages of the *Gorgias*: "Then happiest of all is he who has no evil in his soul, since we have shown that to have it there is the greatest of all evils. . . . In second place, no doubt . . . would be the one who was admonished, and rebuked, and punished. . . . And worst, then, is the life of him who has injustice, and is not delivered from it."[1] ". . . Then it would seem that he who wishes to be happy should pursue and practise self-control, and flee from license, every one of us as fast as his feet will take him, and contrive if possible to have no need at all of chastisement; but if he does require it, either he himself or any of those connected with him, be it individual or state, he must submit to justice and endure correction, if he is going to be happy."[2] "Callicles, I deny that to have one's face slapped wrongfully is the vilest thing that can befall a man, nor yet to have his purse cut or his body. I say it is more of a disgrace, and worse, to strike or cut me or my belongings wrongfully; and that robbing, aye and kidnapping . . . doing me and my belongings any wrong whatever, is worse and more disgraceful, to the doer than to me who suffer it."[3] ". . . Doing wrong must be avoided with more care than suffering it. . . . And let any one despise you as a fool and cover you with abuse if he will, yes, by Heaven, and cheerfully take from him that blow of infamy; for you will suffer no harm from it if you really are an upright man and true (*kalos-kagathos*), pursuing virtue."[4]

[1] *Gorgias*, 478, trans. Lane Cooper, *op. cit.*
[2] *Ibid.*, 507. [3] *Ibid.*, 508. [4] *Ibid.*, 527.

In the *Republic*, Plato writes in the same vein: "And he who lives well is blessed and happy, and he who lives ill the reverse of happy. . . . Then the just is happy, and the unjust miserable."[1] "Need we hire a herald, or shall I announce, that the son of Ariston . . . has decided that the best and justest is also the happiest, and that this is he who is the most royal man and king over himself; and that the worst and most unjust man is also the most miserable, and that this is he who being the greatest tyrant of himself is also the greatest tyrant of his State?"[2]

All this remains strictly true even if, in picturing to oneself the just man falsely accused, one imagines him as "scourged, racked, bound . . . his eyes put out; and at last, after suffering every kind of evil, . . . impaled".[3] There is joy only in the pious and just life.[4]

4. Plato does not only affirm that it is *a worse evil* to commit injustice than to suffer it,[5]—humanity pays little heed to this axiom in practice, but it is quite true that it is fixed in its conscience "with arguments of steel and adamant".[6] Plato also holds that one is *happier*, and that one experiences more joy when one suffers injustice than when one commits it. On the near as well as on the far side of the grave justice is sanctioned by happiness.

Not only the doctrine of the immortality of the soul, but the whole metaphysical idealism of Plato is involved here. The End of human life is to be attained beyond the grave, and it is to be attained beyond that grave which is the body, beginning here below, supra-humanly and mystically, at the summit of the spiritual life, by a divine liberation. The End of human life is expressly, absolutely supra-human, the contemplation of the Forms in which the separate Good shines forth. And the art of conduct, at this heroic moment when Platonic thought first affirms its most radical exigencies, is less the art of conducting one's life than the art of quitting it in order to experience ecstasy in the light of the intelligible Sun.

I am well aware of the fact, moreover, that the heroic moment I just spoke of is not the only moment of Platonic thought. There is the movement of return: the sage, delivered, returns among men to fulfill his mission of leading them to virtue while guiding the legislation and the government of the City by his advice—or better still—by taking the reins in his own hands.

The Morality of Value and Participation

5. The fourth theme is that of value. For Plato as for Socrates, and still more systematically, virtue is knowledge and moral fault is ignorance. But

[1] *Republic*, I, 354, in *The Dialogues of Plato*, trans. B. Jowett, New York: Random House, 1937, Vol. I; London: O.U.P.

[2] *Ibid.*, IX, 580. [3] *Ibid.*, II, 361. [4] Cf. *Laws*, 661–663.

[5] Cf. St. Thomas Aquinas, *Sum. theol.*, I, 48, 6.

[6] Cf. *Gorgias*, 509, trans. Lane Cooper, *op. cit.*

on another point there is radical opposition between Socrates and Plato: no morality in the ancient world was further removed from utilitarianism than the morality of Plato. Socrates recognized virtue in terms of what is expedient, advantageous. For Plato virtue is worthwhile without regard to utility, worthwhile in itself. It bears its value within itself, its measure of goodness is judged by its relation to the absolute, it is intrinsically lovable, it is beautiful. The *kalos-kagathos* acquires a metaphysically founded ethical significance within the treasury of philosophy.[1]

And so another central notion is disengaged from the shadows and appears in broad daylight, the notion of value, or *moral value*. This term is modern (and employed by moderns in senses that are often debatable), but the idea is as old as the world. For the ancients it was enveloped in the classical idea of virtue, since virtue is a stable disposition through which we live *rightly*: a *good* life is a life which occupies a determined place in the scale of values.

Value and End

6. It is well to dwell on these considerations for a moment, in order to bring out a point of central importance for what follows. This point concerns a concept which is quite primary—the concept of the good.

The concept of the good has two typical implications. Let us observe the way people employ it: we see it cleft in twain so to speak (this is the result of its essential analogicity) following two quite distinct lines of signification, oriented in two different directions.

On the one hand the good is a synonym of *end*. Here we have the direction of "final causality". The good, by the very fact of being good, is the goal toward which we aim. And all the rest—that is to say, the whole order of means—is good only in relation to that end, or insofar as it is such as to lead toward that end.

If the philosopher engaged in the domain of moral philosophy—the term "moral philosopher" seems grammatically doubtful to me, let us say rather the ethician—if the ethician considers things solely in this perspective, human acts will appear to him morally good as means, and solely as *means* leading to the end, that is to the ultimate good or sovereign good of human life. Their moral quality will be regarded as consisting entirely and exclusively in their function as *means* ordered to that end. Such will be the standard by which the morality of human acts will have to be measured, and will have to be determined and justified before the tribunal of reason. These remarks are valid for the moral utilitarian, they are valid also for the kind of super-utilitarian represented by a religious morality which would define good actions solely and exclusively as actions which lead to the ultimate eternal end.

[1] Cf. Werner Jaeger, *Paideia*, New York: Oxford University Press, 1943, vol. II, p. 134 and p. 268; Oxford: Blackwell, 1939–1945.

7. On the other hand the good is a synonym of *value*. Here we have the direction of "formal causality". If the good appears to us as good, it is because it appears to us as a certain fullness of being, a certain intrinsic qualitative achievement whose property is to be lovable or desirable: that which is good is worthy of love, worth being loved and desired, has a value in itself and for itself. And in truth this aspect is the primordial aspect of the good; it is by means of it that the good must be primordially described (we should say "defined" if a primary notion could be defined in the strict sense of the word).

If the ethician considers things in this perspective, human acts will no longer appear to him morally good only as means to the end, the ultimate end of human life. Their moral quality will be conceived as an intrinsic value which, by itself and for itself, independently of any consideration of the end, demands approval or disapproval by the conscience. Such was clearly the point of view of Plato.

In fact, in the common judgment of men, is it not in this fashion that good and bad actions are held to be such? I mean, immediately, in themselves, and not as mere means to an end (even the ultimate end). Let us consider some obvious examples, say a coward, an egotist or a debauchee of some kind: if he hears tell of a courageous exploit, or of a life of devotion to others, or of a life of purity, he will know at once and hasten to declare that these kinds of things are good and beautiful. All of us, just by being, all of us know from the beginning, at first glance, that it is a fine thing to tell the truth without fear, or to risk one's life to save a man in danger of death or to care for the lepers, and that it is bad to betray a friend or to let oneself be bought by a suborner. And at that moment we do not ask ourselves whether the act is or is not a means of attaining what we regard as the true end of human life: our judgment is purely and simply a judgment of value; the idea of the supreme Good of man, and of the relation of a given act to that Good, remains foreign to it. This kind of immediate judgment, arising from spontaneous knowledge, moral intuition or moral sense, by whatever name we call it, poses a problem for the philosopher—it is a factual datum whose existence he ought to recognize, not conceal. The discussion of this problem is not within the scope of the present volume. For the moment I wish only to point out that one of the tasks of the ethicist is to try to explain this kind of intuition, after he has applied himself to showing how value, the intrinsic moral quality of human acts, is measured and determined—and reflexively justified—by reason.

Let us remark here in passing that while noting the essential importance of the good *as end*, it was upon this aspect of the good *as value* that Thomas Aquinas was especially to insist in his ethics. For him a human action is good because it conforms to reason. And it is because it is good, because in the first place it has in itself a positive moral *value*, that it is in consequence of such a nature as to lead us toward our final *end*.

The Primacy of Value

8. But let us return to our reflections on the moral philosophy of Plato. What I should like to note is that precisely because the End of human life is, for this philosophy, transcendent and supra-human, it is very difficult to find a common measure between that End and the means which lead toward it, in other words to see how that End could be the measure of our acts as means leading toward it.

Let us place ourselves in the perspective of a non-transcendent or intra-human conception of the end, like that of Socrates: the end is a happiness within our reach—virtue, or wisdom, or power and liberty of spirit. And now suppose that I am inclined to anger—I choose this example because it was the case with Socrates himself, according to Porphyry.[1] It is easy to understand that abandoning oneself to an access of fury against others is not a proper means of arriving at happiness: we lose peace of soul, we call forth the resentment of others, we make a lot of enemies for ourselves. Anger, then, is not a virtue.

But let us place ourselves in the perspective of a transcendent or supra-human conception of Happiness or of the End, like that of Plato, for whom Happiness was the state of the soul which has arrived, here below and then beyond the tomb, at the contemplation of incorporeal reality and the separate Forms. Now I ask: why is patience with others a more suitable means than anger for arriving at that end? Suppose I do not know at first that anger is not good; suppose that the only way I can measure my acts is by their proportion to my ultimate End—what kind of relation can I perceive between the Subsistent Good, transcendent, absolute, ineffable, and my movement of anger or my act of patience? Could I not just as well think that in giving free reign to my anger I shall be co-operating with the effort of nature to expel stupidity and meanness from its bosom; that I shall be avoiding tension or repression and consequently be better preparing myself for union with the divine? I am without a guide and without a compass. The Absolute is too high to serve as a standard for measuring these poor things which are my acts. If the End is transcendent, if it transcends man and the human life, it transcends also the moral measurement and regulation of human acts.

In such a perspective, consequently, moral values will not be reduced to the simple condition of *means* in relation to the end; it is in *themselves* that they will be primarily considered and determined. Thus Plato will define virtue[2] as the order, the harmony and the health of the soul. Virtue makes the soul

[1] Cf. Porphyry, *History of the Philosophers*, III, 10, in *Philosophi Platonici. Opuscula Selecta*, ed. Nauck, Leipzig: B. G. Teubner, 1886, p. 9. A certain Spintharos, whose son Aristoxenus recorded memories concerning Socrates, assures us that "when he was inflamed with anger he became terrible to look upon; there is no action and no word from which he abstained at such moments".

[2] *Republic*, IV, 443–44. Cf. *Laws*, II, 653.

beautiful, it is a participation, on the level of human activity, in the subsistent absolute Good and Beautiful.

9. It is on values in themselves that the accent is placed in the ethics of Plato: an ethic of values, with the intrinsic dignity which inheres in them, rather than an ethic of the final End. This ethic has so to speak an aesthetic character, because nowhere more than in beauty does value appear purely and simply in and for itself, independent of any relation of means to end. Justice is not good because it serves some end, it is purely and simply good, it puts the soul in accord with the standards proper to a rational society, it renders the soul healthy and beautiful. Let us say that with Plato philosophical thought made the discovery, begun by Socrates, of the *bonum honestum*,[1] of the good-and-beautiful, of the good-in-itself; it became conscious of this aspect of the good in a fully explicit way. I know very well that there is no incompatibility between End and Value. What I should like to emphasize for the moment is that the ethic of Plato disengages and underlines, brings the notion of value into relief with an exceptional force and puts it in first place, particularly in regard to the manner in which the morality of human acts is measured or determined.

It is true that when it comes to application Plato's answers too often remain metaphorical and insufficiently precise. He sees quite clearly that every morally good or "virtuous" action possesses an internal value, by reason of which it merits in itself the approbation or disapprobation of the mind. But because of that aesthetic character and that predominance of the beautiful that we noticed above in his moral philosophy, and because in general, as Aristotle and St. Thomas were to observe, his thought operated less in terms of analysis and scientific demonstration than in terms of perception and symbolism proper to poetic knowledge, he had difficulty, in particular cases, in rationally justifying a given value or a given canon of moral conduct, and in offering us a scientific analysis of various virtues. He left us the list of the four great fundamental moral virtues which was to become classic (the cardinal virtues: practical Wisdom or Prudence, Courage, Justice and Temperance).[2] But in order to indicate the nature of these virtues he has recourse to comparisons (with the typical functions of the harmonious City) rather than to definitions.[3]

[1] Alas, this classic tag is not worth much, especially when it is translated literally into our modern tongues; and it seems that philosophical thought has paid dearly, in the course of history, for the poverty of moral vocabulary which is particularly evident in the case at hand. Instead of saying "honest good" we shall say rather *good as right* or good in itself and for itself, *substantial good* of the moral domain.

[2] *Republic*, IV, 427–434; 441; *Laws*, I, 631; III, 688; XII, 963, 965. Plato sees these moral virtues from a civic or political angle. They are divine goods, he says in *Laws*, I, 631.

[3] In any case Werner Jaeger is doubtless right in remarking (*Paideia*, vol. II, pp. 163 and 165) that Plato was not seeking a definition of the virtues, but rather a "vision" or intuitively caught Idea of them.

The Platonic Utopia

10. Dependence and independence with regard to popular norms—that is the fifth characteristic we should like to examine. We remarked in speaking of Socrates that in fact the ethicist depends in large measure on the values and norms commonly recognized in his milieu and time. This remark is applicable in a general way to all philosophers, whatever their moral system may be. Plato is one of those rare philosophers who is to a certain extent an exception. He transcends the mentality of his times when he derides the division of humanity into Greeks and barbarians.[1] He transcends it too, and above all, when he proposes an idea—of the sage fleeing toward the eternal regions—which, in fact, carried the sage beyond and above the city.

But he is caught short immediately by the Greek conviction of the absolute, insurpassable importance of the political order and of the city; and from then on only one way remains to reinstate the sage in the city which he transcends: to crown him, to make him the sovereign of the city. Thus the kingly quality of the sage is a rigorous logical necessity of Platonic thought.

On many other scores Plato, too, depends on the common conscience of his time—he received from it the fundamental notion of the *kalo-kagathia*, likewise the conviction to which I just alluded, that political activity is the highest form of human activity (after his unhappy experiments with tyrants, whose mentor he wished to be, he applied himself to making of the Academy a school for statesmen as well as a school of wisdom); he draws upon the notion of civilization elaborated by the Greece of his time, and upon the aberrant ideal it formulated of a heroic masculine society closed in upon itself; he partakes of the ideas of the reactionary aristocracy with which he had family ties, and he has just that *bit too much* pessimism about human nature which marks those who weep for a lost past.

Finally, if his morality is so inseparably linked to his politics that it can be characterized as a morality of the conscience[2] itself centered on the city and committed to the city,[3] and if he did not perceive (any more than Aristotle did after him) that in every human being, and not only in the sage, there are calls, values and possessions which transcend the temporal city, it is because for him as for Aristotle man is not fully man except as he is a member of the city (at once citizen and non-slave). In short, Plato accepts without question the conception of the City (regarded as a sacred and supreme monad, let us say the hieropolitical conception of the city) which was characteristic of antiquity. But he submits that conception to the inflexible logic of a reason so passionately desirous of perfection and absoluteness that he transforms it into a

[1] *Statesman*, 262.

[2] As opposed to Hegelian *Sittlichkeit*.

[3] One might say "politically extroverted" morality of the conscience, as opposed to "religiously introverted" evangelical morality, where the conscience is centered on the spirit and attuned to the spirit.

utopia in which he is not afraid to reverse the scale of accepted values, to fly in the face of and scandalize the popular conscience, either by installing the community of women in his city or by driving out Homer and the poets after having politely crowned them.

11. To tell the truth, he knew very well, in writing the *Republic* and the *Laws*,[1] that he was too right for anyone to listen to him. And I do not think we ought to embark upon a consideration of the great themes of his philosophy without taking into account the transcendent and extraordinarily refined irony with which he abandons himself all the more freely to the most extreme exigencies of his logic, and is all the more at ease in really believing in them (on the level of pure reason) for the fact that he himself laughs at them on the sly when he thinks of men and what they are.[2]

But what he is quite sure of, in any case, is that if the task consists of obliging men to lead a good life and to be *virtuous*, or irreproachably men, that task can only be accomplished by the city, and only if the city itself is founded and organized on the basis of the science of the supreme verities or upon wisdom. ". . . There might be a reform of the State if only one change were made, which is not a slight or easy though still a possible one. . . . Until philosophers are kings, or the kings and princes of this world have the spirit and power of philosophy, and political greatness and wisdom meet in one . . . cities will never have rest from their evils—no, nor the human race, as I believe."[3] It is for the sake of the virtuous life, to be established here below, that the absolutism of the city is imposed. And looking forward to such an Establishment of moral perfection, it is a small thing to be forced by the rigors of dialectics to sacrifice to the political all those things, interests, possessions, family, which pertain to the private domain of the individual.

I used the term "hieropolitical" above, in speaking of the conception of the city formulated by the ancients. One must be careful not to use the word "totalitarian" here, the more so for having discerned the true nature of the abject totalitarianism whose visage our age has been privileged to see.[4] Greece did not know the totalitarianism of a State which holds itself to be the arbiter

[1] The perspective of the *Laws* is not the same as that of the *Republic*; Plato takes greater account of the historical fact; he discusses the relative merits of the regimes of Sparta and Athens, and the weaknesses, resulting from a lack of culture and education of the Persian monarchy. He has his feet on the ground; if men reject the views of wisdom and reason, at least he will have proposed them in the context of a practical program. (Cf. the long preface to the French translation of the *Laws* by A. Diès, in the Guillaume Budé collection.) It is all the more significant that the theme of the kingly function of the sage, and of his sovereign ethico-political magisterium, should be as strongly marked in the *Laws* as in the *Republic*.

[2] He says himself in the *Republic* (IX, 592) that the city of his choice doubtless exists only in heaven.

[3] *Republic*, V, 473, trans. Jowett, *op. cit.* Cf. *ibid.*, VI, 499.

[4] Cf. Hannah Arendt, *The Origins of Totalitarianism*, New York: Harcourt Brace, 1951; London: Secker and Warburg, 1951.

of good and evil and which laughs at truth because it is itself the insane god of an immanentist world and ideology; its idolatrous cult of the City was a cult of the City which kept faith with transcendental values and subordinated itself to them. Nothing is clearer in the case of Plato. If the Republic must be ruled by philosophers, it is because the Republic itself is measured by wisdom, and because the intemporal truth of the world of Ideas reigns above it. The absolutism of the Platonic city is a kind of theocratic absolutism: the autocracy of wisdom, through law. The philosopher-king is a kind of hierarch who governs a politico-religious society in the name of the eternal Laws.[1]

This city, which imposes adherence to the three articles of its philosophical credo (Gods exist, the universe is morally governed by them, no offering or incantation can seduce them or cause them to betray justice)[2] on pain of punishment by five years' imprisonment, and even, for heretics who are second offenders, on pain of death, is not without some resemblance to the Geneva of John Calvin. A deceptive resemblance however, for it is in nowise a city-church—nothing is more foreign to Greek thought than the concept of a church (the first suggestion of which is found not in any Hellenic notion but in the Hebraic notion of *Qahal*).[3] The Platonic city is strictly temporal and rational. It is at the same time something temporal and rational and something divine; and therein lies the deepest source of utopia and at the same time of serene pride. It is a matter of founding the virtuous life for humanity, of leading man to his perfection through man himself, elevated to the state of a political body in which, as servitor and organ of the gods, he is rendered divine because he participates in the wisdom and sovereignty which emanate from the One and the Good. Plato is the greatest of the Theocrats who in the name of Reason have wanted to force men to be good.

12. It was a vain attempt. And the tyrants will never listen to the philosopher, nor will the people ever crown him. After all, why should Plato be astonished at this? If a rigorous logical necessity of his philosophy is met head on among men by a pure impossibility, is this not simply a confirmation for him of the fact that this world is not the world of truth, but of shadows on the wall and of illusion? "Now human affairs," Plato says in the *Laws*, "are hardly worth considering in earnest, and yet we must be in earnest about them—a sad necessity constrains us. . . . Man . . . is made to be the plaything of God, and this, truly considered, is the best of him. . . ."[4]

It is by his failure, indeed, that Plato offers us his most precious lesson. For

[1] Whether they act with the consent or against the will of their subjects, and with or without written laws, and using violence if necessary, the essential thing, Plato says in the *Statesman* (293–300), is that the government be in the hands of those rare men who possess science and wisdom. The written laws only make up for the absence of the crowned sage.

[2] *Laws*, X, 906–909.

[3] Cf. Henri de Lubac, *Catholicisme*, Paris: Le Cerf, 1938, p. 38.

[4] VII, 803, trans. Jowett, *op. cit.*

he was too great not to perceive this failure with complete awareness, and to disengage its full significance. "If, as everyone seems to agree, the *Republic* was completed around 375, that is, before the last two voyages to Sicily and the definitive failure of his attempts to install philosophy on the throne of Syracuse, it was already before this major setback that Plato foresaw, as though determined *a priori*, the necessary failure of the philosopher. Taking up once again, and this time at his own expense, the sarcasms of Callicles (in the *Gorgias*),[1] he shows us this great soul, too pure, thrown defenceless into a world given over to injustice, too corrupt to trust him: he is sure to perish, profitless if he takes it into his head to want to reform the State; and the philosopher gives up this useless ambition, and, withdrawing into himself, he turns to 'the city which is within him',[2] πρὸς τήν ἐν αὐτῷ πολιτεἰαν, profound and admirable phrase, the last word (if there is ever a last word), bitter and resigned, of the great wisdom of Plato.

"When he wrote the *Gorgias* he had perhaps not yet reached this point, perhaps not yet renounced that will to power which had animated his youthful ambitions (is there not some self-satisfaction in the fiery, life-like portrait he draws of Callicles, that amoral but effusive politician?). Now, the step has been taken: he knows that the philosopher, led essentially by his ideal of inner perfection, is beaten at the start. He will always be a failure among men: a stranger to political, everyday life, his thoughts absorbed by this sublime object, he will cut the figure of a fool, like Thales falling into the well as he looked at the stars, of an impotent; and yet only he is free. . . .[3]

"Now Plato sees clearly into himself: his teaching aims to make *a* man, at the most a little group of men, joined in a school, forming a closed sect, a cultural islet, healthy in the midst of a decayed society. The Sage—for Platonism heads already into a personalist type of wisdom—will spend his life 'occupied with his own affairs', τὰ αὑτοῦ πράττων.[4]

"Thus, Platonic thought, prompted at the start by the desire to restore the totalitarian[5] ethics of the ancient City, comes in the last analysis to transcend definitively the compass of the ancient City and to lay the foundations of what will remain the personal achievements of the classic philosopher."[6]

[1] 486.
[2] *Republic*, IX, 591.
[3] *Theaetetus*, 173–176.
[4] *Republic*, VII, 496; cf. 500.
[5] Henri Marrou used this word improperly here. Cf. above, pp. 28–29.
[6] Henri Marrou, *Histoire de l'Education dans l'Antiquité*, Paris: Ed. du Seuil, 1948, p. 119–120. (Translation ours.)

3

THE DISCOVERY OF ETHICS

Aristotle

The Good and Happiness identified

1. The fundamental question, for Aristotle, is again that of the *supreme good* or sovereign good of man, and that supreme good is, again, *happiness*. It is a question of "living in a blissful and beautiful manner".[1] Happiness, *eudaemonia*, consists in the perfect fulfillment of human nature. We must understand this word nature, not in an empirical sense but in a metaphysical sense, and as a synonym of essence—was not Aristotle the father of the concept of essence? Each being possesses an intelligible structure which constitutes it in its species, and tendencies and inclinations which, unlike the accidental variations found in individuals, emanate necessarily from that typical structure itself. (It will be seen that in the course of time the maxim "follow nature" is given directly opposite meanings, depending on whether the word nature is taken in an empirical sense, as designating only what exists in fact, or in a metaphysical sense, as designating an essence, a locus of intelligible necessities . . .)

Εὐδαιμονία is the state of a man in whom human nature and its essential aspirations have attained their complete fulfillment, and attained it in conformity with the true hierarchy of ends proper to that nature. "Not to have organized one's life with a view to some end is the mark of much folly."[2] In order to determine what happiness is, it is necessary to find out what the ends of our nature are (what is "the meaning of life", the first question to awaken moral anguish in us), and to discover what kind of good above all others man is made for, the good which is uniquely appropriate to a rational being and through which he achieves the fulfillment of his nature.

In order to avoid any misunderstanding, it is important to make the following points clear: (1) Aristotle does not tell us that we *ought* to tend toward happiness—the aspiration toward happiness is a fact of nature. It exists in man necessarily. Aristotle tries to discern or determine *what happiness really consists in*, this happiness toward which we necessarily aspire. (2) This determination of what happiness consists in is the proper task of moral philosophy. But men did not wait for the reflections of moral philosophy and the theories of ethicists in order to begin living and acting. They must, then, have a way

[1] *Eudemian Ethics*, I, 1, 1214 a 31. (Author's translation.)
[2] *Ibid.*, I, 1, 1214 b 10.

of their own—a spontaneous or "pre-philosophical" way—of knowing what is really the meaning of life and what the true supreme good consists in (whether or not the idea of happiness occurs to them explicitly at this point). I mention this problem; it is not within the scope of the present volume. (3) Whether this knowledge be acquired in a practical and spontaneous way or in a speculative and philosophical way, in any case, as soon as we know what the supreme good truly consists in, we know also that we *ought* to tend toward that true good; we are obliged to do so by conscience, not by virtue of some philosophical demonstration, but by virtue of a "first principle" known in an immediate way by each person and self-evident to what Aristotle calls the "intuitive reason" or "the immediate intelligence of principles":[1] one must do good and avoid evil.

When the philosopher has determined what *is* the *true* supreme good of man, he has by the same token indicated the first choice which every man is obliged by conscience to make.

2. We can now outline with some precision the positions Aristotle takes with regard to the basic issues we were able to discern in studying the thought of Socrates and Plato.

First of all, it is clear that the concept of the Good, and that of the supreme or sovereign Good, is as central for Aristotle as for Socrates and Plato and Greek philosophy in general. The observations we have just made only confirm this fact. It is to be noted here that if Aristotle identifies the Sovereign Good with Happiness, it is not that for him the Good is eclipsed by Happiness. For him as for Socrates, the Good remains the Good. It retains its own meaning even though identified with Happiness. It even retains a certain priority over Happiness, for the concept of the Good is in itself a more primitive or primordial concept than that of Happiness—but this priority remains purely implicit in Aristotle's thought.

The fact that Aristotle neglected to elucidate and explain this point in his moral philosophy gives rise, as we shall see, to the kind of amphibology which his system does not succeed in avoiding.

The End—the Aristotelian Sovereign Good

3. In his ethics as in his metaphysics and his philosophy of nature, Aristotle attributes an absolutely major role to finality. All things are, as it were, suspended from the Final Cause. Thus for him the primary aspect of the Good is its aspect as End. And the first question for moral philosophy is the question of the Sovereign Good. This theme was to become classic for centuries in the occidental philosophical tradition, up to the Kantian revolution.

[1] *Nicomachean Ethics*, VI, 1141 a 3–8. (Author's translation.) This corresponds to "synderesis" or the *habitus of first practical principles* in the vocabulary of the scholastic tradition.

But as for the manner in which he conceives the End of human life, or the sovereign Good, Aristotle takes his place mid-way between Socrates and Plato.

In contrast to Plato, the ethics of *eudaemonia* deliberately steps down from the sublime heights of Platonic morality. The supreme good pertains to human life, becomes immanent in that life. It is a happiness which exists here below, a terrestrial happiness. This does not mean that Aristotle failed to recognize its necessary relation to that which is superior to man. He made wisdom, whose object is divine, the principal ingredient of that happiness. He has a theory of good fortune, and, more important, a theory of inspiration, in which he sees a superhuman element intervening in human affairs. We must not forget that, for him, to propose to man only that which is human is to do him disservice, for by virtue of the most excellent part of himself, which is the intellect, man is called to something better than a purely human life.[1] In the *Eudemian Ethics*, whose doctrine we hold to be authentically Aristotelian, we find such a passage as this: "As in the universe, so in the soul, God moves all things. The principle of reasoning is not reasoning, but something better. Now what could be better than even the knowledge of the intellect, if not God? Not virtue, for virtue is an instrument of the intellect. . . ."[2]

In contrast to Socrates, he holds that the practice of virtue does not result in the immediate possession of happiness. The art of living rightly is not the art of being happy through virtue, or of realizing that virtue equals happiness. It is the art of ordering one's life in such a way as to attain the supreme end: happiness—in this earthly life no doubt, in this perishable body, in the midst of the city of men (and not beyond the grave, beyond the prison of this body, by means of a kind of death begun here below, as Plato conceived it)—but not immediately either, as Socrates envisaged, as if happiness were the reverse side of the virtuous act itself. A well-ordered life attains happiness at the end of a long term, after long exercise, at a ripe age, when the hair is beginning to turn silver. Yes, God knows, that is so! Such a view does not arouse great enthusiasm, perhaps—the man who is starving does not like much to wait—but it is eminently reasonable.

4. And now, of what is happiness composed? What are its essential elements? Three things are the principal constituents of happiness: wisdom, virtue, pleasure. For the perfect and happy life is "the most beautiful and best of things, and also that which gives the greatest joy".[3]

[1] *Nicomachean Ethics*, X, 7. Cf. below, p. 47, notes 1 and 2.

[2] *Eudemian Ethics*, VII, 14, 1248 a 26–29. I quote from the *Eudemian Ethics* because I have a predilection for this work and have always thought it authentic. It happens that scholarly criticism now considers it one of Aristotle's earliest works, along with the *Topics* and the *Politics* (Cf. M.-D. Philippe, "La participation dans la philosophie d'Aristote", *Revue Thomiste*, 1949, I–II, p. 269).

[3] *Eudemian Ethics*, I, 1, 1214 a 8–9.

There is an order among the three elements of happiness, a hierarchy of importance. The first place belongs to wisdom, the possession by the mind, however precarious in the case of man, of contemplated truth. Wisdom is essentially contemplative, it is an immanent activity, an activity of repose and fruition. And contemplation is superior to action. The perfect life is above all theoretical, it is the life of knowledge achieved in unity.[1]

In second place comes virtue. The life according to virtue is obviously an integral part of the full accomplishment of human nature.

Pleasure takes third place, and occurs as a surplus, so to speak. It exists as a necessary result. By virtue of a general rule, it is added to the act, as bloom is to youth. And man cannot live without a certain measure of joy or delectation. That kind of interior contentment or that feeling of expansiveness which, in the most profound sense of the word, we call pleasure is the natural recompense of a virtuous life.

But that is not all. The three sorts of good we have just spoken of exist within the soul. There are still other kinds of good, exterior to the soul, which are included in the notion of happiness, if not as integral components at least as indispensable conditions: friendship—a man without friends is not a happy man; health; the possession of material goods (a certain abundance is necessary to the external manifestation of virtue—poverty does not permit munificence, and we may add that poverty is a terrible obstacle to virtue itself); and finally, Aristotle was too much of a realist to be unaware that chance, with its favorable coincidences, the free gifts of good fortune, plays an indispensable role in the happiness of the human being.

The Aristotelian conception of happiness, or of *eudaemonia*, is definitely not hedonistic, since pleasure occupies the third rank in its hierarchy of goods. Rather, it takes the supreme good as it was conceived by Plato and renders it immanent, secularizes it in an eminently humanistic, noble and reasonable way. Like man himself, the happiness of man is complex. It is a compound, made of matter and spirit, of sense and intelligence, of animal conditioning and rational, even super-rational freedom, all of this crowned, and guided, by wisdom and contemplation.

In Aristotle's moral philosophy everything is measured in relation to this complex totality: the best and most beautiful life, the accomplished fullness of human nature, happiness—consisting in the true order of the parts which compose it. It is the end toward which we tend insofar as we are not foolish, insofar as we do not make a mess of the art of living. Herein lies the source of a nuance peculiar to the conception of moral obligation and moral fault which is to be found, if not in the religious thought of the Greeks (witness the great tragedians), at least in their philosophical thought. The idea of duty, as conceived by the Greek philosophers, has less affinity with the idea of a sacred imperative than with that of a masterful ordering of means, something

[1] Cf. *Nicomachean Ethics*, X, 7, 1177 a 12–18.

which is required of man in order to attain his end, and something which is recognized by every reasonable and cultivated spirit anxious to assure his true happiness. Their idea of moral fault is most closely akin to the idea of a badly conducted or senseless action which mars the beauty of life and leads away from happiness. The notion of culpability, rendering man unworthy of existence and bringing down upon him the wrath of the gods, this notion which was so strong in Aeschylus, is now greatly attenuated. As for the concept of the norm, if it still plays an essential role, it also has lost the sacred character it possessed in the beginning. It designates less a divine commandment than a rule of conduct required by the order of nature and of the cosmos. In short, it is not the Kantian "*ought*" that we find here, but "*such is the way to happiness*". It is significant that for antiquity the vocabulary of ethics and that of art remained substantially identical. The artist possesses his virtue just as the prudent man possesses his. The word "sin" is applied as readily to a grammatical or musical error as to a fault against justice or temperance.

The search for an equilibrium between Finality and Value—the primacy of Finality

5. Aristotelian ethics consists of the search for a doctrinal and systematic equilibrium between these two major considerations: that of the End, and that of Values.

Far from neglecting the consideration of values, it deliberately emphasizes their importance: the concept of virtue has a central place in this ethics. One of the great tasks successfully performed by Aristotle was to establish rationally the philosophical theory of virtue: what is the ontological "stuff" of virtue? Virtue is by nature that kind of quality which he calls a *habitus*, a ἕξις; and moral virtue is a ἕξις or stable disposition which fortifies and perfects the powers of the soul in respect to the *right use* of freedom. Now as we have remarked before, the concept of virtue is by its nature inseparable from the concept of value.

But for Aristotle, what dominates the whole field of ethics, and the way in which specific virtues are to be determined, is the consideration of the ultimate End, the primacy of the Supreme Good, or the happy life. At this point he turns away from the positions of Plato to come back to those of Socrates, not, to be sure, with the perspective and to the advantage of that utilitarianism to which Socrates was constrained to limit himself for want of the necessary means to go beyond it, but with the perspective and to the advantage of eudemonism. I mean that in the eyes of Aristotle the good of the virtues is at the same time *bonum honestum* (good worthy in its own right) or good in itself and through itself, and the *means* of arriving at Happiness.

Value and finality—how are these two fundamental aspects of ethics harmonized? Let us recall the famous theory which makes moral virtue consist in a *mean*, a midpoint (μεσότης) between an excess and a deficiency. In each case moral good or moral rectitude is defined by the fact that it strikes the *right note*, a correct, exact and appropriate consonance which is produced by reason. The fundamental notion of the *measurement* or the regulation of our acts by reason makes its appearance here, a notion which was to have a bright future, for it was to become the keystone of moral philosophy in the Christian tradition. Now if my interpretation is correct, we must say that for Aristotle a morally good act is an act which has not only been worked over, brewed, prepared, adjusted, harmonized, concocted, digested, formed, measured by reason—but, more precisely, which has been measured by reason in its very capacity of tending directly toward the ultimate end of human existence, toward Happiness, toward "the good and beautiful life, if one hesitates through a kind of fear to call it by its true name, the blissful life".[1]

On the one hand, then, in virtue of being measured by reason, or conforming to reason, the moral act attains its peculiar configuration, its beauty, its brilliance, the plenitude proper to a human act. It is invested with a quality which makes it good in itself and for itself (*bonum honestum*, good as right). Here the role of *Value* is emphasized.

But on the other hand, it is as *means* to the Happy Life that the moral act is formed and determined, measured by reason. It is in function of its tending directly toward the ultimate End that reason measures the moral act. Here the role of the *End* is emphasized.

It is thus that Aristotle reconciles the claims of Finality and those of Value in ethical theory.

6. But in actual fact, and in a definitive way, the consideration of the ultimate End, or Happiness, plays the major role and carries all before it, since it is by virtue of tending directly toward true happiness that reason regulates human acts. Finality is not only predominant in the order of action, but it is the supreme criterion even in the order of specification, even in the determination of the moral goodness of human conduct. And the result is that the "absolute" or "categorical" character of the moral imperative or of the *bonum honestum* is in some sort relegated to the background. Thence a trace, in spite of all, and more than a trace, of utilitarianism.

All this amounts to saying that the equilibrium sought by Aristotle was not decisively attained. I fear, moreover, that a kind of vicious circle is implied in his procedure: the fact is that virtue appears herein as essentially a *means* toward the good and beautiful life, the blessed life; and yet virtue is also an *integral part* of that blessed life, since without virtue there is no good and beautiful life—the means to the end (virtue) thus enters into the very notion and constitutive of the end to which it is directed.

[1] *Eudemian Ethics*, I, 3, 1215 a 11–12.

Aristotle discovered the right road, but his solution remained imperfect, enveloped in insurmountable difficulties.

When, with the advent of Christianity, the ultimate, the absolute End, and the Beatitude with which it is connected, were to become even more transcendent and supra-human than with Plato, the norm in relation to which reason measures human acts, that norm which must be proportionate with man (as was Aristotelian happiness), was no longer to be supreme Happiness itself—it is too transcendent to serve as a norm for measuring human acts. Beatitude is in fact the end to be attained in the order of action by the righteous human life, but it is not, in the order of specification, the criterion of moral goodness. That criterion (at least in the perspective of nature, which is the basic perspective of the philosopher) was to be the ensemble of primary rules known to us without reasoning (though reflexively justifiable in reason) by virtue of the essential inclinations of our nature, in other words *natural law*, along with all the rules which can be inferred from its principles. At that point the concept of natural law already brought to light, but in a different perspective by the Stoics, was to take its true place in the structure of ethics. And the notion of the *accomplishment of the natural law* was to replace that of *Happiness* as the objective specifying standard in function of which reason measures human acts.

The vicious circle which I just pointed out in speaking of Aristotle no longer exists. For natural law enables us to see what the virtues must be, but the concept of virtue or the virtuous life in no way enters into the notion of the natural law itself. The equilibrium sought by Aristotle is finally attained.

The chart to be found on p. 38 indicates in a diagrammatical way the various positions we have mentioned up to now, and at the same time the kind of trajectory described by the idea of happiness.

Happiness was at first identified with virtue. Then it left this earthly sphere for the transcendent world of subsistent Ideas. In the third stage it came back to earth and to human life. In the fourth stage it is to have its seat in the celestial homeland, as absolutely perfect Happiness, or Beatitude, toward which man tends by the very fact of tending toward his ultimate End, God loved for Himself and above all else.

Ethics and the common Conscience—the theory of the Virtues

7. In the case of Aristotle as in that of Socrates, and even more definitely than in the case of Plato, we can verify the fact that ethical theory works on the basis of moral structures already in existence in the human community and is most often occupied with justifying the scale of values and the rules of conduct accepted by common conscience in a given cultural atmosphere and period. At this stage of our enquiry, the period in question is the fourth century B.C., and it is well known that even slavery, which was one of the

foundations of that society, was regarded by the Philosopher as grounded in reason and required by nature.[1]

Aristotle was fully conscious of the general fact we have just mentioned. The experience of men plays a fundamental role in his ethics. He refers to it constantly. The conduct of the prudent man, the opinion of the elders and

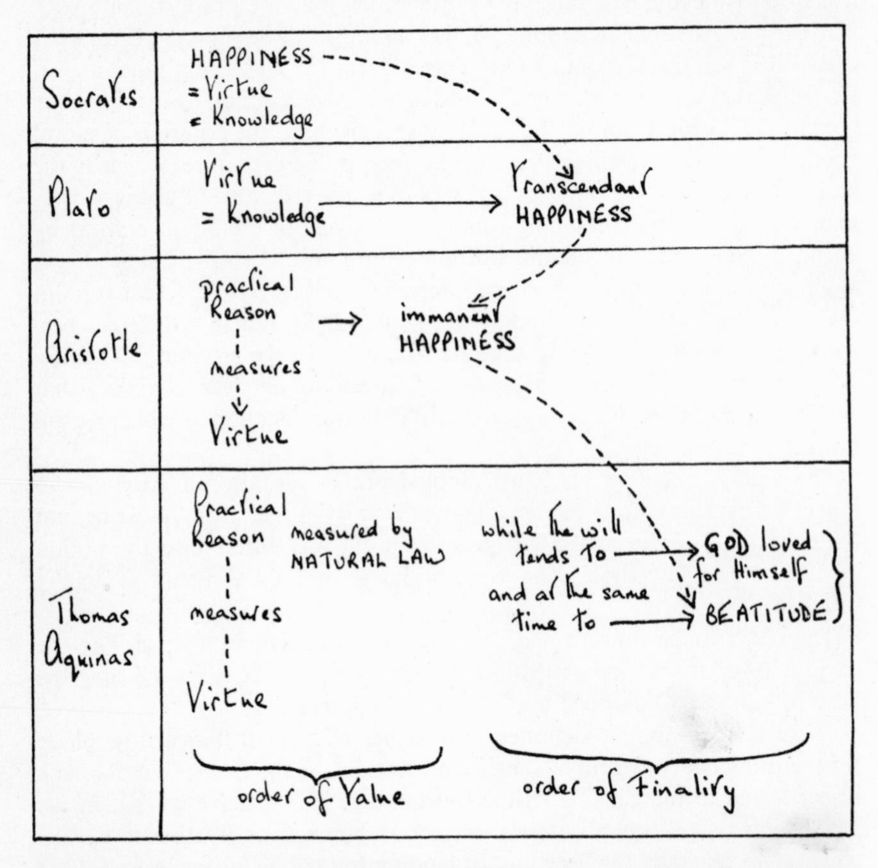

their experience of life, the customs of various cities were, for him, indispensable data for the very construction of moral philosophy. But he uses all this human experience in order to disengage by induction the rational principles with which it is pregnant. Thence the considerable amount of space he devotes to empirical description, the abundant and richly detailed psychological descriptions we find in so many chapters of the *Nicomachean Ethics* and the *Eudemian Ethics*.

[1] Cf. *Polit.*, I, 4, 1254 a 71–77, 1255 b 40—"It is clear," Aristotle teaches, "that certain men are by nature free, and others slaves, and that for the latter slavery is at once just and expedient" (*Ibid.*, 5, 1255 a 2–3, author's translation). On the other hand (ch. 6) he questions the legitimacy of enslaving prisoners of war.

On the other hand, Aristotle was in a position to propose a teleological justification of values and moral rules, in function of the last end, because, as we have seen, that last end found itself humanized in his system, brought back to the level of terrestrial existence and terrestrial standards. Since in the internal hierarchy of earthly happiness theoretical activity or contemplation holds the most exalted place ("Perhaps he thought," Aristotle wrote concerning Anaxagoras, "that he who leads a life without afflictions and free from all injustice, and who in addition is engaged in some divine contemplation, is, insofar as man can be, blessed"),[1] it is in relation to this contemplative wisdom that our various choices and the exercises of the virtues must be ordered. "Whatever choice, then, or the possession of whatever natural goods—bodily welfare, riches, friends or whatever else—is most apt to lead to the contemplation of God, that choice or that possession will be the best. There we have the most noble criterion. . . ."[2] In order to attain to the sovereign good man must, on the one hand, regulate by reason (which is "royal" or "political", not "despotic" government)[3] the lower functions, especially the passions, and, on the other hand, develop the powers of the spirit, and the superior life of the νοῦς.

8. It is here, and still in reference to the good and beautiful life not to be missed, that the theory of virtue as the *golden mean* between opposed vices finds its place—not the golden mean of mediocrity, but the golden mean of eminence, the summit between two contrary depressions, according to that observation so true that it has become trite. It has often been remarked, along the same line, that what Aristotle called prudence is not fear of risk or precautionary timidity; its function is rather to make man master of himself and superior to events, and ready freely to take the risks required by justice, by the dignity of a rational being, and by magnanimity.

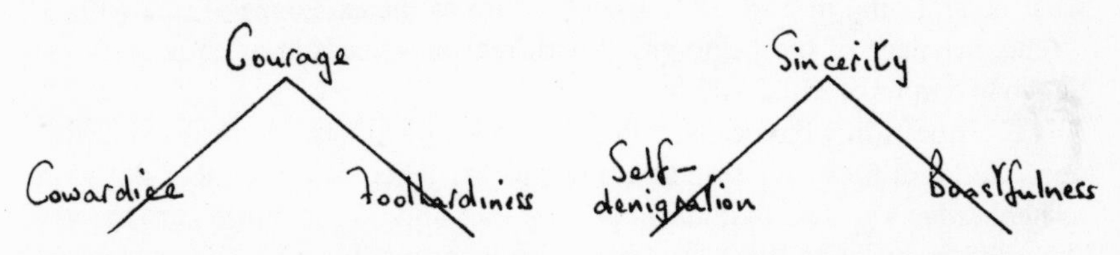

The mean which constitutes virtue is an indivisible thing—it is just a point, the just point; it is what corresponds in the moral order to having a "good ear", to musical or poetic exactitude. The two opposed extremes—by excess or by defect—meet at the summit and fade away, disappear when they come in contact with each other in virtue. To take up a remark of André Gide's, about himself, each virtue could say: extremes touch *me*; and they die of it.

[1] *Eudemian Ethics*, I, 4, 1215 b 12–14; cf. *Nicomachean Ethics*, X, 7.
[2] *Ibid.*, VII, 15, 1249 b 16–19.
[3] *Polit.*, I, 5, 1254 b 4–5.

We find the Aristotelian list of the moral virtues and the contrary vices by excess or defect in the *Nicomachean Ethics*, Book II, chapters 6 and 7, and in the *Eudemian Ethics*, Book II, chapter 3 (1220 b 36–1221 a 12). It should be noted that there is no word in the language for the extreme opposed by defect to envy, and so this vice remains unnamed, although it is a very real thing, as we see in the case of those who do not suffer at all by reason of the prosperity of the unworthy, but who "accept everything, as a glutton swallows no matter what, while those in whom exists the opposed vice are impatient, through envy, at the good of others".[1] There we have an example of Aristotle's method. In this whole analysis of the moral virtues and opposed vices, he relies on the common conscience and refers constantly to the moral judgments men make in the ordinary course of life. But he has disengaged therefrom a universal law, to wit, virtue consists in the proper mean. And armed with this instrument, he corrects common experience and supplies examples of what it fails to notice when "the other extreme, as if it did not exist, escapes our knowledge, remaining unperceived because of its rarity".[2]

Freedom

9. Virtue is not knowledge. In Aristotle's moral philosophy a fundamental characteristic of the ethical theories of antiquity, especially in the heroic age of Greek philosophy, becomes clearly apparent: I am thinking here of the "cosmic" or "ontological" character of this moral philosophy, of the fact that ethical theory presupposes a system of metaphysics and of natural philosophy, and that no ethics can do without prerequisite notions bearing upon the world, man and the supreme realities, in other words, that the universe of freedom (the moral universe) is founded upon the universe of nature.

The ethician must know that there are natures or essences, that there is a human nature, that what pertains to spirit and to reason in man is superior to what is irrational in him. He must be aware of the existence of free will.

This privilege of the being gifted with reason—freedom of choice—is particularly emphasized by Aristotle.

It is a question which caused Plato serious difficulties. He believed in freedom, and had no inclination to contest its existence. But the theory of *virtue as knowledge*, the idea that all sin is ignorance and that it is sufficient to know the good in order to do it, was in reality incompatible with the existence of free will. Plato tried hard to find a way out, for the difficulty was not insurmountable. He sought refuge in a theory of supra-temporal freedom which is not without analogy with that which Kant was to propose—such theories in fact eliminate freedom.

Aristotle, on the contrary, held on to the reality of free will at no matter what cost. This is one of the points at which the existential value of his

[1] *Eudemian Ethics*, II, 3, 1221 b 1–3.
[2] *Ibid.*, II, 5, 1222 a 41–42.

doctrine, which it is fashionable these days to call into question (and in fact he shows many deficiencies in this regard), appears most clearly. As Hamelin has clearly shown,[1] he was so profoundly conscious of freedom that, rather than compromise its existence, he did not hesitate to scandalize the logicians by enunciating his famous theory (so admirable, and so true) of the indetermination of the truth of propositions relating to future contingents.

Of the contradictory propositions relating to a future contingent, he teaches in *On Interpretation*, one will be true when the time in question comes to pass, and the other will by the same stroke be false; but neither can be determined today as true or false, since the truth comprised by these propositions is as indeterminate as the event to which they relate, which itself will not be determined until it takes place. "A sea-fight must either take place to-morrow or not, but it is not necessary that it should take place to-morrow, neither is it necessary that it should not take place, yet it is necessary that it either should or should not take place to-morrow. Since propositions correspond with facts, it is evident that when in future events there is a real alternative, and a potentiality in contrary directions, the corresponding affirmation and denial have the same character."[2]

Similarly, which of the two contradictory propositions is true and which is false remains undetermined until the future moment in question has become present. If this were not the case everything would occur by necessity, and there would be neither contingency nor liberty. "There would be no need to deliberate or to take trouble, on the supposition that if we should adopt a certain course, a certain result would follow, while, if we did not, the result would not follow." A thousand years in advance a prediction concerning the result in question would have had to be necessarily true and its contradiction necessarily false, so that the event itself would arrive necessarily on the date indicated.[3]

10. Since he fully recognized the reality of free will it is not surprising that Aristotle treats of the idea that virtue is knowledge without mincing words. "In regard to virtue," he says,[4] "not to know *what* it is, but to know *whence* it comes (or how to acquire it), that is what is most precious. For we do not want to know what courage is, but to be courageous, nor what justice is, but to be just, in the same way that we want to be in good health rather than to know what kind of thing health is."

He even added that to know is of little use for virtue, or even of no use at all. "As condition for the possession of virtues, knowledge has little or no weight at all."[5]

[1] O. Hamelin, *Le Système d'Aristote*, Paris: Alcan, 1931.

[2] *On Interpretation*, 9, 19 a 30–34, in *The Basic Works of Aristotle*, ed. Richard McKeon, New York: Random House, 1941.

[3] *Ibid.*, 18 b 26–35.

[4] *Eudemian Ethics*, I, 5, 1216 b 21–25.

[5] *Nicomachean Ethics*, II, 4, 1105 b 1–2.

This memorable disillusioned maxim is evidence that Aristotle was possessed of a more profound human experience and a clearer view of moral problems than Plato, or even than those modern little Platonists who no longer believe in the Ideas and install themselves comfortably in the shadows of the cave, but who believe in "scientific" ethics, and think that it is the business of the empirical sciences to lay the foundations of the good life for humanity—just wait a little while until biology, psychology and sociology have completed their discoveries and men will put into practice the laws of good conduct (it will be a long wait, for it is the nature of these sciences to substitute one new approach for another and one new theory for another indefinitely).

The Sage and the City

11. When Aristotle writes that he who escapes social life is either a beast or a god,[1] he certainly intends to reject any kind of solitary life, even that eremitical life so widespread in India and so honored by Christianity,[2] which without doubt does not cut all the bonds linking man and society but where—as far as the essential thing that is the spiritual order is concerned—the "delivered" or "perfect" one is entirely sufficient unto himself and has no need of others. The sage of Aristotle lives no more apart from the city than the sage of Plato.

But there is a profound difference between the two. Carried toward the beyond and the contemplation of separate Ideas, Plato's sage transcended by his own motion, as Sage, the common life of the citizen, and if at the same time it was absolutely necessary for him to bear witness to the ineluctable political vocation of the human being, he could do this only as a prince, as king of the city, wielding political power by a kind of divine right. The sage of Aristotle, on the other hand, is not called to govern the city by virtue of his wisdom, and has neither the mission nor the desire to assume political authority. He is in the city, he does not rule it. And doubtless the immanent activity of contemplation depends to such an extent on what is divine in us that a purely contemplative life "would be too high for man".[3] Life according to the intellect is divine in comparison with human life.[4] But the fact is that if the philosopher participates in a super-human divine life, he is not a god for all that. Because the life he leads is principally, but not purely, contemplative; he remains a man, and thus a member of the city.

[1] *Polit.*, I, 2, 1253 a 29.

[2] Cf. St. Thomas Aquinas, *Sum. theol.*, II, 188, 8: "Sicut ergo id quod jam perfectum est, praeeminet ei quod ad perfectionem exercetur, ita vita solitariorum, si debite assumatur, praeeminet vitae sociali. Si autem absque praecedenti exercitio talis vita assumatur, est periculosissima, nisi per divinam gratiam suppleatur quod in aliis per exercitium acquiritur; sicut patet de beatis Antonio et Benedicto."

[3] *Nicomachean Ethics*, X, 7, 1177 b 26.

[4] *Ibid.*, 1177 b 30–31.

It is quite remarkable that when, in the *Politics*,[1] Aristotle speaks of the too superior man whom the city must either exile or make king (and to tell the truth how could the ostracism of such a man be tolerable in a perfect city? "On the other hand, he ought not to be a subject—that would be as if mankind should claim to rule over Zeus";[2] the city should therefore take advantage of its good fortune and take him as its king)—Aristotle is not thinking here of the sage, or the philosopher, but of the hero of action, the man who is "deemed a God among men"[3] because he possesses preeminently the virtues of command and political genius. (One thinks of Alexander; many centuries later did not Hegel regard Napoleon as "God revealed"?)

Thus the vocation for wisdom and the vocation for political power are separated.[4] And henceforth the question presents itself of knowing whether the philosopher or the statesman leads the most enviable life.[5] Let us say that each excels in his own order, but to be loyal to Aristotle's principles on the superiority of the contemplative life, let us say that the order in which the philosopher excels is higher than that in which the statesman excels.[6]

The fact remains that neither is the philosopher a pure contemplative nor the statesman a pure man of action. The philosopher devotes himself especially but not exclusively to contemplation; he participates in the political life of the city. The statesman devotes himself especially but not exclusively to action; his very virtues require that he participate in some measure in the leisure of contemplation. For he must be wise, even if he is not dedicated to wisdom (this is why he needs the philosopher more than the ordinary citizen does).

The heroic life is therefore at once contemplative and active; and it is normal that all of human life should be drawn to it.[7] This is why, in the perfect city, something of this life—at once contemplative and active—would be the portion of every citizen; to one degree or another, in one form or another, he would have access to contemplative activity concentrated within itself and to

[1] *Politics*, III, 13, 1284 a 3–1284 b 34.

[2] *Ibid.*, 1284 b 30–31.

[3] *Ibid.*, 1284 a 10–11.

[4] Cf. *Eudemian Ethics*, I, 4, 1215 a 34–1215 b 4.

[5] *Politics*, VII, 2, 1324 a 25–34.

[6] In the rest of his discussion Aristotle is chiefly preoccupied with showing that the life of the despot or power-hungry man, who sacrifices virtue and justice to success, is worth nothing compared to the life of the statesman who is eminent in virtue as well as in capacity for action, and who never strays from justice (cf. VII, 3, 1325 b). But if he denounces the error of those who, putting the enjoyment of liberty without care above all else, "place inactivity above action" (1325 a 31), let us not forget that for Aristotle contemplation is the highest form of activity. Thus his apology for the authentic statesman is also, and even more, an apology for the life of the philosopher: to such a degree that since the best life for the city is the same as the best life for the individual, he considers the ideal condition for the city to be one of self-sufficiency, of having all its activity within itself, as it is for "God and the universe". (VII, 3, 1325 b 14–32.)

[7] Cf. *Nicomachean Ethics*, X, 7, 1177 b 19–23 and 1177 b 22–1178 a 2. Quoted below, p. 47.

practical activity turned outward: since these two activities, each in its own place, are integral parts of happiness.[1]

12. The city of Aristotle holds to justice. The "happy city" is the one which "acts rightly", and "neither individual nor state can do right actions without virtue and wisdom". There will be no good life for the city without "courage, justice and wisdom".[2] Political philosophy was to remain attached to this theme of moral rightness and justice as inherent in the common good of the city until the time of Machiavelli.

But Aristotle's city is at the same time—for the individuals who make it up—a good which is purely and simply supreme; the notion of the person has not emerged; and there is no suggestion that the human person—who is a part of the city and must work for its common good, and if necessary give his life for it—might nevertheless transcend the political order of the city according as he is himself directed to supra-temporal goods.

In saying that the good of all, or of political society, is more divine than the good of the individual,[3] Aristotle, like all classical Greek thought, directs the individual in all of his aspects to this more divine good—which St. Thomas was careful not to do[4] (though he liked to repeat Aristotle's phrase,[5] but as a formula to be interpreted freely according to the needs of each particular case). "If all communities aim at some good, the city-state or political community, which is the highest of all, and which embraces all the rest, aims at good in a greater degree than any other, and at the highest good."[6]

[1] The happiness of the city, and of humanity taken collectively, is the same sort of happiness as the happiness of the individual. (*Polit.*, VII, 2, 1324 a 5–7; 3, 1325 b 14–16; 1325 b 23–32).—Cf. *Polit.*, VII, 13, 1332 a 30–38; 14, 1333 a 11–16; 1333 b 36–37; 15, 1334 a 11–40.

[2] *Politics*, VII, 1, 1323 b 30–36.

[3] Cf. *Nicomachean Ethics*, I, 2, 1094 b 6–10: "For even if the end is the same for a single man and for a state, that of the state seems at all events something greater and more complete whether to attain or to preserve; though it is worth while to attain the end merely for one man, it is finer and more godlike to attain it for a nation or for city-states."

[4] Cf. *Sum. theol.*, I–II, 21, 4 *ad* 3: "Homo non ordinatur ad communitatem politicam secundum se totum et secundum omnia sua."—For a more fundamental understanding of the relation between individual and society one must have recourse to the distinction between *individuality* and *personality* which we consider one of the keys to the philosophy of St. Thomas. ("Ratio partis contrariatur rationi personae," *in III Sent.*, d. 5, q. 3, a. 2, resp. Cf. our book *The Person and the Common Good* (New York: Scribners, 1947), p. 61, and note 39 same page.) This distinction has been the source of many misunderstandings because certain intellects who are made uncomfortable by metaphysical "subtleties" took it for a distinction between things, whereas it is a distinction between one *ratio* and another, let us say between two notional aspects or two different poles of intelligibility within the same concrete "thing", which is the individual person. Cf. our books *Three Reformers* (New York: Scribners, 1937; London: Sheed and Ward, 1932), pp. 193–194; *Du Régime Temporel et de la Liberté* (Paris: Desclée De Brouwer et Cie, 1933), pp. 55–65.

[5] Cf. for example *Summa contra Gentiles*, III, 17: "Bonum gentis est divinius quam bonum unius hominis."

[6] *Politics*, I, 1, 1252 a 3–5.

It follows that for Aristotle the ruling, supreme science in the order of practical knowledge is politics;[1] it is to it that all ethics is directed.[2]

On this point St. Thomas Aquinas, while striving to keep using Aristotelian language, adds in his commentary on the *Nicomachean Ethics* that if political science is termed the ruling science, "this is not true absolutely speaking",[3] but only in a certain aspect. As a matter of fact, as he teaches elsewhere,[4] the end which comes under the consideration of politics is an ultimate end in a given order only (in the order of temporal civilization); if it is a question of the absolute ultimate end of human life, in other words of "the ultimate end of the whole universe", "it is the *scientia divina* which considers it, and it is she who is the ruling science in every respect".[5] Here we find ourselves far removed from the perspective of Aristotle himself. In his perspective the ultimate end was temporal: earthly happiness; and man achieved it in and by the city, directing himself to the good of the city as far as all that is in him is concerned.

If, on the other hand, we take the point of view indicated by St. Thomas, it will appear that a reinterpretation—actually a serious recasting—is in order of the division of ethics, classic in the peripatetic school, into "monastic" (concerned with the life of the individual), "economic" (concerned with the life of domestic society) and "political" (concerned with the life of civil society)[6]—with politics having primacy over the two other parts of moral knowledge. For if the ethics of the individual person remain directed to the ethics of the city, or to politics, in this sense that not only in his political activity, but in his private activity itself and his virtues as a private person the individual must take into consideration the common good of the city and direct himself to this end,[7] nevertheless this end is supreme only *secundum quid* or in a given order. It is to the separate common Good, to God Who infinitely transcends the cosmos and human society, that the activity and the virtues of the individual are directed, as to their purely and simply ultimate end. And in this light, which is primordial, the ethics of the individual identifies itself with an ethics of the common good which Aristotle did not and could not know, and which is above politics as the heavens are above the earth, and which one might call the ethics of the kingdom of God. There the supreme common good of the society of men en route toward their final end is identical with the most personal supreme good of the individual person en

[1] *Nicomachean Ethics*, I, 2, 1094 a 27–29.

[2] Cf. *Magna Moralia*, I, 1, 1181 a–1181 b.

[3] *In Ethic.*, I, lect. 2, n. 31.

[4] Cf. *De Virt. in communi*, a. 9; *De Virt. cardin.*, a. 4; *in III Sent.*, dist. 33, q. 1, a. 4, resp.; *Sum. theol.*, I–II, 65, 2; *In Polit.*, Prooemium, no. 7.

[5] *In Ethic.*, I, lect. 2, n. 31.

[6] *Ibid.*, I, lect. 1, n. 6.

[7] "*Virtutes cardinales ordinantur ad bonum civile*," writes St. Thomas, *De Virt. cardin.*, 4, obj. 3 (but "*bonum civile non est finis ultimus virtutum cardinalium infusarum, sed virtutum acquisitarum de quibus philosophi sunt locuti*", *ibid.*, *ad* 3).

route toward his final end: God to be possessed by the vision of His essence; which will be the beatitude of all and which will also be the beatitude of each.[1]

13. I just said that Aristotle could not know such an ethics of transcendent common good: it belongs to the supernatural order, and depends on the revelation progressively made to the prophets of Israel and consummated in the Gospel. But what Aristotle might have known, and did not, is the fact that in the natural order itself the "monastic", as far as it considers the purely and simply final end of human life, identifies itself with a supra-political ethics. For even in the purely natural order (where there is no question of beatific vision) it is not the earthly city but God Who is the absolute final end of man as of the whole universe.[2] And even in the purely natural order there is for human persons, members of the city, a common good which is superior to that of the city, that is the common good of minds,[3] the supra-temporal order of goods, of truths and of intangible laws which reveal themselves to the intellect—and which human life could not do without. The common good of the earthly city itself demands that the city recognize this supra-political common good, and that the persons who are members of the city direct themselves to it, thus transcending the political order of the city by what is eternal in man and in the things to which he is attached. One might say that it took the fracas of revelation and the scandal of grace coming to complete nature to make philosophy see these supreme data of the natural order, which it had been looking at all along, without realizing it.

It is the same here as with the creation, or the immortality of the soul, or the *Esse per se subsistens* and its knowledge of the world. If Aristotle did not know these things, if in his political philosophy he thought that the city was for individuals a purely and simply supreme good, and that there is no way in which the person transcends the city, it is not that his principles obliged him to think so, but rather that he did not follow his principles far enough. What he did not know how to bring out or see explicitly, he held implicitly. We said above that the Greek conception of the city was hieropolitical and not totalitarian. This is especially true of Aristotle's political philosophy; the spirit of this philosophy is profoundly opposed to totalitarianism. And to tell the truth it was at the price of a latent contradiction that Aristotle did not bring out the truths we insisted on above, which his own principles called for.

If the city is committed to justice, it is because without justice there is no "good life" or happiness; doubtless yes, but why is there no happiness or "good life" for the city without justice, if not because the city must recognize

[1] Cf. our book, *The Person and the Common Good*, pp. 75–76.

[2] Cf. below, Chap. V, p. 76.

[3] Cf. our books *The Person and the Common Good*, pp. 52–55 and 71–74, and *Man and the State*, Chicago: Univ. of Chicago Press, 1951, pp. 148–150; London: Hollis and Carter, 1954.

laws which matter more than its own advantage or even its own existence? For there are instances where the city, like the individual, can serve justice only to its own detriment. To say that the city is committed to justice is to say that it is not a purely and simply supreme good.

And what does all Aristotle's teaching on contemplation mean, if not that there are for man goods of another, and better, order than that of political life? In pursuing these goods the individual serves the common good of the earthly city, to be sure—in fact the city needs the impetus given it by those who live according to the intellect, and the wisdom which comes down from their contemplation and incorporates itself in the common heritage; but it is not *for* love of the common good of the earthly city that the individual pursues these goods; it is for love of these goods themselves.

If it is true that "the activity of reason, which is contemplative . . . seems to aim at no end beyond itself, and to have its pleasure proper to itself . . . and the self-sufficiency, leisureliness, untrammelled state" characteristic of perfect happiness;[1] and if it is true that "we must not follow those who advise us, being men, to think of human things, and, being mortal, of mortal things", but must on the contrary "so far as we can, make ourselves immortal, and strain every nerve to live in accordance with the best in us; for even if it be small in bulk, much more does it in power and worth surpass everything"[2]—then it must be said that there are goods and activities for man which depend on an order superior to that of political life; and that with respect to all that which in man concerns these goods and activities, the person emerges above the mortal city, and passes beyond its good, "more divine" as it may be.

The Paradox of Aristotelian Ethics

14. I should like to point out, in conclusion, what one may call the paradox of Aristotelian ethics. There is no moral system more thoroughly and authentically humanistic. And there is no moral system more disappointing for man. At this point it is permissible to speak of the defeats which Aristotelian ethics cannot avoid.

The first Defeat

15. The sovereign good, Happiness, has been brought back to earth, humanized, adapted to the structure and to the essential aspirations of our nature. Yes, but it involves so many ingredients and so many conditions which are hardly attainable—even for a small number of individuals, for a limited aristocracy of philosophers.

It goes without saying that Aristotle had no such consequence in mind. His intentions were generous. He remarked, for example, that "if the beautiful life" consisted "in the gifts of good fortune or of nature, it would be

[1] *Nicomachean Ethics*, X, 7, 1177 b 19–22.
[2] *Ibid.*, 1177 b 32–1178 a 2.

something that not many could hope for and that neither their precautions nor their efforts would permit them to attain; but that if it depended on the individual and on the character of his personal acts, then the sovereign good" would be "at the same time more generally possessed and more divine—more generally possessed because accessible to a greater number, more divine because happiness is then the prize offered to those who impress a certain character on their person and on their acts".[1]

And yet in fact, given the structure of Hellenic society (approved by Aristotle), the philosophical contemplation of truth and of things divine is rendered possible for free men only thanks to slavery and the servile labor of the greatest number; and even then, even at this price, such contemplation, which is the principal ingredient of the good and beautiful life, can only be the privilege of a very limited number of sages among these free citizens.

What is more, those who achieve happiness must also possess the virtues, lead a virtuous life. And they must not only lead a virtuous life but also a life crowned by pleasure. They must know the joys of culture and of art and all the beauty of the world, and not be exempt from an appreciable enjoyment of the corporal pleasures.

And they must have friends whose very presence will intensify their effort toward virtue, and whose society will add charm to existence.

And they must have money, enough worldly possessions to profit by their freedom. And good health is also necessary, in order that the higher activity and peace of the spirit not be troubled or destroyed by bodily ills. And they must not be the victims of misfortune—chance, finally, plays its role. A certain measure of good fortune is required.

There we have the happiness of man. Who, then, as things really go, is capable of attaining the sovereign good, that sovereign good the thirst for which is the source and the fundamental motivation of our whole moral life? It is understandable that Aristotle should ask himself sometimes if, "supposing the choice were offered us, not to have been born would not be the most desirable" thing.[2]

Our whole moral life, all our effort and striving toward rightness and virtue, are suspended from an End which, in fact, eludes us, vanishes within our grasp.

This is the first defeat suffered by Aristotelian ethics.

The second Defeat

16. A second defeat is involved, which derives from the eudemonist conception itself. Aristotle, in agreement with Socrates and all the Greeks, identifies the sovereign Good and Happiness. Now Happiness is, so to speak, the subjective side of the Good; in the concept of Happiness the notion of Good

[1] *Eudemian Ethics*, I, 3, 1215 a 13–19.
[2] Cf. *Eudemian Ethics*, I, 5, 1215 b 20–22.

refers back to the subject. If there is no good which is desired and loved more than Happiness, it is inevitable that Happiness should be desired and loved for the sake of the subject it beatifies.

There are many things, according to Aristotle's conception of happiness, which man loves and desires for their own sake and for their intrinsic goodness—in a way which transcends his own interest, even when his own interest is involved: contemplated truth, wisdom, virtue, all that which depends on the beautiful-and-good (*bonum honestum*). It even happens that he loves them more than his own life. But from the moment that they are included in the overall idea of Happiness, subordinated to that idea, and desired as ingredients of Happiness, from the moment that Happiness takes precedence and becomes purely and simply the supreme End, this whole which is Happiness and which is desired and loved as such can only be desired and loved for the sake of the subject whom it perfects. Even in the case of the philosophic contemplation of truth and of things divine, it would be for the good of my own intellect that I loved them if I loved them only as an ingredient of my happiness. Implicitly, the ethics of Happiness was an ethics of the Good. But this fact remains implicit, veiled. He never makes explicit and precise the distinction between the Good and Happiness which, as a matter of fact, his own metaphysical system requires (since for him it is the Thought of Thought attracting to itself the whole universe which constitutes the absolute End, and thus the supreme Good-in-itself), and which is in a very real way operative in his own ethical judgments and in his moral system. As a result, because this distinction between the Good and Happiness is nowhere clearly elucidated in his moral system, Aristotle leaves us in a state of ambiguity. In spite of everything, in the last analysis his moral teaching leaves us enclosed in love of ourselves. It is *my* good that I love and will in willing and loving Happiness as the supreme Good supremely loved, that is to say the Good taken subjectively, the Good as a perfection of the subject and a resonance in the subject or as a fulfillment of human life. It is a good which I will *propter me*, for my own sake, for love of myself. It is impossible for Aristotelian ethics to escape from the embrace of the Self, from a kind of transcendental egoism. Within the moral perspective of Happiness as the supreme Good, I cannot deliver myself, I can never be delivered of myself, I can never be freed from my egoistical love of myself. And yet in the end it is just such a deliverance that we long for.

The ineffectiveness of the appeal made to Man by the End proposed

17. The two defeats we have just pointed out indicate the practical, existential weakness of Aristotelian ethics. By a curious paradox, it happens that all its principles are true (in particular, the very principle of eudemonism is true, in the sense that Happiness is the last *subjective* End of human life, or the last

end *relative to the human subject*; Aristotle's error was in not going *further*—and could he, with only the weapons of philosophical reason?). All the principles of Aristotle's ethics are true, all its themes are carefully adjusted to what is most human in man. And yet they remain ineffective in fact, they do not come to grips with existence, they do not succeed in taking hold of the internal dynamism of the human will. They ought to have a decisive and imperious appeal for man—they do not at all.

This is the case above all because Happiness as ultimate subjective End did not lead the Philosopher to discover a supreme Good which is loved more than Happiness, a Good worth more than Happiness and for the love of which our Happiness itself is loved. Thus the supreme Good was identified with Happiness. The last End relative to the human subject, the last End as *my* fulfillment or my supreme perfection, or as End in which *my* nature and *my* being are realized, the last End taken subjectively, blocked Aristotle's vision of the last End *in and for itself*, which at the same time he implicitly recognized. It did not totally replace (as was to happen with the Epicureans) but left in shadow the supreme Good to which I and my Happiness are ordered. From this moment the supreme End, remaining essentially human, also remains involved in human complexity. It is proportioned to man and commensurate with man, that is to say with the deception inherent in the human condition, the precariousness and the falsity of human goods. It is the sum and the summit of a collection of goods each of which is uncertain and menaced—a fragile and fleeting supreme End, deprived of all power of *decisive attraction*.

True as they are (but incomplete), the true principles of Aristotle's moral philosophy do not penetrate the concrete existential reality of the human being. They are incapable of stirring his aspirations and his profoundest hopes, which go beyond rational and reasonable happiness, incapable of probing the recesses of his ego and the world of the irrational with its impulses toward death and the void. In a word, what is infinite in man has been forgotten. The *vanitas vanitatum* of the Preacher is the reverse side of Aristotelian eudemonism.

The moral philosophy of Aristotle, which is the truest and the most authentic, the most honest of purely philosophical ethical theories, lacks effectiveness and existential bearing because it is a system of means suspended from an End which does not possess the value of an End *practically* absolute, nor the value of an End *practically* accessible, nor the value of an End *practically* constraining.

Aristotle was right to seek in happiness—I use the word in its most indeterminate sense, the happiness toward which we tend not by choice but by necessity of nature—the point of departure of ethics. But when it comes to the point of arrival, and the determination of what the true happiness of man consists in, the happiness toward which we must tend by free choice, then he sees neither that this true happiness is in fact something beyond purely human happiness, nor that it is itself ordered to a Good which is better and loved more than any happiness. The supreme good which he proposes to us is incapable of a decisive hold on existence.

Aristotelian ethics is *par excellence* the natural (purely natural) ethics and the philosophical (purely philosophical) ethics. And in what concerns the real direction of human conduct it runs aground in inefficacy.

4

ETHICS TRIUMPHANT

Stoics and Epicureans

In search of Effectiveness

1. I have just spoken of the defeats of Aristotle's eminently reasonable and balanced moral philosophy. These defeats, this incapacity of philosophical wisdom to serve as guide and mistress of human conduct, were what the thinkers who followed Aristotle could not accept. They are doctors of the happy life; what they seek above all else is effectiveness. The supreme End and the sovereign Good must be within the grasp of every individual, if only he is sufficiently determined (and if he listens to the new doctors).

But the price of this rush toward moral efficiency was to be a narrowing of the field of vision, total domination by an *idée fixe*, fascination with a single aspect of ethical reality to the exclusion of others and carried to its ultimate extreme.

This tendency constituted a return in the direction of Socrates, but it was accompanied by the passionate fervor for immediate effectiveness which I just mentioned, and it operated within the hardened confines of a system which aspired to exhaustiveness: the supreme good coincides with the ruling quality in human conduct, and Happiness coincides with Wisdom, that is, with the rational organization of life according to the absolute rule of that unique dominating quality—Virtue, or Pleasure.[1]

[1] "Ancient Stoicism" (Zeno, Cleanthes, Chrysippus) which can be traced back to Socrates by way of the Cynics and the Megarians, though it had many other sources also (Ionian and Heraclitean tradition, greco-semitic religious inspiration), developed during the course of the third century B.C.; "middle Stoicism" (Panaetius, Posidonius) took up the end of the second century and the first century B.C.; the third great Stoic branch was the Stoicism of the imperial epoch or the "Roman Stoicism" of the first two centuries A.D. (Seneca, Epictetus, Marcus Aurelius).

The Epicurean school, which goes back to Socrates through Aristippus of Cyrene, and beyond Socrates to Democritus, was founded by Epicurus at Athens in 306 B.C., and remained for a long time one of the four great Athenian schools. It bore its finest fruit in the poem of Lucretius in the first century B.C. (though this work is informed with a grand pessimism quite different from the unavowed, repressed disenchantment of Epicurus himself).

Cf. Paul Elmer More, *Hellenistic Philosophies*, Princeton University Press, 1923 (London: O.U.P., 1924); Emile Bréhier, *Histoire de la Philosophie*, Paris: Presses Universitaires, 1948, vol. II, Hellenistic and Roman Period; R. D. Hicks, *Stoic and Epicurean*, London, 1910; G. Rodier, "Histoire extérieure et intérieure du Stoïcisme" (in *Études de Philosophie grecque*, Paris, 1926); V. Brochard, "La Morale d'Épicure" (in *Études de Philosophie ancienne et moderne*, Paris, 1912); J. Lebreton, "Le monde païen et la conquête chrétienne"

I

THE ATHLETICISM OF VIRTUE—AN ETHICS OF PURE VALUE

For "the Porch" only Virtue is Good

2. The Stoics identified Virtue (moral Force) and the Good. Aristotle distinguished between the virtuous act, which is worthy of praise, and the final Good, or Happiness, to which the epithet "worthy of praise" is not applicable. But Chrysippus taught that the Good itself is worthy of praise, because the only Good is the Noble and the Beautiful (the *bonum honestum*), in other words virtue and the virtuous act. Virtue does not tend toward any external end, it suffices to itself, is desirable in and for itself, *in se tota conversa*, is entirely turned in upon itself, and is perfect as soon as it exists.

For the Stoics it is no longer contemplation, but action, which is at the summit of human life—action, that is, moral virtue. The sage as conceived by the Stoics is a superman, not, as in the Platonic tradition (or even in the Aristotelian tradition), because he participates in the supra-human life of the intellect and of philosophical contemplation (which by the very fact of being supra-human is, as we have noted, eminently human and desirable for man), but he is a superman of Virtue, of moral Action and moral Force. The supreme end of life, the highest good, is virtue. Only virtue is good in the full sense of the word, and virtue consists in the immutable conformity of man with reason and with himself. Virtue is therefore at the same time a completely consistent rational (practical) knowledge, and a supreme force and tension. It signifies that man has become fully master of himself by living in conformity with nature, ὁμολογουμένως τῇ φύσει. By the word "nature" here is not to be understood, certainly, the simple facts and natural events observable by the senses, nor, on the other hand, the essence of the human being, the τό τι εἶναι in Aristotle's sense, but rather the intelligible and rational influx hidden beneath sensible appearances, which at the same time governs the universe and the human being. It is in this connection that the idea of natural law came to be elucidated with particular force by the Stoics. To live in conformity with nature is to live in conformity with the royal law of nature, with the divine will immanent in the cosmos. This in itself implies that one knows that all things happen in virtue of universal Reason, of the immutable Intention which is consubstantial with things and is active in the world, in short, that all things happen through Destiny. That being true, the essential thing is the interior

---

I, La philosophie religieuse du Stoïcisme (*Les Études*, June 1925); Arnim, *Stoicorum Veterum Fragmenta*, Leipzig, 1903, 1905, 1914; *The Discourses of Epictetus*, trans. P. E. Matheson, *The Meditations of Marcus Aurelius*, trans. G. Long, *The Extant Writings of Epicurus*, trans. C. Bailey, in: *The Stoic and Epicurean Philosophers*, ed. Whitney J. Oates New York: Random House, 1940.

disposition of the will, the supreme voluntary acceptance, fully conscious and completely invulnerable, of the world as it is, of every event as it happens, and of every misfortune as it is meted out to us, since all this is an expression of the perfectly inevitable, perfectly rational and perfectly good designs of nature and its God.

The Super-human in moral Virtue

3. Stoicism thus seeks the super-human in that which is in itself most strictly centered upon the human, in moral virtue, moral action, the force and power of the human *subject*—not in some transcendent and supra-human *object* to which man is to unite himself. The result was to be an inflation or hypertrophy of the human subject, and a kind of moral athleticism or human spiritual athleticism, a deification of human virtue, hand in hand with a monist or pantheist conception of the universe.

As far as external things are concerned, some are indifferent, and some are to be preferred, not because they are goods but because they correspond to tendencies which in fact exist in our nature. These preferable things are not goods—only virtue is a good. In other words, the good is entirely confined within the sphere of the voluntary. Consequently, nothing external to man is necessary to man's perfection, and the sage needs nothing but his internal voluntary power, or his Virtue. Virtue suffices for happiness, and is happiness. This does not mean that it renders the sage insensible to pain, but that it makes him superior to pain.

Now this sage, enclosed in his virtue and sovereignly dominating himself and all things, is he superior and indifferent in respect to no matter what line of conduct, as he is superior and indifferent in respect to no matter what event? The Stoics did not fall into quietism, because they admitted, as we noted a moment ago, that certain things are to be preferred as distinguished from certain others; as a result there existed for them a multitude of *officia*, or *advisable* actions (καθήκοντα), which have to do with the ordinary course of life, and which are equally "things to be done" for the sage and for others. These are not precepts or *duties* in the categorical sense of that word, they are rather reasonable directions in the art of right living, *counsels*. Thus there developed a whole Moral System of counsels, with an appropriate casuistry, which covered the whole field of what is ordinarily called Morality, but which for the Stoics was only a secondary or external Morality, an appearance of Morality, the only authentic Morality having to do with saintly virtue, with the voluntary super-power of the sage.

As for the sage, he not only does what is advisable (καθῆκον), he does it with the internal superabundance proper to his Virtue as a superman, to the perfect and indestructible harmony between his will and the fixed will of Nature or God. For it is essential to perfect moral rectitude, or to intrinsically just and right conduct (κατορθῶμα), that all one does be done with the right internal disposition, or through the possession and power of all the virtues concentrated into one, since it is only he who unites in himself all the virtues who can truly be said to possess virtue.

4. The philosophers of the Porch not only conceived that all the virtues are "connected" or related to one another (which is quite true), and that I cannot exercise justice without also being courageous, nor have the virtue of courage if I do not have the virtue of making right practical decisions ("prudence"), nor have prudence if I do not have temperance; but for the Stoics it was necessary to have all the virtues in a state of *full development*, the sage being perfect from the very beginning, thanks to the kind of transmutation which makes of the whole man a personification of Reason.[1] As we have already remarked, virtue consisted essentially for them in a certain interior disposition of the will, constant, immutable, adamantine, in a *super-virtue* which is seen as prudence, courage or justice in its different aspects; and so in the end, at least in the case of Zeno, it is the *unity of virtue* rather than the interconnectedness of the virtues that they taught.

As for the passions and emotions, they result from a failure to bring right judgment to bear upon the problem of what is good and what is bad. No emotion is profitable, or in conformity with the order of nature. The sage has attained the state of *apatheia*; he is without passion, though he is not insensible. He makes room in his soul only for that which is thoroughly rational, he never commits an error, the least of his acts contains as much wisdom as his conduct as a whole, he knows neither fear nor regret nor sadness—he lives in perfect happiness. No delays, no half-measures! Stoic ethics leads us straight away into a state of blessedness. Only the sage is free. He is king and lord; he is not inferior in his internal dignity to any other being, not even to Jupiter. He is the equal of God.

From such a notion of wisdom and virtue, the early Stoics concluded that virtue is something indivisible, in which no distinction of more or less is possible. There is no mean between virtue and vice. A man may be tending toward virtue, approaching it—in reality he is as denuded of virtue as the vicious man. Is not the person who drowns in a bucket of water just as drowned as the one who drowns in the depths of the sea? Both are in a similar state of vice or folly. Consequently, Zeno divided mankind purely and simply into two categories: sages or perfect men, and the bad or foolish—that is, all the others. Such extremism derived, we believe, from the thirst for effectiveness which we pointed out at the beginning. Totally intransigeant, simplist, absolute exigencies have a stronger appeal than a reasonable and moderate ideal (and one which is long-term and seen at once to be difficult of attainment because of its complexity, like the Aristotelian ideal). At least this is true at the beginning, and for those who are persuaded that they fit into

[1] Cf. Clement of Alexandria, *Strom.*, IV, 6 (Migne, *P.G.*, t. VIII, col. 1240).

Zeno's first category, the other category being rightly reserved for my neighbor, not for myself.

But disappointment comes nevertheless, with time. One perceives that it is no joke to make the first category. One wonders if, after all, Stoic perfection is not entirely *too* rare (considering that I myself may be straining for it in vain). What's more, is it even possible? In the end, the last Stoics were to admit that no one fulfilled the conditions of true virtue, and they despaired of the very existence of the sage, of that superman in whom Zeno and Chrysippus had placed all their hope, and the hope of human life.

Emphasis on Value and the aspiration to a heroic moral life

5. Stoicism made a considerable contribution to moral philosophy, not by bringing to light some fundamental new element, but by showing forth at once the grandeur and the harsh demands of the authentically moral life, by insisting on the interior character of virtue, and especially by clearly emphasizing that aspect of the good (the beautiful-and-good, *bonum honestum*) which is value. Stoic ethics is an ethics of pure value, doubtless not excluding happiness and beatitude from the proper realm of morality as Kant was to do, but making them immediately coincide with value. Moral value, being itself the supreme end in this ethical view, brings with it a kind of "salvation"—such as a naturalistic system was able to conceive it: not to be swallowed up in the sea of folly, in which life is wasted, and where it would be better for man not to have been born.

But this whole process depends upon my own effort and my own force. It points towards a complete self-sufficiency, in which the whole energy of the cosmos is concentrated in the energy of the sage. Salvation, and divine autonomy, are to be acquired through my own power as a man, in communion with universal reason. I make myself a member of the family of the gods.

At the root of the Stoic illusion is the *absolutisation*, or rather the deification of moral virtue. As we have already remarked, this amounted to seeking superman in that which by its essence is on a scale with human reason and relates to human action as such, and qualifies the human subject as such; it amounted to seeking the super-human in that which is of itself centered upon the human. Ethics itself is in reality something humbly human, laborious, patient, prudent, which carries the golden rule of reason into the midst of human relativities, and weighs great and little actions in the scales of a diamond-cutter. The Stoics endeavored to make of it something sublime—the high-priest of the deification of man, charged with separating the elect from the damned and pronouncing the condemnation of the mass of fools.

Stoicism was a great attempt at heroic moral living. With Seneca, especially with Epictetus and Marcus Aurelius, and through its insistence on the interior life, its pointing up of the natural law, its idea of the *caritas humani generis*, it was able, in spite of the paganism which animated it and its pantheistic worship of a God who was only Emperor of the world,[1] to manifest a kind of kinship with Christian themes. Many particular insights of Stoic philosophy were to be taken up and utilized by the Christian writers of the first centuries of the Christian era. This fact can only be understood as a result of one of those encounters which occurs between radically opposed perspectives, and one of those fundamental equivocations in which history delights. In this case the equivocation was in a sense a fecund one, providing a fund of conceptual material which Christian thought made use of; but at the same time this very conceptualization was to bear the mark of certain misapprehensions which for a time obscured profounder truths or hindered their expression.

Natural Law

6. We said above that the idea of natural law was stressed with particular force by the Stoics. It might be useful to make a few remarks here about the conception of natural law held by antiquity.

The celebrated fragment 114 of Heraclitus[2] refers both to natural law and to eternal law: ". . . All human laws are nourished by the single divine law: deploying its power as it will, equal to anything and everywhere victorious."

An aristocrat and a conservative, Heraclitus concluded from this that the laws of the city are sacred. "The people must fight for their law as well as for their ramparts."[3]

Later Sophocles, in *Antigone*, was also to invoke natural law, but in an entirely different context: natural law is higher than human law, and the law of the prince has no force when it violates the unwritten laws, the unchangeable laws of heaven.

". . . nor deemed I that thy decrees were of such force, that a mortal could override the unwritten and unfailing statutes of heaven. For their life is not of to-day or yesterday, but from all time, and no man knows when they were first put forth. Not through dread of any human pride could I answer to the gods for breaking *these*."[4]

The views of the Sophists on natural law came up in our first chapter. For them it was a question of opposing the individual to custom and convention. In the same spirit Euripides wrote:

> "If there is aught that causes slaves to blush
> It is the name; in all else than the free
> The slave is nothing worse, if he be virtuous."[5]

[1] Cf. our essay on "The Meaning of Contemporary Atheism", in *The Range of Reason*, New York: Scribners, 1953; London: Bles, 1953.

[2] For bibliography, see G. S. Kirk, *Heraclitus, The Cosmic Fragments*, Cambridge University Press, 1954.

[3] Fr. 44.

[4] *Antigone* II, 452–460. Trans. R. C. Jebb, in *The Complete Greek Drama*, ed. Oates and O'Neill, New York: Random House, 1938, Vol. I.

[5] *Ion*, II, 854–856. Trans. Robert Dotter, in *The Complete Greek Drama*.

For Plato as for Heraclitus it was above all to be a question of making firm the law of the city on an unshakeable foundation. Although neither Plato nor Aristotle treated explicitly of natural law, it was with them that the real philosophical meaning of the natural law took form. In the case of Plato this philosophical meaning is linked with the world of archetypal ideas; a physician is not a real physician, nor a judge a real judge, unless he embodies in some way the idea of Judge or of Physician. Moreover Plato does not hesitate to use the expression "according to nature", κατὰ φύσιν, to designate the conformity of a thing with its idea or type.[1] Thus the notion of normality is brought out.

But it is with Aristotle that this notion is put sharply in relief. With him it is linked not with the archetypal idea, but with the essence or intelligible nature which is within things as the primary "form" by which they exist and act. This essence is within things but it is grasped separately and in its universality by the mind, and it implies ideal exigencies; and things act *normally* only if they respond effectively to these exigencies of their essence and tend straightly to the end it implies. For in Aristotle's dynamic conception all essence is the assignment of an end, a *telos*—which beings endowed with reason pursue freely, not by necessity. Become in your action what you are in your essence—here is the primordial rule of ethics.

From this it follows that one must distinguish between natural justice and legal justice. The latter has its origin in the reason and will of the legislator, the former in what man is. It is defined in terms of what is unalterably demanded by human nature, and it gives authenticity and force of law to human law, brought to bear in such and such circumstances and for the common good of such and such a particular city.

7. By very reason of its intelligible structure the idea of natural law comprises, if I may put it thus, two different and complementary fundamental themes. One of these themes is: obedience in conscience to human law, because natural law itself requires that man live in society, and that what it leaves undetermined be determined by human reason. Plato and Aristotle clung to this theme above all, because it was above all the city which they had in view; if they did not elaborate an explicit theory of natural law (though they laid its philosophical foundations) it was because once the law of the city had been justified in reason, the rest, for them, was secondary.

The other theme is a contrary one: resistance to human law if it is unjust—this is Antigone's theme; or again, and with a universally positive bearing: recognition of the natural dignity of the individual, in the very bosom of the social whole (henceforth to be vaster than the city-state) of which he is a member—this is the theme of the Stoics.

George Sabine insists with reason on the decisively important effect on the

[1] Cf. Werner Jaeger, *Paideia*, II, p. 390, note 48; p. 407, note 202; III, p. 346, note 216.

development of the Stoic doctrine of natural law which resulted from the historical failure of the city-state after the death of Alexander the Great and of Aristotle.[1] Once the bonds of the city had been broken, and the various monarchies where Greeks and "barbarians" were subject to the same power had risen out of Alexander's empire, individuals found themselves isolated, each alone in the great "inhabited world" and "had to learn to live together in a new form of social union much larger and much more impersonal than the city-state".[2] Owing to this new historical situation, Hellenistic man was obliged to take stock of himself as a human being, equal, as such, to the other members of the human race. Thus the equality among co-citizens which Aristotle strongly emphasized—but which for him was limited to the privileged few who were members of the city—extended now to all, even to the slave, to the foreigner, to the barbarian; they were co-citizens of the whole civilized world. . .

The founder of the Stoic school, Zeno of Citium, was a Phoenician; Chrysippus, the second founder, came from Cilicia; and Panaetius, who carried Stoicism to Rome, was a naiive of Rhodes. More cosmopolitan than Greek, Stoicism was especially adapted to the new aspirations we just mentioned.

Already Cleanthes, in the earliest epoch of Stoicism, cried out:

> "Zeus the all-bountiful, whom darkness shrouds,
> Whose lightning lightens in the thunder-clouds;
> Thy children save from error's deadly sway:
> Turn thou the darkness from their souls away:
> Vouchsafe that unto knowledge they attain;
> For thou by knowledge art made strong to reign
> O'er all, and all things rulest righteously.
> So by thee honoured, we will honour thee,
> Praising thy works continually with songs,
> As mortals should; nor higher meed belongs
> E'en to the gods, than justly to adore
> The *universal law* for evermore."[3]

With Chrysippus, in the last quarter of the third century, the idea of the city of the world and of a law valid for all was to come to the fore. A spark of the divine fire which animates the world animates every human being. As Epictetus was to say later: "If a man could only take to heart this judgment, as he ought, that we are all, before anything else, children of God and that

[1] Cf. George Sabine, *A History of Political Theory*, Revised Edition, New York: Henry Holt, 1950, ch. VIII; London: Harrap, 1951.

[2] *Ibid.*, p. 141.

[3] *Hymn to Zeus*, in *The Stoic and Epicurean Philosophers*, ed. W. J. Oates, Appendix, pp. 591–592.

God is the Father of gods and men, I think that he will never harbour a mean or ignoble thought about himself. Why, if Caesar adopts you, your arrogance will be past all bearing; but if you realize that you are a son of Zeus, will you feel no elation?"[1] Chrysippus taught that there is no slave by nature, that a slave is a servant who has been engaged for life. Greeks and barbarians, nobles and commoners, rich and poor, slaves and free men—all are equal. The only real difference is that which separates the wise and the foolish. Gods and men are citizens of the great city of the world, and this city is ruled by right reason alone; its law is the same for all, irrespective of the political power to which they are subject. In order to conciliate the idea that each individual must consider himself proudly as a son of God with the traditional idea, to which the Stoics were faithful, of the major importance of the social whole, to which the individual is essentially subordinate, the Stoic school came more and more to consider the various kingdoms of the earth (and finally the Roman empire) as rough sketches of that divine city of the world, or as roads leading to it. (And henceforth for centuries two notions were to intermingle—the ethical notion of the natural law proper to the human race, and the socio-political notion of the juridical order proper to a universal and truly rational human political community.)

Thus there was interaction between the development of Stoic ethics and the progressive broadening of juridical concepts. The latter were to appeal more and more to the universality of legislative reason, and to a sort of "common law" (imposed by the monarch irrespective of the diversity of customs or resulting from arbitration procedures between cities), and were finally to issue forth in the Roman law of nations (*jus gentium*), produced, like a precious fruit of civilization, from what was originally only laws concerning strangers.

This is why natural law and the *jus gentium*, in Cicero's time, definitely began to cross together the threshold of commonly accepted ideas. Let us say that it was under the protective covering of the juridical idea of *jus gentium* that the philosophical idea of natural law succeeded in imposing itself explicitly on the common consciousness: a phenomenon which was made easier by the pantheist confusion between human reason and divine reason, and which involved fairly damaging confusions between the two ideas themselves of natural law and *jus gentium*.[2]

8. Whatever may be said about this last point, it is to the Stoics that we owe the major theory of natural law elaborated by antiquity, and the

[1] *Arrian's Discourses of Epictetus*, I, ch. III, in *The Stoic and Epicurean Philosophers*, p. 229.

[2] On the distinction between the *jus gentium* (which depends—at least as regards the way in which its laws are known—on the conceptual exercise of human reason) and natural law (which depends on divine reason alone and is known through natural inclinations), cf. our study "Natural Law and Moral Law", in *Moral Principles of Action*, edited by Ruth Nanda Anshen, New York: Harper, 1952—See George H. Sabine, *op. cit.*, p. 157.

explicitly developed philosophical theme of two laws: on the one hand the human law which varies from city to city, and on the other hand the universal and unchangeable law of nature (*non scripta, sed nata lex*) which is innate in the human soul and whose prescriptions we are compelled to recognize. This idea was to remain fundamental to the Romanized and more or less syncretic Stoicism in which Panaetius of Rhodes, prodded by the criticisms of Carneades, tried to absorb the classical tradition of Plato and Aristotle. It was from Panaetius that Cicero received this idea in order to popularize it (the amplifications of an orator were enough for this) throughout the civilized *orbis*.

"There is in fact a true law," he wrote in the *Republic*, "—namely, right reason—which is in accordance with nature, applies to all men, and is unchangeable and eternal. By its commands this law summons men to the performance of their duties; by its prohibitions it restrains them from doing wrong. Its commands and prohibitions always influence good men, but are without effect upon the bad. To invalidate this law by human legislation is never morally right, nor is it permissible ever to restrict its operation, and to annul it is wholly impossible. Neither the senate nor the people can absolve us from our obligation to obey this law, and it requires no Sextus Aelius to expound and interpret it. It will not lay down one rule at Rome and another at Athens, nor will it be one rule to-day and another to-morrow. But there will be one law, eternal and unchangeable, binding at all times upon all peoples; and there will be, as it were, one common master and ruler of men, namely God, who is the author of this law, its interpreter, and its sponsor. The man who will not obey it will abandon his better self, and, in denying the true nature of a man, will thereby suffer the severest of penalties, though he has escaped all the other consequences which men call punishments."[1]

And again, in the *Laws*: "Out of all the material of the philosophers' discussions, surely there comes nothing more valuable than the full realization that we are born for Justice, and that right is based, not upon man's opinions, but upon Nature"[2] . . .

"If the principles of Justice were founded on the decrees of peoples, the edicts of princes, or the decisions of judges, then Justice would sanction robbery and adultery and forgery by the votes or decrees of the populace. But if so great a power belongs to the decisions and decrees of fools that the laws of Nature can be changed by their votes, then why do they not ordain that what is bad and baneful shall be considered good and salutary? Or, if a law can make Justice out of Injustice, can it not also make good out of bad? But in fact we can perceive the difference between good laws and bad by referring them to no other standard than Nature: indeed, it is not merely Justice and Injustice which are distinguished by Nature, but also and without exception

[1] Cicero, *Republic*, III, 22.
[2] Cicero, *Laws*, I, 10.

things which are honourable and dishonourable. For since an intelligence common to us all makes things known to us and formulates them in our minds, honourable actions are ascribed by us to virtue, and dishonourable actions to vice; and only a madman would conclude that these judgments are matters of opinion, and not fixed by Nature."[1]

Later Epictetus was to condemn in the name of natural law those "laws of the dead" which upheld slavery. Marcus Aurelius was to echo Seneca's *homo sacra res homini*,[2] saying: "My city and country, so far as I am Antoninus, is Rome; but so far as I am a man, it is the world."[3]

But for all of them, natural law (where God instructs the conscience concerning its first norms by means of the essential inclinations of human nature) was also the law of the *civitas maxima* (in other words the juridical order proper to a city of the world founded on the *jus gentium*). Doubtless this was because the instinct of the ancient world led them irresistibly to exteriorize the notion of the norms of conduct recognized by the conscience in the notion of the constitutive norms of the political order, and, more profoundly, because in speaking of conformity to reason they had in mind divine reason and human reason pantheistically identified.

It took many centuries to make the necessary distinctions which the Stoics and Cicero had neglected, and to decant the basic truths which they had recognized but at the same time compromised by the simplistic and absolutist nature of their formulations. The Church Fathers took up their doctrine of natural law, purifying it of its original pantheism, and incorporated it into the Christian heritage; in the thirteenth century Thomas Aquinas was to give it a decisive formulation, though some trouble in the expression still remained (as a result of his respect for the juridical tradition, and of the evolution of his own vocabulary).

In the midst of all sorts of vicissitudes, of unwarranted interpretations and tendentious utilizations, the idea of natural law was to persevere in history with singular tenacity.[4] Grotius was for it—in the climate of an increasingly secularized Christianity—what Cicero had been in the climate of stoic pantheism. In the rationalism of the eighteenth century it underwent a dogmatic inflation comparable to the Stoic one, but without serious philosophical content, and destined to end in the completely arbitrary. There followed for this notion an almost total eclipse before it reappeared in our time and once again affirmed its vitality. But there can be no true renascence of the idea of natural law without a vast labor of elucidation and philosophical reformulation, as regards in particular the historical perspective in which it must be placed. There the diversity of moral codes in which its "dynamic schemes"

[1] Cicero, *Laws*, I, 16.
[2] *Epistulae morales ad Lucilium*, XCV, 33.
[3] *Meditations*, VI, 44, in *The Stoic and Epicurean Philosophers*, p. 533.
[4] Cf. Heinrich Rommen, *op. cit.*

have been expressed through the ages will become clear, and, at the same time, the progressive manner in which mankind is bound to learn of its exigencies.[1]

II

THE TECHNIQUE OF PLEASURE—AN ETHIC OF PURE FINALITY

Epicurean Asceticism

9. Epicurus did not have the cosmopolitan background of a Zeno or a Chrysippus. He was a pure Athenian, of refined culture and delicate sensibility. His health was bad. Afflicted by maladies which became more and more painful as he grew older, he held Pleasure, as the Stoics had held Virtue, to be Happiness—a happiness which elevated man to the rank of the gods. But this happiness was essentially an escape or a deliverance from suffering, an internal state of unawareness of suffering, unawareness of fear, unawareness of illness, attained by a free and artistic intelligence. Happiness-as-pleasure was therefore conceived in a supra-emotional, even ascetic perspective. Only sensible pleasure exists, but it is in some way spiritualized by the intelligence, the imagination and the memory.

Pleasure can result either from movement or from rest, but the pleasure of rest is intrinsically superior to the pleasure of movement, more exempt from pain, more stable, that is. There is no other true and authentic pleasure, so that finally, the suppression of pain is the highest degree of pleasure. No longer to be hungry is better than to enjoy tasty foods. Consequently, a state of perfect repose of spirit and perfect indifference, perfect absence of any agitation—an egotistical and sensualist version of the Aristotelian life of contemplation—must be considered as the supreme fulfillment of human life and placed above any kind of action.

Moreover, if this state of abolition of all agitation—without any shows of virtue, without that odor of human sweat exhaled by the Stoic Force—if this calm and serenity in which the soul is empty of all anxiety of desire and of every kind of fear, whether it come from men, from nature or from the gods, if this *ataraxia* is the supreme fulfillment of human life, it is not by virtue of its own merits as an intrinsic good (there is no intrinsic good for hedonism), it is because only in that state is there no more suffering or pain, and therefore supreme pleasure.

The Epicurean distinguishes, moreover, three categories of desires: (1) natural and necessary desires (like eating and drinking); (2) natural but not necessary desires (like enjoying a particular dish); (3) desires which are neither natural nor necessary (like having a crown or a monument); and

[1] We touched on these problems in our book, *Man and the State*, Chicago: University of Chicago Press, 1951, pp. 84–97; London: Hollis and Carter, 1954.

knowing that for the life of supreme pleasure one needs only to satisfy the natural and necessary desires and renounce the satisfaction of the other two categories, he is very nearly independent of external circumstances: "with a little bread and water he rivals Jupiter in happiness".

Epicureanism was thus a kind of asceticism of relaxation and repose, as Stoicism was an asceticism of tension and of action. On the other hand, while Stoicism insisted upon the value of society, and subordinated the individual person to the social and cosmic whole, Epicureanism, on the contrary, was a system fundamentally centered on the self, measuring all things with the advantage of the individual in mind and refusing to any social element any superiority over the individual—although in fact, but always with a view to assuring the maximum of pleasure to the individual, the Epicureans cultivated the social virtues of friendship, hospitality, gentleness and benevolence to a high degree, and according to Plutarch Epicurus himself declared that "there is more pleasure in doing good than in receiving it" (a Christian thinks at once of the saying of Christ reported by St. Paul,[1] "It is more blessed to give than to receive"—there is a world of difference between these two sayings, and yet the former, on the level of egotistical hedonism, resembles the latter, on the level of charity). The disciples of Epicurus also thought, rightly but for reasons of an inferior order, that the most virtuous life is the hidden life, and that it was a good thing, with a view to attaining *ataraxia*, to practise justice, which they regarded, however, as a matter of convention. "Absolute justice has never existed, only conventions arrived at by mutual agreement, according to the country and the times, to provide protection against damage and suffering."[2] As Carneades was to do later, the Epicureans amply exploited in this connection the argument, already put forward by the Sophists, of the diversity of moral codes and customs: a lazy argument, which relies heavily on people's desire to avoid the tiring business of distinguishing and getting to the core of the matter.

The illusion of Pleasure as the supreme End

10. The Epicureans' technique of pleasure was a morality of pure finality, in which everything was judged as a means toward the end, which is pleasure, and at the same time the notion of good was entirely absorbed in that of happiness, which was itself absorbed in the notion of supreme pleasure. It is not that the idea of value was completely rejected; but it was emptied of its proper substance. There is no longer any good in itself and for itself, and value is entirely relativized, and cut down to the status of the means to the end; it is but the quality of means insofar as they lead to the end. There exists thus an Epicurean notion of virtue; but virtue is defined as the sure way through which the state of supreme pleasure is attained. The virtuous man is

[1] *Acts*, XX, 35.
[2] *Sententia XXXIII*, in *Epicurea*, ed. H. Vsener, Leipzig, 1887, p. 78.

the one who firmly and securely possesses the art or technique of pleasure, and who alone, thanks to an accurate calculation and an appropriate practice, is capable of arriving at the maximum of pleasure along with a minimum of pain. Physical suffering? He escapes from it by remembering past pleasures and imagining pleasures to come. He nurses his serenity by a careful and delicate process of auto-suggestion. Death? He knows that at the moment of death the atoms of the soul are dispersed, dissolve into the universe; at that moment sensation ends—death consists precisely in that cessation. Ceasing to be and to feel, we are not affected by death, it does not exist for us. Death is nothing for the sage; he has done away with it. He makes it disappear by a kind of sleight of hand. He has arranged his concepts so as to act *as if* it did not exist. A flight of the intelligence, an artificial and deliberate act of cowardice in the face of the fact of death, is the only possible issue for an ethics of pure pleasure, which is the extreme limit of an ethics of pure subjective happiness.

At the root of the illusion of Epicureanism lies the misunderstanding which substitutes pleasure for moral good, or, to adopt the kind of comparison employed by Epicurus himself, which substitutes the aroma for the roast.

Pleasure is a species of good, but a good by superaddition. We can adopt it as an end in many situations, but then there is always another good, a "substantial" good enveloped in that end, a good to which we customarily refer when we want to justify the pleasure to which we give ourselves over. We go for a nice walk for the pleasure of taking the air; but at the same time the pure air and the relaxation are required for the health of the body. In other words, pleasure can never be the primary and essential aim of our life, nor of any of our powers. There is a pleasure in knowledge; but if in the exercise of intelligence we sought only the pleasure of feeling intelligent, and not truth, we would be perverting within ourselves the function of knowing.

No one can live without delectation

11. Nevertheless, Epicureanism also made a valuable contribution to moral philosophy. It gave the lie to Stoic pride. Above all—and precisely because pleasure is a good by superaddition, a luxury—it preserved better than Stoicism did the element of luxury and artistic superabundance which is indispensable to human life and culture.

Let us note here that pleasure or joy is a sign, and that ordinarily the greatest joy is the sign of the possession of the greatest good (I do not say necessarily of the greatest moral good). And the more noble and spiritual the nature of the plenitude of being or the fulfillment that the joy presupposes, and which it echoes in the sensible or intellectual consciousness, the more closely is the joy in question attached to that plenitude of being and fulfillment. A fruit is *aliquid ultimum et delectabile*, "something which is ultimate in fulfillment and which is also delectable". And if we can define contemplation as the fruition of the absolute, it is because union with the absolute and the joy which comes from this union are consubstantial in it (however masked that joy sometimes may be by suffering and aridity).

These remarks will help us to understand how St. Thomas could say,[1] following Aristotle:[2] "Nobody can do without delectation for long. That is why he who is deprived of spiritual delectations goes over to the carnal." They also make us understand the fact that without a proper appreciation of the value of pleasure, of sensible pleasure and spiritual joy, and of the role of fruition in human existence, a civilization can only with difficulty appreciate those "useless" activities—more necessary to man than the necessaries—which are disinterested knowledge, art, poetry, contemplation.

But these are not the "natural and necessary" pleasures to which the hedonistic asceticism of Epicurus reduced the needs of the sage. Such fruits require a more generous soil than the orchard of Epicurus. They are produced in pain and suffering, and a civilization in which the ideal of *ataraxia*, of the abolition of all agitation, reigned would be unacquainted with them.

III

THE IDEAL OF THE SAGE

Haste to arrive at the supreme End

12. Although fundamentally opposed in their philosophical principles and their inspiration, Stoicism and Epicureanism present us with remarkably similar charts of "advisable actions" in the conduct of the ordinary man—there is nothing astonishing in this, since we know that moral philosophy works on the basis of norms and values previously recognized by the common conscience. But what really interested the Stoics and Epicureans, and what made for the power of attraction of their message, was not the tracing of rules of conduct for ordinary life, but establishing the ideal of the sage. That is what had an immediate appeal for man, mobilized his passion for happiness with a practical efficiency unknown to the morality of Aristotle.

In both cases a certain haste to arrive at the ultimate end seems to me significant. The two systems are the work of philosophers equally in a hurry to attain the end, to bring man to happiness. But in identifying the supreme Good with Happiness, the Stoics (like Aristotle before them) declared identical *in re* two notions which remained distinct in themselves (as if, to make a comparison, I said: the end toward which the activity of knowing tends is "philosophic truth", in which "the complete fulfillment of the intellect" is attained). In this way the Good—which for them was Virtue—was indeed confused with its resonance in the subject, with Happiness, but was not

[1] *Sum. theol.*, I–II, 35, 4, *ad* 2.
[2] *Nicomachean Ethics*, VIII, 5 and 6; X, 6.

effaced or eclipsed by the notion of Happiness. Though the Stoics did not distinguish Happiness clearly from the Good, and though they were not explicitly conscious of the fact (and therein lay the equivocation and the shortcoming), the morality of Happiness was for them a morality of the Good also. This was the case with all of the great Greek schools, except that of Epicurus. For the latter, as we have already remarked, the Good in itself (the properly moral or "honest" good, as well as the supreme Good or Value supremely good in and for itself) was simply done away with, eclipsed by Happiness, because the Epicureans definitely thought *only* in terms of happiness, and happiness for them was pleasure (as if I said, no longer concerning myself with philosophic truth: the end toward which the activity of knowing tends is "the complete fulfillment of the intellect", which consists in "the pleasure of reasoning"). The morality of Happiness was not for them, even implicitly, a morality of the Good, but simply the morality of the perfect state of Pleasure, or of *Ataraxia*.

The fact remains that, in a quite different way than fearless and invincible Force of soul, the state of supreme Relaxation or Indifference also required a kind of heroic asceticism. In both cases the ideal of the sage was a heroic ideal. This was the price of the effectiveness of their appeal to the human soul. But by an unfortunate paradox, the effectiveness of the appeal was to be paid for in its turn by ultimate disappointment in terms of realization. The heroic requirement of perfect virtue ended up in the disabused recognition that Wisdom is too high for man. The heroic requirement of perfect indifference terminated in a dream of evasion of the most profound realities of life, thanks to *tetrapharmakon*, to the quadruple drug of illusion: "God is not to be feared, death is not formidable, good is easily acquired, danger is easy to endure."[1]

Pragmatic displacement of the notion of Wisdom

13. However disappointing it was to appear in the end, the search for pragmatic effectiveness remains the fundamental trait of Stoicism and Epicureanism. We find a very remarkable sign and effect of this in the displacement undergone by the notion of Wisdom. The sage is no longer the man who knows and contemplates, but the one who acts, and in such a way as to grasp happiness, either through perfection or through the complete absence of disturbance. For Aristotle the moral life was centered on prudence; now the art of living well is called wisdom. For Aristotle, as later for St. Thomas, moral virtues were in the service of wisdom; now it is either virtue or the accurate calculation of pleasures which is wisdom itself.

In both Stoic and Epicurean morality the "cosmic" character of Hellenic ethics in general is not only manifest, it is carried to its extreme point (while

[1] This recipe against all evils, mentioned in a fragment of Philodemus of Gadara (first century B.C.), seems to go back to Epicurus himself. Cf. Emile Bréhier, *op. cit.*, p. 410.

taking decidedly the aberrant form of cosmic-without-the-beyond or the closed cosmic—pantheist or atheist). Morality presupposes not only a system of Logic and a Philosophy of Nature, but also that this Logic or Canonics and this Cosmology are identical with Morality. There is no authentic moral life without the dogmas which they teach us. If I do not adhere to the rationalist–immanentist notion or to the atomistic notion of the world, I cannot put the Stoic morality or the Epicurean morality into practice. But if the knowledge of nature and of the laws of discourse have become so indispensable to the moral life, and so arrogant at the same time, it is because thenceforward they are pointed toward action, they are the necessary instruments for right living. Stoic physics and Epicurean physics are thus marred from the very beginning, because they are no longer a disinterested search for the truth of things but an explanation of nature incorporated in a system of happiness dogmatically imposed, and ordered to the primacy of praxis.

Stoic Physics

14. Stoic physics presented itself, in its absolute intellectualism, as an integrally rational knowledge of the world and of its perpetual alternations between birth and dissolution which constitute the very life of the divine Reason: it rendered the force of soul of the sage unshakeable. Identifying the Reason moving through all things with the dynamism of matter in evolution, looking upon movement as "being, at each of its moments, not a passage from potency to act, but an act",[1] this was not a dialectical materialism concerned with the becoming of history, but a materialist rationalism concerned with the cycles of evolution of the world. Moreover, it professed a fervent belief in a God who, immanent in the world as a "forming fire", bound up with nature and the world, charged with the supreme justification of the world and of the evil as well as the good operative in it, was indeed the God of naturalism *par excellence*, the Emperor of the world but not the true God.[2] In his service the Stoics employed any kind of popular theology whatsoever, and a profusion of shameless finalist explanations—the final cause of the existence of flies was to keep us from sleeping too long, that of lice to make us good housekeepers.

It is not my purpose here to examine Stoic theology and cosmology. I should like simply to note that Stoic rationalism ended up in a complete and systematic deification of the world, and that the Stoic notion of Destiny,

[1] Simplicius, *Commentary on the Categories*, 78 b (Arnim, II, no. 499).

[2] If the Stoics spoke of him as different from the world, it was so that he could justify the world and all that happens in the world by his sovereign will and sovereign reason; if they made him immanent in the world and of the same substance as it, it was because he was but the divinization of the world: Emperor of the world consubstantial with the world. "Though they say that the providential being is of the same substance as the being it directs, they also say, nevertheless, that he is perfect and different from what he directs." Origen, *On the Gospel of St. John*, XIII, 21 (Arnim, II, 1122), [Migne, *P.G.*, t. XIV, col. 243].

which linked things to one another much more tightly than the so-called "scientific determinism" of our nineteenth century, absolutely excluded any kind of contingency or chance. Let us add that, as has been remarked,[1] Stoic providentialism seems to point to a Semitic contribution mixed with Greek conceptions, while on the other hand, as we have already noted, the supranational universalism of the Porch was not without relation to the new current of thought provoked by the imperial universalism of the Macedonian kings.

Epicurean Physics

15. In Epicurean cosmology we have to do with an empirical knowledge of nature which cared little about rigorous consistency, which trusted in immediate evidence and was suspicious of rational constructions. Epicurean physics sought neither necessary reasons nor an exact explanation of the detail of things, but was satisfied with no matter what general explanation of a kind that would deliver us from ideas and beliefs engendering fear in us—the fear of meteors, the fear of destiny, the fear of death, the fear of the fate of the soul beyond the grave, the fear of divination and prodigies. The gods existed, but they in no way acted on the world. Made of purified matter, they led a tranquil life in interstellar space, sheltered from atomic collisions, and quite incapable of causing any trouble in human affairs. *Felix qui potuit*. . . . Even the fervor of the poet of *The Nature of Things* is really oriented less toward science as such than toward the state of mind—superior serenity and disdain of vulgar fears—which science is credited with producing in us. And what preoccupied Epicurus above all was to furnish us with an image of the world which rendered a mind free from agitation and oppression by things and by the dangers hidden in things. He was completely at ease in affirming the freedom of the will, which caused the Stoics so many headaches: it is explained quite easily by the *clinamen* (παρέγκλεσις). Do we not know that all atoms fall vertically downward at the same speed, but that at certain moments and in certain entirely undetermined places, certain atoms deviate from the vertical without cause or reason, and so produce the shocks and collisions which engender worlds? Similarly, free will is simply the result of a causeless deviation in the movement of the atoms of the soul.

Epicurus was thus the first to make the indetermination of matter the foundation of the freedom of the will. As far as we are concerned, we believe in freedom of the will, and we have the highest respect for the indeterminist theories of modern physics. But we do not think that the attempts one can make to draw from these scientific theories a metaphysics of free will have any more philosophical value than the Epicurean *clinamen*.

[1] Bréhier, *op. cit.*, II, 297, 298.

F

A supra-philosophical ambition and need—curing the human Soul

16. Let us point out, to bring this chapter to a close, one last trait common to both of the schools of which we are speaking, which in our opinion is highly significant: in reality their moral philosophy is not an ethics, but a super-ethics. The aim is not to determine the guiding principles of an upright human life, but in a single leap to reach the supreme end and supreme happiness, a superhuman state of perfect Virtue or unalterable Pleasure in which the sage leads a divine life (for Epicurus was also a god, according to Lucretius: ". . . a god he was, a god, most noble Memmius, who first found out that plan of life which is now termed wisdom . . .").[1] It is from the heights of this divine life, possessed and experienced, from this state of sublime concentration or sublime indifference, that the Stoic or Epicurean sage descends to the plains of human conduct, that is, to ethics properly so called.

In other words, neither Stoicism nor Epicureanism was a simple system of moral philosophy. We understand nothing of their true significance if we take them for philosophical theories in the ordinary sense of these words. They were practical schools of wisdom and spiritual direction: fundamentally dogmatic schools whose masters and founders were inspired supermen who employed philosophical equipment and works of reason (in one case a supremely intellectualist reason, in the other a sensualist and empiricist reason) to assuage a thirst for deliverance, to appease a deep and burning anguish concerning human destiny, and to satisfy a more or less conscious nostalgia for the blissful life. Some centuries later, and in a quite different intellectual context, the same kind of curers of the human soul were to produce the gnostic sects, already announced in the middle Platonism of Maximus of Tyre and the neo-Pythagorean initiatory rites. If we looked for modern analogies, we should, in order to find them, however degenerated they may be, think of the teachers of a debased Yoga or *dhikr* who have no trouble collecting disciples to-day, or of certain salesmen of happiness and founders of religions who prosper in California.

It is profitable for our inquiry to keep in mind the characteristic of the Stoic ethics and the Epicurean ethics which I have just pointed out. What it seems to us to suggest is that when moral philosophy wants to have an effective hold on the human being, and wants to deal not only with an abstract and simply possible man but with the real man, and with human conduct considered in its real condition of existence, it cannot remain pure moral philosophy and must enter into communication with a world of human data and aspirations more existential than that of philosophy isolated within itself.

[1] *On the Nature of Things*, Book V, trans. H. A. J. Munro in *The Stoic and Epicurean Philosophers*, ed. Whitney J. Oates, p. 163, lines 6–8.

5

CHRISTIANITY AND PHILOSOPHY

The Impact of Christianity on Moral Philosophy

I

THE ANCIENT WORLD AND THE COMPETITION OF WISDOMS

The Wisdom of India

1. As we remarked in another work,[1] the spectacle offered in a general way by the ancient world, the world before Christ, is what might be called the *competition of wisdoms.*

We find in the first place the wisdom of India—a wisdom of deliverance and salvation.

The metaphysical speculations of India have always remained bound up with a practical science of spiritual perfection and sanctity. But it is through a desperate impetus issuing from the depths of the soul, a kind of tidal wave of the divine energies which are diffused in the universe and concentrated in man, that man strives to attain this wisdom. It is nature itself which, freed from illusion and from the constraints of causality, must transcend itself in order to arrive at a perfection which Hindu philosophy called "supernatural", in a quite different sense from the Christian sense of the word. Wisdom was thus the wisdom of salvation, the wisdom of the "delivered ones", to be achieved through the ascetic and mystical effort of human nature. Thence that natural mysticism in which, through the abolition of any particular thought, through total emptiness voluntarily produced, the soul experiences intuitively the existence of the Self.[2]

What is most apparent here is an ascending effort of the energies immanent in our nature, a supreme tension of the energies of our spirit, an *upward motion* by which man is to accede to superhuman conditions, enter into the divine liberty. This effort was capable, in the order of natural mysticism, of leading to the metaphysical experience of the Self of which I just spoke; in certain cases it was supplemented by a grace whose name was not revealed; at the same time that it sought deliverance in a wisdom of salvation it fell

[1] *Science and Wisdom,* New York: Scribners, 1940; London: Bles, 1940.

[2] Cf. our study on natural mysticism in *Ransoming the Time,* New York: Scribners, 1941, ch. X: "The Natural Mystical Experience and the Void". (*Redeeming the Time,* London: Bles, 1943.)

short of the goal, struggling ceaselessly to escape monism, never succeeding in conceptualizing itself without being caught by monism, aspiring ceaselessly to join the divine Absolute and only succeeding, after the Buddhist experiment, in giving an expression to nirvana that was closer and closer to pure negation.

Greek Wisdom

2. In the second place we find Greek wisdom. A wisdom of man, a wisdom of reason, it was turned toward created things and the knowledge of the cosmos, not toward salvation, saintliness, eternal deliverance.

We are aware of the fact that Greek wisdom cannot be called a rational wisdom in a very modern sense of that term. Greek paganism had its roots in magical thought, which continued to furnish the subconscious atmosphere of Greek religion. Sacred traditions did not cease to form an undercurrent beneath Hellenic meditation. Ancient reason was a naturally religious reason. It operated in a climate of natural piety haunted by many terrors. Even at the time when it displayed the most intense rationalism, as in the Stoic school, the rationalism in question remained entirely different from our modern rationalism, and veered toward a kind of magical naturalism, conceiving Reason as a divine fire that permeated matter, and favoring all the pagan superstitions. Greek reason recognized good and bad fortune, believed in higher inspirations, in demonic influences; the idea of destiny, and of the jealousy of the gods, the superstitious fear of admitting happiness, the belief in omens and in divination, even the adoration of the divine similitudes scattered through nature, were evidence of a religious appreciation of the supra-human energies at work in the world and sustained a kind of sacred awe, or fear.

But it was precisely against that fear that Stoic pantheism and Epicurean free thought reacted. More generally, it must be said that Greek philosophy developed from the beginning as a work of reason separated from religion, even when it underwent the influence of the sects and their mysteries, and as a wisdom of this world. Greek wisdom was not elaborated out of the fund of hieratic and sacerdotal traditions, like the wisdom of the Orient, but outside of them and sometimes in opposition to them. It does not start out with the Supreme, with absolute Being, as the Vedanta did, wondering how it is possible that something exists which is not the Absolute, superior to the world. On the contrary, it starts out with things, with tangible and visible reality, with becoming, with movement, with that multiplicity which exercises the act of being with scandalous energy. It bears witness to the existence of that which is not God, and to the intelligible structure of things. In the moral realm it succeeded in establishing in its proper order, and as distinct from speculative philosophy and metaphysics, a practical rational knowledge of human conduct and human acts, which was to fix thenceforth the boundaries of ethics. But the peculiar beauty of Greek wisdom is like that of a rough sketch drawn by a genius, in which the outlines and the essential points are indicated with incomparable artistry. It nowhere came to fruition. In the field of moral philosophy in particular we have seen that neither Aristotelian eudemonism, nor the asceticism of pleasure, nor the asceticism of virtue came to a successful issue.

The Wisdom of the Old Testament

3. Finally, there is a third wisdom, Hebraic wisdom, the wisdom of the Old Testament. It is not a human wisdom like Greek wisdom. It is a wisdom of salvation and of saintliness, of deliverance and freedom, of eternal life—but for it, unlike Hindu wisdom, man does not rise by his own efforts: *quis ascendit in caelum*, who shall go up for us to heaven, and bring it unto us?[1] No effort of asceticism or of mysticism could *force* that wisdom. It must give itself, it must come down and break open the gates of heaven.

The long, the unflagging Jewish impatience beseeches God to give Himself, a God who wants only to give Himself, but who hides Himself. The wisdom of the Old Testament is bound up with the most intransigeant idea of divine transcendence, with the idea of creation *ex nihilo*, and at the same time with a profound sense of human personality and human freedom. This perishable and corruptible flesh, this flesh itself will rise again: an idea that Greek wisdom had no inkling of, and which it was to find scandalous. The history of Israel—and the individual history of each human being—consists in the last analysis of the dialogue between the eternal divine personality and our created persons; it is a love affair between God and man.

Thus we are here in the presence of a supernatural wisdom that gives itself, and that freely descends from the Principle of beings. A wisdom of salvation, a wisdom of saintliness, it is not man who wins it, it is God who gives it; it is not from an upward movement of the creature, it is from a downward movement of the creating Spirit that it proceeds. It is in this opposition of the two movements of ascent and descent that the whole difference between the wisdom of the Ganges and the wisdom of the Jordan must be seen. The wisdom of the sapiential books, like the wisdom of the Gospel, issues from the depths of uncreated love to descend into the most intimate depths of the creature. The New Law, the message of the Word made flesh, will tear away the veil with which the Old Law covered the mystery that the prophets of Israel glimpsed—through the veil—and obscurely foretold.

The Law of the Incarnation

4. The ancient world offers us the spectacle of a competition among three wisdoms; and more specifically, the competition between Judeo-Christian wisdom and Greek wisdom, finally gone to seed and seeking in vain in a syncretism without existential roots, in mystagogy and gnosis, a cure for the great

[1] *Deuteronomy*, XXX, 12; cf. *Baruch*, III, 29–30; *Romans*, X, 6.

pagan melancholy. This conflict was to signalize the disintegration of the ancient world.

Later, in the course of the Middle Ages, there was an extended effort to link together divine wisdom and human wisdom, to recognize and establish the order and hierarchy of wisdom, an effort that continued throughout the Christian centuries. This work of synthesis was to be completed in terms of actual doctrine by St. Thomas Aquinas; but divided as they were against themselves, the culture and the intelligentsia of the late Middle Ages were hardly able to profit by the synthesis, and its dissolution commenced with the beginning of modern times. The fact remains that medieval Christianity was cognizant of the order of wisdom—the wisdom of contemplative experience through the union of love, theological wisdom, philosophical wisdom· Medieval Christianity was dominated by the law of *descending motion* of supreme wisdom to which we called attention in speaking of the Old Testament, and knew its name—it is the law of the Incarnation. Thomas Aquinas formulated it in a text of limitless significance: "In the mystery of the Incarnation," he says,[1] "the descent of the divine plenitude into human nature is of greater import than the ascent of human nature, taken as pre-existent, toward Divinity." Similarly, in the relations between God and humanity, the movement of descent of the divine plenitude into the depths of human nature is of greater import than the movement of ascent by which human nature is fulfilled and mounts toward God. We rediscover here the teaching of St. Paul concerning the law and grace: it is not by our own effort that we are rendered just; it is by the gift of Him who loved us first, and who descends into us through faith and love, that we are born to eternal life and can bear good fruit in our weakness. "And he said unto me, My grace is sufficient for thee: for my strength is made perfect in weakness. Most gladly therefore will I rather glory in my infirmities, that the power of Christ may rest upon me . . . for when I am weak, then am I strong."[2] The moral heroism to which we are in truth called is attained neither by the athleticism of mystical concentration, after the Hindu manner, which claims to draw us into inner solitude in the absolute, nor by the athleticism of virtue, after the manner of the Stoics, which pretends to render us incapable of sin. It is attained through the force of another who descends into us and fills us with His plenitude, and by a love for Him which even in the depths of our weakness removes all obstacles to His love.

[1] *Sum. theol.*, III, 34, 1, *ad* 1.
[2] *II Cor.*, XII, 9–10.

II

THE IRRUPTION OF THE JUDEO-CHRISTIAN REVELATION

5. These very general observations have been by way of preface to the remarks we should like to make concerning the effects produced in the realm of moral philosophy by the irruption in the world of the Judeo-Christian revelation and the impact of Christianity on the tradition of Greek philosophy.

Whether one believes in this revelation oneself, or considers it strictly from without and from a historical point of view, one is obliged to note that in fact the impact in question produced a kind of transmutation of ethical values—a unique phenomenon in the history of humanity, as a matter of fact—and that as a consequence it profoundly transformed the perspectives of moral philosophy.

Such a transfiguration was due to the influence of a religious factor, exterior to philosophy as such—let us say, to speak in terms of its rational formulation, a theological factor—upon a philosophical discipline. In our opinion, that influence was manifested primarily in the way we are now going to try to define—be it understood that these incursions into the theological and religious domain are directed by a philosophical interest, and have as object to mark certain repercussions which occurred in the domain of moral philosophy itself.

"*To-day thou shalt be with me in Paradise*"—*The Absolute Ultimate End and the Subjective Ultimate End*

Beatitude

6. It came as a strange novelty to learn that the final End of human life—not only as supreme Value good in itself and for itself, but as the supreme Object the possession of which constitutes human happiness—is God Himself, the infinite Good, self-subsistent Being. God in His intimate life, the uncreated Glory itself is the end in which our appetite for happiness will be satisfied beyond measure. In this view the transcendence of the final End is affirmed in an incomparably more decisive way than it was by Plato: the infinite transcendence—with which we are called to unite—of a personal God who created the world out of nothing, whom no concept can circumscribe and whom no creature can comprehend, infinite Self, supremely perfect, independent and free, and who is the boundless ocean of being, of intellection, of love and of goodness.

By the same stroke the notion of happiness was transfigured. Happiness is now Beatitude, absolute happiness, absolutely saturating; "Eye hath not seen, nor ear heard, neither have entered into the heart of man, the things which God hath prepared for them that love him."[1]

[1] St. Paul, *I Cor.*, II, 9.

That it is possible for man to attain absolute happiness is not a datum of reason or of philosophy, but of Christian faith. Reason by itself, if we consider not the infinite power of God, of course, but the human condition, would have ample grounds to make us doubt the possibility. The most unhappy of animals necessarily desires happiness, and that is no doubt why it is so unhappy. We are starving for happiness, we make of the *pursuit of happiness* one of our fundamental rights, we seek happiness in everything that is perishable, in the love of a woman or in the conquest of power, and it is almost impossible for us to believe that we can be perfectly, totally, absolutely happy; our experience of life affords too much evidence to the contrary. There are two things in which our nature has not the strength to believe: death, which we see, and perfect happiness, which we do not see. *Verily I say unto you, to-day shalt thou be with me in paradise.*[1] That is an astonishing announcement. Faith, not reason, is the source of it. Men seek beatitude, without believing in it. Christians believe in it, through faith.

In that beatitude, the object of Christian faith, we find, moreover, a supreme verification of the law mentioned above[2]—namely, that joy or delectation is a kind of savor issuing from the possession of a substantial good, and always remains distinct from that possession, but is the more closely bound up with it the higher the nature of the substantial good in question. The essence of beatitude—the possession of the supreme substantial good—is the vision of God: the supreme joy which derives from it is in itself distinct from that vision, but is so nearly identical with it that we can hardly distinguish the joy from the vision.

Absolute Ultimate End and Subjective Ultimate End in the Natural Order and in the Supernatural Order

7. It would be well to pause a moment here to take note of two things. In the first place, as we just pointed out, for Christian faith man is called to an absolutely saturating happiness, and it is the possession or intuitive vision of God Himself which constitutes that happiness; it is the immediate and transforming union with the ultimate End of all creation—to which, unless it is raised by grace, a created nature can only tend or aspire from afar, in fact, from infinitely far—it is the direct union with the absolute ultimate End, good in and for itself, which constitutes the subjective ultimate End of the human being, his final fulfillment, his perfect and eternal happiness.

But in the second place, Christian faith holds at the same time that this beatitude is of a supernatural order; it is a gift of grace, the gift of grace *par excellence*; it does not arise from nature.

If, therefore, man had not been raised to the state of grace, if God had left

[1] *St. Luke*, XXIII, 43.
[2] See above, ch. IV, pp. 65–66.

him in the purely natural order and with only the resources of his own nature, there would be no question for him either of attaining beatitude or of immediately possessing God as object of his perfect happiness. The happiness toward which he would tend, and which would be the subjective ultimate End of human life, or the end relative to the human subject, would be anything one wished, I mean anything philosophy and theology can more or less plausibly conceive, but it would not be God possessed. God would remain the absolute ultimate End, good in and for itself, to be loved above all else, for man as for every creature; but the possession of God would not be his subjective ultimate End, his ultimate end in the line of the subject. Between the absolute ultimate End, the transcendent Good which must be loved above all things, and the subjective ultimate End or the happiness of the human being, there would be in such a case an infinite distance, an infinite abyss. At this point we see clearly and explicitly that distinction between the Good and Happiness which Aristotle missed.

The astonishing tidings brought by Christianity were that in fact, and by the free and gratuitous superabundance of divine generosity, the separation, the cleavage of which we have just spoken between the absolute ultimate End and the subjective ultimate End does not exist for man. The subjective ultimate End or the beatitude of man consists in an immediate and indissoluble union with the absolute ultimate End (to which, as the theologians will put it, man is rendered proportionate through grace and the *lumen gloriae*). But in this very union, this kind of coincidence, the distinction between the subjective End or beatitude of man and God Himself or the absolute ultimate End obviously continues to exist, the distinction between the supernatural plenitude in which the human subject is fulfilled, with the endless joy that goes with that fulfillment, and the divine Essence, the subsistent Good, the vision of which beatifies the human subject. And it is for love of the subsistent Good, loved more than all things, more than the human subject itself and more than his own happiness, it is for love of the absolute ultimate End that man desires the beatitude in which his own being is divinely perfect.

Because the notion of the Good in itself and for itself is no longer related only to the *bonum honestum* (Good as right) in the moral order—or, in the metaphysical order, to the supra-personal Idea of the Good, or to the Thought which thinks itself at the summit of the world—but has its supreme archetype in a subsistent Good which is a living Personality—three Persons in a single nature, one of whom has been incarnated, moral reflection now understands definitively and explicitly that the Good is something other than Happiness, and that the first demand and the first condition of moral rectitude is to love the Good more than Happiness.

Absolute Happiness is desired for love of the Good subsisting of itself

8. In the perspective of Christian ethics three things are to be distinguished: in the first place, the absolute ultimate End. God in His infinite goodness and lovability is the absolute ultimate End, and it is in the vision of God, or the possession of the absolute ultimate End, that beatitude, or the subjective ultimate End of the human being, consists.

In the second place, the subjective ultimate End, in its essential constituent element: that is to say, the vision of God, through which the human being, supernaturally fulfilled, enters into the divine plenitude in knowing God through His essence.

In the third place, the subjective ultimate end in its flowering, in its super-effluence: that is to say, the perfect satisfaction of all the aspirations of the soul in the love of God possessed, the joy or delectation which is a participation in the joy of God itself—as it is said in Matthew, *intra in gaudium Domini tui.*[1]

These three things are distinct from one another. The desire of the second is inseparable from the love of the first; and the desire of the third is inseparable from the desire of the second. But the desire of the second and the desire of the third are for love of the first. Beatitude is loved, but God is loved more; and beatitude, precisely because it is union with the supreme Good subsisting in itself, can only be really and truly loved if it is loved in and for the love of that subsistent Good, supremely loved for itself. The love which the human being naturally has for himself is not abolished, certainly, but it loses first place, it is chased from the primary and royal seat; the absolutely primary love, the love which is above and beyond all others, can and must be torn away from the self and directed toward the uncreated Personality with whom the human person is in a direct relation over and above all the things of this world. The absolutely primary love can and must be fixed in Him whose good we then wish more than our own good—and that is possible, and even, in one sense, easy, since according to Christian faith He is our friend, in the supernatural order of charity.

Thus the egocentricity in which Aristotelian eudemonism remained in fact enclosed is definitely overcome. At the very moment that beatitude is promised to man, he is offered the possibility of finally being delivered from himself and from the devouring egoism which perverts his love of himself.

My happiness, which I naturally and necessarily desire, which I cannot help desiring, and which finally consists in the vision of God, has now been subordinated to something better, subordinated to God—and this is implied, as we remarked above, in the very essence of that happiness, since it consists in the possession of God, who is infinitely better than my happiness. According

[1] XXV, 21.

to a precious saying of Cajetan, "*volo Deum mihi, non propter me*";[1] Christian hope makes me wish that God be *mine*, but it is not *for me* or by reason of myself, it is not for love of myself that I wish God to be mine; it is for God and for love of God, for I love God more than myself and more than my happiness.

Christian morality is a morality of beatitude, but first and foremost it is a morality of the divine Good supremely loved.

9. The theologians are perfectly clear on all this. But popular preaching is often inclined to put the emphasis above all, if not even, exclusively on the joys of the reward and the pains of punishment. These are truths which immediately stir our natural appetite for happiness and our natural fear of suffering. And even if one insists only on them, one can always hope that once the sinner is turned toward the subsistent Good from motives in which love of self hold first place, the living faith will thereafter make him spontaneously subordinate his own interest to God loved first.

After all, one lends only to the rich. And the preachers of the Gospel feel themselves excused in advance if, in the arguments by which they push us toward salvation, they employ without too much scruple a kind of eudemonism, even hedonism, at least ambiguous in character, in the service of the God of love.

It is for the philosophical intelligence—not to speak of the pseudo-philosophical opinions current in popular thought, and sometimes in textbooks of ethics or the history of philosophy—that the final result of this emphasis is dangerous and can be the occasion for serious misconceptions. Even a philosopher like Kant, following a great many others, could imagine that traditional Christian morality (until revised by Pure Reason) was a morality of sublimated egotistic happiness and personal interest, in which it is for love of itself and of eternal pleasure, to which all else is subordinated, that the soul loves the Author of all good and strives to practise his precepts, which in reality is to conceive of Christianity after the model of the idolatrous cults it overthrew.

The Supernatural Order and the Grace of Virtues and Gifts— Divine Charity and Friendship

Theological Virtues and moral Virtues

10. With Christianity a new order in being is made manifest to the human mind—essentially distinct from the order of nature and at the same time

[1] Cf. Cajetan, *in IIª IIªᵉ*, qu. 17, a. 5, no. 8: "Et cum dicitur *quia non potest amari Deus propter nos*, respondetur quod non potest amari *propter nos*, sed *nobis*." (Cajetan goes on to say that what is *secundum se* loved only *mihi*, can nevertheless *secundum effectum suum* be loved also *propter me*. None the less God in Himself is desired by me *mihi, non propter me*.)

perfecting that order—the order of grace and of supernatural realities. This word "supernatural" signifies for Christianity a participation in that which is actually divine, in the intimate life itself of God—something, as we have already noted, which is beyond the possibilities of any created nature through its own capacities, and which is not *owed* to nature, but depends on free and gratuitous divine communication.

From this moment the very concept of nature undergoes a change, opens out, so to speak. Nature is not closed in upon itself, impenetrable by a superior order. It blossoms in grace, is "perfected" or fulfilled by grace, which is not simply added to it like an ornamental façade, but which penetrates its most intimate depths, and which, at the same time that it elevates nature to a life and an activity of another order, of which nature is not capable by itself, heightens it in its own order and in the domain of its own proper activities.

Several remarks may be tendered on this subject. The first concerns the three virtues to which Christianity has given absolutely first rank, and which are called the three *theological* virtues. They do not figure in the Aristotelian list of virtues. It was St. Paul who named them, and who, in a singular reversal of values, gave precedence over the powerful cardinal virtues to interior dispositions—adherence of the intellect to an object which is not seen, confidence in one more powerful than oneself, love—which in the purely human order were too humble to constitute virtues, but which in the divine order, and because they are directed toward God Himself, are henceforward recognized to be the virtues *par excellence*: "And now abideth faith, hope and charity, these three: but the greatest of these is charity."[1]

The object of the theological virtues is the transcendent God, the divine Good with which they unite the human soul. They are a gift of grace. In opposition to them, the term "moral" virtues will be reserved for the virtues enumerated by the philosophers, in the sense that the latter have to do with simply human morality or the conduct of life in relation to goods of the human order. Unlike moral virtues, the theological virtues do not consist in a mean between excess and defect; no excess is possible in the exercise of these virtues—one never believes too much in God, one never puts too much hope in Him, one never loves Him too much.[2] For Christian ethics the theological virtues are superior to the moral virtues. The latter are still required, but they are no longer supreme. The supreme virtues are of a supra-moral order, and the highest of them, on which the perfection of human life depends, is charity.

In order to clarify the distinction between the narrow sense ("moral virtues") and the broad sense ("the moral life", "moral science") of the word

[1] Saint Paul, *I Cor.*, XIII, 13.
[2] "*Circa Deum non contingit peccare per excessum.*" *Sum. theol.*, I–II, 64, 4.

"moral", we may arrange the notions with which we have just been dealing in the following table:

<table>
<tr><td>Supra-moral or theological virtues and rules (proportioned to the divine life)</td><td rowspan="2">The moral life (or the ways in which man makes use of his freedom)—the object of moral science</td></tr>
<tr><td>Moral virtues and rules (proportioned to human life)</td></tr>
</table>

The theological virtues are not the only supernatural energies the notion of which Christianity introduced into our knowledge of the moral life of man. Divine grace, according to the teaching of the Fathers and the theologians, also produces supernatural or "infused" moral virtues in the soul, which are of a higher order than the natural moral virtues or those acquired through the exercise of the will, and which have to do with the life men lead among themselves as members of the city of God and "fellow-citizens with the saints". And the term "gift" is especially reserved for still other capacities that the soul receives through grace and which are the gifts of the Spirit enumerated by Isaiah:[1] they bring the theological virtues to an experimental stage, so to speak, and, like a keyboard in us, touched by divine inspiration, they permit man while he is still here below to have a foretaste of the eternal Life, in other words, contemplative experience through union of love. (This is especially true of the gift of wisdom, the highest of the gifts.) With respect to this contemplative experience of divine things, the moral virtues have only the rank of means for Christian ethics. St. Thomas Aquinas says that the virtue of Prudence "is in the service of Wisdom, introductory to it, and preparing the way for it, like a gate-keeper in the service of the king".[2]

It is thus that Christianity has suspended the moral from the supra-moral in the moral life of man.

Friendship's Love between God and Man

11. All this shook the foundations of the purely philosophical theory of the virtues elaborated by the moralists of antiquity, and singularly transformed it. And all this depended—this is our second remark—on a fundamental change in the notion of the relations between man and God. A *friendship* properly so called, and in the strongest, the most extravagant sense of the word, *a love as between friends* is possible between man and God, and this love between friends—charity, the gift of grace, the highest of the theological virtues—is, over and above the moral virtues, the keystone of the whole edifice of morality. Such a teaching, brought to the ancient world by the evangelic message, was indeed a scandal for philosophy.

[1] *Isaiah*, XI, 2.
[2] *Sum. theol.*, I–II, 66, 5, *ad* 1.

How, asked Aristotle, could any kind of friendship worthy of the name exist between Jupiter and man? And in the purely natural order it is quite true that divine transcendence excludes a friendship properly so called between God and man, because all friendship presupposes a certain equality. It is normal for man to love the First Cause. But he loves God in fear and trembling, as his sovereign, not as his friend. If he loved Him as his friend, it would be because God also loved him in the same way, for love between friends is a mutual love. And how (continuing in the perspective of the purely natural order) could God love man as being His friend, or "another Himself"? If man is loved by God, it is in quite a different way, in the sense that God wishes him well, as He does all that exists, but without having any community of life and interest in common with him, and remaining enclosed in his transcendence.

We find a similar position maintained by the orthodox Moslem theologians, who thought that love from person to person being a passion, and among the most extravagant, it cannot exist in God, and who condemned the mystic al Hallaj to be crucified because he believed in such a love between God and man.[1]

And an analogous position is also to be found in Spinoza, in his great arrogant notion of *amor intellectualis Dei*, of the perfect love with which the sage loves the God immanent in the world without any hope or desire of being loved in return.[2]

As far as Aristotle is concerned, "it would be ridiculous," he says, "to reproach God because the love we receive from him in return is not equal to the love we give him, just as it would be ridiculous for the subject to make a similar reproach to his prince. For it is the role of the prince to receive love, not to give it, or at least to love only in a different way."[3] Here it is philosophical wisdom itself which loses its head, for even in the purely natural order, and even in a love which is not between friends but between sovereign and subject, how could we give more than we received, and love God more than He loves us?

For Christianity, in any case, grace, by raising man to the supernatural order, makes him partake of the very life and goods of God, and by the same token produces that community of life and of goods, and that kind of equality, however scandalous in the eyes of pure philosophy, which are the conditions of friendship properly so called. God is no longer enclosed in His transcendence, He communicates it. Between God and man, as between

[1] Cf. Louis Massignon, *La Passion d'al Hallaj* (Paris: Geuthner, 1922). Al Hallaj was put to death in Bagdad, March 26, 922.

[2] *Ethics*, V, 19: "Qui Deum amat, conari non potest, ut Deus ipsum contra amet".
Spinoza then tries, in vain (*ibid.*, prop. 36, corollary and scholium), to save nevertheless a certain amount of God's love for man (which is no other than His love for Himself working through the human spirit, in other words the *amor intellectualis Dei* itself).—Cf. *ibid.*, 17: "Deus *proprie loquendo neminem amat* neque odio habet" (our italics); and the *Short Treatise*, 2nd part, chap. 24.

[3] *Eudemian Ethics*, VII, 3, 1238 b 26–29.

friends, there can be love from person to person, with all its extravagance, love as between father and son, love as between husband and wife, the love of total giving hailed by the Song of Songs, and to which God was the first to surrender Himself, when He was incarnated. And the mystics will be able to say in this sense that God, because He thus wished it, needed our love as the friend needs the love of his friend, who is "another self". The great news, which is identical with that which promises us absolutely flawless happiness, or beatitude, is that God yearns toward us with love, and that He wishes to be loved by us as His friends.

This news was already contained in the Old Testament. "I love those who love me."[1] It was fully manifested in the Gospel. "He who loves me will be loved by my Father, and I will love him."[2] "Henceforth I call you not servants . . . *but* I have called you friends."[3] And St. Thomas was to define the virtue of charity as the friendship created by grace between man and God, therefore involving mutual love from person to person, and founded on God's communication to man of His own life and finally of His own beatitude.[4]

This charity-love goes out to God first and foremost, and by the same token it goes out to all those who are called to be His friends, it goes out to all men. Love of God and fraternal love are one indivisible charity. And it is on this charity that Christianity makes the whole moral life of the human being depend. The whole law is contained in the precept to love God with our whole soul, and in the precept to love all men as our brothers, and these two form one single precept.

The reversal of Values—the call of the Ultimate End

12. A corollary to all the preceding remarks is the absolute primacy accorded by Christianity to charity-love in the scale of values relating to human life and conduct.

Without it, wisdom and virtue are empty and without value for eternal life. Our good acts are definitely good only by virtue of the charity which animates them. And if it is there it makes up for all the mistakes resulting from our weakness. As St. John of the Cross was to put it, "in the evening of this life it is on love that we shall be judged".

Thus, in the last analysis, mercy fulfills justice; the mercy of God comes to

[1] *Proverbs*, VIII, 17.

Similarly, we read in Isaiah: "Can a woman forget her sucking child, that she should not have compassion on the son of her womb? Yea, they may forget, yet I will not forget thee. Behold, I have graven thee upon the palms of my hands" (XLIX, 15–16); "Since thou wast precious in my sight, thou hast been honourable, and I have loved thee: therefore will I give men for thee, and people for thy life" (XLIII, 4); "I, even I, am he that blotteth out thy transgressions for mine own sake, and will not remember thy sins" (XLIII, 25). Thus does God declare His love to His people.

[2] *John*, XIV, 21.

[3] *John*, XV, 15.

[4] Cf. *Sum. theol.*, I–II, 23, 1.

man's rescue while he is bound to the precepts of the law. God forgives, something the God of the Platonic Republic did not do. And He does not assign to the earthly city the task of forcing men to be good, and irreproachably men; He leaves it to His grace, to His own kingdom, which is universal and above all earthly cities, to work within them to make them His sons and make them good through the very exercise of their most intimate freedom, through the love of charity which animates their acts and which is the form of their virtue, and which also compensates for their weaknesses. As we have already noted,[1] the Christian saint is not a superman formed by human agency, a Hercules of moral virtue like the Stoic sage; he is a friend of God who draws his life from supernatural charity and is formed by the divine hand, and who throws human weakness open to the divine plenitude descending into him. The vainglory of Man is dethroned, and humility, wherein lives the force of God, is exalted.

This reversal of values in relation to the perfection of human life, henceforth conceived as the perfection of charity whose working in the soul no obstacle can stop or restrain, is tied up with a similar reversal regarding wisdom and contemplation. Supreme wisdom and supreme contemplation are no longer the summit of human Science and philosophy, but the abyss in man of the gift of the uncreated Spirit which makes him experience, in faith and through Charity and the union of love, what no effort of the human intelligence can comprehend, and the things of God known as unknown. The very notion of contemplation changes in meaning, because from now on it designates an experience in which love instructs the intelligence, and a veiled communion with subsistent Truth, Life and Goodness, a communion which is the work of charity under the very touch of God. Christian contemplation exists not "for the perfection of him who contemplates, and does not terminate in the intellect, like the contemplation of the philosophers. It exists for the love of Him who is contemplated and does not terminate in the intellect, for the sake of knowing, but passes into the heart, for the sake of loving,"[2] because it proceeds itself from love. And for the same reason it does not terminate in a "theoretical" accomplishment but superabounds in action.

And all are called to such contemplation, from near or from afar, because it does not depend on nature, or on the knowledge of man, but on grace and divine gift—just as all are called to perfection. "Be ye therefore perfect, even as your Father in heaven is perfect",[3] is a precept addressed to all, as indicating the end toward which each one should tend according to his ability and

[1] Cf. above, p. 74.

[2] "Contemplatio philosophorum est propter perfectionem contemplantis, et ideo sistit in intellectu, et ita finis eorum in hoc est cognitio intellectus.

"Sed contemplatio sanctorum . . . est propter amorem ipsius, scilicet contemplati Dei: idcirco, non sistit in fine ultimo in intellectu per cognitionem, sed transit ad affectum per amorem." Saint Albert the Great, *De Adherendo Deo*, cap. IX.

[3] *Matthew*, V, 48.

his condition. The great novelty introduced by Christianity is this appeal to all, to free men and slaves, to the ignorant and the cultivated, adolescents and old men, a call to a perfection which no effort of nature can attain but which is given by grace and consists in love, and from which therefore no one is excluded except by his own refusal.

The same thing is true regarding final Beatitude, the possession of the ultimate End through vision. It is promised to all, if only they really wish it. Impossible to attain through the capacities of nature alone, it offers itself as incomparably more attainable than earthly happiness and Aristotelian eudemonia, for which there is no Penitent Thief.

Thus the moral ideal of Christianity, and the ultimate End it proposes, finally possess that effectiveness of appeal to the human being and his thirst for happiness (now transfigured) which was lacking in the rational ethics of Aristotle, and to which Stoic and Epicurean ethics sacrificed everything, but only to be disappointed in the end. This moral ideal of Christianity is not an easy one; and if one considers only the capacities of human nature, and its infirmities, its propensity to evil, it would seem even more impossible to realize than the Stoic or Epicurean ideal. The fact is that Christianity has only raised the level of human civilizations at the price of bringing about trouble and division in them at the same time, as a result of the yes or no it requires of the heart. It has not put an end to wars. It has activated history—it has not subjugated it (God Himself does not do that). It has evangelized the earth—it has not subdued it. Not only contrary efforts and the rebellions of nature, but the action of humanity's own deficiencies upon the divine leaven itself, when the forces of man have undertaken to serve Christ with their own means, have brought it about that Christianity has increased suffering in our species, at the same time that it brought about all real moral progress and every real increase of goodness. But the evangelic hope has left its mark forever in the depths of humanity. Saintliness has transfigured the heart of man, not only among the saints, but among all the sinners whom a ray of it has touched. And in revealing to us that God is love and makes us His sons through grace, that the ultimate fulfillment toward which our poor life proceeds is to possess Him through vision, Christianity, without giving way to any illusions about the potentialities of nature or underestimating its dignity either, has succeeded in assuring the decisive effectiveness of the appeal to the human soul of the ultimate end which is proposed to it—and this is the crucial concern for ethics.

Philosophy put to the test

13. Where the New Law has been received, the various factors of which we have spoken in the preceding pages have been integrated into the common consciousness and the rule of common morality, which form the proper subject of the moralist's reflection. And thereby moral philosophy is placed in an

embarrassing position. If the moral philosopher recognizes these factors, he makes a place in his philosophy for things which depend on religious faith, not on philosophy. If he fails to recognize them, he is leaving out things which form an integral part of that human reality which he intends precisely to elucidate on the level of reflection, and so he causes moral philosophy to quit the soil of existence and fly off into the void.

In actual fact, not to speak of certain authors of textbooks of Christian philosophy who have naïvely taken the tack, as vain from the point of view of the faith as from that of reason, of making moral philosophy a kind of decalcomania or counterfeit of moral theology, we have seen the philosophers engage first in an attempt at *separation*, seeking with Descartes a more or less Stoic natural morality which Science would establish to ensure happiness in the life here below, while Faith would in addition provide man conceived along the lines of this kind of Christian naturalism with eternal delights for life in the hereafter. Or, like Spinoza, they made of ethics a world apart, reserved for the rationalist sage. Or they followed the theoreticians of natural religion, and reduced all the data issuing from Christian revelation, and even God Himself, to the measure of deist philosophy and its enterprise of rational eviction. Later, with Kant, and particularly with Hegel, in their desire to construct an ethics capable of integrating all values, and the most vital ones, recognized by the common consciousness, the philosophers were to engage in an enterprise of *absorption* and *substitution* of vastly more profound significance, in which philosophy would explicitly assume the whole burden which theology regarded as its own, and finally, in the name of the God of history, would take charge of the destinies and salvation of the human race.

III

REVEALED ETHICS

The Tables of Moses and the Gospel—Moral Law divinely promulgated

14. There exists for man a *natural* knowledge of moral rules—natural, though more or less perfect and developed—a knowledge which presents itself in two quite different modes: in the first place, what can be called a *natural-spontaneous* knowledge of moral rules, which is at work, without words, in the conscience of everyone and which expresses itself socially—at a level which is no longer the level of natural law itself—in the customs and taboos of primitive tribes, then in the laws and customs of political societies. In the second place there is what can be called a *natural-reflexive* knowledge of moral rules, which is the concern of philosophers (it constitutes the object of our present historical analysis). Religious belief, moreover, has always influenced the social expression of the natural-spontaneous knowledge of moral

rules, and in an especially direct way in primitive civilizations and in the great ancient civilizations, in which religion was closely incorporated with the social group as one of the organs proper to it.

When Christianity spread in the ancient world, it brought with it—along with the idea of the distinction between the things that are Caesar's and the things that are God's—what may be called a *revealed knowledge* of moral rules—which did not render the efforts of philosophical reason superfluous in this domain, but relegated them to second place, and, if I may say so, remarkably simplified the task to which the great ethical systems of antiquity had dedicated themselves in their search for the moral ideal to propose to men. This was a change of incalculable significance.

God, the ultimate absolute End, He who Is and whose Name is above all names, God the creator and savior, the personal and infinitely transcendent God of the Judeo-Christian tradition, God Himself speaks and instructs men in His precepts, declares to them what are the right ways in human life.

Through Moses He gave them the Decalogue. Through Christ He gave them the New Law.

The rules of human life are taught from on high. The knowledge of them is brought to us by faith, not by reason. It is a revealed knowledge, even the knowledge of the moral rules which are otherwise naturally knowable by the human intelligence and are, in a more or less obscure, imperfect or warped way, spontaneously perceived by human intelligence (the precepts of the Decalogue are essentially a revealed formulation of the principles of natural law).

Humanity finds itself in the presence of a *revealed ethics*, an essentially religious ethics. It is given to man with the absolute, unquestionable, infallible authority which belongs to the Word of God. Let us recall the thunder and lightning, and the voice of the trumpet, and the flames and the smoking mountain, which made the people tremble and kept them at a distance;[1] and the glory which hindered the children of Israel from fixing their gaze on the face of Moses, because of the brightness of his countenance.[2] Such was the attire in which the Tables of the Law were given to men, and the revealed Ethics enthroned before them.

The moral order in consequence will acquire a fixity, a solidity, a rigor; it will deliver itself in unconditional commandments and in absolute requirements which did not appear in any of the ethical theories elaborated by the reason of the philosophers of classical antiquity. It was under the influence of the Judeo-Christian revelation that these properties of the moral law were inscribed in common consciousness.

The New Law, Thomas Aquinas explains,[3] is less severe than the Old Law, because the Old Law imposed on man a far greater number of external actions and obligations. But the New Law carries its precepts and prohibitions into

[1] *Exod.*, XX, 18. [2] *II Cor.*, III, 7. [3] *Sum. theol.*, I–II, 107, 4.

the very intimacy of the heart, the internal acts and movements of the soul; and in this sense Augustine could say that the New Law is easy for him who loves, but hard for him who does not.[1]

In any case, the Old Law and the New Law have both given a sacred significance, immediately referred to God and the Sanctity of His Justice, to the notion of the precept, as to that of sin and of duty; and this significance was even more profound and more exacting in the New Law.

As a result of the impact of Christianity, the sense of transgression and of obligation were thus to take on a new character, both in common consciousness and in ethical theory.

The sense of transgression and the sense of obligation are both natural to us. They derive from the natural functioning of the practical intellect in each of us (whatever the adventitious part played by the constraints of the group or by social taboos in their development). Yet Greek reason, in its philosophical elucidations, except perhaps in the case of the Stoics, had a rather lowered notion of moral obligation and moral fault, which it considered on a level close to that of art. The Judeo-Christian revelation, on the contrary, raised them to the supra-rational level of divine injunction obeyed or transgressed, and reinforced and magnified them by giving them a sacred status much more profound and purer (because related to a transcendent God, and disengaged from the particularisms of the human group) than the sacro-social regimes of the primitive and ancient religions had been able to do.

Sin is henceforth an offense to God—and according to the Christian faith it is responsible for the death of the Son of God on the cross.

Duty is henceforth a requirement in us emanating from the Creator whom heaven and earth obey, and from the Father whom we love if we do His will.

As for the notion of moral rule or of moral law, it will continue to bear the mark imprinted on it at Sinai, the character of commandment laid down by the hand of God in the radiance of His glory, even if, with the Gospel, it was to be interiorized. The tables of the Decalogue have had the same importance in the history of moral ideas as the words repeated by Moses, "I AM WHO IS," or, according to modern exegesis, "I am who I am,"[2] have had in the history of speculative reason. The rules of human conduct no longer have to be discovered by the gropings of the tribe's collective conscience or by the philosophic reason. They are made manifest by God Himself, in a code of morality fixed from on high.

[1] *De natura et gratia*, cap. LXII.

[2] *Exod.*, III, 14. Actually, in both interpretations "He who is" or "He who alone knows his being and his name" asserts himself equally as Being infinitely transcendent *a se*. In any case it is the interpretation which was accepted for many centuries (He who is) which had a decisive effect on speculative reason and on what Etienne Gilson has called the metaphysics of Exodus.

A reinforcement which may regenerate Moral Philosophy or endanger it

15. Here again it is well to remark on the fact that God is more interested in the salvation of the human race than in the labor of philosophers. No doubt revealed ethics offers invaluable assistance to moral philosophy, if the latter knows how to profit from it; in particular, it was no small matter for philosophy to see the unwritten law written and formulated by its Author. But philosophy does not always know how to profit by divine occasions; they put a purely rational discipline in an embarrassing position, concerned as it is on its own account with primary realities and supreme Laws. If it is not tempted to reject that which it has not itself discovered, and which escapes the grasp of pure reason, philosophy is tempted to bring divine revelation down to its own level, use it to increase its own store by denaturing it in order to bring it within the grasp of pure reason.

The historian of culture has no trouble observing that this divine reinforcement, and, if I may put it so, this sacred aggravation of human morality, have been an immensely valuable help to humanity in its forward movement. But he is also aware that in order correctly to understand the contribution made by the Decalogue and revealed ethics to the moral life of humanity, one condition is necessary: namely, that one also understand that such a reinforcement and such an absolutization of the moral rule must be nurtured in the climate of the supernatural reality of grace given to men, and of the redemptive Mercy in which the Justice of the Author of the Law is consummated, and in the climate of the primary precept—the love above all else of Him who is love itself and who wishes to give Himself, to make the human creature partake of His own life.

If we secularize the Tables of the Law, if we transfer the features of the morality of the Ten Commandments to the natural moral law as it derives from reason alone, and is supposed to operate in the order and climate of pure nature, from which all that pertains to the faith and to grace has been eliminated, then we debase and degrade revealed ethics, the morality of the Ten Commandments, and at the same time we deform and harden, perhaps not in its content but in its attitude, the countenance of natural morality—I mean the spontaneous ethics of the conscience which is guided by the inclinations of nature and the reflective ethics of philosophical reason. We arm natural morality with a thunder which properly belongs only to revealed ethics.

Let us think about the natural rule of morality, that rule of which St. Paul spoke *apropos* of the pagans, whose conscience, with its reproaches and incitements, witnesses that they bear in themselves their own law;[1] one may compare it, in its natural manner and bearing, to a child of man, a young

[1] *Rom.*, II, 14–15.

hunter armed with his bow, who trudges along as best he can in the forest. He has a good eye, he aims straight, but his equipment is humble and primitive. He has a long way to go to become an expert hunter in the years to come. And now suppose that we conceive of this natural rule of morality after the model of revealed ethics. Here is our same apprentice hunter transformed into a king seated on his throne, a crown on his head and a scepter in hand—and giving stern looks, because he is, after all, only a child of the woods.

The last three centuries have been rich in examples of social formations in which the inherited rules of revealed ethics were still to be found in force, but in which the context normally furnished by the order of grace had been lost from sight, and in which a kind of natural religion or decorative Christianity, maintained as a moralizing agency, protected and sheltered earthly interests which were very sure of themselves. If people who shared in this way of thinking were not much interested in God, except as a guardian of order, they nevertheless believed firmly in a code of moral austerity filled with commandments all the more unconditional, with prohibitions all the more rigorous, and with condemnations all the more severely applied because the code was primarily concerned with external acts and aimed above all at the conservation of the structures of the social group. This was a case of a deconsecrated and secularized sacred morality. It was not a Christian morality, which is suspended from the theological order and from love, which knows pardon and pity, and which is attuned to contemplation, and to what St. Paul calls "the goodness and love of God our Savior toward man".[1] Nor was it natural morality, which has its source in our essential inclinations and in reason, and which shares the human mood and the seeking attitude of authentic reason, an attitude in which there is indulgence, curiosity, sympathy, always a little hesitation and a little irony, and always a desire to understand and clarify.

But it is in the realm of philosophy, with Kant and Kantian ethics, that we find the most significant example of the way in which the influence of Christianity and of revealed ethics can impair a reason which in other respects repudiates the most essential content of Christianity. It is always dangerous to be half Christian. The impact of Christianity quickens reason (without rendering it infallible) when reason nourishes itself on the substance of Christianity. When reason fattens itself on the left-overs of Christianity, the impact of Christianity warps it. The sacralization of the moral life becomes a dangerous blessing when we cease to understand what that sacralization means. Then what was a supernatural reinforcement and a sacred promulgation of the moral law, becomes a hardening and an arrogance against nature in an ethics which only retains the imprint of the Tables of the Law in order to make of them the Tables of Pure Reason.

Another historical accident, another misconception for which revealed ethics offered an occasion to human reason, and for which certain theologians

[1] *Tit.*, III, 4.

this time bore primary responsibility, can also be pointed out. I allude here to the line of thinkers (the teachers of Islam above all, but also, on the Christian side, Scotus and Occam in the Middle Ages, Descartes in modern times) who, struck more or less consciously by the grand image of the revelation of the Decalogue amid the lightning and thunder of Omnipotence, believed that the moral law, and finally even the distinction between good and evil, depended not at all on divine Wisdom and Reason, the foundation of eternal necessities, but uniquely and exclusively on the pure Will or the pure All-Powerfulness of God, and on an arbitrary decision of His sovereign Freedom. A kind of divine despotism thus became the source of the moral law, decreed and imposed without reason by the celestial High Command. It seems probable to me that this way of looking at things, which St. Thomas Aquinas considered blasphemy, but which was not without its effect here and there on popular consciousness, or popular ignorance, exercised a serious influence on Kant, and played a double role in his thought. On the one hand, I believe, it made him reject, as subjecting the spirit of man to a despotic heteronomy, any idea of making the authority of the moral law depend on the Creator of nature. On the other hand, it made him transfer this same despotic sovereignty to the pure practical Reason, itself identified with the autonomous Will of Man, taken in its supra-empirical dignity.

6

CHRISTIANITY AND PHILOSOPHY

The Ethics of Kant

I

MODERN PHILOSOPHY BEFORE KANT

Rationalism and Empiricism

1. The classical or pre-Kantian age of modern philosophy did not contribute any basic new departures in moral philosophy. The only thinkers of real stature and lasting historical importance in this field were Machiavelli, Hobbes, Pascal and Spinoza.[1] But the work of Machiavelli is not relevant to the present study, since it bears exclusively on political philosophy, which he separated from ethics (and in so doing appears as one of the fathers of the modern world—and a poor ethician). The work of Hobbes is primarily negative. That of Spinoza, that great solitary column erected by absolute intellectualism from the remains of ancient Judeo-Christian wisdom, is in the last analysis more metaphysical than moral. And the great moral intuitions of Pascal have their origin in mystical experience and religious genius, not in the perspectives and elaborations of philosophy.

From the time of the Renaissance to that of Kant, the spectacle offered by moral philosophy is one of progressive secularization or "naturizing" of the traditional Christian heritage. Let us say, to be brief, that this process took two main forms. First of all, an internal change took place in the universe of thought inherited from medieval Christianity, with its effort (thoroughly compromised as it was by the decadent Middle Ages) to accomplish the synthesis of faith and reason. It was in fact the same universe of thought as regards its material constituents, or the various elements which make up its content. But the lighting changed, as well as the arrangement or internal order of the parts. A phenomenon of cleavage or separation occurred. Reason was isolated from faith, and assumed the task of organizing human life: a process of emancipation from the rationalist point of view; a process of disintegration from the

[1] I would have begun this enumeration with the name of Luther, if his theology were not resolutely anti-philosophical: a fact which did not prevent it from having considerable repercussions on moral philosophy over the years. One should mention in this connection the Lutheran notion of the total corruption of human nature, and the great Lutheran rupture between faith and reason, as between the Gospel and culture, and between the moral order and the politico-judicial order. Kant's (and from another point of view Hegel's) dependence on Luther is evident.

point of view of the organic unity of culture. Montaigne, who had nothing of the rationalist in him, observed human nature with the amused eye of a Christian whose faith was a valid ticket to heaven but of no avail for putting things in order here below. On the other hand, great philosophers like Descartes or Leibniz posed as defenders of religion, either to make of it the celestial crown of a human perfection entirely produced by reason alone, or to reduce it to natural religion (there is not far to go from the Christianity of Leibniz to the gospel of Jefferson). Spinoza, for whom faith was only obedience, involving no knowledge even in an imperfect mode, having only the value of a myth, was to hand over to reason the whole of the ancient empire of religion, bag and baggage, including the matters of salvation and sanctity. But what seems to me especially worthy of notice is that this whole great effort to transfer the values of Christian ethics into a rationalist and naturalistic climate, at the same time retaining insofar as possible their cultural function, generally expressed itself in terms of Christian Stoicism: and there is nothing surprising in this, since, thanks to the historical ambiguity we pointed out in a previous chapter, the Stoic sage lay ready at hand as a substitute ideal for a Christian civilization become anthropomorphic. Thus nothing essentially new was contributed to the proper domain of moral philosophy.

2. What occurred in the second place was a labor of critical laying bare, in which the demands of empiricism and the offensive launched in the name of a pessimistic realism occupy the forefront.

In this connection, one might consider the cynicism of Swift as a counterpart of the scepticism of Montaigne—a scepticism and a cynicism both perhaps more affected than real, but none the less significant.

The greatest thinker to be dealt with here is incontestably Thomas Hobbes. In my opinion his work had an importance in the realm of practical philosophy at least equal to that which the work of David Hume was later to have in the realm of speculative philosophy.

The moral philosophy of Hobbes derives from a radical and decidedly materialistic naturalism which had the merit of refusing all compromises. Hobbes did not seek to reconcile the system of traditional thought with one or another opposed inspiration. He broke with this system of thought. He was a kind of agnostic. Faith, for him as for Spinoza, was a matter of obedience, not at all a matter of knowledge—but obedience to the State (conceived in a frankly despotic perspective). For him, human morality is completely and finally explicable in terms of man's desire for his self-preservation and his pleasure. The condition which makes it reasonable to conform to the fundamental moral rules is the fact that they are generally observed, and the condition on which this general observance depends is the power of the State. Here we no longer have a Christian Stoicism, but rather an Epicureanism controlled by Leviathan or the "mortal God", a policed Epicureanism. At the same time, Hobbes turned upside down the classic notion of natural law, and for the idea of an *ideal order* rooted in human nature he substituted a law of nature conceived in purely empirical terms, and signifying only a *primitive state of fact*—that primitive state whose image, traced by his frank pessimism, is indelibly impressed on the modern imagination. One of the most curious (and least glorious) phenomena in intellectual history is the confusion which was to establish itself between these two concepts of the law of nature, radically opposed as they are.

As Höffding has written, "the naturalistic basis which he [Hobbes] gave to ethics and politics originated in a movement which has been strikingly compared to that inaugurated by Darwin in the nineteenth century."[1] The fact remains, however, that even with Hobbes the moral philosophy of the pre-Kantian era brought no fundamental renewal of ethical perspectives. Hobbes simply reworked the old themes of Cyrenaic and Epicurean ethics, making the latter into something more inflexible and more sombre by subjecting it to the yoke of determinism and incorporating it in the absolutism of the State (which was completely contrary to the spirit of Epicurus). He performed an essentially negative task, chipping away, eroding the already existing body of the classical tradition. He revealed no new constructive principle to moral philosophy.

As for Jean-Jacques Rousseau, whose thought was inconsistent but whose sensibility was prophetic, we have reason to mention him here only because of the influence (more emotional than philosophical) exerted on Kant by his message and his enthusiasm (which was moreover too naturalistic for the philosopher of pure reason) for the liberty of the individual and for moral law.

The English School of the Eighteenth Century

3. I do not believe that moral philosophy has any important lesson to learn from the utilitarianism of Bentham and Mill. This *social-minded* and upright hedonism, which conceived of the end of human life in statistical terms, and which in the case of Bentham had a decidedly mercantile flavor, in Mill was colored by the virtues proper to the gentleman, remained quite inferior to the moral sentiment which furnished its substratum in the popular conscience and which it attempted to rationalize. Moreover, it overlooked the fact that Mandeville had already demonstrated the extreme naïvete of the Benthamite principle according to which "the greatest happiness of the greatest number" results from the sum of pleasures and utility of each individual when they are properly calculated. All that the utilitarianism of the latter part of the eighteenth and the beginning of the nineteenth century succeeded in accomplishing was the complete destruction—even in the very camp of these defenders of virtue—of the idea of moral good properly so called, of the *bonum honestum*

[1] *A History of Modern Philosophy*, London: Macmillan, 1924, Vol. 1, p. 264.

(good as right), which they replaced with the idea of the moral good as equivalent to the advantageous, or the "good state of affairs".

The English school of the eighteenth century, on the contrary, has genuine interest for moral philosophy. Whether, with Shaftesbury, it appeals to an aesthetic sense of beauty and harmony which, with a reassuring spontaneity, harmonizes the impulses of egoism and the requirements of social life; or, with Hutcheson, it appeals to the instinctive judgments of a moral sense distinct from reason and perceiving good and evil as intuitively as the sense of sight perceives colors; or whether in the case of Adam Smith, it appeals to the sympathy which assures us of the goodness of our actions when, duplicating ourselves so to speak in two beings, we feel ourselves sympathizing as benevolent and disinterested spectator with our other self as actor—it abandons all pretension to philosophical profundity, with the candor of an empiricism perfectly satisfied with itself. But the astonishing weakness of their theoretical explanations has at least the merit of bringing into sharper relief the fact which they were struggling to explain, namely, the presence in man of a pre-philosophical moral knowledge, acquired in a different way than that of conceptual discourse and reason, a knowledge whose certitudes seem only the stronger for its being ill-adapted to demonstrating them. Precisely by reason of the flagrant impotence of the systems they propose, without knowing it these philosophers turn out to be witnesses of that *knowledge by inclination* which moral philosophy has to recognize as a fundamental datum, and for which they sought substitutes in vain, retaining all the while an authentic though wretchedly conceptualized feeling for the kind of immediacy which characterizes it.

II

THE KANTIAN REVOLUTION

4. It is with Kant that something really and positively new makes its appearance in post-Renaissance moral philosophy. In the process of summing up and concentrating in himself the complex heritage and the long effort of three centuries of thought, he performed a revolutionary task in the realm of ethical philosophy, as in that of speculative philosophy. Not that he wished to destroy or overthrow anything in the realm of morals—on the contrary, his effort was to restore. But in order to construct his imposing edifice he was in fact compelled to transform completely the whole architecture of ethics. He found himself at the point of convergence of two opposed traditions. On the one hand, the process of rationalist separation which we have mentioned culminated with him in a sovereign cult of Pure Reason and a belief in the absolute hegemony of philosophy as a critical discipline. On the other hand, the influence of Christianity and fidelity to originally Christian convictions left its mark in a similarly absolute and irrevocable way on his moral ideal and

his conception of human conduct (just as Leibnizian metaphysics left its imprint on his critical work in the speculative realm). It was in order to achieve the work of integration which his philosophical genius was undertaking in regard to these two contrasting intellectual heritages, these two conflicting worlds of thought, that he was led to a kind of "Copernican revolution" in the practical as in the speculative order. That is to say that in the practical order he founded the whole moral life not on the good but on the pure form of duty, as in the speculative order he founded knowledge and the object of knowledge no longer on being but on the knowing subject and its *a priori* forms.

The operation which he carried out with singular systematic power thus consisted in the construction of a purely philosophical ethics, an ethics of Pure Reason, which would be at the same time an ultimate completion of—and substitute for—the traditional ethics inspired by the Christian faith. In other words, after having secularized them, he transferred the features of revealed ethics and of Christian morality—as they had come to be understood through the vicissitudes of a secular human experience—into a purely philosophical moral theory, where reason, sovereign organizer and legislator of human life, concerned itself with religious belief (whose fate, in what concerns the renunciation of knowing, was henceforward shared by metaphysics, which was to be saved at this price) only in order itself to determine the legitimacy of that belief and the conditions of its existence and the proper bearing of its content.

It is impossible to understand Kant's ethical doctrine if one does not take into account the convictions and the fundamental inspiration he derived from his pietist upbringing. He prided himself on founding an autonomous morality; he took great pains to that end. But in fact his accomplishment was dependent on fundamental religious ideas and a religious inspiration he had received in advance. That is why, however we may regret not being able to keep the analysis within exclusively philosophical bounds, we are obliged, if we wish to grasp the real significance of the moral philosophy of Kant, to take note of all the points of reference to traditional Christian ethics in its essential structure. It is not with the idea of opposing the two systems to each other that we shall have recourse to this kind of confrontation. We would have preferred to avoid it. But it is forced upon us in spite of ourselves by the exigencies of the subject, and because without it the historian of ideas cannot form an accurate notion of what Kant's moral system really is.

The religious background of which we have just spoken is the source of what characterizes Kantian ethics from the outset, namely, its absolutism, the privilege it assigns to morality as revealer of the absolute to man, the seal of the absolute which it impresses upon morality, the saintliness with which it is clothed. The saintly and absolute value of moral obligation and of the *ought*; the inverse value—sacrilegious and absolute—of moral wrong; the saintly and absolute value of good will; the saintly and absolute value of purity of ethical intention: so many traits whose origin lies in the influence of revealed ethics, and which have been transposed therefrom. But since at the same time the whole universe of objective realities on which that revealed ethics depended in its own order and in the supra-rational perspective of faith had been eliminated, along with the universe of objective realities which metaphysics imagined itself to know, the saintly absolutism of morality required a complete reversal of the bases of moral philosophy and rational ethics. Moral philosophy became *a-cosmic*. The world of morality had to be constituted purely on the basis of the interior data of the conscience, while severing itself from the world of objects—confined in sense experience—which our knowledge attains, and especially from that search for the good, the object of our desires, which also belongs to the empirical order, and to which up to this point the fate of ethics had been tied.

The Good as End excluded as a constituent element of Morality

Elimination of the Subjective Ultimate End—Kantian Disinterestedness

5. The idea of disinterestedness is absolutely central with Kant. In a sense it is one of the elements of his morality which derives from the Christian heritage, for it has obvious historical ties with that search for pure love which had posed so many problems for the Christian conscience, especially in the age of quietism, and which was not without indirect repercussions even on Lutheran pietism. But in another sense Kantian disinterestedness, in which love plays no role, is the peculiar privilege of the ethics of Pure Reason, distinguishing it by opposition both from the morality of Aristotle and from traditional Christian morality. Kant saw the weak point in Aristotelian eudemonism; he also saw the weak point in a great many of the popular expositions of religious morality which were not careful enough to avoid presenting it simply as a transcendent eudemonism. He was deeply aware of the necessity for the moral life to be suspended from a supreme disinterested motive, and to be definitively freed from the supremacy of self-love. For this he deserves the gratitude of philosophers, whom he has put in a position to elucidate this point better than they ordinarily do. This perception also explains the favor with which the Kantian ethics has been received in broad sectors of our culture, and the powerful attraction it exerts on minds in spite of its internal weaknesses: for if the hands of man are egotistical and rapacious, still it is a disinterested ideal (no matter what a great many pseudo-realists think) which has the strongest hold on his dreams and even on his thought.

But Kant formed so exclusive, so excessive a concept of what he perceived so clearly, that in order to have a really disinterested supreme motive he thought it was necessary to reject from morality as such the pursuit (which he supposed to be necessarily interested) of any good as the end of action, and especially the pursuit of the supreme good or of a supreme end, the pursuit of the sovereign Good. In other words, he believed it was necessary to withdraw morality, as far as its basic constituents are concerned, from the order of finality. Yet if it is true that "without an end the agent would not act", a disinterestedness so conceived would only *disinterest*, or cut moral action off from existence itself. It is in the very order of finality that a real disinterestedness can be attained: when a person acts for love of another whom he loves more than himself, because through love the good of another becomes our end. Kant, on the contrary, sought a morality of absolute disinterestedness by cutting off morality as such from the order of love, by the very fact that he cut off morality from the order of finality, and from the pursuit of the good as the end of action, which in his view was merely the pursuit of pleasure.

It would be well at this point to avert a possible misunderstanding. H. J. Paton, in a remarkable book,[1] has defended the ethics of Kant against the oversimplified objections of Schiller. It is not true, he says, that Kant taught that no action can be moral if we have some natural inclination toward it or if we obtain the least pleasure from its performance. In this Mr. Paton is right.

But he goes too far in the opposite direction when he affirms that for Kant self-love, pleasure or happiness can play a role in the moral life as *motives* acting conjointly with the will toward duty for the sake of duty. Kant's texts resist this interpretation.[2]

For Kant the pursuit of happiness, the consideration of pleasure or utility and self-interest, the rational love of self, can no doubt play a role in matters of morality, as being related to certain *things* that a wise man can and even ought to propose to do—for example, he ought to see to the conservation of his health—but always on the condition that the unique *formal reason* or *motivation* be that of duty, of reverence for the law.

These empirical attractions—pleasure, self-interest, happiness—can also play the role of factors which remove obstacles, in counterbalancing the attractions of vice; and even the role of *substitutes* for right intention, which *prepare* man to enter into the moral life.

But they can never be the motives of the moral act itself and as such, even conjoint and secondary motives of the weakest order. Insofar as they intervene in the intention, they taint it and cause it to cease to be moral. They cannot act as motives for the autonomous will, the pure moral will. They have no

[1] *The Categorical Imperative*, Chicago: University of Chicago Press, 1948; London: Hutchinson, 1947. Cf. H. H. Schroeder, "Some Misinterpretations of the Kantian Ethics", *The Philosophical Review*, XLIX (1940), pp. 424–426.

[2] It is enough to refer to what he wrote, in an unequivocal way, in the *Critique of Practical Reason*, Part One, Book I, chap. 3. Mr. Paton himself writes (*op. cit.*, p. 56): "Pure practical reason does not demand that we should *renounce* all claims to happiness, but only that the moment the duty is in question we should not *take it into account*."

place in ethical motivation and in the *formal constituent* or *proper constituent* of morality. An action which satisfies an inclination of nature, which causes joy or pleasure, can be moral, to be sure! But if in my decision to perform it, I adopt that pleasure or that joy as my end—even as a secondary motivation—I fall off to that extent from the moral order. Pleasure, and even the desire for pleasure, can accompany the moral act. But they cannot play any *formal* role, any motivating role, in the intention of the moral act.

Let us add that for Kant what is true of pleasure is also true of happiness. He hardly distinguishes between pleasure and happiness, because happiness is for him an empirical notion and one which derives from the world of sensibility; to seek my happiness is to seek that which pleases me. Moreover, even if like Aristotle and to an even greater degree St. Thomas, Kant had had an ontological notion of happiness—a notion of happiness as the full achievement or perfect fulfillment of the being and powers of the subject and of the desires rooted in his nature—and if consequently he had clearly distinguished between happiness and pleasure, happiness would still have remained for him a state which one can only desire for love of oneself, and the search for happiness would still have been tainted by egoism, and thus incompatible with the disinterestedness inherent in an authentic morality. In short, it is not enough to subordinate the search for one's own good to a higher motive in the order of motivations, because according to Kant it cannot in fact be subordinated; once accepted as a motive, it is sovereign. It must be purely and simply eliminated from moral motivation.

6. Thus we see the peculiar significance of Kantian disinterestedness. The sacredness of good will and moral intention is such that any thought of happiness, any desire for happiness entering into the motivation of our acts can only soil that intention, and cause it to fall off from the order of morality. Good will is good—limitlessly good[1]—precisely because it is a manifestation

[1] Cf. Paton, *op. cit.*, p. 52. Good will is limitlessly good; but in us, finite beings, it is not sacred or all-perfect will as is that of God, because it is subject to the influences of the senses' passions and inclinations, and is good only in submitting itself to a law which constrains these inclinations of the senses and our empirical nature (the "corrupt nature" of Luther). Thus the moral law has for us, and can never lose, an essentially *imperative* and *constraining* character which it does not have in the noumenal world and in the infinite Being.

We were speaking (pp. 96–97) of the saintly and absolute value of good will as well as of moral obligation. This value is saintly, not because the good will of man is saintly, but because it must tend toward—without ever being able to attain—the state of *saintly will*, and because (once the ethical order has been completed by the postulate of the existence of God) it is fitting that our good will be conceived of as a reflection in us of the saintly will of the infinite Being, object of belief (with no proofs whatsoever) for the reason.—Cf. *Critique of Practical Reason*, Part One, Book I, ch. 1, § 7, Remark on the Corollary.

For the same reasons (and without there being any question at all of the existence of God as first known by speculative reason) it was fitting, in Kant's view—especially the Kant of the last years and the unfinished Notes (*Opus posthumum*)—to regard the conscience laying down the law which emanated from Pure Reason as though it were transmitting to us a revelation of God. Cf. *Religion within the Bounds of Pure Reason*, III, *i*, 4; IV, *i* and *ii*.

of the pure practical Reason and performs duty solely for the sake of duty. Duty for duty's sake, such is the only authentically moral motivation; and only one impulse of the heart is permitted to contribute to this pure motivation: respect for the law. Reason admits only one sentiment into moral dynamics: respect for the moral law, reverence for the law[1]—which is an emotion of a unique kind, a sentiment directly engendered by a concept of reason, without the intervention of any sensible object. Still further, if the moral law has nothing to do with happiness, it is because its essential character consists in its being obligatory, and how, asks Kant, could a person be obliged to wish to be happy? There is no moral obligation to be happy. (This is true, as we have pointed out already,[2] because we desire happiness by a necessity of our nature; but there is a moral obligation to choose the true happiness—it is at this point that the universe of freedom inserts itself into the universe of nature—and this is what Kant's perspective kept him from seeing.)

In a word, then, Kant cut the moral life off at the same time from Aristotelian Happiness and from Christian Beatitude, from all impetus toward a supreme earthly felicity and from all impetus toward a supreme transcendent felicity. Neither the natural aspiration toward happiness, which for him had to do solely with the world of nature, not at all with the world of freedom, nor the aspiration to partake of the divine beatitude, which for him derived only from a kind of transcendent eudemonism or even hedonism, was involved in the proper order of morality. What we have called the *subjective ultimate end*, which in the original perspective of revealed ethics was the super-fulfillment of the being and the desires of the human subject through the vision of God, and the joy which derives from it as an inherent property, are definitely banished from this proper order of morality.

It is not that something equivalent to this subjective ultimate end, though exterior to the proper order of morality and superadded to it, was not admitted by Kant. In his doctrine of the postulates of the practical Reason there is a kind of final harmony between the law of the world of freedom (duty for duty's sake) and the law of the world of nature (the desire for happiness), which is rendered possible through those objects of *belief* which are the existence of God and the immortality of the soul. But it is a harmony which is realized *after the fact*, as a final reconciliation between two heterogeneous worlds. The desire for happiness and the choice of true happiness, the aspiration toward beatitude, play absolutely no role and have absolutely no place in the proper order of morality, and in the internal dynamism of the world of freedom. And this final reconciliation of the two worlds, this final achievement of happiness, is not only exterior to the realm proper to morality, which is

[1] Cf. *The Fundamental Principles of the Metaphysic of Ethics*, Section I; *Critique of Practical Reason*, Part One, Book I, ch. 3.
[2] See above, ch. III, pp. 31–32.

entirely constituted and fulfilled without any reference to it, but Kant conceives of it as a "recompense", in the most anthropomorphic and extrinsic sense, a gratification offered in reward for good conduct. For in fact this is only a reconciliation between pure reverence for the law (the world of freedom) and pure eudemonism (the world of nature). In rejecting the desire for happiness from the proper order of morality, Kant renounced the possibility of making it transcend itself, and of freeing it from eudemonism.

Although love has no place in it, the pure disinterestedness of his ethics is really a replica of the doctrines of pure love in their most extreme form. He sought *more* than the disinterestedness of the morality of the saints; he proposes to us the super-disinterestedness of an ethic in whose essential structure the notion of a subjective ultimate end has no part.

In the last analysis this amounts to making of the moral agent an agent who is absolutely self-sufficient, and who acts rightly without needing to perfect or fulfill his being. An expression of the sovereignly autonomous and sovereignly legislating Reason, by the very fact that he belongs to the world of freedom and morality, he has nothing to receive, he is not expecting anything to be given him. It is rather he who gives, who presents to the supreme Being acts whose goodness is entirely independent of that Being. He makes a present of his rectitude and the purity of his intention, to be recorded in the books kept by a God who is a kind of eternal Accountant or Notary charged with establishing the final balance between the absolute Disinterestedness of the moral act and the invincibly interested Appetites of nature.

Elimination of the Absolute Ultimate End—Kantian Autonomy

7. In the same way that he eliminates the subjective ultimate end, Kant also eliminates the absolute ultimate end, which similarly has no part in the proper structure of the Kantian ethic.

It is very difficult for a rationalist philosophy to understand that a being which naturally desires happiness can love another being, even God, otherwise than for its own selfish sake. That is why although the Kantian ethic is, as we have pointed out, a rationalistic replica of the most exaggerated mystical theories of pure love, it is at the same time the extreme opposite of these theories. Love has no place in it. To act for the love of God, whatever the mystics say, would still be to act out of that love of self which in the rationalist way of thinking, consummately formulated in the *Maxims* of La Rochefoucauld, is the reason for all other love. In the last analysis, it would still amount to seeking one's own happiness in a concealed way, to obeying an interested motivation, falling off from pure disinterestedness.

But it is not only in the name of pure disinterestedness of ethical motivation, it is also and above all in the name of the autonomy of the will that for Kant the absolute ultimate end must be eliminated from the constitutive structure of ethics and from the proper domain of the moral life.

God plays no role in this domain. It is true, His existence is one of the postulates of the Practical Reason; but, as we have already indicated, it is only after the fact and outside the proper structure of ethics, once the universe of ethics has already been entirely constituted in and for itself, that this universe requires us to believe in the unknowable objects thus postulated (immortality, free will, God), objects which owe to the universe of ethics the existence we attribute to them. In their intimate origin in the thought of Kant (haunted as he was by metaphysics, which he sought to save in his own way), were these "postulates of the Practical Reason" really present as presuppositions, in particular, and most importantly, the belief in that intemporal Freedom which from the heights of the intelligible world fixes our empirical character once and for all and from which the world of morality is suspended? In any case their function in Kant's system is not at all that of presuppositions.[1] The Kantian postulates are not, like the postulate of Euclid with respect to geometry, indemonstrable assertions which play a necessary role in rationally establishing the ethical theory. They are indemonstrable assertions which, once the ethical theory is rationally established, Practical Reason requires us to believe in order to bring our speculative Reason and the universe of our objects of thought, the picture we have of things, into harmony with practical Reason, and with the already completed edifice of morality. Since everything in this picture which is knowable and is the object of science belongs only to the phenomenal order, constructed or fabricated by our understanding through its *a priori* forms, it is the universe of the practical and of morality which, out of a need for harmony and final unification, makes as it were a present to the speculative universe of that which surpasses the phenomenal and belongs to the order of the absolute, in the form of postulates or objects of belief in which the transcendental Ideas at last find employment, and this in order that the world of thought may be adjusted to moral action. I am quite aware that the Kantian conception of belief is highly debatable, for in opposing "belief" to "knowledge" he opposes it not only to science (that is, to *evident* knowledge) but to all knowing. Belief cannot, consequently, consist in knowledge of a non-evident object through the testimony of somebody who has evidence of it (as faith for the theologians consists in knowledge of divine things through the testimony of the first Truth); it is an adherence by which we affirm without knowing it something which no one attests and in which nevertheless we must "believe" in the name of the exigencies of moral action. That this theory of philosophical or moral belief and of postulates is logically inconsistent, and that in the last analysis it is worth no more, in spite of all the seriousness of Kant's convictions, than the common idea of religion as a "comforting illusion" answering our needs, however, lies outside our present concern. What is important here is that it makes out of God an appendix to morality, not its foundation.

[1] Cf. *Critique of Practical Reason*, Part One, Book II, ch. 2.

8. We have said that the Kantian notion of the autonomy of the will requires that the absolute ultimate end be excluded from the proper and constitutive domain of ethics. It is so because the Practical Reason, or the pure rational will (these two notions are apparently identical for Kant)[1] is absolutely autonomous, that is to say, it is not submitted to any other law than that which it gives itself, or rather, which is one with itself.[2] In other terms, the dignity of the person is such that, in the words of Rousseau, it can only obey itself. This perfect autonomy first of all excludes God as Legislator from the proper and constitutive domain of morality, since in dividing good from evil the eternal reason and will of God as Legislator (or his simple arbitrary will, the popular conception of which St. Thomas held to be a blasphemy[3]) would impose upon us from without the law of Another. The Pure Practical Reason is alone the legislator. And this same perfect autonomy also excludes God as absolute ultimate end from the proper and constitutive domain of morality; it excludes from this order the subsistent Good, which must be loved above all things, and in the love of which the supreme motivation of the

[1] ". . . The will is nothing but practical reason." *The Fundamental Principles of the Metaphysic of Ethics*, trans. by Otto Manthey-Zorn, New York: Appleton-Century, 1938, Section II, p. 29.

[2] "Autonomy of the will is that property of the will by which it gives a law to itself (irrespective of any property of the object of volition). This then is the principle of autonomy: never to choose otherwise than so that the maxims of one's choice be also comprehended in the same volition as universal law." *Ibid.*, Section II, p. 59. Cf. *Critique of Practical Reason*, Part One, Book I, ch. 1, 28, trans. by Lewis White Beck, New York: Liberal Arts Press, 1956, p. 33.

Let us point out moreover these characteristic lines: "The dependence of a will not absolutely good on the principle of autonomy (the moral compulsion) is *obligation*. . . . The objective necessity of an action from obligation is called *duty*." *The Fundamental Principles of the Metaphysic of Ethics*, trans. by Otto Manthey-Zorn, *op. cit.*, Section II, p. 58.

Moral obligation in the practical order—and, in the speculative order, the activity of the mind in knowledge—were (though he promptly deformed them by an extremist conceptualization) the object of the two great philosophical intuitions which we believe must be considered as central to Kant. (That is why he considered moral obligation to be a "fact of pure reason"). What he authentically saw is that moral obligation, while being a constraint *sui generis*, does not violate the "autonomy" essential to the will, or, in other words, is connatural with the will (cf. our remarks on obligation, *infra*, ch. XIV, pp. 418–442). But his conceptualization radically warped this intuition, through two extremely serious errors: instead of regarding the "autonomy" essential to the will as the perfect spontaneity of a nature which dominates its own exercise, and, when necessitated to exert itself, is so necessitated by its own self, and not by its objects (cf. *infra*, ch. VIII, p. 167, note 1), Kant regarded it as a quasi-divine power of being to itself the law of its action;—and at the same time he brought back into the very definition of moral obligation the fact of its imposing itself on a rebellious nature, as though the essence of moral obligation and of duty could not remain in a soul supposed free of all disordered inclinations (or indeed in a human soul effectively elevated to the peak of perfection, like that of Christ).

[3] See above, ch. V, p. 91.—Kant reduced every idea of founding moral law in God to this pure divine voluntarism (cf. *The Fundamental Principles of the Metaphysics of Ethics*, trans. by Otto Manthey-Zorn, *op. cit.*, p. 62); this is one of the reasons why, like Hume, he wanted to cut ethics off completely from any divine foundation; the other reason was epistemological: the God of Kant is given us (as object of belief, not of knowledge) only by morality, and thus God could not found morality without involving a vicious circle.

moral agent must consist. If love is rigorously excluded from Kantian motivation, it is because love, so it seems, is irremediably heteronomous. Is there any worse heteronomy than to do the will of another, and to say to another whom one loves: thy will be done, not mine?

In a "cosmic" ethical theory, or one with an ontological foundation, which takes both the line of final causality and the line of formal causality into account, it is possible to understand, on the one hand, that the moral act can depend on both these lines of causation at the same time: it derives its intrinsic value from its conformity to its formal rule, and it is accomplished in virtue of a motivation which derives from finality (on which its definitive existential value depends, for the end also must be good); in traditional Christian morality a good man does *that which is good* (or in conformity with reason, the formal rule) *for love of subsistent Good* (final causality). And one may understand, on the other hand, that a subordination is possible in the order of ends (a good act can be motivated by love of self and personal interest, by love of the social group, etc., all this being subordinated to a supreme motivation which is the love of God) as in the order of formal reasons (reason constitutes the proximate rule of human acts, itself subordinated to the rule of natural law, which is in turn subordinated to the Eternal law). But Kant constructed his moral system solely in function of the order of formal causality, totally eliminating the order of final causality. He retains (necessarily) the notion of motivation, which in itself derives from final causality; but he can only account for it by referring it to the line of formal causality, and by making of it a unique "feeling", the direct product of a concept of reason—reverence for the law or for the formal rule itself. As a result, the idea of subordination of ends disappears, along with the whole order of finality, which has been eliminated (just as the idea of subordination of formal reasons also disappears, presupposing as it does an ontologically founded ethics). At the same time, any intervention by the love of some end, be it even love of the absolute ultimate End, in the motives which make us act can only violate or destroy the moral character of a motivation which has been conceived exclusively in function of formal causality, and whose purity depends on its unique connection with the formal rule, its unique privilege of manifesting the dignity and sacredness of duty and of the law. The *only* morally valid motivation is reverence for the law.

Briefly, in Kantian ethics respect for the law or reverence for the law has taken the place of the love of God above all things, which is the foundation of traditional Christian ethics—and this in virtue of a transposition of traditional Christian morality into terms of pure reason. Reverence for the law has taken the place of the love for God, just as the unlimited goodness of the will, existing within the moral agent, has taken the place of the infinite goodness of the absolute ultimate End, which exists outside him and above him.

9. If it is true that man is a creature, it is nonsense to claim an absolute autonomy for him as a moral agent. He gains his autonomy progressively, and remains forever subject to the law of another, to a law which depends not on himself but on nature and the author of nature. But this heteronomy is not in itself a servitude, for this law established by another is the law of our own nature—it requires us to act as men, or according to what we are essentially—and it corresponds to our will's radical desire for the good. This heteronomy only becomes a servitude for a will which is in fact turned toward evil. Moreover, it is not incompatible with autonomy, for the autonomy of the moral agent is realized through the interiorization of the law. This process of interiorization is a double one: interiorization through intelligence, and interiorization through love. The only authentic autonomy for the human being is to fulfill the law—the law of another—which he has made his own through reason and through love.

When I have understood, through my reason, that the law is just and good, it is my own reason that I am obeying when I obey the law. That is why reason is the immediate rule of human acts. This is the first degree of autonomy. But insofar as our heart remains evil and our will turned toward evil, this first degree remains imperfect and does not eliminate servitude; it is through fear of this law, which I have made my own through reason and which coerces me, that I refrain from doing what my heart desires and my will inclines to.

But there is a second degree of autonomy, which proceeds from the interiorization of the law through love. Even in its most impoverished forms love brings with it a kind of freedom, because it makes of the one we love another self. A man who renounces his own will in order to do the will of another—even with all the infirmities of passion—because he loves him, and if he truly loves him, has more real autonomy, however weak it be, than a man (if this Kantian fiction could exist) would have who obeyed the categorical imperative through respect for the law and without any love. But when it is a matter of love in its highest form, of love for the absolute ultimate End, who is more ourselves than we are and whom we love more than ourselves, then autonomy makes an end to all servitude, then it is complete freedom that love brings with it. For then, in doing what the law prescribes through love of the law and of the Author of the law, man is following the deepest desire of his whole being—a desire which through his love he has himself rendered more intimate and more natural to his heart than any other desire of his nature. He is following the most personal movement of his will, whose radical aspiration he has himself delivered up to the good, in the freedom of a supreme love. Perfectly interiorized through love, the law has become connatural with him. He is no longer *under* the law, says St. Paul, he is doing what he loves. This is the privilege of those whom St. Paul calls the "sons of God"; they have come to be not above the law but above the constraining imperative that it imposes. There is no higher human autonomy than that of Christ on the Mount of Olives. In saying to His Father: Thy will be done, not mine, He was asking, in an act of supremely free, voluntary and spontaneous obedience, for the fulfillment of a will that was more His than His own—the will of Him whom He loved, as against that which was dearest to Him but which He loved *less*.

As a result of carrying autonomy and disinterestedness to an extreme which was contrary to the human condition, Kant missed the mark and failed to find what he was looking for. He missed the only complete disinterestedness that man can really attain and to which he is really called, and which, like autonomy, is achieved little by little and progressively: the disinterestedness which, following the very channels of our natural desire for happiness, but catching that desire in the trap of love as it were, begins by subordinating to the love of the absolute ultimate End, loved more than ourselves, the search for a supreme happiness that we still desire *for* love of ourselves (although primarily *for* the love of God). This disinterestedness comes to fruition in such a complete love of the absolute ultimate End, loved more than ourselves, that we no longer wish supreme happiness *to* ourselves except *for* love of that End, so complete a love that we even forget (without being able to renounce it) the search for the supreme happiness we wish for ourselves without having to think about it, since we only wish it for ourselves for the love of God, not of ourselves. Because genuine Christianity does not despise the natural desire for happiness and does not reject it from the proper domain of morality but directs it to something better and more loved, genuine Christianity transcends all eudemonism. That Kant did not see.

He also missed, as we just pointed out, the only full autonomy that man can really attain and to which he is truly called. In terms of historical influence, which is subject to all the alterations and accretions of time, the *libertas christiana*, Pauline autonomy, is the remote ancestor of the Kantian idea of autonomy. Kant raised autonomy to an absolute because he separated it from the Absolute on which our being depends, and from the love of that Absolute. One might say that his ethics of Pure Reason is a Christian ethics whose theological root has been severed, leaving only the stiffened moral branches. Thence what could be called the Kantian hypermoralism. There is no longer any order of grace, and consequently no order of charity, of infused virtues and gifts which render man connatural with that which is better than man. There remains only the order of the Law. We have pointed out that for Kant respect for the law takes the place occupied by the love of God above all else in traditional Christian ethics. This means that the Law, respect for which constitutes the only motivation compatible with moral rectitude, can never cease to impose on man its constraining imperative, to subjugate him to its sacred dignity. Man is always *under* the Law. There can be no sons of God nor freedom of the sons of God. Access to supreme autonomy is refused to man.

The Good as a Value inherent in the moral Object excluded as a constituent element of Morality—Kantian Formalism

Primacy of the "you ought", pure of all content

10. The commandments of Sinai, written by the God of Israel on the two tables entrusted to Moses, were like an irruption from heaven, imposing its law on the world of man. They nevertheless had a definite content, expressing with the authority of revelation what are called the fundamental "precepts" of the "natural law", or the fundamental practical judgments which nature and the natural inclinations of the being gifted with reason spontaneously incite the spirit of man to formulate. The Kantian "you ought" is similarly like an irruption from the heaven of the Pure Reason, imposing its law on the empirical world. It is a primary fact, of unique significance, which has no more need of any ulterior justifying reason than did the divine law, justified in itself, for the Psalmist,[1] because it is a manifestation of Reason itself in the practical order.[2] It surges up in us and imposes itself on us, in the thunder and lightning of our conscience, and there is nothing for us to do but yield to it. Kant is the mediator through whom the tables of the Pure Practical Reason are transmitted to us. But nothing is inscribed on these tables, save the form of duty. The Kantian "you ought" has no content, indeed this is the price levied for its supra-empirical character, absolute and unconditioned. It is only the manifestation of Pure Reason's rule over us, without the least reference to intrinsic goodness, to the *good as value* in the object of human acts, any more than to any law outside the moral agent as such, any natural law or law of God. Just as the good as end has been excluded from the motivation of the moral act, the good as *objective value* is excluded from its specification. That which constitutes the value of the moral act is not the goodness of its content or of its object, but its conformity to the formal universality of the pure and primordial "you ought", from the beginning empty of all content.

This results from the fact that the universe of freedom or of morality, the ethical universe, has been totally and absolutely separated from the universe of nature, which, from the point of view of knowledge, is the domain of phenomena, of their laws and their determinism constructed under the unifying power of our *a priori* forms, and, from the point of view of action, the domain of desire and sensibility, of things outside the moral agent as such, the domain of the empirical, therefore of the non-moral. To make the value of the moral act depend on the goodness of its object, or on a quality which intrinsically determined this object in virtue of what things are, and on the ideal order of exigencies of which nature is the vehicle and the witness, would

[1] Psalm 18, verse 10, in the Vulgate.

[2] Kant calls it "the only fact of Pure Reason". *Critique of Practical Reason,* Part One, Book I, ch. 1, § 7, trans. by Lewis White Beck, *op. cit.*, p. 31. (Cf. *ibid.*, § 8.)

not only attribute to us a supra-phenomenal knowledge that we do not possess, but from the point of view of ethics and in its proper order it would cause the moral commandment to lose its absolute dignity and its unconditional authority by making it depend on empirical reasons and specifications. It is the unique privilege of the Pure Practical Reason to transmit something of the intelligible world to man, to procure for him a visitation from the absolute, not certainly in the form of a knowledge but in the form of an injunction, a commandment. And it is only by its form—expressed by the "you ought"—that this commandment is manifested to us as a visitation from the absolute, for it is only in virtue of its form that it derives from the Pure Reason and bears its emblem.[1] It thus impresses the seal of the law of the Pure Practical Reason or of the rational Will (which have their seat in that intelligible world the notion of which Kant inherited from Leibniz) on the life of sensibility and empirical determinations, the world of nature in us; and it does this by means of an imperious and coercive "you ought", because the world of the senses and instincts, of desires and inclinations, the empirical world, is a rebellious world.

Before knowing *what* I ought to do, then, I know, Reason tells me, that *I ought*. Reason submits me to the pure form of moral obligation and unconditioned commandment. In Kant's personal preoccupations and intentions this formalism was attenuated or mitigated by a concrete and authentically human sense of moral realities.[2] In his system it is rigorously pure.

[1] See the famous *hymn to duty* in the *Critique of Practical Reason*, Part One, Book I, ch. 3, trans. by Lewis White Beck, *op. cit.*, p. 89: "Duty! Thou sublime and mighty name that dost embrace nothing charming or insinuating but requirest submission and yet seekest not to move the will by threatening ought that would arouse natural aversion or terror, but only holdest forth a law which of itself finds entrance into the mind and yet gains reluctant reverence (though not always obedience) . . . what origin is there worthy of thee . . .? It cannot be less than something which elevates man above himself as a part of the world of sense, something which connects him with an order of things which has under it the entire world of sense. . . . It is nothing else than personality, i.e. the freedom and independence from the mechanism of nature regarded as a capacity of a being which is subject to special laws (pure practical laws given by its own reason), so that the person as belonging to the world of sense is subject to his own personality so far as he belongs to the intelligible world."

A little before this Kant explains in all rationalistic candor that the Gospel commandment to love God above all else and to love one's neighbor as oneself means no more in reality than this duty to submit oneself to the authority of the moral law emanating from Reason, because on the one hand, since God is not an object of the senses, one could not love Him properly speaking, or experience passion for Him ("pathological" inclination in Kant's sense of the adjective); and because, on the other hand, this sort of inclination may well exist toward men, but could not be commanded.

[2] There is much insistence to-day on the ethico-political works (brought together and translated into French by Piobetta—Paris: Aubier, 1947—under the title: *Kant: La philosophie de l'histoire*) such as the Essay on the different races of men, the Idea of a universal history, etc., where many views relating to the intrinsic content of morality are put forth as a matter of course. But all this does not alter our analysis of the system in any way. One must say the same of certain works of the pre-critical period where Kant distinguishes between the logical opposition of simple contradiction (*more wolfiano*) and real opposition, and considers these two kinds of opposition as irreducible. Cf. *Versuch den Begriff der negativen Grössen in der Weltweisheit einzuführen* (1763), and Roger Kempf's introduction to his

11. I ought; but what ought I? How does this pure form of duty acquire a content, or rather (since its absolute and unconditioned character forbids its undergoing any influence from nature), how does it give itself or determine for itself a content?

Kant is using here the classical notion of *conformity to reason* as a measure of the moral act. But now it can only be the reason in its *purely formal* function, exclusively on the level of the properties and connections which are the object of logic (since any possibility of determination by nature or by the being of things has been suppressed). The essential trait that reason in its pure formal function offers to Kant is the double character of universality and non-contradiction. It is this that Kant adopts as a criterion.

It is sufficient for our purpose to consider the first of the five formulations of the categorical imperative that Kant proposes: "Act only on that maxim which will enable you at the same time to will that it be a universal law."[1] This is the formula of universal law—or of the logically possible (non-contradictory) universalization of the maxim of the act—to which the third formula (the formula of autonomy) is akin: "Act in such a way that the will can always at the same time regard itself as giving in its maxim of action universal law."

In the case of an act such as: not keeping a trust, it would be a logical impossibility or a contradiction to erect the following maxim into a universal law: one must never keep a trust; for if each individual is to receive a trust only with the intention of not keeping it, "trusts would no longer exist". A universal law prescribing that trusts should not be kept would cause its own object to disappear.[2]

French translation (Paris: Vrin, 1949). In Kant's ethical system the formal opposition by virtue of which it is impossible to will that the maxim of an act such as not to keep a trust or put to death an offender be erected into universal law without logical contradiction is itself a real opposition, preventing the will from erecting this maxim into a law of the conscience.

[1] *The Fundamental Principles of the Metaphysic of Ethics*, trans. by Otto Manthey-Zorn, *op. cit.*, Section II, p. 38.

The other formulae of the categorical imperative are:

> Act as if the maxim of your action by your will were to become a universal law of nature [establishing a rational harmony among moral agents] (*Ibid.*, p. 38).
>
> So act that the maxim of your will could always hold at the same time as a principle establishing universal law [or could consider itself as making and promulgating by its maxim of action a universal law] (*Critique of Practical Reason*, Part One, Book I, ch. 7, § 7, trans. by Lewis White Beck, *op. cit.*, p. 30).
>
> Act so that in your own person as well as in the person of every other you are treating mankind also as an end, never merely as a means. (*The Fundamental Principles of the Metaphysic of Ethics, op. cit.*, p. 47.)
>
> ... Each rational being must act as though in his maxims he were at all times a legislating member in the universal realm of ends. (*Ibid.*, p. 57.)

Cf. H. J. Paton, *op. cit.*, p. 180.

[2] Concerning which Hegel was to observe: "If there were no more trusts at all, where would the contradiction be?" But the contradiction would be in the *prescription* which at the same time presupposes and destroys the existence of trusts.

Or to take another example, think of an act such as: killing a man who has trespassed against me. Here the erection of the maxim of the act into a universal law (we must always kill those who trespass against us) involves no contradiction. But what would imply a contradiction and a logical impossibility would be to *will* that the maxim in question be erected into a universal law: for then I should wish that the person whom I happen to trespass against put *me* to death. There is a contradiction involved in willing a law which brings with it the disappearance of the person who wills it. That is why Kant was careful to say: act only in such a way that you *can will* that the maxim of thy act become a universal law.

In one case as in the other Kant deduces the content of the moral law from its pure universality: an act is forbidden, or contrary to the moral law, because it is logically impossible, or contradictory, either to universalize its maxim, or to will to universalize its maxim.

What constitutes the value of the Act is not the good present in its object, but the logical compatibility of its maxim with the Form of the Law

12. As we have just seen, Kant takes into consideration the consequences or results of our conduct: but solely and exclusively in order to determine whether its maxim is compatible or not with the universality of the *you ought*. By virtue of the fact that an act derives from a maxim that is logically compatible with the universality of the form of the law, it is ethically acceptable, it is *moral*, and is made to participate in the absolute goodness of the good will. But the intrinsic moral goodness of the object of our actions, the good and the evil inherent in the things we do, in the reality that we produce in the world, which itself possesses a certain moral quality in virtue of what it is, irrespective of the logical possibility or impossibility of universalizing or willing to universalize our maxims of conduct, has been entirely excluded and eliminated from the structure of ethics. What constitutes the value of an act is not the moral goodness of its object, but the logical appropriateness of its maxim to the requirement of universality of the formal norm.

The fundamental concept of good thus finds itself re-elaborated, re-oriented, and as it were redistributed along new lines. In the first place, the notion of the good as value or of moral goodness obviously has not disappeared—it cannot disappear; but it has been recast, so that it no longer designates anything more than the quality of an act whose maxim is compatible with the universality required by the form of the law. The change in vocabulary here is itself very meaningful: in order to designate this quality or value of the act, one will no longer say that it is "morally good" or "morally bad", but that it is or is not "moral" or ethical. The notion of moral goodness has turned into the notion of ethicalness. An act is ethical or *moral* (a re-worked equivalent of "morally good") because it is *commanded* by the law.

And it is commanded by the law because its maxim can be universalized, or willed to be universalized, without contradiction.

In the second place, as we indicated a moment ago, the notion of an *object* or *content* of the action, which would be considered *good in itself* (by reason of what it is, not physically, doubtless, but morally, or by reason of the value it bears in it, or the being it receives when it is transferred from the physical or ontological order into the proper perspective and the proper order of morality), the notion of the intrinsic moral goodness or moral badness of the object of our acts, in virtue of which the common conscience prescribes an act because it is good and forbids it because it is bad, this notion has been eliminated. The object no longer plays any role in the specification of the moral act. It is of secondary importance, extrinsic to the essential dynamism of morality, it is by a contribution of the act to the object, that in the last analysis the morality (the "moral goodness", in ordinary language) of an act already fully endowed with its value passes over to its content or its object and justifies the object's being itself called (but as a mere factual result, once the act has been decided upon) *moral* (or, in ordinary language, "morally good"). The value of the object is an effect of the value of the act; the object of the act is moral ("morally good") because the act is moral, or derives from a maxim compatible with the universality of the form of the law.

This is to say that the *bonum honestum*, which purely and simply perfects the human subject (the beautiful-and-good of the Greeks), the directly and specifically moral good has ceded the central place it occupied in traditional ethics to the absolute Obligation imposed by the Norm. It has been replaced by a substitute. For the *bonum honestum* is attributed to the object of the act before being attributed to the act itself, and it signifies a *good in itself* (in the proper order of morality).[1] And this "good in itself" is now rejected from the world of ethics just as the "thing-in-itself" is rejected from the world of knowledge. In the same way that the object of knowledge is made an object or "thing" (thing-phenomenon) because it is subsumed under our *a priori* forms, so the object of the act is made moral or "good", receives the seal of pure reason, because it is subsumed under an act whose maxim is appropriate to the universal form of commandment. I do not do right because I am doing the good. What I do is good (is *moral*) because I act according to a maxim which can be universalized without contradiction.

13. A great moral philosophy always has at some point or in some way a connection with the moral feeling of common experience. Popularly considered, and more or less separated from their systematic context, the doctrine and the formulae of the categorical imperative thus find a counterpart in our instinctive sense of the purity and dignity of the moral act, and they furnish

[1] On the *bonum honestum*, see above, ch. II, pp. 24–26; ch. III, pp. 35–37; and below, ch. XIV, Section One, pp. 410–411; Section Two, pp. 432–433.

practical criteria which receive the approval of the common conscience, like other general maxims such as "do unto others as you would have them do unto you". But taken philosophically, the doctrine of the categorical imperative is in itself ruinous, and has done a great deal of harm to ethics.

Just by reason of its formalism it has vitiated the notion of the universality of moral rules and of the law, by transferring that universality from the level of the reality which is human nature to the level of the being of reason which is the object of logic. I am henceforth submitted to the exigencies of a logical universal which imposes its form from without on my individual act without having any contact with my individuality, instead of being submitted to the exigencies of a rational nature which is no doubt common to all men but which is also my nature, individualized in me, a rational nature which no doubt places me under the authority of a general law, but which constitutes in me, and in spite of all my impulses to the contrary, an appeal to that law. The whole process of interiorization of the law, in virtue of which the law is recognized as just and good by the reason, and finally adapted by prudence to particular circumstances and to the singularity of the situations in which the self is involved, this whole process of interiorization is henceforth left out of account. The purely logical universality of the Kantian law, without any roots in nature, keeps it eternally separate from the individual subjectivity and external to it. It is Kant who forced Kierkegaard to seek an outlet for the deepest longings of the moral conscience in a revolt against the generality of the law, and in a "suspension of morality".

In completely separating the world of morality from the world of nature Kant completely destroyed the equilibrium of ethics. Forbidding himself to look for any rational elucidation of moral principles (which would have involved a recourse to being), he suspended ethics from the absolute of a "you ought" which he deprived himself of every means of justifying and which could therefore only appear as entirely arbitrary. He made of ethics a system established *a priori*, on the basis of which, far from relying on the moral experience of men in order reflexively to bring out the principles thereof, the philosopher dictates to them the articles of a legislation of Pure Reason despotically imposed on their life. He centered ethics no longer on the Good but on the Norm, and on "Obligatoriness", and by that very fact he warped the notion of moral philosophy and of its very normative character, detaching this normative character from its foundations in nature and its ties with experience, and making of moral philosophy a purely normative discipline, and normative *a priori*.

A Christian ethics of pure Reason which Christianity was instrumental in warping

14. The Stoic morality was a morality of pure value. But in a sense which this time is absolutely radical, the morality of Kant is a morality of value *only*.

Finality and happiness still played an essential role in the proper structure of ethics for the Stoics; for them happiness and finality were absorbed into value, not opposed to it and excluded in its name. With Kant, the final end, the sovereign good, happiness, are all decisively rejected from the proper world of ethics. Kantian ethics is the irreconcilable enemy of Aristotelian eudemonism, because, in a much more general and more profound way, it is the irreconcilable enemy of Hellenic moral thought, and of the dependence of morality on happiness and on the sovereign good envisaged by the Greeks.

At the root of this enmity there is a kind of purist protest raised in the name of the old conflict between Christianity and paganism. As a result the ethics of beatitude appears as still contaminated by pagan eudemonism; the ethics of Kant, at the same time that it is purely philosophical, will be more Christian than traditional Christian ethics. What is at work at the bottom of this ethics of Pure Reason is a kind of hyper-Christianity without Christ, a Christian ferment deprived of its essence, from which the whole content of faith has been removed, but which continues to act.[1]

Where does the Kantian "you ought" come from, if not, as we have remarked, from a transposition of the revealed ethics of Sinai? Where does the idea of the sacredness of moral obligation and of the moral law, the idea of the supreme disinterestedness of the moral act, of the freedom and autonomy of the will when it identifies itself with the law, of the absolute or "categorical" value of the moral imperative, of the constraint it imposes on rebellious nature, of the dignity of the human person and the duty we have even when we use it as a means always to treat it at the same time as an end, where do all of these ideas come from if not from Christian sources? Kant wished to save all these elements derived from Christianity and to exalt them in an essentially rationalist ethics in which Pure Reason—but a reason which can know nothing of the absolute—takes the place of the God of Moses, in its capacity as Pure Practical Reason and on the condition of imposing an absolute commandment empty of all content. The result was, as we have seen, that he had to replace the Good by the Norm, and so unbalance ethics.

The ethics of Kant is the greatest and most powerful work of genius that modern times have erected in the field of moral philosophy. It is also an extraordinarily significant example of the way in which a moral system which is not only purely rational and philosophical but entirely and supremely rationalistic, can be thrown off balance by a devitalized Christian ferment, a Christianity which this philosophy itself has enclosed "within the limits of pure reason".

[1] Etienne Gilson speaks of Kantian ethics in a similar vein in *The Spirit of Medieval Philosophy*, trans. by A. H. C. Downes, New York: Scribners, 1940, pp. 342, 359–360, 361, 362. (London: Sheed and Ward, 1936.)

Cosmic-Realist Ethics and A-cosmic-Idealist Ethics

15. It will be helpful to recapitulate the results of our long analysis by grouping them into a synoptic résumé.

In the great classical tradition descending from Socrates, moral philosophy can be characterized as a *cosmic-realist* ethics. We say *cosmic* ethics because it is founded on a view of the situation of man in the world;[1] we say *realist* ethics because it is founded on the extra-mental realities which are the object of a metaphysics and a philosophy of nature. This ethics is at once, and essentially, *experiential* and *normative* in character.

We might designate in this way the essential articulations of this cosmic-realist ethics:

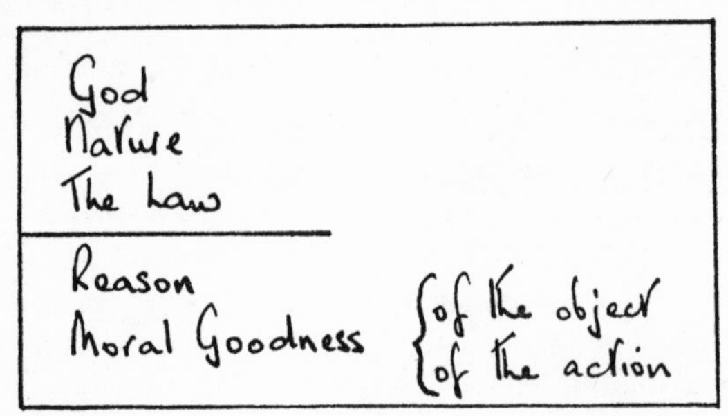

In this table the first three terms relate to extra-mental reality. The Law designates the natural law rooted in the being of things and the expression in them of the creative wisdom.

Reason is the immediate rule or measure of human acts, itself ruled or measured by the natural law and the ends essential to human nature.

In consequence, the moral object is good in itself, intrinsically good, when it conforms to reason. There is an intrinsic *goodness* or *badness*—conformity or non-conformity with reason—in the object of our acts.

And the goodness or rightness of the moral action depends on the goodness of the object.

In this ethical perspective moral goodness has its foundation in extra-mental reality: God, the nature of things, and especially human nature, the natural law. This is the perspective of the common conscience of humanity, and it is also, we think, the authentic perspective of moral philosophy.

16. With Kant everything changed. As we remarked above, Kantian philosophy furnishes the example of a moral philosophy which the influence of

[1] We noted above (ch. IV, pp. 67–68) that the expression "cosmic ethics" can designate a closed-cosmic ethics or an ethics without-the-beyond, like that of the Stoics and of the Epicureans. An authentic cosmic ethics—of which we are thinking here—is an open-cosmic or cosmic-trans-cosmic ethics, where man is considered in his relation to the world and to the transcendent principle of the world,

Christianity—improperly received—helped to warp. It is a Christian moral philosophy, but a falsified one. Kant tried to transpose revealed morality as the Judeo-Christian tradition presents it to us into the register of pure reason. He sought to retain the Judeo-Christian absolutization of morality in an ethics of Pure Reason, which rid itself of any properly supernatural or revealed element in order to replace it with the authority of a Reason not grounded on the real and on nature. He proposes to us an ethics of pure duty, an ethics without a last end, freed from all impulse towards happiness and to-

Cosmic-realist Ethics metaphysically and "physically" based; experimental-normative	A-cosmic idealist Ethics neither metaphysically nor "physically" based; deductive-normative
1. God 2. Nature 3. The Law (natural law)	
4. Reason (measuring and measured measure) 5. Moral Goodness of the object 6 and consequently of the act	1. Reason (measuring only) 2. The Law (merely formal—Categorical imperative) 3. Rightness (or ethicity) of the act (by virtue of the universalisability of its maxim) whence, by superaddition, the moral goodness of the object
Moral good is based in extra-mental reality;	Moral good is based on the universality of pure practical Reason

wards the good; an ethics of the categorical imperative, in which the universe of morality and of freedom is totally separate from the universe of nature, so that the content of the law must be deduced from its form and from the universally normative essence of the Pure Practical Reason. In this ethics the specification of moral acts is freed from any consideration of the *good*, of the goodness-in-itself of the object (that is to say, of its conformity with reason in virtue of the nature of things); and this is logical enough, since things in themselves cannot be reached in Kant's system.

The Kantian revolution thus leads to an *a-cosmic-idealist* ethics, constructed in complete independence of any observation of the situation of man in the world and the universe, wanting to have no foundation either in metaphysics or in the philosophy of nature. This ethics has a *deductive-normative* character.

The first three items of the preceding table are eliminated from this ethics, as having nothing to do with morality.

The initial stage of such a moral philosophy is Reason as the measure of human acts, but no longer in at all the same sense as in the classical tradition, for now we have to do with *Pure* Reason, pure of all knowable matter, reason considered in a purely formal manner, solely from the point of view of the exigencies of logical universality.

The second stage is the law, no longer the natural law, but law in the sense of the categorical imperative, the absolute "you ought" of Sinai imposed in the name of Pure Reason as the *a priori* form of human acts.

The third stage is the rightness or morality (the moral goodness) of the action. For Kant the action is moral when its maxim is a maxim that it is possible to will to universalize, to erect into a rule of universal commandment over the conduct of every human being. It is this universalizability of the maxim of the act that constitutes its ethicalness, or, in ordinary language, its moral goodness—a goodness which depends in no way on the goodness of the object. There is no intrinsic goodness in the object on which the goodness of the act might depend. On the contrary, if in the end and as a by-product one can speak of the goodness of the object, it is only as depending on the morality of the act. The morality of the act makes its object morally good. Moral good no longer has any foundation in extra-mental reality, it is founded solely on the universality of Pure Practical Reason, the content of the moral action having to be deduced from this universal form and from the exigencies of universality essential to the reason. We have noted that Kantian ethics is an ethics of *value only*. Let us add that this value itself is henceforth the value of the moral act, not of the object, which no longer specifies the value of the act but, on the contrary, receives its own value, as a by-product, from the act itself.

PART TWO

THE GREAT ILLUSIONS

Post-Kantian Dialecticism

7

HEGELIAN IDEALISM

Hegel and Wisdom

I

HEGELIAN DIALECTIC

After the Kantian Revolution

1. After Kant moral philosophy entered into a period of utter confusion, a state of permanent crisis. Three principal lines of evolution can be discerned in the history of the systems elaborated by the philosophers of the time. The first line is that of dialectical philosophy—either dialectical idealism, involving an a-cosmic (pseudo-cosmic) ethics, or dialectical materialism, involving a cosmic (pseudo-cosmic) ethics. The second line is that taken by positivist philosophy, which (after having, with Comte himself, asked morality to regulate individual conduct in accordance with the needs of sociocracy and the religion of Humanity) reduces morality to a "science of mores" deprived of any normative character, and finds its most significant expression in terms of "sociologism". The third line embraces various reactions against positivism, inspired by philosophies that differ widely among themselves but for one reason or another made the attempt to return to a cosmic ethics, by which I mean a science of human acts and of the universe of freedom grounded in the universe of being.

The great German idealist systems took their point of departure from the Kantian revolution. But the critical philosophy of Kant was for them only a kind of chrysalis, to be shed once philosophy had found its wings. Their inspiration was fundamentally different. If the Kantian revolution had freed the mind from the regulation exercised upon it by things, it had done so, originally, in order to limit the field of knowledge and restrain the ambitions of reason. Now it was necessary to bring this revolution to its logical conclusion, enable it to bear its full fruit, and, by freeing the mind of the regulation exercised upon it by things, to break down every barrier restricting the domain of philosophic knowledge, in short, to liberate the metaphysical ambitions of reason at last from any possible limitation. For this to be accomplished, the Kantian dualism of phenomena and the thing-in-itself had to be overcome, since the thing-in-itself, by virtue of its very unknowability, still belonged to the world of extra-mental being and remained a reality independent of the mind. No more "things"! The mind itself was to abolish the thing-in-itself by taking its place, whereupon phenomena would become manifestations of mind.

Breaking the moorings which by virtue of its own nature attach philosophy to the existential datum with its irreducible diversity, emancipating itself from the now outmoded concern with piercing and tapping the depths of extra-mental being, philosophy embarked under full sail toward the supreme affirmation of itself and its own power. Its self-assigned goal was to bring the universe of knowledge into a supreme Unity, and to comprehend it in and through its Totality. Ἓν καὶ πᾶν: in one way or another, the mind was to be the principle of this absolute unity, itself engendering its own differentiations.

The idealism of Fichte, primarily moral in inspiration, made everything proceed from the Self by a process of development in which things posit themselves through their mutual opposition. The ethical life is conceived as a progressive realization of the sovereign independence of the Self, that is to say, of the transcendental and supra-individual Self (since concerning individual subjects he says, "for he who still has *a self*,—in him assuredly there is nothing good").[1] In the idealism of Schelling we already find the principle of the triad (thesis, antithesis and synthesis), but in terms that are still superficial and too closely allied to human discourse. Schelling makes everything proceed from the Absolute—from an Absolute of pure indetermination which, as Hegel was to put it, is "as the night in which, as we say, all cows are black".[2]

It is possible to consider the attempts of Fichte and Schelling as preparations for the philosophy of Hegel, but only in the form of imperfect approximations, unsuccessful rough drafts, since Fichte's Self and Schelling's Absolute, although they are interior to thought, still appear as something distinct from it. They are posited by thought, but they are in a certain way *looked at* by it, so that they still retain a vestige of the thing-in-itself. Hegel's stroke of genius was to make the Absolute out of thought itself, or out of the spirit.[3]

[1] *The Way towards the Blessed Life*, Lecture XI, in *The Popular Works of Johann Gottlieb Fichte*, trans. by W. Smith, 4th ed., London, 1889, Vol. II, p. 494. Cf. p. 445 (Lecture IX): "So long as man still desires to be something on his own account, the True Being and Life cannot develop itself within him, and hence he likewise remains inaccessible to Blessedness; for all personal, individual Being is but Non-Being, and limitation of the True Being."

[2] Preface to *The Phenomenology of Mind*, trans. by J. B. Baillie, 2nd ed., New York: Macmillan, 1931, p. 79; London: Allen and Unwin, 1931. As a general rule, the title of the work to which we will refer in the following notes will be given in English when the citation is taken from the English translation, and in German when the citation is taken from the German text. Unless otherwise specified, these latter are taken from Hegel, *Sämtliche Werke* (hereafter called *Werke*), ed. G. Lasson, 21 vols., Leipzig: Felix Meiner, 1920–1940.

[3] "*The Absolute is Mind* (Spirit)—this is the supreme definition of the Absolute. To find this definition and to grasp its meaning and burthen was, we may say, the ultimate purpose of all education and all philosophy: it was the point to which turned the impulse of all religion and science and it is this impulse that must explain the history of the world." *The*

The thing-in-itself was thus liquidated;[1] and instead of a universe of phenomena unified under our *a priori* forms, it was the real universe which came within our grasp, real not in the sense of being a manifestation of thought, but real in the sense of being a manifestation of thought within itself.[2] Being is thought; there is nothing beyond reason; it is the Idea which makes the reality of things. A dynamic Absolute, a God in motion, thought encloses within itself all that arises out of it, being a process of immanent activity. Thought is the Whole which, engendering its own differentiations and present in them, alone can furnish the ground of each of them, in its very capacity as the Whole.

One of the inconsistencies of the Kantian doctrine has often been noted: Kantian Reason was the ordinary human reason present in each individual human being, and at the same time it belonged to that intelligible world which Kant conceived as above time and space, and endowed with a universality dominating the empirical world. Draped in its capital letter like the other personified Abstractions the eighteenth century used so extensively, it was there like a supra-personal Power lodged in the Absolute. Hegelian "Thought"

Encyclopaedia of the Philosophical Sciences, Hegel's Philosophy of Mind, § 384, trans. by W. Wallace, Oxford: Clarendon Press, 1894, p. 7.

See also the Preface to *The Phenomenology of Mind*, on the *true* as *subject*, pp. 80 ff. (cf. below, ch. VIII, p. 150, note 1).

At this point we meet a great difficulty in vocabulary. Hegel says that the Absolute is *der Geist*; now in the English translations of Hegel's work, it is customary to translate *geist* by *mind*. This is in my opinion quite questionable. In reality *geist* means both *mind* and *spirit*.

As James Collins observes in his excellent *A History of Modern European Philosophy*, "The very term *Geist* enjoys a strategic ambivalence, since it signifies what we mean by both 'mind' and 'spirit'. As Hegel employed the term, it is not so one-sidedly cognitive and contemplative in import as 'mind', and not so exclusively associated with the immaterial and religious spheres as 'spirit'. *Geist* includes will and the passions, along with the knowing powers; it embraces the structure of the material world and the whole range of man's secular interests, as well as his religious attitude and his direction toward immaterial goods. The term has the further advantage of applying to both the human mind and the divine spirit. It suggests both that the human mind is an aspect of the divine spirit and that the divine spirit is fully rational and self-conscious." *A History of Modern European Philosophy*, Milwaukee: Bruce Publishing Co., 1954, pp. 609–610. Yet the metaphysical connotation of *spirit* has more importance in the Hegelian system than the psychological connotation of *mind*. So that James Collins himself, and quite rightly in my opinion, uses the word *spirit* preferably to the word *mind*. And so shall I.

[1] At least assuming that the thing-in-itself may ever be *truly* liquidated—I am speaking in regard to the real functioning of the intellect. Here is the root of ambiguity in every idealist metaphysics. *In the exercise* (repressed) of the intellect the Hegelian Thought itself, even as it abolishes the thing-in-itself *in the system*, plays the part, despite all, of that same thing-in-itself, which the intellect, be it against its will or without admitting it, cannot get along without.

[2] Thus the *absolute Idealism* of Hegel returns in a way to realism (in this sense that nature, history and the world—but as manifestations of the development of Thought—have a consistence independent of our knowing activity as thinking subjects). What the spirit of the Sage (or the Spirit in the Sage) thinks is just what the Spirit, in the circular process wherein it thinks itself discursively, does as nature, history and the world, and is as Logos.

is Kantian "Reason" decidedly deified.[1] Hence the supreme ambiguity that characterizes it. It retains the properties of human reason; it deals with universal notions and lives on their multiplicity; it unites and divides concepts and ideas; it is discursive, advances by reasoning, is subject to logical becoming. And at the same time it is absolute Thought: human reason emancipated from itself as finite and set up as divine Reason, as νοήσις νοησέως, as "the Idea that thinks itself" and in thinking itself engenders in itself the phases of a discourse which is reality.[2]

Dialectic as Knowledge or Science[3]

2. In the light of these considerations we can understand the necessity of *Dialectic* in the Hegelian sense (I am thinking here especially of the Hegelian

[1] For a detailed discussion, which would be out of place here, of the relation between the Hegelian Reason and the Kantian "unity of apperception", and more generally between the positions of Kant and those of Hegel, cf. *The Encyclopaedia of the Philosophical Sciences*, The Logic of Hegel, § 40–60, trans. by W. Wallace, 2nd ed., Oxford Univ. Press, 1892, and Jean Hyppolite, *Logique et Existence, Essai sur la Logique de Hegel*, Paris: Presses Universitaires, 1953 (especially pp. 69–118 and 167–208). Some very just observations on this question are to be found in James Collins' *A History of Modern European Philosophy*.

[2] This is why finite reason and infinite Reason can be reconciled. Cf. R. Kroner, *Von Kant bis Hegel*, Tübingen, 1924, II, p. 403: "The finite or phenomenal spirit is itself only the becoming of the absolute spirit, the absolute spirit becoming conscious of itself."—The reference to the God-Thought of Aristotle was underlined by Hegel himself, who concludes the *Encyclopaedia* with a citation from Book XII, ch. 7, of the *Metaphysics*.

Alexandre Kojève has understood very well that the Spirit for Hegel is Discourse and Power of abstracting or separating (*Scheiden*) just as the human spirit (cf. A. Kojève, *Introduction à la lecture de Hegel*, Paris: Gallimard, 1947, pp. 538–549, dealing with a very characteristic passage from the Preface to the *Phenomenology*). The Spirit "implies human discourse" (p. 536), because Hegel has put Discourse into things; "the Spirit is the Real revealed by Discourse" (p. 546; cf. pp. 528–529). Kojève concludes from this that in reality the Spirit for Hegel is nothing other than Man. "The Spirit, that is to say the Being which manifests itself to itself, is not God but Man-in-the-World" (p. 548). This interpretation, which makes Hegel the great founder of modern atheism, throws a good deal of light on the system; and it has the merit of putting things in an eminently clear and univocal perspective. But just because of this—without mentioning other considerations (see below, ch. X)—we cannot regard it as authentically Hegelian. It is in fact essential to Hegelian thought to refuse the simple *yes* and the simple *no* (this is why, as soon as it is a matter of a truly philosophical position, Hegel feels assured of the truth of what he expresses only while experiencing the rending and the power of the Negative in his own mental word, and while using a language so stretched by the expanding emphasis as to maintain the No under the Yes and the Yes under the No).

The Spirit for Hegel is the human Reason, yes, but the human Reason deified. It is Man-in-the-World, but it is *also* and at the same time God; it is God, the Thought of Thought, becoming Himself through and in the Man-in-the-World.

[3] A special difficulty, which deals with the language, must be mentioned immediately. In Latin, in German, in French, there are two different words, *cognoscere* and *scire*, *kennen* and *wissen*, *connaître* and *savoir*, to designate, on the one hand any kind of more or less imperfect knowing or awareness, and on the other hand that "perfect" or consummate knowing which is demonstrative knowledge. Now in English there is only one word for the two things, namely *to know*. And this is especially embarrassing in the present case, for our discussion of Hegelian dialectic presupposes the distinction between the act of knowing in the most general sense (sense-awareness, tentative approach, opinion, belief, etc.) and the

dialectic in its definitive form, the Hegelian dialectic of the Logos). Thought engenders within itself a universe which remains Thought itself; it can only do this through the logical development which is the law of the *discursus* of reason. "Everything is a syllogism."[1] Idealism hereby entails a consequence which is in reality more profoundly characteristic of the work of Hegel, and which was to have a much more decisive historical importance, than idealism itself: the transformation of dialectic into a *science of the real*, or, to put it in another way, the substantialization of the logical process, and the idea of the absolute immanence to itself, as the Whole of reality, of the logos in movement, or of the evolution of concepts in interdependence, in other words, of the evolution of Reason in its logical development: let us say, the immanentism of endogenous logical becoming. We find ourselves now in the presence of a process of pure logic, and we remain enclosed in the world of logic; and yet this world is the world of reality.

The ancient notion of logic as the science of the "second intentions of the mind" presupposed a realist conception of the world. The concept was first of all a grasp of extra-mental reality, and afterwards logic considered it apart, in terms of the state of being and the properties it had in the mind. Reasoning, whose laws were the subject-matter of logic, was used as an instrument by the science of reality, but this very science was by its nature distinct from logic; and the highest form of this science of reality, distinct in nature from logic, was philosophy. Dialectic, on the contrary, *formed part of logic*; and any attempt to remain within logic in order to possess the knowledge of reality and to construct the *opus philosophicum* was pure nonsense for the ancients (I mean for traditional occidental thought, dominated by the *Organon* of Aristotle); in their eyes such an attempt tried to make of dialectic a *Knowledge*—and a supreme Knowledge—whereas in reality dialectic is not Knowledge (*scientia*) but only a tentative sort of knowing, only a first attempt at the exploration of things, preliminary to knowledge and incapable by its nature of procuring knowledge (because, far from seeking the proper structures and reasons of things, in dialectic we content ourselves with submitting things to logical frameworks, beings of reason which are extrinsic to things and exist only in our mind).

One might say that dialectic is a kind of reflection or reversion of the logical upon the real. This is a point of crucial importance,[2] whose special difficulty

---

act of knowing in the strict sense of demonstrative or unshakeably established knowledge, *scientia*, genuine science. As a result, I would like to stipulate (it's a mere matter of conventional vocabulary) that in the first, broad or undetermined sense, we shall say simply *knowing*, whereas in the second, strict, or consummate sense, we shall say *knowledge*, or genuine knowledge.

[1] *Encyclopaedia*, Logic, § 181 (Wallace trans.), p. 271.

[2] One would doubtless see this point of doctrine better if one tried to understand why, in a healthy Aristotelian philosophy, it is in logic, not in metaphysics, that the treatise on the supreme genera or categories is to be found. (Substance, quantity, etc., are real beings; but

derives from the nature of the human mind, obliged as it is to manipulate abstract ideas and to fabricate beings of reason. (Plato let himself be caught in the trap, but without completely losing sight of the authentic notion of knowledge; he did not erect dialectics into a supreme knowledge; he simply believed that it opened on to the supreme knowledge.) Perhaps a metaphor would be of some help to us. Let us imagine that logic is a kind of control tower where reason manipulates its signs and figures and symbols as an engineer manipulates his instruments to verify their accuracy and their perfect construction.[1] Sometimes the logician happens to go out on the platform of the tower and to lean over the balcony of logic to look down, through his measuring instruments and the figures and symbols shown by them, at the real world, in the midst of which the philosopher and the scientist busy themselves with trying to see *into the interior of things*, how they are made, what their hidden properties are. When they succeed, they possess *Knowledge* (science). As for the logician, he sees inside his equipment certain schemas which, *from without*, he tries on things, and into which things fit more or less well. The approach he thus attempts toward the real, by means of entities which (whether in themselves, or by virtue of the state of generality at which they are taken) exist only in the mind, and not by virtue of the proper reasons or causes of things, constitutes dialectic—which, not scrutinizing the nature of things, and applying to them only extrinsic frameworks, is a kind of sketch, a first draft of knowledge, inevitably uncertain, fleeting and contestable, and by its very nature separated from genuine Knowledge (science) by an impassable distance.

In order to help clarify our ideas it will be useful to cite here a major text from St. Thomas Aquinas' *Commentary on the Metaphysics of Aristotle*.[2] "The dialectician, like the metaphysician," he says, "considers all things. And that could not be unless he considered them in virtue of their sharing in a

---

as supreme genera or considered precisely in the condition of generality which they have in the mind, they are the object of the science of discourse, not of the science of the real. And whereas to know the real is to know it through its proper or specific causes, to approach a problem of the real on the contrary by means of a *genus generalissimum* is to attack the real from the outside, to assay or survey it dialectically, not to know it.)

It is one of the misfortunes of modern philosophy to have forgotten or misconceived this distinction between true *knowing* and simple dialectical surveying or assaying. Many of Bergson's criticisms of the intelligence bear in fact not on the intelligence but on the purely dialectical use of it. And, to tell the truth, it is with this difference between knowledge and dialectics that the opposition which he so likes to insist on between *the thing cut to measure* and *the ready-made* coincides.

[1] Should we push this comparison into greater detail? We might say that the fixed equipment of the cabin (*logica docens*) serves to control the proper functioning of the rational instruments (*logica utens*), which savants and philosophers make use of at the base of the tower, at the level of the real, to scrutinize things. But some of the apparatus in the cabin is portable and can be taken out on the balcony by the logician, who aims it at things when he wishes (*dialectica*) to test his ciphers on them and thus to know them in his fashion.

[2] *In Metaphys.*, IV, lect. 4, Cathala ed., nos. 573 ff.

certain unity. . . . Now the only unity in which all things share is the unity of being; it is obvious therefore that the matter of dialectic is being, *ens*, *et ea quae sunt entis*, which is also the matter of the metaphysician; so that the philosopher, the dialectician, and the sophist, all three, deal with the same thing: being." But the being the philosopher deals with is real being, while that which the dialectician deals with is the being of reason, or de-realized being.[1] "The philosopher's way of considering things is of greater potency than that of the dialectician. For the philosopher proceeds demonstratively in relation to all things included in being, and that is why he possesses the science or the Knowledge of them, and knows them by way of certainty, since certain Knowledge, or *scientia*, is the result of demonstration; while the dialectician proceeds by way of probability in relation to all these same things, and that is why he does not arrive at knowledge (*non facit scientiam*), but only at opinion. This is so because being is twofold in nature: it is divided into being of reason and real being, or being of nature; and being of reason (that is, being which cannot exist outside the mind, which can only exist in the mind) . . . is properly the subject of logic." Now any "lining" is of the same width as the cloth; "the intelligible intentions of the logician [his beings of reason] are counterparts of the beings of nature, by virtue of the fact that the latter fall under the consideration of reason. That is why the subject of logic extends to all the things to which real being is attributable. The subject of logic has the same amplitude as that of philosophy, whose subject is the being of nature." The subject of logic, however, is only that *ens rationis*, in which logical properties and relations consist, and it can only exist in the mind. And the dialectician, in dealing with things, proceeds not according to reál causes, as the philosopher does, but "according to merely ideal entities", or logical beings of reason, "which are extrinsic to the nature of things, *extranea a natura rerum*".

So the dialectician is not a philosopher; he is a logician, and if through dialectic he approaches the real and knows it after a certain manner (in terms of opinion), still he never achieves knowledge (science) or philosophy. He remains a logician, who looks at the real from without, by means of logical beings of reason and logical generalities, more precisely, through a kind of "idea-montage" consisting of the patterns and arrangements executed in the mind upon generalities and categories separated from the real or taken in the state in which they exist in the mind and can exist only in the mind.

3. But now all is changed. Idealism has broken the barrier which divided logical being from real being. Now here (expressed in language that is doubtless not Hegelian but is nevertheless exact) is the great discovery, the philosopher's stone of Hegel—in order to render conceptual thought co-extensive

[1] Cf. our work, *A Preface to Metaphysics*, New York: Sheed & Ward, 1939, pp. 33 ff.; London: Sheed & Ward, 1939.

with concrete reality, or convertible with it, it is the logical being of reason which provides us with the science of reality. Dialectic becomes *knowledge*—and absolute knowledge.

In the first stage of the system—let us say rather in the non-temporal stage, since in an essentially circular system there is no first stage—which is the stage of Logic itself, in which the pure Logos[1] has not yet issued forth into Nature in order to return into itself as Spirit, Hegel declares that logic is the science of the real, and that it is "one with metaphysics".[2] His absolute knowledge is, as has been remarked,[3] an ontologic—I mean to say: an ontology in which the *ontic* has been reduced to that kind of being which is the logical being of reason, in which, in other words, real being is conceived in terms of logical being and is explained by it.[4]

There are no longer any extra-mental things, whose sign is the concept (in the ordinary sense of the word);[5] the function of the concept being to transfer extra-mental things into the mind, to be known there. Now therefore, on the contrary, the concept must be taken in the intra-mental state in which it appears to the logician, as the subject of logical properties and relations, the concept as a being of reason—become (since it is no longer the sign of things) the self-affirmation of the very thought that engenders it. And it is this concept thus taken as a being of reason that dialectic has to use in order to deduce *a priori*, by a kind of creative knowledge, the totality of the real (henceforth conceived as interior to thought and a manifestation of thought).[6] The "intentions of reason" (*intentiones rationis* or merely ideal entities), the *principles extrinsic to the nature of things* of which St. Thomas spoke, thus become the generative principles of the real, which is known down to its ultimate elements, in the very process of its generation into existence.

[1] "The Idea in and for itself" (*Encyclopaedia*, Logic, § 18, p. 28); "the pure Idea; pure, that is, because the Idea is in the abstract medium of Thought" (*ibid.*, § 19, p. 30).

[2] "Logic therefore coincides with Metaphysics, the science of things set and held in thoughts—thoughts accredited able to express the essential reality of things." *Ibid.*, § 24, p. 45. Cf. Hegel's *Philosophy of Right*, § 31, trans. by T. M. Knox, Oxford: Clarendon Press, 1942, p. 34.

[3] Jean Hyppolite, *Genèse et Structure de la Phénoménologie de l'esprit de Hegel*, Paris: Aubier, 1946, p. 554. Cf. *ibid.*, p. 562: "This Logic which is the Absolute's thought of itself is therefore an onto-logic; it reconciles Being (hence its ontic character) and the Logos (hence its logical character); it is Being as Logos and the Logos as Being."

[4] Thus "a corpse," Hegel will say for example, "is still an existent, but its existence is no true existence; the concept has left it; and for this reason a dead body putrefies." *Philosophy of Right*, Addition to § 21 (inserted by Gans from the philosopher's oral teaching), Knox trans., p. 232.

[5] Synonym of notion (νοήμα, *conceptus*). The Hegelian meaning of Concept (*Begriff*) is much more specialized. See below, 145–146.

[6] Nothing is more suggestive from this point of view than the way Hegel transforms the *logical* process of the syllogism into the basic "ontic" process of the real in development. Cf. *Science of Logic*, Book III, last chapter, trans. by W. H. Johnston and L. G. Struthers, London: George Allen & Unwin, 1929, Vol. II; *Vorlesungen über die Geschichte der Philosophie*, ed. J. Hoffmeister, II, pp. 410–415, in *Werke*, XVa. A similar operation was performed at the start on the theory of judgment (see below, p. 129, note 2).

The Real introduced forcibly into the logical Being of Reason does violence to Logic

4. At this point a radical reformulation of the dialectic itself was necessary.[1] How can the logical being of reason, and the network of "ideal"

[1] The great precursors whom Hegel recognizes here are Zeno, Heraclitus, Plato, Kant, Fichte and Schelling. He notes (cf. *Encyclopaedia*, Logic, § 48) that in the preparation of his own conception of dialectics the Kantian theory of the antinomies of reason played a specially important role. (And in fact Kant had thereby already introduced contradiction into the heart of reason.) But now the antinomy is no longer only in the reason speculating on the object, it is in the object itself, and it completely impregnates both being and knowledge.

Would that an author animated with a true philosophic spirit may some day give us a good History of Dialectics! There are few questions more controverted, and more obscured by the quantity of confused ideas, than those which touch on the nature of dialectics and on the varying conceptions which have been made of it. To limit ourselves to a few very summary remarks, let us say that before coming to no matter what particular theory or conception of it, dialectics can be described in a formula designedly very indeterminate and one whose unity is purely analogical, as *a discipline which takes ideas or concepts as its object according as they are linked together and opposed to each other in discourse and which proposes to judge the real by this means.*

For Plato, since the separate ideas were the true reality, dialectics was not only, in a very general way, "the reasonable conversation of the mind which has an eye to truth in ideas", as Mr. Blackmur says so well (*The Lion and the Honeycomb*, New York: Harcourt, Brace, 1955, p. 177; London: Methuen, 1957); dialectics was identified with philosophy and philosophic knowledge. But the reality attained by this knowledge was not itself dialectical, in this sense at least that it was not itself submitted to the logical becoming and to the movement of discourse (the archetypal Ideas were eternal and immutable). And the supreme knowledge was not dialectics, being rather the supra-conceptual union to the One and to the Good.

Aristotle's realism obliged him to distinguish between the idea or the concept as *pure sign* of the real and pure means of grasping it (*prima intentio mentis*) and the idea or the concept as *object* itself reflexively grasped by the mind (*secunda intentio mentis*). As a result dialectics is no more than a part of logic, and the sort of knowledge of the real which it achieves remains at an impassable distance from true understanding. Aristotle's own texts underline only the more or less secondary aspects of this Aristotelian conception of dialectics (logic of controversy, of critical argumentation, of refutation, reasoning based on the opinion of competent judges or on commonly accepted opinions . . .); it is Thomas Aquinas who has exposed its absolutely essential and characteristic core (commentary on the *Metaphysics*, Book IV, ch. 2, 1004 b 19–27). We have expounded above this Aristotelian conception as rethought by Saint Thomas. This, in our opinion, is what illumines the whole discussion.

Kant refers to the classical conception of dialectics (logic of controversy). But for him dialectics becomes consubstantial with the activity of Reason. It is the only way whereby judgments can be formulated on the subject of the Ideas of Reason, and this way leads to fundamentally necessary and inevitable antinomies.

With Hegel these antinomies are no longer mere antinomies of Reason, they belong to the real itself (which is Thought). Whence the Hegelian revolution: dialectics is no longer identified simply with philosophical knowledge as in Plato, it passes over to the object, becomes the essence of Reality, which is logical self-movement.

A curious displacement (which doesn't help to clarify ideas) then took place: it is through the notion of internal opposition in the world of things, of self-contradiction of the extra-mental real, and of self-movement in which the antagonisms immanent to exterior nature are surmounted and reconciled that dialectics will be above all characterized for Hegel's non-idealist heirs. It is thus that Marxism will present itself as a dialectical materialism (see below, ch. X). To be sure, it always uses the oppositions of discourse to account for

generalities with which the dialectician envelops things from without, provide that science of the real which is now demanded of them? On the condition that things, with all their natural behavior, enter into the very tissue of the network, even at the risk of shattering it in order to take their place in it; on the condition that the world of logic be violated by the world of the real in order to be made to coincide with it, and to account for it, to furnish the intrinsic principles of this real world which has entered into the world of logic by force.

In the world of logic the first law of thought is the principle of contradiction. Logical movement, the movement of discourse or of reasoning, takes place from concept to concept or from notion to notion, each one remaining what it is, since it is the sign by which an aspect of the real is grasped; and it is by means of notions whose meaning does not change once they are defined in a given manner, that the movement of the real is known to us.

In the real world the first law of being is, correspondingly, the principle of identity. But the world of the real is the world of the multiple and the world of becoming. The principle of identity presents no obstacle either to the multiplicity of being and the interaction of the multiple or to change and becoming, because being is analogous and beings exercise a reciprocal causality on one another, and because that which changes becomes other in another respect than that in which it "is". And the world of the real, I mean the world of experience, of time and of matter, which is the world of becoming, obeys two characteristic laws: the law of universal interaction and the law of change.

In order to attain *a priori* knowledge of the real by means of the dialectic and the logical being of reason, Hegel violated the world of logic by making these two laws penetrate into it and subjecting it to them. Since an idea is henceforth a self-affirmation of thought itself and of the universe of thought, it has meaning only in relation to the whole which reverberates in it, and by virtue of enveloping within itself what is outside it. "Every position is a negation" (every concept includes its opposite) and "every negation is a position" (every "opposite" includes that to which it is opposite). And the very idea or notion itself changes, undergoes a metamorphosis, ceases to be what it is in

---

the real. But for it the oppositions of discourse are only the "reflection in our brain" of the oppositions of matter.

Let us add that if the formula submitted at the beginning of this note (a discipline which takes ideas or concepts as its object according as they are linked together and opposed to each other in discourse and which proposes to judge the real by this means) satisfactorily expresses the most general idea which one may have of dialectics, one ought to say that it was Descartes, from the fact that for him ideas are the immediate *object* of the mind (theory of the idea-pictures), who effectively, although without knowing it, impressed a dialectical orientation on his own thought—and on modern philosophy in general. More and more one will look at the real through the opera glasses of some idea-object (*secunda intentio mentis*).

order to become something else, is subject to the vicissitudes of birth and death. "Die and become", one must die in order to live. *Except a corn of wheat fall into the ground and die, it abideth alone: but if it die, it bringeth forth much fruit:*[1] this law of extra-mental reality in its most fundamentally, most irreducibly existential aspect, becomes the law of ideas themselves and of the world of logic, as a result of which logical becoming coincides with real becoming, or rather absorbs real becoming into itself.[2]

5. So the essence and the life of the absolute is revealed: the fundamental and ubiquitous process by which thought, thinking itself, engenders itself, and by which the notion, which is the real, surmounting the limits of finitude, develops itself in order to re-enter into its own infinity, is the process which proceeds from simple and immediate identity, through negation, alienation and conflict, to super-identity and super-interiorization reconciling the contraries within itself—from the immediate *in-itself,*[3] through the *negative of self* or the *other-than-self* which is also the *for itself,*[4] to the mediatized *within-itself* or *in and for itself.*[5] Every true concept is a structure in evolution, in transit, in

[1] *John*, XII, 24.

[2] Let us note here, by way of parenthesis, that in the simplest case of logical movement, in the judgment, *subjectum et praedicatum sunt idem re, diversa ratione*: the subject and the predicate, which are different with respect to the concept or notion, are declared by the mind to be identical with respect to the extra-mental reality, of which these different notions each grasp an aspect. (See our works *The Degrees of Knowledge*, new trans. by G. B. Phelan, New York: Scribners; London: Geoffrey Bles, pp. 97–98—p. 97, last line read "Lask" instead of "Locke"—and *Réflexions sur l'intelligence*, Paris: Nouvelle Librairie Nationale, 1924, pp. 68–74.)

If now one abolishes the extra-notional being and makes the world of the real enter the world of logic, one must maintain that in the judgment the subject and the predicate, originally posited as different with respect to the notion, are declared identical with respect to the notion itself as well. In other words the subject will alienate or deny itself in the predicate in order to identify and then to reintegrate the predicate in itself. Thus the Hegelian Concept will be the universal which denies itself while remaining itself—hence the *restlessness* which Hegel attributes to it, when he speaks of the "notions in restless activity, which *are* merely in being inherently their own opposite, and in finding their rest in the whole" (*Phenomenology*, p. 767). Cf. Hegel, *Encyclopaedia*, Logic, § 167, p. 300: "all things are a judgment"; and § 171, p. 302: "At first, subject, predicate, and the specific content or the identity are, even in their relation, still put in the judgment as *different and divergent*. By implication, however, that is, in their notion, they are *identical*."

[3] *An-sich-sein.*

[4] *Anders-sein* or *Für-sich-sein.*

[5] *An-und-für-sich-sein.*

If we are looking for more complete elucidations of the famous triad, one of the commentators imbued with the thought of the master who can help us is Alexandre Kojève. The concrete real Being, he writes, "is not only Identity-or-equality-with-itself (Sichselbstgleichheit), but also Being-other (Anderssein) or negation of itself in so far as given and creation of itself in so far as other than this given. . . . Now, to be other than one is (Negativity) while remaining oneself (Identity), or to identify oneself with another while distinguishing oneself from it—this is at once *to be* (and *to reveal* by discourse) as much what one is as what one is not. To become other than one is—this is to take a position vis-à-vis itself, it is to exist (as one was) for itself (as one is now). . . . The being simply identical, on

discursive movement. As soon as it is posed, a concept departs from itself and loses itself in another in order to return into itself, enriched by the spoils of the other. Does not the freedom of the child alienate itself in the discipline of education in order to be reborn in the freedom of the adult, just as the freedom of the adult alienates itself in the discipline of the law to be reborn in the freedom of a member of the state? Yes, no doubt in the real world the human subject passes through these stages; but it is in the world of concepts, become now the real world, that the very idea of freedom burns and is reborn from its ashes. So it is that the old good, decent concept of classical philosophy finds itself transformed into the Hegelian concept.[1]

Because in the world of the real everything we see is related to everything else and by that very fact is not simply itself but also something else—because this flower is not just a flower but also illuminated by the sun or wet by the rain, and is thereby something other than flower—we must say that in the world of concepts, now become reality, the idea which posits A also by the same token posits something other than A, and, to that extent, not-A; we

---

the contrary, exists only *in itself* and *for others*, that is to say, in its identity with itself and by the relations of difference which bind it to the rest of the identical beings in the bosom of the cosmos: it does not exist *for itself*, and the others do not exist *for it*.

"Thus, the Being which is at once *Identity* and *Negativity* is not only *Being-in-itself* (Ansichsein) homogeneous and immutable and *Being-for-another* (Sein für Anderes) fixed and stable, but also *Being-for-itself* (Fürsichsein) divided into real being and revelatory discourse, and *Being-other* (Anderssein) in perpetual transformation which liberates it from itself in so far as *given* to itself and to others."

However, "the (revealed) concrete real Being is neither pure *Identity* (which is Being, *Sein*) nor pure *Negativity* (which is nothing, *Nichts*), but *Totality* (which is becoming, *Werden*). Totality then is the third fundamental and universal onto-logical category. . . . The Being which reaffirms itself in so far as Being identical to itself after having denied itself is neither Identity nor Negativity but Totality. . . . In other words . . . Being is neither *Being-in-itself* only nor *Being-for-itself* only, but the integration of the two in *Being-in-and-for-itself* (An-und-Für-sichsein). This is to say that Totality is Being revealed for Being conscious of itself (which Hegel calls 'absolute Concept', 'Idea', or 'Spirit'). . . . In spite of the *Negativity* which it includes and presupposes, the final *Totality* is wholly as one and unique, homogeneous and autonomous, as the first and primordial *Identity*. In so far as *Result* of the Negation, the Totality is just as much an Affirmation as the Identity which has been denied in order *to become* totality." (A. Kojève, *op. cit.*, pp. 473–475.)

In the course of this process of mediatization of the immediate and of suppression-sublimation (*Aufhebung*) the Negativity *suppresses* that which it denies and at the same time *conserves* it (since it is A, and not anything else, which is denied in non-A) and *super-elevates* it—according to the three connotations of the word *aufheben*.

Thus is built the dialectical Knowledge of the Real—because the Real itself is dialectical, ". . . the process of positing itself (Sichselbstsetzens) or . . . mediating (Vermittlung) with its own self its transitions from one state or position to the opposite (Sichanderswerdens). . . . True reality is merely this process of reinstating self-identity, of reflecting into its own self in and from its other (Anderssein). . . . It is the process of its own becoming, the circle which presupposes its end as its purpose (Zweck), and has its end for its beginning; it becomes concrete and actual only by being carried out (Ausfuhrung), and by the end it involves." Preface to the *Phenomenology*, Baillie, pp. 80–81 (Hoffmeister ed., *Werke*, Vol. II, p. 20).

[1] See below, p. 145, and note 3, p.145.

must say that from the point of view of Thought as the Whole, an idea only affirms itself by denying itself at the same time. Since in the realm of real becoming a thing is at the same time itself (in one respect) and not itself (in another respect), now, in order to engender Becoming ideally, there is nothing left but to declare that Being is at the same time Nothing. Simply by the fact of positing itself as being—its only determination being not to have any determination—Thought denies itself; "In fact, Being, indeterminate immediacy, is *Nothing*, neither more nor less."[1] This assertion (thanks to which the philosopher can engender becoming as concrete totality, and as the reconciliation between Being identified itself with nothing and Nothing rediscovering itself as being) is not at all surprising in a philosophy which confuses the being of metaphysics with that of logic—where, as merely logical entities, "what is not" and "what is" exist equally (in respect to real existence); moreover, and still more characteristically, this same philosophy, emerging from three centuries of pure essentialism during which the primordial intuition of *esse*, of the act of existing, was misunderstood,[2] gives its full and final weight to the Kantian conviction that "there is no more in a hundred real thalers than in a hundred possible thalers", no more in the existent than in the non-existent. "These beginnings"—Being and Nothing—"are nothing but these empty abstractions, one as empty as the other."[3] "But this mere Being, as it is mere abstraction, is therefore the absolutely negative: which, in a similarly immediate aspect, is just *Nothing*"[4]—being is *nicht mehr noch weniger als Nichts*.

Thus the absolute rule and dominion of Logic and of Thought will be established on the wreck of the first law of logic and of thought, and on the ruins of the principle of contradiction.[5] The real will be transported, along with the behavior proper to it, into the world of pure logical thought, into the world of ideas taken in a separated state within the mind and as objects of reflexive logical attention, as logical beings of reason. Well, the real will enter therein—by force and violence—at the cost of violating thought.

[1] Hegel's *Science of Logic*, trans. by W. H. Johnston and L. G. Struthers, London: George Allen and Unwin, 1929, I, p. 94. "Das Sein, das unbestimmte Unmittelbare, ist in der Tat Nichts, und nicht mehr noch weniger als Nichts" (Lasson ed., I, p. 67 in *Werke*, III).

[2] Cf. E. Gilson, *L'être et l'essence*, Paris: Vrin, 1948, ch. VII, "The Deduction of Existence." Citing article 51 of the *Encyclopaedia* (Logic, Wallace trans., p. 109: "For, if we look at the thought it holds, nothing can be more insignificant than being. And yet there may be something still more insignificant than being,—that which at first sight is perhaps supposed to *be*, an external and sensible existence, like that of the paper lying before me. However, in this matter, nobody proposes to speak of the sensible existence of a limited and perishable thing.") Gilson correctly writes (*op. cit.*, p. 210): "This doctrine which recognizes nothing more lowly than being, unless this be existence itself, seems to announce the most extreme devaluation of the act of existing that is conceivable."

[3] *Encyclopaedia*, Logic, § 87, p. 162.

[4] *Ibid.*, § 87, p. 161.

[5] This principle is henceforth only a law of formal thought operating on the empirical level; it still has value for the finite understanding and for the specialized sciences, but in the face of being and concrete thought (which is reason itself, cf. *Vorlesungen über die Geschichte der Philosophie*, Einleitung, J. Hoffmeister ed., in *Werke*, XVa, p. 95) its power vanishes.

This is inevitable, and Hegel had at least the merit of pushing the operation to its local conclusion, if dialectics is truly and definitely the *science or knowledge of the real*, and provides us with absolute knowledge.[1]

The Great Sophistry

6. At this price it is possible to deduce all of the real from thought, since one has placed it there to begin with. Before finding himself decisively in the dialectic of the Logos, Hegel first looked for logical self-movement in the tragic process of Consciousness. And he knew perfectly well, when he deduced his categories, that it was experience and the empirical sciences that had disclosed them to him; but he deduced them nevertheless—just as he reinterpreted in his philosophy of nature all that the science of his time offered him—translating all the data "into the form of thought"[2] from the superior point of view of the absolute and of creative knowledge. He will thus dialectically engender all of the mutations of being, as if he and Thought were producing them together.

His dialectic, he tells us, is not an "adventitious art",[3] exterior to things, lodged in the mind of the logician and used by the logician to advance toward a (non-scientific) knowing of things. It is lodged in things, and it is within the real itself that the sage, with that perfect knowledge proper to absolute science, contemplates its movements and its conflicts. But the fact still remains that if the real itself is dialectical, the dialectic thus conceived as immanent in things and in knowledge is still, and more than ever, a kind of logic in the hands of man, that is, a method or logical procedure, which man henceforth uses as an instrument of knowledge only because it is also the very logic through which things and their processes are brought into being.

Two extremely effective stratagems of the Hegelian dialectic should be pointed out here. In the first place, it does not possess any fixed center of perspective. By virtue of the principle set forth in the Preface to *Phenomenology*, that "truth is the whole", and that "pure thoughts", become "fluid", in other words become "concepts", are self-movements refusing any fixity, the center of perspective of the system is constantly displaced, following the movement

[1] Cf. *Encyclopaedia*, Logic, § 81, p. 147: "But by Dialectic is meant the indwelling tendency outwards by which the one-sidedness and limitation of the predicates of understanding is seen in its true light, and shown to be the negation of them. For anything to be finite is just to suppress itself and put itself aside (sich aufheben). Thus understood the Dialectical principle constitutes the life and soul of scientific progress, the dynamic which alone gives immanent connexion and necessity to the body of science."

[2] He himself notes in the *Encyclopädie* (Einleitung, § 5, Lasson's 4th ed., *Werke*, V, p. 35) that what he proposes is "the translation of the true content of our consciousness into the form of thought and concept". As Emile Bréhier writes (*Histoire de la philosophie*, Paris: Presses Universitaires, 1949, II, 3, p. 757), "let us not forget that Hegel's philosophy is a 'translation' into speculative language; there must be a text to translate, and this text can be provided only by experience."

[3] *Encyclopaedia*, Logic, § 81, p. 147.

of the idea passing through the stages of the triadic process, so that the philosopher, by reason of the change of the center of perspective, is free at any moment to recast what he has enunciated at another moment, changing its meaning or its bearing, since all contradictions are reconciled in advance and pardoned or, rather, are required in advance. This is what might be called the stratagem of focal displacement.

The second stratagem derives from the fact that all that experience, science, history, the efforts of men to scrutinize the things of nature and of the mind, all that the philosopher himself has been able to decipher in things (and with what brilliant perceptiveness in the case of Hegel) by force of intuition and power of observation and actual contact with that extra-notional being whose existence he denies in theory, the whole universe of the knowledge of things is surreptitiously transferred into the world of pure thought, there to be re-engendered and camouflaged into beings of reason and the conceptual conflicts of a logic which has been itself remodelled and mobilized for this purpose. This is what might be called the stratagem of disguising the real as logical process.

Thus equipped, the Hegelian dialectic is always right. Not only is it able to deduce *a priori* all the things it began by stealing from experience, but it can justify no matter what conclusion (those of Hegel himself and those of any other system employing it) by preparing in advance an appropriate logical process. It can at every moment invoke reality in confirmation of its conclusions, by hand-picking in advance the evidence offered by reality. Extra-notional things no longer being the measure of thought, the dialectic is pushed off center, as it were. The "extrinsic principles" by means of which it offered to the logician a "tentative" knowing of the real, a knowing of pure opinion, have been cut off from any relation to extra-notional things, which are themselves totally eliminated; and as a result these very principles will henceforth be recast according to the fancy of the philosopher, in such a way as to provide him with a science of the real known—in illusory terms—from within and in the very process of its own engendering, and to furnish him with an essentially *arbitrary* absolute knowledge. With the instrumentality of logical generalities and logical categories, either founded in fact upon things or invented and patterned to fit the needs of the moment, and in both cases manipulated according to the procedure we have described, this off-center dialectic leads wherever one wants to go. And since the real is no longer the rule and measure of thought, but simply the furnisher of materials for the *a priori* exercise of thought, this off-center dialectic can make the real say anything it wants it to, provided only that the materials in question are chosen with sufficient astuteness and perspicacity.

In a passage cited above, Thomas Aquinas remarked that the philosopher, the dialectician and the sophist, all three consider the same subject-matter, the universality of being, but from three incompatible points of view. He would doubtless have said that in transforming dialectic into metaphysics Hegel made of it a supreme sophistry. Schopenhauer, applying the famous legend to Fichte, Schelling and Hegel, called them *The Three Impostors*; the phrase is eminently applicable to the genius of Hegel. He forged his dialectic as an instrument of extraordinary power—an organon as perfectly designed for dogmatic trickery as Aristotle's logic was designed for knowledge, a machine for deluding the intellect whose effectiveness modern times and modern philosophy (submerged in opinion-as-knowledge) will continue to feel for a long time to come.

7. Smuggling into his logical beings of reason all the riches perceived in things by his encyclopaedic mind and his astonishingly profound poetic vision, Hegel used the constantly renewed and constantly surmounted dialectical conflicts of his philosophy of Pure Knowledge,[1] his philosophy of Nature, and his philosophy of Spirit, to re-do the work of creation. However marred his philosophy of history may be by arbitrariness and his penchant for system, it is to him that the philosophy of history owes the conquest of its place among the philosophical disciplines. His primordial intuition finds its natural place in the philosophy of history.[2] Moreover, in the very world of extra-notional being, history itself, whose being, like that of time, is not fulfilled without memory and without mind, enables us to watch the development of idea-forces or intentional charges at work in the collective psyche and incarnated in time. These historical ideas, forms immanent in time, presuppose nature, the being of things, and the being of man, which have nothing to do with the procession of ghosts of Hegelian metaphysics. And they are far from constituting the whole of history. But nevertheless, when we consider their proper role in history, we can say that each one only realizes itself fully, in time, by giving rise to its contrary and denying itself, because its very triumph exhausts the potentialities which called it forth, and by the same token it generates and reveals the contrary potentialities in the abyss of the real.[3]

But this is only one of the partial aspects of history, and history reveals its intelligible significance to the philosopher under a great many other aspects, and through many other laws, which are more important and more closely allied to the real. Hegel did not want to admit that the philosophy of history is an inductive discipline in which analysis of the empirical concrete and philosophical knowledge illuminate one another. As a result of absorbing matter

[1] On *Logic* as philosophy of knowledge not yet alienated from itself in nature and history, or as philosophy of the Logos which is the Spirit or the Whole abstracting from itself insofar as Logos, cf. the conclusion ("Phenomenology and Logic"), especially pp. 580–582, of the already mentioned work of Jean Hyppolite, *Genèse et structure de la phénoménologie de l'esprit de Hegel.*

[2] See below, p. 139; ch. VIII, pp. 153–155; ch. IX, pp. 194–196.

[3] Cf. our work *Raison et raisons*, Paris: Egloff, 1947, pp. 95–96. *The Range of Reason*, New York: Scribners, 1952, pp. 45–46; London: Bles, 1953.

into idea, he failed to recognize the fundamental fact that matter as such is one of the essential components of history. He confused the general laws at play in history, and the factual necessities in the course of history, with the supposedly essential necessities, or realities by right, of an arbitrary dialectic into which he absorbed all that which depends in history on contingency and chance, as well as on the freedom of human agents, thus saving it all "within the form of thought". In virtue of the principle that "Reason is the sovereign of the world", and that "the history of the world, therefore, presents us with a rational process",[1] he made of history a theogony of logical entities springing up and dying by turns, the perishable avatars of the sovereign Reason.

Even though for Hegel only spirit is history, and nature has no history,[2] his whole philosophy, even when it prescinds from time, as in the Logic, can in a certain way be called a philosophy of history, or rather, an absolute identification of Science and History, in the sense that it is a supreme conceptual knowledge in terms of pure becoming, becoming being the prime truth of intellection just as it is the prime concrete reality. "Where the primary concrete reality is not being because being is posited as absolute abstraction, primary concrete reality can only be becoming, because, being at the same time being and not-being, becoming is the primary contradictory."[3] Only that which makes or creates itself is *real*, all else being "abstract" and not (yet) intrinsically true. Made up of events and advents, reality is nothing but action and process of transformation, offering no fixed locus to thought. But this ceaseless movement is not an aimless movement. It has a final goal, but it also starts off from that goal, because it is a circular movement, in which the Absolute, by going beyond itself insofar as Nature, raises itself to supreme consciousness of itself (in man), while at the same time, it goes beyond itself insofar as Logos, in order to alienate itself in Nature and reascend therefrom toward its supreme reintegration. This is why Hegel's system itself is not an edifice with a definite configuration but rather an uninterrupted series of windshifts in which everything is called into question at each moment, a "bacchanalian revel", as Hegel said of the true,[4] "where not a member is sober", and where the only element of permanence derives from the *Erinnerung* or the "interiorizing memory". But the very trajectory of such a sequence of windshifts is circular, so that the Philosophy of History issues into Logic, but only in order that Logic may extend beyond itself by means of the Philosophy of Nature and that of spirit, and of the Philosophy of History, which in turn extends beyond itself by means of logic.

[1] Hegel, *Philosophy of History*, Introd., trans. by J. Sibree [1857], New York: Collier and Son, 1901, p. 52.
[2] *Phenomenology*, p. 326.
[3] Etienne Gilson, *L'être et l'essence*, Paris: Vrin, 1948, p. 215.
[4] Preface to the *Phenomenology*, p. 105.

And this system of continuous displacement, this philosophy of absolute Becoming is indeed a gnosis, in which, it must be admitted, the element of delusive pride inherent in all forms of gnosticism is carried to its ultimate extreme. A knowledge of the world which is also an engendering of the world, the wisdom of the philosopher is confused with creative wisdom. *When He established the heavens, I was there.*[1] In its primary and ultimate stage, the stage of logic, does not this wisdom reveal to us the triadic development of Pure Knowledge and of the divine thought "before the creation of Nature and of a Finite Spirit"?[2] The dialectician transformed into a philosopher and sage has been promoted to the position of confidant of God. In a man named Hegel, who, having appeared at the end of history, nourished himself with all the experience of history and assumed the whole substance of the development of thought, Spirit revealed itself to itself. The temptation to smile at this pretension has not been resisted, but it would be quite superficial to reproach Hegel for it without realizing that it was in fact the result of the three centuries of history he had behind him. Karl Barth is right when he remarks that if Hegel considered his philosophy to be the highest possible summit, a definitive conclusion to philosophy, it was because it was in truth the consummation of the whole effort of specifically modern Reason, or what regarded itself as such, as it was effected in a Protestant Christian climate.[3] In a sense, the times were fulfilled. And the fact of taking his messianic role with absolute seriousness was an indication of the philosophical greatness of a Hegel, as of an Auguste Comte. The history of modern rationalism is not, in fact, an endless development along an indefinite line in time; it is the history of an organic and articulated development whose lines of force converged toward a summit, a final point. Hegel had the audacity to declare that he constituted this summit because it was really so. His error was to have believed that what thus achieved its supreme height was the immense Himalaya of

[1] *Proverbs*, VIII, 27.

[2] "This content shows forth God as he is in his eternal essence before the creation of Nature and of a Finite Spirit." (*Wissenschaft der Logik*, Lasson ed., I, p. 31, in *Werke*, III; trans. by W. H. Johnston and L. G. Struthers, *Science of Logic*, I, p. 60.) The word "creation" is here only a poetic or symbolic way of speaking, *an imaginative representation*, as Hegel himself says. For it would be "absurd to imagine any causality of the Logos whatsoever which would produce nature" (Jean Hyppolite, *op. cit.*, p. 580).

[3] Cf. Karl Barth, *Protestant Thought: From Rousseau to Ritschl*, New York: Harper & Brothers, 1959, ch. VII, Hegel. "Hegel's philosophy," Barth writes, "is the philosophy of *self-confidence*." And "Hegel's brand of self-confidence is also confidence in mind [spirit] which for its own part is one with God and the same with God. The characteristic thing about this, however, is that the confidence in mind or in God must also to the fullest extent and in ultimate seriousness be self-confidence, because there is likewise and in the same sense a final identity between Self and mind, as there is in general between thinking and the thing thought" (p. 275). "Self-confidence, qualified as confidence in God, confidence in God given concrete form as self-confidence—where is the man who, with the blood of this modern man in his veins, would not listen to this and hear the finest and deepest echo of his own voice? If we wish to take this modern man seriously . . . then Hegel also must be taken seriously" (p. 281).

human thought: it was only a little bulge, the molehill of modern Reason trying to be the measure of all things.

"The keen, even super-human attempt . . . at becoming one in human philosophizing with the Divine Mind, was one of the most exciting experiments" that thought can undertake, an historian has said.[1] It was certainly an exciting experiment, and even an instructive one, in which the rationalism born of Descartes was carried to its ultimate extreme, making the irrational consubstantial with reason, and ending up with the mirage of dialectic as the supreme science and wisdom.

II

THE INTEGRATION OF THE IRRATIONAL INTO REASON

The primordial intuition of Hegel

8. I have just said that Hegel carried modern rationalism to its ultimate extreme, by rendering the irrational consubstantial with reason. It is relevant to note that the very word *irrational*, in its modern usage, belongs to the conceptual vocabulary of rationalism. For a rational but not rationalist philosophy, like that of Aristotle for example, there were different degrees of intelligibility; there were in particular, at the very bottom of the scale of intelligibility, realities which were not intelligible directly in themselves (*per se*), although intelligible through other things—but there was nothing irrational. Intelligibility in pure act was found only in Intellection in pure act, and intelligibility went hand in hand with being, so that things contained a certain intrinsic element of unintelligibility (non-intelligibility directly in themselves) to the extent that they involved potency, and especially matter, or to the extent that they freely "nihilated" (swerved toward nothingness) by choosing evil. This element of opacity, essential to things insofar as they are not God, is only surmounted, St. Thomas was to hold, by the divine Intellect, which utterly and exhaustively knows potency through act, matter through form, evil through good, because it knows all things in and through its own uncreated essence and intelligibility. For our human reason this element of intrinsic opacity constitutes a mystery in things into which our reason penetrates but which it will never surmount; it exists outside our reason, in

[1] Siegfried Marck, "Dialectical Materialism", in *A History of Philosophical Systems*, edited by Vergilius Ferm, New York: The Philosophical Library, 1950, p. 307.

As Alexandre Kojève, candidly enough, explains in his own perspective of Hegelian atheism, "on first sight it is extremely simple. It suffices to read a handbook of Christian theology . . . in which God is in effect a total and infinite Being, and to say after having read it: the Being in question there—it is myself. . . . However, even today . . . it is very difficult to affirm it (seriously, that is). And it is a fact that philosophic thought went on for several millennia before a Hegel came forward and dared to say it." (A. Kojève, *op. cit.*, pp. 318–319.)

extramental reality, which for that reason will forever remain obscure to us in some degree, and will not permit our reason to know the whole of anything.

But what is the position of rationalism? For rationalism this element of radical opacity, of non-intelligibility-through-itself inherent in things, becomes an unintelligibility pure and simple, an absolute nothingness of intelligibility, in short a defiance to reason. That is what "irrational" means in modern philosophical language. And it is clear that for every rationalist philosophy this element of opacity in things must be overcome. What every rationalism demands, in the last analysis, is that Reason, as human reason, be capable of achieving the status of Reason as divine reason. The world must therefore contain no element which is *in itself* an irreducible, definitive deficiency in intelligibility.

And on the other hand the world must contain no element which is irreducibly and definitively supra-intelligible in some degree *for us*. We must be able to attain the real in the light of a reason from which nothing is hidden, our real eyes not being those owl's eyes of which Aristotle spoke and which are blinded by too pure a light.[1]

Given these premises, it was natural that rationalism began by regarding the irrational as an appearance to be dissipated, and that it undertook first to reject the irrational by denying it, or by constructing a knowledge of the world that was purely rational from beginning to end. The enterprise was a failure. Reality escaped in every direction from the great rationalist metaphysical systems of the classical age and from the sterile rationalism of the *Aufklärung*.[2]

It is at this point, then, that Hegel inaugurates a completely new phase of modern rationalism, in which the rationalist demand is more cogent than ever, but in which the irrational, instead of being denied and rejected by reason as an appearance to be dissipated, becomes itself consubstantial with

[1] "Man, because he is Spirit, should and must deem himself worthy of the highest; he cannot think too highly of the greatness and the power of his spirit. . . . The Being of the universe, at first hidden and concealed, has no power which can offer resistance to the search for knowledge." Hegel, *Lectures on the History of Philosophy*, trans. by E. S. Haldane, London, 1892, I, p. xiii (translation modified). "There is only one reason; there is no second, super-human one. It is the divine in man. Philosophy is reason grasping itself under the form of thought. . . ." *Vorlesungen über die Geschichte der Philosophie*, Einleitung, J. Hoffmeister ed., *Werke*, XVa, pp. 123 f. "What we call knowing is not merely knowing that an object *is*, but also *what it is*, and not knowing what it is only in general and having a certain knowledge or certainty thereof, but rather having knowledge of its determinations and content, being a knowledge which in its sound and achieved character is conscious of the necessity holding these determinations together." *Vorlesungen über die Philosophie der Religion*, Lasson ed., I, p. 50, in *Werke*, XII. And it is thus that philosophy knows God, it is thus that "reason is the place of the spirit where God reveals Himself to man". *Ibid.*, I, p. 49. "De Deo scire non possumus *quid sit*", said Saint Thomas Aquinas, *Sum. theol.*, I, q. 3, prol. (Cf. our work *The Degrees of Knowledge*, new trans. by G. B. Phelan, New York: Scribners, 1959; London: Bles, 1959. Appendix III.)

[2] Cf. *Vorlesungen über die Geschichte der Philosophie*, Hoffmeister ed., *Werke*, XV^{a}, pp. 191–199.

reason, as a reality we must reckon with—and pass beyond—and as the *other of reason,*[1] which reason will surmount by reconciling it with itself. Using his language, one might say that with Hegel rationalism loses itself or alienates itself in its own negation, irrationality, in order to triumph over it by means of the supreme negativity, the negation of negation.

9. In order to understand the genesis of this radical recasting or transformation of rationalism—and by the same token to appreciate more fully the significance of what has been explained in the preceding section concerning the Hegelian dialectic—it is necessary to go back to the primordial intuition which, dating from the philosopher's early years, preceded and governed the constitution of the system and the invention of the dialectic of the Logos and of the Idea.[2] This intuition, like every authentic intuition, bore on reality. It has been described as the intuition of the mobility of life,[3] or rather the intuition of the mobility and the disquietude essential to the being of man, "who is never what he is, and is always what he is not".

This, Hegel was to write (in the first edition of the *Logic*), is the distinguishing character of being when it is dominated by the category of Negativity, or when given over to the "prodigious power of the Negative", which is "the energy of Thought, of the pure Self", as he said in the preface to the *Phenomenology*. And he adds,[4] "Death, as we may call that unreality, is the most terrible thing, and to keep and hold fast what is dead demands the greatest force of all. Beauty, powerless and helpless, hates understanding, because the latter exacts from it what it cannot perform. But the life of the mind is not one that shuns death, and keeps clear of destruction; it endures death and in death maintains its being. It only wins to its truth when it finds itself utterly torn asunder. It is this mighty power, not by being a positive which turns away from the negative, as when we say of anything it is nothing or it is false, and, being then done with it, pass off to something else: on the contrary, mind is this power only by looking the negative in the face, and dwelling with it. This dwelling beside it is the magic power that converts the negative into being." I quote this remarkable passage because it is deeply imbued with the

[1] Reason "seeks its 'other', while knowing that it there possesses nothing else but itself: it seeks merely its own infinitude". *The Phenomenology of Mind*, trans. by J. B. Baillie, 2nd ed., New York: Macmillan, 1931; London: Allen and Unwin, 1931, p. 281. "What is not rational has no truth, or what is not comprehended through a notion, conceptually determined, *is* not. When reason thus speaks of some other than itself, it in fact speaks merely of itself; it does not therein go beyond itself." *Ibid.*, p. 566. It is with the same movement that Hegel renders the irrational consubstantial with reason and proclaims the empire of absolute rationalism.

[2] Cf. Jean Hyppolite, *op. cit.*, pp. 143–145; also Paul Asveld, *La pensée religieuse du jeune Hegel*, Paris: Louvain, 1953.

[3] H. Marcuse, *Hegels Ontologie und die Grundlegung einer Theorie der Geschichtlichkeit*, Frankfurt, 1932. Whatever the value of Marcuse's general theses, this view which he expressed in 1932 is of central interest for us.

[4] *Phänomenologie*, Hoffmeister ed., in *Werke*, II, pp. 29–30; Baillie trans. p. 93.

fundamental equivocity of the Hegelian conceptualization. Spirit has no fear of death, and bearing death is what requires the greatest strength, that is true; yes, but in order to be purified by death, not to nourish oneself on it. It is by being utterly torn asunder that the spirit attains truth, but the spirit does not tear itself asunder by discovering, and breathing in, the No in the bosom of the Yes, and by identifying the one with the other; it tears itself asunder by separating the Yes and the No so perfectly that all the being and truth that is trapped in the No is freed and assumed by the Yes. It is not in order to transpose the Negative into Being, but in order to save and to recuperate all the Being from which the Negative draws its apparent force, that the spirit sojourns with the Negative and diligently contemplates it.

The fact remains that back of the notions put forth here in so profoundly equivocal a manner there lay a true intuition, that of the contrasts and the mobility of our being, or of the perpetual being what one is not and not being what one is that is at the heart of human life. But instead of being expressed as the revelation of the ambiguity of a heart and a history divided between the yes and the no and passing from one contrary to the other, this intuition is conceptualized by Hegel as the presence of the no in the yes and of the yes in the no, a conception dear to Jacob Boehme, with the difference that in the case of Boehme it applied to a mystical experience, whereas for Hegel it was a primordial axiom of reason: the identity of identity and non-identity.[1] The task consisted then ("to think pure life, that is the task", he had written in his youth), in thinking life as "the anxiety of the Self which has lost itself and finds itself again in its otherness",[2] and as a perpetual non-coincidence with itself, "For life is always other in order to be itself; it always posits itself in a certain determination, and always denies itself in order to be itself, because this determination, as such, is already its first negation."[3] Here the irrational is introduced into thought itself, rendered immanent in reason, which only finds itself by losing itself in it and by surmounting it in order to integrate it in itself, from phase to phase. So rationalism changes its face, undergoes a mutation, a complete metamorphosis.

This is what we see happening, already at the time of *The Phenomenology of Spirit*, in the form of a dialectic of Consciousness. But this first kind of dialectic, still dominated by a tragic vision of the agonies of human becoming which remains close to Hegel's primordial intuition, this dialectic cannot

[1] *Differenz des Fichte'schen und Schelling'schen Systems der Philosophie in Erste Druckschriften*, G. Lasson ed. (*Werke*, I), p. 77. I note in passing that this formula, which marks the instant of the self-awakening of Hegel's thought and which signifies for him the irrational in reason, could, in the perspective of transcendence, signify at the summit of being the highest supra-rational truth (but free of all irrationality and able to be assented to by theology without any violation of the principle of contradiction; cf. John of Saint Thomas, *Cursus Theologicus*, I. P., disp. 12, a. 3, Vivès ed., IV, pp. 52 ff.), namely the identity between the identity which is the divine Nature and the non-identity constituted by the three divine Persons, non-identical among themselves.

[2] Jean Hyppolite, *op. cit.*, p. 145. [3] *Ibid.*, p. 145.

conceal the degree to which it depends on a certain analysis of experience and of happenings (and this is what makes for the authentic philosophical interest of the *Phenomenology*). Thus this first dialectic is only imperfectly rational, still blemished with empiricism; it is only a rough draft, a passing stage.

For the victory of reason to be complete it will be necessary to pass from the tragic to the logical, to integrate "pantragism"[1] into "panlogism"; the primordial intuition of Hegel will have to be definitively conceptualized into what will properly constitute Hegelian dialectic—into that dialectic of Logos which we considered in the preceding section, and in which all becoming of the real, which is the dialectic itself, takes place or is supposed to take place as a result of the internal demands of opposition, going beyond, and returning upon itself, of Reason alone, in its *self-movement*.

Thus reason has achieved its total victory. The irrational no longer exists in a reality exterior to reason and opposing reason from without; and Reason no longer undertakes to deny or reject the irrational (admitting by the same token its incapacity to grasp the real). The irrational (and I am speaking not only of the phenomenal and the contingent, I am speaking of the very ways in which concrete thought transcends them), the irrational now *is* Reason's and within Reason, which is itself Reality. Reason has taken over its enemy to the point of making of it a necessary element of its own substance and of its own becoming. And there, in its own becoming, Reason devours the irrational, nourishing itself thereon within its own bosom, advancing by means of it, from act to act of the drama, toward the supreme reconciliation which will be its supreme fulfillment. Rationalism has thus been carried to its ultimate extreme, but only at the price of introducing contradiction into thought, of placing the irrational within reason, and of renouncing not only all purism but all purity of the reason.[2] The irrational lies from the very beginning at the heart of reason, and in the most flagrant form: being is nothingness. Rationalism has won everything, the world and God, the integrity of the real, thanks to the triumphant acceptance of the impurity of reason. The saying attributed to Luther, *pecca fortiter, et crede fortius*, could now be translated: prostitute reason to the irrational, and depend more strongly than ever on the invincible courage of the reason. At this price the rationalist ambition, the equalization of the Reason as human reason with the Reason as divine reason, will achieve its fulfillment, but not before the final groaning of the world, of history, and of the Reason in their travails of engendering themselves through themselves.[3]

[1] H. Glockner, *Hegel*, II, p. 566 (a study contained in the 21st and 22nd volumes of the jubilee edition of the Works of Hegel, Stuttgart: Frommann, 1929–1940, reprinted, 1954).

[2] Thus R. Kroner has been able to say, *op. cit.*, II, p. 271, that Hegel is "the greatest irrationalist that the history of philosophy knows".

[3] In order, therefore, to comprehend Hegel's thought, we believe it necessary to insist on these two fundamental moments: (1) the primordial intuition of the mobility and unrest essential to human life; (2) the invention of dialectics (the dialectics of the Logos)—that is to say, the transformation of dialectics into knowledge—in order to express this intuition in the perspective of absolute rationalism.

The Hegelian requirement of Overcoming and of Affirmation-Destruction, or the ritual murder of Realities that are elevated to the skies

10. Far from denying or neglecting Individuality or Singularity, Personality, Freedom, in his system, Hegel constantly insisted on their crucial value for philosophy. His genius was too perspicacious, his perception of the things of experience too keen, for him not to discern the primary importance of these treasures of existence. The task of his dialectic was to appropriate them to itself, for it was to live on them. And his philosophy presents itself above all as a philosophy of freedom, a metaphysical epic of the progressive realizations and the supreme fulfillments of freedom.

But leaving the Hegelian system aside and considering the truth of things, where do singularity, personality and freedom have their reality? In man as an individual, finite and distinct from the universal Whole, in the human atom. It is he who is the seat of their real signification, of *what they are* in the created universe; it is in him that we grasp them.

For the Hegelian dialectic, on the contrary, they exist in the individual man only in their least true, most disappointing, most inapprehensible form, only acquiring consistency little by little as they extend beyond the human atom and make it go beyond itself. And they are only truly realized in the superior totalities and in the assumption of the individual by these totalities in the various stages of progress of consciousness through which the universal Self realizes itself. The infinite that is immanent in the finite forces the finite to lose itself, in order for it to re-integrate itself only at the progressive moments of its equalization with the infinite. The rational value and dynamism with which singularity, personality, freedom, are invested, press with their whole irresistible weight toward what is *beyond* each one of the still self-divided moments reached in the course of the development. By virtue of the kind of "horizontal transcendence" of which we have spoken,[1] they run after their own concept, and they will only overtake it at a stage beyond what they are in man as a finite individual.

Hegel venerates singularity, personality and freedom in the course of their realization in the world as much as St. Thomas venerated them in God; but while St. Thomas also venerated them in the human individual, where they are a deficient participation in these divine perfections, Hegel expels them from the individual to restore them to him only in the measure that the individual escapes from his finitude and contingency by integrating himself in a whole which extends beyond him. In short, at the level or stage of man as a finite individual, singularity, personality and freedom are still nothing more than the irrational to be *conquered and overcome*. It is only beyond the

[1] Cf. Jean Hyppolite, *op. cit.*, p. 525, note 1.

individual that they win their rationality, and hence their reality, by dint of conflicts and reconciliations.

This amounts to saying that in order to elevate them to the skies, it is necessary to begin by immolating them in the place where, within the created universe, what they really are finds its seat, in the place where they truly have their reality and their signification.[1] This ritual murder is the propitiatory sacrifice of the Hegelian liturgy. At the very instant that he invokes singularity, personality and freedom, and sends up toward them the incense of absolute rationalism, and wears himself out trying to follow up into the clouds of heaven the phases of their realization, the philosopher kills them on earth, I mean in man as a finite individual—his very affirmation is a destruction—in the name of the principle, "all that is real is rational", and in the name of the dialectical transfigurations by which the irrational introduced into reason must arrive at rationality.

11. Let us consider individuality or singularity, personality and freedom as they truly are. For every reason that is not divine reason they involve a certain obscurity, a certain non-intelligibility by excess or defect, a non-intelligibility that is definitively and irreducibly present in them. In the universe of the purely spiritual, they are only knowable to us by analogy, and are too intelligible in themselves to be immediately grasped by us. In the universe of sensible experience, we touch them through shadows.

Thus the positive reality which is individuality or singularity (unity-incommunicability of being) escapes our direct apprehension by excess of intrinsic intelligibility in the universe of "pure forms"; the individuality of God is as incomprehensible as His essence. And in us, in our own human universe, it is because of an intrinsic defect of intelligibility that individuality is only imperfectly and indirectly apprehensible to our reason. *Omne individuum ineffabile*. The individuality of things here below is non-intelligible in its very nature (*non intelligibilis per se*) because it has its root in matter.

Personality and freedom are intelligible *per se*, but they are too purely intelligible relative to our intelligence. They exist in us as something obscure *for us*. This is true of personality because it implies the possession of the self by the self which is proper to spirit.[2] It is true of freedom, taken as freedom of independence or of autonomy,[3] because it resides in the depths of the

[1] And indeed is not all *Begreifen*, as stated in chapter VII of the *Phenomenology*, a species of murder?

[2] And more basically (for this applies to the *suppositum* in general as well as to the person), because it is founded on subsistence, which is added to the essence without forming part of what reason can decipher therein, and which is that whereby the essence, under the creative influx, passes into the state of subject. Cf. our "Note sur la subsistence", *Revue Thomiste*, 1954, no. 2, 242–256; English trans. in *The Degrees of Knowledge*, *op. cit.*, Appendix IV, 434–444.

[3] Liberty of independence or of autonomy is not only a higher degree of the liberty of spontaneity (*libertas a coactione*) but differs *by nature, essentially*—in virtue of the spirituality which it implies—from simple liberty of spontaneity.

determination of the self by the self which is proper to spirit, and implies that existence as the simple fact of existing should superabound in a superexistence of intellection and a superexistence of love (or is even identical with that superexistence, as happens in the case of the divine aseity, the infinitely transcendent example of freedom of independence or autonomy). It is true of freedom taken in the sense of free will (*libertas a necessitate*) because the will itself renders efficacious the motive or the reason that determines it, and because the will thus manifests a primacy of exercise over specification.[1] Our intelligence grasps them without comprehending them. Even more than the universe itself, individuality, personality and freedom are known by us and intelligible to us as mysteries, and in the mystery of existence.

Such is the true notion of these things, and it derives, not certainly from what the modern vocabulary calls an irrational element, but from the secret hidden in extra-mental being, outside our reason and of such a nature that Reason as human can *never* succeed in completely penetrating it. The secret is definitively and irreducibly obscure to human reason. Therefore Hegel can only reject the notion, because it is incompatible with the primary claim of rationalism. He recasts the notions of individuality, personality and freedom in such a way as to integrate them into the Reason at work, to make of them, insofar as they still contain what must now be called an irrational element, and especially insofar as they are considered in the finite individual, the human atom—dialectical moments to be traversed in the self-movement of thought. But the ideas of individuality, of personality, of freedom, are not thereby eliminated. On the contrary, they are affirmed more strongly than ever. They will be realized *elsewhere* and otherwise—on the ruins of their authentic signification, and very far from the *only* point (the human atom) where they truly have here below their seat and their reality.

12. For Hegel, the individual posited *hic et nunc* in his immediacy, the individual, that is, as he was known before Hegel, the individual as given, the born individual, let us say, possesses only a shadow of singularity; he has no true singularity at all. He is only a kind of simple abstract point—the logical opposite of the abstract universal. And in this very opposition he denies himself, for in fact he is identical with the universal, is nothing but the most abstract universal. "If nothing is said of a thing except that it is an actual thing, an external object, this only makes it the most universal of all possible things, and thereby we express its likeness, its identity, with everything, rather than its difference from everything else. When I say 'an individual thing', I at once state it to be really quite a universal, for everything is an individual thing."[2] In other words, the single thing, the "pure this", the *individuum*

[1] Cf. our work *Principes d'une politique humaniste*, Paris: Paul Hartmann, 1944, chap. I, "La conquête de la liberté"; English trans. in *Freedom: Its Meaning*, New York: Harcourt, Brace & Co., 1940, pp. 631–649; London: Allen & Unwin, 1942.

[2] *Phenomenology*, p. 160.

ineffabile of the ancients, is for Hegel an ἄλογον, the irrational at its most extreme point of irrationality, and something which the reason overcomes without difficulty because it declares its own unreality insofar as it is singular.[1] Far from having its proper place in extra-notional reality, I mean in the *act of existing*, itself incommunicably exercised, individuality or singularity in its distinctive character results from the contradictory fusion of two logical beings of reason, *intentiones secundae* par excellence: it is the synthesis of the Particular and the Universal, and is truly realized only when the Particular is raised to the Universal or loses itself in the universal in order to receive from it a new life, as the Universal's other in which the universal determines itself. Individuality is only really authentic or true in the Concept (Begriff), "which is nothing other than the subject".[2] In the concrete Universal which is at the same time itself and its other (the particular or the determined), and in which the particular, denying and overcoming its particularity by its reflection in itself, is equalized with the universal, and by this process of mediation makes the universal return to immediacy.[3] Such a return of the universal to

[1] For Hegel animal individuality is only a sort of betrayal of the genus (organic life in general being moreover irremediably inadequate for the thought which extraposes itself in it: "The *immediacy* of the idea of life has the result that the notion as such does not exist in life," *Encyclopädie*, Naturphilosophie, § 368, trans. from G. Lasson's 4th ed., *Werke*, V, p. 325). Speaking of the animal as individual, Hegel writes: "Its inadequacy for the universal is its original sickness and the innate germ of its death" (*ibid.*, § 375, p. 331).

The self, on the other hand, is spiritual, it consists in thought. The self of each of us exists as finite and distinct from the universal Self, but it has its substance and its reality in the universal to which it returns, and in the final analysis in the universal Self. One might say that the individual Self is Thought or Subject *not yet become* concrete Self (God) by a supreme reflection of the fully actualizing and universalizing consciousness. While waiting, it is the veritable Self only insofar as thought thinking the necessary (cf. below, ch. VIII, p. 169, n. 5). Need one be astonished that Hegel accumulates obscurities when speaking of the Self? In fact this is one of the sore points of the system. *Who* really thinks when I think? If it is the universal Self who thinks in me, then I no longer have any distinct existence as a finite self. And if it is I who really think, then it is the individual Self insofar as finite and contingent which is subject, substance and reality. The two positions are equally untenable in the Hegelian system.

[2] Jean Hyppolite, *Genèse et structure de la phénoménologie de l'esprit de Hegel*, p. 81. Cf. p. 143: "The concept is omnipotence but is such only while manifesting itself and affirming itself in its Other; it is the Universal which appears as the soul of the Particular and is completely determined in it as the negation of negation or authentic Singularity. . . ." See also *Hegel's Philosophy of Right*, Introd., § 1, trans. by T. M. Knox, p. 14: Philosophy shows "that it is the concept alone (not the mere abstract category of the understanding which we often hear called by the name) which has actuality, and further that it gives this actuality to itself".

[3] This concrete Universal, often regarded as Hegel's great discovery, is, to tell the truth, only a being of reason made up of mutually repugnant elements. It is a being of reason *cum fundamento in re*, its extra-mental foundation is something eminently real: an idea as incarnated in history, more precisely an idea (a *universal*, but *abstract*) insofar as by both conscious and unconscious modes it animates and directs *concrete* and singular (but extra-mental) formations, for example this or that collective whole (this people, as when one speaks of the spirit of a people; this religious communion, as when one speaks of the genius of Christianity; etc.). It nevertheless remains that the Hegelian concrete Universal itself, conceived as it is in an entirely intra-notional manner, is a patent *self-contradiction*

immediacy, such a universal individuality, in a whole which is outside the singular thing and superior to it, or in the identification of the individual consciousness with this whole, constitutes the only real singularity for Hegel, and the only real concrete,[1] and the only rationally possible solution to the problem of individuality, which, as has been said,[2] is the central problem of his philosophy.

13. Personality, for Hegel, is not distinguished from individuality. It is rather individuality itself in the superior degree which is characterized by consciousness and therefore by the properly historical kind of development. Personality is the superior limit toward which nature tends, but because it is now defined as consciousness directed back to its own interiority for the purpose of disengaging it, or as the reflection by means of which the Concept knows itself as Self, personality is no longer an ontological perfection inherent in the human individual, with which he is born into the world, a perfection of his immediate being. It necessarily presupposes the mediation of consciousness (that is, of the universal "I", taking consciousness of itself through the medium of the finite). That is why in the individual man considered as such (apart from the Whole or the community) it is still no more than the abstract form of the Self juxtaposed with a miserably contingent content; and in the periods of history[3] in which the community ceases "to be the un-selfconscious substance of individuals", the latter "count as selves and substances with a being of their own", they "all count for as much as each, i.e., have the significance of *persons*"—the universal, "split up into the atomic units" is no longer anything but a "lifeless spirit".[4] In short, the only

---

(the universal-singular), a being of reason of the unthinkable type erected into the rational-and-real, just as the Concept in the Hegelian sense ("That which remains itself in its being-other").

For minds curious about fortuitous rapprochements one may note that there is in Thomism also, but in a wholly different sense, a sort of concrete universal—that which the angelic intellect uses, and which is not, as ours, a universal abstracted and drawn out of things. Rather it contains in act all its singulars and takes knowledge directly to the singular, because it represents things according as they proceed in their very individuality from the universal causality of God, inasmuch as the infused ideas of the angel are participations of the creative Ideas and attain things by the very ways which make them be, i.e. by the confidence of the Artist (cf. John of Saint Thomas, *Cursus Theologicus*, disp. 21, a. 3, § 29, Vivès ed., t. IV, p. 755b). But the concrete universal of the angel *makes* the singular *known*, while the Hegelian concrete universal *is* the singular.

[1] Cf. *Encyclopaedia*, Logic, § 164, Wallace trans., p. 295.

[2] Jean Hyppolite, *op. cit.*, p. 53, n. 1.

[3] In fact, for Hegel, in the epoch of the Roman Empire.

[4] *Phenomenology*, p. 501. "The person is the self devoid of substance" (*ibid.*, p. 645). Cf. *Philosophy of History*, Sibree trans., Collier, 1901, p. 406: "The living political body—that Roman feeling which animated it as its soul—is now brought back to the isolation of a lifeless Private Right. As, when the physical body suffers dissolution, each point gains a life of its own, but which is only the miserable life of worms; so the political organism is here dissolved into atoms—viz. private persons."

personality that Hegel attributes to the individual as such, the individual-born, is the "abstract and formal"[1] juridical personality, "lacking spirit",[2] which "gives itself reality in the existence of private property",[3] and has nothing to do with real and authentic personality but is only a blank mask applied to everyone indifferently.

This false personality of the individual must give way to the subsequent developments of spirit. Personality—or, to employ a more nearly Hegelian language, subjectivity—begins only after the stage of the individual taken as such, and it develops by stages that are further and further removed from the contingency of the finite as such, from the contingency that characterizes "that which does not have the foundation of its being within itself",[4] and whose presence in nature and in history Hegel affirms only in order to go beyond it. From negation of negation to negation of negation, subjectivity is to be realized progressively in the supra-individual human "I" which sums up within itself the whole spirit of its time: in the "Ego that is 'we', a plurality of Egos, and 'we' that is a single Ego";[5] in the inter-subjectivity which is the consciousness of the universal self; and finally, in the absolute Knowledge of self which is characteristic of the absolute Self, of God mounting the throne of His own divinity. And the individual possesses real subjectivity only insofar as he equalizes himself with this supra-individual subjectivity by denying himself at one or another moment of his development, and so expires in one way or another—to become—in the infinity of spirit. In the last analysis, it is the Absolute that is Subject. There is no true Self in the human atom, but only in the "authentic singularity" of the Concept and of the concrete Universal, of the Whole which is immanent in each of its determinations and which, after denying itself reaffirms itself, and brings itself and all of its parts back into itself.

14. In short, it is above and beyond the individual man that the drama of freedom is enacted, as we shall see more explicitly in the section which follows. Freedom of choice is an illusory moment. The only freedom that interests Hegel is the freedom of autonomy. But this freedom is acquired at the price of going beyond the individual personality in man, and sacrificing it. Freedom will be truly realized first of all in the State, then in the absolute Spirit, which needs finite spirit in order to know itself, but which by the same act causes finite spirit to vanish as individual personality.

Freedom is identical with the Spirit. Just as the essence of matter is gravity,

[1] *Phil. of History*, p. 409. Cf. *Philosophy of Right*, § 35 ff.

[2] *Phil. of History*, p. 420.

[3] *Ibid.*, p. 366.

[4] Cf. *Philosophie der Religion*, Lasson ed., in *Werke*, XII, p. 211. (On contingency, *Zufälligkeit*, see *Encyclopaedia*, Logic, § 145, pp. 263 ff.; *Wissenschaft der Logik*, Lasson ed., in *Werke*, IV, pp. 171 ff. and Johnston and Struthers trans., II, pp. 174 ff.; *Beweise vom Dasein Gottes*, Lasson ed., in *Werke*, XIV, lectures 11 and 12.)

[5] *Phenomenology*, p. 227.

the essence of spirit is freedom.[1] All of the qualities of spirit exist solely by virtue of freedom. Spirit "has its center in itself", "it exists *in* and *with itself*", it is existence contained within itself. And that is freedom.[2] In other words, freedom, which is spirit, is the sovereign freedom sought itself in Nature. And so freedom is coextensive with all that is. It is everywhere, and the fact is that it precedes Nature, because, in absolute terms, Spirit precedes Nature. If "from our point of view Mind [Spirit] has for its *presupposition* Nature, of which it is the truth", on the other hand and for this very reason it is the absolute *prius* of Nature, "the *absolutely first* principle. In this its truth Nature is vanished, and . . . spirit has resulted as the 'Idea' entered on possession of itself".[3] Thus the whole dialectical process, in the course of all its conflicts, is the development of freedom. Diffused and alienated from itself in Nature—in which gravitation is its first prototype, and sensation, "the culminating point and end of Nature",[4] its ultimate preparation—freedom finally emerges with the appearance of the concrete spirit in man. Once it has emerged, freedom is realized through new dialectical conflicts and new developments of subjective Spirit, objective Spirit and absolute Spirit.

In the realist perspective of a St. Thomas, the spontaneity (*libertas a coactione*) inherent in nature as an internal principle of activity attained higher and higher degrees of perfection as one passed from inanimate matter to vegetative life to sensitive life, and finally became autonomy—infinitely above simple spontaneity—in the human person. But these were specifically distinct degrees in being. With Hegel it is no longer a question of specifically distinct degrees in being, but of phases of development of the Idea-Reality. And it is the idea of freedom conceived as total autonomy, perfect and absolute independence—a replica of the divine aseity seen through the eyes of a pantheist immanentism[5]—which, starting with its own negation, realizes itself from stage to stage by losing itself and refinding itself dialectically, up to the point where it refinds itself in total plenitude at the stage of the Spirit, which preceded itself in forms which were not entirely itself.

[1] *Phil. of History*, Introd., p. 61.

[2] "Spirit is *self-contained existence* (Bei-sich-selbst-seyn). Now this is Freedom, exactly. For if I am dependent, my being is referred to something else which I am not; I cannot exist independently of something external. I am free, on the contrary, when my existence depends upon myself." *Ibid.*, p. 62. "The Will is Free only when it does not will anything alien, extrinsic, foreign to itself (for as long as it does so, it is dependent), but wills itself alone—wills the Will." *Ibid.*, p. 552.

[3] *Encyclopaedia*, Phil. of Mind, § 381, Wallace trans., p. 6.

[4] *Vorlesungen über die Philosophie der Religion*, Lasson ed., I, p. 170, in *Werke*, XII.

[5] Likewise it is only if one relates it to the aseity of the infinitely transcendent Pure Act and to its infinite liberty of independence, that Hegel's formula—"Liberty is the truth of Necessity"—finds a decidedly true meaning. Cf. *Vorlesungen über die Geschichte der Philosophie*, Einleitung, ed. J. Hoffmeister in *Werke*, XVa, p. 116: "We have to say that the spirit is free in its necessity and only in it does it have its freedom, as its necessity consists in its freedom." Is there any need to observe that the attribution of aseity, or the equivalent of aseity, to the self-movement of a spirit which engenders itself and everything else through its losses and recoveries of self is pure absurdity?

8

HEGELIAN IDEALISM

Hegel and the Human Person—*Sittlichkeit*

I

THE DIALECTICAL IMMOLATION OF THE PERSON

The Individual Person

1. In the previous chapter we considered the Hegelian dialectic of negativity and *Aufhebung* (suppression-superelevation) in its various aspects. What does all this mean for the human person? And what becomes of the person itself?

For Christian realism the person, by the very fact of being an individual substance, was a whole; independence was one of its defining characteristics; and the notion of personality was an analogical notion, which was realized, in essentially different ontological degrees, in God, in pure spirits and in man. Here below, then, the person—"that which is most perfect in all of nature"[1]—was the individual human subject (composed of soul and body and subsisting by the subsistence of the soul) which, superexisting spiritually in knowledge and in love, constituted a whole universe in itself but was at the same time a part of the universe and a part of the social group, and possessed a very characteristic independence of personality but possessed that independence only potentially, in the midst of all the servitudes to which matter and the world, heredity and environment, subjected it. The drama of human life consisted in rendering the limited, fragile and menaced independence more and more effective and vigorous in itself, and in passing through deaths to self in order to conquer its freedom of autonomy, as far as that is possible for a created being—for a creature made of flesh and spirit—and with the restrictions proceeding from the human condition.

But limitation is precisely what Hegel cannot accept, unless it be to go beyond it. Hegelianism claims to *go beyond* all limitation. In the Hegelian perspective, finitude and contingency can only occur as immediate data (irrationals), which it is the object of the processes and conflicts of development, phase by phase, to deny and surmount, or sublimate. The limitlessness of freedom of autonomy is posited from the beginning in the very definition of Freedom, which is Spirit, and the only thing that matters is finally to recover that limitlessness by the losses of self and the reintegrations of self

[1] Saint Thomas, *Sum. theol.*, I, 29, 3.

through which the Idea of Freedom works its way. The human person is not a mysterious center subsistent in itself, a substantial existent obscure to itself precisely by reason of its ontological richness which is inexpressible in any object of thought, an individual in which is contained and consummated the metaphysical reality of personality and in which the destiny of the personality is worked out—for Hegelianism this destiny is achieved outside the individual. The individual personality constitutes a first point of reflection, emerging from Nature, in which the spirit begins no doubt to turn back upon itself—but it will only really return to itself by investing the individual personality with the personality of a superior whole; and as individual (individual-born), the personality is not really a whole, it is only a contradictory moment in which the abstract form of personality hides the absence of and the waiting for true subjectivity. It can only overcome the afflictions of the particular and the contingent by escaping from itself. In short, all the limitations and the miseries in the midst of which, as we remarked above, the human person struggles to become what it is and to conquer its freedom of autonomy now come to be contained in its very notion, making of it nothing but a moment to be surpassed.

2. Hegel knows that the Absolute is Subject.[1] And he glorifies subjectivity and the depths of subjectivity, but for him it is "infinite subjectivity"[2]—"pure certainty of itself"[3] which "the individual attains not in virtue of his particular idiosyncrasy, but of his essential being".[4] He does not know how to recognize

[1] This proposition, put in a perspective wholly opposed to Hegel's, signifies that God is Personality, Intelligence, and Love. For Hegel it signifies that the Absolute (Spirit) is Discourse through which it reveals itself (to itself and to Hegel). When he says, "Everything depends on grasping and expressing the ultimate truth not as Substance but as Subject as well" (Preface to *The Phenomenology of Mind*, trans. by J. B. Baillie, 2nd ed., New York: Macmillan, 1931, London: Allen and Unwin, 1931, p. 80), he intends to affirm from the beginning the dialectic structure of Being: "The living substance [that is to say, neither static nor given] . . . is that being which is truly subject, or, what is the same thing, is truly realized and actual (*wirklich*) solely in the [dialectical] process of positing itself, or in mediating with its own self its transitions from one state or position to the opposite" (*ibid.*, p. 80; cf. above, ch. VII, p. 129, n. 5 *sub fine*). Here Hegel was directly attacking Schelling and his Absolute conceived only as Substance—although one may be able to say that Schelling himself had prepared the way for him, when, under the inspiration of both Spinoza and Kant, but without suspecting anything of the absolutely new meaning which such a formula could take on for Hegel, he had written to him in 1795 that "God is nothing other than the absolute I" ("Gott ist nichts als das absolute Ich" in *Briefe von und an Hegel*, J. Hoffmeister ed., I, Hamburg, 1952, p. 22). Cf. the analysis of Hegel's position vis-à-vis Schelling (1794–1796) in Paul Asveld, *La pensée religieuse du jeune Hegel*, Paris-Louvain, 1953, pp. 75–99.

[2] *Philosophy of History*, J. Sibree trans., New York: Collier, 1901, p. 317; f. p. 330.

[3] *Ibid.*, p. 317.

[4] *Ibid.*, p. 520. Hegel explains there that "the specific embodiment of Deity—infinite subjectivity, that is true spirituality, Christ", whom "Christendom had formerly sought in an earthly sepulchre", was found by the Lutheran reform, thanks to "the time-honored and cherished sincerity of the German people", "in the deeper abyss of the Absolute Ideality of all that is sensuous and external" (*ibid.*, pp. 518 f.). Elsewhere he speaks of subjectivity as "the Human Will as intrinsically universal" (*ibid.*, p. 413).

subjectivity and the depths of subjectivity where they exist here below—in the "particular individuality" of each one, in the poor human atom pursuing its quarrel with the servitudes of limitation, of matter and of contingency which overwhelm it from every side. In spite of his profound insight into the tragic rendings and the progressive moultings of human consciousness, he is ignorant of the abyss of subjectivity in the individual person, because this abyss, though it certainly involves the reversion of the spirit upon itself, is a substantial abyss which, far from being defined by consciousness of self, defies consciousness of self, which is for it a night which becomes darker as it penetrates into it. That is why it is indeed a night that Hegel contemplates in others, but a very different night from that substantial abyss, or universe to itself proper to each individual. "Man is this night, this empty Nothingness which contains all in its simplicity: a store of an infinite number of images, of pictures, none of which he perceives clearly, or which do not exist as really present. It is the night, the interiority of Nature which exists here: pure Self" —an interiority *of Nature*, Hegel says (and not: of the singular subject itself) because for him the pure I-personal or the pure Self is *universal*, and Nature is the first avatar in which, by alienating itself from itself, it lets itself be glimpsed obscurely, as a Void and Negation of itself. And Hegel continues: "In phantasmagoric shows there is night all around; here a bloody head suddenly rises up, there a white phantom; and both as suddenly disappear. It is the night that one sees when one looks men in the eyes: one plunges then into a night which becomes terrible; it is the night of the world which presents itself then to us."[1]

Thus for Hegel the night of subjectivity is only an empty shadow where the ghosts of dreams rise up and where the multiple and the apparent slumber. When he *looks a man in the eyes* he is not fascinated by the mystery of *this soul*, of the unique *you*; it is the *night of the world* that he sees in these eyes, this alone that fascinates and disturbs him.

Hegel knows that Christianity has had the privilege of bringing to light the value and the dignity of the individual.[2] He took over from Christianity, in

[1] *Jenenser Realphilosophie*, II, *Die Vorlesungen von 1805/06*, J. Hoffmeister ed. in *Werke*, Lasson ed., XX, pp. 180 f.

[2] "It was through Christianity that this idea came into the world. According to Christianity, the individual *as such* has an infinite value as the object and aim of divine love, destined as mind to live in absolute relationship with God himself, and have God's mind dwelling in him"; and Hegel indicates immediately the philosophic or real meaning of these religious assertions: "i.e. man is implicitly destined to supreme freedom" (*Encyclopaedia of the Philosophical Sciences*, Philosophy of Mind, § 482, W. Wallace trans., Oxford: Clarendon Press, 1894, p. 101). Cf. *Phil. of Hist.*, p. 426: "Under Christianity Slavery is impossible; for man as man—in the abstract essence of his nature—is contemplated in God; each unit of mankind is an object of the grace of God and of the Divine purpose: 'God will have *all* men to be saved.' Utterly excluding all speciality, therefore, man, in and for himself —in his simple quality of man—has infinite value." In the Hegelian reconceptualization of Christianity, as later in Marxist humanism, it is the belonging to the human race, and to the human community, not the human person, which is considered in the individual.

order to reinterpret it, the idea that each human being is "unique in the world" and that this uniqueness is of infinite value. More important than that, he took over while denying it the Christian idea of man to such an extent that while he rejected as mythical the notion of grace and the supernatural order he embodied at the very heart of his thought the Christian idea of man's accession to the divine life and his transformation into God. As a result, the human as such consisted of a rendering oneself other, of changing radically, and there was no longer, properly speaking, any human nature;[1] human nature henceforth gave place to the historical auto-genesis of humanity, and it is thus by his own action that man acquires his being, makes himself at the same time Man and God. "The true being of man is . . . his act."[2]

But toward what does the action of man tend in the course of history, if not to the appearance of the highest forms of social Community and the supreme revelation of absolute Knowledge? The infinite value of the individual and his uniqueness are only a shadow, a promise, a frustrated aspiration or a vain presumption, so long as they do not pertain to these high universal Totalities, taken either in their own superindividual unity-indivisibility or as the soul and substance of the individuals integrated into them.

And no doubt it is quite true that personality only grows in man to the degree that he leaves the closed world of simple material individuality in order to open out spiritually, through intelligence and through love, toward the outside world and toward others, toward the common good of the family and that of the city, toward the boundless sea of truth, of the suffering of his brothers, of the charity of his God. But this is a process taking place on the moral level, produced out of the anguish of each one's free choice; and Hegel substitutes for it an onto-logical development, produced by the dialecticity of being—in such a way that there is nothing higher than Individuality when at last it finds itself and realizes itself in the Universal, and nothing more miserable while it remains in its own individual being-there. The human individual, eminent as he appears in relation to the world of Nature, in reality only achieves *concrete personality* and *subjectivity*[3] beyond himself as a particular individual; what we call the human person is interesting only by virtue of the destiny which carries it beyond itself; it must in its turn be surpassed and sacrificed so that personality or self-consciousness may be re-established at a higher level, in the individual which is really Totality—the Totality of the universal come back *to its original self* with all the spoils of its differences reabsorbed into itself. This is so because, in fact, what Hegel posited from the very beginning, and what governs his whole perspective, is that the Self is a

[1] "For Hegel there is no 'human nature': man *is* what he *does*; he creates himself by his action; the innate in him, his 'nature', is what he is as an animal." Alexandre Kojève, *Introduction à la lecture de Hegel*, Paris: Gallimard, 1947, pp. 89 f.

[2] *Phenomenology*, Baillie trans., p. 349 (*Phänomenologie des Geistes*, chap. V, 3rd ed. by G. Lasson in *Werke*, II, p. 236: "Das *wahre Sein* des Menschen ist vielmehr *seine Tat*").

[3] And value and dignity that are *real*, and not merely symbolic or *represented* by religion.

universal Self, and that it is essential to Spirit to deliver itself from the dictatorship of the singular (which will become authentic again only in the universal).

3. Kant, affirming the absolute dignity of the person as an end in itself, had deified it by transporting it (I mean transporting, by the touch of a magic wand, the sensible singular *I*'s themselves, inseparable from the universal I and belonging to the same tribe) into an intelligible world where empirical singularity, the differences deriving from space and time, disappeared. Hegel undertakes the inverse operation. Faced with the great idols of superindividual personality engendered by the movement of the Idea, he completely relativises the individual person. The human person is only a wave which traverses the ocean of History, and thinks it is propelling the water while in reality it is being carried along by it. And no doubt it is quite true—it is one of the great apperceptions by which Hegel was dazzled—that most often what the individual performs on the stage of the world is really something quite different from what he thinks he is doing,[1] and that while they seem to be carried away by their passions and their particular interests the great men of history are really accomplishing a work which manifests the majesty of destiny, because, given the pressure exerted by the tide of life and the needs of the human race, it was indeed necessary that a decisive change of that sort should occur. But Hegel believes that just as it occurred in fact, so the act in question was required by Reason at work in history; he does not see that this work—which no doubt *had* to be done—*might have been* done *otherwise* (for every great historical event, ambivalent though it be, can emerge into existence with the mark of better or of worse upon it, as a substantially healthy fructification or as a worm-ridden and rotten fructification), and that this properly moral quality, this *how* of the work, depends largely on the great figure himself who makes history while remaining dependent upon it. He sees neither that the courses taken by human personality in history are freer of the instant than is history itself (the great figures of history are not only those who are received by their own time because they bring about what was already about to

[1] Cf. our remarks on *masks* and *roles* in *Religion and Culture*, London: Sheed and Ward, 1931 ("Theatrum mundi", pp. 63 ff.).

Let us note in passing, to avoid any misunderstanding, that for Hegel it is not as *individual* but as *incarnation* of the Universal that "the great man is what he has done and one ought to say that he has willed what he has done just as he has done what he has willed" (cited by Jean Hyppolite, *Genèse et structure de la phénoménologie de l'esprit de Hegel*, Paris: Aubier, 1946, p. 283). Insofar as he is an individual his ends remained enveloped in the Idea, of which he himself "had no consciousness", for he derived his ends and his vocation "from a concealed fount—one which has not attained to phenomenal, present existence—from that inner Spirit, still hidden beneath the surface, which, impinging on the outer world as on a shell, bursts it in pieces, because it is another kernel than that which belonged to the shell in question" (*Phil. of Hist.*, pp. 76 f.). Cf. Hegel's *Philosophy of Right*, § 348, T. M. Knox trans., Oxford: Clarendon Press, 1942, p. 218.

happen, but also those who struggle against their time and are broken by it, like the prophets);[1] nor does he see that the individual element that counts most in the individuality itself of the great man is not that which is seen by the "psychological valets"[2]—his passions and his egoistic interests; it is what they cannot see—his conscience (if he has one). And especially he fails to see that in relation to the human person and what it accomplishes there is another dimension than that of history (there are events and works, and a duration, which are meta-historical, because they derive from the purely spiritual).[3] For Hegel the whole grandeur of the great figures of history—"these agents of the World-Spirit"[4]—is to have been the accomplices of the exigencies of the time, to have foreseen what the time had made "ripe for development"[5]—*Ripeness is all*, as Edgar says in *King Lear*.

Few passages show more clearly the sort of profound Hegelian mistrust and aversion regarding individuality as such (native or "given" individuality) than that in which the philosopher explains that one must expect individuality to pervert the course of history. If this is not the way things go, it is thanks to one of the mysteries of the dialectic, and because this very individuality which was to make the course of the world into a "perversion of the good" serves the Universal as a point of insertion and realization in history.[6] The individual is good for this and for this alone; the individual person can be tolerated by reason only insofar as it is *not* taken as individual, insofar as it is the actualization of the Universal which surpasses it. It is not surprising that in such a perspective the human person, as we shall notice a little further on, only finds

[1] Cf. what we wrote about the "temptation" of history (*On the Philosophy of History*, edited by J. W. Evans, New York: Scribners, 1957, p. 59; London: Bles, 1959): "Those who make it their first principle to advance with history, or to make history advance and to march in step with it, thereby bind themselves to collaborate with all the agents of history; they find themselves in very mixed company.

"We are not co-operators with history; we are co-operators with God.

"No doubt, to absent oneself from history is to seek death. Spiritual activity, which is above time, does not vacate time, it holds it from on high. Our duty is to act on history to the limit of our power: yes, but God being first served. And we must neither complain nor feel guilty if history often works against us: it will not vanquish our God, and escape His purposes, either of mercy or of justice. The chief thing, from the point of view of existence in history, is not to succeed; success never endures. Rather, it is *to have been there*, to have been *present*, and that is ineffaceable."

[2] Cf. *Phil. of Hist.*, Introd., p. 79.

[3] Cf. our book *Approaches to God*, New York: Harper & Brothers, 1954; London: Allen and Unwin, 1956, pp. 77–78.

[4] *Phil. of Hist.*, Introd., p. 77.

[5] *Ibid.*, p. 77. Cf. *Philosophie der Weltgeschichte*, Lasson's ed., I, p. 76, in *Werke*, VIII: "Und eben die weltgeschichtlichen Individuen sind diejenigen . . . in deren Innerem sich geoffenbart hat, was an der Zeit, was notwendig ist."

[6] "The world process was supposed to be the perversion of the good, because it took individuality for its principle. But this latter is the principle of actual reality, for it is just that mode of consciousness by which what is implicit and inherent is for an other as well. The world process transmutes and perverts the unchangeable, but does so in fact by transforming it out of the nothingness of abstraction into the being of reality." *Phenomenology*, Baillie trans., p. 409.

itself by losing and annihilating itself as every individual does in the community; and the supreme autonomy, that which is won by merging with the Absolute, belongs not to the human person as person, but only to the Knowledge by which and in which the finite spirit is superindividually reconciled with the infinite spirit.

Freedom of Choice

4. In his doctrine of the subjective Spirit and in that of the objective Spirit, Hegel gives us as it were a dialectical recasting of the whole subject matter of Psychology and the whole subject matter of Ethics in their broadest extension. The three fundamental stages of development of the subjective Spirit are that in which the spirit of man is still immersed in the impulses and inclinations of nature; that in which it begins to free itself by the negation of that given being; that in which, by giving to itself a superior being through consciousness of self and elevating self to universality, it definitively passes the threshold of freedom (and, by the same token, of the world of objective Spirit).

What does this mean? At the second stage free choice appears. The will is concerned with impulses which come from outside or from nature. Yet at the same time, possessing the abstract certitude of its autonomy (not yet really and concretely realized at this stage), it envelops in this empty form of self-determination a content which it has not given to itself, and which is composed of the pressures exerted by nature; and what appears to it as a "choice" among these diverse pressures is from now on nothing but an event which, because it "is not the fact of the activity of self-determination", derives from nature while at the same time being contingent or without internal necessity within the sphere of the will: in short, free choice is nothing other than "contingency manifesting itself as will".[1] And since there is no real freedom, but only contingency posing as freedom, one must say that in the judgment of philosophy free choice implies an inevitable illusion.[2] Hegel, who was neither

[1] *Phil. of Right*, § 15, Knox trans., p. 27. Cf. *Encyclopaedia*, Phil. of Mind, § 478, Wallace trans., pp. 98 f.

[2] "Instead of being the will in its truth, arbitrariness is more like the will as contradiction. . . . Since, then, arbitrariness has immanent in it only the formal element in willing, i.e. free self-determination, while the other element is something given to it, we may readily allow that, if it is arbitrariness which is supposed to be freedom, it may indeed be called an illusion" (*Phil. of Right*, § 15, pp. 27 f.). Free choice is not *free will* (cf. *ibid.*, § 22, p. 30). Let us not forget that for Hegel "the point of view from which things seem pure accidents vanishes if we look at them in the light of the concept and philosophy, because philosophy knows accident for a show and sees in it its essence, necessity" (*ibid.*, § 324, p. 209; cf. Gans' additions to § 15 of the same work, pp. 230 f.).

One sees very well in these texts from the *Philosophy of Right* that Hegel cannot grasp the reality of free choice because he conceives freedom in only one of the two forms which this notion admits of, in the form of freedom of independence or autonomy. It is in the light of the latter (*libertas a coactione*) that he seeks to understand freedom of choice (*libertas a necessitate*). Not having the idea of *self-determination* proper to free choice (by which the will, in virtue of its active or dominating indetermination, itself renders efficacious the motive which determines it), authentic motivation (inherent in the practico-practical

a determinist (because he is interested only in the self-movement of the Idea) nor an anti-determinist (for the same reason), does not hesitate to talk about free choice. Free will, or freedom of choice, has its place in the development of the subjective Spirit—but as an illusory moment.[1] This is the maximum of effective recognition that Hegelian rationalism can bestow upon it.

In the third stage of the development of subjective Spirit freedom of choice is superseded. The way is now clear for true freedom, which is a perfect spontaneity of the spirit without dependence on anything exterior, or autonomy, finally realized.[2] There is no longer choice. The will has brought

---

judgment) escapes him, and is replaced for him by impulses, instincts, and inclinations which derive from nature (and which therefore—in non-Hegelian language—depend upon the determinism of nature). On the other hand, the *self-determination* which he seeks and which is proper to freedom of independence or autonomy (and by which, according to him, a being acts in dependence upon itself alone—but since this formula really applies only to divine freedom, let us say rather: by which a being acts without anything exterior preventing it from following its own law)—this *self-determination* can exist only where the content of the will is *given* by the pressures of nature. Hegel can thus conceive of free choice only as the application of the abstract form of the freedom of autonomy to a content which derives from nature (that is to say—in non-Hegelian terms—which in reality remains in submission to the determinations of nature) and which in relation to the will itself is only *contingent* and arbitrary (in other words is not, as in "true" and "concrete" freedom, that which the will cannot not will—for let us not forget that according to Hegel this "true" and "concrete" freedom is for the will *to will itself*).

[1] As Jean Hyppolite remarks (*op. cit.*, p. 147, note 1), abstraction, for Hegel, is not a mere operation of our minds, it belongs to being and characterizes certain phases of being. One must say the same of appearance or *phenomenality*. There are abstract existences and phenomenal or apparent existences (and in an idealist philosophy it is certainly possible to speak in this fashion). "Experience, as it surveys the wide range of inward and outward existence, has sense enough to distinguish the mere appearance, which is transient and meaningless, from what in itself really deserves the name of actuality," Hegel writes in the *Encyclopaedia*. In defending his famous formula: "What is reasonable is actual; and, What is actual is reasonable", he explains that "as regards the logical bearings of the question, that existence is in part mere *appearance*, and only in part actuality", and that "even our ordinary feelings are enough to forbid a casual (fortuitous) existence getting the emphatic name of an actual". And he adds: "As for the term Actuality, these critics would have done well to consider the sense in which I employ it. In a detailed Logic I had treated amongst other things of actuality, and accurately distinguished it not only from the fortuitous, which, after all, has existence, but even from the cognate categories of existence and the other modifications of being." *The Encyclopaedia of the Philosophical Sciences*, Logic, § 6, W. Wallace trans., 2nd ed., Oxford: O.U.P., 1892, pp. 9 ff.; cf. *Phil. of Right*, Introd., § 1.

Thus the contingent belongs to being but not to *reality*; it is a *phenomenal* or apparent existence. And the apparent which passes itself off as real, as in the case of free choice, is properly the *illusory*.

[2] "The contradiction which the arbitrary will is comes into appearance as a dialectic of impulses and inclinations . . ." (*Phil. of Right*, § 17, Knox trans., p. 28). This contradiction ceases only at the moment in which the will has "universality, or itself *qua* infinite form, for its object, content, and aim"; then it is "free not only *in* itself but *for* itself also". This will which exists in itself and for itself "has for its object the will itself as such, and so the will in its sheer universality". In it are absorbed "the immediacy of instinctive desire and the particularity which is produced by reflection", in other words, the conditions to which free choice was still bound. "This process of absorption in or elevation to universality is what is called the activity of thought." *Ibid.*, § 21, pp. 29 f.

everything under the universal. It is very significant that for an instant Hegel gives as an indication of this true freedom, inclined toward the universal, the will to happiness,[1] in which in effect the spontaneity of the will is complete—along with necessity. But happiness is only an abstract and imagined ("represented") universality of things desired. True universality, the concrete universality of the will, is only attained when the entire content of the will depends uniquely on the will itself, in other words is the very essence, reflexively thought, of the will as object of itself. Then the will is truly free, by which is to be understood that having gone beyond freedom of choice it enjoys a freedom of independence or autonomy which coincides with the necessity of that which is willed in the pure and purifying consciousness of self which "grasps itself as essence through thought"—it is only "as thinking intelligence" that the will is authentically a will, and free[2]—and in that reassumption and repatriation in the concrete Universal and the common Will which make it adhere to the supreme obligations manifested by the objective Spirit.

The morality of Conscience

5. It is only with the rise of the objective Spirit (when in virtue of that degree of intensity which Subjective Free Spirit has attained, "it is elevated to the form of Universality")[3] that Freedom is truly made concrete and realized. In short, "it is only in consciously willing the State that the individual goes beyond the contingency of free choice to enter upon the native soil of Freedom".[4]

Freedom acquires body in external institutions as in a world that Spirit has created for itself. Then freedom presents itself *in the form of necessity*,[5] and this necessity can impose constraint upon the individual if he refuses to be free, but in itself it is only the visage of freedom, or of the self-determination of mind. The three stages of development of the objective Spirit—in which it is actualized first exteriorly, then interiorly, finally completely (exteriorly and interiorly at the same time)—are those of abstract Law, the Morality of Conscience, and the Ethicity involved in the social group and above all in the State.

Abstract Law[6] is the world of relations between juridical persons as proprietors of things. We will only concern ourselves here with the typical separation, already affirmed by Kant (and whose source must be sought in Luther)

[1] Cf. *Encyclopaedia*, Phil. of Mind, §§ 479, 480, p. 99.

[2] "The self-consciousness which purifies its object, content, and aim, and raises them to this universality effects this as thinking getting its own way in the will. Here is the point at which it becomes clear that it is only as thinking intelligence that the will is genuinely a will and free." *Phil. of Right*, § 21, p. 30.

[3] *Phil. of Hist.*, p. 521.

[4] J. Hyppolite, Preface to the French translation of *Philosophie des rechts* (Paris), 1940, p. 18.

[5] "Freedom, shaped into the actuality of a world, receives the *form of Necessity*. . . ." *Encyclopaedia*, Phil. of Mind, § 484, p. 103.

[6] *Phil. of Right*, First Part.

between the juridical order and the moral order: Law, for Hegel, comes before the stage of Morality and is entirely independent of it; the rules of Law, and the external obedience they require, belong to a sphere completely separated from that of the exigencies which work on the conscience in matters of good and evil. We should add that the symmetrical arrangements of the system ought not to conceal the very close relation which exists between this first stage of the development of the objective Spirit and the second of the three phases[1] of the third stage, that is, between Law and "civil Society". The abstract world of Law, of private property and private needs, finds its concrete realization and its own collective spirit, its sociality, in civil Society (*bürgerliche Gesellschaft*),[2] which Hegel distinguishes from the State, while misconstruing the significance of this distinction in the worst way: instead of taking political society or the body politic (which is to be identified with the authentic concept of civil society) for the political and social whole of which the State is only the central organ, he makes the State itself the political whole, and reduces what he calls civil society to an atomistic collection[3] of individual rights which have to do solely with the economic order and with the relations between private interests. In other words, it is the *homo oeconomicus* of classical economics (in whom the *homo juridicus* assumes a concrete shape, takes on muscles and a stomach) that we find here lodged at a certain point in the system—in civil society, which among the concrete social forms is that in which the abstract or contractual law has its *locus naturalis.*

Moralität,[4] in which man follows the dictates of his own conscience, and "free will penetrates the interior particular",[5] is a manifestation or outgrowth of Spirit—deeper but more disturbed and perilous than Law, and finally deceptive, destined to annihilate itself—in the contingency and insufficiency of the individual.

With morality the idea of the good emerges. Thus the good, which Kant had rejected from the formal structure of ethics, regains its place with Hegel at the stage of the Morality of Conscience, which might equally well be designated as the Morality of good and evil. This was quite inevitable from the moment that Hegel re-established, after his fashion, the connection between the universe of morality and the universe of being. But he conceives of the good in a way that is at the same time thoroughly metaphysical (with no distinction between metaphysical good and moral good) and thoroughly voluntaristic; it is nothing other than "the essence of the will in its substantiality and universality"[6] or "the universal of will".[7] And as we shall see, it

[1] Family, Civil Society, State.

[2] Cf. *Phil. of Right*, Third Part, sub-section 2.

[3] Cf. *Encyclopaedia*, Phil. of Mind, § 523, p. 122.

[4] Cf. *Phil. of Right*, Second Part; *Encyclopaedia*, Phil. of Mind, Section II, sub-section B; and the chapter on Conscience in the *Phenomenology*, Baillie trans., pp. 642–679.

[5] J. Hyppolite, Preface to the French translation of *Philosophie des rechts*, p. 14.

[6] *Phil. of Right*, § 132, p. 87.

[7] Cf. *Encyclopaedia*, Phil. of Mind, § 508, p. 116.

completely fails in the end, like the conscience which appeals to it, to put us in possession of the principles of human conduct.

6. *Moralität*—which made its historical debut with the advent of Christian conscience insofar as it was connected with the myths inherent in religion and with the regime by which the Church affirmed the supremacy of the spiritual over the temporal, but whose principal manifestation occurred with the individualistic disintegration of that conscience during the age of rationalist criticism and especially of romantic liberalism—*Moralität*, or the Morality of Conscience, is a necessary stage because it is indispensable that in the development of the objective spirit the latter should manifest itself in the very heart of subjectivity and subjective freedom, and that man should thus obey the moral commandments transmitted by the social group and by religion because he recognizes them himself in "his heart, sentiment, conscience, intelligence", and possesses "a personal knowledge of the distinction between good and evil".[1] To will the good prescribed by conscience is for the individual to have the intention of according his particular designs with the universal Will. The effort by which an individual thus seeks to render effective the dictate of his own conscience and his own conception of the good represents a higher degree of moral development than purely external conformity to the rules characteristic of the sphere of Law. Yes, no doubt. But what firm criterion of conduct can a morality of the good furnish? Absolutely none, in fact, from Hegel's point of view. Because for him, though the good is "the universal element of the will, determined in itself" (precisely insofar as it is good in general), it in no way suffices to determine the particular it contains, because this particular is still abstract and so not concretely designated in the universality of good. I want to perform the good, but what is the good *here and now*? The notion of the good does not tell me. Consequently, "there is no principle at hand to determine it".[2] In other words, every rational criterion of conduct is absent, because Hegel neither admits, with perennial philosophy, the objective rule furnished by the natural law as an ideal norm of human action,[3] nor admits, with Kant, the purely formal rule of the possibility of willing to universalize without contradiction the maxim of the act; and because, on the other hand, it is only in the succeeding stage of development, in

[1] *Encyclopaedia*, Phil. of Mind, § 503, pp. 113 f. [2] *Ibid.*, § 508, p. 116.

[3] Is it because of the old Lutheran aversion for the Mosaic Law that a philosopher who takes as much pleasure as Hegel in invoking Holy Scripture and religious imagery does not say a word about the Decalogue when he treats morality of conscience? The only writing, to our knowledge, in which he alludes to the Decalogue is one of the products of his youth (translated into English under the title "The Spirit of Christianity and Its Fate" in G. W. F. Hegel, *Early Theological Writings*, T. M. Knox trans., Chicago, 1948; Cambridge: C.U.P., 1949), and it is for the purpose of laying the blame on Judaism and on "the God of the Jews". (It is well known that the titles of these youthful fragments do not come from Hegel himself, but were proposed by their editor, H. Nohl, *Hegels theologische Jugendschriften*, Tubingen, 1907.)

the stage of *Sittlichkeit*, that the objective rule furnished by the social community and above all by the State will appear. Thus the morality of the good or of conscience is, for Hegel, because he has deprived it of its objective rational consistency, nothing more than the morality of private inspiration, of good intentions and good sentiments, in which "the heart, the feelings, the conscience, prudence", in short the purely subjective according to him, are the principle of distinction; and it is a morality without a compass. Why should we be surprised to see the conscience laboring and hesitating in the midst of conflicts and collisions between the multiple goods and duties, determined from outside the universality of the substantial will,[1] which its abstract aspiration toward the good in general causes to crowd up before it? There are only vain gropings of the individual conscience where the firmness of an objective criterion, which only the majesty of the concretely manifested universal can furnish, is lacking. So long as it does not give way to voluntary submission to the social whole of which man is a member, the will to act according to one's own conscience exposes human conduct to illusion and contradiction. More than that, very little is needed for it to slip into moral evil, for it lives close to evil and has the same root.[2] In fact it is by virtue of the same movement that the self-assured decision of the individual buries itself in the solitude of the conscience and—if it goes just a little further—into the supreme retirement into self which is characteristic of evil. When, solely in virtue of his free individual and subjective decision, and because the weight of his good intentions bears him toward the universal, man accepts the rules of good and evil recognized by his fellows, taking his conscience as the arbiter of his conduct, he is still submitting himself to a general law by making the content of his act a particular case under the general law; but in revolting against the universal he is going still further in the assertion of his free individual and subjective decision—he is making the content of his act depend upon it alone.[3] It is thus that Hegel sees the individual finally falling into evil,

[1] Cf. *Encyclopaedia*, Phil. of Mind, § 507, p. 115.

[2] "To have a conscience, if conscience is only formal subjectivity, is simply to be on the verge of slipping into evil; in independent self-certainty, with its independence of knowledge and decision, both morality and evil have their common root." *Phil. of Right*, § 139, p. 92.

Between holding that an order does not oblige me because it is contrary to the moral law and holding that it does not oblige me because it displeases me (because I am "the master of law and thing alike") no distinction is possible in the Hegelian perspective. Every rebellion against the will of the social super-individual is the deed of "beautiful souls" who believe they are above the law and take "the culminating form of this subjectivity" for the "final court of appeal", while considering themselves as "the arbiter and judge of truth, right, and duty". *Ibid.*, § 140, pp. 102 f.

[3] Cf. *Encyclopaedia*, §§ 511, 512, pp. 117 f. "Wickedness is the same awareness that the single self possesses the decision, *so far as the single self does not merely remain in this abstraction, but takes up the content of a subjective interest contrary to the good*" (*ibid.*, § 511, p. 118; italics ours). This view of Hegel's may serve to explain why, in existentialist literature after the second World War (whose morality remained precisely at the level of a wholly subjective *Moralität*), the heroes of conscience were usually criminals.

as a result of following his own conscience—a phenomenon in which *Moralität* overthrows and annihilates itself.

It is at this point that the profound significance—and the historical importance—of Hegel's moral philosophy becomes evident. Just as Hegel has completely relativized the individual person, and made of freedom of choice an illusory moment, so he has completely relativized the morality of conscience,[1] and made of it a moment to be got over, in which the moral life, not yet having come into possession of its rational foundation, tries itself out in a subjective effort of self-affirmation of individuality as such—an effort which is subject to the pernicious instability of the contingent and is immediately exposed to the contagion of evil, to the tendency whereby man thinks to exist for himself by opposing his miserable individuality to the law. And the worst occurs when conscience and evil lend each other support, and when the rebellion derives from the very commandment of conscience, which by seeming to justify it confers upon it a perverse obstinacy. If the conscience tries "testing the laws . . . moving the immovable"[2]—in other words if it declares that an unjust law is not a law and does not deserve obedience, or claims the right to obey God rather than men—if it says *no* to the State,[3] it deviates into unpardonable illusion, it resists Mind, which is the only real evil, it is guilty.

There is no real and rational morality or ethicity except when the force of the individual, integrated into the interiority of the common conscience where the universal Self affirms itself, moves of itself toward the object willed by the social superindividual and above all by the State.

[1] It can happen that the conscience is in error, and if my conscience errs *through my own fault*, it is also wrong to commit the act, in itself bad, prescribed by it. But the absolute principle remains that *it is always and in every case a fault to act against one's conscience* (even in the case where I would be at fault unless I reformed the judgment of my conscience: either in following my culpably erroneous conscience, or in acting against it). Hegel fails completely to understand this absolute principle. And he also fails to understand the fact that the conscience can be objectively and with good reason certain of not being mistaken, if it enlightens and instructs itself, does not erect itself into a supreme judge of the truth when it affirms its certitude about a precept any more than the speculative reason does when it affirms its certitude about a self-evident axiom or about a demonstrated conclusion.

[2] *Phenomenology*, Baillie trans., p. 450. The law by definition is no longer held to be just, it is henceforth defined only by the will of the State. "The law is . . . the pure and absolute will of all which takes the form of immediate existence. This will is, again, not a command which merely *ought to be*; it *is* and *has* validity; it is the universal ego of the category, ego which is immediately reality, and the world is only this reality." *Ibid.*, p. 451.

[3] One of the reproaches which Hegel addresses to Catholicism is that "in the Catholic Church . . . it is nothing singular for the conscience to be found in opposition to the laws of the State". On the contrary, in the holy interiority of German Protestantism "the Rational no longer meets with contradiction on the part of the religious conscience; it is permitted to develop itself in its own sphere without disturbance, without being compelled to resort to force in defending itself against an adverse power". *Phil. of Hist.*, p. 529.

II

ETHICITY

The State as the Objectivication of Mind and the Incarnation of Freedom

7. If the Family is in fact already an individual, in which the notion of individuality is realized at a higher level than in the individual person,[1] then the State, itself, collective Man as a living unity, is the Super-individual, the human Person or Super-person *par excellence*, because it is Spirit thoroughly objectified—not yet Spirit conscious of itself as infinite Spirit and divine subjectivity, but Spirit sovereignly affirming itself as Action, Will and practical Imperium, in a particular consciousness or certitude of itself raised to universality (the personality of the State).[2]

Kant thought that ethical conduct, imposed by duty, was the realization of the free and reasonable Will which, in the intelligible world, is essentially one and the same, and common to all men. Hegel departs from this point, but he reproaches Kant for having left it to each individual to determine the content of this Will by applying subjectively the formal condition of acting according to a maxim that he can without contradiction will to universalize. Kant's trouble is not having seen that the universal Will is concrete, and is identical with Freedom in its effort to realize itself. It is objectively actualized in the laws and the institutions and the common moral psyche of the supra-individual whole. It is fully actualized only in the State. "The basis of the State is the power of reason actualizing itself as Will."[3] Then there finally appears in its definitive manifestation the content of the universal Will, the universal triumphant. The historical age of this definitive manifestation is that in which Hegel himself appeared (for the very purpose of revealing this age to itself), the age of Napoleon and of the Napoleonic State (at the time of the *Phenomenology*—but they did not fulfill their promises), then (for the system decisively constituted) of the Germanic-Christian State, in the form of the Prussian State, or some other form to come, called upon to impose itself one day

[1] "The Family may be reckoned as virtually a single person." The parents have "mutually surrendered their individual personality". *Ibid.*, p. 90.

[2] *Phil. of Right*, §§ 258 and 279. "Hence it is the basic moment of personality, abstract at the start in immediate rights, which has matured itself through its various forms of subjectivity, and now—at the stage of absolute rights, of the state, of the completely concrete objectivity of the will—has become the personality of the state, its certainty of itself. This last reabsorbs all particularity into its single self, cuts short the weighing of pros and cons between which it lets itself oscillate perpetually now this way and now that, and by saying 'I will' makes its decision and so inaugurates all activity and actuality" (§ 279, p. 181). Hegel adds that the monarch is necessary for the full, concrete reality of the personality of the State.

[3] *Phil. of Right*, § 258, Gans' addition from Hegel's oral teaching, Knox trans., p. 279. The German original reads: ' Sein Grund ist die Gewalt der sich als Wille verwirklichenden Vernunft." *Philosophie des Rechts*, 3rd ed., in *Werke*, VI, p. 349.

upon the entire world as the "universal and homogeneous State", in the phrase of M. Kojève.

The State is the supreme realization of universal reason in the practical sphere, the terrestrial incarnation of Freedom. "The State is the actuality of concrete freedom",[1] "mind present on earth",[2] "a self-consciously rational and ethical organization";[3] "The State is the realization of Freedom, *i.e.* of the absolute final aim, and . . . it exists for its own sake."[4] That is why "man must venerate . . . the State as a secular deity",[5] "the march of God in the world, that is what the State is";[6] "The State is the Divine Idea as it exists on Earth."[7] It follows from this that the rational end of man is life in the State. "The State is absolutely rational inasmuch as it is the actuality of the substantial will which it possesses in the particular self-consciousness once that consciousness has been raised to consciousness of its universality. This substantial unity is an absolute unmoved end in itself, in which freedom comes into its supreme right. On the other hand this final end has supreme right against the individual, whose supreme duty is to be a member of the State."[8] In the complete organic unity of the social Whole, individuals come to achieve that reality for which the necessary beginnings were conferred on them by the family and intermediary social groups; they only truly exist as members of the State. Only within the State are they really *recognized*, and is it not in being recognized by others (a theme dear to Hegel) that individuality is born into its true nature and its supra-contingent reality? That recognition of his uniqueness that the man of uneasy conscience received only symbolically from the transcendent God of religion, here at last I have actually obtained it![9] Yes, recognized by the Whole, but let it be clearly understood on what conditions: on the condition that in return I recognize the Whole for what it is (that is, my entelechy), and on the condition that I am become *recognizable* to all—with no longer anything in me which is not exposed to all and to myself—each one in the uniqueness of his empirical being-there no longer having any soul or spiritual interiority other than the very soul of the Whole. Thus it is that "Man is not . . . truly human, that is to say 'individual' except in the degree to which he lives and acts as a 'recognized' citizen of a State".[10]

"Everything that man is, he owes to the State. He has his being only in it." . . . "All the worth which the human being possesses—all spiritual reality, he

[1] *Phil. of Right*, § 260, p. 160.
[2] *Ibid.*, § 270, p. 166.
[3] *Ibid.*, p. 174.
[4] *Phil. of Hist.*, Introd., p. 87.
[5] *Phil. of Right*, § 272, Gans' addition, Knox trans., p. 285.
[6] *Ibid.*, § 258, Gans' addition, Knox trans., p. 279. The German original reads: "Es ist der Gang Gottes in der Welt, dass der Staat ist" (*Phil. des Rechts* in *Werke*, VI, p. 349).
[7] *Phil. of Hist.*, § Introd., p. 87.
[8] *Phil. of Right*, § 258, pp. 155 f.
[9] "This is why Hegel says that the 'absolute' State which he has in view (the Napoleonic Empire) is the *realization* of the Christian kingdom of heaven." A. Kojève, *Introduction à la lecture de Hegel*, p. 193. [The Napoleonic Empire at the time of the *Phenomenology*; the Germanic State at the time of the *Philosophy of History*.]
[10] Kojève, *op. cit.*, p. 505.

possesses only through the State."[1] "Since the State is mind objectified, it is only as one of its members that the individual himself has objectivity, genuine individuality and an ethical life"[2]—this is the very formula, the original formula of political totalitarianism.

8. With Hegel German Protestant thought took an historical turn of crucial importance. Following the initial act of rupture effected by Luther, concerning which so many dithyrambs have been chanted in honor of the conscience of the individual, Protestant thought, by dint of insisting on the interiority of the conscience, had veered to the doctrine of freedom of conscience. Now, on the contrary, individualism was finished; the necessity for an objective rule and for a supra-individual authority was again recognized; but since one cannot demand these things of the Protestant Churches, which have decisively renounced them, they will henceforth be the rule and authority of the sovereign temporal community, the State—not in order to transmit to men the word of God, but in order to make them act as they ought to act. The characteristic functions of the Protestant spiritual community pass over to the Germanic State. The collective subjectivity which Christ inhabits is to be found in the State in the form of reason, constituting the *nous* of Spirit, and it is therein that it is reconciled with the objectivity of the Law. The mystical operation by which, for Rousseau, individual wills died in the general will to be resurrected in unity, passes for Hegel from the social level to the metaphysical level. And it is in virtue of a fundamental requirement of the dialectic that when the State arises the will of each individual dies to itself in order to relive—transfigured—in the common will, where it finally achieves its reality and its freedom. It is of its own accord, then, and with all the spontaneous force of its subjective freedom, that the individual does what the State wishes. As a crowning piece of political hypocrisy, this mythology guaranteed by the dialectic gives complete security to the sovereign power of the State, which, far from exercising restraint upon me, *is* my freedom, and consequently has a right not only to my obedience, but also to my enthusiasm and to a warm glow in my heart. Thus we see how, now that the true religion has revealed to itself the interiority of the common conscience, the State, understood according to its authentic idea, assures subjective freedom[3] and does not impose itself from without by enslaving individuals as did the despotic empires of long ago, but subjects them to itself all the better—without submitting them

[1] *Philosophie der Weltgeschichte*, Lasson ed., I, p. 90 (*Werke*, VIII), (Sibree trans., p. 87).

[2] *Phil. of Right*, § 258, p. 156. (*Philosophie des Rechts*, § 258, Lasson's 3rd ed., *Werke*, VI, p. 196: "Er [der Staat] hat aber ein ganz anderes Verhältnis zum Individuum; indem er objektiver Geist ist, so hat das Individuum selbst mur Objektivität, Wahrheit und Sittlichkeit, als es ein Glied desselben ist.")

For Hegel, as Jean Hyppolite has noted (*Genèse et structure de la phénoménologie de l'esprit de Hegel*, p. 376), the general will is the "intrinsic self of individuals", their substance, which at first appears to them as alien, but which they must become through culture.

[3] Cf. *Encyclopaedia*, Phil. of Mind, § 552, Wallace trans., p. 165.

to the least heteronomy—because it is the very substance and truth of their will.

At this price they are free, they have attained their freedom of autonomy, because they are moved by the freedom which has become embodied in the Whole in which they are annihilated in order really to relive. And they are truly moral agents, because they are no longer subject to the uncertainty of subjective reflection. The abstract categorical imperative has been replaced by the concrete *imperium* of the State. They see their duty. Its authority is over them, and it is by themselves willing this authority that they fully realize their freedom.[1]

Departing, as we remarked above,[2] from the Lutheran separation between the juridical and the moral, Hegel has now succeeded in tracing his curve and closing the circle: it is the law—not certainly the purely formal law of abstract Law, but the living and concrete law of the divinely real State—that defines duty. The legal—the concrete legal—has become the moral.

At this stage in which objective will and subjective will interpenetrate each other in a superior identity "and present one identical homogeneous whole",[3] and in which freedom and necessity are reconciled in unity, we are no longer dealing with *Moralität*, but rather with *Sittlichkeit* or *Ethicity*,[4] which constitutes the moral life in its pure and authentic, stable and consistent, or completely rational form, and which, developing from its origin in the familial community, has for its keystone the State. Then I am no longer obliged to "reflect on the object of my activity" in order to form my "own conviction"; I do my duty "as it were from instinct", because it is my "second nature".[5] The rule of conscience is finally transcended.

[1] "The laws of *real* Freedom demand the subjugation of the mere contingent Will." *Phil. of Hist.*, p. 569. "Law, Morality, Government, and they alone", are "the positive reality and completion of Freedom" ("die positive Wirklichkeit und Befriedigung der Freiheit"). *Ibid.*, p. 86 (Lasson ed., I, *Werke*, VIII, Leipzig, 1930, p. 90). Cf. *Phil. of Right*, §§ 146–147, pp. 105 f.: "This ethical substance and its laws and powers are on the one hand an object over against the subject, and from his point of view they *are*—'are' in the highest sense of self-subsistent being. This is an absolute authority and power infinitely more firmly established than the being of nature. . . . On the other hand, they are not something alien to the subject. On the contrary, his spirit bears witness to them as to its own essence. . . ."

[2] See above, pp. 157–159.

[3] *Phil. of Hist.*, Introd., p. 88.

[4] The expressions "objective morality", "social morality", or "customary morality" which are sometimes used for the word *Sittlichkeit* are worthless, because they overlook the essential Hegelian connotation of interiority or subjective depth of the moral life.

[5] *Phil. of Hist.*, Introd., p. 88. Cf. *Phil. of Right*, §§ 151, 152, pp. 108 f.: "But when individuals are simply identified with the actual order, ethical life (*das Sittliche*) appears as their general mode of conduct, i.e. as custom (*Sitte*), *while the habitual practice of ethical living appears as a second nature* which [is] put in the place of the initial, purely natural will. . . . In this way the ethical substantial order has attained its right, and its right its validity. That is to say, *the self-will of the individual has vanished together with his private conscience which had claimed independence and opposed itself to the ethical substance*" (italics ours).—*Encyclopaedia*, Phil of Mind, § 514, pp. 119 f.: "The consciously free substance, in which the absolute 'ought' is no less an 'is', has actuality as the spirit of a nation. . . . But the

It is easy to see what all this means in the reality of human experience. Faced with an order of the State, my conscience may experience scruples, and the thing prescribed may appear to it inhuman, unjust and criminal. No matter! This uneasiness and these scruples of the conscience have only a subjective value, and I reject them with the courage of authentic morality, which has become my second nature, and without troubling myself with the kind of reflection that deliberates. I know that I am fulfilling the absolute requirement of a truly ethical mode of conduct, *absolute duty—that which is*—by doing that which the State, that is Spirit, prescribes for me, and I know that the State itself, including within itself the sphere of abstract law and that of morality but superior to both, is subject neither to the rules of law nor to those of good and evil as the conscience understands them. In willing what the State wills as if it were my own being, I possess my *real freedom*, and I am covered, not only by my hierarchical superior but by the unshakeable certitude of the objective and universal order in which God manifests Himself. In practice, *Sittlichkeit* is the morality which consists in the sacrifice of the conscience, made joyously and spontaneously to the State. It is this morality that Hegel, after having invested it as the Spirit of the world, made a present of to the Germano-Protestant community and to occidental civilization in its decline.

Freedom of Autonomy and the Hegelian system

9. The points made in the preceding sections permit us now to try to elucidate the Hegelian conception of freedom of autonomy.

Taken according to its true notion, freedom of spontaneity signifies not the absence of necessity but the absence of constraint or coercion; and freedom of autonomy, or the perfect freedom of spontaneity proper to the spirit, can coincide with intrinsic necessity, by no means in virtue of some dialectical opposition and reconciliation, but in virtue of the very nature of things. Is not the Pure Act at the same time, and precisely because it exists *a se*, supremely free (independent) and supremely necessary? Does not the will will its happiness by a necessity of its nature and in a completely spontaneous manner, or without the least constraint? And when it is in the presence of the subsisting Good seen face to face, in the beatific vision, does it not live it at the same time necessarily and with the perfect spontaneity or the perfect independence of an agent which nothing constrains—nay, of an agent which absolutely nothing other than itself, not even the object that fulfills all its desire, but only

---

person, as an intelligent being, feels that underlying essence to be his own very being—ceases when so minded to be a mere accident of it—looks upon it as his absolute final aim. In its actuality he sees not less an achieved present, than somewhat he brings it about by his action—yet somewhat which without all question *is*. Thus, without any selective reflection, the person performs its duty as *his own* and as something which *is*; and in this necessity *he* has himself and his actual freedom."

its own nature[1] necessarily determines to action? In other words, if there is a self-determination free of all necessity (which is the self-determination of free choice), there is also another self-determination free of all constraint, even of all extrinsic necessitation to act, which is not free choice nor the absence of necessity, and wherein the agent determines himself not in the freedom of his choice but in the independence of his being.

But if freedom of autonomy can exist without the exercise of free choice, it always presupposes in the subject the power or faculty of free choice, the existence of free will. It only comes into existence in the process of distinguishing itself from simple freedom of spontaneity, at that level of being where the threshold of the spirit is crossed and where reason brings freedom of choice along with it. And more than that, when freedom of autonomy designates a *state* or an existential condition of human life, in which man fulfills the law while being free from its constraint—the condition proper to the life of the perfect citizen, free in the state, or the condition proper to the life of the sage, free in the world, or the condition proper to the life of the saint, free of everything but God—then it embraces, as contributing to the condition in question, everything in which human life expresses itself, notably that very exercise of free will and the flux of acts which proceed from it; the state of freedom involves the joint exercise of freedom of choice and freedom of autonomy: because it is the highest state of that universe-to-itself which is the human person.

Hegel, on the contrary, makes of freedom of autonomy definitively acquired a stage of the development of the spirit in which freedom of choice has been superseded, and in which there is no longer any choosing to be done, because the performance of duty has become a second nature. There is no longer any question of freedom of choice—it has annihilated itself to rediscover itself in freedom of autonomy. This is true, in the last analysis, because the individual man, as a singular entity (what we call a person),[2] far from being really and by his nature a *whole*, only becomes a *whole* by becoming in a certain way—in the now recognized uniqueness of his empirical *Dasein—the Whole* itself, therefore the State. For Hegel, as we have already seen, human

[1] Taking into account the disposition or existential state in which it finds itself. Cf. Cajetan on Thomas Aquinas, *in Sum. theol.*, I–II, q. 10, a. 2: "Aliud est dicere, Voluntas necessario movetur ab objecto ad exercitium actus; et dicere, Voluntas *sic disposita* necessario movetur ad exercitium actus. . . . Nullum objectum, ut sic, et quantum est ex sua efficacia, potest naturali necessitate compellere voluntatem ad exercitium actus. . . . Voluntas Deum clare visum necessario amat: est enim tunc in dispositione tali, quod ex natura sua actu provenit amor et delectatio talis objecti. . . . Quandocumque voluntas necessario movetur ad exercitium, necessitas illa nunquam est ab objecto, sed a natura et naturae Datore."

[2] For Hegel the individual as a particular individual, or as a human atom, is a whole or a person only in a purely abstract and formal sense; but the individual renounces even this and then goes beyond it. In the family he exists "not as an independent person but as a member" (*Phil. of Right*, § 158, p. 110); it is the same, and for all the more reason, in the State.

individuality in its quality of humanness (personality) is only acquired by the human atom if he universalizes himself, rejoins his true substance, his being-in-itself in the general will, if he effaces himself like every other individual consciousness in the shadow of the glory of the State. Napoleon is the individual *par excellence*, hence the Autonome *par excellence*, *der erscheinende Gott*,[1] because as creator and maintainer of the State he embodies the social entelechy itself, the very whole of the State. Ordinary citizens are authentic individuals, really autonomous beings, because insofar as they are and will themselves to be true members of the State, they make of themselves pure parts of the whole of the State, each having this whole itself as his entelechy. In immersing himself in the depths of freedom of autonomy the individual has renounced his being as an individual whole, and has actively annihilated himself as a person in order to be *only a part*, which as such exists only in the existence of the Whole, but which, knowing this and willing it, thus equalizes itself with the superior individuality of the Whole, and gains for itself by this self-consciousness as part of the Whole, the superior personality and the superior freedom of the Whole itself. Such is the meaning of Hegelian self-determination.

10. This is really a determination of the self by the self no longer to be a particular self—by virtue of which the will confers upon itself its content, which is only its own because it is that of the Universal Will. Then each individual, *recognized* by the Whole in its very uniqueness, feels itself definitely a self and definitely autonomous, not indeed because its own interior glance in some way penetrates the substantial night of its subjectivity, but because, henceforth perfectly universalized, it sees itself in the eyes of all others and receives from the millions of looks which recognize it the satisfaction it was looking for, and by the same token the certitude of being itself and free (by doing what it wills because it wills what the Whole wills). From this it becomes apparent that what finally perfects and consummates truly human individuality (personality), and the freedom to which citizens are raised by the State, is to die for the State, because it is in dying for the Whole that they attain supreme recognition by the Whole. "In the last analysis it is because man can *die* that he can be an individual."[2] As Hegel expresses it,[3] "In death the absolute power, the *master* of the *particular*, that is to say the common will, has become pure Being-as-given [which is the corpse of the citizen who died for the State]." "This condition of universality, which the individual *as such* reaches, is mere being, death . . . death is the fulfillment and highest task which the individual as such undertakes on . . . behalf [of the community]."[4]

[1] *Phänomenologie des Geistes*, 3rd ed., in *Werke*, II, p. 472.
[2] A. Kojève, *Introduction à la lecture de Hegel*, p. 561.
[3] *Jenenser Realphilosophie*, II, *Die Vorlesungen von 1805/06* in *Werke*, XX, p. 225, n. 3. (Translation based on Kojève, *op. cit.*, p. 563.)
[4] *Phenomenology*, pp. 470 f. (Lasson ed., 1928, pp. 321 f.)

In the last analysis, the consciousness of self in which, as we remarked above, autonomy is realized, this "self-consciousness which justifies its object, content and aim", and raises them to universality, because it is "thinking getting its own way in the will",[1] is nothing but the "self-contained existence of which 'spirit' consists".[2] It appears when "the particular . . . by its reflection into itself has been equalized with the universal".[3] Then there is self-determination, in other words, "the *self*-determination of the ego . . . means that at one and the same time the ego posits itself as its own negative, i.e. as restricted and determinate, and yet remains by itself, i.e. in its self-identity and universality. It determines itself and yet at the same time binds itself together with itself."[4] It remains itself and bound only to itself because it has its substance in the Self of the spirit, in "infinity as negativity relating itself to itself, this ultimate spring of all activity, life, and consciousness".[5] To be free is, without having to choose, to will something definite by virtue of the simple fact that I am myself, that is, that I have denied myself as an individual entity in order to return to the universal and will that which is willed by the universal Will, thereby equalizing myself with an individuality and a totality which belong to the concrete Universal, or to the Spirit.[6] The real person, the individual person, has been done away with; not by a simple negation, but by inclusion in an essentially ambiguous dialectical pair, and as the result of an inevitably misleading attempt to retain the multiple in a completely univocal view of being-becoming. In reality, and when we consider the final issue of this system, the only authentic freedom of autonomy that remains in Hegelianism—that freedom in which "the will [is] by itself without qualification, because . . . it is related to nothing except itself and so is released from every tie of dependence on anything else"[7]—is that of the super-individual Spirit, and that of the State, the incarnation of Spirit.

11. Hegel rejected the fundamental truth of political philosophy, which is that the body politic (by him perniciously confused with the State) is a Whole made up of parts which are themselves wholes, a Whole composed of wholes. His State is a Whole whose parts are nothing but pure parts, that is, parts

[1] See above p. 157, note 2.
[2] *Phil. of Hist.*, Introd., p. 62.
[3] *Phil. of Right*, § 7, p. 23.
[4] *Ibid.*, p. 23.
[5] *Ibid.*, p. 24. Let us recall (cf. above, ch. VII, p. 144) that the finite, contingent, phenomenal self is entirely abstract and general and attains true individuality only while denying itself in order to reintegrate itself in the concrete universal. The true self is "liberation existing for itself", which owes its existence to thought thinking the necessary and which "consists in that which is actual having itself not as something else, but as its own being and creation, in the other actuality with which it is bound up by the force of necessity" (*Encyclopaedia*, Logic, § 159, p. 285). Cf. *ibid.*, § 20, pp. 38 f.; and *Phil. of Right*, Gans' addition to § 7, Knox trans., pp. 228 f.
[6] Thus it is that in order to liberate itself in the truth the subjective spirit "*abnegates its particularity* and comes to itself in realizing the truth of its being". *Phil. of Hist.*, p. 521 (italics ours).
[7] *Phil. of Right*, § 23, p. 30.

which are not persons, and which only acquire personality insofar as they are and wish themselves to be integrated into the supra-individual Self of the State. Then they cease to be mere clouds of atoms, and are recognized and dignified, invested with authentic morality and personality (that is, for Hegel, with rational necessity) *as members and uniquely as members* of an organic whole or concrete universal which is the State. There is no place here for the freedom of autonomy which on the level of social life we attain to as persons in the body politic of which we are members, or as individual wholes possessing their own rights within the political whole and surpassing it by virtue of that which is eternal in them, bound to that whole by mutual relations of justice and by civic friendship, obeying its laws because their personal conscience commits them to the common good,[1] which flows back upon or is redistributed among them as members of the community.

It behooves us at this point to examine matters very closely, and not be taken in by false appearances. The true, or authentically human, common good is a reduplicatively common good (reflecting upon the social Whole and upon its parts as persons or as individual *wholes*); in other words, it is redistributed to those persons, it is a supra-organic common good. Hegel, for whom despotism, controlling a swarm of non-integrated individuals from without, is an inferior and outmoded stage of development, unworthy of Christian times, strove to maintain the dignity of the individual within the State, but he did this only *through* the State, and in virtue of the individual's having his very substance in the State, as a member of the organism. Because his genius was the genius of immanence and immanentism, he failed in this way to go beyond an organicist conception, which he carried to its logical extreme with unparalleled thoroughness. He replaced the transcendence of the person as derived from its supra-temporal values and under the formal aspect of personality[2] (and as, in this respect, it constitutes an end for the State) by a dialectical relation between the individual and the State as concrete universal, in which the individual is only dignified in receiving from the State all its human value. Instead of being a *redistributed* and *supra-organic* common good, the common good of the Hegelian State is, then, no more than a so-called *organic* common good, and *irreversible* to other wholes than the Social Whole itself; we may say that it is the private good of the Whole, which is

[1] If it is true that "only that will which obeys law is free" (*Phil. of Hist.*, Introd., p. 87), it is in virtue of the interiorization of the law thus effectuated by the individual conscience and reason which see that it is right to obey and decide accordingly. For Hegel, on the contrary, this will then "obeys itself—it is independent and so free" (*ibid.*, p. 87), because in reality it has its true *independence* in "the common interests of the members generally" (*ibid.*, p. 91). "The Rational has *necessary* existence, as being the reality and substance of things, and we are free in recognizing it as law, and following it *as the substance of our own being*" (*ibid.*, pp. 87 f.).

[2] On the difference between the formal aspect of individuality and the formal aspect of personality in the human person, see our book *The Person and the Common Good*, New York: Scribners, 1947; London: Geoffrey Bles.

not redistributed to individual persons as to other wholes, but is shared by them uniquely as *parts* and *members* of the Whole. Clearly it follows from this that except in cases where the Whole requires some part to sacrifice itself for it, it is in the interest of the Whole that its own private good (the good of the hive, or of the organism) should take advantage of the parts as such (of the bee, of the hand) to the degree that the parts are means for it, or rather moments and elements of its own life. This is the full import of the notion of the Hegelian State as *Tun Aller und Jeder*, and all Hegel means when he assures us that in the fulfillment of his duty toward the Whole the individual must at the same time find his own compensation.[1] And this is essentially

[1] *Phil. of Right*, § 261, p. 162.

Whenever one has to do with a *great* error (great not only in gravity, but also in courage, significance, and logical consistency), one naturally finds subtle *attenuators* or *extenuators*, intelligent and erudite, who think that a simple declaration of fact is lacking in elegance, and exaggerates.

In his book *Hegel et l'Etat* (Paris: Vrin, 1950, p. 117), Eric Weil assures us that the Hegelian conception of the State is not totalitarian but liberal. To show this it suffices for him to neglect Hegel's actual philosophy and all its doctrinal apparatus and to take into consideration only the constitutional form which he in effect recommends. But to tell the truth, all that one can conclude from this is that Hegel's totalitarianism was too profound, and too consubstantial to his very notion of the State, to have any need of the appearances of absolutism.

Canon F. Grégoire, in a communication to the Académie Royale de Belgique ("Une semi-légende, la 'divinité' de l'Etat chez Hegel," *Bulletin de la Classe des Lettres et des Sciences morales et politiques*, 5e serie, Tome XLI, 1955—VI, pp. 315 f.), assures us, for his part, that for Hegel in the pair State-individual "each of the two terms is an end for the other"; in such a way that "for one part—a preponderant part, moreover—the State is the ultimate end of the individuals, considered in their exterior advantages, and for one part—a smaller part—the individuals are the ultimate end of the State". In support of this interpretation Canon F. Grégoire refers us to "two capital passages" which he does not quote at all though he does provide references (*Philosophie der Weltgeschichte*, Lasson ed., I, p. 91 in *Werke*, VI; *Geschichte der Philosophie*, II, in H. Glockner's Jubilee edition, *Sämtliche Werke*, Vol. 18, Stuttgart, 1929–40, reprinted 1959, pp. 394–400). When one turns to the pages cited, one finds absolutely nothing to justify the interpretation in question.

Hegel considers as inferior stages, on the one hand (thesis), the Greek city and the Aristotelian theory of the city (in which the individual is subordinated to the whole, but without being "recognized" by it), because this whole itself remains abstract, and on the other hand (antithesis), the modern liberal State, in which the individual is enclosed within his natural singularity like a worker who makes only parts which others will assemble and who is ignorant of the whole (cf. *Gesch. der Phil.*, II, Glockner ed., Vol. 18, p. 400). In his own conception, it is not only because of his immediate or natural singularity and in relation to the State taken as abstract whole that the individual is a part of the State; it is in spirit and in truth (as raised to the rational level) and in relation to the State as concrete universal that the individual, through his consciousness of this whole which is his real essence, wishes to become part of the State and at the same time equates itself with it, and receives from it, along with his true individuality and liberty, his unique value at last concretely realized. There is no trace of any higher recognition accorded to the individual in the lines which constitute, so far as one can judge, one of Canon F. Grégoire's "two capital passages", and in which, after having noted that the "bürgerliche Freiheit"—"principle of isolation"—is a "necessary moment" (on the way to a higher synthesis, the Hegelian state) "which the ancient States did not know", Hegel adds that neither did they know "diese vollkommene Selbstständigkeit der Punkte, und eben grössere Selbständigkeit des Ganzen,—das höhere organische Leben. Nachdem der Staat diess Princip in sich empfangen, konnte höhere

different from the redistribution of the good of the Whole to parts which are themselves not only parts but also wholes.[1] For in this case—the case of a Whole which aims only at its private good—the rights of individuals and their dignity as persons derive solely from the State and are only taken into consideration insofar as the good of the State requires it, or even, in the name of

---

Freiheit hervorgehen". (*Ibid.*, p. 400.) It is in and through the independence of the whole that each "point" possesses its own independence, the higher organic life being that in which each part is raised to the being of the whole through an active communion with it. The more so as that which this "higher freedom", higher than "civil freedom", makes us see is—instead of simple "Naturspiele und Naturprodukte" or of "individual fantasy"—"das innere Bestehen und die unzertörbare Allgemeinheit, die real, *konsolidirt in ihren Theilen* ist". (*Ibid.*, pp. 400 f.; italics ours.)

As for the second "capital passage" to which Canon F. Grégoire refers us (*Phil. der Weltgeschichte*, Lasson ed., I, p. 91, in *Werke*, VI), we read: "Der Staat ist nicht um der Bürger willen da; man könnte sagen, er ist der Zweck, und sie sind seine Werkzeuge. Indes ist dies Verhältnis von Zweck und Mittel überhaupt hier nicht passend. Denn der Staat ist nicht das Abstrakte, das den Bürgern gegenübersteht; sondern sie sind Momente wie im organischen Leben, wo kein Glied Zweck, keines Mittel ist. Das Göttliche des Staats ist die Idee, wie sie auf Erden vorhanden ist." Hegel is explaining to us here that the State might be said to be the end and individuals its instruments, but that the relation of means to end is inappropriate in this context, because the State is not an abstract whole opposed to the individuals; the latter are moments as in organic life where all the members are for one another. This does not mean at all, as Canon F. Grégoire suggests, that the part is for the whole and the whole for the part, but that *the parts* exist for one another. As for the State, its divinity comes from the fact that it is the Idea manifested on earth; in other words, it is the concrete universal in which the individuals exist for one another and which is not an end separated from them because it is their unity itself and the substance of the rational in them. On the previous page (*op. cit.*, p. 90) Hegel has taken care, moreover, to note that man has no rational existence except in the State, and that *all that he is, all his worth, all his spiritual reality* he owes to the State and only to the State. "Im Staat allein hat der Mensch vernünftige Existenz. . . . Alles, was der Mensch ist, verdankt er dem Staat; er hat nur darin sein Wesen. *Allen Wert, den der Mensch hat, alle geistige Wirklichkeit, hat er allein durch den Staat.*" (Italics ours.)

Hegel reproaches the Greek city for *not having sufficiently integrated* the individual, and therefore for subjecting him to itself without at the same time freeing him. In the Hegelian State the individual is integrated in a manner so organically superior that his submission is his freedom and he derives *all his worth* from the State. It is an absolute and totalitarian spiritual-State-community. To say that for Hegel individuals have "distinct emergence, so to speak, outside this whole" which is the State (cf. the already cited communication to the Académie Royale de Belgique, p. 327), is one of those subtle paradoxes, one of those pleasant jokes of which certain cultivated and smiling ecclesiastics seem to be masters. For Hegel the absolute spirit and absolute science are certainly more divine than the State, and through them the sage, a member of the State, reflexively justifies the State and reveals it to itself, but even the sage has no "distinct emergence" outside the State, which is absolutely supreme throughout the whole practical or ethical order.

[1] A few examples will make this distinction clearer. Take a manufacturer who makes his factory psychologically and technically attractive for the sole purpose of obtaining better production from the workers: the workers certainly benefit, and all is for the best, but it is only by accident that their dignity as persons is benefited at the same time. Now take an army which organizes for its soldiers, according to the best rules of hygiene, facilities for the use of prostitutes and the violation of the sixth commandment; or a State which crams its citizens with controlled culture in order to domesticate their ideas and their minds. In both these cases the individual finds himself in a certain way benefited, but his dignity as a person is disregarded and insulted.

the good of the State, flatly disregarded; and the whole (the Hegelian State) has an absolute and unlimited right over the individuals and groups that are its members. In the last analysis, the only concern of such a State, in spite of all the real but unavailing efforts of dialectical immanentism to establish after its fashion the double value of the individual and of the State, and in spite of the resounding declarations by means of which it deludes itself, is to have the machinery in good working order, or happy slaves persuaded that they are enjoying a superior freedom. It is to Hegel that the totalitarian States peculiar to the modern age owe the perverse and fundamentally anti-political notion of the common good as a good pertaining to the Whole, whereas in reality, as we noted above, it is the good common to *the Whole and to the parts*, which are themselves individual wholes, or persons—the only real persons on this earth.

12. But let us return to the Hegelian conception of freedom of autonomy. It is really impossible to talk about this freedom without going back to the archetypal idea of it which, as we have previously pointed out, is presented to us in the texts of the Apostle Paul on the freedom of the sons of God. Hegel tried to carry over from the religious level of obedience to the law of God to the political level of obedience to the law of the State the notion of *libertas christiana* that Protestant thought had developed in the course of interpreting the texts of St. Paul according to its own perspective. In a much more general way, and because his whole system is geared to the idea of freedom of independence or autonomy, he tried to recast in purely philosophical terms the Pauline notion of the freedom conferred by the Spirit. The attempt failed, because the *Weltgeist* is not the Holy Spirit, and because the whole reality of that which love accomplishes in making man one in spirit with the infinitely transcendent God becomes pure mirage when a so-called onto-logic tries to find its equivalent in the auto-negation in which the individual, seeking his own essence, comes upon it in the concrete universal, which is itself traversing history toward its own divinity.

Those whom St. Paul describes as being conducted by the Spirit which bloweth where it listeth are free not only because they are no longer under the law (in achieving this state they are following their own inclination, an inclination which is doubly personal since they have of their own accord voluntarily assumed it out of love), but because, having passed beyond the stage where there is any question of observance of the law, embarking upon a terrain where there is no longer any path marked out, what means everything to them is the person-to-person dialogue and the mutual expression of love in which they are engaged with Him who is infinitely beyond all created necessity, and in whose own freedom they participate, in the perpetual unforeseeability, superior to any historical *fatum*, of that state of being in which, as we said above, freedom of choice and freedom of autonomy are exercised together. But all human freedom consists for Hegel in grasping and fundamentally realizing the truth of necessity, in other words, in recognizing the rational and its necessity as law and in obeying it as one obeys the substance of one's own being. The individual is only free when of himself, and as if it were a second nature he fulfils the laws of the State, the objectification of the Spirit; and it is finally in *amor fati*, in reconciliation with destiny, with the history of the world, that in Hegel's view resides the supreme consciousness of freedom.[1] Finally, in the Pauline conception man, moved by the Spirit of God, of the separated Whole, remains himself and is more than ever an individual whole, a person; and love itself requires that within the unity of spirit the duality of persons be maintained. At the very moment that the saint says to Him whom he loves: *thy will be done*, he says in the same breath: *and not mine*, which indicates that his own will is still in existence: it subordinates itself and gives itself, it does not abolish itself. But in the Hegelian conception —we have insisted on this point in our previous analyses—man only achieves freedom by giving up being a person, a self-consistent whole as born individual.

It is thus quite in vain that Hegel tries to carry Pauline freedom over into the political order as a designation of the individual's freedom in relation to the State. Whatever he does and whatever he says, he still leaves no place at all for the inferior but authentic freedom of autonomy of which man is capable on the level of social life. Nor, when we go on to the stage which he calls that of absolute Spirit, does he leave any place for that superior freedom of autonomy which, on the level of the spiritual life, Greek wisdom looked for in the accomplishments of reason, the natural mysticism of India in intellectual concentration attaining through negation the existence of the self, the supernatural mysticism of Christianity in a union of love with a supremely personal transcendent God. He leaves no place for that supreme freedom of autonomy in which the person is moved, not by the Spirit of the world incarnate in the State, but by the Spirit of God, and precisely in its quality as a universe to itself in which free choice is present under grace.

Aristotle's sage was a whole contemplating a Whole. For Hegel philosophy is not so much the work of the philosopher as "the reconciliation of the Spirit with itself",[2] "the knowledge of Spirit by Spirit".[3] He de-personalizes the

[1] Cf. Jean Hyppolite, *Genèse et structure de la phénoménologie de l'esprit de Hegel*, p. 343.

[2] ". . . of the Spirit which has grasped itself *in seiner Freiheit und in dem Reichthum seiner Wirklichkeit.*" *Geschichte der Philosophie*, K. L. Michelet ed., III, in *Sämtliche Werke*, XV, Berlin, 1936, p. 684.

[3] *Phenomenology*, p. 86. Cf. Hyppolite, *op. cit.*, p. 312. Further on (p. 574), after having cited the following lines from the *Phenomenology* (p. 793): "Herein it is established, at the same time, that the third moment, universality, or the essence, means for each of the two opposite factors merely knowledge. Finally they also cancel the empty opposition that still remains, and are the knowledge of Self as identical with Self: this individual self which is immediately pure knowledge or universal," the same author remarks: "The reconciliation of the finite and the infinite spirit which is expressed in this last text is absolute knowledge itself, a knowledge which is at the same time the knowledge which the Absolute has of itself and that of this finite spirit which is raised to the universal consciousness of self."

philosopher as he does the citizen, the latter in the collective Self of the community, the former in the Self of thought in historical self-motion and finally in the Self of the spirit reintegrated into itself in absolute Knowledge. His philosopher no doubt belongs to an age, and inevitably bears the marks of it.[1] And also he has had to await the modern age in order to become a Sage and have absolute knowledge revealed to him.[2] But the moment he becomes the consciousness of the spirit of his time, and restores his thought to the realm of the universal in order to infinitize it therein, the philosopher in his contingent particularity is no longer anything more than a point of actualization of the universal Whole or the universal Spirit, which at a given moment of time becomes conscious of itself as "Philosophy" in its historical development, and expresses itself therein—still inchoately and partially—as in a medium in which pure thought thinks itself and all things. As for the Sage, he suppresses himself even more perfectly as an individual person or as an individual whole. "The True is the essence of the thing, the general. . . . In thinking the general, we are the general; this is why only philosophy [the Knowledge of the Sage] is free . . ."[3]

13. Philosophers have followed one after another down through history, the Sage arrives when all is accomplished: not only because he sums up within himself all the philosophy of the whole of history, but because the absolute Spirit can only be actualized in a man through reflection on the supreme achievements of the objective Spirit. The pre-condition of the existence of the Sage is that he be a citizen of the absolute State, and himself enjoy the

[1] See the Preface to *Phil. of Right*, Knox trans., pp. 11 f. Cf. *Geschichte der Philosophie*, Einleitung, J. Hoffmeister ed., in *Werke*, XVa, p. 149: "Philosophy is identical with the Spirit of the epoch in which it appears; it is not above it, *it is only the consciousness of what is substantial in its time or knowledge thinking of what is in time*. An individual likewise does not dominate his time, rather is he its son; *the substance of this time is his own essence; he merely manifests it under a particular form*. An individual can no more get outside the substance of his time than he can get outside his skin. Thus from the substantial point of view philosophy cannot go beyond its time." (Italics ours.)

One will notice that for Hegel not only does philosophy inevitably bear the mark of its time, but it is entirely bound up in time; in his thought there is no region above time; he merely *manifests the substance of his time*. And philosophy itself is entirely bound up in time, there is nothing supra-temporal or non-temporal in it; *it is only the consciousness of what is substantial in its time*. None of the truths which it perceives dominates the ages; at each period in history they all have to be not only re-thought anew (which is true), but recast in a new doctrinal substance proper to the spirit of the time (until the arrival of absolute Knowledge at the end of history).

[2] J. Hyppolite, *op. cit.*, p. 48.

[3] *Geschichte der Philosophie*, Einleitung, Hoffmeister ed., *Werke*, XVa, p. 84. In philosophy "we find ourselves by ourselves (*bei uns*) without depending on anything else," because in philosophy (in absolute knowledge) we are the Spirit thinking itself and hence we depend neither on an extra-notional reality nor on a Spirit which transcends us. "Philosophy having the general as its object is not liable to the variability of the subject. It is possible that someone may have ideas about essence, he may know this or that about truth; but thoughts or knowledge of this kind is not yet philosophy. . . ." (*Ibid.*)

freedom proper to a citizen who is a member of the absolute (Napoleonic or Prussian) State, in order to achieve absolute Knowledge and the freedom that goes along with it. This freedom is of a superior kind, it is complete autonomy, because it is the freedom of Spirit itself. The Sage is more of an emperor than Napoleon, more completely the Individual *par excellence* than he, because it is the Sage who reveals to the State and to Napoleon what they are, and who transforms the *Bewusstsein* of Spirit objectified in the State into the *Selbst-bewusstsein* of the absolute Spirit, fully reconciled with itself in Knowledge. He makes himself equal with the Whole not by becoming a pure part of the whole which is the State, but by identifying himself dialectically with that Whole which is the absolute Spirit in its very function of being the Whole. Thus, like the ordinary citizen, he fully retains his empirical existence and his empirical singularity, his existential particularity. But while the citizen in his activity as a member of the State exercises real and rational supra-contingent individuality, received from the State, which has become his entelechy, the Sage, on the other hand, in his comprehensive contemplation, does not exercise the supra-contingent individuality that he has arrived at by means of absolute Knowledge, but rather abandons it, divests himself of it in that very Knowledge. For the Sage is nothing other than Knowledge, *begriefendes Wissen*.[1] Insofar as he is Knowledge, he is the consciousness of self of the Spirit; but insofar as he remains at the same time an empirical singular in his contingent particularity, he surrenders up to the Spirit that supreme consciousness of self, and thus the supreme Individuality (Personality) it constitutes. "The whole sphere of finitude, of the fact of being one's self a part of the sensible world, is engulfed in the true-or-veritable Faith before the thought and the intuition (*Anschauung*) of the Eternal, and becomes here one and the same thing. The swarming gnats of the subjectivity are burned in this devouring fire and *the very consciousness* of this gift-of-oneself (*Hingeben*) and this annihilation is annihilated."[2] Though Hegel found it very hard at first to bear the idea of such a surrender, and such an annihilation[3]—which have no relation, by the way, to an "ecstasy" like that of Plotinus, but which are rather, in a completely immanentist perspective, the price of a discursively articulated Gnosis in which the work of the Reason is distilled into philosophy—he ended up by finding the complete satisfaction (*Befriedigung*) proper

[1] A. Kojève, *Introduction à la lecture de Hegel*, p. 324 (*à propos* of *Phänomenologie*, 4th ed., by J. Hoffmeister, in *Werke*, II, p. 556). "There where the Sage is," Kojève writes once more (*ibid.*, p. 418), "there is no more Man properly speaking. There is only the Concept."

[2] *Glauben und Wissen* (1802) in *Werke*, I, pp. 303 f.

[3] "Hegel knows and says it [that it is necessary to undergo this annihilation]. But he says also, in one of his letters, that this knowledge cost him dearly. He speaks of a period of total depression which he experienced between his 25th and 30th years: a 'hypochondria' whose effect extended 'bis zur Erlähmung aller Kräfte,' 'to the paralysis of all his strength' and which derived precisely from the fact that he could not accept the necessary abandonment of *Individuality*, that is to say in fact of humanity, which the idea of *absolute* Knowledge demands. But, finally, he overcame this 'Hypochondria'. . . ." Kojève, *op. cit.*, p. 441.

to the Sage in this renunciation of being a whole in the face of the Whole, in this death to self as an individual person, thanks to which supreme Knowledge is in him as it is in God. It is the same kind of satisfaction he found in accepting total and final death for himself: for in dying completely man bears witness that there is no Transcendence[1]—no other God than the Spirit immanent in nature and in history which realizes in the end all the attributes of its divinity, its divine personality and its divine freedom of autonomy through the ephemeral unity with it of the princes of humanity who are its manifestations—and on their ashes. For Hegel's Sage as for his citizen it is in death, and in the acceptance of death with nothing after, that autonomy is consummated.

[1] It is *in this sense*, and thus modifying them considerably (by putting them into a perspective which sees Hegelian thought as anthropo-theist, certainly, but not atheist) that we subscribe to Kojève's remarks in his study on "The idea of death in the philosophy of Hegel" (*op. cit.*, Appendix II). The conscious acceptance of death (as definitive) and the absolute liberation which it implies with regard to any idea of a *transcendent* God "satisfies", Kojève writes (p. 570), "the infinite pride of man, which constitutes the very basis of his human existence and which is the last irreducible motive of his act of self-creation". Yes, that is authentically Hegelian.

9

HEGELIAN IDEALISM

Hegel's God

I

THE HEGELIAN GNOSIS

Religion captured by Philosophy

1. The Spirit objectifies itself in the State—according to a process of generation and destruction of nations and empires which reaches its ultimate stage with the advent of the Christian-Germanic State; and so, in and through the concrete super-personality of the State, it reveals to man the unconditional rule of the ethical life, obedience to which constitutes freedom for man. But the State remains a limited thing; it is the supreme objectification of the Spirit, but it is not the Spirit in-and-for-itself. The Spirit itself (or Freedom itself) is infinite. The return of the Spirit into itself, by means of which it transcends the opposition between subjective Spirit and objective Spirit, and restores the finite to the infinite, occurs on a level above that of ethical conduct and regulations, the level of pure Knowledge—either masked in the delights of beauty, or mythically "represented", or directly attained. Nothing is superior to the State on the practical level and as far as duty is concerned. That is why the Church, or religion in the form of a finite organization, is subordinated, like every particular society or community, to the State.[1] But religion in its spiritual essence is infinite and belongs, like the chrysalis of Philosophy, to a more elevated order of manifestations of the spirit. In short, the summit of dialectical development is the development of the absolute Spirit, with its three essential stages: Art, Religion, Philosophy. At this point in our analysis, the positions Hegel takes concerning the last two of these stages are of primary interest to us.

Thanks to the dialectical revolution which made all the irrational flow back into reason, the rationalism inaugurated by Descartes has now achieved its ultimate triumph. Everything is subject to the dominion of Reason, which, in the most decidedly univocal sense, is "the Positive Existence [*Wesen*] of Spirit, divine as well as human".[2] Philosophy is knowledge purely and simply supreme. When it attains absolute Knowledge, it coincides with the Science which God has of Himself. But in seizing first place in the degrees of

[1] See the following section.

[2] *Philosophy of History*, J. Sibree trans., New York: Collier and Son, 1901, p. 427.

knowledge, philosophy charged itself, like it or not, with the burden of all the enigmas in the midst of which the human spirit had been struggling. It was not enough to deny or reject everything that derived from faith and from theology, as the tragic prattle of the eighteenth century had bravely attempted, in the candlelight of the *Aufklärung*. It was necessary to integrate and reinterpret it all. With Hegel as with Auguste Comte, under the label of Christianity as under the label of the religion of Humanity, modern philosophy perceived that in overthrowing theology it had taken over the whole heritage of theology. Henceforth it was up to philosophy to furnish men with the final answers and the ultimate certitudes, and with what will serve in the place of transfiguration, the communion of the saints, the Paraclete, and of the good news of salvation and redemption which they had expected from revelation. In seeking to build up a purely philosophical morality that would work better than Christian morality, and to enclose religion within the limits of pure reason, Kant had remained honestly a philosopher. That is why he had failed. Now it was necessary to make religion enter into the very substance of philosophy. The Auguste Comte of the *subjective synthesis* was to attempt a lay counterfeit of Catholicism, intended to supplant the Christian message. As for Hegel, by religiously absorbing Protestantism into his philosophy, it was the Christian message itself and the salt of the gospel, it was Christ and His redemptive passion, the Trinity, the Incarnation and the *felix culpa* that he installed in the dialectic and restored with his pious hands: "Philosophy . . . to-day is essentially orthodox; it is what conserves and maintains the articles of faith that have always carried authority, the fundamental truths of Christianity."[1] "The content of philosophy, its needs and its interests, it holds in common with religion; *its object is eternal truth—nothing other than God and his explanation.* Philosophy does nothing but explain itself in explaining religion, and in explaining itself it explains religion. . . . Thus religion and philosophy coincide."[2] Consummate philosophical knowledge, which is absolute Knowledge—"the spirit knowing itself as spirit"—does not, then, leave religion behind. It integrates religion in itself and constitutes the full comprehension of it. The forms that precede philosophy are the organic constituents of the empire of absolute Spirit, of which philosophy is the fulfilment. ". . . they are the recollection and the Golgotha" of its history, and at the same time "the reality, the truth, the certainty of its throne, without which it were lifeless, solitary and alone".[3]

Is there any philosophy more Christian than Hegelian philosophy? It is religious at its very foundation, animated from the beginning by the theme of a God suffering passion and given over to death. It "preserves many more

[1] *Philosophie der Religion,* Lasson ed., III (*Werke,* XIV), pp. 26 f.

[2] *Ibid.,* I (*Werke,* XII), p. 29.

[3] *The Phenomenology of Mind,* trans. J. B. Baillie, 2nd ed., New York: Macmillan, 1931, p. 808; London: Allen and Unwin, 1931.

elements of dogma than the dogma itself, than theology itself";[1] "it is itself, in reality, a devotion offered to God".[2] Here is, to be sure, a Christian philosophy, a hyper-Christian philosophy, in the sense that it has taken all that it could from Christianity in order to thrive on it. At the same time it has completely emptied Christianity of its own substance, and this in the name of a radical requirement of the historical meaning and destiny of Christianity itself, as it conceives them. For Christianity came to reveal to man an unheard-of freedom and dignity which are his, and the fact that he is called to participate in the very life of God. But at first this revelation could only be formulated in the unreal images and the myths proper to religion, by elevating above the world the idea of a transcendent God who, from heaven where he dwells, "recognizes" each man and his dignity, and calls each one to enter after the death of the body into his own divine life and freedom. But what is the good of being "recognized" above if I am not here below, of entering into the divine life once I am dead and not while I am living here below? The real meaning of such a revelation is that each one must be recognized, not by a Whole who is imagined as separate, but by that very Whole which is the World (and primarily in the form of the State), and that man must enter into the possession of his divinity in this very world and in this very life, when the travails of history are concluded, Jesus having been the first among us to know that He was God, because God and man make themselves God in man. And so it is that Christianity comes to be what it is, to realize itself truly, only by ceasing to be Religion (or represented under the form of myths) in order to become Philosophy (in the sense of absolute Knowledge), and by understanding that there is neither hereafter (*Jenseits*) nor afterlife, and no *other world* than the World. We must concur with M. Kojève on this point, when in his commentary on the *Phenomenology* he shows so clearly that for Hegel Christianity can only realize itself through the suppression (*Aufhebung*) of Christian theology and Christian dogmatics.[3]

2. It is not, then, by virtue of some more or less subjective and purely theoretical allegorical interpretation, but following the very dictation of history, and by virtue of the internal requirements of a *Christianity-without-hereafter*, forcing itself into being, that Hegel knows that Christianity, or religion having attained "its true or absolute form", is "an anticipatory representation of philosophical thought",[4] a system of myths preparatory to philosophy. Its content is nothing more than the very content of philosophy, but obscured by symbols.[5] It is philosophy which reveals the truth that

[1] *Philosophie der Religion*, Lasson ed., I, p. 40 (*Werke*, XII). [2] *Ibid.*, I, p. 29.
[3] Cf. A. Kojève, *op. cit.*, pp. 156, 182–184, 192–195, 294. [4] J. Hyppolite, *op. cit.*, p. 514.
[5] "In religion and philosophy there is thus one substantial content, and only the manner of formation is different. . . . Philosophy is thus not opposed to religion; it comprehends it." *Vorlesungen über die Geschichte der Philosophie*, Einleitung, Hoffmeister ed. (*Sämtliche Werke*, Lasson ed., XVa, Leipzig, 1940), pp. 185, 192.

revelation still veiled and that religion attained only imperfectly: because philosophy is the "highest, freest, wisest phase"[1] in the union of subjective spirit with objective spirit, and the final goal of the whole development. "What was formerly revealed as a mystery, and remains in the purest forms, and still more in the obscure forms of revelation, a mystery for (merely) formal thought, is (finally) revealed for (genuine, concrete) Thought itself, which, exercising the absolute right of its freedom, affirms its obstinate determination to be reconciled with the content of the real only if the latter knows how to give itself the form most worthy of thought, that of the concept, of the necessity which binds all things together and thus liberates them."[2]

The Incarnation of the Word thus signifies the fundamental law of the dialectic: thought must enter into the abyss of its own negation in order to find its plenitude through return into itself and abiding with itself; the redemptive passion signifies the process by which human consciousness makes an end to its separation from the universal and in which the finite and the infinite are reunited and reconciled. For the only begotten Son, in His phase of "disintegration"[3] appears as the finite world of nature and of man, which far from being one with the Father, begins by being in a state of alienation and division from Him, and where the finite mind "completes its independence till it becomes wickedness".[4] And the history of Christ is that of the reintegration of this finite world into unity. The remission of sins[5] (which was no doubt as central a problem for Hegel as for Luther) signifies that the fall is the necessary condition of the advent and triumph of Spirit. The Trinity

[1] *Philosophy of History*, Sibree trans., p. 99.

[2] *Encyclopädie der philosophischen Wissenschaften*, Preface to the 2nd ed. in *Werke*, Lasson 4th ed., V, p. 21.

[3] Cf. *Encyclopaedia of the Philosophical Sciences*, Philosophy of Mind, § 568, trans. by W. Wallace, Oxford: Clarendon Press, 1894, pp. 177 f.

[4] *Ibid.*, p. 178.

[5] In an immanentist philosophy such as Hegel's this expression takes on a special import. Is it enough for sin to be pardoned? And by what transcendent God would it be pardoned? Is it not necessary, rather, that it be blotted out of existence, in short that God perform the impossible by making what has been not to have been? Hegel thus found himself preoccupied with a problem which, in a wholly anti-Hegelian perspective, was going to play a central role in Chestov's thought. "The Spirit," he writes, "can make what has happened not have happened. The action remains, to be sure, in the memory, but the Spirit strips itself of it; the finite, evil in general, is denied." "Der Geist kann das Geschehene ungeschehen machen; die Handlung bleibt wohl in der Erinnerung, aber der Geist streift sie ab, . . . das Endliche, Böse überhaupt ist vernichtet." (*Phil. der Religion*, III, in *Werke*, Lasson ed., XIV, p. 173.) "The wounds of the spirit heal and leave no scars behind. The deed is not the imperishable element; spirit takes it back into itself. . . ." (*Phenomenology*, Baillie trans., p. 676.) Cf. Hyppolite, *op. cit.*, p. 479: "In this dialectic the spirit reconciles evil within itself and becomes absolute spirit. The Christian dialectic of the remission of sins is the symbolic representation of a tragic philosophy of history, in which the finiteness of the acting spirit is ever converted into the ascensional movement of the spirit, wherein the past awaits its *meaning* from the future. It is in this transcending, this 'Aufhebung,' that the spirit takes hold of itself as absolute, not in the consciousness of sin, but in the consciousness of the forgiveness of sins."

signifies that the life of the Spirit consists of Reason's self-interior movement and reflection on itself. This dogma lets us into the secret of Hegelian metaphysics, and the triadic structure of Being. In short, the whole message of the religion of Christ is the absolute Knowledge of the philosophy which deciphers it, by explaining to us, for example, concerning the "infinite return, and reconciliation with the eternal being", or "the withdrawal of the eternal from the phenomenal into the unity of its fullness",[1] that "the *universal* substance, as actualized out of its abstraction", is realized "in an *individual* self-consciousness", which is identical with the "essence—(in the Eternal sphere he is called the Son)— . . . transplanted into the world of time", in Him the universal substance shows evil as suppressed in itself. But furthermore, the concrete absolute, in "this immediate, and thus sensuous existence", "of its own expiring in the pain of *negativity*", becomes—as "infinite subjectivity . . . [keeping] himself unchanged"—an "absolute return" and "universal unity of universal and individual essentiality" for itself—this is "the Idea of the Spirit eternal, but alive and present in the world".[2] Hegel's philosophy is centered on the Christian idea of the mediation of the Son of God, understood in the sense that humanity is its own mediator and that history is the very process of mediation by which God realizes Himself and manifests Himself in incarnation—making Himself God and man at the same time.

So the Christian faith, like everything else, is "put in the form"[3] or "translated into the form of thought".[4] Everything is there, and everything is a corpse. All the truths of the faith are hanging up in the slaughterhouse of pure reason. This is quite inevitable, since philosophy has become so Christian that it has usurped the place of the revealing God.

Philosophy has caught Christianity and even God in its dialectic, in order to extend the supreme protection of Reason over them. It lavishes its care on a dead Christianity. It is a dead God that it causes to reign over men and charges with sanctioning the power of the State. Once again Hegel has killed what he affirmed and exalted. In proclaiming the death of God,[5] Nietzsche will only unveil what had been covered by the cloak of dialectical idealism. The atheism of Nietzsche and Marx will unmask the religiosity without faith

[1] *Encyclopaedia*, Philosophy of Mind, § 566, Wallace trans., p. 177.

[2] *Ibid.*, § 569, p. 178.

[3] *Encyclopädie*, Einleitung, Lasson ed., § 5, *Werke*, V, p. 35. Cf. above, ch. VII, p. 132, note 2.

[4] The same passage, Wallace trans., p. 8; Lasson ed., p. 35: ". . . dass der wahrhafte Inhalt unseres Bewusstseins in dem Übersetzen desselben in die Form des Gedankens und Begriffs erhalten, ja erst in sein eigentümliches Licht gesetzt wird. . . ."

[5] Hegel had already said: "God Himself is dead" in a totally different sense from that in which Christian theology speaks of the death of Christ. For Hegel this "hard word" means that God Himself or *insofar as He is God* is dead—in the reversion of the universal consciousness of self into the depths of night—in order to rise again insofar as God, that is to say, in order that this consciousness at last become *for itself* in the knowledge the community has of the spirit, which is the advent of Paraclete or the concrete spirit who lives in the community. Cf. Hyppolite, *op. cit.*, pp. 546 f.

of Hegelian reason by rising up against Christianity. The faith of Kierkegaard will avenge itself upon it by rising up against reason.

The Spiritual captured by the Temporal

3. We have just seen how religion is captured by philosophy in the Hegelian dialectic. By virtue of the same operation the spiritual is captured by the temporal. The evangelical distinction between the spiritual order (the things that are God's) and the temporal order (the things that are Caesar's) vanishes with the advent of the Idea of the State finally actualized in its truth, that is, with the advent of the Christian-Germanic State. When "the end of days is fully come",[1] and thanks to the Protestant Reformation and the developments which followed, the fourth stage of universal history, the Germanic empire, arrives at its final outcome, then "the antithesis of Church and State vanishes. The spiritual becomes reconnected with the secular, and develops this latter as an independently organic existence. The State no longer occupies a position of real inferiority to the Church . . . and the spiritual is no longer an element foreign to the State."[2]

In protesting against the distinction between the spiritual and the temporal,[3] Hegel was following in the footsteps of Hobbes and Rousseau.[4] But his State is more deeply imbued with religion than theirs, because it is the social body of the Spirit—it is to the Church what philosophy is to religion, it envelops and protects it by absorbing it into itself.[5] The fact is that Religion, as

[1] *Phil. of Hist.*, Sibree trans., p. 435. [2] *Ibid.*, pp. 170 f.

[3] The fact that "the Religious element was regarded as utterly alien to the secular"—in other words, that man has been "driven into the Inward, the Abstract"—is connected for Hegel to the belief "in *Evil*, as a vast power the sphere of whose malign dominion is the Secular" and depends on the same *wunderbar* historical phenomenon as the horrors of the trials for witchcraft (*Phil. of Hist.*, p. 531; Lasson ed., II, in *Werke*, IX, 2nd ed., p. 891). Cf. *ibid.*, p. 568: "There is no sacred, no religious conscience *in a state of separation from*, or perhaps even hostility to, *Secular Right*" (italics ours). Cf. also *Encyclopaedia*, Phil. of Mind, § 552, p. 160: "The precept of religion, 'Give to Caesar what is Caesar's and to God what is God's' is not enough: the question is to settle what is Caesar's, what belongs to the secular authority." And doubtless Hegel does not blink the fact "that the secular no less than the ecclesiastical authority have claimed almost everything as their own". But "the divine spirit must interpenetrate the entire secular life: whereby wisdom is concrete within it, and it carries the terms of its own justification".

[4] "Of all Christian authors, the philosopher Hobbes is the only one who has clearly seen the evil and its remedy, and who has dared to propose a reunion of the heads of the eagle and the complete restoration of political unity, without which no State or government will ever be well constituted." Jean-Jacques Rousseau, *The Social Contract*, Bk. IV, ch. VIII, trans. by H. J. Tozer, London: Swan Sonnenschein & Co., 1905, p. 223.

[5] "The distinction between Religion and the World is only this—that Religion, as such, is Reason in the soul and heart—that it is a temple in which Truth and Freedom in God are presented to the conceptive faculty: the State, on the other hand, regulated by the selfsame Reason, is a temple of Human Freedom concerned with the *perception and volition of a reality, whose purport may itself be called divine*. Thus . . . moral rectitude in the State is only the carrying out of that which constitutes the fundamental principle of Religion." *Phil. of Hist.*, pp. 427 f.

"This is the sense in which we must understand the State to be based on Religion. States

Hegel conceives it, is resolved and absorbed, on the one hand, into Philosophy and absolute Knowledge (and as we saw above, it is in this role, as the chrysalis of Philosophy, that religion belongs to a higher order than the State), and, on the other hand, it is resolved and absorbed into the State, in the sense that by nourishing men with the symbols of truth it was like the maternal bosom where the State took possession of its proper principles and established its divine authority. But once this authority is established, the whole substance of Religion passes into the ("Christian") State, as far as the regulation of conduct is concerned, just as its whole substance passes into ("Christian") Philosophy as far as knowing is concerned. The temporal State in its ultimate form is the spiritual community *par excellence*, "secular life is the positive and definite embodiment of the Spiritual Kingdom".[1]

"There is nothing *holier* than the ethical element and the law of the State."[2]

---

and Laws are nothing else than Religion manifesting itself in the relations of the actual world." *Ibid.*, p. 522.

"For in affirming that the State is based on Religion—that it has its roots in it—we virtually assert that the former has proceeded from the latter; and that this derivation is going on now and will always continue; that is, the principles of the State must be regarded as valid in and for themselves, which can only be insofar as they are recognized as determinate manifestations of the Divine Nature." *Ibid.*, p. 101.

Cf. *Philosophy of Right*, § 270, trans. by T. M. Knox, Oxford, 1942, p. 166: "If religion is in this way the groundwork which includes the ethical realm in general, and the state's fundamental nature—the divine will—in particular, it is at the same time only a groundwork; and it is at this point that state and religion begin to diverge. The state is the divine will, in the sense that it is mind present on earth, unfolding itself to be the actual shape and organization of a world."

Cf. also *Encyclopaedia*, Phil. of Mind, § 552, Wallace trans., pp. 154 ff.

[1] *Phil. of Hist.*, p. 552.

[2] "That harmony which has resulted from the painful struggles of History, involves the recognition of the Secular as capable of being an embodiment of Truth. . . . It is now perceived that Morality and Justice in the State are also divine and commanded by God, and that in point of substance *there is nothing higher or more sacred.*" *Phil. of Hist.*, p. 528.

After the crises of the modern world and the "run of the Church", whose "corruption" provoked the Lutheran Reform and which was henceforth in "a position of inferiority to the World-Spirit" (*ibid.*, pp. 516 f.), "Spirit, once more driven back upon itself, produces its work in an intellectual shape, and becomes capable of realizing the Ideal of Reason *from the Secular principle alone*". *Ibid.*, p. 170 (italics ours).

The following texts, which offer the totalitarian State a breviary of its right to persecute the Church, are in perfect accord with those principles:

"When individuals, holding religious views in common, form themselves into a church, a Corporation, they fall under the general control and oversight of the higher state officials." *Phil. of Right*, § 270, Knox trans., p. 169.

"On the other hand, the doctrine of the church is not purely and simply an inward concern of conscience. As doctrine it is rather the expression of something, in fact the expression of a subject-matter which is most closely linked, or even directly concerned with ethical principles and the law of the land. Hence at this point the paths of church and state either coincide or diverge at right angles. The difference of their two domains may be pushed by the church into sheer antagonism since, by regarding itself as enshrining the content of religion—a content which is absolute—it may claim as its portion mind in general and so the whole ethical sphere, and conceive the state as a mere mechanical scaffolding for the attainment of external, non-mental, ends. It may take itself to be the Kingdom of God, or at

What Hegel introduces here into modern history is a principle which, in its direct opposition to the Gospel, constitutes the mystical root of the deification, no longer of the Emperor, as in ancient Rome, but of the totalitarian State: that is to say, the claim of *sanctity* for the world and the temporal power.

II

THE ETHICS OF DIALECTICAL CONNIVANCE WITH HISTORY, IN "CHRISTIAN" SUBMISSION TO THE EMPEROR OF THIS WORLD

Hegel's God

4. In the proper philosophical order itself, what is the Hegelian notion of God? God is the infinite Spirit insofar as it makes itself personal or suprapersonal by becoming conscious of itself (in man), that same infinite Spirit which only realizes itself by first denying and alienating itself in the finite, and which posits itself as Idea and then exteriorizes itself as Nature before returning into itself as Spirit.

---

least as the road to it or its vestibule, while it regards the state as the kingdom of this world, i.e. of the transient and the finite. In a word, it may think that it is an end in itself, while the state is a mere means. These claims produce the demand, in connexion with doctrinal instruction, that the state should not only allow the church to do as it likes with complete freedom, but that it should pay unconditional respect to the church's doctrines as doctrines, whatever their character, because their determination is supposed to be the task of the church alone." *Ibid.*, p. 170.

"Now it is, of course, a matter of history that in terms and under conditions of barbarism, all higher forms of intellectual life had their seat only in the church, while the state was a mere mundane rule of force, caprice, and passion. . . . But it is far too blind and shallow a proceeding to declare that this situation is the one which truly corresponds with the Idea." *Ibid.*, p. 171.

"It is philosophic insight which sees that while church and state differ in form, they do not stand opposed in content, for truth and rationality are the content of both. Thus when the church begins to teach doctrines (though there are and have been some churches with a ritual only, and others in which ritual is the chief thing, while doctrine and a more educated consciousness are only secondary), and when these doctrines touch on objective principles, on thoughts of the ethical and the rational, *then their expression* eo ipso *brings the church into the domain of the state*. In contrast with the church's faith and authority in matters affecting ethical principles, rightness, laws, institutions, *in contrast with the church's subjective conviction, the state is that which knows*. Its principle is such that its content is in essence no longer clothed with the form of feeling and faith but is determinate thought." *Ibid.*, p. 171 (italics ours).

"It is only thereafter that the state, in contrast with the particular sects, has attained to universality of thought—its formal principle—and is bringing this universality into existence. . . . Hence so far from its being or its having been a misfortune for the state that the church is disunited, it is only as a result of that disunion that the state has been able to reach its appointed end as *a self-consciously rational and ethical organization*." *Ibid.*, pp. 173 f. (italics ours).

Hegel denied being pantheist because pantheism,[1] he said, consists of affirming "the identity of God and the world",[2] while in Hegel's system the world is necessarily other than God: but in what way? Because in its very otherness the world is necessary to God as an extraneation of God, and in order that God may become Himself in the world. Whether He be taken in the state of alienation from self or in that of reintegration into self, God is nothing but the eternal process, painful or victorious, of a Thought which has been raised to the absolute, not as a pure act of intellection but as discursive reason. He is but the eternal process of an infinite Whole which is not "separate", nor transcendent, but consubstantial with becoming and with the swarming of the forms of the finite. Such an absolute immanentism is more pantheistic than common pantheism.[3] And how does this God of Hegel become conscious of Himself and personalize Himself, how does He acquire His divinity, starting from His own negative? In order to accomplish this He needs the finite. It is through man and man's thought that He brings Himself and all things back into Himself. "God must be apprehended as spirit in his community."[4] "Not only is God not independent of the spiritual community, but he exists *qua* God, or as knowing himself, only in this community."[5] The development of the absolute Spirit thus coincides with the history of the human spirit. "Both [the divine and the human spirit] have in common what is in-itself and for-itself—the universal, absolute Spirit."[6] "The divine nature

[1] Cf. the long developments in § 573 of the *Encyclopaedia*, Phil. of Mind, Wallace trans., pp. 181–196.

[2] *Ibid.*, p. 194.

[3] It would be too easy—and hardly philosophical—to avoid the question, as Jean Hyppolite does (*op. cit.*, p. 524), by writing: "It is impossible to accuse Hegel of pantheism in the popular sense, if pantheism makes one of the terms of the opposition disappear in the other." Besides, it is not a matter of accusing but of stating. The same author abounds in assertations which reveal Hegelian doctrine as the most authentic pantheism, not popular but highly and learnedly elaborated, when he tells us, for example, that according to this doctrine "all consciousness of self is for itself double: it is *God and man* in the bosom of a single consciousness" (*ibid.*, p. 183); "the infinite essence is realized in finite existence and the finite existence raises itself to essentiality", in such a way that a God who would be "above the battle"—that is to say, who would not be Himself engaged in the agonies of the finite—would be only an "abstract God" (*ibid.*, p. 473); "God is not beyond the knowledge which religion has of him. . . . He is knowledge of self in man and by man who thus shares in the divine life" (*ibid.*, p. 523); "the absolute spirit goes beyond the finite spirit, but is, however, only through it, if it is true that only in this reconciliation (which supposes separation and unity) is the spirit authentically absolute because it becomes so" (*ibid.*, p. 525); "in creation God becomes Self" (*ibid.*, p. 544); etc.

[4] *Encyclopaedia*, Phil. of Mind, § 554, p. 168.

[5] Emile Bréhier, *Histoire de la philosophie*, Paris: Presses Universitaires de France, 1946, II, 3, p. 778. "As those primitive gods who would die without the offerings of their faithful," the same author notes (p. 781), "one may literally say that the God of Hegel owes his existence to religion."

[6] *Geschichte der Philosophie*, Einleitung in *Werke*, XVa, p. 175. Hegel adds (pp. 175 f.): "We ought to conceive of the Spirit as free; the freedom of the Spirit means that he is by himself, that he understands himself. His nature consists in encroaching on the Other, where he refinds, reunites, possesses, and enjoys himself."

is itself only this: to be the absolute Spirit, that is to say, the unity of the divine nature and human nature."[1] "God is God only so far as he knows himself: his self-knowledge is, further, his self-consciousness in man, and man's knowledge of God, which proceeds to man's self-knowledge in God."[2]

This means that the reconciliation of the Spirit with itself, and the final realization of its divinity, or its final conquest of an "infinite interiority", take place in man and through man. If God is "spirit in its community", it is because He becomes conscious of Himself, as we noted above, through the community of minds, and realizes Himself as God thereby. And even this occurs in a consummate way—no longer under the shadow of sense perceivable beauty or under the veil of myths which nourish feeling, but in full rational splendor—only in and through absolute Knowledge of Philosophy, in which the reintegration of the finite into the infinite is accomplished, and which is the ultimate interior sanctuary, the Word formed in time, in which God at the same time, and in a totally pure way, becomes conscious of Himself and of the world and becomes, insofar as He is thought, an infinite personality or supra-personality. Suppress philosophy and its history, and God is no longer God. In other words, suppress man and his history, and God is no longer God. For "the owl of Minerva begins its flight only at nightfall"—the Knowledge of the sage is none other than a supremely comprehensive reflection in which is revealed, in the "interiorizing-memory", what has been accomplished, what the real has become. At the same time and by the same token such knowledge reveals God and Man having attained the plenitude of their being, as one being, God become true God in Man and Man become God in becoming truly Man.[3] This is not "common pantheism", it is anthropo-theistic immanentism.

5. But Hegelian pantheism has consequences which have no less significance and which it is important to point out. They have to do with the problem of evil (or evil *par excellence*, sin)[4] in its relation to God.

[1] *Phil. der Religion*, Lasson ed., III in *Werke*, XIV, p. 38.

[2] *Encyclopaedia*, Phil. of Mind, § 564, p. 176.

[3] The "element of existence" "in which absolute knowledge becomes possible" is "universal self-consciousness present in 'the universal divine man' ". J. Hyppolite, *op. cit.*, p. 574.

[4] Of the two kinds of evil—sin, the evil of free will or of the person, and suffering, the evil of nature—the second is evil in a less detestable sense. This is why Plato said he would rather be punished, even unjustly, than guilty. It is of the essence of the material universe to entail suffering, and more generally privation. From the very fact that He creates the world God is also the cause of the suffering which matter renders inevitable—*generatio unius corruptio alterius*—but He is the cause of it only *per accidens*, or in a manner extrinsic to His intention. What He intends are the existence and good of the world—to which, however, suffering and privation are bound. (And it is only in Him, because of the transcendent simplicity of His willing, that such a *per accidens* causation can be purely *per accidens* or extra-intentional: willed, but without being even in a secondary way an object of intention.) But the evil *par excellence*, moral evil or sin, God does not will in any way,

In the authentic perspective of Christianity, the innocence of God is a corollary of His transcendence. God is absolutely innocent of evil. More than that, He wages war against evil, and against its companion, death. He took them upon Himself when he was incarnated in order to suffer, as if He sought thus to console His glory for having created a world in which evil is permitted, because it is in the nature of everything that is not God to be capable of failing.

A philosophy of transcendence[1] knows that God is innocent of evil: because the primary origin of evil lies in a universe—the universe of created existence—so completely *other* than that of the uncreated Unity that this universe of created existence can isolate itself from God (that is, it can nihilate, it can do nothing). Since God is self-subsistent Being itself, and since things exist in their own nature, absolutely distinct from the divine *esse*, those among them that are free agents or persons produce *by themselves alone*, or *without God*, the rupture or nihilation which is at the root of the evil act. They alone initiate evil; they are the *primary cause* of evil. Evil is the only thing (but it is not a thing—it is a privation) that God knows without having caused it. And certainly nothing happens without His having willed or permitted it. But to permit is not to will. And the permission for the creature to slip away from the influx of God *if it wishes* is but one with the fact that the influx the creature receives in the ordinary course of things is a "breakable" influx, as befits the peccability natural to created agents. As for the permission of the act itself which is infected with this nihilation, if God, the uncreated Freedom, thus suffers to have the wound of evil that He has not willed pass into being, it is because in the duel with created liberties in which He is engaged, and in the adventure in which His love has staked all, He will draw from this evil that He does not will a greater good which will be His reply to it. Only the uncreated Freedom is capable of winning such a game with infallible art, a game played at breakneck speed, in which the losses are terrifying because the gains are divine: namely the final entry of the creature (free, at each moment of the drama, in relation to prevenient grace) into the very joy of self-subsistent Being, which it becomes by participation, by virtue of the vision of the divine essence. Whatever created freedom may do, however far it may sink into evil, God will produce from His treasures supercompensations better than all the good that would have existed, had

---

even extra-intentionally. He is not the cause of it, even *per accidens*; He is *absolutely not* the cause of it.

Let us add that according to the Judeo-Christian revelation man was created in a state above nature, in which he did not know suffering. For man suffering—the evil of nature—came after sin—the evil of free will—for which the created agent is alone responsible. It is the consequence of the first sin, of the fall, and, moreover, of the whole backlog of sin accumulated in the human race since then. God did not make man to suffer, but to be happy.

[1] Cf. our work *Existence and the Existent*, New York: Pantheon Books, Inc., 1948.

this not happened. The "fair play" of God is the first law of the philosophy of history. He plays a fair game with free agents. From the moment that He decided to create the world, He decided to let them have their way, even though they might undo His work, and say *no*, even though they might, either in the manner of angels or in the manner of man, raise, like gods from below, nothingness against His love. He enlists us along with Himself in this enterprise. Our collaboration is required for its progress. This is the unheard-of paradox of the first three petitions in the Lord's Prayer, that, as has been said,[1] they are prayers we address to God for God, for His Name, for His Kingdom, for His Will, for His own victory over the evil that He permits, that He does not will. He is the sovereign master and governor of history (in which He nevertheless has partners—the created free agents). And He is the cause only of the good, not of the evil of history. He is pure of the impurities of history, innocent of its crimes. Absolutely innocent.

All this is the A, B, C of Christianity. But for the "Christian" immanentism of Hegel, things are quite otherwise. The distinction between permitting and willing has no meaning when there is no Person dealing with other persons, but rather a Process which tends toward unity and consciousness of self through its own differences. God is now immanent in the becoming of things; he and they are univocally Thought—it is his own self that he negates and reassumes in the engendering of the universe and time and in the progress of history. His entire being, "the complete richness of the Spirit",[2] is contained in each of the Worlds or historical Spirits which succeed each other in the movement of human becoming. His eternity does not transcend time—before considering it in itself, in the dialectic of pure thought, the philosopher contemplates that eternity within the most intimate workings of time—eternity is the other of time immanent in time; it alienates itself in time and reinstates itself through time.[3] God's freedom is nothing other than the "truth of necessity" and the spontaneity of dialectical development. He makes himself through the conflicts and oppositions of this development, and through all the losses of self and the annihilations into which the "work of the negative" must descend for the sake of ulterior resurrections. Is it not so that Schelling's and Fichte's idea of God "sinks into insipidity", because

[1] We refer here to private notes which were kindly communicated to us by their author.

[2] The "succession of spiritual shapes (*Geistern*)" which constitutes universal history is "a gallery of pictures, each of which is endowed with the entire wealth of Spirit". *Phenomenology*, Baillie trans., 2nd ed., p. 807.

[3] On this re-establishment of eternity by time, cf. Jean Hyppolite, *op. cit.*, pp. 548–549: "That the effective spirit, that of history, become its own self-knowledge, and that this self-knowledge show itself to its consciousness in history, this certainty implies the dialectical reconciliation of finite human existence and essence, but that this reconciliation be apprehended as *our work*, this double exigency leads to a divine Humanity which states in a temporal way an eternal truth. Do not all the difficulties of the Hegelian system come together in this last relation of the finite and the infinite, of the singular and the universal, under the form of time and eternity?"

"it lacks the seriousness, the suffering, the patience, and *the labour of the negative*"?[1] It is a necessity of being, to pass through the negative and through evil. God also must pass through it. Without the Golgotha of Absolute Spirit, which history forms, spirit would be "lifeless, solitary and alone".[2] If the fall and the experience of evil are, as we noted above, the necessary conditions of the advent and triumph of the Spirit, this means they are an integral part of the history of God.[3] It is at this price that "God posits himself in his alterity, in order to find himself as Self and Spirit".[4] Similarly, what religion depicts as the original fall was a metaphysical necessity. It was necessary that man desert his animal innocence in order to become spirit-for-itself, through the rending which is the knowledge of good and evil procured through the experience of evil.[5] In short, evil is dialectically or metaphysically necessary. And God, by virtue of His own existence and His own process of self-realization, is the primary (immanent) source of evil as of good, and ultimately responsible for it. He is the source of evil with all its fruits as He is the source of good with all its fruits in the history of the human race; and He is the supreme justification of evil as of good, of evil with all its fruits as of good with all its fruits.

6. Hegel speaks frequently of the spirit of the world, and it is as Spirit of the world that his God enters into history in order to realize Himself. It would be very naïve not to understand this expression *Spirit of the World* as bearing all the implications involved in the strangely ambiguous word which designates at once the *cosmos* of the Greeks and the *hic mundus* of the Gospel ("the world cannot receive the spirit of truth," Christ said.[6]) Absolute Knowledge has made the Spirit of God emigrate from the Trinity, as conceived by the Faith, into the *cosmos* and into *this world.* The divine Spirit is henceforth the Entelechy of the World and the Spirit of this World. In other words, the God that Hegel asks us to adore is God conceived as the Emperor of this World.[7]

[1] *Phenomenology*, p. 81 (italics ours).

[2] *Ibid.*, p. 808.

[3] "The infinite Spirit should not be thought of as beyond the finite spirit, beyond man who acts and sins, for he is himself eager to share in the human drama. His true infinity, his concrete infinity, is not realized without this fall" (Hyppolite, *op. cit.*, p. 507). "One must learn that this fall forms a part of the absolute itself, that it is a moment of the total truth. The absolute Self cannot be expressed without this negativity; it is an absolute Yes only while saying No to a No, only while overcoming the necessary negation" (*ibid.*, p. 509).

[4] *Ibid.*, p. 545 (cf. *Phenomenology*, p. 770).

[5] "Knowledge, as the disannulling of the unity of mere Nature, is the 'Fall', which is no casual conception, but the eternal history of Spirit. For the state of innocence, the paradisiacal condition, is that of the brute. Paradise is a park, where only brutes, not men, can remain." *Phil. of Hist.*, p. 411; cf. Hyppolite, *op. cit.*, p. 545.

[6] *John*, XIV, 17.

[7] Here is the true "master and lord of the world" (*Phenomenology*, p. 505), the true "living God" (*ibid.*), the true "*monas monadum*" and "Person of Persons" (*Phil. of Hist.*, pp. 409 f.), to take up the terms which Hegel himself used concerning the miserable exemplar

We had occasion to allude to the idea thus designated in connection with the Stoics. It was latent in Greek tragedy (though man as the victim of the gods, who punished him for a crime into which they had themselves made him fall, began to assert himself against them); but it was more clearly delineated in the *fatum* of the Stoics. This was one of the faces of the God of pagan antiquity, but this God had a double visage. He was at the same time the true God of nature and of reason; and thus the idea of God as Emperor of this world was in this context counterbalanced and partially held in check by that of the true God. With Hegel, the idea of God as Emperor of this world is finally invested with full philosophical authority.

It is important to understand the significance of this idea clearly. Imagine, we have written elsewhere,[1] a notion of God which, while recognizing the existence of the One and Supreme, of the Spirit on which everything depends, at the same time misunderstood that which St. Paul called His glory, denied the abyss of freedom that His transcendence signifies, shackled Him to the world He had made; imagine a notion of God shut off from the supernatural, and which rendered impossible the mysteries hidden in the love of God and in His freedom and in His incommunicable life. Then we should have the false God of the philosophers, the Jupiter of all false Gods. Imagine a God tied to the order of nature or to the evolution of the world; a God who is nothing more than the supreme guarantee and justification of that order or of that evolution; a God who is responsible for this world but without the power to redeem it, and whose inflexible will, that no prayer can reach, is pleased with and condones all the evil as all the good of the world, all the deceit and the cruelty as well as all the generosity which are at work in the world; a God who blesses iniquity and slavery and misery, and who sacrifices man to the cosmos, and who makes of the tears of children and the agony of the innocent a mere ingredient of the sacred necessities of the eternal cycles or of evolution—with no after-life where His goodness mends the ravages made in His work by created freedom. Such a God would doubtless be the One and Supreme, the Spirit on which everything depends, but changed into

---

of the idea offered by the Caesar of imperial Rome—"titanic self-consciousness, which takes itself to be the living God" but which, being only a wretched "solitary single person", a merely "formal" and abstract self incapable of subduing the unleashed forces which emerge within him, finds "his procedure and his self-enjoyment" only in "titanic excess" (*Phenomenology*, pp. 504 f.). The veritable *Herr der Welt*—what we are calling the Emperor of the world—is the concrete personality, the Self of the infinite Spirit in process of fully possessing itself. It will also be noted that if, for Hegel, Faith "is an escape from the real world . . . and yet is the same substance which, as in a mirror trick, appears here in the aspect of the powers of this world, in the form of absolute being, of God" (Hyppolite, *op. cit.*, p. 405), this is because for Hegel God only realizes Himself through the world and the powers of this world and only *comes into His own* there.

[1] Cf. *La signification de l'athéisme contemporain*, Paris: Desclée De Brouwer, 1949, pp. 26 f. (text modified); an English translation of this essay appears in *The Range of Reason*, New York: Scribners, 1952; London: Geoffrey Bles, pp. 110 f.

an idol, deprived of his essence and profaned, "the *naturalistic God* of nature, the Jupiter of this world, the great God of the idolaters of the powerful on their thrones and of the rich in their earthly glory, of lawless success, and of the pure fact exalted into law".

This is the God of Hegel, to be sure, except that by descending further into immanence than the God of the Stoics and of ordinary pantheism, who without being transcendent was still superior to time and to becoming, he is no longer, properly speaking, the One and Supreme. But he is still the Spirit on whom everything depends. And no doubt he does not dominate the world *from on high*, as that empty and degraded skeleton of a *Herr der Welt*, the Roman Emperor, pretended to do, and as the transcendent God of the Christians did, "represented" as He was in mythical terms; but it is from the very *bosom of the world* and from the groans of the world, it is from the profoundest depths of time that in the process of making himself and of consummating or realizing his own limitless freedom Hegel's God extends his power over all things. Thus involved in the world by the very requirements of his own divinity, needing the world in order to be, and leading it, in Man, to that same ultimate freedom which is his, this God eminently deserves the title of Emperor of this world, in an incomparably more decisive way than the God of the Stoics (because he has undergone the influence of Christianity, and is a Christian God turned inside-out, or an anti-christic God). Moreover, if, as Hegel puts it in the *Phenomenology*, the Christian God was a celestial sublimation of the Roman Emperor, it is another Emperor, Napoleon, the God revealed, *der erscheinende Gott*, who was the first real manifestation of the supremely immanent God of Hegel.

Emperor of this world and Emperor of history, this God is only free, infinitely free, insofar as he manifests and knows his own infinite necessity. The freedom of the creation, the freedom of the redemption, the freedom of revelation, all these have completely disappeared. It is in virtue of the very necessities of the dialectical process that he deploys himself in the world, that he reconciles the world to himself, that he manifests himself to the world. This God, the God of Hegel, is not innocent of evil—he passes through evil himself in order to win his own divinity. And everything that happens, evil as well as good, is his own work.[1] He has on his head the blood of all the victims immolated since the beginning of the world by the blessed harrows of the dialectical development, more inexorable than those of the sacrifice machine of Kafka's *Penal Colony*. He is in our midst, πόλεμος πατὴρ πάντων, the Principle of War, which is the father of all things. He does not command men to love; he is not so naïve as that. He is not interested in what ought to be, but only in what is. And it is certainly not of him that it was said, "God is

[1] Cf. the last lines of the Lectures on the *Philosophy of History*, Sibree trans., p. 569: "What has happened, and is happening every day, is not only not 'without God', but is essentially *His Work*" (italics ours).

Love." He knows, and makes real, the fact that crime has its necessity, as does war, which is a "crime *for the Universal*", and one in which the particular, giving and receiving death "in the void, impersonally", "contemplates itself as absolutely free, as universal Negativity for itself and really against another".[1] He fosters war in men, and the sacred will to victory; he sanctifies war as the great breath which "keeps the waters of the lake from stagnating" and keeps individuals from sinking into security. Thanks to war, nations and empires replace one another and succeed one another at the head of humanity, up to the advent of the people definitely chosen, the Christian–German community. (For "the pure inwardness of the German nation was the proper soil for the emancipation of Spirit";[2] it is the Germanic nation which, at "the last stage in history",[3] will cause the spirit to reign over the world.) "In order not to let particular systems get rooted and settled . . . and thus break up the whole into fragments and let the common spirit evaporate, government has from time to time to shake them to the very centre by War. By this means it confounds the order that has been established and arranged, and violates their right to independence, while the individuals (who, being absorbed therein, get adrift from the whole, striving after inviolable self-existence . . . and personal security), are made, by the task thus imposed on them by government, to feel the power of their lord and master, death. By thus breaking up the form of fixed stability, spirit guards the ethical order from sinking into merely natural existence, preserves the self of which it is conscious, and raises that self to the level of freedom and its own powers."[4] In *The Philosophy of Right* of Berlin, Hegel was to write: "The state is an individual, and individuality essentially implies negation.[5] Hence even if a number of states make themselves into a family, this group as an individual *must engender an opposite and create an enemy.* As a result of war, nations are strengthened, but peoples involved in civil strife also acquire peace at home through making wars abroad. To be sure, war produces insecurity of property, but this insecurity of things is nothing but their transience—which is inevitable. We hear plenty of sermons from the pulpit about the insecurity, vanity and instability of temporal things, but everyone thinks, however much

[1] *Jenenser Realphilosophie*, II, *Die Vorlesungen von 1805/06* (*Werke*, XX), pp. 261 f.

[2] *Phil. of Hist.*, p. 526.

[3] *Ibid.*, p. 552.

[4] *Phenomenology*, p. 474.

[5] Let us not forget that for Hegel in the dialectic of the particular striving towards individuality each makes itself known only by being ready to "injure" the other "unto death". "Each particular ought to put himself as a totality in the consciousness of the other in such a way that he engages against the other, for the preservation of some particularity, his entire phenomenal totality, his life: and similarly each should necessarily have as his end the death of the other. I can know myself in the consciousness of the other as this particular totality [that is to say, as individual or human person] only to the extent that I put myself in his consciousness as being in my exclusion [from him] a totality from exclusion, [that is to say, as] having his death for end. In having his death as my end I expose myself to death, I risk my own life. . . ." *Jenenser Realphilosophie*, I, *Die Vorlesungen von 1803/04*, J. Hoffmeister ed. in *Werke*, XIX, pp. 228 f.

he is moved by what he hears, that he at least will be able to retain his own. But if this insecurity now comes on the scene in the form of hussars with shining sabres and they actualize in real earnest what the preachers have said, then the moving and edifying discourses which foretold all these events turn into curses against the invader. Be that as it may, the fact remains that wars occur when the necessity of the case requires. The seeds burgeon once more, and harangues are silenced by the solemn cycles of history. . . ."[1]

In regard to what we have called the Jupiter of all the false gods, or the Emperor of this world—"who is an absurd counterfeit of God but who is also the imaginary focus whence the adoration of the cosmos radiates, and to whom we pay tribute each time we bow down before the world",[2]—in regard to this false God Christianity is an act of total rupture and absolute rejection. "Thus are we even called atheists. We do proclaim ourselves atheists as regards those whom you call gods."[3] But Hegel proposes this God to us as the very God of Christian philosophy, no doubt, because meditating on the history of Christ in order to feed the "absolute knowledge", with it, Hegel saw from the beginning, in the black fires of his immanentist gnosis, the image of the Lamb of God who bears the sins of the world—the immaculate Logos who although he is "in the form of God" has freely consented to take on the "form of a servant"[4] in order to save us—Hegel saw this image turn into that of a God who had fallen, by virtue of the very law of His being, into the condition of the slave and who, in order to achieve the form of God, and to emerge as Emperor of the world with all the riches of the world integrated into him, had Himself to live through the sins of the world and slave among its crimes, and to bless the fecundity of the negative.

History as the supreme Law of Good and Evil

7. But let us return now to the order of human conduct, to ethics. It is the State that reveals to us the content of the categorical imperative. Yet the State emerged from originally imperfect forms of society and is itself subject to historical development. In reality, it is the dialectical movement of history that determines the substance of *Sittlichkeit* at the various stages of development, even after the State has made its appearance. In other words, if the most obvious characteristic of Hegel's ethics is the voluntary submission to the State which it requires of man, and which for Hegel constitutes freedom, its deepest and most essential characteristic is the obligation it places upon the human will to put itself in unison with history, or to do the will of history

[1] *Phil. of Right*, Addition to § 324, Knox trans., pp. 295 f. (italics ours).

[2] " The Meaning of Contemporary Atheism", in *The Range of Reason*, New York: Scribners, 1952, p. 111; London: Bles, 1953.

[3] Saint Justin Martyr, *The First Apology*, ch. 6, trans. by T. B. Falls in *The Fathers of the Church* ed., New York, 1948, pp. 38 f.

[4] Saint Paul, *Philippians*, II, 6 and 7.

earnestly, patiently and fervidly. It is this full interior consent to, or this full identification with, the universal will expressing itself in history which marks even submission to the State with the seal of Christian freedom. Is not the history of the world, the history of "national spirits",[1] the history of that "series of external forms each one of which declares itself as an actually existing people",[2] is not the history of the world the very history of the city of God, the history of "the divine, absolute development of spirit in its highest forms",[3] *sacred history*? "The carrying out of his [God's] plan—is the History of the World."[4] "The History of the World, with all the changing scenes which its annals present, is this process of development and the realization of spirit—this is the true *Theodicoea*, the justification of God in History."[5] It is through history that the universal Self progresses toward the perfect freedom in which it no longer knows anything beyond itself, and possesses "in the strength of its certainty of itself" "the majesty of absolute self-sufficiency, of absolute αὐτάρκεια, to bind or to loose".[6] And it is the history of humanity "which alone decides the truth of an action emanating from an individual Self".[7]

It is to Hegel that we owe the new attributes and the new connotations by which history has been enriched for the last hundred years, along with the ethical coefficients which they involve. What makes the force of these *entia rationis* or of this kind of mythology is the fact that they have a foundation in reality. For human history does possess an intelligible structure. It passes through typically different periods or climates which have a rational significance. And the factual conditionings on which it depends, and the collective forces or tendencies which are at work in it, determine lines of necessity which limit the field of human freedom while at the same time furnishing it with possibilities and means of action of tremendous breadth. All this is true. But there has been grafted onto this a mythical identification of the movement of history with the will of God (which is natural in Hegelianism, since for it

[1] *Phil. of Hist.*, Sibree trans., p. 104.

[2] *Ibid.*, p. 134.

[3] *Ibid.*, p. 104. Bréhier, *op. cit.*, p. 773: "the history of the degrees of the coming of the spirit." *Phil. of Hist.*, p. 125: "the development of Spirit in *Time*"; cf. *ibid.*, p. 107: "Universal History exhibits the *gradation* in the development of that principle whose substantial *purport* is the consciousness of Freedom."

[4] *Ibid.*, p. 84: "God governs the world: the actual working of his government—*the carrying out of his plan—is the History of the World*" (italics ours).

[5] *Ibid.*, p. 569. Cf. p. 60: This theodicy, attempted by Leibniz "metaphysically in his method, *i.e.*, in indefinite abstract categories", consists in a "harmonizing" of "the thinking Spirit" with "the ill that is found in the World", attained by perceiving "the ultimate design of the World" and "the fact this design has been actually realized in it, and that evil has not been able permanently to assert a competing position".

[6] *Phenomenology*, p. 658.

[7] Hyppolite, *op. cit.*, p. 479. It is history, as Kojève (*op. cit.*, p. 459) writes from his point of view, "which judges men, their actions and their opinions, and in the final analysis also their philosophic opinions".

God makes Himself through and in the course of history). Instead of signifying simply the fact that certain changes or certain needs whose pressure has become irresistible oblige collective life to find a means of adjusting itself to them, the expression "historical necessity" has come to designate a so-called essential necessity (by right) according to which the directions taken by the collective life are supposed to be entirely predetermined. And a mythical relation between man and history has been conceived according to the pattern of the relation between man and God. I would note here that to call upon man's freedom to cooperate with divine grace posed difficult problems for theology but did not involve a contradiction, while to call upon human freedom to cooperate with the necessities of history sounds like complete nonsense. However that may be, the movement of history understood as the will of God, the designs or purposes of history, the inflexible necessities of the development of history which nevertheless require the free gift and the full cooperation of all the energies of man, the sanctions of history, the supreme moral importance of historical efficiency and historical success, these constitute the apparatus of concepts which the schools of thought tributary to Hegel will depend upon for the major regulations of human conduct.

8. *All that is rational is real.* The implication is clear: there is no exigency of reason that is not realized in being, no *ought to be* that is distinct from what really *is.* "The real world is as it ought to be."[1] For Hegel the very notion of an "ought to be" which remains in this state and does not push itself forward into being is an offense to philosophy and condemns itself. "Philosophy speculates on nothing which does not exist. Only that which is is rational. '*Philosophy does not deal with a being so impotent that it lacks the force to push itself forward into existence.*' "[2]

In short, there is no *natural law* in the sense that the whole long tradition of Greco-Roman civilization and Christian civilization understood that word.[3] (Kant had already made a clean sweep of it, while trying unsuccessfully at the same time to restore what he had destroyed. And Hegel as well was to have a theory of natural Right, but founded solely on the freedom of the will

[1] *Phil. of Hist.*, p. 84.

[2] Bréhier, *op. cit.*, p. 772. The citation from Hegel is taken from *Phil. der Religion*, Lasson ed., I, *Begriff der Religion* in *Werke*, XII, p. 73.

[3] It is in a totally different sense that Hegel speaks of the divine or unwritten law. The latter is for him the subterranean law of nature which expresses the non-self-conscious immediateness of that which merely is, and that which it is incumbent on woman (Antigone) to manifest. Cf. *Phenomenology*, pp. 452, 478 f. Elsewhere (*Phil. of Hist.*, p. 87) in order to confirm the supreme rationality of the laws of the State Hegel refers to "the divine commands . . . not of yesterday, nor of today" invoked by Antigone. It is rather surprising for the latter to find herself thus in the long run being made responsible for sanctifying Creon.

To see how far the traditional notion of the natural law was foreign to Hegel's mind (the more so since for a long time, but especially since Hobbes, the notion of the natural law as an ideal order had been lost in that of a state of nature taken as a situation of fact) cf. *Encyclopaedia*, Phil. of Mind, § 502, Wallace trans., p. 112.

which wills itself.)[1] There is no ideal order which, distinct from concrete existence, imposes itself upon the latter as deserving to be realized in it, and which, spontaneously or instinctively knowable to reason in virtue of the essential inclinations of the human being, exists in us as a participation in that order which the Christian Doctors properly called the eternal law, lodged in the uncreated wisdom. For them—and this is quite evident—if, on the level of thought (judging *per modum inclinationis*, and even though slowly advancing in the discernment of particular rules[2]) an *ideal* law is perceived which is superior to fact, or to temporal existence, and which requires of fact and of temporal existence, that they conform to it, it is because that law is founded and rooted in the *real* eternity of the transcendent God, directing all things according to an order which it behooves free agents, just because they are free, to accomplish freely, and which therefore prescribes what they *ought* to do or what *ought* to be. But now with Hegel the eternity which is transcendent to time has vanished. What takes place in time is part of the very internal process of the divine eternity. There is all the more reason that the ideal order founded in this eternity, the ideal order which, as naturally known to us, constitutes the natural law, should vanish also. Everything that is rational is real. It is just what reason prescribes that has or will have the force to be, to impose itself into existence.

It follows from this that the most mysterious and the most certain right is the right exercised by the "stewards of the genius of the Universe", by the great figures of History. They obey moral laws which are above the laws of Morality of the conscience, and which justify these "historic individuals". Judged according to Kantian moralism and romantic liberalism, Napoleon was Evil personified, *das Böse*, but in reality no one has the right to accuse him, for, to express the true thought of Hegel without circumlocution, "Every action is egoistic and criminal, as long as it does not succeed;—but

[1] "The Will is Free only when it does not will anything alien, extrinsic, foreign to itself (for as long as it does so, it is dependent), but wills itself alone—wills the Will. This is absolute Will—the volition to be free. Will making itself its own object is the basis of all Right and Obligation—consequently of all statutory determinations of Right, categorical imperatives, and enjoined obligations. The Freedom of the Will *per se* is the principle and substantial basis of all Right—is itself absolute, inherently eternal Right, and the Supreme Right in comparison with other specific Rights; nay, it is even that by which Man becomes Man, and is therefore the fundamental principle of Spirit." *Phil. of Hist.*, p. 552.

In virtue of this notion of natural law one must say that "the authority of ethical laws is infinitely higher" than that of the laws to which natural objects are subject (*Phil. of Right*, § 146, Knox trans., p. 106), but the moral laws in question are those of *Sittlichkeit* and of obedience due to the State. As Hegel makes clearer further on (*ibid.*, § 148, p. 107) "an immanent and logical 'doctrine of duties' can be nothing except the serial exposition of the relationships which are necessitated by the Idea of freedom and are therefore actual in their entirety, to wit in the state".

[2] Cf. Raïssa Maritain, "Abraham and the Ascent of Conscience" in *The Bridge*, I (1955), pp. 23–52, and our work, *Man and the State*, Chicago: Univ. of Chicago Press, 1951, ch. IV; London: Hollis and Carter, 1954.

Napoleon succeeded."[1] This does not mean that *Moralität* is rejected; it has been sufficiently relativized to cede its place to a superior ethics, at the same time remaining intact in its subjective and uncertain sphere, where it still believes in good actions. But the obligations that it imposes and all its claims are dominated and set aside by a duty which is incomparably more sacred because the ought-to-be is therein possessed of an irresistible potency to push itself forward into being. Men who have been the instruments of history (their whole merit, as we noted previously, was to divine the fact; and in following their ambitions or their personal passions, they were without knowing it the objects of the "cunning of reason"[2]) may have been condemned by the morality of their time, may seem to have been contemners of the moral law,[3] even criminals; but they were all these things in appearance only, for in reality none of that counts. They were preparing the future, they are absolved and justified by history, it makes them white as snow. Their actions "thus appear not only justified in view of that intrinsic result of which they were not conscious, but also from the point of view occupied by the secular moralist".[4] It remains for the virtuous conscience and the envy characteristic of the sphere of *Moralität* to find consolation in seeing that such men were unhappy, that they were as much victims as heroes.[5]

9. But what about the other men, the men of ordinary humanity, insofar as they also are engaged in the movement of history and furnish to it the indispensable material of their energies? No doubt the "inner focus . . . the abstract sphere of conscience—that which comprises the responsibility and moral value of the individual, remains untouched; and is quite shut out from the noisy din of the World's History".[6] But universal history still has the last word, in concrete reality; and once it is no longer a question of the purely private sphere, once the interests of the people are involved, and those of the future of humanity, the ultimate criterion of what must be done is

[1] Kojève, *op. cit.*, p. 153 (*à propos* of *Phenomenology*, Baillie trans., pp. 667 ff.). See below, pp. 206–207.

[2] Cf. *Phil. of Hist.*, p. 81.

[3] "A World-historical individual . . . is devoted to the One Aim, regardless of all else. It is even possible that such men may treat other great, even sacred interests, inconsiderately; conduct which is indeed obnoxious to moral reprehension. But so mighty a form must trample down many an innocent flower—crush to pieces many an object in its path." *Ibid.*, pp. 79 ff.

[4] *Ibid.*, p. 120.

[5] "Their whole life," Hegel writes in a specially eloquent passage, "was labor and trouble; their whole nature was naught else but their master-passion. When their object is attained they fall off like empty hulls from the kernel. They die early, like Alexander; they are murdered, like Caesar; transported to St. Helena, like Napoleon. This fearful consolation—that historical men have not enjoyed what is called happiness, and of which only private life . . . is capable—this consolation those may draw from history, who stand in need of it; and it is craved by Envy." *Ibid.*, pp. 77 f.

[6] *Ibid.*, p. 85.

provided by victory, I mean *historical* victory or success, that of the community, with the destiny of which the individual must identify his own destiny. It is in the measure that he shares that victory that the individual proves and at the same time realizes his mission in respect to the movement of history.[1] History is the judgment of God. The history of the world is the tribunal which judges the world, *Weltgeschichte ist Weltgericht*. To cooperate in the victory of the community, which in virtue of its historical success will be absolved at this tribunal, that is the only requirement that the higher ethics makes of the individual, the ethics which has to do with the destiny of peoples. It was when the one-party systems, the organized prophetic Minorities of the totalitarian type appeared, that this implication of the Hegelian *Sittlichkeit* became fully manifest, an implication more secret but even more deeply rooted than that which has to do with the State. At the same time it became clear that this same *Sittlichkeit* had opened the doors of the modern world to what can best be called absolute Machiavellianism.

"We must then combine justice and might," said Pascal,[2] "and for this end make what is just strong, and what is strong just." But "we cannot give might to justice, because might has gainsaid justice, and has declared that it is she herself who is just. And thus being unable to make what is just strong, we have made what is strong just." This is precisely what Hegel did, but in an incomparably more thorough-going manner than is possible through the force of custom or the social apparatus. In the very truth of things as they are revealed to philosophy, in the sacred scales of infallible Reason, in the judgment of God, it is *just*—in that higher realm where the destinies of States are played out and the necessities of universal history unfolded—it is *just* for injustice to triumph, if it is strong.

Machiavelli made of politics an art absolutely separate from morality, but he never called evil good or good evil; he was content to teach that since politics aims solely at power or success, good politics used good and evil means indiscriminately—honesty and perfidy, justice and injustice, and as things actually go, this results most often in the use of evil, injustice and perfidy. Now, on the contrary, in the perspective established by Hegel, it must be said that the politics which forms the will of history and triumphs because the force of history is invested in it is the higher expression of ethics. It is ethically right, it has God on its side. And the means it uses to guarantee victory, even if they must "necessarily crush many an innocent flower",[3] are for that very reason ethical too, and sacred. The Hegelian critique of the

[1] "For Hegel, the individual judges himself by *success*. In order 'to be right', he has to impose his idea on others, in other words to *realize* it. This is why there are absolute values. States judge themselves in a similar way, by universal history. The true 'test' is action: one criticizes himself by putting his idea to work; one criticizes others by fighting them unto death." Kojève, *op. cit.*, p. 92.

[2] *Pensées*, § 298, trans. by W. F. Trotter, New York: Modern Library ed., 1941, p. 103.

[3] Cf. above, p. 198, note 3.

"moral vision of the world"[1] is not inveighing simply against the kind of moral purism which separates the universe of freedom from the universe of nature after the Kantian fashion, and in which conscience, busy justifying itself by condemning existence, falls in the end into hypocrisy and envy; in the last analysis the Hegelian critique implies that efficiency and purity are only reconciled in the "self-certitude" of "mind" when mind actualizes itself in terms of the truth of what *really is*, in the sacred course of history which constitutes its epiphany. We said a moment ago[2] that the God of Hegel gave His sanction to all the evil as well as to all the good in the world, to all the deceit and all the cruelty as well as to all the generosity which are at work in the world, and that in the name of the sacred necessities of historical development he blessed iniquity, slavery, misery, and the agony of the innocent. Let us add now that the word evil was employed in this connection only as signifying what appears to men engaged in the illusions of the vulgar conscience. These things are no doubt bad from the point of view of *Moralität* and when they concern only the private life of individuals, or—in the higher realm we are dealing with now—when they thwart the purposes of history; but they are good, they are only bad in appearance, we must greet them with all the inner respect, all the *seriousness* of a profound and religious ethical conviction, when they serve the purposes of history and of God who is making Himself through history. When it struggles against the course of the world, the virtuous conscience is without knowing it confronting "actually real good" and "always hits upon places where goodness is found to exist; the good, as the inherent nature of the world's process, is inseparably interwoven with the manifestations of it, with all the ways in which the world's process makes its appearance, and where it is real the good has its own existence too".[3] In short, "The History of the World occupies a higher ground than that on which morality has properly its position."[4]

[1] *Phenomenology*, pp. 615–641.
[2] See above, pp. 191–194.
[3] *Phenomenology*, p. 407.
[4] *Phil. of Hist.*, p. 119. This is why "Moral claims that are irrelevant must not be brought into collision with world-historical deeds and their accomplishment. The Litany of private virtues—modesty, humility, philanthropy and forbearance—must not be raised against them" (*ibid.*, p. 120). Cf. *Phil. of Right*, § 337, Knox trans., p. 215: "At one time the opposition between morals and politics, and the demand that the latter should conform to the former, were much canvassed. On this point only a general remark is required here. The welfare of a state has claims to recognition totally different from those of the welfare of the individual. The ethical substance, the state, has its determinate being, i.e. its right, directly embodied in something existent, something not abstract but concrete, and the principle of its conduct and behaviour can only be this concrete existent and not one of the many universal thoughts supposed to be moral commands. When politics is alleged to clash with morals and so to be always wrong, the doctrine propounded rests on superficial ideas about morality, the nature of the state, and the state's relation to the moral point of view." From the viewpoint of objective morality, of *Sittlichkeit*, "the so-called injustice proper to politics" is thus fully justified. Hegel writes further: "Justice and virtue, wrongdoing, power and vice, talents and their achievements, passions strong and weak, guilt and

10. When it is a matter of any private end, and of "subjective opinion about what is good and better", Hegel can only condemn and reject with contempt the principle that the end justifies the means.[1] But how could the same thing be true in regard to the absolute end? Where the ultimate—and divine—criterion is the achievement of the ends of history, how could the supreme rule of the higher ethics dealing with the destiny of peoples be anything other than that for him who is accomplishing the ends of history the end authorizes and consecrates the means? They are fully consecrated, rendered ethically good. So it is that for the absolute Machiavellianism which our age has witnessed, evil is called good and must be consciously recognized as such, if it has served the ends of history and those who are taken to be the standard-bearers of history. And good is called evil and must be consciously recognized as such, if it has not served the ends of history and the standard-bearers of history.

From the same point of view it must be noted that the judgment of the moral value of human acts varies as history passes through different phases. And no doubt it is true that some ethical rules which are obligatory today could be innocently broken in ages when the moral consciousness had not yet perceived them. But here we have to do with quite a different matter: in the Hegelian perspective it is the ethical rule itself that history causes to vary. History condemns in one epoch what it blessed in another. Yet the great man of action whom history would oblige us to consider a malefactor today, played the role expected of him at the time he lived. At that time he deserved well of history, he was worthy of praise, a hero perhaps. And to-day, even if we disapprove of his conduct when we imagine it as taking place in our own time, he still deserves our full moral approbation for this conduct when we refer to the past.

To tell the truth there is only one residue of evil that is irreducibly bad, unassimilable by the Hegelian "theodicy", and with which the thinking mind cannot *reconcile itself*.[2] That is the illusion and perversity of the particular will presenting itself as universal, or of the individual conscience when, in its contingency and its "subjective opinion", in its radical weakness and its

---

innocence, grandeur in individual and national life, autonomy, fortune and misfortune of states and individuals, all these have their specific significance and worth in the field of known actuality; therein they are judged and therein they have their partial, though only partial justification. *World-history, however, is above the point of view from which these things matter*. Each of its stages is the presence of a necessary moment in the Idea of the world mind, and that moment attains its *absolute right* in that stage. The nation whose life embodies this moment secures its good fortune and fame, and its deeds are brought to fruition" (*ibid.*, § 345, p. 217; italics ours). And still further: "In contrast with this its absolute right of being the vehicle of this present stage in the world mind's development, the minds of the other nations are without rights, and they, along with those whose hour has struck already, count no longer in world history" (*ibid.*, § 347, p. 218).

[1] *Phil. of Hist.*, § 140, pp. 97 f.

[2] Cf. above, p. 195, note 5.

solitude, it presumes to oppose itself to the State or to History, to the universal Will. As the consciences of certain Communist leaders brought to trial by their Party were to feel so keenly, in so profoundly Hegelian a way, the man who gives way to this illusion and to this perversity is irretrievably lost (separated from the spirit of the community, therefore from the very substance and truth of his very being), unless he confesses himself guilty and condemns himself. The others, however dark their deeds may appear to us, have been justified at least at some particular moment—they have done what they had to do.

The higher ethics that Hegel called *Sittlichkeit* is in the last analysis the rationalization and philosophical normalization of the type of morality that some people have permitted themselves in order to justify as good and permissible any act whatever that served (or was thought to serve) the interests of God. (In the perspective of traditional Christianity this type of morality has sometimes been employed, but it was held to be an aberration.) Now it is the glory and the power of the God of Immanence that must be served, by fulfilling the purposes of history. This ethics can be defined as an ethics of dialectical connivance with history, in a so-called "Christian" submission to the Emperor of this world.

Characteristics of the Hegelian Ethic

11. Hegelian ethics may be called *acosmic* in the sense that for absolute idealism there exists no world having extra-mental consistency and reality. But at the same time it is a *pseudo-cosmic* ethics in the sense that, dealing with a world which is not the world, a world taken as a development of the Idea, it brings to an end the Kantian separation between the universe of being and the universe of freedom; and even further, it somehow merges them into each other, since being is nothing but the manifestation and the progress of freedom in search of itself, and since, on the other hand, it is in the communion with the mind of the world, or in the accomplishment of the universal Will expressing itself through the State and through History that freedom for man on the practical level exists. The super-disinterestedness required by Kant is still there, but it no longer consists in pure devotion to duty, it consists in the sacrifice of the individual self, making itself into a pure part, and through this very loss equalizing itself with the supra-personal Whole.

This ethics is as normative, and as imperiously normative as that of Kant. But now the *you ought* of the categorical imperative, its content and its form, are delivered from the heights of the Sinai of the State (or of History). And woe to him who transgresses it! He is thrown on the scrap-heap, expelled from history, *in tenebras exteriores*. As far as the motivation of the subject is concerned, it is only in the imperfect and contradictory stage of *Moralität* that an act is dictated (by the conscience) because it is good; on the level of *Sittlichkeit*, an act is good because it is dictated (by the State, or by History), and its ethical quality or its rectitude (what we call its moral "goodness") depends not on the intrinsic nature of the object but on the fact that this object is prescribed by the universal Will.

And yet (contrary to what is the case with Kant) the notion of the Good is for Hegel part of the very structure of ethics: because his is a metaphysical or metaphysically based ethics.

Is it a question of the Good as Value?—The notion of value is present at every stage of the dialectical development, and the supreme values are revealed to us in the stages of the development of the absolute Spirit. And in the specifically moral sphere the notion of value is also present. But if (on the level of *Sittlichkeit*, or the ethical properly so-called) the value of human acts still has an unconditional character as far as the extrinsic criteria on which it depends are concerned (historical success is an absolute, on the level of events), it is entirely relative as regards the intrinsic nature of these acts, what they are in themselves. In respect to the divine ends of the State and of History, they have a moral value only as means to the end. And if philosophical reflection declares them to be good or bad, it is no longer in virtue of a quality intrinsic to them (conformity to reason), but in virtue of their consequences relative to the ends of the State or the designs of History, or in virtue of their impact on the social community in a given historical context, briefly, in virtue of their results or their effects of a collective nature. By the same token the notion of *bonum honestum*, of the good as right, which is essentially connected with value, and which is maintained in connection with the judgment of acts (by the community—and by the Sage in whom the supreme consciousness is embodied), is also completely relativized as far as the nature or intrinsic quality of the act is concerned.

Thus an essential displacement occurs in relation to the morality of Kant. Finality has become the crucially important thing. The question, "what is the ultimate design of the World?"[1] is primordial for Hegel.

12. Considering the Good as End, then, it must be said that in Hegel's ethics the end has not only been reintegrated, but has primacy over value. It is so thoroughly an ethics of finality that everything in it is justified in the last analysis by the ends of history; and the value of human conduct, at the authentically ethical stage (*Sittlichkeit*) is measured, as we have just seen, by the fact that its results serve or betray the ends (supra-individual, but immanent in time) of the historical process. Moreover, there is in this ethics no

[1] *Phil. of Hist.*, p. 60. This end of the universe is "the *consciousness* of its own freedom on the part of Spirit, and *ipso facto*, the *reality* of that freedom" (*ibid.*, p. 64). Cf. *Phenomenology*, pp. 137 f. Elsewhere in the same work (p. 808) Hegel writes that "the goal of the process [that is to say, of World History] is the revelation of the depth of spiritual life, and this is the Absolute Notion.... The goal ... is Absolute Knowledge or Spirit knowing itself as Spirit."

ultimate subjective end, properly speaking[1] (a corollary of what we have called the dialectical immolation of the person): for if, to use the symbolical language of religion, man is, as Christianity holds him to be, destined to eternity and to "his true home in a supersensuous world—an infinite subjectivity",[2] it is only insofar as he surrenders his own personality in the "consuming fire" of Knowledge, through which God achieves being in him. But there is an objective ultimate end—the self-realization of God (and the whole of humanity) through the dialectical development—to which man-in-history and all things are subordinated and towards which they are borne. But it is not that man-in-history has a relationship of love with this objective ultimate end (one wishes well to an existing person, not to the final stage of a development): before being equalized with it at the end of history, man's relationship with it is one of self-oblation, of voluntarily accepted death and annihilation, in that recognition of the truth of necessity which is the essence of our freedom.

Although, as we have just remarked, Hegelian ethics is essentially an ethics of finality, it must be observed that the very notion of end has lost its rational authenticity and its intelligibility in this system. For in itself the notion of end implies design or intention: before it is attained, the end is known by an intelligence that directs toward that end either the action of the intelligent agent itself or the activity of other agents that are subject to it. Surely there is an immanent finality in the living organism; but since the organism itself is not aware of the end of its activity (the perfecting of its own being), there must be a separate Intelligence that does know it, and that made the organism and activated it toward that end, as it has made and activates the whole of nature. Hegel, on the contrary, doing away with this separate and creative Intelligence, attributes to being as a whole, because it is spirit, an immanent finality that, while it is finality, still presupposes neither previous knowledge nor previous intention of the end. It follows from this that if the end is at the heart of the very process that tends toward it, it is because the end draws the process toward itself as a force which operates within it and moves it; the end is not a terminus to which an essence, with its tendencies and its aspirations and its intrinsic necessities, is preordained in virtue of deriving its very intelligibility from the Primary Intelligence; the end is rather a terminus that *actively*[3] and by itself determines the process of development and its dialectical

[1] The notion of happiness plays a role in *Moralität* but without constituting a real ultimate end, for it is purely abstract and empirical. Cf. above, ch. VIII, pp. 156–157, and *Encyclopaedia*, Phil. of Mind, §§ 505 f., Wallace trans., p. 115.

[2] *Phil. of Hist.*, p. 425.

[3] Cf. *Geschichte der Philosophie*, I, Michelet ed., in *Sämtliche Werke*, XIII, Berlin, 1833, pp. 395 ff. In this passage Hegel gives as an example the immanent finality characteristic of living beings, but without seeing that it poses exactly the same problem as the finality observable in the material world generally, even in the non-living part of it. If "the animal is its own end", this is because it is the product of a creative Intelligence which has thus established its essence, the "form" of which is a "soul" or entelechy.

necessities, in the manner of a magnet (as if a magnet not already realized could by itself perform an action!). What we have here is a hybrid or bastard concept in which the end conceived by the intelligence of the spectator (the philosopher who contemplates things) is by him transported into the very process of efficient causality that the spectacle offers him, there to burgeon in tendency and aspiration. Such an operation has been rendered possible by the transformation of things into Thought; for there, in thought, the end that attracts does exercise a real causation, but through the medium of knowledge and of desire,[1] and not through who knows what pseudo-efficient activity.[2]

But the dangerous ties between Hegelian philosophy and Finality involve still more serious perils, and this time for the philosophy itself. We noted previously[3] that for Hegel self-creation of the real is a ceaseless movement but not a movement without an end, because it is a circular movement whose final terminus is also its point of departure. This is a necessary characteristic of the laws of purely logical (onto-logical) movement: on the one hand, purely logical movement actually takes place in that completely formal eternity proper to Spirit which has returned into itself and is acting as pure thought or denying itself as Nature.[4] But Spirit cannot deny itself as Nature, except because, on the other hand, it is alienated from itself into Nature, in other words because, passing beyond itself, the Logos extrapolates itself into Nature, which is the Whole denying itself as Logos: from this point onward it is in its other—in Time—and as immanent in Time (in the Time of nature in which it is alienated from itself, and in the time of man in which it is reintegrated into itself) that eternity becomes real and concrete; and it is in the circularity of the phases Spirit-Nature-History-Spirit—the spasms of the old serpent that bites its tail—that the law of its own proper discourse or logical (onto-logical) movement is accomplished. We must now add an additional remark, concerning a great difficulty in the system:[5] it is that while the circular movement of the eternal process by which God loses and regains His divine condition goes on without ceasing, on the other hand, as far as man and his life in time (his only life) are concerned, in short, as far as the Time of man (History) is concerned, once the final end of history is reached it is not followed by a relapse and a new beginning, as taught in the ancient schools fascinated by the myth of the eternal return. What should one say then? That once the terminus of history is reached the times are accomplished and remain accomplished for man, who will no doubt always live in time but

[1] Cf. John of Saint Thomas, *Cursus Philosophicus*, Nat. Phil., I pars, quaest. XIII (Reiser ed., 1949, II, pp. 270–287).

[2] Cf. *Geschichte der Philosophie*, I, Michelet ed., *Sämtliche Werke*, VIII, p. 397. "*This activity which determines itself*, which is then also active towards something else, which enters into opposition, but finally abolishes it, dominates it, reflects therein upon itself, this is *the end*, the *νοῦς*, thought" (italics ours).

[3] Cf. above, ch. VII, p. 135.

[4] Hyppolite, *op. cit.*, pp. 568–583.

[5] This difficulty is of the same type as that to which attention was called in the passage from Jean Hyppolite cited above, p. 189, note 3.

who will then live in the perfect autonomy of definitively victorious Reason, with no more dialectical transformations henceforth, and no more self-creation? Will this life, then, be in the nature of a *state*? Are stability and permanence, which had been excluded by definition, restored at the end of all ends, and is becoming then abolished? If this were so, one would have to say that Finality had finally triumphed over Becoming, and that the affirmation of a last End is, for any dialectical philosophy of the Hegelian type, the source of an inevitable incoherence.

13. In view of all this, what happens to obligation in Hegelian ethics? Obligation is no longer the kind of completely interior and completely spiritual constraint exercised upon the will in the depths of the soul by the grasp of universal law, by intelligence of what is intrinsically and in itself good or bad, a constraint which is effective because the will is incapable of willing the bad insofar as it is bad; obligation is now the constraint—disguised as freedom and therefore retaining its character of *moral* obligation—exercised by the commandment of an infinitely more powerful will, that of the State, and still more fundamentally that of History, upon the feeble and precarious will of the individual, which the latter must consent to under pain of being annihilated, separated forever from its own essence and its own truth. This is still another bastard concept, but a concept thanks to which there can exist an "ought to be" which possesses the additional merit and power of "pushing itself into being".

Finally, the same may be said of the notion of culpability.

On the one hand, in the general perspective of the metaphysics or the dialectics of action, a very correct philosophical view of the endless repercussions of our destitution—in the sense that into the best of our actions there slips some element, I do not say of sin, but of impurity—is confused with the idea that every human operation is culpable and involves a species of crime (*Verbrechen*) because it is inevitably tied in with finitude and the affirmation of finitude as such, in other words, because it disturbs being, breaking into it with effectivity and the law of the opposite.[1] Where one ought to say "Only God is holy", Hegel declares: only the stone is innocent—"innocence is an attribute merely of the want of action . . . a state like the mere being of a stone".[2] He thus pushes the positions of Luther to the extreme—and follows in Luther's train as healer, freeing us from the sting of conscience; for if the fault is to this extent universal and inevitable, why torment ourselves with the feeling of culpability, even on those occasions when we might have the best reasons for experiencing the feeling.

On the other hand, within the perspective of *Sittlichkeit*, and of our

[1] Cf. Hyppolite, *op. cit.*, pp. 348 f., 479, 501 ff.

[2] *Phenomenology*, p. 488. Elsewhere (*Phil. of Hist.*, p. 81): "The brute alone is simply innocent." The God of Hegel certainly is not.

obligations toward the State and towards History, the notion of culpability becomes noticeably tougher, and is falsified at the same time. For it no longer designates the state of an agent responsible for having transgressed the moral law that his conscience revealed to him. It designates the state of an agent responsible for having set up his particular judgment against that of the Whole (of the community, of the State, of History), and of having separated himself, isolated himself from the spiritual community, and by that very fact of having cut himself off from the universal Reason at work in the world. Such a notion of culpability retains within a concept which is really social in nature the ghost of a properly moral concept which the former has dismissed and replaced. It follows from this that, by a kind of regression toward the situation of primitive societies, intention counts very little in the evaluation of the fault: if in fact a man is mistaken when he believes, and wills, to act in communion with the spirit of the Whole, this means that he has already broken with it. Finally, the very content of the notion of culpability has been displaced, for henceforth there is no greater crime than to break the absolute right of the State, the objectification of Mind, to be and to increase and to fulfill its historic mission. The "Organic Law"[1] which was to develop later on in Germany, and according to which a man innocent of such and such particular crimes he is accused of, but engaged in activities subversive of the sovereign Whole, deserves punishment all the more (is really all the more guilty) because the innocence in question renders him more dangerous to the State, has thoroughly Hegelian sources. We noted above that *Sittlichkeit* amounts in practice to joyfully offering up the conscience in sacrifice to the State. It amounts also to virtuously offering up to the State (or to the community elected by history) the sacrifice of the innocents, because they are, if they do harm to State (or the community elected by history), guiltier than criminals.

14. Why not end this chapter with a quotation from an author particularly devoted to Hegelian studies, and to the Hegelian philosophy?

"What is, finally," asks M. Kojève,[2] "the morality of Hegel?

"True moral judgments are those made by the State (moral = legal); States themselves are judged by universal History. But for these judgments to have a meaning, it is necessary that History be finished . . .

"What exists is good just in that it exists. Every action tending to negate

[1] The expression comes from Hegel himself, from the Jena period. The *organic natural Law*, he taught at that time, is based on the supreme moral value and the supreme law of the beautiful totality (*die schöne Totalität*), of the "absolute moral totality" which "is nothing other than a people". Cf. *Phenomenology*, pp. 377 f., and *Schriften zur Politik und Rechtsphilosophie*, 2nd ed., *Werke*, VII, p. 371 (cf. Hyppolite's preface to the French translation of the *Philosophie des Rechts*, Paris, 1940, pp. 12 f.) and also p. 415 and *Phil. of Hist.*, pp. 102 ff.

[2] A. Kojève, *op. cit.*, p. 95.

the existing given is therefore bad: a sin. But sin can be pardoned. How? Through its success. Success absolves the crime, because success—is the new reality that *exists*. But how is success to be judged? For this it is necessary that History be terminated. Then we see what maintains itself in existence: definitive reality.

"Christian (Lutheran) origins: every action is a sin; only Hegel (= God) can absolve sins, by pronouncing the judgment of completed universal History (= Christ)."

10

DIALECTICAL MATERIALISM

Marx and His School

Realism and Materialism—Marx Turns Hegel Over

1. It was by breaking completely with idealism that Marx and Engels initiated their celebrated "turning over" of the Hegelian dialectic. ". . . The dialectic of the concept itself became merely the conscious reflex of the dialectical motion of the real world and the dialectic of Hegel was placed upon its head; or rather, turned off its head, on which it was standing before, and placed upon its feet again."[1]

A return to realism, that is the primary significance of this rupture with Hegelian idealism: what first motivated the Marxist "turning over" was the realist instinct inherent in the intelligence, a strong reaction of common sense, convinced of the primacy of the thing over the idea, and not doubting that the object of the human intellect was extra-notional reality. But from the very beginning, and without the least suspicion of the philosophical problem involved therein, this realism was conceived as a materialism; extra-mental reality was confused with matter.[2] What was the source of this confusion?

[1] Engels, *Ludwig Feuerbach and the Outcome of Classical German Philosophy*, in Karl Marx, *Selected Works*, ed. V. Adoratsky, English ed. C. P. Dutt, New York: International Publishers, s.d., Vol. I, p. 453. Cf. Marx, Afterword to the Second German Edition (1873) of *Capital*, Moscow: Foreign Languages Publishing House, 1954, Vol. I, pp. 11–20. The figure of speech used here is itself Hegelian in origin. Hegel had written, for example, in the *Phenomenology of Mind* (trans. J. B. Baillie, New York: The Macmillan Co., 1931, pp. 87–88; London: Allen and Unwin, 1931): "For the naïve consciousness, to give itself up completely and straight away to science is to make an attempt, induced by some unknown influence, all at once to walk on its head. The compulsion to take up this attitude and move about in this position is a constraining force it is urged to fall in with, without ever being prepared for it and with no apparent necessity for doing so"; and in the *Philosophy of History* (Section III, chapter III, trans. J. Sibree, revised ed., New York: The Colonial Press, 1899, p. 447), speaking of the French Revolution: "Never since the sun had stood in the firmament and the planets revolved around him had it been perceived that man's existence centres in his head, *i.e.* in Thought, inspired by which he builds up the world of reality."

Let us note that if the words "dialectical materialism" were not employed by Marx himself, yet they are clearly a description of the "turning-over" pointed out by Engels, and the Marxist school has quite properly adopted them as the stock formula to designate the doctrine of Marx-Engels.

There is a rather detailed discussion of Marxist realism in H. B. Acton, *The Illusion of the Epoch*, London: Cohen and West, 1955, chap. I.

[2] In *Materialism and Empirio-Criticism*, Lenin was to distinguish rightly between "matter" in the sense of the physicist and "matter" in the sense of the philosopher; but as a faithful disciple of Marx and Engels he was to define matter in this second sense as that which

In a general sense, its source lies in the evolution of philosophy in the two preceding centuries, philosophers having got into the habit, beginning with Malebranche and Spinoza, of regarding the subject-object opposition or dichotomy as equivalent to the thought-matter opposition or dichotomy. But in a much more specific sense the confusion in question derives in the case of Marx "from a kind of vengeful apperception of the importance of *material* causality, that is to say, in a general way, of the role of material factors in the course of nature and of history. This material causality takes first place, becomes, while being integrated into the dialectic, the mother-activity."[1] The apperception of which I am speaking, taken in itself, could have been conceptualized in a kind of Aristotelian form-matter or hylomorphist perspective. And who knows what role a certain Aristotelianism, with its notion of a material causality and a formal causality in interaction, may have played in the background of Marx's thought, but without ever being accepted or crossing the threshold of conceptual formulations accepted by him. For Marx, a conceptualization of this kind was simply impossible: because, on the one hand, his aversion for any transcendence forbade him to recognize the autonomy of the spiritual element in man and human history; and because, on the other hand, in injecting the Hegelian dialectic into extra-notional reality, it was in the perspective of the self-movement of discourse

---

exists independently of our consciousness, and so from the very beginning confuse the concept of matter and that of extra-mental reality. "The concept of matter . . . epistemologically implies *nothing but* objective reality existing independently of the human mind and reflected by it." (*Materialism and Empirio-Criticism*, New York: International Publishers Co., Inc., 1927, p. 268.)

There is no "third way" possible, half-way between idealism and realism. In this sense, the criticisms that certain Marxist authors like Georges Lukacs (*Existentialisme ou Marxisme*, Paris: Nagel, 1948), inspired by Lenin's polemic against Mach, direct against the phenomenologist *Wesenschau* or against existentialism, are perfectly well-founded. But they confuse everything by saying *matter* instead of *reality*, and by pretending that materialism is the only conceivable realism (Lenin, *op. cit.*, p. 128), which is a serious error simply from the point of view of the history of philosophy: neither Aristotle nor St. Thomas Aquinas was a materialist. Moreover, Marxist philosophy abstains completely, and with reason, from asking itself any questions concerning the nature of knowledge as such (that is dangerous ground—knowledge implies immateriality), and contents itself with speaking as Engels did of "*reflections* of objective reality in consciousness" (Lukacs, *op. cit.*, p. 263), without defining the precise activity of knowing.

Let us add that the work of Lenin mentioned here furnishes a curious example of dialectical mystification. We are told that the relative or approximative character of scientific truths—partial and in a process of perpetual renewal—concerning the "essence" (the rationally established laws) of things is in harmony with the absolute character of the total truth towards which we are thus progressing and which embraces the cosmic ensemble of all "Immediate phenomena". These views have nothing of the dialectical in them but derive from ordinary, even very ordinary, philosophical reflection; but they are quickly translated into the idea that *the relative is a moment of the absolute*, and offered as a triumph of the dialectical method (cf. Lukacs, *op. cit.*, pp. 272–292).

[1] See our work, *Humanisme intégral*, nouvelle edition, Paris: Fernand Aubier, 1946, p. 53. There is an English translation of this work under the title *True Humanism*, New York: Scribners, 1938 (London: Bles, 1939), with later reprintings.

that he sought to understand the dynamism of reality. Therefore the relation of reciprocal causality in the Aristotelian sense was eliminated, replaced by the dialectical relation in which matter is the term originally posited and the factors pertaining to human consciousness simply an answer, a response whose action can only be secondarily determinant. Moreover, in the Marxist perspective, the dialectical process itself is concerned principally and above all with matter, or the infra-structure, that is, the contradictions and antagonisms engendered by the system of production. And although there may be reciprocal action between the infra-structure and the super-structure, the latter—from the moment that all transcendent reality and all transcendent value from which it might derive an autonomous consistency are eliminated—has its first principle of determination only in the infra-structure to which it reacts, and only therein finds its real meaning for human life. "Morality, religion, metaphysics, all the rest of ideology and their corresponding forms of consciousness, thus no longer retain the semblance of independence. They have no history, no development; but men, developing their material production and their material intercourse, alter along with this their real existence, their thinking and the products of their thinking. Life is not determined by consciousness, but consciousness by life."[1]

If, then, the economic factor is not the unique factor, it is nevertheless the significant and primarily determinant factor, and the one which the will of the collective Titan keeping pace with history must first of all take hold of. "The materialist conception of history, according to which the conditions and forms of production determine the formation and the evolution of human societies, constitutes the capital element of the doctrine of Karl Marx."[2] As we have written in another work,[3] what distinguishes Marxism is not only the fact that it teaches the preponderance of the economic, but the fact

[1] Marx, *The German Ideology, Parts I & III*, ed. R. Pascal, New York: International Publishers, 1947, pp. 14–15 (Marxist Library, Vol. VI). Cf. *A Contribution to the Critique of Political Economy*, trans. N. I. Stone, Chicago: C. H. Kerr and Co., 1904, Author's preface, pp. 11–12: "The mode of production in material life determines the general character of the social, political and spiritual processes of life. It is not the consciousness of men that determines their existence, but, on the contrary, their social existence determines their consciousness"; *A World Without Jews*, trans. Dagobert D. Runes, New York: Philosophical Library, 1959, p. 3: "Respective religions" are "as different stages in the evolution of the human spirit, as successive snake skins shed by history—man being the snake that bore them all".

[2] Auguste Cornu, *Karl Marx, l'homme et l'oeuvre. De l'hégélianisme au matérialisme historique* (Paris: Alcan, 1934), Introduction, p. 1.

Cf. Henri Chambre, *Le Marxisme en Union Soviétique* (Paris: Seuil, 1955), pp. 33–34: "The economic is therefore primary and essential in the thought of Marx. Politics comes back finally to the economic, and sociology is reducible to it. It was this reduction of the social to the economic that was to vitiate the whole analysis of Karl Marx. It is not accidental. It is to be found in *Capital* as well as in *German Ideology* and the *Economico-philosophical Manuscripts of 1844*."

[3] *Humanisme intégral*, pp. 58–59. The views presented in this work and those we are proposing here on the philosophy of Marx are complementary.

that it makes all forms of human life, with all their values and all their efficacy, not denied but vassalized, depend on this material absolute (this human material absolute) in dialectical movement. Hence the singular degradation which Marxism imposes upon philosophical controversy. Instead of offering the fecund insights which it would have been possible to propound in analyzing the real but *accidentally* determining dependence of philosophical doctrines (and especially of their success with the public) upon social behavior and the "economic basis", it holds this dependence to be not only real but *essentially* determining. As a result, it can do nothing more than reconstruct these doctrines and their history from without and as a dependent variable of social conditions, with an incredibly arbitrary naïveté. And in order to register its disagreement with one philosophical school or another, Marxism finds no other supremely critical characterization than the label *reactionary* (or "counter-revolutionary", or "in the service of bourgeois interests"), which is pinned, moreover, quite inevitably, upon everything which is not consistent with the particular Marxist orthodoxy of the moment.

To return to the notional lexicon of Aristotle, let us say that material causality has become purely and simply primary causality.

Marxist Atheism

2. Thus Marx opens his mouth to say "realism" and he pronounces "materialism". A mistake of the same kind can be observed at a more vital and profound juncture in Marxist thought.[1] I refer to the moral revolt which gives the Marxist "turning over" of the Hegelian dialectic all its importance and all its significance.

It will be useful to return to Hegel for a moment here. We know that because history for him was the growth of truth, Hegel held that philosophy was intrinsically measured by history, since in itself philosophy consisted of the achievement of self-consciousness and the manifestation of the spirit of the time. He thus erected into the supreme rule of the effort towards wisdom, to the great relief of our thinkers, that inner whispering which the zeal of philosophers obeys so willingly: you are a child of time, bow down to time, take as the substance of your thought whatever recent authors have said that is most conformable to the coming moment, with the sole view to making it still more conformable. But Hegel believed that he came at the end of all the ages, as a consummation of human history. In fact, he came at the end of an age, as a consummation of three centuries of European history. And there is no philosophy of which one can say so truly as one can say of his that it fulfills his own requirement that philosophy must be the becoming aware and the manifestation of the spirit of the time. Hegelian philosophy was

[1] We use the word "Marxian" when we are thinking of Marx himself *more* than of his school, and the word "Marxist" when we are thinking of his school *as much as* or *more* than Marx himself.

the mirror and the guiding light of all that was to be victorious, imperial, and sure of itself in the period following the French Revolution, when the science of phenomena and capitalism in its golden age launched anthropocentric humanism on its conquest of the earth. Hegelian idealism was perfectly adapted to a state of the world in which the Sign everywhere took precedence over Reality, and which, in an absolute self-confidence of order and of the State, guaranteed in heaven by God—and here below by the armies—still cherished the vastest and firmest hopes in the imperative of an unshakeable *Sittlichkeit* or social morality. It was a philosophy in which the final satisfaction of conscience and of thought was to be found in the world such as we make it; "as a justification of the principle", this philosophy was, as he put it, "general appeasement and general reconciliation".[1] Everything was maintained—for the comfort of man, that is, for the comfort of those among men who enjoyed the privileges of freedom and could play an active role in the movement of history—in so-called "Christian" submission to the immanentist God who justified evil as well as good.

No doubt this philosophy recognized the "working of the negative". It was a philosophy which included disquieting possibilities, and its dialectic of the master and the slave was to be interpreted later in a revolutionary way. But for Hegel himself, who detested revolutionary impatience, this dialectic signified rather that, because the slave did not dare to face death in order to achieve "recognition", he deserved his fate and had not yet crossed the threshold of authentic humanity. If at the same time it was true that the future belonged to him, it was because he was in his turn to emerge victorious by suppressing and surpassing the master, to arrive finally at the superior synthesis of the soldier-citizen. Thus Hegel was like the bird of Minerva, looking at all this dialectic in the evening twilight—in other words from the point of view of what had come about at each successive stage, as memory contemplates it (whereas Marx was to look at it from the opposite point of view, in order to act upon what will come about). Hegel is always on the side of the winner, and at each stage sanctions the success of the strongest, because it is real, and therefore necessary in itself: *Was wirklich ist ist in sich notwendig.*[2]

It is quite true, moreover, that Hegelian optimism has nothing in common with a *Christian Science* point of view. It does not deny the existence of misery and tears, doubt, deception, anguish, or the agonies of the unhappy conscience, or the tragic element in life. It rather feeds upon these things. It is from these things that it takes its departure and by means of them that it makes its way: but only in order to absorb all this victoriously into *the peace which the world gives*, to have done once for all with the infirmity of pity, of revolt, or of scruple. No one succeeded better than Hegel in inducing the

[1] *Philosophie der Religion*, ed. Lasson, I, p. 53 (in *Werke*, XII).
[2] *Philosophie des Rechts*, § 270, Addition (Ed. Lasson, *Werke*, VI, p. 354).

sleep of the just in the powerful and prosperous who might be tormented by a vague anxiety concerning evil done or consented to, in reassuring the troubled conscience, and, by causing it to renounce any wish for an illusory "ought to be", in setting it up in a state of perfect self-confidence, armed and ready for combat, in the actually existing order of things, which will perish to-morrow and be succeeded by another order and then another, all equally blessed by God in their turn, up to the final order to which man will accede when History shall be accomplished (or, as Marx would say, when man shall have mastered his History). Perfect *Befriedigung* is the mark of the sage, and his supreme conquest.[1] *Say to the just that all is well:*[2] it is when he looks at the world and the Emperor of this world that Hegel's sage hears these words, or rather addresses them to himself. After having swallowed the world, the serpent of dialectical gnosis digests it; he is free, sated, desirous only of himself. Having arrived at the stage of absolute knowledge, the spirit returns into itself enriched by all its falls and alienations and by all the misery and all the wars of the contingent, and feels *at home* in the low places as in the high places of human existence. Not without effort, but at last, and by dint of courage, the spirit is content, with itself and with everything.

3. It was against this universe of idealist satisfaction and its implacable Jupiter, wounded and triumphant, that Kierkegaard revolted in the name of subjectivity (in other words, in the name of the human person), and by placing himself at the center of its spiritual anguish. Marx revolted in the name of human work, and the dispossessed human masses, in the name of the "proletariat of all times", by placing himself at the center of its economic and social claims. But it is not just a certain system of production that he denounces; it is the whole world with which Hegelian idealism is in complicity from the beginning, and the full *acceptance* of this world demanded by a wisdom which thinks history *after the fact* and which believes it has already arrived at the final achievement. Marx wants none of the *Befriedigung* meted out by the God of this philosophy.[3] It is against the God of Hegel, against the Emperor of this world that he, like Kierkegaard, is in rebellion. And this rebellion was in itself a protest of human dignity, an act of breaking away from resignation to evil, to injustice, to the false order by which oppression and eternal slavery are maintained. This rebellion might have been Christian —and who knows what messianic passion, rooted in the Judeo-Christian tradition, it obscurely stirred in Marx? In fact, it was atheistic with him.

If the Kierkegaardian rebellion against the false God of Hegel was the

[1] Cf. A. Kojève, *Introduction à la lecture de Hegel*, pp. 110, 272–282. This is why the Hegelian sage "limits himself to *understanding* all, without ever *denying* or *modifying* anything". *Ibid.*, p. 561.

[2] *Isaiah*, III, 10.

[3] "German idealism . . . has but given a transcendental sanction to the rules of existing society." Marx, "Capital Punishment—Mr. Cobden's Pamphlets—Regulations of the Bank of England," New York *Daily Tribune*, Friday, February 18, 1853, p. 3, col. 5.

rebellion of faith, the Marxist rebellion was that of atheism, pure atheism, positive and absolute. Here is the second great and irreparable misapprehension: Marx mistook the God of Hegel for God. In rejecting the God of Hegel, it was God Himself, the true God, whom he rejected, as explicitly, as decisively, as totally as possible, thus tapping the spring from which the paradoxical religion of militant atheism was to flow out upon modern history.

For Marx, atheism is a primary datum, the philosophical elaboration of which he derived from Feuerbach,[1] but which had for him the value of an axiom. We have pointed out in *True Humanism* the essential part played by resentment against the Christian world in Marxist atheism—and not only against the Christian world but against Christianity itself. Thoroughly instructed by Hegel to dismiss as null and void the saying of Christ concerning the coin marked with the effigy of Caesar, how would Marx have distinguished between Christianity—which, pertaining to the spiritual order or the "things that belong to God", transcends every form of culture or civilization—and the Christian world, which pertains to the temporal order or the "things that belong to Caesar", and acquires its character from the collective comportment of the peoples or social strata of Christian denomination in the social and cultural realm at such or such given moments? During twenty centuries of history the Christian world has had numerous opportunities to be false, more or less generally, to its own principles, and it can be said that it has rarely failed to take advantage of them. In the nineteenth century it did so in a peculiarly striking manner, doubtless because by then it was hardly Christian except nominally, or "decoratively". But for a mind nourished on Hegel, the fact that a world composed of sinners is, as a rule, false to that very Christianity whose articles of faith it still professes or seems to profess (and which has its own *city* elsewhere) is a sure sign that Christianity is nothing but an ineffectual ought-to-be which has not been able to thrust itself into *being*, a kind of compensatory superstructure.

Hence the accusation hurled by Marx against Christianity and the Christian love of one's neighbor. ". . . When experience teaches that in 1800 years this love has not worked, that it was not able to transform social conditions, to establish its own kingdom, then surely it clearly follows that this love which could not conquer hate does not offer the vigorous energy necessary for social reforms. This love wastes itself in sentimental phrases which cannot do away with any real, factual conditions; it lulls men to sleep by feeding them lukewarm sentimental pap."[2]

[1] On the atheism of Feuerbach and its relation to the atheism of Marx, cf. Henri de Lubac, *Le drame de l'humanisme athée*, Paris: Spes, 1945, chap. I (English trans.: *The Drama of Atheist Humanism*, New York: Sheed and Ward, 1949; London: Sheed and Ward, 1949).

[2] "Der Volkstribun Redigiert von Herman Kriege", in Marx-Engels, *Historisch-Kritische Gesamtausgabe*, ed. N. Riazanov and V. Adoratski (Berlin-Moscow: Marx-Engels Verlag G.M.B.H., 1927–1935), Abt. I, Band 6, p. 7, note. (Hereafter, *MEGA*).

One may know very well that Christianity has a primary object which does not pertain to the terrestrial order and which has nothing to do with the temporal structures of the world; one may know very well also that Christianity, however, has unceasingly worked gradually to transform these structures by its repercussion on them and by its impact on secular consciousness;[1] yet one cannot help being hurt by Marx's diatribe, however vile the rhetoric it employs—not only because one thinks of the inhuman material conditions in which a tremendous mass of human beings have languished from time immemorial and about which we shall never do *enough*, but also because one thinks of the opportunity which Christianity tragically lost at the very period in which Marx was writing. I refer to the period of the first great crisis of growth of the industrial revolution, when there appeared at the same time the worst abuses to which the social-temporal structures of the modern world had subjected human life, and the forces which at long last afforded the means of changing these very structures, thanks to resources of technical organization and especially to the development of the labor movement. The fact remains, however, that the lines we have quoted from the young Marx indicate a curious ignorance or a curious blindness.[2] Marx did not know, and never came to know, that whereas the lukewarm sentimental pap of which he speaks was the specialty of the domesticated religion of the Hegelian-Christian-State, it is, on the contrary, the sword and the fire which Christ came to bring among us, and that love is the only force *active* enough not to allow what it brings into existence to be corrupted. He did not know, and did not want to know, that his own anger was aroused (we shall return to this point) by a desire for justice,[3] and that this desire for justice which devoured

[1] Cf. our study "L'Eglise Catholique et le progrès social", in *Raison et raisons*, Paris: Egloff, 1947, pp. 289–326; and our book *Christianity and Democracy*, London: Geoffrey Bles, 1945.

[2] In another work of the same period ("Der Kommunismus des Rheinischen Beobachters" [*Deutsche Brusseler Zeitung*, 12 Sept. 1847, No. 73], in *MEGA*, I, 6, p. 278), Marx presents a pure caricature of the "social principles of Christianity", to which, it must be admitted, a certain kind of so-called apologetic literature of the period lent itself only too well, a literature which was also responsible in part for the violence of Proudhon. Consider, for example, the *Dissertation* of the Rev. J. Townsend *On the Poor Laws, by a Well-wisher of Mankind* (1817); this minister of the Gospel, who held the stimulus of hunger in the lower classes to be a providential disposition necessary to the social order, was fair game for Marx.

[3] One thinks of the often-quoted lines from a letter written after the publication of *Capital*, in which Marx excuses himself to a friend for not having written sooner: "I was perpetually hovering on the verge of the grave. Therefore I had to use *every* moment in which I was capable of work in order that I might finish the task to which I have sacrificed my health, my happiness in life and my family. I hope this explanation requires no further supplement. I laugh at the so-called 'practical' men and their wisdom. If one chose to be an ox one could of course turn one's back on the agonies of mankind and look after one's own skin." Marx to S. Meyer, April 30, 1867, in Marx-Engels, *Correspondence, 1846–1895*, trans. Dona Torr, new edition, New York: International Publishers, 1936, Letter no. 95, p. 219.

Louis Gardet has written (in "L'homme Marxiste", *Nova et Vetera*, Oct.–Dec. 1955, p. 259) concerning the chapters in *Capital* which treat of the working day of the worker: "They [these chapters] follow highly technical analyses of absolute and relative surplus-

him, and which he warped by incorporating it into the Manichean myth of the Revolution, and by substituting war for justice, had been awakened in the heart of modern anguish by the ancient faith of Israel and by the Christian faith making their way in the underground of history. He had no idea of the intrinsic forces of the spiritual, or of its law of action.[1] He never glimpsed that which constitutes the mainspring of human history, that struggle between God and evil of which we have spoken above, and in which man's freedom either co-acts with God, being activated by Him, or, through its lapses, condemns history to have the tares grow along with the wheat up to the end of time.

But when Marx reproached Christianity for not having been able to "establish its kingdom here below", what he was thinking of was a kingdom of God on earth which, in his perspective, was the kingdom of Man become the ultimate end in place of God. It is here that we come upon the deepest root of Marxist atheism. On the intellectual level, this root is an immanentism, doubtless not more profound (that is impossible) but less equivocal than that of Hegel, and frankly taken to its logical extremes, an immanentism for which the very God of Hegel is intolerable because, while needing man in order fully to realize Himself, He still dominates man by His majesty and His infinity. For though the God of Hegel be the prince of all false gods, he was still God for Hegel: Hegel's seriousness is never more pronounced than when he is speaking of God. M. Alexander Kojève offers us an atheistic exegesis of the system only because he sees with devastating clarity what Hegel did not see at all—that is, that a God who has absolutely lost all transcendence is absolutely not God. He has thus disengaged one of the most fundamental *virtual* meanings of Hegelian philosophy. But as for its actual and real meaning in the mind of Hegel himself and those who listened to him, this exegesis is untenable. It is clear that for Hegel the Spirit is Freedom (Autonomy), on which everything else depends, and which is infinite; and while in his view man dies forever, the Spirit only passes through death for a series of metamorphoses in which it continues endlessly to be and to act. We must agree with Karl Barth when he writes: "It is a question of whether the definitions with which Hegel surrounded his method allow us to recognize that which

---

value. It would have been sufficient, for the purposes of the demonstration in question, to to give one or two examples and some statistical data. Instead, Marx describes the day (or night) of the worker and of the child laborer in British industry as it existed in his day, and one senses in these lines a kind of shudder which can come only from the heart. No doubt Marx sought thereby to convince his reader. But nothing permits us to think that he was not himself as it were carried away by his indignation and his compassion. With good reason, moreover! . . ."

[1] For Marx, thought exerts no real action in the world except as it is changed into material force. "Material force must be overcome by material force, but theory too turns into material force as soon as it takes possession of the masses." "Zur Kritik der Hegelschen Rechtsphilosophie. Einleitung" [Aus *Deutsch-Franzosische Jahrbucher*, Paris, 1844], in *MEGA*, I, 1/1, p. 614.

he intended and achieved, as knowledge of God. There can be no denying that knowledge of God was what he meant, and that he was speaking from very close to the heart of the matter."[1] "Its intention is to give the honour as expressly as possible to *God* and not to man; and this it expresses quite directly and consistently not *only* in the form of a most naïve human *self*-confidence, but *also* in this form, as explicitly as possible."[2]

At the same time it is true that the system of Hegel is anthropotheistic, and that when God shall have consummated His divinity in and through man, man will have succeeded in making himself man and in making himself God. But in the meantime, the historical labor by which he helps God to make Himself subjects man to a universal Will which, for all that it inhabits not heaven but the web of becoming, must nonetheless either be worshipped in the popular and symbolic perspective of Religion, or, finally, be recognized in the real and veridical perspective of Philosophy as possessing and exercising absolute and infinite rights; and man must bend himself to the will of a master who, while losing all his transcendence in order to become Emperor of the world, requires that everything be sacrificed to his own becoming. There is an appearance of transcendence here, of a false transcendence, which Marx was logically determined to reject. And what, after all, is a God who becomes conscious of Himself in man? In reality, it is man who will free all things, by becoming the sovereign master of nature and of history. It is man and not God who is the final goal of the development. The anthropotheism of Hegel and the a-theism of Marx are both tributary to Judeo-Christian eschatology. But for the latter, time and history are in ontological discontinuity with the beyond-history; they give way to a new earth and new heavens, to the universe of the resurrection. The anthropotheism of Hegel, on the contrary, signifies that Man finally becomes equal with God at the end of History—on the seventh day of History, when, having succeeded in engendering God, History will rest, in a beyond-history in continuity with history, in which time will continue. And the a-theism of Marx signifies that Man has taken the place of God as the ultimate goal of History, and that there is no beyond-history, even in continuity with History. History will continue, like time,[3] but Man will direct it as his reason pleases.

4. It was thus the logic of immanentism, followed out to the end without equivocation or compromise, that was at the root of Marxist atheism on the

[1] *Protestant Thought: From Rousseau to Ritschl*, New York: Harper & Bros., 1959, p. 298.

[2] *Ibid.*, p. 279. Further along (p. 304), Barth remarks, however, that the identification of God with the dialectical movement "implies a scarcely acceptable limitation, even abolition of God's sovereignty, which makes even more questionable the designation of that which Hegel calls mind, idea, reason, etc., as God. This God, the God of Hegel, is at the least his own prisoner."

[3] Concerning History and time, still another typical contrast between Hegelian idealism and dialectical materialism may be noted. For the latter, it is not for Man only, as Hegel said, that the notion of History is valid, but for Nature also.

intellectual level. I believe, however, that the intellectual level is not the only one involved here, and that it is necessary to dig deeper. Everything leads one to think that, on the moral level, a certain primary option of the will, which appears to me generally characteristic of absolute atheism, must have played a decisive role in the case of Marx himself. "If," as I have written elsewhere,[1] "at the moment when he takes stock of himself and decides upon the whole direction of his life, a man confuses the transition from youth to manhood with the refusal not only of childhood's subordinations but of any subordination whatsoever; if he thus considers the rejection of any transcendent law as an act of moral maturity and emancipation; and if he decides to confront good and evil in a totally and absolutely free experience, in which any ultimate end and any rule coming from above are cast aside forever—such a free moral determination, dealing with the primary values of existence, will mean that this man has entirely excluded God from his own universe of life and thought. Here is, in my opinion, the point at which absolute atheism begins in the depths of a man's spiritual activity. But what is this I have just been describing if not a kind of act of faith, an act of faith in reverse gear," whose content is a refusal of God and a decision for combat against God in which the whole soul is engaged?

It is in the light of this act of atheist faith that the Marxist theory of alienation must be viewed (in its Feuerbachian form, alienation of man by the idea of God into which he projects his own essence, and then, in its properly Marxist form, alienation of man by private property, which appropriates the fruits of his labor in order to subjugate him, and which is the real alienation of which the other is a reflection). It is in this light also that we must view the declaration with which Marx began his whole work, and which his youthful enthusiasm only renders more profoundly significant: "In the philosophical calendar, Prometheus is the most eminent saint and martyr";[2] "as long as a drop of blood pulses in its world-vanquishing, absolutely free heart, philosophy will never cease to cry out, with Epicurus, against its adversaries: 'The blasphemer is not the one who holds the gods of the crowd in contempt, but the one who adheres to the idea that the crowd has of the gods.' Philosophy does not conceal the fact. The credo of Prometheus is its own: 'In a word, I hate all the gods.' And this is its proper motto against all the gods of heaven and earth who do not acknowledge human self-consciousness as the supreme divinity."[3]

"Man is the supreme being for man," Marx wrote two years later.[4]

[1] "The Meaning of Contemporary Atheism", in *The Range of Reason*, New York: Scribners, 1952, p. 105; London: Bles, 1953. This article is a translation of *La signification de l'athéisme contemporain* (Paris: Desclée De Brouwer, 1949).

[2] Doctoral thesis: *Differenz der demokritischen und epikureischen Naturphilosophie*, Vorrede, in *MEGA*, I, 1/1, p. 10. [3] *Ibid.*, p. 10.

[4] "Zur Kritik der Hegelschen Rechtsphilosophie. Einleitung", in *MEGA*, I, 1/1, p. 615. The chapter on Marx was already completed and in the hands of the publisher when Père Cottier's book appeared (Georges M. M. Cottier, *L'athéisme du jeune Marx, ses origines*

I

THE ETHICS OF DIALECTICAL CONNIVANCE WITH HISTORY, IN THE ATHEIST REBELLION AGAINST THE EMPEROR OF THIS WORLD

The Marxist Dialectic

5. If Marx turned Hegelianism over, it was at the price of a reaction against Hegel that was doubtless more profound and more violent than is ordinarily admitted; but he remained deeply attached to the dialectical conception of becoming, which he accepted as a definitively acquired discovery, and he carried Hegelian immanentism and anthropocentrism to certain of their most radical extremes. Marx never freed himself of Hegel, remained always under his spell.[1] And in the vital depths of his thought, it is from dialectic as recast by Hegel[2] that he derived his essential weapons and his combat strength; this dialectic is the never-resting genius of Marxism.

It would be well to note here the particular importance of what went on in Marx's mind at the moment of what might be called his incomplete emancipation from Hegel. In his *Critique of Hegel's Philosophy of Law* (1843—Marx was then twenty-five years old), Marx saw clearly that in causing realities like the family, society, the State, and the "political constitution" to be derived

---

hégéliennes, Paris: Vrin, 1959). On many occasions we would have liked to cite this work, of such superior quality historically and philosophically. Let us note at least that his analyses of the thought of Hegel and of the writings of young Marx are of special interest with regard to certain themes met in the present chapter. On the dialectic of the master and the slave and on Marxian atheism, as on the notion of *Gattungswesen*, with the confusion that this implies between every solicitude of the person as such and egotistical interest; on the ethico-eschatological requirement enclosed in the Marxian idea of alienation, on the definition of man by work, on the primacy of the ethical point of view in the young Marx, on all these the author's observations are particularly enlightening. We believe, moreover, that Père Cottier is quite right to translate *Entäusserung* and *Entfremdung* by *kénose* and *aliénation* respectively (Jean Hippolyte translates them by *aliénation* and *extranéation*).

[1] The influence of Darwin on Marx was also very profound (Cf. Jean Hyppolite, "De la structure du '*Capital*' et de quelques présuppositions philosophiques de l'oeuvre de Marx", *Bulletin de la Société française de philosophie*, 42e Année, no. 6, Oct.–Dec., 1946, pp. 169–196. It remained secondary, however, in comparison with that of Hegel.

[2] When Marx wrote in the second edition of *Capital* (1873) that his dialectic was the "direct opposite" of that of Hegel (Afterword to the Second German Edition, Vol. I, Moscow: Foreign Languages Publishing House, 1954, p. 19), it was insofar as one is realist-materialist and the other idealist. But the conception of the dialectic as a method and as knowledge—and as immanent in the real—passed directly from Hegel to Marx. It is thus that Plekhanov can write: "the dialectical method is the most important scientific legacy that German idealism left to its heir, modern materialism", and regard Marx as the "true successor" to Hegel. (*Les questions fondamentales du Marxisme*, Paris: Edit. Sociales, 1950, pp. 128–129.) Cf. V. I. Lenin, "Frederick Engels" (1895) in *Marx-Engels-Marxism*, 2nd English edition, Moscow: Co-operative Publishing Society of Foreign Workers in the U.S.S.R., 1937, p. 52: "*Retaining Hegel's idea of the eternal process of development*, Marx and Engels rejected the preconceived idealist point of view." (Italics ours.)

not from the nature of things but from the logical movement of concepts, Hegelian dialectic was performing a kind of "mystification".[1] But he believed that it was only by virtue of its being *idealist* that the Hegelian dialectic was responsible for this "mystification"; he did not see that it was precisely in virtue of being *dialectic* that Hegelian dialectic was responsible for it.[2] And thus in transporting the Hegelian dialectic into his own materialist realism, he also, without realizing it, transported the "mystification".

The great secret, the supreme arcanum, is always to seek *knowledge* in dialectic, that is, through the logical *ens rationis* or being of reason. This time, it is true, the operation no longer consists in forcing the logical being of reason by inserting the real and experience into it; it consists rather in forcing reality, by inserting the logical being of reason and the process of discourse into it, like a ghost by which it will be possessed. But the result remains the same: it is always the self-movement of the logical being of reason which is supposed to explain the real. Marxist "realism" only adds a new ambivalence. "We comprehended the concepts in our heads once more materialistically—as images of real things instead of regarding the real things as images of this or that stage of development of the absolute concept. Thus dialectics reduced itself to the science of the general laws of motion—both of the external world and of human thought—two sets of laws which are identical in substance, but differ in their expression insofar as the human mind can apply them consciously, while in nature and also up to now for the most part in human history, these laws assert themselves unconsciously in the form of external

[1] "He [Hegel] transformed the subject of the Idea into the product, the attribute of the Idea. He does not explain his thought by the object, but the object following a completed thought fixed in advance and situated in the abstract sphere of Logic. It is not a question of explaining the concrete Idea of the political constitution but rather of relating the political constitution to the abstract Idea, classifying it as a link in the development (*Lebensgeschichte*) of the Idea—an obvious mystification." *Aus der Kritik des Hegelschen Rechtsphilosophie.* Kritik des Hegelschen Staatsrechts (§§ 261–313), in *MEGA*, I, 1/1, pp. 414–415.

[2] In his *Economic and Philosophical Manuscripts* (1844), Marx continues his critique of Hegelian idealism, and insists upon it, but remains at the same time, and always, subjugated to the Hegelian dialectic. "The outstanding thing in Hegel's Phenomenology and its final outcome—that is, the dialectic of negativity as the moving and generating principle—is thus first that Hegel conceives the self-genesis of man as a process, conceives objectification as loss of the object, as alienation and as suppression (*Aufhebung*) of this alienation, that he grasps the essence of *labour* and comprehends objective man—true because real man—as the outcome of man's *own labour*." *Economic and Philosophical Manuscripts of 1844*, trans. M. Milligan, Moscow: Foreign Languages Publishing House, s.d., p. 151 (translation modified).

In the Afterword to the Second German Edition of *Capital* (1873), at the very moment when he declares that his dialectical method is the "direct opposite" of that of Hegel, Marx will continue explicitly to refer himself to the Hegelian dialectic. "The mystifying side of Hegelian dialectic I criticized nearly thirty years ago, at a time when it was still in fashion. . . . The mystification which dialectic suffers in Hegel's hands by no means prevents him from being the first to present its general form of working in a comprehensive and conscious manner. With him it is standing on its head. It must be turned right side up again, if you would discover the rational kernel within the mystical shell." (Vol. I, Moscow: Foreign Languages Publishing House, 1954, p. 20.)

necessity in the midst of an endless series of seeming accidents."[1] The dialectic was reduced to the science of the general laws of movement, Engels says, and he no doubt believed it,[2] but only by dint of fooling himself, and not without assuring us that the laws of the real and those of thought are in the last analysis *the same laws*. In other words, the "ideas of our brains" being the "reflections" of "real objects", if there is a dialectical process in our thought, it is the reflection therein of a dialectical process in extra-mental reality, or matter: the self-movement of the real world, caused by the internal contradictions and oppositions of matter, is the primary fact to which the self-movement of thought, caused by the internal contradictions and oppositions of concepts or ideas, corresponds in the mirror of our brain. There we have the dialectic carried over into extra-notional reality. But by the same token we see the weakness of the system, I mean the lack of critical spirit, the surprising simplism which is at the origin of the operation. Unlike any philosophically authentic realism, Marxist realism has no conception of the mind's own activity in the accomplishment of knowledge, or of the freedom of movement with which the intelligence produces within itself, composes, divides, manipulates its concepts in order through them to bring itself into conformity with what is. He is content with the metaphor of "reflection", or even, in the language of Lenin,[3] of the "copy" or "photograph", and reduces everything involved in the knowing process of thought to the simple parallel, or the simple replica in a mirror, of what is in things. The fact that objects known, *by the very fact of being known*, have in the mind a life of their own, which belongs to the universe of logic, is thus completely ignored. As a result, this life of logic, whose proper place is in thought, and which Hegel had violated in order to introduce reality into it (a reality identified with the Idea), is now in the object before the object is known, in the real as it exists originally, independent of our thought; the life or movement of logic is an intrinsic principle of reality; and if it is also found in the world of ideas or concepts—like a replica of what it is in things—it is that the world of ideas or of concepts is

[1] Engels, *Ludwig Feuerbach*, in Marx, *Selected Works*, Vol. I, pp. 452–453.

[2] In the same way, with a similar objectivist zeal, he was to write: ". . . principles are not the starting point of the investigation, but its final result; they are not applied to Nature and human history, but abstracted from them; . . . principles are only valid insofar as they are in conformity with Nature and history." Engels, *Herr Eugen Dühring's Revolution in Science* (*Anti-Dühring*), trans. E. Burns, New York: International Publishers, 1939, p. 42. However, and here the counterpart is immediately evident, with its illusory themes, "history" not only shows that a process has been realized, but it "demonstrates" that it must necessarily be realized in the future; and it is the *dialectical law* which finally accounts for what happens: ". . . after he [Marx] has proved from history that in fact the process has partially already occurred, and partially must occur in the future, he then also characterizes it as a process which develops in accordance with a definite dialectical law." *Ibid.*, p. 147.

[3] Cf. V. I. Lenin, *Materialism and Empirio-Criticism*, p. 237; see *ibid.*, pp. 240, 274, 285, 359. Professor V. Adoratsky writes similarly: "Our knowledge contains an absolute (unconditional and unquestionable) truth, *viz.*, that it reflects the external world." *Dialectical Materialism*, New York: International Publishers, 1934, pp. 66–67.

the reflection of the real in the mirror of our brain. All possibility of recognizing the being of reason for what it is, and of eliminating it from the explanation of things, is henceforth excluded from the very beginning.

6. It is worth remarking here the peculiar situation created in the history of thought by a philosophy which, for extra-philosophical reasons and in virtue of political and social events of major importance, was to impose itself upon considerable masses of population, but which in itself was so hastily put together that its own characterization of itself consisted of two incompatible terms. It is acting out a contradiction to pretend at the same time to scrutinize reality scientifically ("scientific Socialism", in the manner of the natural sciences) and to explain it dialectically ("dialectical Materialism"). In the first place, the very notion of dialectic loses its proper sense in actual use. One result is that, by making the dialectic pull in its claws and by covering over its distinctive attributes with a magic veil, Marxist doctrine will claim to absorb it entirely into the realm of the real, declaring for example that the three laws of the dialectic are the generalization by Marx and Engels of the data of natural science[1] and that the dialectic is nothing but "the doctrine of evolution".[2]

[1] Cf. *A Soviet History of Philosophy*, extracts translated by William Edgerton, Washington, D.C.: Public Affairs Press, [1950], p. 38.

[2] V. I. Lenin, "The Three Sources and Three Component Parts of Marxism", in Marx, *Selected Works*, Vol. I, p. 35: "The main achievement [among those of classical German philosophy] is *dialectics*, *i.e.*, the doctrine of development in its fuller, deeper form, free from one-sidedness." Elsewhere Lenin writes: "A development that repeats, as it were, the stages already passed but repeats them in a different way, on a higher plane ('negation of negation'); a development, so to speak, in spirals, not in a straight line; a spasmodic, catastrophic, revolutionary development; 'breaks of gradualness'; transformation of quantity into quality; inner impulses for development, imparted by the contradiction, the conflict of different forces and tendencies reacting within a given society; interdependence, and the closest, indissoluble connection between all sides of every phenomenon (history disclosing ever newer and newer sides); a connection that provides the one world-process of motion proceeding according to law—such are some of the features of dialectics as a doctrine of evolution more full of meaning than the current one." "Karl Marx" in Marx, *Selected Works*, Vol. I, p. 28. This passage seems highly significant to us. It has the air of offering an objective or "scientific" description, derived from observation and generalization, while in reality the notion of dialectical self-movement is presupposed, as the key by means of which all of the objective material is interpreted. What appears to be simply a description of the comportment of things derived from observation and generalization remains an application of the dialectic of Hegel, which is the all-purpose weapon. "The contributors to the magazine *Under the Banner of Marxism* must arrange for the systematic study of Hegelian dialectics from a materialist standpoint, i.e., the dialectics which Marx applied practically in his *Capital* and in his historical and political works. . . . Taking as our basis Marx's method of applying the Hegelian dialectics materialistically conceived, we can and should treat this dialectics from all sides, print excerpts from Hegel's principal works in the magazine, interpret them materialistically and comment on them with the help of examples of the way Marx applied dialectics, as well as of examples of dialectics in the sphere of economic and political relations, which recent history, especially modern imperialist war and revolution, is providing in abundance." V. I. Lenin, "On the Significance of Militant Materialism", in Lenin, *Selected Works*, London: Lawrence & Wishart, Ltd., 1939, Vol. XI, pp. 77–78.

The following passage from Stalin shows very clearly how in the official orthodoxy of

Another result is that in the ordinary language of to-day every opposition and every passage from one opposite to another, any process involving phases of action and reaction, ends up being baptized "dialectic". In the second place, when one considers the manner in which Marxist philosophy operates in fact, one notices that while the really objective study of given junctures in history imposes a determined content and restrictive conditions on the explanation by logical entities, the element of objectivity in question serves in reality only to render the peculiar procedures of the dialectical pseudo-knowledge more specious. The "general laws of movement", the play of causes in action and interaction in the world, the processes of the real, these are not neglected, far from it! It is even supposed that everything is being reduced to them, and in fact they are examined with the most arduous attention. But insofar as dialectic is involved in the analysis, these real causes and processes are possessed by logical entities that have been breathed into them, and they are subjected to the explicative power of these entities; in other words, they are in practice dummies, and furnish a "scientific" camouflage for the properly dialectical (Hegelian-dialectical) process of the logical being

---

Marxism the sleight of hand by which the word "dialectic" jumps from logical contradictions in discourse to real contrarieties in nature is executed as something wholly natural and posing no problem, and how by the same means the essential operation—the injection of the logical being of reason and of the movement of human discourse into the reality of nature and of matter—is completely concealed: "Dialectics comes from the Greek *dialego*, to discourse, to debate. In ancient times dialectics was the art of arriving at the truth by disclosing the contradictions in the argument of an opponent and overcoming these contradictions. There were philosophers in ancient times who believed that *the disclosure of contradictions in thought* and the clash of opposite opinions was the best method of arriving at the truth. This *dialectical method of thought, later extended to the phenomena of nature*, developed into the dialectical method of apprehending nature, which regards the phenomena of nature as being in constant movement and undergoing constant change, and the development of nature as the result of the development of the contradictions in nature, as the result of the interaction of opposed forces in nature." Joseph Stalin, "Dialectical and Historical Materialism", written in September 1938 for the *History of the Communist Party of the Soviet Union* (chapter IV), in Stalin, *Selected Writings*, New York: International Publishers, 1942, p. 407. (Italics ours.)

The essential operation that we have mentioned, however, retains all of its importance, and it is not difficult to recognize it underneath its "scientific" disguise. After having in a completely fallacious way indicated the opposition between the dialectic and "metaphysics" in terms of three points (as if "metaphysics" were not the first to point out the universal interdependence of nature, its state of movement and change, the qualitative leaps occasioned in it by quantitative modifications: long before Hegel, Aristotle, in his analysis of the category of measure, exemplified this "dialectical law" of the passage from quantity to quality, in his theory of substantial changes and of ultimate disposition, or in that of organic growth, or that of the "golden mean" of virtue), Stalin goes on to a fourth point, where he affirms (and this time it is quite exclusively a matter of dialectical explanation) that the "internal contradictions" implied in "all things and phenomena of nature" are "the internal content of the process of development", and declares, following Lenin (*Filosofskie tetradi* [Philosophical Notebooks] in *Leninskii Sbornik* [Lenin Miscellany], Moscow, 1929–1930, Vol. XII, p. 263) that dialectic is "the study of the contradictions in *the very essence* of things", and (*Selected Works*, London: Lawrence & Wishart, Ltd., 1939, Vol. XI, pp. 81–82) that "development is the 'struggle' of opposites". (*Ibid.*, p. 410.)

of reason which has been incorporated into the real and from which the system derives its true and essential principles of explanation. This is why on the same page in which he criticizes the Hegelian notion of the dialectical movement of the Idea, Engels concludes with an affirmation of the *dialectical movement of the real world.*[1] The "general laws of movement" of "the external world" are the laws according to which the "external world", the "real world", moves itself *dialectically*, with the very movement by which (Hegelian) logic passes from negation to the negation of negation and from the loss of self to reintegration.

This means that the logical being of reason no longer reigns in the Idea, but in the thing. But while emigrating from the aprioristic universe of the Idea to the experimental universe of matter, and installing itself there as in a conquered country, Marxist dialectic retains the essential traits of the Hegelian dialectic, even though, unlike the latter, it is henceforth directed toward Action, and no longer toward Contemplation.

7. This last point requires some elucidation. It is clear, first of all, that the Marxist dialectic fundamentally presupposes the "theoretical" conception of knowledge which is that of common sense as it was that of Aristotle and of Hegel himself, and which, without feeling the necessity of any philosophical explication, Marx simply uses instinctively, like everyone else. The laws of dialectic development, notably those which determine the movement of history, were in his view the object of a true knowledge because they were consonant with what is. But on this "theoretical" basis a quite different comportment of the knowing intelligence was to develop, simply from the fact that the Marxist approach is at the same time realist-materialist and dialectical. Extra-mental things really exist now, and they are what thought observes and analyzes; yet while they nourish and orient it, they do not furnish it with its formal rule of intelligibility. They are not any more than with Hegel the *measure* of thought, because it is still and always its own logical entities and its own logical process that thought seeks in them. Logic thus retains its primacy over the real (and in a more insidious way, being henceforth fixed within the real itself). Nevertheless, it is in the extra-mental real that the dialectical "knowledge" thus obtained terminates. And what can be the final objective of a knowledge which *terminates* in the real without being *truly measured* by it, if not to *act* on the real and to modify it? That is why *praxis* is consubstantial with philosophy for every dialectical philosophy that wants to be realist. This notion of *praxis* is perhaps idealist in origin, as Gentile held it to be.[2] But in Marxism it takes on a meaning which no longer has anything

[1] "The dialectic of the concept itself became merely the conscious reflex of the dialectical motion of the real world." Engels, *Ludwig Feuerbach* . . . in Marx, *Selected Works*, Vol. I, p. 453. See above, p. 209, note 1, and p. 222, note 1.

[2] Cf. George M. M. Cottier, "La Philosophie de la *praxis*," *Revue Thomiste*, LV, no. 3 (1955), pp. 582–614.

of idealism in it, for it is precisely with respect to the relation of knowledge to things in their most crudely extra-notional existence that it has assumed such an importance.

But let us continue our analysis. If realist-dialectical knowledge, because it terminates in things without being measured by them, has as its final objective to prove its truth only by transforming things, if in the last analysis it is a demiurgic knowledge, then it necessarily follows that what finally determines and fixes the work of the reasoning-that-ends-in-knowledge must be the action to be realized, the change to be effected in the world. By declaring that what is important for philosophy is not to interpret the world but to transform it, and that it is in *praxis* that man must demonstrate the truth of his thought,[1] Marx probably intended especially to attack the Hegelian attitude of contemplative acceptance, and this declaration has even been interpreted as an expression of the most banal platitudes concerning the practical verification of our acts of knowledge.[2] Considered in its own right, however, it goes much further, and casts a great deal of light upon the way in which the Marxist dialectic, even though it may not admit it to itself, really proceeds; its deeper meaning, relative to the very constitutive process of philosophical knowledge, is that *praxis* has the function of furnishing the truth of knowledge. This is by no means a mere pragmatic conception which, in order to define truth, would replace adequation with the real by practical efficiency. What really takes place is at the same time more subtle and more radical than that. It is truth as adequation with the real which is itself made dependent on *praxis*, and which inclines one way or another depending upon the practical end which the dialectical process is moving toward at the moment.

It follows from this that the kind of adaptability-to-all-ends which we pointed out as characteristic of the Hegelian dialectic[3] passes over into Marxist dialectic not simply with the result that Marxist dialectic bears the inevitable mark of arbitrariness characteristic of every dialectic of the Hegelian type (even though it be realist, and, to that very extent, concerned about

[1] "The question whether objective truth is an attribute of human thought—is not a theoretical but a practical question. Man must prove the *truth,* i.e. the reality and power, the 'this-sidedness' of his thinking in *practice*. The dispute over the reality or non-reality of thinking that is isolated from *practice* is a purely scholastic question." "The philosophers have only interpreted the world differently, the point is, to change it." *Theses on Feuerbach*, II and XI, as an Appendix in Marx-Engels, *The German Ideology*, *Parts I & III*, pp. 197, 199. (Italics ours.) Cf. the common translation based on Engels' edition of the *Theses* in Marx, *Selected Works*, Vol. I, pp. 471, 473.

[2] It is thus that in his *Ludwig Feuerbach* . . . (in Marx, *Selected Works*, Vol. I, pp. 432–433) Engels explains that our knowledge concerning the chemical constitution of a given coloring matter is only verified when we are capable of producing the agent in question, and that it was the discovery of a hitherto unknown planet, whose position had previously been computed, which verified the Copernican theory. He might just as well like many a "practical man" who considers himself clever, invoke the example of Diogenes proving the reality of movement by walking.

[3] Cf. above, chap. VII, p. 133.

objectivity),[1] but also with the quite special result that in Marxist dialectic "certitude" and the "demonstration" of "knowledge" are established and determined, even as to primary principles but more especially as to particular conclusions and assertions formulated at a given moment, by reason of revolutionary *praxis* and of the practical end to be attained. Concerned with engendering God when it was waltzing on its head, concerned with transforming the world when it now waltzes on its feet, dialectic turned into *wissen* leads its leader wherever he wants to go, and puts him in a position to make the real say whatever the collectivity which speaks in the name of the proletariat judges in any given context of facts and causal connections to be most advantageous in the struggle of history. This is the case because all of the conflicts, the crises, the causal interactions of the world of real existence, and all the vast materials seized upon by objective observation and analysis and by an attentive and penetrating view of social realities, remain subordinate to the movement, to the conflicts and to the oppositions of the logical entities constructed by the dialectic, as a consequence of which they only receive their decisive rational significance from this movement, from these conflicts and from these oppositions. They can thus serve to "prove" and justify any conclusion (within the limits of a given historical context) toward which either a superior interest discerned by a crudely realist view or the action which the consciousness of the historically chosen community demands, will determine the mind to direct the ever-adaptable mobility of the play of its *entia rationis*.[2]

[1] Cf. above, pp. 223–225. The way in which Marx and Engels, each in his own manner, explain the dialectical law of the transformations of property is a remarkable example of the inevitable arbitrariness we are speaking of here. (Cf. Karl Kautsky, *Materialistische Geschichtsauffaussung*, Berlin: 1927, I, pp. 133–134; Serban Voinea, *La Morale et le Socialisme*, Gand: La Flamme, 1953, p. 301.)

For Marx (*Capital*, Book I, vol. II, part viii, chapter xxxi, Moscow: Foreign Languages Publishing House, 1954, Vol. I, pp. 761 ff.; cf. *Value, Price and Profit*, VII, in Marx, *Selected Works*, Vol. I, pp. 313–314), the historical and dialectical point of departure is small enterprise, with private ownership by the worker of his means of production. Then comes the negation (primitive capitalist accumulation dissolves this form of private property and replaces it with concentrated capitalist private property). Then finally, the negation of the negation (ownership by the worker of the means of collective production).

For Engels on the contrary (*Anti-Dühring*, p. 151), the point of departure is common ownership of land; then comes the negation (transformation into private property); then the negation of the negation (returning to common property of a superior type).

The subsequent developments of Marxism have amply illustrated this inevitable arbitrariness of the Hegelian *organon*. The work of M. Maurice Merleau-Ponty, *Les aventures de la dialectique*, Paris: Gallimard, 1955, is particularly suggestive from this point of view.

[2] Cf. Andrei Zhdanov, in his Speech to the Philosophers (on the subject of Professor Aleksandrov's *History of Philosophy*), *Bolshevik*, 16 (1947), pp. 7–23. In this address Zhadnov recalls that, according to the teaching of Lenin, dialectical materialism "carries the party spirit with it, so to speak, obliging us in every evaluation of events to take directly and openly the point of view of a definite social group". Paragraph 42, quoted in "Andrei Zhdanov's Speech to the Philosophers: An Essay in Interpretation", by J. and M. Miller, *Soviet Studies*, Vol. I, no. 1 (June, 1949), p. 45, note 8.

Insisting more than Marx and Engels had done on the importance of ideology, and on showing in the "philosophy of praxis" "the ideology of the revolutionary workers'

This play of logical beings-of-reason, this dialectical development which a flick of the wrist can deflect in the desired direction, is the Hegelian heritage from which Marxist "science" derives its tools, as well as its astonishing power of adaptation, of mutation and readjustment, every time a new phase in the struggle demands a new application of the fundamental laws.

In order to appreciate to what extent Marx remained a Hegelian in spite of his polemic against Hegel, it is sufficient to consider these fundamental laws which reality obeys in history, according to dialectical materialism as codified by Marx's disciples. There is the law of the unity of opposites reciprocally penetrating each other or being transformed into each other (*Selbstbewegung* caused by internal contradictions), the law of the passage of quantity into quality and of quality into quantity, the law of the negation of negation. By means of such laws we are told how, through a spontaneous process of division necessarily followed by a process of conflict which leads to a phase of integration, man's alienation from himself pursues its history from stage to stage on the familial, economic, political and religious levels, up to the final reconciliation of man with himself, which will be like a return to the original state of evolution in an infinitely richer and more perfect form. What are presented to us here are not processes of real causality, but logical entities, either logical relations or utterly generalized notions, supreme genera through which the real is seen from without, but which are employed in the guise of real factors of explanation, and which are the more easily taken to be real factors from the fact that every ideal entity founded in reality may be mirrored in seemingly actual instances when we pass to the level of the real (such was the case with the beings of reason which ancient physics did not hesitate to use). It is to the manipulation of such logical entities, or of categories like the couples: essence and phenomenon, foundation and condition, form and content, etc., or other cruder ones of a polemical character which mark the enemy with a defamatory stigma, that dialectical materialism owes its remarkable fecundity in myths adapted to action, in the creation of which it utilizes with great success the Manichean instinct characteristic of the myth-making function—the villains of the piece being here those who oppose the inevitable movement of history. And is it not in fact the mark of an intolerable perversity to hinder that which is inevitable?

There is a further tremendous advantage afforded to Marxist materialism

---

movement" (H. Chambre, *op. cit.*, p. 45), it is not surprising that Lenin turned out at the same time to be the prophet of "party spirit". It is in this same perspective that a Marxist author of recognized authority could write: "Every philosophy is a 'politics', and every philosopher is essentially a politician." A. Gramsci, *Il materialismo storico e la filosofia di Benedetto Croce*, Turin: Einaudi, 1949, p. 45, quoted by H. Chambre, *op. cit.*, p. 44.

On the power of the Marxist method to captivate minds, once they agree to "play the dialectical game", see the searching remarks of Louis Gardet in "L'homme Marxiste", *Nova et Vetera*, Oct.–Dec., 1955, pp. 252–254.

by the unlimited flexibility of the dialectical procedure such as we have analyzed it: it permits the system to make room for the true as well as the false when it is necessary, and thus to make all the readjustments it needs in relation to the real, and to reintegrate, even while leaving aside their most profound implications, all kinds of elements of the common treasure of humanity—the primacy of quality over pure quantity, for example, the value of moral energy and of moral discipline, of family stability, of the heroic gift of the self to a higher cause, or (under suitable controls, it is of course to be understood) of freedom itself, of free research and individual rights—values which other brands of materialism find it very difficult to justify. Some of the developments of Marxism in the climate of Soviet Russia are very significant from this point of view.[1] It is because Hegel had identified reality (which for him was thought) with logical process that Marx was able to conceive the idea that *matter* moves itself in a *dialectical* movement, without seeing therein a flagrant contradiction. At the price of sacrificing the principle of contradiction, he thus found himself in possession of matter which—if not living, animated, full of gods, activated from within by an intelligence somewhat like that of the old hylozoists of Greece—was at the very least a matter inhabited by discourse, galvanized in its self-movement by the logical entities which human thought infuses into it, and pregnant with the resources of *our* mind.

Connivance with History

8. It is in the light of the conception of matter which we have just mentioned that the inevitability of the movement of history in the Marxist system must be considered. This inevitability has nothing in common with the strict determination of the course of events as conceived by a mechanistic materialism. It is a functional equivalent of what for Hegel was the will of God incarnated in history. In fact, it is related to the *entia rationis* which, lodged by Marxist dialectic in the core of the infrastructure (economic factors and relations of production), activate or galvanize this matter of history.

The Marxist conception of history runs counter to the Hegelian conception in this, that for Marx " 'history' is not a person apart, using man as a means for its own particular aims; history is nothing but the activity of man pursuing his aims".[2] As he will write in his critique of Proudhon, "man is the actor and the author of his own history".[3] History is not "a person apart, a

[1] Cf. Gustavo A. Wetter, *Il materialismo dialettico sovietico*, Turin: Einaudi, 1948 (there exists an English translation of a later and much revised German edition of this work: *Dialectical Materialism*, trans. P. Heath, New York: Frederick A. Praeger, 1958); Henri Chambre, *Le marxisme en Union Soviétique*, Paris: Editions du Seuil, 1955.

[2] *The Holy Family, or Critique of Critical Critique*, chapter VI, trans. R. Dixon, Moscow: Foreign Languages Publishing House, 1956, p. 125. This title refers to Bruno Bauer and his colleagues.

[3] *Poverty of Philosophy*, chapter II, ed. C. P. Dutt and V. Chattopadhyaya, New York: International Publishers, n.d., p. 98.

metaphysical subject of which real human individuals are but the bearers".[1] History is the action of the masses,[2] it is incarnate in the human multitude, in "real living man".[3] He makes it. But he makes it according to the ineluctable laws of the dialectical movement which is the life of his life; the Hegelian self-motion has emigrated from the Idea-in-evolution to concrete Humanity-in-evolution. This is why capitalism engenders its own negation, socialism, with "the inexorability of a law of nature" as it is said in *Das Kapital*.[4] And this is why "the question is not what this or that proletarian, or even the whole of the proletariat at the moment *considers* as its aim. The question is *what the proletariat is*, and what, consequent on that *being*, it will be compelled to do. Its aim and historical action is irrevocably and obviously demonstrated in its own life situation as well as in the whole organization of bourgeois society to-day."[5] "The working class is revolutionary or it is nothing."[6] "They [the working class] know that in order to work out their own emancipation, and along with it that higher form to which present society is irresistibly tending by its own economical agencies, they will have to pass through long struggles, through a series of historic processes, transforming circumstances and men. They have no ideals to realize, but to set free the elements of the new society with which old collapsing bourgeois society itself is pregnant."[7] If then, the working class has a "full consciousness" of its "*historic mission*" and if it has the "heroic resolve to act up to it",[8] this is because it is fully conscious of the demands of concrete history which make of it (because at the height of the negative it endures the "abstraction of all humanity, even of the *semblance* of humanity",[9] in short it is the "total loss of humanity"[10] and is, in its servitude and in its dispossession, a concentration of the "scandal" and of the "*notorious crime* of the whole society"[11]) the necessary mediator of the "*total redemption* of man",[12] the author of that laicized salvation of the human race represented by "the begetting of man through human labour",[13] the autocreation of the human totality, or of man deified.

It is true that Marx took care to criticize the illusion wherein "later history is made the goal of earlier history" or its "destiny".[14] But in this case as in

[1] *The Holy Family*, chapter VI, p. 107. [2] *Ibid.*, p. 110. [3] *Ibid.*, p. 125.

[4] *Capital*, Book I, vol. II, part viii, chapter xxxii, *ed. cit.*, Vol. I, p. 763.

[5] *The Holy Family*, ch. IV, p. 53. "It cannot abolish the conditions of its own life without abolishing all the inhuman conditions of life of society today which are summed up in its own situation." *Ibid.*, p. 52.

[6] Marx to J. B. Schweitzer, February 13, 1865, as quoted by Marx in his letter to Engels, February 18, 1865, in Marx–Engels, *Correspondence, 1846–1895*, Letter no. 80, p. 190.

[7] *The Civil War in France*, in Marx, *Selected Works*, Vol. II, p. 504.

[8] *Ibid.*, p. 504. (Italics ours.) [9] *The Holy Family*, ch. IV, p. 52.

[10] "Zur Kritik der Hegelschen Rechtsphilosophie. Einleitung", trans. in Bottomore and Rubel, *Karl Marx. Selected Writings in Sociology and Social Philosophy*, London: Watts & Co., 1956, p. 182.

[11] *Ibid.*, p. 180 ff. [12] *Ibid.*, p. 182.

[13] *Economic and Philosophical Manuscripts of 1844*, p. 113.

[14] *The German Ideology, Parts I & III*, p. 38.

many others his effort toward a purely "scientific" conceptualization does not succeed in covering up his messianism. For what he is really criticizing here is again the idealist conception of history, and the attribution to history of "particular goals", as for instance when it is claimed that "the discovery of America is to further the eruption of the French Revolution".[1] If, on the contrary, it is no longer a question of such "abstractions" but of the concrete march toward self-emancipation and total human emancipation which is identical with the very being of the working class, then one sees the idea—or rather the dynamic image, in the unconsciousness as well as in the consciousness of the mind—of the historic mission of the proletariat and of the irresistible demands or exigencies of history, manifestly exercising its sway over Marx's thinking. And among the general run of Marxist thinkers (who will no longer trouble themselves at all about the scruples which in Marx himself were the result of training in philosophical disciplines inherited from the past and of his still fresh break with Hegelian idealism) we shall see this idea of the irresistible demands or exigencies of history reach the height of its mythical power, not only as a theme of propaganda but as a basic conviction.

It is true that there are irreversible proclivities and determinate directions in history which any sound philosophy must recognize. But a *demand* or an *intention*, a *requirement of history*, this is a being of reason which the mind constructs therefrom and which it infuses into the texture of the real (and which in fact Marxism constantly makes use of, even while making a great show of rejecting any notion which too clearly connotes finality). For dialectical materialism it is not the course of particular events, it is this requirement of history which is insurmountable, irresistible, all-powerful. It may pass through a host of accidents—it will inevitably end by being realized. Man can oppose himself to it, then he is guilty and condemned, must be and will be broken. Man can cooperate with it and hasten its realization; and in that case, pending the day when he will become the master of history, he is making history in the degree that he puts his energies in the service of the exigencies of history. He is a chained Titan who is pulled by his very chains in the direction of deliverance and who acts upon history by forging ahead in precisely the direction in which history carries him along.[2]

[1] *The German Ideology, Parts I & III*, p. 38.

[2] It is a rationalization, effected after the fact and wholly superficial, to seek, with Charles Andler or Sidney Hook for example, to reconcile in Marx the inevitability of the historic process and the essential role attached to the will of the masses and their thinkers by saying that the inevitability in question reduces itself to that of a dilemma or of a double possibility: either *this* (communism) or *that* (barbarism), such that it is ethically (but only ethically) necessary to choose *this* (cf. Maximilien Rubel, *Pages choisies pour une Ethique Socialiste*, pp. xxii–xxix). One then disregards Marx's faith in the rationality immanent in the movement of history. When Marx writes (*Poverty of Philosophy*, ed. C. P. Dutt and V. Chattopadhyaya, New York: International Publishers, s.d., p. 147): *le combat ou la mort, la lutte sanguinaire ou le néant* [George Sand—"battle or death, bloody struggle or extinction"], he understands quite well that in reality there is neither death nor extinction, but the combat and the bloody struggle which the historical process inevitably requires and produces. As

Thus, by reason of the Marxist reversal, the role of the human will with regard to history and its irresistible exigencies appears to be greater in historical materialism than in Hegelian idealism. Under the influence of *praxis* Marxism, unlike Hegelianism, has understood the necessity of a "pathetic appeal to the individual",[1] and is more prepared to make a place in its view of things for the action of individuals, which it regards as more decisive in proportion as the situation is more revolutionary.[2] (Nevertheless, the accent is no longer on the great historical individuals, the great men of history, but rather on collective formations and classes, notably on the proletarian class, of whose conscience and will a particular collectivity, the Party, is held to be the organ and the expression.) Man's obedience to the movement of history and man's effect on history are two terms which rather than being in opposition are bound up with each other. One is the direct reason of the other. Human effectiveness has been itself annexed to, and incorporated into, the sovereign power of history—which it will one day annex to itself and reincorporate into the human essence.

The fact remains that in spite of all the differences I have just pointed out, differences which originated in the passage from idealism to dialectical materialism, Marx's idea of history is fundamentally the same as that of Hegel. In both cases history is made into a self-subsisting process, and it develops dialectically, by means of a *Selbstbewegung* whose various phases correspond to exigencies which cannot be denied; passing through alienations and conflicts, these phases tend toward a supreme reintegration or ultimate reconciliation. For both of them "force is the midwife of every old society pregnant with a new one",[3] and it is force and war, with the will to annihilate the enemy of the moment, which are the necessary instruments of progress. Marx simply transferred to social war, the war of the classes, the sacred mission which Hegel laid upon war between nations and empires. For both of them history and its exigencies are raised to a supreme criterion of good and evil, and the primary moral imperative for man is to conform willingly to the

---

we have indicated in the text, what the Hegelian dialectic reset upon its feet taught Marx is at once and by the same means the inevitability of the heroic engagement itself of the proletariat in combat, and the essential role of this willing engagement in the very inevitability of historical movement. In the absence of any philosophical affirmation of freedom of choice (*liberum arbitrium*) and of any philosophical doctrine of moral obligation, obviously no valid theoretical solution of the antinomy was possible. Understandably the solution for Marx was, and could be, only practical. From the Marxian point of view, as Maximilien Rubel correctly writes (*Pages choisies* . . ., p. xxxi), "the solution of theoretical antinomies is indeed possible only in a *practical* manner" and this is precisely what the theses on Feuerbach state, notably thesis III: "The coincidence of the changing circumstances and of human activity or self-changing can only be comprehended and rationally understood as *revolutionary practice*." As an Appendix to *The German Ideology, Parts I & III*, p. 198 (cf. the translation in Marx, *Selected Works*, Vol. I, p. 472).

[1] Maximilien Rubel, *Pages choisies* . . ., p. xliv.

[2] Cf. Georges Lukacs, *op. cit.*, p. 235.

[3] *Capital*, Book I, vol. II, part viii, chapter xxxi, *ed. cit.*, Vol. I, p. 751.

designs of history (they say modestly, the "necessities" of history,[1] but charge the latter word with all the content of the former), to be in heart as in action in connivance with history.

The obligation to be in connivance with history is just as strong, as total, as fundamental for Marx as for Hegel. It is difficult for the observer who is determined to maintain the freedom of the critical mind not to conclude from this that in the last analysis Marx was vanquished by the false God of Hegel, of whom it must be asked that his will be done on earth not *as* it is done *in heaven* but *as* the *earth* exhibits it, and asked while bowing the knee to history.

We remarked on this fact, which seems to us to be of capital importance in the analysis of contemporary atheism, in another study from which we shall quote several passages here, and in which we showed that the atheism of historical materialism condemned to failure its own original rebellion against the Emperor of this world. What is, we said, in effect, the "actual end-all of the philosophy of absolute Immanence which is all one with absolute atheism? Everything which was formerly considered superior to time and participating in some transcendent quality—either ideal value or spiritual reality—is now absorbed in the movement of temporal existence and the all-engulfing ocean of Becoming and of History. Truth and justice, good and evil, faithfulness, all the standards of conscience, henceforth perfectly relativized, become radically contingent: they are but changing shapes of the process of History, just as for Descartes they were but contingent creations of divine Freedom. The truth, at any given moment, is that which conforms with the requirements of History's begettings. As a result truth changes as time goes on. An act of mine which was meritorious to-day will be criminal tomorrow. And that is the way my conscience will pass judgment on it. The human intellect and moral conscience have to become heroically tractable."[2]

Thus the rupture with God, which "began as a claim to total independence and emancipation, as a proud revolutionary break with everything that submits man to alienation and heteronomy", "ends up in obeisance and prostrate submission to the all-powerful movement of History, in a kind of sacred surrender of the human soul to the blind god of History".[3] Instead of hurling against the Emperor of this world "the strength of the true God, and of giving himself to the work of the true God, as the saint does, the atheist, because he rejects the true God, can only struggle against the Jupiter of this world by calling on the strength of the immanent god of History, and by dedicating himself to the work of that immanent god. It is indeed because he believes in the revolutionary disruptive power of the impetus of History, and because he

[1] It is curious to note that, according to Wetter (*op. cit.*, p. 327), the way in which Soviet philosophers explain the category of necessity (as opposed to the fortuitous) allows us to glimpse a certain appeal to finality.

[2] "The Meaning of Contemporary Atheism", in *The Range of Reason*, pp. 106–107.

[3] *Ibid.*, p. 108.

expects from it the final emancipation of man, that the atheist delivers over his own soul to the blind god of History. Yet he is caught in a trap. Wait a while, and the blind god of History will appear just as he is—yes, the very same Jupiter of this world, the great god of the idolaters and the powerful on their thrones and the rich in their earthly glory, and of success which knows no law, and of mere fact set up as law. He will reveal himself as this same false god in a new disguise and crowned by new idolaters, and meting out a new brand of power and success. And it is too late for the atheist. . . . He is possessed by this god. He is on his knees before History. With respect to a god who is not God, he is the most tractable and obedient of the devotees."[1]

II

MARXIST HUMANISM

Towards true Man or deified Man as Human Species or Human Community

9. "Man is the supreme being for man." For Marx it is only in Man—and not, as it was for Hegel, in God (in God in Man)—that history has its ultimate end. The end toward which the flow of becoming moves is the engendering not of God but of Man as having finally reconquered the plenitude of his essence and his freedom—the engendering of "deified man or *true man*, who apprehends himself as the creator of his own history and who *makes* his own history".[2] It is in this way that communism is at the same time a "fully-developed naturalism" and a "fully-developed humanism", and that it brings "the *genuine* resolution of the conflict between man and nature and between man and man—the true resolution of the strife between existence and essence, between objectification and self-confirmation, the individual and the species. Communism is the riddle of history solved, and it knows itself to be this

[1] "The Meaning of Contemporary Atheism", in *The Range of Reason*, p. 112.

[2] "As proletarian, man becomes the produce of his own product, he is reduced to the state of a simple cog in the immense machine which is greater than he is, and whose overall workings Marx is determined to grasp. Capital produces itself, or rather reproduces itself and grows; it is Capital which determines men, which determines the conditions of reproduction, of the nourishment or life of men as a group. But a moment comes when this alienation becomes a living contradiction. This moment is the moment of the proletariat. In the proletariat, and especially in the general proletarianization of society, man is no longer anything but the inert product of his own product. Now according to Hegel, the consciousness of man is 'absolute elasticity'. It cannot reconcile itself to perceiving itself as a mere thing. Its final state of inertia is therefore the condition of its own resurgence. That is why human consciousness regrasps itself in the proletariat and in the proletarianized Society. This class consciousness is at the same time a human consciousness, a consciousness which becomes creative of a new order. Communism . . . is the active negation of its negation, capitalism, but this negation of the negation is authentically affirmative. It is the idea realized, man deified or *true man*, who grasps himself as the creator of his history and the one *who makes it*." Jean Hyppolite, "Marxisme et Philosophie", *Revue Socialiste*, November, 1946, pp. 548–549.

solution."[1] After all the alienations and all the antagonisms, it causes history to open out into the final realization of the divinity of man; for the "true end of the quarrel between existence and essence" is none other than that absolute independence which the theologians call *aseitas*, and of the conquest of which man's mastery over his history will be the sign and the manifestation.[2] Marx, like Hegel, is not at all interested in free will, but only in freedom from coercion. Independence and power, which man gains little by little in the course of his struggle with nature, in passing through diverse forms of society,[3] is the only kind of freedom he recognizes, and this freedom, which consists for him of *necessity understood or recognized*[4] (and put to work), will reach its peak in "deified man" or "true man".[5]

It is clear that the Man in question in all this is and can only be collective man, humanity (at the same time in the sense of the human species and of the universal social community). The divine attributes, and the government of history, are obviously too heavy a burden for individual man. Every philosophy of the deification of man (in whatever form it may occur: the State of Hegel,[6]

[1] Marx, *Economic and Philosophical Manuscripts of 1844*, p. 102.

It is on this dogmatic theme that the Marxist philosophy of history depends—and it is this which keeps it from being an authentic philosophy of history. If contemporary Marxists had an authentically philosophical view of history they would understand that all the uproar and all the agitation concerning the advent of the communist revolution into the world in the second half of the twentieth century only proceeds in reality from an ideological fixation. In actual fact, their revolution is no longer ahead of them, it is behind them, it has *already taken place—in* Russia. And having taken place at this point in the world, it has taken place *for* the world, just as, having taken place in France, the French Revolution has taken place not only for France but for the world. No doubt the communist revolution can be *extended*, as has happened in China, but this process of extension is necessarily limited by the resistance of the areas of noncommunist civilization whose reactions of self-preservation have been awakened. Under these conditions, the historical process which will really take place is that according to which the noncommunist peoples must henceforth assimilate, each according to its own spirit and its own structures, the effects, the recoils, and the general results of the revolution of 1917, while the communist peoples, on their side, must stabilize themselves and evolve new internal structures proper to themselves.

[2] Cf. G. V. Plekhanov, *Les questions fondamentales du marxisme*, Paris: Editions sociales, 1950, p. 83: "In his *Philosophy of Religion, Oeuvres Complètes*, vol. xii, p. 98, Hegel says: 'Die Freiheit ist dies, nichts zu wollen als sich,' that is to say: *Freedom consists in willing nothing other than oneself*. . . . It would be the same for the proletariat, which would transform the means of production into social property and organize social production on new bases: *it would will nothing but itself*. And it would feel itself completely free. . . ." (Italics ours.)

[3] Cf. Georges Lukacs, *op. cit.*, p. 183.

[4] "Freedom is the appreciation of necessity." Engels, *Anti-Dühring*, p. 125. The saying is taken up by Lenin—"Karl Marx" (1914), in Marx, *Selected Works*, Vol. I, p. 26—and is classic in Marxist authors.

[5] Cf. above, p. 234, note 2. This "deified man", or "true man", is what Marx called *whole man* ("Man appropriates his total essence in a total manner, that is to say, as a whole man." *Economic and Philosophical Manuscripts of 1844*, p. 106)—the "supreme instance", as H. Lefebvre says (*Le matérialisme dialectique*, Paris: P.U.F., p. 149), of communist humanism.

[6] And even his absolute Knowledge: for the Hegelian Sage, who moreover abandons his subjective individuality, "consumed like a gnat", through the intuition of the eternal, is only the point of convergence of the history of man and the whole of philosophy.

or the Great Being of Auguste Comte, or the Communist Society of Marx) leaves the individual person out of consideration, and concerns itself only with social man, in whom history is made and consummated.

Before going any further we must make a brief digression to clear up a question of vocabulary, which, like several other similar questions, owes its existence to the fact that Marx's philosophy, as systematic as it is, remained in many ways insufficiently elaborated—the price of *praxis*, and of perpetual polemic aggressiveness, had to be paid. The question which occupies us here concerns the notion of human nature. In one sense, there is no longer any human nature, in the philosophical sense of this term, for Marx any more than for Hegel, because for him as for Hegel man is action and makes himself or creates himself by an unlimited process of transformation.[1] The classical notion of nature as an intelligible structure immutably defined in itself must therefore be rejected; let us say that for Marx there is no human *nature*, underlining the word "nature".[2] But nevertheless, man is for Marx (as he was for Hegel, but in a perspective at once ontological and idealist which is not that of Marx) a being distinct from every other, recognizable by certain typical characteristics,[3] and even so far set apart that he is on the march toward his own deification. And it is his very capacity for infinitization which distinguishes him most profoundly from every other being. It should be noted that for Marx man

[1] "M. Proudhon does not know that all history is nothing but a continuous transformation of human nature." Marx, *Poverty of Philosophy*, p. 124.

Marx will similarly write in *Capital*, that in acting on the external world and changing it, man at the same time changes his own nature.

[2] This does not keep the essence of man, from which man is now alienated and which he must reconquer in the end, from being an important part of the Marxist system. But this essence (the word still had a completely Hegelian signification for the young Marx) is not at all a synonym of human nature: indeed it is nothing other than freedom in the Hegelian sense, the autonomy which will be fully realized in true man or deified man. "Freedom is . . . the essence of man," wrote Marx in the *Rheinische Zeitung* in 1842. ("Debatten uber Pressfreiheit und Publikation der Landstandischen Verhandlungen" [*Rheinische Zeitung*, 12 (May, 1842), no. 132] in *MEGA*, I, 1/1, p. 202.

[3] Cf. *The German Ideology, Parts I & III*, pp. 7 ff.; *Economic and Philosophical Manuscripts of 1844*, pp. 75–76. Some Marxist authors will speak, for example, of the three distinctive traits of man, which are articulated language, abstract thought, and the fabrication of tools (cf. A. Pannekoek, *Marxismus und Darwinismus*, Leipzig, 1914. Marx himself, in *Capital* (Book I, vol. I, part iii, chapter vii, *ed. cit.* Vol. I, p. 179), described man, following Franklin, as a tool-making animal). But these characteristics have only a purely empirical significance for them, and are not the properties of a *nature* in the philosophical sense of that word.

Let us add that Marxism seems to be totally ignorant of the authentic concept of nature (as an intelligible object immutable *in its specific characteristics* but *existing in time*); he regularly confuses this concept with that of a thing *absolutely immutable* and *existing above time* (like a separated Platonic type, or like the Kantian "thing in itself") and which can neither evolve, transform itself, nor progress inside its specific limits, nor permit a substantial transformation as a result of which the specific nature of the descendants of an organism will be other than the specific nature of the organism itself, as happens according to the transformist view. In fact, when Marxist authors attack the notion of nature, they most often appear to do so in the name of a transformism whose philosophical import is childishly conceived.

becomes infinite not, as for the ancients, in the "intentional" order of knowledge and love, but in the very order of entitative being, through the series of self-creative moultings through which he passes in the course of history. We shall say then that for Marx (as for Hegel) man has a human specificity or a specific-human-being,[1] but one which is not immutable in any respect; and that in this sense, from which not only every Platonic but even every Aristotelian, and even every philosophically consistent connotation has been banished, the notion designated by the words "human nature"—which Marx no more refrains from using than does ordinary language—occupy a central place in his thought, as central as the notion of man.

10. Having closed this parenthesis, we may return to our discussion of Marxist humanism. Could one speak of a *humanism* if there were not a human specificity or a specific-human-being? A feeling for the dignity of the specific-human-being—or of human nature—played a role of crucial importance in the formation of Marx's thought. It is thus that he is everywhere seeking to discover the real texture of human relations, which is concealed by what appears at first glance as mere relations among things. His great reproach against present society is that it is a *dehumanized world*.[2] Was not his central intuition, "the great ray of truth which traverses his whole work",[3] that of the dehumanization with which both the propertied man and the proletarian are simultaneously stricken in a world subjected to the sovereign rule of pure capitalist profit and the fecundity of money? His habits of Hegelian thought made him conceptualize this intuition in a philosophy of dialectical antagonism, in which the proletariat became the Antithesis invested with the creative power of Negation, and by the same token the instrument of Reintegration; at the same time his atheism made him conceptualize the same intuition in the philosophy of deification of man of which we have just spoken. And in such a perspective, "if the economic serfdom and the inhuman condition which is that of the proletariat are to cease, it is not in the name of the human person—whose dignity has a spiritual basis, and which in respect to economic conditions has such imperious needs only because it is ultimately ordered to transcendent goods and rights—it is in the name of collective man, so that he may find in his own collective life and in the free disposition of his collective work an absolute liberation (*aseitas*, in reality), and finally deify in himself the titanism of human nature".[4]

We know what Marx himself owed to the humanist tradition, and the value he attached to the works of the mind; he was a great reader of Goethe and

[1] I.e., *Gattungswesen*. Cf. *Economic and Philosophical Manuscripts of 1844*, pp. 76, 105, 158 (and the German text in *MEGA*, I, 3, pp. 87, 88); "Zur Judenfrage" [*Deutsch-Franzosische Jahrbuch*, August–November, 1843] in *MEGA*, I, 1/1, p. 584.

[2] Marx to Ruge, May, 1843, in *MEGA*, I, 1/1, p. 562.

[3] Cf. *Humanisme intégral*, pp. 54–55.

[4] *Ibid.*, p. 55.

of Heine (he formed a friendship with the latter in Paris), and he could not dispense with the tragic visions he found in Aeschylus, Shakespeare and Dante—this atheist was a fervent admirer of the *Divine Comedy*.[1] Although Bakunin was able to reproach him with much "vanity", and with "petty hatred",[2] the mutual attachment and the constant collaboration between Engels and himself enabled Lenin, waxing elegiac for the occasion, to place their relationship alongside the great examples of friendship celebrated by the classic tradition.[3] It would seem that a recollection of Aristotelian felicity, and the exalted feeling he had for the nobility of human thought, are reflected in the kind of golden age he dreamed of as the result of the advent of communism, in which, now that humanity would finally take the "leap from the realm of necessity into the realm of freedom",[4] not only would men make their history themselves in full consciousness, but the enjoyment of the treasures of culture and knowledge would be the lot of the whole community. And if Marx objects to the Hegelian cult of the State, if after the use that the dictatorship of the proletariat will inevitably have to make of the State (of the State in the full Hegelian sense), the State is to disappear in the end,[5] it is because at the end of the development there must be nothing and there will be nothing above man, not even human power separated from man and deified in the State. It is man himself (the human species and the human social community, henceforth identified with each other in communist humanity) which in the end will be deified, or restored to the full truth of his essence. Marxism is a humanism —an atheistic humanism in which the anthropocentric humanism of the rationalist centuries reaches its full realization.[6]

But this humanism is a humanism of the generic-human-being, a humanism of human nature expanded and consummated in human society—it knows nothing of the human person as such. Because it does not want to recognize anything which carries with it a reflection of the divine transcendence, it is purely and simply ignorant of what distinctively constitutes the person (the fact of being a whole, a universe in itself). While it sees correctly that man is only man in society, it does not understand that in the last analysis this is only

[1] Cf. Paul Lafargue, "Reminiscences of Marx", in Marx, *Selected Works*, Vol. I, p. 84.
[2] Cf. A. Cornu, *op. cit.*, p. 346.
[3] Lenin, "Frederick Engels" (1895), in *Marx-Engels-Marxism*, pp. 56–57.
[4] Engels, *Socialism: Utopian and Scientific*, III, in Marx, *Selected Works*, Vol. I, p. 186. Cf. Engels, *Anti-Dühring*, p. 310.
[5] "The first act in which the State really comes forward as the representative of society as a whole—the taking possession of the means of production in the name of society—is at the same time its last independent act as a State. The interference of the State power in social relations becomes superfluous in one sphere after another, and then ceases of itself. The government of persons is replaced by the administration of things and the direction of the processes of production. The State is not 'abolished', *it withers away.*" Engels, *Anti-Dühring*, p. 307. Cf. Engels, *Socialism: Utopian and Scientific*, in Marx, *Selected Works*, Vol. I, p. 182; *The Origin of the Family, Private Property and the State*, New York: International Publishers, s.d., p. 158.
[6] Cf. our work *Humanisme intégral*, chapter I ("La tragédie de l'humanisme"), pp. 16–42.

in order to transcend society (the society of creatures). In short, it conceives of the individual only as a *social being*;[1] the individual is in no sense a whole and in no way emerges above the social whole. The social whole is not composed of wholes. Not only is the individual a part of society, but he has no reality and no true human dignity except insofar as he is a part of society. All of this is pure Hegel, wrenched out of the Hegelian metaphysical perspective. No more than in *Tun Aller und Jeder* is there the least element of personalism in the formula of the Communist Manifesto: "In place of the old bourgeois society, with its classes and class antagonisms, we shall have an association, in which the free development of each is the condition for the free development of all",[2] or in the old fighting slogan, "one for all, all for one". The meaning of these formulae is that in the communist society the good of the whole will necessarily be the good of the parts because the integration of the parts into the whole and of the parts among themselves will be so perfect that all the old conflicts will have been surmounted. They do not mean at all that the good of the social whole will flow back upon its parts in virtue of the fact that they are themselves wholes or persons, having their inalienable rights, and a destiny superior to that of the social-temporal whole. This notion of the necessary redistribution of the common good to persons (it is only on this condition that it is the *common* good)[3] makes no more sense for Marxism than for Hegelianism. And so thoroughly do the Marxist theoreticians ignore the human person that when they are trying to formulate a conception of the ultimate flowering of the human individual in the completely realized communist society, what they imagine is nothing more than an individual who is in a position to fulfill equally well all of the social functions, an encyclopedically and polytechnically social individual, capable of doing anything in the society. Communism is marching toward "the education, training and preparation of people who will have an all-round development, an all-round training, people who will be able to do everything".[4]

[1] "The individual *is the social being*." Marx, *Economic and Philosophical Manuscripts of 1844*, p. 104. Cf. *ibid.*: ". . . the *human* essence of nature first exists only for *social* man; for only here does nature exist for him as a bond with man. . . . Thus *society* is the consummated oneness in substance of men and nature—the true resurrection of nature—the naturalism of man and the humanism of nature both brought to fulfillment." Cf. also *Theses on Feuerbach* (thesis VI): "In its reality it [the essence of man] is the *ensemble* (aggregate) of social relations." As an Appendix in *The German Ideology, Parts I & III*, p. 198.

[2] *Manifesto of the Communist Party*, in Marx, *Selected Works*, Vol. I, p. 228.

[3] Cf. our study *La personne et le bien commun*, Paris: Desclée de Brouwer, s.d. [1947] (English trans.: *The Person and the Common Good*, New York: Scribners, 1947; London: Bles, 1957).

[4] V. I. Lenin, "*Left-Wing*" *Communism: An Infantile Disorder*, revised trans., New York: International Publishers, 1934, p. 33 (cf. Lenin, *Selected Works*, London: Lawrence & Wishart, 1947, Vol. II, p. 594). Marx had written in *Capital* (Book I, vol. II, part iv, chapter xv, section 9, *ed. cit.*, Vol. I, pp. 487–488): "Modern Industry, on the other hand, through its catastrophes imposes the necessity of recognizing, as a fundamental law of production, variation of work, consequently fitness of the labourer for varied work, consequently the

In the last analysis, what we have here is the perpetuation in atheistic Marxist humanism of that dialectical immolation of the human person which Hegel undertook. As we wrote in the essay already referred to in speaking of atheism, "What of the self, the person, the problem of human destiny? . . . There is nothing eternal in man; he will die in the totality of his being; there is nothing to be saved in him. But he can give himself, and give himself entirely, to the whole of which he is a part."[1] By virtue of the primordial moral choice—against all transcendence—which we spoke of above,[2] "the absolute or positive atheist hands himself over, body and soul, to the ever-changing and all-engulfing whole—be it the social or the cosmic totality. It is not only that he is satisfied to die in it as a blade of grass in the loam, and to make it more fertile by dissolving in it. He is also willing to make of his own total being, with all its values and standards and beliefs, an offering given . . . to that great Minotaur that is History. Duty and virtue mean nothing else to him than a total submission and immolation of himself to the sacred voracity of Becoming."[3] There is an element here of mystical "pure love"—giving up every hope for personal redemption—a real unselfishness and self-sacrifice, but a self-sacrifice in which man gives his soul in such a way that he can no longer ever find it, an unselfishness achieved at the price of the Person itself, at the price of that which is in us an end in itself, and the image of God. The dialectical immolation of the person is as complete in the spiritual order as in the social order.

In spite of the passionate ardor of the original impulse, Marxist humanism—like the Marxist revolt against the Emperor of this world—ends up in a failure.

The latest Christian heresy

11. This humanism could be described as a theology of Man as the "supreme being for man" and the ultimate end of History. The atheism which dominates it, and which is more exactly described as an anti-theism (a "militant atheism"), must not blind us to the fact that for Marx as for Hegel philosophical reason remains a reason which has to bear the whole burden taken over from revelation and theology.

---

greatest possible development of his varied aptitudes. It becomes a question of life and death for society to adapt the mode of production to the normal functioning of this law. Modern Industry, indeed, compels society, under penalty of death, to replace the detail-worker of today, crippled by life-long repetition of one and the same trivial operation, and thus reduced to the mere fragment of a man, by the fully developed individual, fit for a variety of labours, ready to face any change of production, and to whom the different social functions he performs, are but so many modes of giving free scope to his own natural and acquired powers." Cf. *The German Ideology, Parts I & III*, pp. 74–75; Engels, *Anti-Dühring*, p. 320.

[1] "The Meaning of Contemporary Atheism", in *The Range of Reason*, p. 107.

[2] Cf. above, pp. 218–219.

[3] "The Meaning of Contemporary Atheism", in *The Range of Reason*, p. 107.

The pursuit of the kingdom of God in history, the redemptive mission of the proletariat, the universalism of the revolutionary gospel, the nostalgia for communion (not the "communion of the saints" but communion in social life and in the work of history), the march toward the transformation or transfiguration of man finally achieving his true name, not to speak of the kind of political simulacrum of the Church offered us by the Party and the conscience of the Party—all these features derive from ideas of Christian origin, distorted and recast.

But there is more; and in a sense there is to be found in Marx a real though vitiated Christian element not to be found in Hegel, all of whose Christianity was translated into illusory terms. Hegelianism was a pseudo-Christian gnosis. Hegel took Christianity over whole, without omissions, in the universality of its affirmations, and he saved the whole of it through pure reason, by emptying it of all its reality and by completely suppressing-transposing it. With Marx, on the contrary, the original impulse of revolt against the God of Hegel emanated from a real instinct deriving from the Judeo-Christian tradition—immediately captured by atheism. I spoke above of the fire of justice with which Marx was consumed. Yet justice has no place in the conceptual vocabulary of the Marxist system;[1] no role is assigned to it in the Marxist-revolutionary dialectic. The notion of justice is good enough for a pseudo-revolutionary, like the author of *Justice in the Revolution and in the Church*—it smells of idealism and of "petty bourgeois" romanticism which have nothing to do with "scientific socialism". This is the theory, but only because, as a result of a censorship exercised by the system, Marx did not want to admit to himself a psychological stimulus which was intensely real and active in him. M. Auguste Cornu has very clearly shown[2] how it was an impulse of a moral order, indignation against egoism and injustice, the will to defend the oppressed, which pushed Marx toward communism and historical materialism, in which precisely such reasons can no longer be invoked. In his youthful

[1] It was simply as a stylistic device and as a pure concession to current ideas (see his letter to Engels, November 4, 1864, in Marx–Engels, *Correspondence, 1846–1895*, Letter no. 71, p. 162) that Marx employed the words moral and justice in the "Address and Provisional Rules of the Working Men's International Association", and in the *Preamble* to the statutes (in Marx, *Selected Works*, Vol. II, 432–445).

[2] *Op. cit.*, especially pp. 183–186, 294–306. On p. 308 the author writes: "Thus Marx's conception of communism, born, like that of Hess and that of Engels, of a feeling of moral reprobation toward social injustice, evolved from idealism toward materialism, passing from the philosophical and moral level on which Hess operated to the economic and social level. . . ."

Karl Popper, in *The Open Society and Its Enemies* (Princeton: Princeton University Press, 1950; London: Routledge and Kegan Paul, 1952), pp. 385–388 and 392–397, insists with great force upon the essential role of this background of moral indignation in Marx, however deeply he repressed it owing to his aversion to idle phrases and moralism, and however incompatible it was with the pretension to pure "objectivity" of a materialist "science".

Maximilien Rubel also recognizes in Marx the existence of "powerful ethical motivations". (*Pages choisies . . .*, p. xv.)

writings Marx drew arguments from moral considerations. Once he became a communist, he excluded from his doctrine all moral and juridical argumentation, henceforth admitting only economic and social considerations. But it is clear that although justice and the defense of the oppressed were no longer to play any role in his doctrine and argumentation, they did not for all that cease to nourish the ardor and the desire of his will. In reality, not only in the thought of the masses to whom the agitator-propagandists address themselves, but also in the thought of Marx himself, the feeling for justice, as an emotional charge which could not be integrated into the theory but whose importance in the birth of the theory cannot be overrated, plays a decisive role, however unavowed.

If one fails to see that, one does not understand a great deal about the concrete dynamism of Marxism. In particular, one cannot understand why the master-slave dialectic took on an entirely different meaning in the thought of Marx than it had for Hegel. Marx, in his dialectic, ranged himself not on the side of the stronger at the present moment, but on the side of the one who would one day become the stronger. But what *is* a force which does not yet exist? Marx is on the side of the weaker, whom he actively endeavors to make conscious of his latent power, to organize, and to launch into the battle. He is on the side of the "exploited and oppressed class",[1] on the side of the "labourers, who must sell themselves piecemeal" like "every other article of commerce",[2] on the side of those who are alienated from themselves, from their work and from their proper human substance, by the regime of "private property": why is this so, if not because for him this very concept of alienation, which for "science" connotes only the laws and necessities of the dialectical movement, is at the same time loaded with an emotional dynamism which makes it function in unconscious thought as a practical equivalent of those notions of unjust frustration and infringed rights which are proscribed by historical-materialist orthodoxy, and which there is all the less need to employ since the idea of alienation has in fact alienated them to its own benefit? Thus in using the words "social claim" one is spared the use of the words "justice" and "right", but what is the fighting value, the persuasive force of a claim if it is not just?[3] Yet this justice which no longer knows how to say its own name cannot efface the mark of its Judeo-Christian origins. And how can we fail to recognize in the sense of the dignity of human nature and

[1] Engels, Preface to the German Edition of 1883, *Manifesto of the Communist Party*, in Marx, *Selected Works*, Vol. I, p. 193.

[2] *Manifesto of the Communist Party*, *ibid.*, p. 212.

[3] In his article on Engels, Lenin notes that "Marx and Engels were *democrats* before becoming socialists, and their democratic feelings, which made them *hate* the arbitrary in politics, were extremely strong." (V. I. Lenin, "Friedrich Engels", in *Karl Marx et sa doctrine*, p. 48.—Cf. the translation in Lenin, *Marx-Engels-Marxism*, 2nd English edition, Moscow: Co-operative Publishing Society of Foreign Workers in the U.S.S.R., 1937, p. 57.) One would like to know the name of this "democratic feeling" which makes one hate "the arbitrary in politics".

the dignity of the offended and humiliated masses, however deformed it may be by a materialist conceptualization and an anthropocentric messianism, a really Christian residue isolated from all the rest of the Christian heritage—the only residual element (on the purely human level) which remains from Christianity, and which will be turned against Christianity when an implacable resentment has banished all Christian truths from the soul save that one from which this residue derives its explosive power. This is to say that Marx is a heretic of the Judeo-Christian tradition, and that Marxism is a "Christian heresy", the latest Christian heresy.[1]

One sometimes hears very young students in theology—or rather in apologetics—wishing that a new Angelic Doctor would do with Hegel's philosophy what Thomas Aquinas did for the Christian faith with the philosophy of Aristotle. They do not realize that the latest Christian heresy, the atheist faith of Marxism, is precisely the only faith in which a real vestige of Christianity has found and could ever find a rational systematization in terms of the Hegelian dialectic.

III

MARXIST ETHICS

The implicit moral content and the theory of Morality

12. Hegel's way of looking at things was above all metaphysical, that of Marx, above all social. Neither of them wrote an Ethics, a treatise devoted to human conduct as constituting the object of a separate philosophical discipline. Yet the problems and the doctrine of conduct occupy a central place in the thought of Hegel, and there is an Hegelian ethics, however mixed up it may be with Hegelian metaphysics and dialectic. And although Marx, unlike Hegel, was not very much interested in focusing his reflections on the philosophical problems of human conduct, there is nevertheless also a Marxist ethics, growing by implication out of Marx's social thought.[2] Whole books have been written to show that there is a "socialist morality"[3] or a "communist morality", but the fact is that it was hardly necessary, for it is clear from the very beginning that there is a morality, a conception of human conduct and its rules, in every doctrine for which men are ready to suffer and to give their lives. Benedetto Croce's remark that "to write on the principles of ethics according to Marx seems to be a somewhat hopeless undertaking",[4] is true

[1] Cf. our study *The Person and the Common Good*, p. 88. Toynbee has also characterized Communism as a "Christian heresy".

[2] Cf. the anthology collected by Maximilien Rubel, *Pages choisies pour une éthique socialiste*, Textes réunis, traduits et annotés, précédés d'un introduction à l'éthique marxienne, Paris: Marcel Rivière, 1948.

[3] Cf. Serban Voinea, *La morale et le socialisme*, Gand: La Flamme, 1953. The author is a disciple of Kautsky.

[4] Benedetto Croce, *Historical Materialism and the Economics of Karl Marx*, chapter III, trans. C. M. Meredith, London: George Allen and Unwin, Ltd., 1931, p. 115.

only insofar as it relates to the theory of morality, and signifies that if it is a matter not of *having a morality* but of *treating of morality*, then Marxist authors who venture onto this terrain prove to be so poorly equipped for such a task[1] that any attempt at philosophical conversation with them is a hopeless enterprise. But we may leave that question aside, since what is important for us in any case is less to know if Marx had an ethics than to know what that ethics is worth.

One of the paradoxes of this Marxist ethics is that in making the ideological superstructure simply a reflection of the economic infrastructure, it seems to deny any intrinsic value to moral concepts themselves. In reality, however, not only is the reflection in question in reciprocal action with the infrastructure, but intrinsic value is denied it only in Marxist polemic against such notions as justice, natural and inalienable law, love of one's neighbor, eternal verity and immutable precepts, which are held to be tainted with Platonism and hypocrisy. If dialectical materialism does not make use of these notions, nay more, if it seems to think that to invoke moral reasons or obey moral motives is by the same token to renounce all action other than moral action, it still does not hesitate to appeal to standards of an ethical order,[2] and it does not refrain from employing the most energetic moral qualifications (deception and fraud,[3] monstrosity,[4] infamies committed by the oppressors against the oppressed,[5] naked, shameless, direct, brutal exploitation)[6] in order to stigmatize capitalist society. We have seen, in addition, that moral concepts like that of the dignity of human nature occupy a central place among the originating principles of Marxism, and that absolute atheism and connivance with history entail a system of quite specific ethical norms, in the type of conduct and self-immolation, even immolation of the claims on individual conscience, as

[1] The absence of a moral philosophy as a particular philosophical discipline ("l'assenza di una qualsiasi filosofia morale come disciplina filosofica a se stante") in Soviet systematization, pointed out by G. Wetter (*op. cit.*, p. 237), is very significant from this point of view.

[2] "Only the marriage based on love is moral . . ." Engels, *The Origin of the Family, Private Property and the State*, chapter II, New York: International Publishers, s.d., p. 73. "If Marx had a horror of the moralising verbalism of doctrinaire socialists, if he avoided employing in his writings such words as 'justice', 'duty', 'morality', etc. . . .—terms which Proudhon had constantly abused—it remains none the less true that the most objective sequences of his thought are embellished with value-judgments under their diverse forms. . . ." Maximilien Rubel, *Pages choisies* . . ., p. xxvii. Cf. *ibid.*, p. xlvi.

[3] Engels, *Anti-Dühring*, pp. 307–308.

[4] Marx, *Capital*, Book I, vol. I, part iv, chapter xiv, *ed. cit.*, Vol. I, p. 360; cf. Engels, *Anti-Dühring*, p. 324.

[5] Marx, "Der Kommunismus des Rheinischen Beobachters" [*Deutsche Brusseler Zeitung*, 12 Sept. 1847, no. 73], in *MEGA*, I, 6, p. 278. Cf. *Aus den Exzerptheften* [Review of J. R. MacCulloch, *Discours sur l'origine, les progrès, les objets particuliers et l'importance de l'économie politique*] in *MEGA*, I, 3, p. 558: "The infamy of political economy . . ."; or again *Capital*, Book I, vol. II, part viii, chapter xxxii, *ed. cit.*, Vol. I, p. 762: "The expropriation of the immediate producers was accomplished with merciless vandalism, and under the stimulus of passions the most infamous, the most sordid, the pettiest, the most meanly odious . . ."

[6] *Manifesto of the Communist Party*, in Marx, *Selected Works*, Vol. I, p. 208.

well as in the first moral choice that they involve. Doubtless no trouble is taken to justify these norms philosophically, but that is because they do not require justification, they form a part of the exigencies of historical becoming, according as, on the one hand, they express the kind of behavior required by the state of war in which the proletariat finds itself, and, on the other hand, they manifest the fact that man is the supreme being for man. Marxism is animated by a moral flame without which the indignation and resentment on which it feeds would generate only a passing violence, and it is shot through with functional equivalents of the Platonizing moral concepts which it repudiates. (Since most of these functional equivalents have no names in philosophical language, it is in terms of the outrages inflicted upon the enemy that Marxism prefers to express them.)

13. At the same time, as we noted a few moments ago, when Marxism undertakes to treat of morality, its philosophical equipment, ill-adapted to grasping the things of the spirit and to perceiving, and dealing with, the distinctively ethical problems involved in the conduct of an agent who is master of his actions, enables it to take only the poorest exterior views of moral conduct. The indications left by Marx and Engels themselves are but few in number and unsystematized. The only moral imperative they really recognized is the revolutionary categorical imperative, resulting from the fact that man is "the supreme being for man"[1] and prescribing the heroic effort toward the self-emancipation of the proletariat and at the same stroke the emancipation of all men. It is an ethical imperative because it is the supreme necessity of history. Did not Hegel teach that there is no ought-to-be distinct from being? Here we are dealing with the holy of holies, the Hegelian soul of Marxism. Apart from that, Marx and Engels drew upon the mediocre ideology of Holbach and Helvetius; they believed in "the natural equality of human intelligence, the unity of progress of reason and progress of industry, the natural goodness of man and the omnipotence of education";[2] all that was wrong resulted from social conditions; from which they concluded that it was from the radical alteration of these conditions that one must expect in man the free blossoming of his humanity and of his original goodness (whence the Marxist utopia).

They criticized the "hypocrisy" of bourgeois morality, its self-righteousness, its legal sanctions treating the criminal as a pure abstract free will;[3] they insisted upon the commonplace that the moral conceptions of men are

[1] "The critique of religion ends with the theory that man is the supreme being for man, therefore with the categorical imperative to abolish all conditions in which man is a degraded, enslaved, abandoned, despised being." Marx, "Zur Kritik der Hegelschen Rechtsphilosophie. Einleitung", in *MEGA*, I, 1/1, pp. 614–615.

[2] *The Holy Family*, chapter IV, p. 174.

[3] Cf. Marx, "Capital Punishment—Mr. Cobden's Pamphlets—Regulations of the Bank of England", New-York *Daily Tribune*, February 18, 1853, p. 3, col. 5.

variable and conditioned by their social status—in order to conclude therefrom that there are no "eternal verities" governing human conduct. Marx's diatribes declaring that morality is "impotence in action"[1] and making fun of Christian repentance as killing "human nature . . . in order to heal its illnesses" are no doubt strongly colored with polemic—he had his work cut out for him in attacking the moronic morality of the French novelist, Eugène Sue, author of a big popular novel, *Les mystères de Paris*, and in reproaching him for his ignorance of all the inhuman social conditions which form the background of crime and prostitution. And yet there is a great deal more than this in those two chapters of *The Holy Family*: one sees reflected there that passionate faith in Man which inclined Marx to views closer to Fourierist utopias[2] than to "scientific" sociology, but which also made him say in a true and moving way: "Man seems to be a mystery for man: one knows only how to blame him, one does not know him."[3] As for Engels, Robert Tucker[4] is right to call attention to the importance of the passage in which, turning against Feuerbach the sovereign contempt—of Hegelian inspiration—with which he and Marx had always treated the notion of moral good and that of love, he declares that "according to Hegel, evil is the form in which the motive force of historical development presents itself", and insists on "the historical role of moral evil":[5] which would be simply a platitude if in that assertion there were not implied the notion that the use of this moral iniquity and of the "wicked passions of man: greed and lust for power", so clearly displayed by "the history of feudalism and of the bourgeoisie", must be fully accepted and exploited by anyone wishing to make history, at least until the final coming of the new man; one has only to think of the author of *The Prince* to realize that such a position itself has nothing original about it. Apart from that, Engels' contribution consists above all in remarking that in the course of

[1] *The Holy Family*, chapter VIII, p. 265. The remark is taken from Fourier's *Théorie des quatre mouvements et des destinées générales*.

[2] Cf. H. B. Acton, *op. cit.*, pp. 209–215, 235–236.

[3] Marx, "Peuchet: vom Selsbstmord" [*Gesellschaftspiegel*, Bd. II, Heft VIII (Jan. 1846), pp. 14–26] in *MEGA*, I, 3, p. 394.

[4] "The Cunning of Reason in Hegel and Marx", *The Review of Politics*, Vol. 18 (July, 1955), pp. 269–295.

[5] Engels, *Ludwig Feuerbach* . . ., in Marx, *Selected Works*, Vol. I, pp. 446–447: "He appears just as superficial, in comparison with Hegel, in his treatment of the antithesis of good and evil. 'One believes one is saying something great,' Hegel remarks, 'if one says that "man is naturally good". But one forgets that one says something far greater when one says "man is naturally evil".' According to Hegel, evil is the form in which the motive force of historical development presents itself. This, indeed, contains the twofold significance that while, on the one hand, each new advance necessarily appears as a sacrilege against things hallowed, as a rebellion against conditions which, however old and moribund, have still been sanctified by custom; on the other hand, it is precisely the wicked passions of man—greed and lust for power—which, since the emergence of class antagonisms, serve as levers of historical development—a fact of which the history of feudalism and of the bourgeoisie, for example, constitutes a single continual proof. But it does not occur to Feuerbach to investigate the historical role of moral evil."

history "there has on the whole been progress in morality, as in all other branches of human knowledge", in noting that in the most advanced countries of Europe three kinds of morality can be seen to co-exist, Christian feudal morality, bourgeois morality and proletarian morality, and in affirming that class morality, which has been the only morality in force since mankind emerged from the primitive state, will give way to a "really human"[1] morality only after the advent of the communist society, in which the very memory of the opposition between classes will have been abolished. Later, conflicts were to develop among the disciples of Marx. Certain ones will tell us (1) that at "each general stage of human development" there is a certain level of collective conscience and of "understanding of good and evil" which is the highest level attainable "in the historical conditions" (how this level is to be measured, however, they do not tell us); (2) that "since we needs must love the highest when we see it" (is this by any chance an 'eternal verity'?), "it is the duty of each individual not to aim lower in his own morals than the ethical ideals of his society" (still another eternal verity?), and "a society or social group which falls short in its ethical ideal of those ideals previously established is morally retrogressive"; and finally (3) that a community whose "stage of organization" is higher possesses by that very fact a "higher stage of morality" in its social functioning, so that that "exact knowledge—('science')" which is provided by sociology suffices to furnish the foundations of ethical studies.[2] If one is not satisfied with these views, nor with those of other communist authors, who think, for their part, that "morality can only be truly socialized by renouncing the metaphysical opposition between good and evil, that dualism which is nothing but the earthly shadow of religion",[3] then the best one can find, by turning to Marxist authors of a quite different school,[4] is a theory which recognizes the distinction between good and evil as natural and necessary and makes an effort to maintain the validity of ethical concepts within the perspective of dialectical materialism, but which finds the origins of morality solely in the "social instincts" of the animal and of man, and, at least as concerns present times, adopts the conception of "class morality", which has become an article of socialist faith. The term "class morality" does not refer simply to the fact that the class, like every special group, develops a particular moral behavior, but implies that, given the state of war which exists between the classes, the man who either by birth or by chance is a member of the proletarian class is morally obligated only in respect to that class and its interests. This would make sense if the propertied man were a serpent or a

[1] "A really human morality which transcends class antagonisms and their legacies in thought becomes possible only at a stage of society which has not only overcome class contradictions but has even forgotten them in practical life." *Anti-Dühring*, p. 105.

[2] "*Voprosy Filosofii* (Problems of Philosophy), 3 (1948)", summarized by J. and M. Miller in *Soviet Studies*, Vol. I, no. 3 (January, 1950), p. 227, note 20.

[3] Roger Garaudy, *Le communisme et la morale*, Paris, 1945, p. 17.

[4] Serban Voinea, *La morale et le socialisme*, Gand: La Flamme, 1953.

spider and the proletarian a hedgehog, but it is absurd from the moment that one recognizes the value of universal notions like that of loyalty, for example, or of respect for others, and yet at the same time regards the conscience as obliged to loyalty or respect for others only within the limits of the class and its combat discipline. The application of moral laws is proportioned to the diversity of circumstances and cases, but the fact remains that a morality whose precepts are not universally valid and which does not recognize our obligation to *act rightly* toward every man whoever he may be is not a morality at all. To ask us to wait for the advent of the communist society in order to enter into possession of a *really human* morality is to condemn us until then to take as our inwardly and freely accepted rule an infra-human code of conduct, inferior in reality to that of the animals, which, in following no rule other than their "social instincts" (not to speak of other instincts in them), do not betray their nature, since they are without reason.

The foregoing considerations explain, in the last analysis, why one cannot be astonished that the theories advanced by Marxism on the subject of morality prove to be incapable of accounting for the moral content of Marxist *praxis* itself as it is lived out in concrete existence.

14. As for the idea that the advent of the communist society will also be the advent of a "really human" morality, it shows, we believe, that what we have written elsewhere[1] concerning "the putting aside, the disdainful rejection of all metaphysical ideology as a transitory expression or reflection of an economic moment" applies as well to the putting aside of all "superstructure" of moral judgments and universally valid moral norms. It is this putting aside which, in a sense, "is an illusory theoretical appearance, or, like the arguments of the old Greek Sceptics, a drastic theme intended to purge the opposing thought. I believe that in good Marxist doctrine this putting aside applies to a certain metaphysics, a certain ideology: bourgeois ideology. When the bourgeois invokes metaphysical values, this is nothing but a vain superstructure. But Marxist metaphysics, for its part, is not a momentary superstructure, because it is to be found incarnated, in an immanent and lived manner, in the proletariat and its movement. And it is thus that after the great day of the universal revolution we shall see metaphysical and 'mystical' values, such as those expressed by the words 'justice' and 'freedom', reappear with an infinite plenitude of reality and legitimacy, because then they will not be

[1] *Humanisme intégral*, pp. 61–62. A certain confirmation of these views is to be found in the rehabilitation of "ideology" accomplished by Lenin, and in the restitution of moral concepts (recast in dependency on the absolute primacy of the social) which is taking place in Soviet Russia. Although the realization of communism in Soviet society remains extremely far from the full realization promised to the human race by Marxism, what we have there is nevertheless a "third phase", which "corresponds to the victory of socialism in the U.S.S.R. It is that phase in which the conscience of Soviet men is radically modified, in such a way that 'communist morality has become the morality of the whole Soviet society' [V. N. Kolbanovski, *O Kommunisticeskoj morali*, p. 109]." (H. Chambre, *op. cit.*, p. 267.)

signified in philosophical systems or opinions but *lived* in a complete, integral immanence, through and in humanity, in the very practice of humanity delivered by the proletariat."

In other words, it can be said (and this is no doubt the most exact formulation) that Marxist morality is an eschatological morality. It will only be fully itself in the final state of human development, and it is in relation to that final state that the progress of morality of which Engels spoke is meaningful. In this way Marxist ethics thinks it can at the same time banish all "eternal verity" and disclaim ethical relativism[1]—and herein appears its inconsistency. It is caught in an insoluble contradiction; for it knows perfectly well that it is not the business of the science of phenomena, concerned uniquely with facts, to establish for men unconditional norms of conduct; it must therefore turn to philosophy. And Marxism is armed with a philosophy which possesses a domain of its own and precisely by virtue of which it goes beyond simple positivism; but it happens that this very philosophy consists only of formal logic, theory of knowledge and, first of all, dialectical interpretation of the very phenomena which are the objects of various sciences, an interpretation according to laws of a superior degree of amplitude and generality.[2] The dimension which ethics requires, and according to which reason grasps intelligible realities which are of another order than the phenomenon in things, is entirely absent from this philosophy and its special domain.[3] And finally, it is upon the sciences of phenomena, in particular on sociology, that Marxist ethics must consequently fall back to demand of them, as a kind of window dressing, a rational objectivity which the sciences in question can give only to

[1] "Marxist ethics [has] objective and rigorous norms and principles derived from a scientific understanding of society", and "ethical relativism was important in the thought of Rosenberg and Goebbels", wrote H. Shiskin in the Soviet periodical *Voprosy Filosofii* (cited by J. and M. Miller in *Soviet Studies,* Vol. I, no. 3 (Jan. 1950), p. 227). "Communist morality is just, because scientific, that is to say, founded on Marxism. It excludes all 'subjective relativism'." H. Chambre, *op. cit.*, p. 268 (summarizing G. M. Gak, *Voprosy etiki v marksistiko-leninskoj morali*). "In the sphere of morality, there is no duality of truth" writes Mr. Gak.

[2] "L'oggetto del materialismo dialettico coincide perciò con l'oggetto delle singole scienze positive. La differenza consiste in ciò: che la dialettica materialistica (cioè la filosofia), si occupa di quest' oggetto in un senso molto piu universale . . .

"La dialettica materialistica ha un duplice oggetto: le leggi universalissime del pensiero umano e, nello stesso tempo, le leggi universalissime della realtà . . .

"Il materialismo dialettico è l'unità della logica, della dialettica e della teoria della conoscenza. Principio che fu già definito da Lenin 'della massima importanza'." G. Wetter, *op. cit.*, pp. 234–236. These pages on philosophy and the positive sciences in the Soviet conception of philosophy are of major importance.

[3] The way in which Marxist philosophy understands the notion of essence is very significant in this perspective. "Essence" does not belong to a different order from "phenomenon", is, indeed, identical with it, being nothing other than the connection and internal necessity, expressed through the laws of science and those of dialectic, among phenomena, which, as simple empirical data and before being treated by science, are characterized as external, apparent, and fortuitous. Cf. G. Wetter, *op. cit.*, pp. 302–306 on the categories Essence and Phenomenon.

assertions of fact, not at all to unconditional norms of conduct. Let us say that in the absence of eternal verities any condemnation of ethical relativism vanishes into thin air. And if there are eternal verities (such as are all truths bearing upon what things are in themselves),[1] one is still able to understand, in terms of the actual human condition, the variability of moral codes, and "truth on this side of the Pyrenees, error on the other", and the progress of moral conscience in the course of history. But if there are no eternal verities, then one cannot understand the common traits and the discoverable constants in the moral codes of humanity, however diverse they may be, nor can one understand why the final stage of development should be a qualitatively superior state in relation to which there is progress of moral conscience.

However this may be, until the advent of the communist society, it is with respect to that advent and the preparations for it that the morality of the proletariat is defined. "When people talk to us about morality," Lenin declared in 1920, "we say: for the Communist, morality lies entirely in this compact, united discipline and conscious mass struggle against the exploiters. We do not believe in an eternal morality, and we expose all the fables about morality. . . . We subordinate our Communist morality to this task [the class struggle of the proletariat]. . . . We say: morality is what serves to destroy the old exploiting society and to unite all the toilers around the proletariat, which is creating a new Communist society. . . . Morality serves the purpose of helping human society to rise to a higher level and to get rid of the exploitation of labour."[2] Some twenty years later, Messrs. Rosenthal and Yudin concluded the article on "Ethics" in their *Short Philosophic Dictionary* by saying, in a similar vein: "Communist morality takes the position that only that which contributes to the abolition of human exploitation, poverty and degradation, and to the building and strengthening of a system of social life from which such inhuman phenomena will be absent is moral and ethical."[3] Class morality, but unconditionally imperative, by reason of the work to be accomplished.

But when humanity shall have arrived at the goal, it will morally and socially have entered into the realm of freedom; it will no longer need a moral code, or sanctions, or repressions. How could it be otherwise, since then essence and existence will be reconciled, and the true man, the deified man finally made manifest? Once human nature has reached its perfect social achievement, one may say—borrowing a phrase from Jean-Jacques Rousseau —that "all the primary movements of nature" will be "right"; "really human"

[1] Cf. below, chapter XI, pp. 287–289 and p. 288 note 1. Let us add that every truth, from the instant it is true, is eternal in a sense, even if it bears upon a temporary event or state. "Robespierre will be overthrown tomorrow" is a proposition which was true one day, but which has ceased to be true. But once the event has occurred, it will remain eternally true that Robespierre was overthrown on the 9th Thermidor, in the year II.

[2] V. I. Lenin, "The Tasks of the Youth Leagues," Speech delivered at the Third All-Russian Young Communist League, October 2, 1920, in Lenin, *Selected Works*, London: Lawrence & Wishart, 1947, Vol. II, pp. 669, 670.

[3] New York: International Publishers, 1949, p. 42.

morality will be a spontaneously lived morality, and will no longer impose any constraint. We shall be finished not only with the division of labor (especially the division between manual labor and intellectual labor), but with all the other cleavages and mutilations from which Marx wished to free man. Such a flowering of the human being, all of whose fundamental needs will henceforth be satisfied and who, having finally reintegrated the totality of his essence, "leads a complete life", this is what Marx had in mind when he declared that in the communist society, which will itself take charge of regulating and planning general production, "nobody has one exclusive sphere of activity, but each can become accomplished in any branch he wishes"; and when he described the communist man as free "to do one thing today and another tomorrow, to hunt in the morning, fish in the afternoon, rear cattle in the evening, criticize after dinner, . . . without ever becoming hunter, fisherman, shepherd or critic".[1] It is no doubt difficult for a materialist thinker to picture to himself in any other way the freedom of the sons of God. Without being aware of it himself, he remains tributary to St. Paul. And the testimony thus rendered to the nostalgia which inhabits us is the more remarkable.

The golden age of which Marx dreamed in his youth, as he made a sort of Hegelian idealism into an absolute and into a somewhat rapturous plenitude of human communion, remained his permanent nostalgia. One may see an allusion to it in those lines of *Das Kapital* where, after having argued that "the realm of freedom does not commence until the point is passed where labor under the compulsion of necessity and of external utility is required", he adds: "Beyond it begins that development of human power, the true realm of freedom."[2]

The writings of Marx's youth show us how he conceived this reign of

[1] *The German Ideology, Parts I & III*, p. 22. It is likewise the division of labor which is responsible for the concentration of artistic talent in certain ones only, and of "the subordination of the individual to a given art so that he is exclusively a painter, a sculptor, etc. . . . In a communist organization of society there are no painters; at most there are people who, among other things, also paint." Marx–Engels, *Literature and Art*, New York: International Publishers, 1947, p. 76 (from *Deutsche Ideologie*. Das Leipziger Konzil, III, Sankt Max, in *MEGA*, I, 5, p. 373).

[2] *Capital*, Book III, part vii, chapter xlvii, trans. E. Untermann, Chicago: Charles H. Kerr & Co., 1907, Vol. III, p. 954.

On the level of work imposed by need and external necessity "freedom in this field cannot consist of anything else but of the fact that socialized man, the associated producers, regulate their interchange with nature rationally, bring it under their common control, instead of being ruled by it as by some blind power; that they accomplish their task with the least expenditure of energy and under conditions most adequate to their human nature and most worthy of it. But it always remains a realm of necessity. Beyond it begins that development of human power, the true realm of freedom, which, however, can flourish upon that realm of necessity as its basis. The shortening of the working day is its fundamental premise." *Ibid.*, pp. 954–955. To this fundamental condition another is added in the communist society of Marxian utopia, namely, the interchangeability of functions in such a way that "nobody has one exclusive sphere of activity", and that the basis constituted by the realm of necessity is reduced to the fact that "society regulates the general production". *The German Ideology, Parts I & III*, p. 22, see above, pp. 250–251.

liberty. It is the final goal. In relation to it communism, which "as the negation of the negation . . . is hence the *actual* phase necessary for the next stage of historical development in the process of human emancipation and recovery", remains itself a necessary condition: "communism as such is not the goal of human development".[1]

At present "man himself alienates himself", "his activity appears to him as torment, his proper creation as a foreign potency . . . the essential tie which binds him to other men as an unessential tie and, even more, separation from other men as his true being, his life as sacrifice of his life . . . he, the lord of his creation, appears to be the slave of this creation".[2]

But finally, in the reign of liberty, in the kingdom of the total man or of man deified, I will not work merely to live; my work will be my life.[3] Production become human will be but an objectification of the individual,[4] that is, of the "social being";[5] in my activity and in its object I shall experience the joy of recognizing myself;[6] and in the use which others will make of what I have created I shall enjoy having "objectified human nature and thereby supplied for the need of another human being his appropriate object". And I shall have also "the joy of having been for you the mediator between yourself and the species, therefore of being recognized and experienced by you as a complement to your proper nature and as a necessary part of you yourself, therefore of knowing myself affirmed as well in your thought as in your love, the joy of having produced in the individual manifestation of my life the immediate manifestation of your life, therefore of having affirmed and realized in my individual, immediate activity my true nature, my human nature, my social being".[7] Our productions will be "so many mirrors" in which "our being is reflected".[8] I shall contemplate myself in the world I myself shall have created.[9] Instead of developing myself "in a unilateral, mutilated"[10] way, I shall pursue an omnilateral activity and thus realize all my possibilities.[11] And

[1] *Economic and Philosophical Manuscripts of 1844*, p. 114.

[2] *Aus den Exzerptheften* [Review of J. S. Mill, *Elements d'économie politique*] in *MEGA*, I, 3, p. 536.

[3] *Ibid.*, p. 547.

[4] "In my production I objectified my individuality . . ." *ibid.*, p. 546.

[5] *Economic and Philosophical Manuscripts of 1844*, p. 104.

[6] *Aus den Exzerptheften*, in *MEGA*, I, 3, p. 546.

[7] *Ibid.*, p. 547. [8] *Ibid.*, p. 547.

[9] Cf. *Economic and Philosophical Manuscripts of 1844*, p. 76: "It is just in the working up of the objective world, therefore, that man first really proves himself to be a *species-being*. This production is his active species life. Through and because of the production, nature appears as *his* work and his reality. The object of labour is, therefore, the *objectification* of man's species life: for he duplicates himself not only, as in consciousness, intellectually, but also actively, in reality, and therefore he contemplates himself in a world that he has created." (From *MEGA*, I, 3, pp. 88–89.)

[10] *Deutsch Ideologie*. Das Leipziger Konzil, III. Sankt Max, in *MEGA*, I, 5, p. 242.

[11] "This last [the development of a totality of desires] depends on whether we live in circumstances which permit our omnilateral activity and, with that, the development of all our abilities." *Ibid.*, p. 235.

the transformation of the social being, his reconquest of himself in his social communion with his fellows, will be such that "need or enjoyment" themselves will "have completely lost their egotistical nature" and that "nature" will have lost "its mere *utility* by use becoming *human* use".[1] And not only the object of our productive activity, but the object of our senses itself will have been transformed, will have become a pure objectification of man in his social being. "Man is not lost in his object only when the object becomes for him a *human* object or objective man."[2] "The suppression [*Aufhebung*] of private property is therefore the complete *emancipation* of all human senses and attributes; but it is this emancipation precisely because these senses and these attributes have become, subjectively and objectively, *human*. The eye has become a *human* eye, just as its object has become a social, *human* object —an object emanating from man for man, the *senses* have therefore become directly in their practice *theoreticians*. They relate themselves to the *thing* for the sake of the thing, but the thing itself is an *objective human* relation to itself and to man, and vice versa."[3] Marx, in other words, expected from the communist Jerusalem, where deified man reveals himself to himself, such a fulness of humanity that the senses and work will have come to belong to sorts of glorified bodies in a materialist eschatology, exulting at one and the same time in self-communion, and in the autonomy and the pure selflessness of their finally reconquered, or rather self-created generic essence.

Characteristics of Marxist Ethics

15. If we seek to characterize the ethics of dialectical materialism, we must observe on the one hand that this ethics is only preoccupied with the acts of man insofar as they have a bearing upon distinctively human life, that is to say, in good Marxist doctrine, insofar as they enter into the sphere of the social and influence the movement of history. It is certainly true that one finds Marxist authors uttering judgments of morality touching the sphere of private life, but either these judgments remain on the pre-philosophical level of common sense and instinctive moral reactions, or they refer to the social impact of the conduct in question. The fundamental virtues are those that are required by the struggle for the advent of the communist world: class solidarity, discipline, inexorable hate of all oppression and exploitation, the enthusiastic gift of self to the construction of the communist society, etc.[4]

We must observe on the other hand that Marxist ethics presents two quite different, indeed incompatible, traits. In the first place, it is a fundamentally relativistic ethics insofar as we consider the content of its precepts, its rules and its norms, which exclude any "eternal verity" and are dependent variables

[1] *Economic and Philosophical Manuscripts of 1844*, p. 107.
[2] *Ibid.*, p. 107.
[3] *Ibid.*, p. 107 (translation modified).
[4] Cf. G. Wetter, *op. cit.*, p. 238.

of historical becoming and of the interests of the social whole at any given moment. "Marxism believes that ethics is a human creation. . . . It holds that men's moral conceptions change as the material conditions of life, the forces of production and the production relations change, and that they are limited at any given time by the economic structure of society."[1] Yet in the second place—and in this, in spite of itself, it remains thoroughly Hegelian—as far as the way in which the duties it prescribes obligate us, Marxist ethics is a categorical ethics, imposing its precepts (however variable according to the phases of the development) in an unconditional manner. In this sense it does not admit of any "ethical relativism",[2] and holds that certain acts are *absolutely* moral or *absolutely* immoral.[3]

We have pointed out above[4] the inconsistency that is thus manifested. Let us add now that the views expressed by certain Soviet theoreticians,[5] according to which Marxist ethics is a *scientific* ethics based on sociology, are doubtless nothing more than a subsequent rationalization—quite ineffectual, moreover, for so long as a principle of value (foreign by nature to positive science) is not discovered, the best established scientific and sociological facts will never suffice to create in me an obligation of conscience. In reality, materialism has betrayed the dialectic here. On a much deeper level than this "scientific" rationalization which smells of positivism, Marxist ethics is a *dialectical* ethics based on the Hegelian onto-logic become atheist and materialist, and on a metaphysics of history for which development tends toward a final end which will be the total emancipation and deification of man. The trouble is that through a kind of materialist *pudeur* or modesty Marxist ethics dares not admit to itself the true nature of the foundation on which it thus rests. And from the properly ethical point of view, the fact remains in any case that to ask man to feel himself *absolutely* obligated in conscience to follow lines of conduct whose object, being cut off from any relation to a transcendent and immutably true element, involves in itself *no intrinsic goodness* and answers only to a momentary social interest or to a moment of history,[6] is in defiance

[1] M. Rosenthal and P. Yudin, article on "Ethics", *Handbook of Philosophy*, p. 41.

[2] Cf. above, p. 249, note 1.

[3] After having quoted this assertion from P. Kolonickij, *Kommunisticeskaja i moral' religioznaja* (Moscow, 1952), p. 18: "Everything that serves the cause of the people, the interests of the liberation of the workers, and the building of a classless communist society is *absolutely* moral," Father Henri Chambre writes: "Let us underline this adverb *bezuslovno*: absolutely, without reserve. It is repeated in the next sentence, which tells us what is '*absolutely* immoral'." (*Op. cit.*, pp. 280–281.)

[4] Cf. above, p. 250.

[5] Cf. above, p. 247.

[6] Is such an ethical conception in incipient contradiction with Marxist morality as Engels characterized it in *Anti-Dühring*, as Father Chambre (*op. cit.*, p. 282) maintains? We do not think so. Engels rejects all "eternal, ultimate and forever immutable moral law" (*Anti-Dühring*, pp. 104–105), but that does not mean at all that he rejects the *unconditional* character of the commandment prescribed for the individual at a given moment of development by class morality, and therefore the *absolutely* immoral character of the act in discord with this commandment.

of reason as well as the dignity of conscience: conscience, as we have remarked above,[1] must henceforth become heroically tractable.

Here it is well to take note of the effects of a curious play of misunderstandings which is due to our inherent psychological structure. When, as happens most notably under the pressure of human realities in Soviet society in process of stabilization, Marxist ethics exalts such moral themes as Fatherland, Work and Family, themes that are very well known, and even extensively exploited by many reactionary regimes, but which it recasts in the purely immanentist perspective of the absolute primacy of the revolutionary task, of the "collective" and of society,[2] then the great mass of the indoctrinated to whom this morality is proposed accept it the more willingly in that, far from realizing its real significance, they interpret it in the light of the absolute and unconditional notions of good and evil which they naturally bear within them.[3] Caught in the trap of their own natural morality, it is enough for them to see the good and true elements which the ethics in question contains in large number because without them the social group would waste away, but which are only tricks through which the social whole tries to seize upon individuals more completely, the precious human *capital* of which Stalin spoke—immediately their moral instinct fastens upon these elements in order to integrate them; and thus it is that the mass of the indoctrinated, without even being aware of what they are doing, recast and re-establish in a perspective worthy of man what is taught them—but at the same time they are sold an ethical system which in reality rejects both the existence of that natural morality which is at work in them and the philosophical realities which are its objective basis.

And the indoctrinators themselves, the Marxist theoreticians—in the very moment that they reject any scale of values, and so make of the ethical life of man a pure instrument of history and of social becoming—the secret instinct of natural morality in them slips surreptitiously into their doctrinal declarations, causing an echo therein from time to time of absolute ethical values, either as an almost imperceptible note stealthily introduced (I think, for example, of the purely and simply reprobatory connotation of the words "exploiting society" or "inhuman phenomena" in the writings of Lenin and in the *Little Philosophical Dictionary* quoted above),[4] or in the form of more explicit affirmations, like that concerning the "monstrosity" of human relations inherent, according to Marx, in the regime of capitalist property, or

[1] Cf. above, p. 233.

[2] Concerning this point, see the penetrating remarks of Father Henri Chambre, *op. cit.*, pp. 269–281.

[3] In connection with another subject (the Soviet theory of Law), Father Chambre, citing these lines from Hauriou: "An established social order in practice always contains a certain amount of justice which is incorporated in it", adds: "The amount of justice incorporated in the Soviet order comes not from Marxist ideology but from the voice of natural law which subsists in the depths of the Russian human conscience in spite of every effort to destroy it." (*Op. cit.*, p. 241.)

[4] Cf. above, p. 250, notes 2 and 3.

that concerning the final necessity of a classless society assuring the free development of each and of all, or that concerning what one Marxist author calls "the universal message of redemption, of the oppressors and of the oppressed" announced by Marx.[1]

If some neo-classical painter undertook to represent allegorically the phenomena of which I have just been speaking, he could entitle his painting: "The Natural Law Avenged." We owe to dialectical materialism, and to the double psychological experience it provokes—in the indoctrinators and in the indoctrinated—one of the most remarkable testimonies that can be rendered to the presence and to the tenacity of the natural law in the depths of the human intellect.

16. But let us return to our analysis of the characteristics of Marxist ethics. At least as long as the ultimate end of the development has not been reached, the dialectical movement of history remains the ultimate rule of morality for Marxist materialism as for Hegelian idealism. The idea of an *ought to be* distinct from *what is* having no more meaning for one than for the other, the notion of natural law elaborated by the Greco-Roman and Christian tradition is excluded from Marxist ethics as from Hegelian ethics. Kant had submitted man to the absolutism of a moral imperative which depended in no way on the intrinsic goodness of the object. Once the purely logical artifice by which Kant gave content to this empty form is laid aside, there remains nothing but the decree pronounced *hic et nunc* to determine the content of the moral commandment, and the decree is no longer pronounced by the will of of the State, as with Hegel, but by the conscience of the proletariat and of the community (the Party) which is its incarnation. The absolute and unconditional character of the moral imperative remains with respect to the commandment itself,[2] and with respect to the extrinsic criteria of the value of the act (conformity to the requirements of history, to the interests of the class

[1] Galvano della Volpe, "Originalita dell'Umanismo socialista", in *Studi filosofici*, fasc. 1 (1948).

One might ask oneself if the repudiation of Stalin to which the Soviet government proceeded after the dictator's death will not have repercussions in the moral realm and is not the symptom of a significant evolution in Soviet ethics. This historical condemnation of Stalin does as a matter of fact very definitely involve questions of the crimes and injustices of which his regime was guilty, and these words seem to be employed in the sense in which they are normally understood by those who believe in absolute and universal moral values. Is this a sign that in spite of everything a rehabilitation of these values is going to occur, in keeping with the fact (pointed out above, p. 248, note 1) that the morality taught in the name of the Communist Party must henceforth, in Soviet Russia, be addressed not simply to the militant members of the proletariat in their class struggle, but to all the members of Soviet society? It is difficult to imagine that, under such circumstances, this morality would not tend to pass from the state of class morality to that of simple morality, or "human morality".

[2] Hence the "absolutely moral" or "absolutely immoral" acts which were spoken of above, p. 254, note 3.

struggle of the proletariat, and to those of the consolidation of the communist society . . .); but it has disappeared with respect to the nature or intrinsic quality of the object of the act. It is true that in a sense the role of the object has been restored, since, in terms of connivance with history, it furnishes the explanation of the rational superiority of the decisions of the collective conscience and its organs. But this role of the object of the act has nothing to do with any value or intrinsic quality inhering in the object by its very nature; it is its *social content* or its *social results* which are in question. Thus, strictly speaking, it is as a morality of result that Marxist ethics opposes itself to moralities of pure intention like that of Kant (and it is so thoroughly opposed to them that intention, as in the case of Hegel, really loses absolutely all interest). And the unique value which the result itself possesses in the last analysis, its social impact, is that of a means appropriate or not to the end envisaged by the collective conscience and toward which the requirements of history point; in other words, value is henceforth completely relativized. As Berdyaev correctly noted, "Marxism is a philosophy of goods and not of values. You cannot talk with Marxists about the hierarchy of values, for they do not understand your putting the question: for them only necessity, 'good', usefulness, exist."[1]

This is to say that, like Hegelian ethics, Marxist ethics—we remarked above that it was essentially an eschatological ethics—gives crucial importance to the perspective of finality. As in the case of Hegelian ethics, historical success is for it the sole decisive criterion.[2] The very logic of absolute immanence requires that, since the object of our acts submits to no measure superior to the flux of the real, their moral quality must needs derive completely from the end toward which they are ordered as means within this flux. Thus (and taking into account the way in which Marxism renders dialectical the relation between means and ends), the good as end entirely absorbs the good as value. No doubt because in the purely individual sphere, like everyone else, they recognize the natural rules of common morality (without being able to justify them), perhaps also because they believe the formula is of "Jesuitical" origin, Marxist authors are very careful to repudiate the maxim: "The end justifies the means." Even so, at the level of the social struggle and with respect to what is really useful to the self-emancipation of the working class, i.e., the emancipation of humanity, this maxim is logically called forth by their system. As a matter of fact, Marx is probably the only Marxist who refused obeisance to it because his task as thinker of the revolution forbade him the freedom of revolutionary politics, and because on the other hand his idea of the messianic

[1] Nicolas Berdyaev, *The Realm of Spirit and the Realm of Caesar*, chapter V, trans. Donald A. Lowrie, New York: Harper & Bros., 1952, p. 89; London: Gollancz, 1952.

[2] "The only sense in which it is possible to show that something is good or bad, right or wrong, is by demonstrating that it accords or disaccords with the historical process, assists it or thwarts it, will survive or will inevitably perish." Isaiah Berlin, *Karl Marx*, 2nd ed., London: O.U.P., 1948, p. 140.

mission of the proletariat rendered sacred for him, according to a scale of values which was a relic of the past, the honor of the working class and of the "workers' party".[1]

Let us make no mistake, in spite of everything in the system that goes counter to it (we shall come back to this point later on), the historical process has a certain ultimate end (the advent of the universal communist society), and this ultimate end (in respect to which all other ends are means) is held to be *good*: because it is the end toward which historical development really and truly tends, and because the movement of history is essentially progressive (a heritage of Hegelian metaphysics, the messianic hope and an extrapolation of Darwinism, all thrown together). In fact, nothing shows better to what degree dialectical materialism is the heir of Hegelianism, and of the dialectic whereby the God of Hegel made himself: its "matter" has divine attributes, its "historical process" is in reality the Hegelian God deconsecrated. And at the same time, nothing shows better the irreducible contradiction between "scientific" materialism and "dialectical" materialism. But let us pass over that. What is important to the present discussion is the fact that in the Marxist perspective the ultimate end of the historical process of humanity in its state of historical movement is good, because it is the final end toward which the process really tends. Just any historical success does not suffice to justify a line of conduct, far from it! The success of counter-revolutionary forces only renders their action more condemnable. Marxist authors experience no embarrassment in castigating the cynicism of reactionary *Realpolitik* and venerating the memory of the vanquished heroes of the Commune.[2] But it is so because they are in the confidence of history, because they know where it is really going, and that the success of reactionary forces is opposed to its real movement, while the effort of vanquished revolutionary heroes contributes to it. The cynicism of those who take simple success (no matter what success) as the supreme criterion has its root in their *historical agnosticism*.[3] The great thing is the "correct understanding of history".[4] What does this mean if not that the criterion is not simple success, but the success which is intended by history? There is no use trying to play the role of a pillar of virtue, one must finally recognize that "it is, then, in a very large measure, the objective

[1] It is indeed significant that despite the hopes which he had put for a time in the Communist League, then in the Workers' International, the "party" in the name of which Marx spoke was in his eyes not a party in the ordinary sense of the word but a kind of invisible church whose self-constituted prophets were Engels and himself (cf. Maximilien Rubel, *Pages choisies* . . ., pp. xl–xliv).

"I am not a '*Realpolitiker*'," Marx indignantly wrote against the agreement which Lassalle tried to conclude with Bismarck (Marx to Kügelmann, February 23, 1865, in Marx–Engels, *Correspondence, 1846–1895*, Letter no. 81, p. 197). "The honour of the workers' party demands that it should reject fancy pictures of this kind even before their hollowness is exposed by experience." Marx to J. B. Schweitzer, February 13, 1865, as cited by Marx in his letter to Engels, February 18, 1865, *Ibid.*, Letter no. 80, p. 190.

[2] Cf. Georges Lukacs, *op. cit.*, pp. 211–212.

[3] *Ibid.*, p. 211. [4] *Ibid.*, p. 212.

content and the real direction of history which determine whether the character of individuals acting historically is heroic or ignoble, tragic or comic",[1] and that the value of the moral qualities exerted in the struggle is determined "in the last analysis by the objective pace of history itself".[2] In other words, it is historical success in conformity with the truth of history or with its real movement which is the decisive criterion of morality.[3]

17. It is relevant to add that no more in the Marxist perspective than in the Hegelian perspective does the human person have a subjective ultimate End. The super-disinterestedness required by Kant is better assured therein than in Kant himself, for it is complete, as we have seen, and requires the total gift of the individual immolating himself for the sake of the immanent god of becoming. Nor is there for dialectical materialism any objective ultimate end at the summit of a hierarchy of means and ends, since the relation between means and ends is no longer held to be a relation of hierarchized subordination, but one of dialectical interaction, ends and means succeeding each other interchangeably throughout the indefinite spiral of which Lenin spoke, and every end is in its turn a means. But if the advent of the universal communist society can in its turn become the means to another end (for example, full freedom of independence or the flowering of the total man, and so on), yet the fact remains that this advent is the ultimate end toward which the dialectical movement of history tends.[4] In this sense, or as the limit of the dialectical self-movement of humanity on the march toward the reign of freedom, it must be said that for dialectical materialism, taken in terms of its actual thought-processes,[5] and regardless of the officially recognized formulations, there is, as for Hegelianism, an objective ultimate End—the reintegration of man into the plenitude of his essence, the accomplishment and final emancipation of human nature, the epiphany of Man deified, true Man. In view of the fact

[1] Cf. Georges Lukacs, *op. cit.*, p. 213.

[2] *Ibid.*, p. 214.

[3] "The Marxist criterion of morality is the conformity of morality with the actual phase of development of the society in question." Chambre, *op. cit.*, p. 268. "The supreme criterion of communist morality is the struggle for communism." V. Prokof'ev, *Dve morali, Moral' religioznaja i moral' Kommunisticeskaja* (Moscow, 1953), cited by Chambre, *op. cit.*, p. 280. All of these formulae are equivalents.

[4] Once the end is attained, there will still be history (cf. above, p. 218), but will there still be dialectic? Must it be said that since all opposition will have disappeared, that will be "the death of the dialectic" (cf. Chambre, *op. cit.*, pp. 284, 508)? We think not. For though all opposition should have disappeared as among humans, still opposition, and therefore dialectic, could still reappear under other forms, as between humanity and nature, for example (particularly in view of the fact that nature carries with it the necessity of death).

[5] Cf. A. Cornu, *op. cit.*, p. 405 (on the doctrine of Marx): "In spite of its objective appearance, *his doctrine is actually penetrated with finality*; one feels in him as in Hegel a mystical faith which leads him to bend the fact towards the end which he assigns to them, and, though he likes to proclaim with Hegel that the march of history is an inevitable march, it is because he knows that this necessity constrains the fact to realize an ideal which is his own." (Italics ours.)

that, since any Intelligence directing things to ends has been eliminated, the movement of history is thus regarded as directing itself toward immanent ends and tending of itself toward an ultimate End, and that a profusion of exigencies, aspirations and purposes has been blown into it, the notion of finality has lost all claims to authentic intelligibility in the system of Marx as in that of Hegel. Let it be added that Marxism is indeed perfectly aware of this fact; and all the while that it is, in actual fact, ceaselessly using, and profiting by, such an idea of the (onto-logical) goal of history, it does so only without admitting it, and without admitting it explicitly to itself. Unlike Hegelianism, and in its character as materialism, it can reject this use of finality in theory and in its officially recognized formulations, and pretend that what it deals with is only the final term at which it knows by observation that the movement of history will arrive in fact, not the end to which this movement tends—so that in good Marxist orthodoxy the category of end can only be admitted in the social order and as dependent upon human consciousness.[1] This denial of immanent finality in the dialectical development is, however, nothing but a formality of protocol and cannot deceive anyone. As if an end which is the Reconciliation of essence and existence and the Reintegration of man in his own truth were not a goal and an end!

Let us note, in conclusion, that Marxist ethics is an ethics at once naturalist and normative (implying the same recasting of the notions of obligation[2] and of guilt[3] that we pointed out in connection with Hegelian ethics). More precisely, it is a socio-normative or politico-normative ethics. And it is a cosmic (pseudo-cosmic) ethics: cosmic, by reason of the realist-materialist reversal performed by Marx; pseudo-cosmic, in the sense that the universe on which the ethics of dialectical materialism essentially depends is not the world of nature and of matter in their authentic extra-notional reality, but the world of a nature and matter haunted by the logical being of reason and animated by the self-movement proper to discourse.

[1] Cf. G. Wetter, *op. cit.*, pp. 324–328. (But see also, in the same work, the remarks on page 327 concerning the element of finality which in spite of everything slips into the idea of the category of necessity as formulated by Soviet authors.)

[2] Cf. above, chapter IX, p. 206.

[3] Cf. above, chapter IX, pp. 206–207.

11

POSITIVISM AND HUMAN KNOWLEDGE

Auguste Comte and the Age of Relativism

The anti-Kantian reaction and purely Scientific Positivism—Positivism and Kantism

1. We shall not discuss here a school of Kantian or neo-Kantian inspiration which was important in Austria and Germany in the nineteenth century, the school of "value philosophy" (Franz Brentano, Meinong, Lotze, Ritschl, Windelband), because it does not bring any truly original element to our critical investigation. (It might be said, it seems to us, that just as in the ontological domain Husserl's phenomenology was to seek a middle course between realism and idealism, so in the moral domain value philosophy sought a middle course between a conception which held values to be objectively and intrinsically founded, and a conception which held values to be merely subjective; such a quest, however profitable the analyses one owes to it may have been, was doomed to veer in the direction of one or the other of the two pure positions between which it hoped to maintain itself, and between which there is really no middle position.) The positivist movement, on the contrary, in spite of the poverty of its properly philosophical content, is of major interest to us.

In the speculative order positivism is in reaction against Kant in this sense that Kant, while making the task of philosophy *critical* and no longer *doctrinal*, remained a philosopher in the royal tradition; that is, he held philosophy to be a discipline of superior rank, a queen-discipline, centered on an object which belonged to it in its own right and which constituted for it an independent noetic domain or territory. Even when he was convincing himself of the impossibility of any metaphysics as a science, he remained haunted by metaphysics and applied himself to restoring it in its truth by belief. The idea of the activity of the mind, however wrongly he may have understood it, was at the base of his inquiry. And if he limited our knowledge to phenomena and the world of experience, nevertheless he admitted, in the regions where science does not reach, the existence of the noumenon or of the thing-in-itself.

All this is repugnant to Auguste Comte, whose philosophy is profoundly and deliberately acritical, and for whom it is pure nonsense to think that the mind could itself analyse itself, could proceed to the examination of its own power of knowing and of the value of this power. Lévy-Bruhl[1] was right when he objected to Renouvier that this absence of critique was fully intended by Comte and logically demanded by his system. Renouvier, however, was right when he reproached Comte for both this absence of critique and the very positions which made it logically necessary for him. Comte was the first of those philosophers—whose species has become common—who philosophize all the more arrogantly as they chase philosophy from its own realm and forbid it its own proper territories, and for whom it has no independent object nor independent domain, having no other domain or object than those of the sciences (I shall return to this point later). In pushing to the extreme the idea of the essential unity of science—a notion so dear to Descartes—and in assembling at the sole level of phenomena all human science henceforth completely homogeneous, Comte thus inaugurated in a systematic way what might be called epistemological Jacobinism or sans-culottism, for which philosophy is an ex-noble, now door-man and guardian-in-chief of the Museum of Science. Rejecting metaphysics, it was only normal that he should also reject the critique of knowledge. He uses the mind without seeking in the least to know what it is. As for the thing-in-itself, he is immunized against all the headaches it caused the German idealists: it is enough for him to realize that the world of science is being constituted without it. Finally if belief plays in his system a role still more prominent than in Kant's, it is not to introduce us to realities which are beyond science; it is to nourish us on fables invented by "Auguste Comte our father",[2] and to have us practise a holy auto-suggestion.

2. The disagreement between positivism and Kantism as far as the speculative order is concerned is therefore profound. It does not prevent, however, a sort of friendly understanding and real convergence between them on the level of commonly circulated opinions and of popularized philosophical ideas, and to the extent that it is a question only of excluding the possibility of any other science than that for which we are indebted to the positive sciences.[3] Melted into a same notion, the phenomena noted by one system and the phenomena constructed by the other were to mark for a horde of thinking beings of the species "modern man" the limit at which human knowledge stops, and on which is written in all the languages of the world: out of bounds.

On the contrary, as far as ethics is concerned, positivism is opposed to Kantism in an entirely irreducible manner; and in proportion as it has extended its empire the anti-Kantian reaction—which takes its most extreme

[1] Cf. Lévy-Bruhl, *La philosophie d'Auguste Comte*, Paris: Alcan, pp. 398–399.

[2] Cf. chapter XII, p. 326.

[3] This is why Comte could write: "While Hume is my main philosophical precursor, Kant plays only a secondary role; his fundamental notion was really systematized and developed only by positivism." *Catéchisme positiviste* (1852), 3rd edition, 1890, Paris, 10 Monsieur-le-Prince St., p. 10.

form in positivism—could only become more pronounced and stronger. Kant's apriorism itself called for such a reaction and made it inevitable. The positivist state of mind rightfully resists this apriorism, is outraged by the theory of the categorical imperative and its purely formal exigencies as well as by the arbitrary character of its *you ought*. Ethical absolutism and purism, and the commandments of Sinai transferred to the noumenal Will of man, say nothing to it of any worth. And above all, it is rightly scandalized by the firm Kantian resolve to cut any link between the world of morality ("the world of liberty") and the world of nature. Despotic norms of conduct prescribed for human life in the name of a universal Will inhabiting a supratemporal world whose existence cannot be proved, and in the name of a supratemporal law devoid of all content—this is the picture which this disaffected Christian ethics that is the ethics of Pure Practical Reason presents to an age for which nothing has any meaning outside of experience, and on which the influence of Darwin will come along to complete that of Auguste Comte. What is there astonishing in the fact that in reacting against Kantian morality this age has reacted at the same stroke against all morality called "normative"? We have here but a new chapter in the history of errors which merges in so many points with the history of philosophy.

The idea that not only the minds formed by positivism but also the great mass of our contemporaries were thus to form of all *normative morality*, is consequently that of a theory elaborated *a priori* according to which human nature is a simple bit of matter—an ungrateful and rebellious bit of matter, clay or marble of poor quality—on which a law descended from the heaven of pure reason imposes itself just as the art of the sculptor imposes on his matter the form that pleases him: to such a degree was the Kantian morality to be considered as the type of every doctrine regulative of conduct, and so much were the sheep-like fever of the philosophers, and their need to belong to their time, to push them to forget that in the eyes of all the "normative moralities" with an ontological base which have held the stage in the East as in the West, the kind of "normative morality" proposed by Kant can appear only as a grandiose aberration, *magni passus extra viam*. . . . The very notion of normative ethics was thus to be rejected along with the normative ethics of Kant, and from then on can only designate an attempt made by theorists ignorant of the real, and ambitious to legislate, to submit human life to an arbitrary code of their own making.

However, one was not to come immediately to the remarkable efforts accomplished in little more than the past half-century to conceive a morality which would not be a morality or to have morality vanish either into sociology or into semantics, and into the irremediable so-called subjectivity proper to every judgment about value.

Purely scientistic or secularized Positivism

3. The efforts we have just mentioned spring from what can be termed *purely scientistic positivism* or *secularized positivism.* This form of positivism had been denied in advance by Auguste Comte, who called its partisans "incomplete positivists", but it is this positivism which flourished everywhere in the second half of the nineteenth century and which continues to exercise a considerable influence on many minds. Let us say that it constitutes positivism in the current sense of the term.

Its influence has been felt in the most varied areas. And it is not only a doctrine; it is also, and perhaps first of all, a state of mind. It is not surprising, then, that on the level of everyday life, and by virtue of the diversity of temperaments and circumstances, this state of mind is found among men animated by practical convictions which are not only different but diametrically opposed. Thus there is a positivism of the left, liberal, humanitarian, naïve and inconsistent, which fights for justice, human brotherhood and human rights while holding as null and void all that roots these notions in reason. And there is, on the other hand, a cynical and articulated positivism of the right—as utopian, moreover, as the positivism of the left, but under the sign of order and force—which in the name of nature and its necessities, and of a so-called scientific realism, nourishes a profound aversion for justice and moral values.

But what interests us is positivism as a philosophy. If we consider secularized or purely scientistic positivism from this point of view, we can discern in it three principal aspects, or three doctrinal attitudes clearly distinct, and yet naturally related to each other. The first doctrinal attitude is that of historicism, which goes back directly to Auguste Comte (in whose eyes, however, historical relativism did not apply, of course, to his own doctrine, regarded as definitively established); historicism holds that all human thought is conditioned by history, not only as to its accidental modalities, but also as to its very relation to the object; it is so, because, it is held, all knowledge "presupposes a frame of reference; it presupposes a horizon, a comprehensive view within which understanding and knowing take place. Only such a comprehensive vision makes possible any seeing, any observation, any orientation. The comprehensive view of the whole cannot be validated by any reasoning, since it is the basis of all reasoning. Accordingly, there is a variety of such comprehensive views, each as legitimate as any other: we have to choose such a view without any rational guidance",[1] and which varies with the era. Wherefore it follows that no judgment whatsoever—and in particular no moral judgment—is universally valid, and that all norms of conduct are essentially relative to time and to the diversity of the moments of history.

[1] Leo Strauss, *Natural Right and History*, Chicago: University of Chicago Press, 1953, 26–27; Cambridge: C.U.P., 1954.

The second doctrinal attitude is that of logical positivism and its substitutes, which, carrying certain of Comte's views farther than he did himself, consider as alone endowed with meaning and capable of intersubjectivation those statements (proper to the sciences of phenomena) which have to do only with the data and the methods of observation and measurement. The consequence (although, even toward the different scientific disciplines, as well as toward "phenomena" more or less "noble" or more or less "coarse", Comte never showed himself sparing of value judgments) is that the domain of facts is the only one to allow of objective certitude, and the domain of values is purely subjective. The same conclusion, reached by a totally different way, follows from philosophico-sociological systematizations such as those of Max Weber, which admit fact alone as matter of science and profess a complete agnosticism on the subject of value.[1] Let us add that logical positivism is not without presenting varied and even opposed aspects, depending on whether those who invoke it or appear to invoke it regard it as a system where one stops (and with what dogmatism) or as a methodological moment through which one passes. It can happen that some may see in it only a sort of catharsis or "therapeutics" demanded by a will for clarity and coherence in language, and through the illusion that a sufficiently rigorous Socratic examination, not of thoughts and *Denkmitteln*, but of words and the stock of verbal tools, will be able to renew philosophy. Once this approach is attempted—an attempt thanks to which the confusional complaisances between science and philosophy are at least brushed aside—these thinkers, if the sense of being exists in them at all, will perceive that in reality they have never been *logical* positivists; and with an equipment of their own choice (in which the analysis of common or pre-scientific language is of major importance) they will turn toward a rediscovery of the ontological order and of that which is based on it, in particular of value. Such has been, we believe, the case with Ludwig Wittgenstein.[2] He associated himself with logical positivism for a time, only to abandon it. The fact remains that the orthodoxy of the school is just as we have stated.

The third doctrinal attitude is that of sociologism, which is no more to be confused with sociology than historicism with history, and which holds (this was especially Emile Durkheim's position) that all that relates to human conduct, the behavior of individuals as well as that of the group, and the ideas, beliefs and rules which preside therein, belongs to a unique knowledge which is sociology, a pure science of observation of social facts or social phenomena. Wherefore (and if the principle is purely Comtian as concerns the exclusion of all ontological knowledge of man, the consequence is contrary to the Comte of the *Politique positive* as concerns ethics[3]) it is necessary

[1] Cf. Leo Strauss, *op. cit.*, chapter II.

[2] On this point I refer to the studies of Peter Geach who is an authority on ethics as found in the works of Wittgenstein.

[3] See chapter XII, pp. 327–329.

to declare that no ethics is possible apart from sociology. Either, then, one will look to sociology itself for an ethics,[1] as one looks to medicine for a hygiene, presupposing, without confessing it to oneself, and without critical examination, the most rudimentary—and the most equivocal—philosophy of social utility.[2] Or, one will recognize that it is impossible for a science merely occupied with phenomena to be observed, and with their laws to be constructed, to furnish an ethics by itself alone, and one will content oneself with the facts and laws of sociology, holding as vain all search for a moral knowledge suited to direct conduct; one will content oneself with studying as variables dependent on the successive states of the various societies and cultural areas, the various moralities in which men have believed or believe; and in the absence of every objectively founded ethical value and ethical rule there will remain only to suggest to each one a melancholic choice between *adjustment to the environment* and suicide.

Auguste Comte and Messianic Positivism

4. According to Comte, as we were pointing out above, purely scientific positivism was only an incomplete positivism, and one unfaithful to its mission. Before secularized or purely scientific positivism there was sacral or messianic positivism, the positivism of Auguste Comte himself, the study of which, as much from the point of view of the "objective synthesis" as from that of the "subjective synthesis", is particularly instructive. The present chapter and the following one are devoted to this positivism taken in its original state.

Oppositions and convergences

5. Auguste Comte (1798–1857) was twenty years older than Karl Marx (1818–1883). If we have examined Marx's doctrine before Comte's, it is because of Marx's close connection with Hegel, and because our critical investigation must give precedence to the order of ideas over mere historical chronology.

Marx and Comte represent tendencies of mind clearly hostile to each other. Comte, who continued the French Revolution but in order to found a new order, detested revolutionary theories and movements; and Marx detested the social tendencies, which he found hopelessly bourgeois, of

[1] Such is the position—so it seems—held by Lévy-Bruhl in his book *La morale et la science des mœurs*, 9th edition, Paris: Alcan, 1927.

[2] As if it were obvious that just as health is the good of the body, so what profits society—but in what would this consist? in the domination of the whole over the individuals? in the free development of these individuals? in the power of the State and its expansion all over the world? in its imperial mission? in the economic productivity of the nation? in peace or in war?; all the ethical problems are already seen coming in through the window—as if it were obvious, I say, that what profits society is the good of the whole of man.

positivism, which he scorned as a philosophy.[1] The fact remains that in the course of time, Marxism, however different it may be from positivism, was to undergo in spite of itself the general influence of the latter, without the contrary being true, except by accident. As for Hegel, he seems to have noted with some interest one of the writings of the young Comte,[2] but Comte was nothing for him. Besides he had only in an indirect manner, as subtle as air, the least real influence on Comte, and nothing is more obvious than the radical opposition between the Hegelian onto-logic and the anti-metaphysics of Auguste Comte. If John Stuart Mill found that frequenting the writings of Hegel "tends to deprave one's intellect",[3] any Hegelian could have replied that to seek light in the Course of positive philosophy and the System of positive Politics was a sign of mental anaemia.

This opposition between the two doctrines only makes more curious the accidental convergences which have with good reason been pointed out between Auguste Comte and Hegel.[4] Mr. Hayek, for example, notes[5] that in spite of the fundamental difference in perspective, for both of them every theory of society must aim at "constructing a universal history which shows

[1] Cf. his letter to Engels, July 7, 1866: "I am also studying Comte now, as a sideline, because the English and French make such a fuss about the fellow. What takes their fancy is the encyclopaedic touch, the synthesis. But this is miserable compared to Hegel. (Although Comte, as a professional mathematician and physicist, was superior to him, i.e. superior in matters of detail, even here Hegel is infinitely greater as a whole.) And this positivist rot appeared in 1832." *Selected Correspondence*, 1846–1895, London, 1934.

Similarly, in a letter to Professor Beesly of University College, London, June, 1871: "I as a Party man have a thoroughly hostile attitude towards Comte's philosophy, while as a scientific man I have a very poor opinion of it." *Ibid.*

The very notion that Marx had of the economic basis of historical development reflects this opposition between historical materialism and positivism. It has been rightfully said that economic factors, in the name of which material-efficient causality dominates Marxist thought, are not "economic factors in the raw state, as they were in that other materialism (positivist materialism) which in fact is the classical liberal economy. The Marxists, with much more penetration, will insist on the productive forces of society on the one hand, and the relationships of production between men on the other hand; the latter and their relations to the former dominate the laws of social evolution." (Louis Gardet, "L'Homme marxiste", *Nova et Vetera*, October–December 1955, p. 248). It is so because dialectics goes beyond the "phenomenon" and the "laws among phenomena" in Comte's meaning. Cf. further on, p. 291–294.

[2] *Le Plan des travaux scientifiques nécessaires pour réorganiser la société*, preface by Saint-Simon (1822). Gustave d'Eichtal says that Hegel lauded this little work to him. Cf. Georges Dumas, *Psychologie de deux messies positivistes*, Paris: Alcan, 1905, p. 157.

[3] To A. Bain, Nov. 4, 1867—*The Letters of John Stuart Mill*, ed. H. S. R. Elliott, London, 1910, II, p. 93.

[4] Cf. F. Dittmann, "Die Geschichts-philosophie Comtes und Hegels", *Viertellforsschrift fur wissenschaftliche Philosophie und Sociologie*, XXXVIII (1914) and XXXIX (1915); F. A. Hayek, *The Counter-Revolution of Science* (The Free Press: Glencoe, Ill., 1952) Third Part. —From the view-point of epistemology, Emile Meyerson insisted upon the resemblance between Hegel's and Comte's attitude in regard to science. Neither one, when he speaks of science, means what his contemporaries understood by that term. For Comte science is a science remade according to his principles, without microscopes and astral astronomy. For Hegel it is his own *Naturphilosophie*. (Cf. *De l'Explication dans les sciences*, pp. 453 ff.)

[5] *Op. cit.*, pp. 196 ff.

the necessary development of humanity according to determined laws", and that Comte, too, holds that only the social whole is real, the individual being nothing but an "abstraction"[1]—regards, he too, the great men of history as instruments or "organs of a predetermined movement"[2]—and, just as Hegel identified liberty with the recognition of necessity,[3] makes also "true liberty" consist in "a rational submission to the sole preponderance, suitably noticed, of the fundamental laws of nature".[4] However equivocal may be the word "liberty" (which has an essentially metaphysical meaning in Hegel, and a merely moral meaning in Comte), the fact remains that for both it is only by knowing and utilizing necessity that man attains freedom of independence (the only kind of liberty which is important to them). Finally, in their philosophy of history, both set themselves the task, not only of understanding the past and rendering it full justice, but of justifying indiscriminately, as good and necessary in the moment of their prevalence or of their historic success, all the human works of which it is made;[5] isn't history for one the true theodicy, and for the other "the sacred history" of the Great-Being? After this it is not surprising that one can observe a powerful convergence between the influence of Hegel and that of Auguste Comte in the domain of the social sciences;[6] this merely shows that men are more interested in results than in principles, and that the great philosophical systems exercise their impact on a thought in general too mediocre even to think of discerning its origin.

The mission of Auguste Comte

6. We know that from the awakening of his philosophical vocation Auguste Comte intended to reorganize the West by replacing Christianity—the failure of which had been manifested by the French Revolution—by a complete system of intellectual, moral and religious life. "Humanity is not made to

[1] *Discours sur l'esprit positif* (ed. 1918), p. 118; *Cours*, VI, p. 590—"This whole is the only reality, and the individual exists only by an abstraction, an abstraction which is moreover indispensable." *Correspondance inédite*, III, p. 114 (to Mr. de Tholouze, 15 Gutenberg 64).

[2] *Cours*, IV, p. 298. "They are the very organs of a predetermined movement."

[3] "The rational, in so far as the substantial, is necessary, and we are free if we recognize it as law and if we obey it as the substance of our own being; then the objective and the subjective wills can be reconciled, and they form the same calm totality." *Philosophie de l'histoire*, Introd., trans. Gibelin, p. 46.

[4] *Cours*, IV, p. 147. Cf. *Catéchisme positiviste*, p. 86: "Our real liberty results essentially from a worthy submission"; *Ibid.*, pp. 209–210: "If human liberty consisted in following no law, it would be even more immoral than absurd, since it would make impossible any regime whatsoever, whether individual or collective. Our intelligence shows its greatest liberty when it becomes, following its normal purpose, a faithful mirror of the exterior order in spite of the physical or moral impulses which would tend to disturb it. . . . Thus, real liberty is found everywhere inherent and subordinated to order, human as well as exterior."

[5] Cf. *Catéchisme positiviste*, pp. 344–345: "No regime could deserve such censure except during its decadence. It would never have arisen nor prevailed if the major part of its dominance had not been sufficiently in conformity with our nature, and even quite favorable to our progress."

[6] Cf. F. A. Hayek, *op. cit.*

dwell in ruins"—he was convinced of this as was Saint-Simon, and he liked to repeat that "one destroys only what one replaces".[1] His final goal then was practical, and even religious, from the outset. We know too that to proceed to an operation of such amplitude Auguste Comte, who had read Joseph de Maistre a great deal, took as model that "political masterpiece of human wisdom"[2] that was medieval Catholicism, the twelfth century in particular.

Moreover, he had a remarkably over-simplified idea of the Middle Ages. On the one hand, ignorant of what the transcendent unity of theological faith is, and what diversity it admits, and even incites, on the level of rational researches, he attributed to the Middle Ages a complete intellectual homogeneity which never existed. On the other hand, in his admiration for the depth of the mental combinations and the matchless sagacity of a clergy which, according to him, devoted itself to throwing off without crisis that Gospel in the name of which it spoke, and for which Comte himself nourished a solid aversion, he believed that the Catholic Church, at the time when it was giving its form to medieval Christendom, had no other final goal than the political organization of the earth and the coming of a temporal theocracy superlatively ordered[3] (thanks to the distinction between the two powers). We may say that Auguste Comte has brought this imaginary Middle Ages and this imaginary theocracy to their ultimate achievement. He has been the supreme theorist of clericalism—which could be extolled to this extreme exaltation only at the moment when it was abandoning all pretenses of being Christian, and when the priesthood of Aaron and of the Roman pontiffs was passing over to the high-priest of Humanity. At the same time he has been the supreme adversary of pluralism and the last herald—but at the moment when it was becoming atheistic—of the idea proper to the sacral regime, according to which unity of faith is an indispensable prerequisite for political unity. It was in order to restore to their unity the political city and temporal civilization on their way to anarchy, and in order to establish a Christendom without Christ even more perfectly a whole unit than medieval Christendom, that he undertook to establish intellectual unity among men on new bases—a unity of philosophical conviction first of all, a unity of religious belief next—and that consecutively he had "to be" first "Aristotle", then "Saint Paul".

The lesson of Auguste Comte is very valuable here. What will happen,

[1] In his opinion this was "the most profound political statement of the nineteenth century". He found it in a speech of the Prince-President. "The author of this admirable maxim," he added, "as well expressed as it was thought out, yet offers nothing outstanding from the intellectual aspect." *Catéch. positiviste*, p. 8.

[2] *Cours*, V, p. 205.

[3] "To theology as dogma, corresponded theocracy as regime and theolatry as cult. Similarly, to sociology as final dogma, must correspond sociocracy as regime and sociolatry as cult." *Corresp. inédite*. 2, p. 42 (to Pierre Laffitte—1st Guthenberg 61).

What Comte sees in medieval Catholicism is above all "the general perfecting which the *social organism* received in the Middle Ages, under the *political* ascendancy of Catholic philosophy". *Cours*, V, 3eme Edition, p. 231. (Italics ours.)

indeed, if, in a world to cement the unity of which Christianity is decidedly too high, this heroic attempt at unification of men by the sole virtue of Reason without God, of Science and of consciously elaborated Myth should fail even before it starts? The meaning will be clear. Either civilization will have only to wait, in order to establish its temporal unity, for that kind of spiritual unity which some totalitarian Holy Empire, as atheist as Comtian reason, will try to impose over men, or civilization will have to give up the utopia of integral unity, the old myth of the Holy Empire, and explicitly forego making spiritual unity—be it philosophical or religious—the condition and foundation of the unity peculiar to social *living together*.

7. In his book on Auguste Comte and Saint-Simon, Georges Dumas observes that between 1800 and 1848 Messianism was rife. "By its criticism the eighteenth century had destroyed Catholicism and kingship; the Revolution had marked the end of a religious regime, the end of a political regime. In the eyes of many contemporaries, too close to the collapse to be able to see what was left standing, nothing of the past any longer existed, the future was to be made, and a number of enthusiasts believed themselves called upon to preach the moral or political gospel of the new age. . . . Saint-Simon assumes the title of the scientific pope of humanity and God's vicar on earth. . . . Fourier . . . declares that for three thousand years mankind has been mistaken in its philosophies and religions, and that he was the first to discover the secret of making the human race happy, by freeing its passions. . . . Enfantin, having deified Saint-Simon, proclaims himself the new Isaac, the new Jesus and the new Gregory VII." He writes to Duveyrier: "When you have learned how to speak to Moses, to Jesus, and to Saint-Simon, Bazard and I will welcome your words. Have you fully realized that Bazard and I have no one above us, no one except he who is always serene, because he is everlasting love". . . .[1]—"Bonaparte's influence," Georges Dumas notes besides, "is apparent in the majority of the romantic heroes; it is obvious in Comte, in spite of the anathemas with which he pursues 'the retrograde genius' and perhaps even because of these anathemas . . . and Comte considers him a rival as much as enemy."[2]

Auguste Comte, therefore, was "neither more extravagant" perhaps, "nor more bizarre" than many of his contemporaries. But, unlike many of his contemporaries—and this fact is indeed more bizarre, if not more extravagant —he was at the same time a philosophical genius of considerable importance

[1] Georges Dumas, *op. cit.*, pp. 1–3.

[2] *Ibid.*, p. 5. "After repeatedly stigmatizing him," continues the author, "after having expressed the wish to dedicate a day in the positivist calendar to cursing his memory, in 1854 he ended up by demanding that the Vendome column be demolished, that it might be replaced by the statue of Charlemagne, whom he considers as one of the most eminent precursors of the positive regime. 'This parody of a Roman trophy,' he said (*Syst. de politique positive*, IV, p. 397) 'must be replaced by the worthy effigy of the incomparable founder of the Western republic'."

and the founder of this dwarfed, correct, and exceedingly narrow rationalism, entrenched in the relative and enclosed in the ante-rooms of positive science, which is called positivism, and which offers us definitive guarantees against the anti-social tendencies and the empty ambitions of metaphysics and theology.

Christian philosophers, those odd amphibians who as philosophers belong to the world and as Christians are not of the world, find, on the whole, in the spectacle the history of philosophy offers them, few occasions for rejoicing (the ancient Boethius is indeed the only one who considered philosophy *consoling*). How could they let such occasions escape when they occur? It is a powerful stimulant and a source of joy for the mind to consider that Rationalism was born in a "heated room in Germany" where Descartes, fired with enthusiasm, was the recipient of his famous dreams which a genius had forecast to him, and where the Spirit of Truth had descended upon him, so that he might make a present of the *scientia mirabilis* to modern centuries;[1] to consider that Positivism, the final landing of this *scientia mirabilis*, was founded by a regenerator of the West imbued with the grandeur of his "incomparable mission", who, when he will devote himself to organizing love after having organized the mind, and will have become the high-priest of humanity ("I publicly seized the pontificate which had naturally fallen to me"[2]), will each day carry out the meticulous rites of his "private cult" before the armchair, exalted as a "domestic altar", of his "holy colleague" Clotilde,[3] promised, as he was, to immortality "in the most distant memories

[1] Cf. my *Le songe de Descartes*, Paris: Corrêa, 1932, pp. 3–31. In his summary of the *Olympica*, Baillet writes that Descartes had noted that "the genius that heightened in him the enthusiasm which had been burning within him for the past several days, had forecast these dreams to him before he had retired to his bed", and that "the human mind had no part in them".

[2] "Far from arousing the least protest, this event soon caused to appear among several of my Western correspondents the external address: *To the reverend high-priest of humanity*—a manifestation especially decisive under the papal coat of arms, in the monthly letters sent to me from Rome by your former Polytechnic class-mate, Alfred Sabatier, whom you would in no way dare accuse of servility, although you may never realize to what degree he surpasses you in heart, mind and even character." Auguste Comte, *Lettres inédites à C. de Blignières*, Paris: Vrin, 1932, p. 136—June 27, 1857.

[3] This armchair, "since it had always been Madam de Vaux's chair during her holy Wednesday visits, I set it up as a home altar, even during her life, and especially after her death. . . . It will be able to fulfil this office as long as it lasts, along with the flowers that my holy colleague especially made for me, which, though long since faded, I have at our public rites steadfastly put in their vase." *Testament*, p. 19.

Three times a day, for thirteen and a half years, Auguste Comte performed the exercises of the cult rendered to Clotilde.

"As soon as he arose, at half-past five, he prayed for an hour, a prayer made up of a commemoration and a great pouring forth of sentiments.

"The commemoration lasted for forty minutes. Comte, kneeling before the armchair-altar, would evoke Clotilde's image, recite some verses in her honor and relive in thought, and in chronological order, the whole year of happiness he had lived with her. . . .

"The pouring forth of sentiments would last twenty minutes. Comte, kneeling before Clotilde's flowers, would first of all evoke her image and would recite some Italian verses,

of grateful humanity".[1] We must admit, however, that the very reading of Auguste Comte adds to these edifying images a still rarer pleasure due to the quality of a style unique in its kind, the magnificent candor and touching fun of which are those of a "Providence-man"[2] who takes himself infinitely and *absolutely* seriously[3] (everything is relative, of course—*except Auguste*).

I

THE REORGANIZATION OF THE MIND

The Law of the Three Stages

8. The first part of the career of Auguste Comte consisted in his reorganization of knowledge. At the root of this great effort there was a genuine

---

then he would arise and come closer to the altar and, standing, he would address invocations to his beloved in which he mixed the language of the mystics with the expression of his love. He would say to her: '*One*, union, continuity; *two*, ordering, combination; *three*, evolution, succession . . . man becomes more and more religious—submission is the foundation of authority.—Good-bye, my chaste eternal companion.—Good-bye, my beloved pupil and worthy colleague. Good-bye sister. Good-bye dear daughter. Good-bye chaste spouse! Good-bye holy mother! Virgin mother, daughter of your son, good-bye. Addio sorella. Addio cara figlia. Addio casta sposa! Addio, sancta madre! Virgine madre, figlia del tuo figlio, addio.' Then he would kneel again and with open eyes would repeat some sentences from the beginning of the commemoration. Finally, on his knees before the altar-chair in its slip-cover, he would invoke Clotilde again, speak to her, and would repeat three times: 'Amem te plus quam me, nec me nisi propter te!' At ten-thirty, the same ceremony would begin again and would last twenty minutes; this was the prayer for the middle of the day. . . .

"Finally, in the evening, a new commemoration which he made sitting up in bed, a new pouring forth of sentiments once he had lain down, and always the same thanksgiving, the same verses, the same mystical sentence from the Imitation of Christ." Georges Dumas, *op. cit.*, pp. 214–216.

[1] "As the main personal recompense for the noble works which remain for me to accomplish under your powerful invocation, I shall perhaps obtain that your name will finally become inseparable from mine in the most distant memories of grateful humanity." *Système de politique positive*. Dedication to Clotilde de Vaux.

[2] "From the age of twenty-five, he thinks as a Providence-man." Georges Dumas, *op. cit.*, p. 3.

[3] "When he reflected on himself—and he often did—it was his social life, his work as a reformer and as a founder, his 'incomparable mission', that he considered; he never descended into his intimate self to analyse and discuss himself; he accepted himself as he accepted science, without asking any complex questions about the origin and value of his deep propensities; examination of conscience was foreign to him; he seems never to have had the least remorse or the shadow of a doubt. It was as social projection that he saw himself, under the form of a new providence; he was the one, he thought, who, by the positive philosophy, was to end forever the period of crisis inaugurated by the negative philosophy of the Revolution. He would be, not the new God, but the high-priest of the new power, the spiritual father of men, the undisputed head of the Western republic, and later, when 'his objective life' would have been long since terminated, he promised himself an endless 'subjective life' in the most distant memories of humanity. Great visions filled these dreams of social glory: the banner of humanity waving over his tomb, Clotilde representing humanity on the pavilion of the West, the Pantheon resounding with the sound of the organs and the singing of the faithful, and the women, worthy daughters of humanity, lauding the Founder." Georges Dumas, *op. cit.*, pp. 248–249.

observation,[1] which deserves to be clearly isolated at the very beginning. This very genuine and very simple observation was merely the *prise de conscience* of a factual situation already long in existence, though more or less badly recognized because it ran contrary to the traditional ideas, and whose decisive bearing Comte (after Kant, but in an entirely different perspective) grasped. No observation is more commonplace today, for Comte it was a flash of light. It was the observation that, as they have developed since the Renaissance, the sciences of nature, in their gradual separation from philosophy, have made a clean break with the manner of thinking appropriate to philosophy, so that their way of approaching the real and the way of approaching the real which is characteristic of metaphysics, and, more generally, of philosophy as an independent way of knowing, constitute two modes of thinking which are specifically and irreducibly different. So much is true, and so much is fundamental.

Comte never knew what metaphysics was. He did know what science was.

I am well aware that, with this in mind, he was able, in his more and more fanciful claims to "reform" science, to make it his business to do outrageous violence to it. Similarly, and from the very beginning, when he undertook to characterize the mode of thinking proper to science, he could be seriously mistaken, by his extreme simplification of things and by his yielding to the mania for rhetorical construction and oratorical symmetry peculiar to what are called "clear ideas". Everything was falsified by going to the extreme, and through the passion for system, when Comte insisted that science seeks nothing but *laws* or invariable relations between phenomena, whereas metaphysics seeks *causes*—asks only the question *how* without ever asking the question *why*—and rises above simple empirical observation only in order to *foresee facts* or *phenomena* in a deductive manner, having not the slightest concern for the essence or the intimate structure of beings. The achievements of the sciences themselves, particularly the profound renewals of physics in the twentieth century, have shown that science is as much anxious about the mystery of being as philosophy—though it avoids meeting it head-on, and it is less concerned with making it rationally known than with seizing and handling it as unknown. And modern epistemology, especially the works of Emile Meyerson,[2] has shown that in the way in which they

[1] We have tried to indicate the nature of both Hegel's (chapter VII) and Marx's (chapter X) primitive intuition. This term "primitive intuition" is not applicable to Auguste Comte. His original discovery was not the revelation of any reality seized in the density of what is, but only a *prise de conscience* concerning the proper course of the science of phenomena. That is why we here use, purposely, the word "observation" rather than "intuition". No philosopher was less intuitive than Comte. No light shed on things in his whole work. A mind with a thirst for organization, not for seeing.

[2] Cf. Emile Meyerson, *Identité et Réalité*, 3rd ed., Paris: Alcan, 1926; *De l'Explication dans les sciences*, Paris: Payot, 1927.

"Science," writes Meyerson, "is not positive and does not even contain positive data, in the precise sense, as given this term by Auguste Comte and his followers, of data *deprived*

actually carry on their investigations, scientists in no way conform to the Comtian code, and that they are tormented like everyone else, and like philosophers (although they react to the stimulus in a very different manner), by the idea of cause and why. The positivist asceticism as Auguste Comte conceived it, involves imposing on scientists honest but futile rules, whose rigor proceeds from the spirit of system and from an inflexible and conscientious bureaucratic ideal.[1] It is not surprising that as early as the *Cours de philosophie positive*, but more and more as his undertaking of regeneration extended, Auguste Comte claimed to govern scientific research itself with dictatorial authority.[2]

---

of any ontology. Ontology is one with science itself and cannot be separated from it. . . . The positivist plan then is truly fanciful." *Identité et réalité*, p. 438; cf. *De l'explication dans les sciences*, pp. 32–39.

When he uses the word ontology in this way, Meyerson merely means that there are *things*, a reality independent of the mind and of our sensations, a reality that the scientist does not doubt in the least, and that he undertakes to scrutinize in his own manner. But this does not at all mean (and on this point Meyerson remains equivocal) that this manner itself aims at being as such, or to put it another way, this does not at all mean that science approaches the mystery of being in becoming, via an ontological approach in the strict sense of the word (resolving concepts in the intelligible being). This ontological approach is proper to philosophy; the approach proper to science is empiriological, it resolves concepts in the observable and the measurable as such. Cf. my work *Les degrés du savoir*, First Part.

Let us note again that in a purely positivist theory of science (such as Mach and Kirchhoff, and, to a more or less degree, Poincaré and Duhem, were to adopt), science, having no interest whatsoever in the processes of causation at work in the real, has for goal only to describe in the most suitable or the most economical fashion what appears to our senses, or to "save phenomena". That is what Greek astronomy proposed to do, in a spirit certainly very different from Auguste Comte's but with equivalent epistemological positions. Alexander Koyré observes that these positions were those of Proclus and Simplicius, and that Averroës adhered to them. "Positivism," he writes, "is the son of failure and renunciation. It was born of Greek astronomy and its best expression is Ptolemy's system. Positivism was conceived and developed not by the philosophers of the thirteenth century [as A. C. Crombie claims in his book on Robert Grosseteste], but by the Greek astronomers. . . ." Alexander Koyré, "Les origines de la science moderne", in *Diogenes*, no. 16, October 1956.

[1] In his chapter "Figures et Traditions familiales", Henri Gouhier remarks: "Auguste Comte's father seems to have been a model functionary whose life was divided up with administrative precision. When the aging philosopher will set up a systematic use of his time, he will know again, without suspecting it, the regular rhythm that had punctuated the exemplary existence of an office manager. Pierre Laffitte wrote: the master 'inherited from his father habits of order and regularity that the latter described at the beginning of his brochure, and that his very duties as book-keeper were to perfect'. Perhaps we should add that certain pages of *Politique positive* and *Synthèse subjective* will call to mind a large cash-book meticulously kept." Henri Gouhier, *La jeunesse d'Auguste Comte*, Paris: Vrin, 1933, t. I, p. 33.

[2] As Lévy-Bruhl observes, "positive philosophy aspires to nothing less than directing them [the sciences] and 'regenerating' them". (*Op. cit.*, p. 195.) We know that in the sixth volume of the *Cours* Comte proscribed the "alleged sidereal astronomy, which to-day constitutes the sole serious scientific aberration proper to the celestial studies". (*Cours*, VI, p. 751.) "Ten years later, in the first volume of the *Politique positive*, he 'regenerates' astronomy from the synthetic point of view. He is no longer satisfied to restrict it to the knowledge of the solar system. He encloses the particular study of our world between narrow limits. . . . Comte ends up by saying, in the fourth volume of the *Politique positive*,

Comte, then, has defined much too summarily and much too simply the characteristics which distinguish the mode of thinking proper to science from the mode of thinking proper to philosophy as an independent knowledge. It remains that he saw that there is an irreducible difference between these two modes of thinking. To have seen that is of primary importance—and is what constitutes the merit and the historical strength of Comte. This truth should be formulated in another manner than his. But one must recognize it.

And not only was he right in affirming the irreducible originality of the way of approaching the real which is proper to science; he was also right in wishing to extend this way of approaching the real to the things of man as well as to the things of nature, to physico-chemical and biological phenomena. For it is very clear that wherever there are phenomena to be observed and to be grouped under explanatory[1] schemes, we should be able to apply the way of knowing in question; a "science of phenomena" is possible in the domain of what is to-day called human sciences as well as in the domain of the natural sciences. The mode of thinking which consists in observing and measuring, and in organizing the results in a mathematical construction or in some other sort of symbolic construction, which is itself verifiable by experience, has to assert its validity for the entire universe of experience. There you have the authentic "discovery" of Comte. To make that discovery there was no need to dig deeply into things, but only to see what was obvious. At least, Comte was able to open his eyes—although he hadn't the slightest idea of what were, after him, to be such sciences as ethnology and psychology (so far as psychology is concerned, he favored phrenology and thought it

---

that, if need be, it would be enough to study the sun and the moon. We may add the ancient planets, but not the little telescopic planets. (*Pol. pos.*, IV, 212). . . . The Newtons and the Laplaces of the past have fulfilled a necessary function. . . . But, now that their efforts have led to the foundation of positive philosophy, and this philosophy itself to the 'final religion', there is no longer any reason for continuing research which mankind can henceforth do without. We must even 'prune many trifling acquisitions' (*Pol. pos.*, I, 508–513). In a word, from the religious point of view, Comte, in order to remedy the 'anarchy' of science, suppresses its liberty." L. Lévy-Bruhl, *op. cit.*, pp. 174–176. Comte is very hard on the use of mathematical analysis in physics (*Cours*, II, 317). He rejects as useless the theory of undulation in optics. He forbids to physicists the hypotheses of ethers and of fluids in the theory of heat, light and electricity. "Every hypothesis should bear exclusively on the laws of phenomena, and never on their modes of production." He condemns organic chemistry and biological chemistry (*Cours*, III, 186–195). Similarly he condemns microscopic investigations (cf. Meyerson, *Identité et réalité*, pp. 6 and following), doubtless because he believes that microphenomena are subject to laws inaccessible to the human mind (cf. Meyerson, *De l'explication dans les sciences*, pp. 99 and following), but also because with the sure instinct of a high-priest he mistrusts investigations which threaten to shake the dogmatic edifice and the definitive security of science such as he wishes it.

[1] I use this word purposely, for the claim to exclude from scientific knowledge every element of *explanation* whatsoever (that is, every effort in any way to-render-intelligible-the-datum) is one of the untenable *over-simplifications* of Comte.

scientific. Moreover, in his solid mistrust of that mark of spirituality that is the inward look, he thought that "sociological inspiration controlled by zoological appreciation": such is the general principle of the biological construction of the "cerebral theory".[1]) But he did have the idea of sociology. After having first called it social physics, he gave it the name it was to retain; he introduced it into the family of scientific disciplines, as Hegel introduced the philosophy of history into the family of philosophic disciplines. It is true that he attributed an excessive importance to it, and this completely warped its meaning. It is true also that so far as properly scientific investigation is concerned, he left the field completely fallow, satisfied as he was with his law of the three stages, his claim to derive from this law a philosophy of history, and his (quite valid) distinction between social statics and social dynamics. The fact remains, however, that thanks to him we have the rare example of a new science of phenomena springing from the head of a philosopher, and established, not by someone whose works and investigations have revealed to him its fecundity, but by one who has stated in advance its idea and its necessity.

Yet, despite all that, Comte has set forth as a principle and codified one of the most serious errors of the nineteenth century. The foolish mistake was to think that the mode of thinking proper to the sciences of phenomena annihilated the mode of thinking proper to metaphysics, and more generally, to philosophy as an independent way of knowing; in other words, that the second mode of thinking was illusory, only the first constituting a valid approach to reality; in short, that instead of being ranged on several different levels, where they coexist in the human mind, the various types of knowledge are all spread out on the same level, where they compete with each other, because, finally, *to give an account of phenomena* is the sole and unique object of theology, of metaphysics, of philosophy of nature, and of the science of phenomena: this was an extraordinary begging of the question, for the question was precisely to know if there isn't something to be known beyond the phenomenon. As a result, astronomy, physics, chemistry and biology would necessarily eliminate every other knowledge of reality, whether it be obtained by philosophy of nature, metaphysics or theology: and sociology was not only to be constituted as the science of social phenomena, it was necessarily to eliminate every other science of man, whether pertaining to theology, to metaphysics, to psychology, or to authentic ethics: man was but a sociological phenomenon, or a grouping of sociological phenomena bound by laws. Every philosophical knowledge of things, distinct from the knowledge which the sciences give of them, was henceforth void. Such was the clearest result of the law of the three stages.

[1] *Politique positive*, I, 673. In consideration of which the "cerebral chart" of Comte will contain 18 irreducible faculties, 10 for the heart, 5 for the mind and 3 for character, a special organ being assigned to each one.

9. It was this famous law that Comte cherished as his great discovery. It was for him the key to sociology, to positive philosophy, and to the moral and political reorganization of the West. In reality, it was a perverted and highly sophistical systematization of the authentic insight I mentioned above about the irreducible originality of the mode of thinking appropriate to the sciences of phenomena. Now this mode of thinking is going to become the only valid one, is going to define the "positive" stage of human thought and civilization, and is going to appear as the ultimate term of the historical progress of humanity. For with Auguste Comte, as with Hegel, we have arrived at the end of time.[1]

As early as 1822, in the *Prospectus des travaux nécessaires pour réorganiser la société*,[2] Comte wrote: "By the very nature of the human mind, each branch of our knowledges[3] is necessarily required to pass successively, in its progress, through three different theoretical states: the theological or fictitious state, the metaphysical or abstract state, and finally the scientific or positive state." He formulates his law in the same way in the first lesson of the *Cours de philosophie positive*, adding: "In other words, the human mind, by its nature, successively uses in each of its researches three methods of philosophizing whose characters are essentially different, and even opposed: first, the theological method, then the metaphysical method, and finally the positive method. Thence there are three sorts of philosophies, of general systems of conceptions about the totality of phenomena, which mutually exclude each other. The first is the necessary starting point for the human intelligence, the third is its fixed and definitive state; the second is destined solely to serve as a transition."[4]

One sees that this law is requested by "the nature of the human mind". One sees also that the three stages it mentions characterize the conceptions man forms "about the totality of phenomena". In the theological state the human mind explained phenomena by "supernatural agents" and by arbitrary wills conceived in the image of man. In the metaphysical state it explained them by abstract entities and hidden causes ("abstract forces inhering in bodies, but distinct and heterogeneous"). In the positive state it does not seek to explain them, it observes them as facts and unifies them by laws, and so makes itself capable of rational prediction (it restricts itself to "considering

[1] Cf. *Synthèse subjective*, p. 39: "We must, therefore, establish the *final regime* . . ."; p. 43: "It has, however, prepared the *final regeneration* . . ."; *Catéchisme positiviste*, p. 379: ". . . A truly steadfast philosophy, which would lead to the establishment of the *final religion*. . . ."

[2] This "fundamental opuscule" was inserted in a volume of Saint-Simon (*Suite des travaux ayant pour objet de fonder le système industriel*), whose secretary Comte was at that time. Comte reproduced the opuscule in question under the title *Plan des travaux scientifiques pour réorganiser la société*, in the appendix of volume IV of his *Système de politique positive*.

[3] "Each branch of our knowledges" here means each of the fundamental sciences, astronomy, physics, chemistry, physiology. . . Cf. Henri Gouhier, *op. cit.*, vol. III, p. 290.

[4] *Cours*, I, p. 3.

them as subjected to a certain number of invariable natural laws which are nothing else than the general expression of the relations observed in their development").

10. It is appropriate to make some remarks at this point. In the first place, even if we suppose (which is highly debatable from many points of view) that the interpretation of the phenomena of nature has actually passed through these three stages, the essential question, that of knowing whether the interpretation of the phenomena of nature is the only object to which human thought can legitimately apply itself, would still remain. Comte neither asks nor discusses this question. On the contrary, he maintains *a priori* that the law of the three stages is purely and simply *the fundamental law of the intellectual evolution of humanity*,[1] the law of the history of human thought integrally taken (whence it follows that on this fundamental law depends the whole history of arts, of institutions, of morals, of law, of civilization in general)[2]; which implies that there is for human thought no other sphere of genuine knowledge than that of the knowledge of phenomena. It is to this abrupt surreptitious passage from a particular level of knowledge to human intelligence in its entirety—entirety flattened down, by the same stroke, on this single level of knowledge—that is primarily due the deceiving ambiguity of the law of the three stages (without speaking of the other deceptions and elements of trickery it involves). This famous law is but an example, a very remarkable one, of the mirages that can be produced, at the end of prolonged concentration,[3] by a clear idea passionately grasped and spreading all over the field of vision. Not only is it contradicted by concrete historical situations (in India, for example, "theology" and "metaphysics" have had their great

[1] *Syst. de polit. pos.*, III, p. 28. [2] L. Lévy-Bruhl, *op. cit.*, p. 43.

[3] The event took place in February or March 1822. Comte was twenty-four years old. "I have heard Auguste Comte say," writes Pierre Laffitte, "that the law of the three stages was discovered one morning, after a long night of continuous meditations; and that it was almost immediately afterwards that he discovered the law of the scientific hierarchy, which is, really . . . absolutely inseparable from it." *Revue occidentale*, 1895, vol. I, pp. 4–5.

We know that the sources of this "discovery" have given rise to numerous discussions, and that Comte's originality has been disputed. But in actual fact, as far as his fundamental law is concerned, he owes nothing to Burdin, Saint-Simon, or Turgot. It is true that a passage of Turgot in the *Plan* of his *Second discours sur l'histoire universelle* (written about 1751, published by Dupont de Nemours in 1807) seems to announce a similar law. But, on the one hand, Comte did not know this passage. On the other hand, this passage is only an observation on the history of our knowledge of nature and has none of the universal bearing that characterizes the pseudo-intuition of Auguste Comte. Cf. Henri Gouhier, *op. cit.*, vol. III, pp. 395–403; Henri de Lubac, *The Drama of Atheist Humanism*, trans. Edith M. Riley, New York: Sheed and Ward, 1950; London: Sheed and Ward, 1949, p. 82: Turgot had formulated his statement "only for one category of phenomena, with no thought of extending it 'to conceptions of a moral and social order' and, above all, with no thought of ever fettering the whole of our intellectual activity with the shackles of the positive state. That is what several disciples of Auguste Comte—Dr. Audiffrent, Dr. Robinet and E. Semerie—rightly pointed out in opposition to Renouvier and Pillon. They adduced this simple and incontestable proof; Turgot believed in God."

developments simultaneously; in the West the domination of "metaphysics" in the Hellenic and Hellenistic world, from Plato to Plotinus, preceded the "theological" domination characteristic of the Christian Middle Ages), but it pays no heed to the essential fact that from the beginning and at each period of history, the observation of phenomena, metaphysical thought, and religious thought with its myths or its theologies have coexisted, I mean to say as ways of knowledge or of grasping reality: originally confused, then progressively differentiated,[1] and with domination alternating from one to the other, the historical rise of positive science being, moreover, a characteristic of modern times. If one wishes to make use, in an authentically philosophical way, of the notion of a succession of states, an entirely different historical law must be formulated, the one according to which human thought, with all its specifically diverse activities, functions first of all in the *magical* or "nocturnal" state, from which it passes to the *logical* or "solar" state.[2]

It can be pointed out in the second place that, in Comte's eyes, the "metaphysical" state is no more than a transitory compromise, lacking any power of its own, between the final "positive" state and the "theological" state, which at least provided some satisfaction for real needs. Not only is the mode of thinking proper to metaphysics and to philosophy as an independent knowledge necessarily destined to be eliminated by the mode of thinking proper to the sciences of phenomena, but it is merely a degradation of the theological method, considered primarily in its full primitive vigor and under the form of fetishism, for which Auguste Comte always had a weakness, even before the period of his own supreme pontificate. Rather any kind of religious faith and the ecstasies of the tom-tom or the cult of the plumed serpent than philosophical and metaphysical knowledge is a typical trait of the positivist state of mind, and not only in Auguste Comte. The reign of metaphysics could be considered only as a sort of transitory chronic sickness.

And finally a third remark: it is in a specially altered sense, extremely remote from the ordinary meaning of these words, that Comte uses the terms "theology" and "metaphysics". For him the sensualists of the eighteenth century, because they manipulated abstractions and because their work was principally negative, provide us with a good example of the metaphysical method, and the theological method is at its best with the rain-conjurors. But we must not forget that the ordinary meaning of the words "theology" and "metaphysics" is still included, as a special case, in the altered meaning

[1] "Again, where Comte saw three successive states, it is actually a case of 'three coexistent modes of thought', corresponding to three different aspects of things; thus progress consists in an increasingly clear distinction between these three aspects, at first perceived in a kind of chaotic unity. If, then, it is true to say that 'physics' (in the sense of the whole of science) began by being theological, it would be just as true to say that theology began by being physical, and the law of evolution does not tend to expel theology any more than science, but to 'purify' both by differentiating them." H. de Lubac, *op. cit.*, p. 82.

[2] Cf. our essay "Signe et symbole", in *Quatre essais sur l'esprit dans sa condition charnelle*, 2e ed., Paris: Alsatia, 1956.

used by Comte. In leaving behind the explanation of the phenomena of nature by the four qualities, by antiperistasis or the horror of the void, the human mind has by the same stroke left behind and definitively liquidated the metaphysics of Aristotle and any hope of grasping a spiritual reality by means of a metaphysical understanding. In leaving behind the explanation of the phenomena of nature by the evil eye or by the vengeance of the gods, the human mind has by the same stroke left behind and definitively liquidated the theology of St. Augustine and that of St. Thomas, and any hope of entering into the mystery of a revealed datum by means of a theological understanding. And that is all self-evident, without the slightest need of examination or of critical discussion. This procedure by which one condemns without judging reveals an unconscious dishonesty which is particularly significant when it occurs in the mind of one who was as honest and candid as Comte was. His attitude toward a theological idea such as that of Divine Providence is not, moreover, unlike that of the officials who guard the doors at anti-religious museums; it is clear to him that the idea in question can neither withstand Franklin's lightning-conductor, which shows that lightning is a natural phenomenon,[1] nor the observation that the world is not perfect (But then? Would it be necessary that it be God?), nor the fact that optical apparatus is conceivable alongside which the human eye does not deserve even satisfactory mention.[2] These and similar bits of nonsense, which Comte is pleased to repeat in order to jeer at the "stupid admiration" of those for whom the heavens speak of the Creator, have also their meaning, which depends on the psychology of the unconscious. The truth is that the law of the three stages was as dear as it was to Auguste Comte only because, by its complete obliteration not only of theological knowledge but also of metaphysical knowledge, leaving not the slightest trace of them, it was a perfectly sure protection against any possibility of an offensive return of God.

"*Everything is relative, that's the only absolute principle*"

11. Similar remarks can be made about the way in which Comte has raised relativity to an absolute law. He had a genius for apparent clarity, and for mottoes to be inscribed in town-halls or borne by marching bands. "Everything is relative, that's the only absolute principle" is one of those statements which seem clear at first glance—it was to provide a deep visceral satisfaction for generations of bourgeois—but are dark as night when they are examined. Looked at more closely, it appears that it requires a serious effort of exegesis, and that the *quid est veritas* of a man who was likewise remarkably gifted at phrase-making was at least clearer.

Everything is relative, that's the only thing absolute, Comte had written in his youth, when, at nineteen, he and Saint-Simon were writing the third

[1] Cf. *Cours*, II, 2e ed., 1864, p. 293.
[2] Cf. *Cours*, III, 2e ed., pp. 321 sq., and Footnote 1.

volume of *L'Industrie*. Much later, when he had become the high priest of humanity, he took up again,[1] with a slight modification of its form, "this characteristic sentence" which had sprung forth in 1817, "in the middle of a useless publication", out of those "untimely writings to which I was inspired by the disastrous relationship through which my spontaneous debut took place". From that time on the "characteristic sentence" is: *Everything is relative, that's the only absolute principle.*

If we look again at the text of 1817, we notice that it deals with the necessity of taking into account time and its ripenings if right judgments about social institutions are to be made—a necessity which is forgotten both by the reactionaries who believe that time is reversible and by the revolutionaries who want to "set the time on fire". Here again we have an authentic insight which is wrongly conceptualized. "It is no longer a matter of carrying on endless discussions to determine which is the best government; absolutely speaking, there is nothing good, there is nothing bad; everything is relative, that's the only thing absolute; so far as social institutions are concerned everything is especially relative to time."[2]

Comte saw very clearly that time is not a formless medium, that the ages and periods it bears constitute frames of reference that the mind cannot neglect, and that the dimension of time, once recognized by thought, requires us to consider many things as justified and based on reason—in relation to a given historical situation—instead of becoming indignant with them and condemning them. Time is the great relativisor.

The question is to know whether *everything* is subject to time and measured by it, and consequently whether all things are made relative by time and justified by time. And that is exactly what Comte takes at once for granted. Absolutely speaking, there is nothing good, there is nothing bad; everything is relative, that's the only thing that is absolute. The conceptualization has gone far beyond the insight; it has made the relative absolute.

Certainly a writer—and particularly a nineteen-year-old writer—not infrequently forces the expression of his thought and says more than he means. And was not Comte writing, at the same period: "Very few people have paid enough attention to the march of the human mind and the generation of events to know that the best in itself is not always what best suits"?[3] And does not this seem to indicate (unless it is a manner of speech used in passing and inadvertently) that he had not yet completely rejected the notion of "best in itself"? As a matter of fact, it is quite clear that there is not the least incompatibility between defining *what is*, absolutely speaking, *the best government*, and thinking that in relation to different historical situations there are only forms of government *which best suit*, in reference to a given period. But

[1] *Système de politique positive*, vol. IV, Appendix, p. ii.
[2] *Revue Occidentale*, May 1884, p. 331.—Cf. Henri Gouhier, *op. cit.*, vol. III, p. 184.
[3] *Ibid.*, September 1884, p. 169. (Gouhier, *op. cit.*, vol. III, p. 184, note 5.)

in spite of its being required by common sense, such a recognition of the twofold and concordant necessity of the category of the absolute and of that of the relative was just what the impetus of his thought, at the moment he wrote the lines just quoted, led Comte to deny. If he was to hold so precious the "characteristic sentence" of 1817, it was because he had at that early date felt dawning within him, in the perspective of history and social institutions, the idea which was for him decisively liberating, the idea of the necessity of excluding the absolute absolutely and everywhere.

Thus the first, the original, meaning of the Comtian formula concerns the relativity of "everything", particularly of "good" and "evil", in relation to the dimension of time. "All is relative especially to time"; all values are relative to time. There is absolutely nothing absolute, that is, nothing intemporal or above time. All things, and in the first place all our values, are engulfed in time, subject to time and measured by time. And everything that time has produced is justified by time. "Everything that develops spontaneously is necessarily legitimate for a certain time, as fulfilling by that very fact some need of society."[1] The older Comte grows, the more he will insist on the fundamental character of his principle and the more he will extend its application. It applies to every order. The positive mind requires of us that we "substitute *everywhere* the relative for the absolute".[2] Still, the original meaning, the one we have just indicated—relativity in respect of time—will always remain the predominant one.

12. In a second meaning, to which Comte will devote a good deal of time, it is the relativity of science and truth that will be affirmed—relativity of every truth in respect of the state or the situation[3] of the human subject (and so also, in the last resort, in respect of time). "Absolute" means immutable and ultimate; "relative", provisory and awaiting something better.

It is correct to say that the view of the world offered us by the science of phenomena is always an approximation, that no scientific theory is a definitive acquisition, and that scientific progress takes place by a succession of total recastings of such a sort that the old theory is completely eclipsed by the new, which has reinterpreted in its own way and reassimilated all the viable elements of the old. Thus one must say that not only are there many things that we hold to be true to-day which will not be held to be true to-morrow,

[1] *Opuscules*, p. 240; 5th opuscule, March 1826: *Considérations sur le pouvoir spirituel.* [Reprinted in *Pol. pos.*, IV, App.]—cf. above p. 268, n. 5.

[2] *Discours sur l'esprit positif*, p. 53.

[3] Science, says Auguste Comte, and the truths that it states are necessarily relative to "our organization" and to "our situation". (*Discours sur l'esprit positif*, p. 15). But, as Lévy-Bruhl (*op. cit.*, pp. 84–85) points out, since, according to Auguste Comte, human nature, and therefore our "organization", does not change, it is in terms of our "situation", that is, in terms of the moment in history in which we find ourselves in the evolution of the species, that the system of our ideas, and our science, necessarily vary; it is then the relativity of science in regard to our "situation" that matters above all.

but also that in the domain of the science of phenomena nothing that we hold to be true to-day is assured of being held true to-morrow.

This is the proper situation of the science of phenomena. But on this authentic datum Comte performs an operation which warps everything. Instead of thinking: relativity of the state of our knowledges or of what we hold as true, he thinks: relativity *of truth*. It is not simply an assertion which we thought to be true which will be recognized as not being true to-morrow. It is to-day's truth which will be false to-morrow. In short, one must not say that there are assertions purely and simply true (absolutely true), and assertions true in a certain respect (relatively true), and that the explanatory or theoretical assertions of the sciences of phenomena are true only when compared to the whole ensemble of known facts: one must say that there is no assertion which is absolutely true. Truth as such is relative; truth is not immutable;[1] truth changes. These words have no meaning (for even if a statement is true only under given conditions, the fact that it is true in this way, in a certain respect, remains something purely and simply true); but they dazzle thought and insidiously get themselves accepted by it because of the authentic datum to which they refer, and which they distort while claiming to express it. We should not be surprised that Comte has consequently felt the need to define the truth in his own way—a completely "sociological" and subjective way—as the coherence between our conceptions and our observations at each period of time.[2]

The *everything is relative, that's the only absolute principle* thus has a twofold result. In the first place it causes the science of phenomena to lose its soul. For what is it that first and foremost moves the scientist, whatever one may say, if it is not truth and the desire for truth? It is truth he wants, or the adequation of the mind with being.[3] He knows that in virtue of its very nature, the science of phenomena, as a whole, could provide us with absolute certitude, with knowledge immutably and unshakeably true—and therefore attain to that "perfect" knowledge in which, according to Aristotle, scientific knowledge consists—only at a final term at which it will never arrive, and where the immense collective work by which it progresses from generation to generation would come to completion.[4] But he dedicates himself to making

[1] Positive philosophy "abandons the chimera of unchangeable truth. It does not consider today's truth as absolutely true, nor yesterday's truth as absolutely false. It 'ceases to be critical towards the whole of the past'." Lévy-Bruhl, *op. cit.*, pp. 87–88.

[2] "Truth, then, in every epoch, is 'perfect logical coherence', or the agreement of our ideas with our observations." Lévy-Bruhl, *op. cit.*, p. 87.—Cf. vol. VI, p. 675.

[3] This classic formula "adequation of the mind with being" is itself analogically true, and is not to be understood in the same sense for the truth of philosophical assertions and for the truth of scientific assertions. In this last case, the case of the science of phenomena, it signifies the adequation of our mental constructions founded on observation and measurement, with observable and measurable reality as such.

[4] Auguste Comte saw very clearly (cf. Lévy-Bruhl, *op. cit.*, pp. 82–86) that the science of any sector of nature can be unshakeable only if it would be complete, which it will never

his contribution to its progress to this term. And so long as science remains on this side of that limit, which it unceasingly approaches and which it will never attain, it is at each instant "true and relative at the same time",[1] or true in a certain respect, only because it is moving toward the absolute ideal term I just mentioned, and at each instant is offering us, in its totality, an anticipated likeness of it which is less and less imperfect. To overthrow, as Auguste Comte does, the Aristotelian notion of scientific knowledge, to exorcise the idea of knowledge which is immutably and definitively true, is, by depriving the science of phenomena of the end or the beyond-itself toward which it tends, to deprive it of its direction, of its motion, and of the kind of truth itself (truth in a certain respect) which is appropriate to it at each moment of its history.

13. The second result of the *everything is relative, that's the only absolute principle* is, from another point of view, the very one to which the law of the three stages leads: the abolition of any science superior to the science of phenomena, and particularly of any independent philosophical science.

It is undoubtedly true of philosophy as it is of science that it will never be completed; but philosophy progresses in time in a way entirely different from that of science—by growth and deeper penetration, not by recasting and substitution. And undoubtedly in its sphere, too, things which were one day held as true (e.g. Aristotle's views on the first moveable or on the legitimacy of slavery) will not be held as true to-morrow. But what is proper to the scientific knowledge which is philosophy, in contrast with the science of phenomena, is that it cannot be said that in its domain nothing that we hold as true to-day is assured of being held as true to-morrow. On the contrary, there are in philosophy, even if only one philosopher in a thousand sees them, certitudes which are definitive acquisitions and assertions which are true forever. For what philosophy by its nature demands is the attainment of a knowledge which is immutably and necessarily true, of scientific knowledge. (The quarrels between the philosophers precisely bear witness to this: philosophers' reason for being is but the pure and simple truth, the absolute truth, the mark of which their doctrine is supposed to bear. And it is so for

---

be on any point, and that thus science, not only as a whole but in each of its assertions and theoretical elaborations, is a "progress", not a "state". What he refused to see is that if the term to which it tends is a limit which will never be reached, nevertheless the validity in itself of this final term, ideally considered, is necessarily implied in the movement of science toward it. And, to tell the truth, the term in question is not only ideal. One day all will be known—but infinitely beyond this ideal term, and by an intuitive knowledge that transcends to the infinite all human science. By a curious paradox the very relativity of the positive sciences and the fact that they are in continuous recasting (I do not mean as regards the real observation they gather, nor even many a theoretical view, more or less complete, I mean as regards what is related to their most general and comprehensive explanations) manifests in them a kind of eschatological aspiration.

[1] L. Lévy-Bruhl, *op. cit.*, p. 88.

Auguste Comte as well as others, even the most skeptical among skeptics. Thus these doctrines are inevitably opposed to each other so long as what all the philosophers have grasped of the real has not been conceptualized in the completely exact perspective, which in itself is unique—but which for each philosopher is his own.)

What is true in philosophy is true not in a certain respect but purely and simply, or absolutely—true to-day, and true to-morrow—because philosophical truth is above time. If the absolutely true knowledge to which the science of phenomena tends is the asymptotic limit of the historical development of this science—as a knowledge in which the totality of all phenomena would be completely known—in short, if science can be absolutely true knowledge only if it is a total knowledge, it is because the object of the science of phenomena is completely immersed in experience and time, and hence can give rise to an absolutely true knowledge only if this knowledge exhausts both experience and time. On the contrary, the object of philosophy rises above experience and time, and it is because of this emergence of its object above experience that philosophy has no need to know everything in order to be an absolutely true knowledge—absolutely true as regards certain special entities grasped in the immensity of the knowable real; and it is also because of this emergence of its object above time that, at each instant of time, philosophy, insofar as it is true, is a knowledge independent of time. This freedom with respect to time, and hence the possibility of saying *hic et nunc* what is true forever is so essential to philosophy that philosophers for whom nothing rises above time are compelled to locate themselves at the end of time, as Hegel did, and as Comte himself did at the cost of the most flagrant contradiction.

14. This digression was not useless. It shows us clearly in what way the "only absolute principle" of Auguste Comte, understood in its second sense—the relativity of truth—is simply the negation of philosophical knowledge. It shows us also that this principle has a third meaning, no longer related to truth, but to what is. There is indeed a correlation between the object of knowledge and the truth of knowledge. If no knowledge is absolutely true it is because there is no absolute in the unconditional sense, in other words, because no object possesses any determination, is this or that, except by reason of circumstances or by dependence on certain conditions given in the world of experience—our methods of observation and measurement in the case of a scientific phenomenon (it is defined by them); the dispositions of the subject due to the times and the environment, the taboos of the social group, etc., in the case of a value (it is believed to be measured or determined by them). Relativity (in respect of conditions in effect in the world of experience), phenomenality of everything that is. Nothing has being in itself or for itself. We simply posit an *ens rationis*, an imaginary and illusory entity, if we posit

a being or some sort of intelligible structure which would be "heterogeneous", in Comte's term, to the phenomenon, and, it is supposed, hidden behind it—let us say, a being or an intelligible structure which would be reached by the intelligence *within* the sensible and the observable, but without itself falling under the senses or observation, in short, which would be of a different order than the phenomenon. There is neither substance nor nature nor cause nor quality nor action nor matter nor form nor potency nor act—not even *being*, except as a word in the language. With even greater reason there is no reality to be grasped by the understanding (analogically) *beyond* the sensible and the observable: no soul, no mind, no spiritual powers such as intelligence and will, no free will, no personality.

And with still greater reason there is no first transcendent Cause or self-subsisting Being. Since nowhere and on no level is there anything absolute or unconditioned, it is clear that the absolute has been thoroughly eliminated. At last we have arrived at the end of our labors. If relativity as the only absolute principle has such a fundamental importance it is because this principle delivers us absolutely from God. What miracles of grand surgery! But the price to be paid was much higher than was thought, and Comte has had the merit of seeing more clearly than any other atheist what the price had to be. Everything had to be made relative, made phenomenal, and the denial of philosophical knowledge had to be erected into a philosophy. An absolutely clean sweep had to be made.

What is unfortunate is that all of this involves a contradiction. The idea of relativity is a very great, a very fertile, and a profoundly philosophical idea. But relativity has no meaning but in being relative itself; it is meaningful only in relation to the absolute. That is why there is no vision of universal relativity more intense and more comprehensive than the Hindu vision of Maya. *Nieti, nieti!* Without Atman, there is no Maya. If one denies any reality to the absolute, all that is left is to make the relative absolute. Comte thought he could escape it with a witticism. But in *everything is relative, that's the only absolute principle* there is a great deal more than a simple verbal paradox. For if everything is relative it is strictly true that there cannot exist even *one* absolute principle. And on the other hand if it is not absolutely true that everything is relative there is room for and a possibility of the absolute.

Moreover, as a matter of fact Comte could not and did not hold to his principle. For him it is an absolute truth that the positive state is the definitive state of humanity.[1] He holds as an absolute truth the law of the three stages,

[1] "Not being universal, theological philosophy could only be provisional. Alone will be definitive the philosophy, that is to say, the method of interpretation of natural phenomena, which will apply itself to all phenomena, without exception, from the simplest to the most complicated. For only this philosophy will realize the unity demanded by the understanding." L. Levy-Bruhl, *op. cit.*, p. 49.

whose necessity derives from *the nature of the human mind*[1] and is demonstrated on that basis. He holds it as an absolute truth that the edifice of the positive sciences must be crowned by sociology. He holds as an absolute truth the necessity of completing the objective synthesis with the subjective synthesis, and the positivist reorganization of knowledge with the positivist reorganization of religion. He holds it as absolute truth that political unity is chimerical unless it is based on intellectual unity,[2] and that every reform of social institutions has as a prior condition the reform of philosophy, of religion and of education.[3] There is not the least trace of relativity in his certitude that future generations will bless his name and his work. Always he is dogmatizing, retrenching, regenerating, excommunicating, reconciling, pontificating. As a matter of fact no one is more absolutist than this herald of relativity.

15. If the discussion of the positivist absolutizing of relativity has occupied us so long, it is because this discussion touches on a point which is crucial for moral philosophy, one of the principal historical effects of positivism having been to introduce into the minds of a great many men the idea that moral values are relative like everything else. Now moral philosophy could never admit such an idea without betraying itself, since this idea ignores a primary datum of the moral life in its existentially given reality.

What is implied in the moral decision of a man to do nothing contrary to the judgment of his conscience, if not that, rather than commit an act which his conscience judges to be criminal, he is ready to sacrifice all kinds of things however precious in themselves, he is ready to suffer and to cause suffering if need be, he is ready to die if he has to? He may fall short of this decision, yet he will feel that then he was wrong. Now to suffer and to cause suffering—is this not to hurt my own being and somebody else's being, everything I have, everything he has? To give my life—is this not to give what is uniquely mine, to give all that I have, my own particular absolute? And

[1] "By the very nature of the mind. . . ." "The human mind, by its nature. . . ." Cf. above, pp. 277–278.—Comte "is not satisfied" with historical verification. Moreover, he claims to deduce the law of the three stages from the nature of man. He will thus give a direct demonstration of it. . . . "This demonstration shows . . . that the successive passage through the three stages, in an invariable order, was the necessary form of the progress of the human mind in the knowledge of phenomena. It is founded on the nature of the mind." *Ibid.*, pp. 44–52.

[2] "I consider all discussions on the institutions as utter nonsense, until the spiritual reorganization of society is brought about or at least well advanced." Letter to Valat, December 25, 1824 (*Lettres à Valat*, pp. 156–157). "Real science, envisaged from the highest point of view, has no other general aim than to establish or unceasingly fortify intellectual order, which is the indispensable foundation of every other order." *Cours*, IV 147.

[3] On the reorganization of education as necessary prerequisite, cf. *Politique positive*, I, pp. 169 seq., and *Synthèse subjective*, p. vii. See also Lévy-Bruhl (*op. cit.*, p. 381) and Georges Dumas (*op. cit.*, p. 192).

can I be ready to do so save for a reason which is itself absolute and unconditional, in other words, because the malice of the act which I refuse to perform is something absolute and unconditional in the ethical order? It is because this act is in itself objectively and intrinsically evil, according to his own conscience's absolute conviction, that a man will die rather than commit it. But if it were judged evil only because of a purely subjective disposition deriving from heredity or education, or because of the stage of evolution of the social group at a given moment, if, in short, its moral value were purely relative, I should be a fool to die rather than commit it; indeed it would be immoral to sacrifice my life or my happiness or the happiness of others for something which is not their equal in value. Moral life is possible for the human being only if the value of his acts is an ethical absolute which stands forth like a rock from the river of facts, events, phenomena, time and history. And because every knowledge whose object is something absolute and superior to time stands forth above time and, so far as it is true, is immutably true, this ethical absolute must be the object of immutable truths bearing on the value of our acts, unless the moral life of the human being is no more than a mirage or a mystification. That is why every moral theory, whether it be relativist or materialist, which makes fun of the "eternal truths" (the expression is not appropriate,[1] let us rather say supra-temporal truths), betrays the moral life it undertakes to explain. That man makes progress only with the greatest difficulty in the knowledge of these truths which are immutable by nature, that he can occasionally more or less lose consciousness of them, that at the various moments of evolution what he knows of them may be mixed with all kinds of elements which depend on infinitely variable social conditions and historical situations, that is quite another story. But it is a sign of childishness to think that a truth ceases to be true because the myopic see it badly or the blind do not see it at all.

It is worth noting, moreover, as a particularly striking mark of progress, that ethnology, which for a long time refused to bear the slightest value judgment on the various cultures it studied, is now beginning to reject ethical relativism and moreover recognize the actual universality of the primary moral notions which are developed by the various human groups, if,

[1] As Saint Thomas teaches (*Sum. theol.*, I, 16, 7), it is only in the divine intellect, which is subsisting Truth, that truth exists with an eternal existence like that of God Himself. Saint Augustine called mathematical truths eternal, but (*ibid.*, ad 1) "dicendum quod ratio circuli, et duo et tria esse quinque, habent aeternitatem in mente divina"—"it must be said that the *ratio* of circle, and that two and three are five, have eternity *in the divine mind*". The truths present in the human intellect are no more "eternal" than this intellect itself, even when they bear on an object that is unchangeable or superior to time and are therefore themselves non-temporal or supra-temporal, and unchangeable.

It is not without reason that those who claim to reject all truth that would be non-temporal or unchangeable in itself, should instinctively resort to an incorrect and obviously exaggerated expression like that of "eternal truths". In this way they manage for themselves a more advantageous position before their public.

at least, these notions are considered in their most general and basic state.[1] So we have the beginning of that rapprochement between anthropology and moral philosophy which answers, so I believe, a particularly pressing exigency of contemporary thought.

II

SCIENCE AND PHILOSOPHY

The Positivist conception of Philosophy

16. As we noted at the beginning of this chapter, the central thesis of Auguste Comte is that there is but a single authentic knowledge, the one we get from the positive sciences, the sciences of phenomena. These form a homogeneous whole, of which mathematics are a part (for Comte they are natural sciences like the rest),[2] and which constitutes the integrity of knowledge. There is knowledge only of phenomena.

As a result, philosophy is not a distinct and independent knowledge. There is no reality whatsoever of such a nature that the knowledge of it is not brought by some one of the sciences of phenomena and brought by philosophy. In the immensity of the real, philosophy has no object distinct from the object of science, nor has it any domain distinct from the domain of science.

This thesis is not established by any consideration deriving from the critique of knowledge (which would be to admit, by the very fact, that philosophy has a proper object and a proper domain, to draw thence the conclusion that it hasn't). It is not established at all, it is posited. Its only justification is the Comtian absolutization of relativity—a contradiction in terms—and the law of the three stages whose necessity Comte (again a contradiction) demonstrates "by the nature of the human mind".

In the universe of the knowable, philosophy has neither *object* nor domain

[1] Cf. the excellent article by Clyde Kluckhohn, late professor of anthropology at Harvard University, "Ethical Relativity: Sic et Non", in *The Journal of Philosophy*, vol. 52 (November 10, 1955), pp. 663–677.

We are particularly pleased to note the significant affinity between what the author writes about *ethical universals* (pp. 671–672) and our own observations on the "fundamental dynamic schemes of natural law" (*Man and the State*, p. 93).

[2] "Far from saying with Plato or with his successors that there is no science of the phenomenon, or of what passes, Comte thinks on the contrary that science has for sole object phenomenal reality, as subject to laws. . . . If for a long time the mathematical sciences were the only sciences properly speaking, and if today they are still the most advanced of all the sciences, the fact is that geometric and mechanical phenomena are in reality the simplest of all, and the most naturally linked to each other. . . . But the difference between the mathematical sciences and the other sciences remains nonetheless a difference of degree, not of nature. The mathematical sciences are ahead of the other sciences; they are not on another terrain. In short, the mathematical sciences, like all the other sciences, are natural sciences." L. Lévy-Bruhl, *op. cit.*, pp. 143–144.—Cf. *Cours de phil. pos.*, I, 101, sq.

distinct from those of science. Yet Comte is a philosopher and "positive philosophy" is a philosophy. How is this possible? Philosophy has a *point of view* of its own,[1] which is not that of the sciences, for sciences are particular. The point of view of philosophy is the point of view of the whole, or of the greatest universality. Thus it is a reflection upon the sciences (it teaches us, for instance, that the fundamental sciences are at the same time homogeneous and irreducible to each other), but it is much more than that; it states "encyclopaedic" laws which are more general than those of the sciences in this sense that they make converge in a single formula laws which the particular sciences establish in their own orders but which are found in the various orders of phenomena;[2] it organizes and systematizes the sciences, and it regenerates them: it unifies them, not by reason of their object—every attempt at unification on these terms is chimerical, and indeed the sciences tend of themselves to anarchy—but by reason of the universal subject that is humanity, and in view of having this subject come to intellectual unity, which is itself the basis of religious unity and finally of political unity.

It is in this manner—from the point of view of the whole, itself related to the human subject—that Comte claims to found a philosophy at the same time he is denying to philosophy any independent object and domain. For the moment I shall not discuss that claim. Neither is it my concern whether, contrary to his thesis about the relativity of truth, Comte did not believe that the sciences regenerated by him, so reached a final stage and thence were to advance only on the basis of definitively acquired certitudes; nor whether Comte has actually been true to his theoretical positions; nor whether in fact his philosophy of the sciences is not inseparable from his philosophy of history and progress[3]—which goes far beyond phenomena and their verified relations, since its laws are conceived not only as abstract regularities which throw light upon some particular aspect of history, but as a network of necessities which govern the march of history and the movement of mankind in a concrete way, a kind of operative fate (with which, moreover, man co-operates, and which allows him to modify, within certain limits, the course of things).[4] Nor am I considering whether, as already discussed above, he

[1] Cf. Lesson 58 of *Cours de philosophie positive*; and Lévy-Bruhl, *op. cit.*, pp. 124–129, 139, 402–403.

[2] Cf. *Cours*, VI, pp. 667, 670; *Polit. pos.*, I, pp. 494–495; IV, pp. 173–180; and Lévy-Bruhl, *op. cit.*, pp. 113–116.

[3] "In Comte's eyes, the philosophy of the sciences is inseparable from the philosophy of history and the theory of progress." L. Lévy-Bruhl, *op. cit.*, p. 137.

[4] This notion has a superficial resemblance to Marx's notion (although the idea, central for Marx, that man is one day to become master of his history is lacking here). But it has a very different origin. We think that it is due to that confusion between the necessity of laws and the necessity of the course of events that we pointed out in *Les degrés du savoir* (pp. 48–54) and which is so general to-day. In spite of his principles, Comte did not escape that *hypostasierung* of scientific law, especially when it is a question of social dynamics and philosophy of history. And if he observes rightly that we must not confuse "the subordination of any events whatsoever to invariable laws with their irresistible, necessary accomplish-

himself does not abound in absolute assertions; whether he does not derive, as Lévy-Bruhl has pointed out, his notion of the unity of the understanding from Cartesian ontology; and whether even an idea as "metaphysical" as that of finality does not play a role in his thought as fundamental as it is unacknowledged.[1] All these things are important, but what is of primary interest to us at this time is the fact that Comte intended to found a philosophy which is in no way a knowledge independent of the sciences, in other words, which has neither proper object nor proper domain in the universe of the real, a philosophy which is entirely on the level of the positive sciences, without the slightest elevation to rise above the plain.

All the other more subtle and refined forms of positivism which will develop in the future will pursue the same goal and will have the same fundamental conception in common. If Comte himself carried out his enterprise only with the help of gross violations of his own program, and if on the other hand his mission required Messianic dimensions and an ultimate religious destination for his work, other doctors were to come after him who, without needing recourse to prophethood, will have at their disposal perfected equipment and a superior operating technique to permit them to proceed to the scientific castration of the human intellect.

Positivism and Dialectical Materialism

17. It is of interest to note that on this problem of science and philosophy, the positivist and the Marxist positions are clearly different. Historical materialism and positivism have in common a great number of negations, but historical materialism can, in the long run, only nourish a solid aversion for positivism, because historical materialism is itself the end product of an entirely different current of thought and constitutes a *Weltanschauung*, a philosophical view of the real with very fixed dogmas; it is derived from Hegel

---

ment" (*Cours*, III, p. 564), that means for him that the more the phenomena are "noble" or complex, the more the laws that *render the event necessary* leave it at the same time, from the very fact of their interlacing, a certain margin of contingency, so that the necessity in question is not "irresistible". Wherefore that bastard idea of a non-rigid historical determinism or of a "modifiable fatality" (*Polit. pos.*, II, p. 427), which translates into a poorly conceived philosophical language an obvious truth of fact.

[1] Consider for example the law of the three stages, the idea of which flashed into Comte's mind in an incontestably finalist perspective, as Henri Gouhier has well noted (*op. cit.*, vol. III, p. 395, note 2), or the idea that he had of his own mission in the history of mankind. . . .

As for "the principle of the conditions of existence", it offers a pretty example of a functional equivalent masking simply the notion that it is supposed to replace. To say: "from the moment that I have lungs, I can breathe", or: "it is necessary and sufficient that I have a good beef-steak on my table, and the phenomenon called nutrition will actually take place in me", is exactly the same thing—less the intelligible clarity—as to say: "I have lungs in order to be able to breathe", or "I have ordered a good beef-steak to appease my appetite". The principle of the conditions of existence, which Comte valued so highly, but which was scarcely to survive him, is the principle of finality turned inside out—and is of as little use as a glove turned inside out.

whose dialectic it could not deny without at the same time bringing about its own ruin.

No doubt Marx and Engels had declared in *Ideologie Allemande* that "when reality is depicted, philosophy as an independent branch of activity loses its medium of existence",[1] adding, in order not to be outdone in finesse by Feuerbach, that "philosophy and the study of the real world are related to one another as are onanism and love between the sexes".[2] Yet all this was nothing but a flash of wit. In reality philosophy retained an essential importance in their eyes—it was philosophy which accounted for Marx's prestige among the other socialist theorists of his time. Lenin will remain faithful to the thought of Marx and Engels when he rehabilitates ideology; and when Soviet Marxism grants philosophy its own domain, however limited it may be, in the universe of the real, this is quite in accordance with their principles.[3] This domain, distinct from that of the sciences, embraces, as has been noted in the preceding chapter,[4] first of all theory of knowledge, which establishes the absolute truth of materialist realism in opposition to every kind of idealism—secondly, logic—thirdly, and particularly, materialist dialectic, which deals with both the most universal laws of reality and the most universal laws of human thought. We know that Auguste Comte, on the contrary, excommunicated logic[5] and the theory of knowledge—he had good reasons to mistrust them, and from the strictly phenomenist and relativist point of view he was more consistent than the Marxists. His

[1] Marx and Engels, *The German Ideology, Parts I & III*, ed. R. Pascal, New York: International Publishers, 1947, p. 15.

[2] *MEGA*, I, 5, p. 216.

[3] Thus Engels wrote: "As soon as each separate science is required to get clarity as to its position in the great totality of things and of our knowledge of things, a special science dealing with this totality is superfluous. What still independently survives of all former philosophy is the science of thought and its laws—formal logic and dialectics. Everything else is merged in the positive science of Nature and history." *Herr Eugen Dühring's Revolution in Science* (*Anti-Dühring*), trans. E. Burns, New York: International Publishers, 1939, p. 31.

[4] Cf. above, chapter X, p. 249, notes 2 and 3.

[5] "With what would one observe the mind itself, its operations, its way of proceeding? One cannot divide up one's mind, that is to say, one's brain, into two parts, one of which acts while the other watches it act, to observe the way it proceeds. The so-called observations made of the human mind considered in itself and *a priori* are pure illusions. What is called *logic, metaphysics, ideology*, is a chimera and a dream, when it is not an absurdity." Letter to Valat, September 24, 1819 (*Lettres à Valat*, pp. 89–91). It may be remarked that if our mind were *our brain*, Comte would be right; his materialism is on this point more coherent than Soviet materialism. Perfect self-reflection is a privilege of spirituality; and if our mind were our brain there would be no logic.

On the rejection of formal logic by Auguste Comte, cf. Lévy-Bruhl, *op. cit.*, pp. 117–120.

There is however a "positive logic" (cf. Lévy-Bruhl, *op. cit.*, pp. 121–136), but one which has nothing to do with logic properly speaking. It results from the historical and sociological observation of the functioning of the human mind, and in the end this "true logic" will appear to Comte, not as the logic of the mind, "guided above all by artificial signs", but as the logic of the heart, "founded on the direct connection of emotions" (*Polit. pos.*, II, pp. 101–102). "True logic, in which emotions dominate images and signs, has a fetishistic origin." *Catéch. posit.*, p. 337. See *Synthèse subjective*, pp. 26–55.

encyclopaedic laws, on the other hand, remained of the same type, in all respects, as those of the positive sciences; these laws of Comte merely brought together in a single formula, but a more general one, certain laws of the positive sciences, and every *explanatory* claim was excluded from them, just as it was excluded from the scientific laws. On the contrary, the supremely universal laws which for Marxism are the property of dialectics are of another type than the laws of the positive sciences and they give us an explanation which goes much further and which has—to the extent that it renders intelligible such or such a moment of the development—a definitive value. In order to characterize in a more precise manner the opposition between Marxism and positivism, we may note that Soviet Marxism admits a dialectic between *essence* and *phenomenon* which has no meaning for positivism. Doubtless, for Soviet philosophy, essence is not of another order than the phenomenon, it has nothing of an intelligible structure attained through eidetic visualization at a level of the real with which positive science is not directly concerned, it is but the rational texture of mutual relations and intrinsic necessities immanent in the phenomena themselves. Nevertheless, it is very significant that the term *essence*, detested by positivism,[1] should be given to the rational texture in question, and even more significant that the mutual relations and the intrinsic necessities dealt with, should be expressed not only by the laws of positive science, but also, and *par excellence*, by the laws of materialist dialectic. We might say consequently that, if Marxism and positivism are in agreement in denying that philosophy has in the universe of the real an *object*, in the precise meaning of the word, distinct from the object of the sciences of phenomena and situated on a deeper plane of interiority or at a higher level, still they are opposed to each other in this respect: for positivism philosophy has in the real no *domain* distinct from that of the sciences; whereas for Marxism philosophy, while attached in the real to the same object as the sciences, and while remaining at the same degree of knowledge (there is only one, that of the phenomenon), nevertheless possesses its own *domain* within this order—which follows in the last analysis from the fact that, at the very degree of the phenomenon, the real splits dialectically into phenomenon and essence and thus admits of two different dimensions.

Let us say that Marxism grants to philosophy the strict minimum conceivable of independence with regard to science, and takes the greatest care to reduce the difference of level which for classical philosophy separated the domain proper to the sciences of phenomena from that of philosophical knowledge (and in truth metaphysical knowledge can reach infinite heights by analogical or ananoetic intellection) to the simple differences between the amplitudes of two dialectical oscillations (whether dialectic of the phenomenon and essence takes place in the perspective of the experimental sciences

[1] In spite of all the "essentially"'s that stud Auguste Comte's language.

or in that of dialectics itself). The minimum, however, has considerable significance. Marxism does not reduce and cannot reduce human knowledge to a uniformly flat level of knowledge; it is not, and cannot be, a pure phenomenism. Thus it even admits, however minimal, however carefully circumscribed and delimited it may be, a possible beginning for independent philosophical knowledge. Thus too, its atheism is less serene and less smug than positivist atheism. It is an absolute atheism, but one which knows how threatened it is; it needs to defend itself and to attack; it must be militant; whereas Auguste Comte, having deprived human thought of the very idea that it might rise above the science of phenomena, by the same token entrusts the simple natural process of *disuse* with the care of eliminating God. He can count on such a process, he has not the least anxiety.

Thus it appears that, if Marxism is much more deeply and more efficaciously in agreement with the historical energies of modern atheism than is positivism insofar as these energies move toward the Deification of man (what is the mythification of the Great-Being in comparison with the revelation of "the true man, the deified man"?), on the other hand, positivism is much more deeply and efficaciously in agreement with the historical energies of modern atheism than is Marxism insofar as these energies move toward the definitive Resignation of the human intellect (what is a materialism still preoccupied with the theory of knowledge and with dialectical certitudes, however invested they may be in the phenomenon, in comparison with the fixation of the mind in the peace of full philosophical impotence erected into the final philosophy?).

We see at the same stroke that modern time's atheism, let us say atheism which claims to be the ultimate phase of evolution, is a house divided against itself.

Homo Positivus

18. We see, also, that in turning up his nose at Auguste Comte, Marx made a rash judgment, or rather he still remained (does not Tawney call him *the last of the Schoolmen*?) in the "outdated" perspective of the intrinsic values of the intelligence, he himself forgetting that for modern man and especially for Marxist man the sole valid criterion is that of history and of historical efficacy. From this point of view we must recognize that Comte has been, if not properly speaking the author, at least the prophet and the formulator of a revolution which doubtless has directly affected only the domain of ideas, but whose power of diffusion and (for that very reason) the index of universality are certainly more considerable than those of the Marxist revolution in the social domain. Positivism has exercised its influence throughout the entire world, East and West, in countries now communistic as well as in non-communistic countries and especially in the Western democracies, and it has done so on all the levels of culture. Doubtless it is quite

true that, taken in its original form and its original codifications, we can speak of it only in the past tense. But, if the principal philosophical movements of the twentieth century have reacted powerfully against it and have discredited it as a philosophy, if the metaphysics that was thought to be dead and buried has indicated its own rights anew, the fact remains that under new forms and with new shoots positivist philosophy itself shows its vitality and pursues its process of development. It is true, too, and this is what is essentially important, that the state of mind that positivism or neo-positivism undertakes to formulate and to justify (but which has sources deeper than any philosophical theory, and the advent of which it was the stroke of genius of Auguste Comte to foresee), the *anti-sapiential* state of mind, is taking on in our age of civilization an extension so typical that no one need exert his imagination very much in order to ask himself whether we are not progressing toward a cleavage of the human species into two sub-species, *homo sapiens* and *homo positivus*, or toward the pure and simple hegemony of the second.

It is this hegemony of a new human sub-species that Comte announced, and it is in this—at least, and I do not wish to say anything else, as concerns the direction of the forces which in his time were just beginning to make their appearance and which were later to have such great developments—that he was somehow a prophet.

In order to describe in non-Comtian terms the way in which things seem to be moving, unless powerful contrary forces gain the upper hand, let us say that the sub-species *homo positivus*, such as it is developing before our eyes, has roughly three varieties: (1) an important number of specialists dedicated to the sciences of phenomena; (2) a large portion of the mass of common humanity; (3) a certain family of philosophers.

The men who belong to the first variety do not realize that science as such, mainly in its present highest and most ingenious form, theoretical physics, enjoys an overwhelming authority to rebuild the universe of observable and measurable facts into greater and greater syntheses of signs, definitions and mathematical deductions (or at least, as far as sciences of nature not yet mathematized are concerned, into syntheses of symbolic entities, worked out toward an explanation similar to mathematical explanation); they do not realize that science is thus not only entirely distinct from philosophical knowledge, but also distinct from any refusal of its validity. They are so disposed not by scientific inclination but by a very human, too human trend, to consider as null and void what is outside one's own field. Without, however, being doctrinal positivists (they are less and less so, it seems), these men dedicated to a certain kind of knowledge of nature which demands rigorous disciplines and has a formidable yield are quite naturally inclined to consider this kind of knowledge of nature as the only kind of knowledge possible; moreover the highly specialized training that scientific research demands, the natural talents which it presupposes and which are related to poetic imagination of the most adventurous kind, disciplined only by the exactitude of mathematical formulations and methods of experimental control, finally the mental habits it involves and sustains—all of these together cause a great number of scientists to become "spontaneously freed", as Comte would say, from any idea that a philosophical and metaphysical knowledge of realities of a more profound order could complement the knowledge of nature gained through the science of phenomena. In short, they hold for what can be called an exclusivist concept of science.

I don't say it is the case of all scientists. There are scientists who recognize, without any limitation, the validity of the natural apperceptions of the intellect, and understand that a child has such a spontaneous grasp of the principle of causality for example, taken in its original and integral (ontological) meaning, only because in the primordial intuitions of childhood the human being is awakening to the life of human intelligence as such.[1] These scientists whom we can call *liberals* by opposition to the *exclusive* scientists (this distinction has nothing to do with science itself, for in both categories can be found men endowed with the highest scientific capacities), are ready not only to try to grasp reality far beyond phenomenon, but to recognize the necessity of using toward this end the properly philosophical equipment. We may expect that a day will come when such scientists' state of mind[2] will prevail. But as long as scientists do not devote more time to philosophy and philosophers do not meditate on science, the research people for whom the only authentic knowledge to be attained by reason is the domination of phenomena, will remain the most numerous group in the world of sciences.

We come back now to the group of scientists we were speaking about previously. These exclusive scientists will be able (this is something Comte had not foreseen) to adhere to one or the other of the traditional religions, to have a fervent faith and a lofty spiritual life; they will not be atheists as far as religion is concerned; they may also have and even recognize irrepressible metaphysical aspirations, which they will endeavor to satisfy by extrapolations, always more or less arbitrary, of their science—every kind of metaphysical or philosophical *wisdom* will remain a dead letter for them; they will be atheists as far as reason is concerned.

[1] Cf. the epilogue, as anti-positivist as possible, written by the well-known physiologist, Dr. Andrew Conway Ivy, to the book *The Evidence of God in an Expanding Universe*, ed. J. G. Monsma (New York: Putnam, 1958, pp. 229–231), where are collected testimonies of scientists belonging to the most different fields of specialization. The remarks made by Dr. Ivy on children's intelligence are in relieving contrast with *Les ages de l'intelligence* by Léon Brunschvicg.

[2] I must name here, to speak only of those I have personally known, the renowned geologist Pierre Termier, the eminent chemist Sir Hugh Taylor, the mathematician Marston Morse, the physicists Robert Oppenheimer and Léon Brillouin, the aerodynamics specialist Luigi Crocco, biologists Hans Driesch, Rémy Collin, Hans André, W. R. Thompson, the zoo-psychologist F. J. J. Buytendijk, the already mentioned Dr. Ivy, and, connected in particular with the existence of God—of a personal God—as required by the intelligibility of the universe, the testimony of Einstein himself.

This variety (*homo scientificus exclusivus*) of *homo positivus*, moreover—in spite of its fundamental importance in our technological age—faces the danger of abdication within. For, on the one hand, the scientist, in his deepest inspiration, lives only on truth and for truth; and yet the science of phenomena, once cut off from all vital connection with philosophical and metaphysical wisdom, to which the intellect tends as to the supreme natural accomplishment of the desire and the joy of knowing, inevitably loses (I say, in the very mind of the scientist, the "exclusive scientist") the strength to affirm against the pressure of social needs its essentially speculative and disinterested character, and passes under a yoke alien to its nature, that of utility, and of practical finalities. This passage is evident in Auguste Comte himself who never stopped manifesting his scorn for knowledge for the sake of knowledge;[1] in thus denying Aristotle and the great contemplative tradition of humanity he betrayed not only philosophy, he also betrayed science and submitted it (his own attempts at regimentation have showed this clearly) to the arbitrary rule of the practical interests of the human community. Facing the danger of seeing modern States subjugate some of the major fields of scientific research to their own practical and military purposes, all the more powerfully since the advancement of sciences requires in these fields immense financial resources, we understand Einstein's joke, declaring that if he had known, he would have chosen to be a plumber rather than a physicist. He was a liberal scientist, he had enough philosophy to hold above all for the spiritual dignity of physical science, and its goal to know for the sake of knowledge. Confronting a factual situation which seems helpless as long as humanity does not pass to a supra-national organization of the world, he was left at least—with sadness and anguish—with the chance to refuse to bend within, and the immovable conviction that science lives on freedom as well as truth.

19. In the sub-species *homo positivus* there is a second variety—let us call it *homo gregarius*—made up of vast portions (and I don't say portions only that

[1] The maxim "*Know, so as to foresee, so as to provide for*" shows clearly that for Comte the contemplative finality of knowledge, truth to be seen and to be cherished for itself, was completely eliminated. Doubtless he was not unaware that science cannot do without researches that are speculative and without immediate application, but it is then only *forgetting* temporarily its essentially practical end (cf. Lévy-Bruhl, *op. cit.*, p. 70). As Meyerson notes (*Identité et réalité*, p. 36), Comte recognizes the existence of the need for understanding, but he makes it "one of the least imperious needs of our nature".

"I would have very little esteem for scientific works", Comte wrote to Valat in 1819, "if I did not think perpetually of their utility for mankind; I would then just as much amuse myself in working out very complicated riddles. I have a supreme aversion for scientific works whose utility, whether direct or remote, I do not perceive." (*Lettres à Valat*, September 28, 1819, p. 99.) "To know for the sake of knowing seems to Comte to be a culpable use of the human intellect." L. Lévy-Bruhl, *op. cit.*, p. 175. "Under the positivist regime, one will have to abstain from every exercise of thought which will not have some real utility, whether material or moral; 'science for the sake of science' is a principle not only contemptible but criminal." G. Dumas, *op. cit.*, p. 163.

are of Marxist or positivist persuasion) of the common mass of humanity. In this variety, as in the preceding one, many who believe in God can be found. But, believers or non-believers, all who belong to this group are characterized by their unresisting adaptation to, and their complete conformity to, the cultural environment proper to the scientific, technological or industrial age, and they are gregariously engaged in the system of thought and mental habits which predominate in such a culture. From this point of view Herbert Butterfield was not wrong in considering as a fact of central importance in human history the general diffusion and the cultural preponderance of a manner of thinking which is the popularized version of the way of thinking required by the science of phenomena, and according to which nothing is accessible to us and nothing has interest except what can be the object of a manipulation by means of symbolic formulas.[1] One of the consequences is the "Promethianism of science" and the confusion, the old magic confusion between knowledge and power. Invested with the power of the signs by which he masters nature and utilizes the unknown, "man the Manipulator takes charge of the Manipulated world" (here positivism and Marxism join forces).[2] The other consequence is the phenomenalization of thought. In his remarkable essay on "The Secularization of Culture", Thomas O'Dea points out, using the terminology of Martin Buber, that thenceforth, in the manner in which man envisages things, other men, and the mystery of being, the "technical relation" (in which he manipulates things by controlling them from the outside, and in which the other is nothing but an "it", a phenomenon) takes predominance over the "essential relation" (in which man responds interiorly to things as to subjects, and in which the other is a "thou", a being-for-itself).[3] In an essay on the *Chemins de la Foi*[4] I have pointed out two other typical aspects of this phenomenalization of thought: mental productivism or "fixation in the sign", and the primacy of verification over truth.

Such a manner of thinking, when it becomes preponderant, does not preclude religious faith (although it offers it a weakening climate). But it

[1] "Science regards the object of its studies precisely as object, an 'it' undefinable without reference to the operations—the manipulations—necessary to observe or measure it, and given meaning within mathematical schemata where it is treated as the object of abstract 'handling', of symbolic manipulation. This way of seeing reality, which Herbert Butterfield regards as sharing with the rise of Christianity the position of greatest significance in Western history, was the result, in his words, of our putting on a new thinking cap, rather than of new facts. It derived from the new ability to see the world in terms capable of mathematical expression and manipulation." Thomas F. O'Dea, Professor at the Massachusetts Institute of Technology, "The Secularization of Culture", *The Commonweal*, April 20, 1956, p. 69.

[2] Cf. Max Raphaël, *La théorie marxiste de la connaissance*, French trans., Paris: Gallimard, 1938, p. 121; and our *Quatre essais sur l'esprit dans sa condition charnelle*, 2e ed., Paris: Alsatia, 1956, pp. 211–213.

[3] Cf. Thomas F. O'Dea, article cited, p. 67.

[4] Cf. *Le philosophe dans la cité*, Paris: Alsatia, 1960.

is strictly incompatible with the natural exercise of the intelligence—preliminary to philosophy but in continuity with it—by which the great mass of men spontaneously possess the treasure of certitudes on which a truly human life feeds. *Homo gregarius*, the human product resulting from a total adjustment to the manner of thinking with which we are now dealing, is, just as were the exclusive scientists we considered above, an atheist in the domain of reason, even when he is not at all an atheist in the domain of religion. And how could he still admit according to reason that there are ethical values which are objective and unconditionally founded? As far as values are concerned, he knows the value of the dime, and he knows that it is certainly relative.

Finally, the third variety of *homo positivus* is made up of those philosopher descendants of Auguste Comte (neo-positivists, logical-positivists, logical-empiricists, neo-empiricists, or whatever other name they call themselves) who in one way or another strive to complete the intellectual and cultural work begun by Comte, and to justify in reason the loss of the sense of being that is manifest in the world of to-day. This is the variety *homo in-sipiens*. In actual fact it is far from having the importance with which Comte saw his disciples invested. It is not its representatives who are called to form the new spiritual power. There is no high-priest of humanity, no "positivist clergy" among them. They are prosaic atheists, atheists who do not even try to replace what they destroy, incomplete positivists, as Comte said. Moreover, it was not really to philosophers that Comte entrusted supreme authority. It was rather to the scientists—to those scientists inspired with his spirit, and capable of "synergy", whom "a true encyclopaedic initiation"[1] will have made capable of understanding "the mutual harmony" of "fiction" and "demonstration",[2] and capable of proceeding to the two indispensable "successive constructions: the one philosophical, the other poetic".[3] No desire, however, to serve humanity in this fashion has seemed to manifest itself yet among our most advanced scientists. In fact, on the day when the development of *homo positivus* would demand a religion according to his measure, it is the State in its openly or hypocritically totalitarian forms which, with the assistance of its technicians in Propaganda, means of mass communication, Collective Psychology and Depth Psychology, would provide—and doubtless not with "love as

[1] Cf. *Lettres inédites à C. de Blignières*, pp. 102, 110; *Lettres à divers*, I, 2, pp. 93, 117, 159–160; *Catéch. positiv.*, p. 22: "The positive priesthood . . . in virtue of its immense encyclopaedic preparation . . ."; *ibid.*, p. 274: "during the seven years which separate him from the complete priesthood, each curate has practised all the encyclopaedic steps . . ."; *Testament*, pp. 21–22: "I have recently determined, for the priests and curates, the encyclopaedic conditions which will be a guarantee for the public, as also for the High-Priest, of the theoretical aptitude of philosophers, when their moral qualities will be sufficiently established. . . ."

[2] *Synthèse subjective*, p. 12.

[3] *Lettres à divers*, I, 2, 58 (to Thales Bernard, 28 Aristotle 62).

a principle"—for the production and distribution of the myths necessary for the consumption of its citizens.[1]

Impossibility of the philosophy of Anti-philosophy

20. On the fundamental truth systematically misunderstood by Auguste Comte, and in practice ignored by the scientist when he entrenches himself entirely in the knowledge of phenomena—I mean, on this fact that other ways, typically different, of approaching and knowing the real are equally valid, and form with science an ensemble at once heterogeneous and coordinated, and that in particular the "ontological" approach to reality, the mode of knowing proper to philosophy and metaphysics, keeps, in the face of the science of phenomena, its superior legitimacy and its superior necessity—I have insisted many times in several works.[2] The only point I would like to make here in this respect is the logical inconsistency of the position according to which the "empiriological" approach proper to the sciences of phenomena (resolution of concepts in the observable and the measurable as such, so as to construct thereon beings of reason that permit of a rational manipulation of the data of experience by means of well-founded symbols) is the only approach which attains to authentic knowledge of the real. Three remarks, we hope, will make our position sufficiently clear.

First: it is highly significant that positivism feels the need of justifying rationally (by the law of the three stages, for example) the anti-philosophical stage to which it destines culture and thought, and of presenting

[1] To-day we see science in the service of the State threatening human liberty in a much less problematic and more tangible form—that of integral planning. The "integral" or omnilateral plan, as it has begun to be used here and there, is an organic group of reforms, spread out over a certain period, which cover, altogether and in interrelation, the most diverse areas of economic, social and cultural life. The unavoidable result is a general transformation of the living conditions, the customs and the collective psyche of a given population. And the efficacy of the method is such that, though its application in the beginning was limited to under-developed regions, it seems destined inevitably to spread. But such plans can be implemented only by the most painstaking work of numerous teams of experts and scientists, and the State only is in a position to subsidize such an undertaking. That the State should thus have the power to model human life according to the wishes of its planning experts, constitutes a most serious threat to democratic liberties.

As far as we can see, there is only one solution, namely, that, through the intermediary of political parties, the people might be able to choose from among *several* omnilateral plans (elaborated according to varying perspectives and in the light of differing ultimate objectives) proposed by the various political parties. For this to come true, we would have to hope, on the one hand, that the parties (whose existence is indispensable to the proper functioning of a democratic society) would be regenerated in such a fashion as to become real schools of social and political thought (cf. *True Humanism*, pp. 157–158); and on the other hand that *the State itself* would put its planning teams at *the disposal of the parties*, each one of which would establish an omnilateral plan inspired by its particular conception of the common good. The part the State should play in the de-statization of the life of our modern societies was suggested in our *Man and the State*, p. 22.

[2] Cf. *Réflexions sur l'intelligence et sur sa vie propre; The Degrees of Knowledge; Quatre essais sur l'esprit dans sa condition charnelle* (Chapter IV); *Raison et raisons* (Chapter I); *Philosophy of Nature.*

itself as a philosophy—as definitive philosophy. But from the moment that there is a philosophy, it is necessary that it have in the universe of reality an object distinct from that of the sciences: to believe with dialectical materialism that without having a distinct object it at least has a distinct domain, or with positivism that without having either a distinct object or a distinct domain it at least has a distinct point of view, is to dupe oneself. Philosophy can have neither a domain distinct from that of the sciences nor a point of view distinct from theirs, except insofar as there is in what is, a certain knowability to which it is adapted, in other words, insofar as it has in the universe of the real an *object*, which is proper to it. However reduced, however one may diminish it, it is there in spite of everything (and even a pure logical empiricism[1] which seeks only to bring out the meaning of what the sciences themselves are doing, ascribes to itself, not perhaps in the extra-mental real, but at least in the mental real, in the very universe of the sciences as they are in the mind, an object which is not the object of the sciences). Finally, if we look closely at the object in question, then however much materialism, positivism, or empiricism may impoverish it, we come to realize that, in fact, the only way of designating it which has any sense is to designate it as a residual aspect of *being*—ah yes, here is that ancient one again, with his faithful Parmenides. And if being is there and is recognized as such, there is no reason not to give it all its dimensions . . . (Here we may note parenthetically that already in the *Tractatus logico-philosophicus*[2] one of the maxims of Wittgenstein: "Not *how* the world is, is the mystical, but *that* it is", can receive a fully philosophical sense, and can be regarded as a valid assertion of the metaphysics of *esse*. As to the principle put forth in the same work: "What can be said at all can be said clearly", it can be understood in the sense of the most narrow scientific univocation, according to which that only is "clearly said" which is defined by a means of mathematical or experimental verification. But it can be understood also in a sense truly worthy of the intelligence, signifying that, on the one hand, we can formulate statements "clearly said" about things obscure in themselves (such as the *materia prima* of Aristotle) or obscure for us (such as the divine perfections), and that, on the other hand, the clarity of a statement is something essentially analogical, and that there are as many different ways of "clearly saying" as there are distinct steps in knowledge—why should a philosopher accuse a physicist of not speaking clearly when he speaks of *anti-matter*? And why should a physicist accuse a philosopher of not speaking clearly when he speaks of *being in potency* or of *contingent being*?)

[1] I am thinking in particular of the positions of Alfred J. Ayer. Cf. *Language, Truth and Logic*, 2nd Ed., 1950, London: Victor Gollancz.

[2] This book was published in 1923. We know that in his posthumous work *Philosophische Untersuchungen* (*Philosophical Investigations*, ed. Elizabeth Anscombe, 1954) Wittgenstein abandoned much of his radicalism and made his way in a direction clearly incompatible with logical positivism.

Second: the object proper to philosophy as an independent knowledge, which we were just now considering, that *being* seized (by the humbly human means of eidetic abstraction) beyond the observable and the measurable as such, seized as something determined in itself—whether it is a question of the act of existence or of its determinations, intelligible natures or structures which are definable not through our operations of measurement but through their own intrinsic characteristics—the very sciences of phenomena demand it. Indeed they presuppose that there is a reality independent of our perception or of our mind, and yet knowable to our mind, and this truth can be critically established and defended only in terms of philosophical knowledge.

Moreover, in the very operation of research and discovery, the mind of the scientist, even when it is taking for object only the observable and the measurable as such, can seize new relationships between phenomena or glimpse the possibility of a new global arrangement of explanatory symbols, only if the guiding idea surges up in it while it struggles obscurely, at the outer gateways of science, in the mystery of a certain reality which is not phenomenon but being, and of a certain rationality which is not that of its explanatory constructions but of the universe of things: this mystery remains for it a vast unknown; but that this unknown is there, it knows very well, in a prescientific or common-sense knowledge which only philosophy can bring to the level of science. And it is indeed by reason of this indispensable ontological background that (contrary to Comtian interdicts) the scientist does not deprive himself of making use of a whole lexicon of notions (substance, matter, nature, cause, energy, power, action . . .) which he has inherited from the philosophy of nature and from metaphysics, but (and this time in agreement with the most profound views of Auguste Comte) which he totally *recasts* in a purely phenomenalist perspective.

In the third place: scientific work is inseparable from a whole natural and human conditioning (in particular the human relationships of the scientist with his collaborators, his rivals, his laboratory personnel . . .) in which are involved processes of non-scientific knowledge, which stem from the natural intelligence, and which are valid processes, although not bearing on the phenomenon as such. And it belongs to philosophy (to the critique of knowledge) to establish and to elucidate the validity of these processes of knowledge, at the level of a knowledge of an order other than that of science.

21. Finally it must be noted that while the development of the sciences draws them to a state of ever greater specialization, the desire for unity and integration grows proportionately in the mind of the scientist. But at the same time science itself, which prospers only in adventure, refuses all unification which would come from constraint, even were it in the name of the exigencies of the heart and of the interests of humanity; it does not want to

be "regenerated" by any clergy, even a positivist one. The only unity which is worthy of it is a unity attained in the very order of knowledge. Does this mean that the unity in question must be expected from a kind of bastard philosophy which, on the one hand, would be, as Comte's philosophy was, on the same level with the sciences and deprived of any independent domain, and which, on the other hand, would claim, however, to know more than the sciences themselves do, so as to unite them in some object more fundamental than theirs? Those who foster such notions are not even good positivists. If the supreme objects proposed to metaphysical or religious thought have for centuries fulfilled the function of *poetic integrator*, as Julian Huxley says,[1] that has never been on the level of the explanation of phenomena; and to wish to find to-day this *poetic integrator* in the notion of some "self-transforming and self-transcending reality" would be only to adulterate the science of phenomena by mixing with it an ambiguous Hegelianism. In general the philosophical theories that certain scientists rightfully preoccupied with universal problems and anxious to attain to some unified conception of the world, like to build up without recognizing the proper instruments of philosophical thought, and with the aid only of an extrapolation of their scientific concepts, can finally only be disappointing for the mind; they bring it a momentary, sometimes vigorous, stimulation, but they feed it with confusions.

The only solution satisfactory both for science and for philosophy is to hold that the unity and the integration to which the scientist aspires in the very order of knowledge are attained not at the level of the sciences themselves, but *beyond them and their domain*, and *higher*, at the level of philosophical knowledge and of the realities which constitute its proper and independent object—while each science goes its own way as the wind blows. It is the business of metaphysics, and still more of the philosophy of nature, to reinterpret in the proper perspective and the proper universe of philosophical knowledge, and to unify therein, the vast and perpetually changing material of facts and theories elaborated by the various sciences.[2]

To conclude, may I be permitted to reproduce a few lines from an essay in which I insisted upon the irreducible diversity of the intellectual virtues and of the types of knowledge which together constitute the integrity of human knowledge. "In the history of human knowledge we see now one, now another of these intellectual virtues, now one, now another, of these types of knowledge, trying, with a sort of imperialism, to seize, at the expense of the others, the whole universe of knowledge. Thus, at the time of Plato and Aristotle, there was a period of philosophical and metaphysical imperialism;

[1] Quoted by Thomas F. O'Dea, *article cited*, p. 69.

[2] Cf. our essay on "La philosophie et l'unité des sciences", Annex II to Chapter IV of *Quatre essais sur l'esprit dans sa condition charnelle*, 2e ed., Paris: Alsatia, 1956; and our essay "God and Science", in *On the Use of Philosophy*, Princeton: Princeton University Press, 1961.

in the Middle Ages, at least before St. Thomas Aquinas, a period of theological imperialism; since Descartes, Kant and Auguste Comte, a period of scientific imperialism which has progressively lowered the level of reason while at the same time securing a splendid technical domination of material nature. It would be a great conquest if the human mind could end these attempts at spiritual imperialism which bring in their wake no less serious damage, to be sure, than that which results from political imperialism; it would be a great achievement if the human mind could establish on unshakable foundations the freedom and autonomy as well as the vital harmony and the mutual strengthening of the great disciplines of knowledge through which the intellect of man strives indefatigably toward truth."[1]

The atheism of Comte

22. Comte became an atheist at the age of thirteen. "From the age of thirteen I have been spontaneously freed from all supernatural beliefs," he wrote in his Testament.[2] And in a letter to his father: "From the age of fourteen I had naturally ceased to believe in God."[3] Henri Gouhier tells us[4] that according to Dr. Robinet[5] this "emancipation" was "undoubtedly due to the vigor of a very superior cerebral organization" but might be "additionally explained" by the system of education to which the child was subjected.[6] Comte's violent reaction against the military regime which prevailed in the Montpellier lycée[7] in which he was enrolled as a resident student when he was barely nine years old, and in which a decorative religion was imposed by consular decrees and regulations on youth still imbued with the Jacobinism of the preceding generation, was able indeed to play an accidental role in the spiritual event under question. Such explanations, however, are not only secondary, they are obviously futile. The rupture with God mentioned by Comte—the very way he speaks of it shows this clearly—was an eminently personal decision, and one which derived, if not from a "very superior cerebral organization", at least from a power of moral self-determination

[1] *The Range of Reason*, p. 11.
[2] *Testament*, p. 9.
[3] January 26, 1857. *Revue Occidentale*, 1909, vol. I, p. 15. Cf. Henri Gouhier, *op. cit.*, vol. I, p. 71, note 5.
[4] *Op. cit.*, vol. I, p. 71.
[5] Robinet, *Notice sur l'oeuvre et la vie d'Auguste Comte*, Paris, 1864; 3e éd., Paris: *Société positiviste*, 1891, p. 100.
[6] "Brought up in one of those lycées in which Bonaparte tried in vain to restore, at great expense, the ancient mental preponderance of the theologico-metaphysical regime, I had scarcely reached my fourteenth year when, surveying spontaneously all the essential degrees of the revolutionary mind, I experienced already the fundamental need of a universal regeneration, at once political and philosophical, under the active impulse of the salutary crisis whose principal phase had preceded my birth, and whose irresistible influence over me was the more assured because, in complete accordance with my own nature, it was at that time everywhere about me." *Cours*, vol. VI, Preface, p. ix.
[7] Created by a decree of May 6, 1803, the Montpellier lycée opened its classes the 12th of Brumaire in the 13th year of the first French Republic (November 3, 1804).

which was remarkably sure of itself, since this decision was definitive and sufficed to keep Comte, during his whole life, in an atheism which he never questioned.

In all probability the major decision thus made at the age of thirteen coincided in Comte with that first act of freedom through which, in the moment that he leaves the regime of childhood and deliberates for the first time about himself, man chooses the end to which he makes his moral life tend and the good on which he makes it depend. It seems also that the observations on the first springing forth of atheism in the soul which we made previously[1] in regard to Marxist atheism are equally applicable to the atheism of Comte. Here, as there, it is a question of a first option in which the soul regards the refusal of any transcendent law (any "supernatural" law, to use Comte's term) as an act of moral maturity and emancipation, and decides to approach good and evil *absolutely by itself alone*, and therefore without any God in heaven and on earth before Whose will it would have to bend.

But between Marx's atheism and Comte's atheism there are two notable differences. On the one hand, it was through confusing Hegel's God with God that Marx rejected God, whereas in Comte there is no confusion of this kind: it was simply from the catechism that the schoolboy of Montpellier held his idea of God—he was too young to know anything of the false gods of philosophy. On the other hand, Marxist atheism at its origin entails a rebellion (in the end a failure, as we have seen) against the Emperor of this world, and it is inseparable from a revolt against the world and the social order such as they are *hic et nunc*. Comte's atheism, on the contrary, was from the beginning a private affair between God and him and does not entail the shadow of a revolt against the world. As the whole career of the philosopher will show (and even more strongly in his second period), this atheism will be an atheism as conservative[2] as the theism of Hegel, and one which will not even have to justify the world, but will only have to note its laws by reason, and to venerate it with the heart.

This atheism, at least as far as its psychological dominants are concerned, puts us very far from Marx and Feuerbach, and even from Diderot, very far too from Kirilov. It is absolute, certainly—as absolute as the "everything is

[1] Cf. above, chapter X, pp. 218–219.

[2] "During the thirty years of my philosophical and social career, I have always felt a profound scorn for what is called, under our various regimes, the opposition, and a secret affinity for builders of whatever kind. Those even who sought to build with materials obviously worn out, always seemed to me better than mere destroyers, in a century in which general reconstruction is everywhere becoming the principal need." *Catéchisme positiv.*, p. 6.

"We must regard the mass of conservatives or reactionaries as the true milieu of positivism. . . . Positivism will become for them the sole defense against the communist or socialist subversions." *Correspondence inédite*, II, pp. 167–168 (to Pierre Laffitte, 8 Gutenberg 65).

It was in 1855 that Comte published his famous *Appel aux conservateurs*.

relative"—but it is not revolutionary,[1] it is neither militant nor argumentative, nor wishful of self-proof—so surely and comfortably installed that it is not even conscious of an adversary (its Adversary has disappeared). It has a quality of ease and naturalness, of proud tranquillity, which makes it unique in its kind. It has no need for Prometheus, it does not insult the gods, and does not raise against God the claim of the enslaved or alienated man—the old slavery and the "long minority of mankind" have spontaneously come to an end with "the irrevocable exhaustion of the reign of God".[2]

And this atheism does not want an eschatological effort of history thanks to which the human species will finally reach its divinity. Out of the human species the Great Being will be fashioned, and under this title it will substitute itself "definitively for God".[3] But originally, in the generative movement of Comtian atheism, it is not mankind that is the concern, but Comte himself. And Comte does not feel the need of being God, it is enough for him to be Comte. What happened in him when he became conscious of himself was a simple phenomenon of internal shiftings. He "spontaneously" and "naturally" recognized that the central place which God was thought to occupy really belonged to himself, Comte, and he slipped into that place as into the hollow of his bed, never to move from it. It was a psychological operation which could be accomplished with such irreproachable assurance only through that infinite self-esteem he indulged in from the very moment of his reaching the use of reason, and which he possessed from his constitutional egocentrism, symptomatic of the mental diathesis which was to appear later.[4]

23. Nor did Comte, who never deigned to use any other argument than the law of the three stages against the validity of metaphysical assertions and belief in anything absolute, ever pay God the honor of discussing His existence. This attitude has great significance. The problem did not arise for him, and was not to arise. Why? Because it was already resolved, not by way of rational inquiry and philosophical examination, but in virtue of an ethical private option—in virtue of the wholly personal and incommunicable act of non-faith accomplished at the moment when he deliberated about his own life.

Thus, therefore, for Comte—and it will be the same for Marx (although in the young Marx the decisive option was made more slowly, and in a mind caught up in the heady excitement of philosophy)—atheism came from outside of philosophy, from a more personal and more profound source; and for both it is also through something outside philosophy that belief in God will disappear from the minds of men—not through the effect of any rational

[1] He is not revolutionary as regards the world and the social order. "The great Western revolution" for which Comte received the mission is essentially a spiritual revolution.

[2] *Polit. positive*, IV, p. 531.

[3] *Catéch. posit.*, p. 380; *Testament*, p. 9; *Polit. posit.*, III, pp. 618–623.

[4] Cf. further on, Chapter XII, p. 314, note 2.

examination of the problem, but as the consequence automatically precipitated by an inevitable radical change, either (for dialectical materialism) in the economic and social regime, or (for positivism) in the general regime of thought.[1] It is not surprising that both[2] showed little sympathy for the demonstrators of atheism, and that Comte, in particular, clearly separated himself from doctrinaire atheism, with which he has nothing in common, as he writes to John Stuart Mill, *except "not to believe in God"*,[3] and whose "proud musings on the formation of the universe, the origin of animals, etc."[4] he strongly condemns. Those who wish to prove the non-existence of God are only wrong-way theologians and the most inconsistent theologians.

It is nonsense to wish to conclude from this that Comte was not an atheist, but only an agnostic. As Father de Lubac has very well shown, Comte does not remain on this side of atheism, he goes beyond it. "We have it on Comte's own authority that he wished to go beyond atheism, considering it a position that was over-timid and not proof against certain counter-offensives."[5] For him doctrinaire atheism "does not go far enough, it does not pluck out the root of the evil".[6] In brief, Comte's atheism is that of an anti-Church which wishes to be triumphant and sees itself as already triumphant. He knows that one does not get rid of God by reasoning against Him, but by forgetting Him, by losing sight of Him, by exercising the function of thinking in such a way that the question of God cannot even appear.

The ideal would be never to have to pronounce His name. History, however, obliges us to do so—and on the occasions when he thus encounters the idea of God, Comte reveals by his violence to what degree he is affronted by it. We know that he reserved favored treatment for polytheism in order the better to belabor monotheism. Monotheism, however necessary it may have been at a certain period in history, now "more and more deserves the reprobation its advent inspired for three centuries in the noblest practitioners

[1] "No one, doubtless, has ever demonstrated logically the non-existence of Apollo, Minerva, etc., nor that of the Oriental fairies or of the different poetic creations; but this has not at all prevented the human mind from inevitably abandoning the ancient dogmas, when they have finally ceased to fit in with the ensemble of its situation." *Disc. sur l'esprit positif.*, 1844, p. 52. [Comte purposely ignores that many Arabian and Christian philosophers "demonstrated logically" the unicity of God, which logically dismissed Apollo, Minerva, etc.]

"Sound philosophy," Comte says, "sets aside, it is true, all insoluble questions; but, 'in explaining their rejection, it avoids denying anything in their regard, for this would be contrary to that systematic obsolescence through which alone incontestable opinions must die out.' (Comte means: opinions which escape positive discussion.) The problems connected with the essence of the soul or with first substance will vanish as have vanished already most of the metaphysical problems of the Scholastics." L. Lévy-Bruhl, *op. cit.*, p. 80. [A prophecy denied by the course of events.]

[2] Speculative atheism, which to reject God stays on the level of rational argumentation, "is only a [useless] abstraction", Marx affirmed in *Economie politique et philosophie*. Cf. *Revue marxiste*, February 1, 1929, p. 125.

[3] *Lettres d'Auguste Comte à John Stuart Mill* (1841–1845), Paris, 1877, pp. 252–253.

[4] *Ibid.*, p. 352. [5] H. de Lubac, *op. cit.*, p. 95. [6] *Ibid.*, p. 96.

and theorists of the Roman world."[1] It leads man to adore a being who, if he existed, would degrade himself by a "puerile vanity".[2] It is incompatible with the sound equilibrium of the social order and progress. "The sincere and judicious conservatives . . . have remarked that the motto of the anarchists is *God* and the people, just as that of the reactionaries was already *God* and the king."[3] "Catholics, Protestants and deists" are all "slaves of God" "at once backward-minded and disturbers".[4] They "adore an absolute Being, whose power is without limits; so that His wishes necessarily remain arbitrary. If they were really consistent, they would then consider themselves real slaves, subjected to the whims of an impenetrable power. Only positivism can make us systematically free, that is, subject to immutable and known laws, which emancipate us from all personal rule."[5] Finally (and how deny the consequence if the *first and constitutive* function of religion is of the human order: to bring mankind here below to a state of consummate concord and unity?)[6] God is contrary to religion; and the supreme benefit of the positive religion will be "to finally brush God aside as irreligious"—a perspective capable of softening even M. Littré.[7]

[1] The passage deserves to be quoted in its entirety, for it is doubly instructive, both through the violence which animates it and through the flagrant falsity of its accusations, which, since in Comte they are not imputable to bad faith and deceit, can only derive from a characteristic blindness. "Henceforth abandoned spontaneously to its natural corruption, monotheistic belief, whether Christian or Musulman, more and more deserves the reprobation its advent inspired for three centuries in the noblest practitioners and theorists of the Roman world. Being able at that time to judge the system only according to doctrine, they did not hesitate to reject, as an enemy of the human race, a provisional religion which placed perfection in a heavenly isolation. The modern instinct rejects still more an ethic which proclaims benevolent inclinations as foreign to our nature, which ignores the dignity of work to the point of having it derive from a divine malediction, and which sets woman up as the source of all evil." *Catéch. positiv.*, p. 12.

[2] *Syst. de politique positive*, I, p. 353. [3] *Lettres à divers*, I, 1, p. 75.

[4] *Syst. de politique positive*, IV, p. 533.—On the expression "slaves of God", first used by Comte in one of his lectures in 1851, see H. de Lubac, *op. cit.*, pp. 100–101.—The preface to the first edition of *Catéchisme positiviste* begins with the following lines: "'In the name of the past and of the future, the theoretical servants and the practical servants of HUMANITY are arriving to take over deservedly the general direction of terrestrial affairs, in order to build at last the true providence, moral, intellectual, and material; while irrevocably excluding from political supremacy all the various slaves of God, Catholics, Protestants, or Deists, as being at once backward-minded and disturbers.' Such was the decisive proclamation with which, at the Palais-Cardinal, I ended, on Sunday, October 19, 1851, after a summary of five hours, my third *Cours philosophique sur l'histoire générale de l'humanité.* Since that memorable closing. . . ." *Catéch. posit.*, p. 5.

[5] *Lettres à divers*, I, p. 520 (to H. D. Hutton).

[6] "Nolite arbitrari quia pacem venerim mittere in terram: non veni pacem mittere, sed gladium. Veni enim separare hominem adversus patrem suum, et filiam adversus matrem suam, et nurum adversus socrum suam: et inimici hominis, domestici ejus." *Matt.*, X, 34–36. "Think not that I came to send peace on the earth: I came not to send peace, but a sword. For I came to set a man at variance against his father, and the daughter against the mother, and the daughter-in-law against her mother-in-law: And a man's foes shall be they of his own household."

[7] "In a free talk before dinner, in the midst of Saint-Germain forest, I was able to observe at last that the systematic use of the compulsory word: religion and its derivatives,

Christianity is essentially "antisocial" (and therefore "immoral"),[1] not only because the seeking of salvation is pure egoism, and to love others for the love of God a "gasconade" which excludes any "human sympathy"[2] and covers a reckoning which is culpably selfish (positivist altruism lives on a disinterestedness no less sublime than that of the categorical imperative) but first and above all because, by "giving rise to purely interior observations", the Christian faith "consecrated the personality of an existence which, binding each one directly to an infinite power, profoundly isolated him from Humanity".[3] "There (it may be said) lies the radical evil: this linking-up of each man to God, which has the effect of 'exaggerating the human type', making every man an absolute like God Himself, and leading him to subordinate the world to himself. This accounts for the 'shamelessness' of 'monotheistic aspirations' and the 'anarchic Utopias' from which we are suffering to-day. For theology has infected metaphysics. In other words, on the plane of concrete facts, it is the personalism of the Christian religion that has given birth to the personalism of modern philosophy—that philosophy whose 'dominating thought is constantly that of the ego', all other existences being hazily shrouded in a negative conception, their vague sum total constituting the non-ego, while 'the notion of we' secures no 'direct and distinct place in it'."[4] "The man who believes he is in direct touch with an Absolute Being can only be a ferment of social disintegration."[5] God is anti-social as He is *irreligious*, and the two condemnations make but one.

The reasons which prompted Auguste Comte to admire the apostle Paul and to insult Jesus are not very difficult to discern. Saint Paul, who was only a man, could (on condition that he first undergo a good cleaning up) be considered as the precursor—just like Aristotle, Caesar and Charlemagne—and even as the greatest precursor, of Auguste Comte. But how could one consider Jesus as Comte's precursor? He said He was the Son of God, there was nothing to do but to brush Him aside, Him and His Father, and deny Him even the smallest place in the positivist calendar. He was nothing but a

---

no longer offends M. Littré, who is very affected even by the hope of brushing *God* aside as irreligious." *Correspondance inédite*, II, p. 89 (to Laffitte, 17 Shakespeare 61). Cf. *Ibid.*, p. 107 (to Lafitte, 11 Descartes 61): "Whereas the Protestants and the Deists have always attacked religion in the name of God, we must, on the contrary, finally brush God aside in the name of religion."

[1] "Since the Western priesthood has become irrevocably reactionary, its belief, given over to itself, tends to develop freely the immoral character inherent in its anti-social nature." *Catéch. positiv.*, p. 13.—Cf. *Polit. positive*, III, pp. 411 seq.

[2] *Lettres à divers*, I, 1, p. 169; *Corresp. inédite*, II, p. 371.—"Pursuing the least good only under the bait of an infinite reward and out of fear of an eternal punishment, their hearts appear to be as degraded as their minds obviously are, seen the absurdity of their beliefs." *Catéch. positiv.*, p. 30; cf. *ibid.*, p. 281.

[3] *Catéch. positiv.*, p. 166.

[4] H. de Lubac, *op. cit.*, p. 107.

[5] *Ibid.*, p. 109.

"bogus founder",[1] "whose long apotheosis henceforth gives rise to an irrevocable silence",[2] and whose real work was purely subversive and disruptive.

To speak the truth, the "construction of western monotheism" presupposed a "divine revealer", but Saint Paul, "the true founder of what is improperly called Christianity", was too great to assume such a role, which demands "a mixture of hypocrisy and spellbinding". With "sublime abnegation", then, he contented himself with the role of an apostle, leaving the first place "to some one of the adventurers who were then often to attempt the monotheistic inauguration".[3] "It is clear," Father de Lubac comments in this regard, "that the imagination of the novelist was not totally lacking in Auguste Comte. Saint Paul finally adoring Jesus sincerely because it spares him that obligation always odious for an upright man of having to adore himself—it's quite a pretty finding!"[4] All this, and the care that Comte takes, each time he has the opportunity, to disparage the Gospel, simply means that Jesus, not being a precursor, can only be a rival, and therefore an impostor by essence.[5] The analysis of an envy-complex so curiously significant would be the joy of the psychiatrists, if they did not reserve for Comte, even when they dissect his case, a kind of reverence (for, after all, was he not subject to "theopathic" states, and can he not be classified as a mystic? . . .).

[1] *Catéch. positiv.*, p. 11.—"A false founder", *ibid.*, p. 353; a "supposed founder", *ibid.*, p. 358.

[2] *Lettres à divers*, I, 1, p. 513.

[3] *Syst. de pol. pos.*, III, pp. 408–410.—Cf. *Catéchisme positiv.*, pp. 353, 358.

[4] H. de Lubac, *Le drame de l'humanisme athée*, Paris: Spes, 1945, pp. 196–197. (Author's translation.)

[5] Cf. H. de Lubac, *The Drama of Atheist Humanism*, p. 110.

12

POSITIVISM AND HUMAN CONDUCT

Auguste Comte—The High Priest of Humanity

I

THE SYSTEMATIZATION OF THE HEART AND THE POSITIVE RELIGION

The subjective synthesis

1. Why is unity better than dispersion? One can hardly see how this question could pertain to scientific knowledge such as Comte conceived it. It seems, however, that for philosophers who reduce all our knowledge to phenomena and turn away from being, unity becomes, as it were, a functional substitute for being—the more they forget the metaphysical significance of unity, the more they cling to this transcendental. At any rate, no other philosopher had more nostalgia for unity than Comte. "As the principal characteristic of our existence is unity, our growth is essentially bound to develop human harmony."[1]

Moreover Comte saw very well that unity of the intellectual and spiritual order is the highest and the most precious kind of unity for us, and that without it unity in man—unity of each man with himself and unity of men among themselves—shall never be perfect.

It was also quite clear to him that the science of phenomena cannot satisfy the need for unity of the human intellect. And since for him no other science was possible—in other words, since he had completely *de-ontologized* knowledge and denied philosophy any right to an independent domain and way of knowing—it was clear to him that intellectual unity could not have its source in the object, or in the "objective synthesis". It is in turning to the subject—the universal subject, humanity—that Comte claims to have discovered the hierarchy of the sciences, and, in general, the possibility of regulating scientific research and unifying the work of the intellect. No wonder that sociology, the peak of the objective synthesis, will become—but in a new and regenerated perspective[2]—the starting point of the "subjective synthesis", which,

[1] *Catéchisme positiviste* (1852), 3rd ed., 1890, Paris, 10 rue Monsieur-le-Prince, p. 336.

[2] "It suffices then that an angelic impulse came to regenerate morally the founder of sociology, in whom aesthetic appreciation thus serves as a link between the preparation of the mind and the supremacy of the heart." *Synthèse subjective* (1856), 2nd ed., Paris, 1900, Fonds typographique de l'exécution testamentaire d'Auguste Comte, p. 5.

from the viewpoint of humanity as center, will forcefully submit "the theoretical spirit", naturally anarchic, to an "irresistible discipline, first by regenerating its mathematical source, then by establishing its moral destination".[1] Besides, the laws proper to sociology are those of the most complex and noble phenomena and, as such, easiest to modify. They reveal that mankind inevitably marches toward unity; at the same time, being "modifiable fatalities",[2] they allow man, especially the great Western founder, Auguste Comte, actively to accelerate this movement toward unity and, above all, toward the final spiritual unity.

2. The fact remains that since it is not by integrating themselves to a higher objective truth that the sciences can be unified, it can only be by their subordinating themselves to the needs and practical utility of the subject. It is also clear that unity of the understanding alone is in no way enough. The whole man must be unified. In other words, intellectual and spiritual unity, really capable of reaching the entire man, cannot be the work of the intellect all by itself, even if it coordinates and directs the sciences from the point of view of the subject. Only in becoming entirely subordinate to feeling (and this is quite logical, because no truth superior to phenomena—whether the suprasensible truths of metaphysics, or the first truth of the revelation—is accessible to intelligence) can the intellect become a real instrument of human unification. This means then that the intellect leaves the objective or scientific domain and passes to the subjective, poetical or religious realm. There, under the guidance of love, it will work out the cult and the (mythical) dogma through which feelings themselves are to be systematized—that is to say taken away from the robber which is our natural and inextirpable individual egoism (a sort of substitute for original sin in Comte's view), and led back, in a powerful convergent reflux, to the supreme unifying principle which must be developed and consolidated before everything else—namely, sympathy. "So far as relatively grounded, the synthesis may wholly consist in extending and consolidating sympathy, which is both the source and the destination of the supreme existence. Sympathy disposes the intellect to assist feeling in a more direct manner and to a deeper degree than by merely unveiling the order of the world. Having to depict this order only approximately in the degree adapted to our wants, the mind, after having sufficiently discharged its passive

[1] "Western anarchy mainly involves the intelligence, the disorder of which is the principal source of the alteration of feeling and the deviation of activity. My *Synthèse subjective* is therefore in special harmony with the essential needs of the modern situation, in which the theoretical spirit has alone become a direct source of disturbance. It must make our time undergo an irresistible discipline, first by regenerating its mathematical source, then by establishing its moral destination." *Synthèse subjective*, p. 5.

[2] "Thus the natural order always constitutes a modifiable fatality, which becomes the indispensable basis of the artificial order. Our true destiny is therefore a compound of resignation and action." *Catéchisme positiv.*, pp. 56–57.—Cf. above, chap. XI, p. 290, note 4.

function, may assume an attitude of activity by rising from philosophy to poetry, in order to develop worship, the main component of religion. This second domain is to be looked on as the normal complement of the first; for when the intellect passes into the *direct service of feeling*, it by no means ceases to serve activity, ultimately destined to the perfecting of our moral constitution."[1]

Thus religion, the task of which is to assure supreme human unity,[2] is, to the same extent to which it is distinguished from science and philosophy, essentially subjective, and founded uniquely on feeling. In contrast to the maxim of the ancients, "*the will needs to be guided by the intellect in all its actions*" (incidentally, by no means incompatible with the doctrine of the supremacy of charity), the heart has now to guide and regulate the intellect, even in theoretical matters. "Act from affection, and think to act."[3] "Under this regime, feeling . . . takes therein an irrevocable ascendancy",[4] and if the intellect "acquires a dignity previously unattainable", it is so because of "its religious consecration to the ceaseless service of sociability, the sole source of its own growth".[5] Thus are assured the "worthy subordination of male reason to female feeling",[6] and the "constant predominance of the heart over the mind", which is "the sole basis of our true unity".[7] Briefly, "the normal solution of the human problem" can be found only "by devoting the reason to the service of feeling",[8] and submitting it to a discipline that will fix its objects and direct its efforts in the name of human needs and the primacy of the heart.[9]

Here we have a double abdication of intelligence—in favor of praxis and in favor of feeling. This is, no doubt, the deepest reason why Littré was scandalized by the second career of his master. But, despite an evident difference in emphasis, this abdication is coherent with the positions taken by Comte from the beginning. "On the question of the unity of his doctrine Comte wins

[1] *Synthèse subjective*, p. 36. (Italics ours.)—The "supreme existence" is the existence of Humanity.

[2] "In itself, [the word "religion"] denotes the state of perfect unity which characterizes our existence, at once personal and social, when all its parts, moral as well as physical, converge habitually towards a common end. . . . Religion, then, consists in *regulating* each individual nature and in *rallying* all the separate individuals." *Catéchisme positiviste*, p. 44.

[3] Cf. *Catéchisme positiviste*, p. 64.

[4] *Synthèse subjective*, p. 40.—Cf. p. 26: "Restored and disciplined by such a connection the intelligence is again freely subordinated to feeling, against which it had been in increasing opposition since the beginning of the flight into abstraction."

[5] *Ibid.*, p. 38.

[6] *Catéchisme positiviste*, p. 34.

[7] *Ibid.*, p. 59.

[8] *Synthèse subjective*, p. 47.

[9] In fact, "in the 'final structure' sympathy was to rule synthesis and fashion it to its own liking. Criticism of the 'empty presidency of the mind' tended more and more to become distrust of the understanding, the mere exercise of which was to be regarded as a manifestation of egoism and vanity." H. de Lubac, *The Drama of Atheist Humanism*, trans. Edith M. Riley, New York: Sheed and Ward, 1950, p. 146; London, Sheed and Ward, 1949.

the case against Littré."[1] Since the days of his youth, he affirmed that philosophy was only a preamble, and that the final end was the positive religion erected on this philosophy. As he wrote to John Stuart Mill in 1845 (the year of his fourth and last brain crisis,[2] and the year which opened the "second half" of his "philosophical life"), he considered his fundamental work (the *Cours*) as only preparatory, because the systematization of feelings was "the necessary continuation of the systematization of the ideas", and the "indispensable basis for that of the institutions".[3] If he had first to put an end to mental anarchy by changing science into philosophy, it was in order that he might put an end to moral and political anarchy by changing philosophy into religion. "I have systematically devoted my life to making real science provide, at last, the necessary bases of sound philosophy, in accordance with which I had, in a second step, to construct true religion."[4]

3. Comte is essentially an organizer. From the very start, his end is practical, and he attributes to praxis no less importance than Marx—with this difference, that Marx was down-to-earth, whereas Comte remained content with pontificating and changing the world on paper.

His ultimate aim is the reorganization of social and political institutions. To reach this goal, religious organization is needed, the construction of the true and definitive universal religion is necessary. I previously pointed out

[1] L. Lévy-Bruhl, *op. cit.*, p. 15.—"Then we do not have the right to speak of contradiction when we follow the logical development of Comte's thought; he aimed only at the subjective synthesis, this is to say social, of our knowledge; he has written his philosophy of science only to prepare the way for his politics and the establishment of the new spiritual power. . . ." Georges Dumas, *op. cit.*, pp. 172–173.

[2] The first crisis (1826) was an "attack of well-characterized insanity" (Georges Dumas, *op. cit.*, p. 127). The three other crises were rather threats of relapse. "Without any doubt Auguste Comte was insane for a time, and he rightly sensed he was liable to relapses. But once free of the mania, he avoided it by all possible means, he cheated it, and in the last analysis he vanquished it." And Georges Dumas rightly concludes that "this fight against insanity speaks much more for his will than for his intellect". (*Ibid.*, p. 159.)

It is, therefore, false to claim with Madame Comte and Littré that he fell into insanity during his second career. But it remains a fact that his congenital psychopathic disposition revealed itself more and more with the years and made him beyond any question a medical case (Henri Gouhier has shown that Comte's heredity was worse than Georges Dumas thought it was). This pathological background stimulated certain tendencies and emphasized certain characteristics of Comte's intellectual work, but it could not play an essential and formally determining part in an elaboration which remained under the control of the mind.

[3] *Lettres d'Auguste Comte à John Stuart Mill*, pp. 356–357.

[4] *Polit. pos.*, II, xx.—The following text shows well how Comte conceives the mutual relation between "establishing the true religion" (subjective synthesis) and constructing the "sound philosophy" (objective synthesis): "Guided by the heart, we adhere directly to Humanity, and then to the universal order which serves as the basis of Its existence. But the intellect, substituting for the order of dignity the order of simplicity, submits in the first place to external laws, and through them it subsequently recognizes human laws. Extended to their legitimate limits, these two methods converge spontaneously, since the Great-Being constitutes both the main element and the necessary summary of universal order." *Synthèse subjective*, p. 39.

that Comte saw very well that intellectual and spiritual unity was the highest and most precious unity for us. Yes, this is so. But in another respect Comte was lacking in perspicacity; for he made this highest and most precious unity, and in its strictest form, the indispensable condition of all other kinds of unity. Two reasons account for this. On the one hand, he craved unity too much and too deeply to be satisfied with anything less than total and faultless unity. On the other hand, as we observed in the preceding chapter, he had read Joseph de Maistre too well,[1] and believed that mediaeval Christendom with its sacral regime (he mistook it for theocracy) offered the only possible type of political unity and organic civilization. Comte held, therefore, that unity of religion was the indispensable foundation and the condition *sine qua non* of political unity. Hence, for him there were only two conceivable solutions: either a return to mediaeval Christendom, which was impossible; or the establishment of a sort of atheistic Catholicism which, universal as reason itself, would organize, regenerate and discipline, both morally and politically, first the West, then the rest of civilized peoples. God, who in the last analysis is irreligious, will have been only a precursor[2] of the supreme, though relative, object of love and adoration—Humanity.

What strikes Comte above all in mediaeval Christendom, is "the miracle of the papal hegemony".[3] In contrast to Hegel, he considers the distinction between the spiritual power and the temporal power as an essential progress and a marvel of wisdom, but of *political* wisdom, because for him the order and progress of the social organism remain the only aim to which everything is related.[4] It is this order and progress of the terrestrial society which demands that the priest who governs minds should direct the prince who governs the State. Hence it is that the distinction between the two powers is justified *in view of the temporal.* Therefore, frankly speaking, Comte who exalts this distinction is less remote than one would think from Hegel who rejects it. We must completely secularize Catholicism—eliminate from it God, Christ and the Gospel; reject its faith and doctrine, but restore its morals thoroughly purged from any supernatural beliefs; re-establish its institutions and authoritative structure on a wider and stronger basis furnished to us by positive

[1] After pointing out that "the eminent Condorcet" was his "essential precursor", Comte writes: "So, under the political aspect, Condorcet required, for me, to be completed by De Maistre, from whom, at the commencement of my career, I appropriated all his essential principles, which now find no adequate appreciation except in the Positive school." *Catéch. positiv.*, p. 10.

[2] "The growing struggle of Humanity against the fatalities which weigh upon it, presents to the heart as well as to the mind a better spectacle than the omnipotence, necessarily capricious, of its theological precursor. . . ." *Catéch. positiv.*, p. 59.—"Our emancipation should mainly consist in the substitution of the true Great-Being for its fictitious precursors. . . ." *Synthèse subjective*, p. 36.

[3] L. Lévy-Bruhl, *op. cit.*, p. 330.

[4] Cf. *Catéch. positiv.*, pp. 248–250.—Briefly, socio-temporal progress constitutes "the ultimate goal of dogma and worship, thus preserved from any ascetical or quietist deviation, according to the impulse of true love". *Polit. pos.*, II, p. 77.

philosophy. Thus the "government of souls" will pass into the hands of the positivist clergy. "The more I scrutinize this immense subject, the more I am confirmed in the feeling which I already had twenty years ago, at the time of my work on the spiritual power, that we systematic positivists are the true successors of the great mediaeval men, taking over the social work from where Catholicism has brought it."[1] "In a word, except for the dogma, Comte borrows from the Catholicism of the Middle Ages almost everything, its organization, its *regime*, its worship and, if he could, its clergy and its cathedrals. His religion will be a desecrated Catholicism."[2]

4. It seems to me that we can neither fully see the historical significance of the task undertaken by Comte, nor understand how he could have dreamed of carrying it out, without taking into account the religious degeneration in certain social strata of his day, which furnished him with an already distorted image of Catholicism. Comte is an extravagant, but singularly representative, phenomenon of the French bourgeoisie. We must consider his physiognomy against the background of the French bourgeois society of his time. Thomas Huxley said that positivism is "Catholicism without Christianity". It is a fact that at Comte's time a noticeable part of the French bourgeoisie had already inaugurated this kind of Catholicism. If Comte could dream of founding an atheistic Catholicism, it was because the class in question had among its most solid members a number of practical atheists, more or less brought up by Voltaire and Béranger. They called themselves Catholic, though in all their principles of conduct they denied God, Christ and the Gospel, and upheld religion for merely temporal and political reasons—preserving social order and prosperity in business, consolidating their economic power, and keeping the lower classes in obedience by means of a virtuous rigor sanctioned from on high. The existence of this type of so-called Catholics made the idea of creating an atheist version of Catholicism less impossible; at the same time, the sort of inconsistency and hypocrisy which affected them was for the founder of positivism an incitement to endeavor to regenerate them. The religion of humanity was, so to say, a reply to their negativeness. It told them: Admit what you are—and instead of adoring God with your lips without really believing in Him, and instead of being socially useless, because you despise the commandment given to you to love each other, adore the Great Being which is made known to you by sociology, and make yourselves useful by serving it with that atheistic love which is called altruism.

Such an appeal was bound to remain unheard, because no matter what love and devotedness one spoke of, this was precisely what the persons thus addressed did not want at any cost; besides, they had no desire to deprive

[1] *Lettres d'Auguste Comte à John Stuart Mill* (1841–1845), Paris, 1877, p. 359.
[2] L. Lévy-Bruhl, *op. cit.*, p. 332.

themselves of the slim chance offered to them by a Christian death, in case the priests were prating more than fairy tales.

The appeals Auguste Comte made to conservatives, even to the "Ignatians",[1] were equally bound to remain unheard, but for quite different reasons. In approaching the Jesuits, he was not dealing with profiteers in the religion of façade which I just described, and which he wishes to regenerate by making them positivists. But this made Comte happy: the men with whom he sought an alliance did not interest him unless they were authentic Catholics and real believers. However led astray by their belief in God they might be, he regarded them as reasonable and open-minded enough to consider that the moral and political reorganization of earthly society mattered first and foremost. They disappointed his expectation. Fond as they were of social order and stability, positivist alliance was for them not even, as it was to be for some Catholics later on, a temptation to repel.[2] They did not take Comte seriously.

5. Although, in Comte's eyes, worship and "regime" (that is, discipline of conduct) together are of a much greater importance for religion than dogma,[3]

[1] On Comte's hope of seeing the Jesuits "regenerated into Ignatians" ally themselves to him in order to help him "to reorganize the West", and on the amusing history of the visit of Alfred Sabatier, as ambassador of positivism, to the General of the Jesuits, see Georges Dumas, *Revue de Paris*, Oct. 1, 1898, and H. de Lubac, *op. cit.*, pp. 124–127.

[2] "Auguste Comte", writes Father de Lubac, "is here the instrument of a temptation which, always latent, becomes particularly strong when Catholicism *seems* to have its back against the wall. What he proposes to the Church, with the utmost naivete, is a betrayal. . . ." In another passage the same author rightly observes: "Can it at least be said that the positivist menace is not very formidable? To my mind it is, on the contrary, one of the most dangerous that beset us. At any moment the failure of other nostrums, with greater outward attractions, may suddenly send its stock up. Many of the present campaigns against individualism already derive their inspiration from the ideas of Comte and his disciples, too often at the cost of the human person. They may loudly proclaim their agreement with traditional philosophy, but what they understand by that term, too, is often nothing but a traditionalist philosophy—completely heterodox in some of its fundamental propositions—which is actually one of the sources of Comtian thought. They lead believers astray by ambiguous pronouncements. They pay homage to Catholicism; but, in varying degrees and often without being clearly aware of it, their purpose is to rid it more effectually of the Christian spirit. They stress the elements of superstition which still subsist in a body so large as the Church, and which it is so easy to exacerbate, especially in periods of unrest. It sometimes happens that churchmen, paying too little heed to the Gospel, let themselves be caught by this. Positivism is gaining ground, as its founder repeatedly predicted, far less by any conquest over former 'metaphysicians' or 'revolutionaries', than by a slow and imperceptible dechristianization of a large number of Catholic souls. The 'accommodations' and 'alliances' favoured by Comte have actually borne fruit. They were followed by a period of spontaneous assimilation, and the faith which used to be a living adherence to the Mystery of Christ then came to be no more than attachment to a social programme, itself twisted and diverted from its purpose. Without any apparent crisis, under a surface which sometimes seemed the reverse of apostasy, that faith has slowly been drained of its substance." *Op. cit.*, p. 127; pp. 157–158.

[3] In *Catéchisme positiviste* (pp. 76–77), dogma, as theoretical, is declared to be inferior to worship and regime, which are both practical and depend on love. But in *Politique positive* (IV, pp. 86–91) Comte affirms the essential primacy of worship over both dogma and regime.

nevertheless religion founded by him cannot lack a dogma and a faith. The positive faith (even after passing to the stage of myth) will be first of all a faith in human science and philosophy constructed on it; briefly, a faith in the system of Auguste Comte.

It is true, as he takes pleasure in insisting, that every one of us, not being able to repeat for himself the work of all the scientists of the world, in fact believes (except as regards the minute point in which he may happen to specialize, if he is a scientist) the things which in all the fields of science competent men hold to be true. We believe these things—but certainly without putting our hand into the fire to prove them, and without other advice than that of our own reason. Moreover, when we deal with philosophers and their authority, that is quite another matter, all the more so because they are in mutual opposition. Universal in its object, philosophy is an eminently personal matter as to our approach to it. Even if one is not a philosopher, one adheres to a philosophy only because one has tested it oneself and judges that it is well-founded. To ask of those who have competence neither in science nor philosophy (that is, of the great majority of people) an act of faith, a morally obligatory adherence to the *dicta* of scientists and philosophers, even to those of the founder of positivism,[1] is both an insult to the intellect, upon which no purely human authority has the least claim, and a violence done to science and philosophy, which live on the freedom to criticize. It is reasonable for me to hold that the earth turns around the sun: what, in this case, for modern astronomy is a scientific certitude, for me who am not an astronomer, is a sensible opinion. But if it were made into a dogma to which I must adhere or commit a fault against the Great Being, and to which I must adhere because the astronomers-priests-of-humanity who teach me this have a right to require the adherence of my mind, I would prefer to believe that the sun rises each morning to run after the moon. Comte plays with words when in his famous passage on the freedom of conscience, written in 1882 and reproduced in the fourth volume of the *Cours*,[2] he declares that "there is no freedom of conscience in astronomy, physics, chemistry, psychology, in the sense that everyone would find it absurd not to believe with confidence in the

[1] Cf. *Politique positive*, IV, General Appendix (*Considérations sur le pouvoir spirituel*, March, 1826), pp. 207–208: "Faith, that is to say the disposition to believe spontaneously, without previous demonstration, in dogmas proclaimed by a competent authority", is, as "Catholic philosophy" had realized but in an "essentially empirical" manner, "a *fundamental virtue, the immutable and necessary basis of private and public happiness*". And this is more true than ever in the positive age, "for in this new state, characterized as it is by a more complete and ever increasing separation of the various functions, each person, whatever may be his capacity, can, unaided, grasp but a very small portion *of the Doctrine which he needs for his guidance*". (Italics ours.)

"In other people he [Comte] increasingly preferred the faith of the heart to 'scientific faith', and that is one of the reasons why he increasingly dissuaded would-be readers from studying his *Cours*." H. de Lubac, *op. cit*., p. 143.

[2] *Cours*, IV, p. 40.—On the opuscule of 1822 (*Prospectus des travaux nécessaires pour réorganiser la société*), see above, chapter XI, p. 277, note 2.

principles established in the sciences by competent men". Science itself advances only by constantly questioning the "principles established by competent men"; nay more, if a man who is not a physicist is not free to disbelieve the law of gravity, it is only because he has understood the proofs given for this law in the textbooks of physics. Otherwise he is not obliged to believe even Newton or Einstein. He is equally free to remain, if he wishes, ignorant of physics altogether.

When religion teaches divine truths, it can leave the domain of human truths to our free investigation. But if a so-called religion teaches a scientific or philosophical dogma, there can no longer be a free investigation in the realm of human truths. The refusal to leave room for error in the believers' minds must necessarily extend to the entire field of thought. Even before assuming the chief priesthood, Comte manifested a naïve and proud intolerance which only grew with years. This intolerance is of great interest to us, since it was manifested by a man for whom the idea that *everything is relative* was the supreme truth. This shows us that intolerance is not a privilege of those who believe in the absolute, and that, contrary to a widespread prejudice which is a shame for the intellect, mutual tolerance is not tied up with a cast of mind in which every conviction would be affected by a note of relativity. There is real and genuine tolerance only if we fully respect the right to exist, and to speak his mind, of him who we are fully convinced is in error. Intolerance is created not by the sense of the absolute, but by the instinct of domination and the loss of the sense of transcendance.

6. The Church of Auguste Comte is not in charge of a revealed deposit which it has only to transmit to men. It is the spiritual power itself which constructs faith, because the content of faith is but scientific-sociological-philosophical truth, relative as it is. Comte prides himself that the positive faith thus is a "demonstrated faith", that is, a faith by which those who do not know, believe what for those who know is rationally demonstrated. In Catholic faith man, without seeing them, believes, on the word of God, things which God sees; in the same way, in the positive faith, the ignorant one, without seeing them, believes, on the word of the *clergy and people who know*, things which are seen by the latter, and by Auguste Comte.

But, as a matter of fact, the "demonstrated faith" is only the first stage of the positive faith. If Comte sometimes gives the impression of forgetting this, it is so because his confidence in himself is so great that the demonstrability in question seems to him to extend to the poetical elaboration itself to which he submits the contents of this faith—is this elaboration not justified by such evident reasons that everyone must necessarily recognize it as well-founded? The second stage of the positive faith is no longer "demonstrated faith", but what we might call fabled or mythified faith. This second stage is indispensable: since the scope of religion is to bring about moral and political unity and regulate human conduct, its essential mission is to systematize the heart, or feelings, by which alone it can have a hold over action. Thus the primary object of the "construction of the positive synthesis" is to bring us to a state in which sympathy must irrevocably prevail, or, as Comte put it, to the "most sympathetic state. We may affirm beforehand that such a state will be, as a direct consequence, the most synthetic and the most synergic."[1]

Hence it is absolutely necessary that the demonstrated assertions of the positive dogma satisfy the hearts both of the ignorant and the learned, as well as the minds of the learned, and exert on feeling and the sympathetic inclinations a powerful, irresistible appeal. This is possible only if these assertions are transformed into myths ceaselessly echoing in our affective faculties, or into well-founded poetical fictions, by regenerating the most primitive and most venerable form of the theological state, which is fetishism. In the intellectual regeneration required by the "final regime", "Positivism absorbs fetishism whilst discarding theologism",[2] and, in this way, "accomplishes the universal integration by regenerating fetishist dispositions".[3] "Rallying the advanced portion of the white race with the larger portion of the yellow and the whole of the black race, the incorporation of fetishism into Positivism can alone give its full consistence to the universal religion."[4] Thus is brought to a close and consummation the construction of the true faith; thus was instituted, by the efforts of Auguste Comte, the Trinity of the positive religion.

The religion of Humanity

7. The concept of humanity is, as it were, the hinge on which the positive faith turns in order to pass from the "demonstrated" to the fabled stage. Humanity is the object of a science—the highest science of phenomena, sociology—which studies, after the manner of other natural phenomena, moral and social ones. They are the most "complex" and "noble" of all; their laws are established by social statics and dynamics. On this plane of science and philosophy, the human person has already been sacrificed—nothing, moreover, is less reducible to phenomenon. According to Auguste Comte, man is man only through society; the human intellect, as such, is a purely biological object. The properly human functions of intelligence and morality "are essentially social things".[5] In other words, the human species must be considered an "immense organism" resulting from the social *consensus* and growing through history, or "a single 'immense and eternal' individual".[6] The human species forms a higher collective unity, an undivided whole; the

[1] *Synthèse subjective*, p. 26.

[2] *Ibid*, p. 39.—Cf. *Catéch. positiv.*, pp. 327 and 337. See also on *fetishistic incorporation* the Appendix (composed by Pierre Laffitte) to *Catéchisme positiviste*, pp. 391–395.

[3] *Ibid.* p. 771.

[4] *Ibid.*, p. 23.

[5] L. Lévy-Bruhl, *op. cit.*, p. 386.

[6] *Ibid.*, p. 384.—Cf. *Cours*, III, pp. 232 ff.

individual is elevated to human quality by participating in it. Man is man only by his participation in humanity as a social whole and universal subject.

Consequently it is enough—and this is no longer the job of science or philosophy—to personify this immense organism by making it the principle of all moral, intellectual and affective values, of every effort of progress and devotedness, of all the accumulated good deeds which constitute the treasury of human history: the immense organism in question will be transformed into an object of love and adoration and, by the same stroke, brought onto the plane of myth or well-founded fiction. Humanity is far from being perfect, she is not eternal, one day she will end like the planet on which she lives. But she is the noblest thing in the world (Saint Thomas said this of the human person; now this must be said of the historical social whole); we are and live through humanity; we must love her more than ourselves; we are born in order to serve her. "The necessary basis of human order" is "the entire subordination of man to Humanity."[1] Thus the human race is transformed into the Great Being (Hobbes would have said, into the mortal God). To this "new Supreme Being",[2] "composed of" its "own worshippers",[3] "who is for us the only true Great Being, and whose necessary members we consciously are, every aspect of our life, individual or collective, will henceforth be directed. Our thoughts will be devoted to the knowledge of Humanity, our affections to her love, our actions to her service."[4] "In a word, Humanity definitely substitutes herself for God, without ever forgetting *his provisional services.*"[5]

This very process calls for a definition of humanity no longer by the simple criterion of fact, but rather by the criterion of quality. Hence it requires, to the extent to which humanity is the Great Being, that there be cut off from it everything which is dead dregs and useless tare. Not every man is a member of the Great Being. "All those who are not or were not 'sufficiently assimilable', all those who were only a burden to our species, do not form a part of the Great Being."[6] The sword of the positive religion divides the elect from the reprobate, and rejects into the outer darkness the simple "digesting machines",[7] so that only those may have life in humanity who have lived for her. Thus at once appear both the mythico-moral unity of the Great Being, and the sort of consoling paradise which everyone can hope to find in it. For,

[1] *Synthèse subjective*, p. 31. [2] *Catéch. positiv.*, p. 73.

[3] *Politique positive*, I, p. 354; cf. *ibid.*, II, p. 59. [4] *Ibid.*, I, p. 330.

[5] *Catéch. positiv.*, p. 380. (Italics ours.)—Thanks to the contempt for historical exactness natural to every philosophy of history which reconstructs the past by means of necessary laws, Comte was persuaded that this substitution had begun in the Middle Ages with the cult of the Virgin, image of Humanity. "After inaugurating admirably the worship of Woman, the necessary prelude to the Religion of Humanity, the feudal feeling really brought about, in the century of the Crusades, the change which Western monotheism underwent when the Virgin tended therein to take the place of God." *Ibid.*, p. 363.

[6] L. Lévy-Bruhl, *op. cit.*, p. 389.—Cf. *Polit. pos.*, I, p. 411.

[7] *Catéch. positiviste*, p. 69.

through "subjective immortality", all the worthy members of the Great Being will subsist in it, insofar as they will be remembered for generations—in much the same way as, during our existence, everyone of us, heir of the generations past, lives by remembrance, gratitude and veneration, more with the dead than with the living. To tell the truth, the mortal God is not the God of the living, as the God of Abraham, Isaac and Jacob:[1] he is the God of the dead. In fact, not only is humanity composed more of the dead than of the living, but, "as the conduct of each one can only be finally judged after his death, humanity is essentially made up of the dead",[2] and, "if the living are admitted it is, except in rare instances, only provisionally".[3] Hence, once dead with the dead, and entirely dead as they are, I shall find myself, if I was an altruist, inseparably incorporated into the Great Being by the remembrance which others will have of me.

Let us not insist on the risk which the good positivist runs by counting in this way on the memory of his neighbor, and entrusting his posthumous existence to the image which man is supposedly keeping of man. (Moreover, since the unfortunate is not judged by God who does not exist, his fate will be "irrevocably fixed", seven years after his death, by priests; they shall place him, in the memory of the people, among the elect or the reprobate.)[4] I find something else to be noted here: man has such a raging thirst for perpetual existence, that the Comtian faithful, when he thinks of future centuries honoring him, does not actually envision that the whole matter will have lost all interest for him—he rather acts *as if* he should then possess just enough existence to keep enjoying the tender self-satisfaction with which this saintly perspective provides him at present. However that may be, it is curious to see how the same Comte who stigmatizes the egoism of Christians because they hope to see God, promises as reward to his faithful the delights, not despicable, I admit, but somewhat suspect as to the forgetting of oneself, which stem from the good reputation they will have in the opinion of men, and from the positive incense which the recognition of the servants of humanity will send up toward their name.

8. The institution of the Great Being was the primordial step. The same process, extended and completed, achieves the positivist Trinity. Comte's intention, we remember, is to fix the understanding and imagination in a system of representations and incitements which will make sympathy, "the only principle of Positive unity",[5] irrevocably prevail. For this purpose he uses the very

[1] "De resurrectione autem mortuorum non legistis quod dictum est a Deo dicente vobis: Ego sum Deus Abraham, et Deus Isaac, et Deus Jacob? Non est Deus mortuorum, sed viventium." *Matt.* XXII, 31–32.

[2] L. Lévy-Bruhl, *op. cit.*, p. 390.

[3] *Polit. positive*, I, p. 411.

[4] Cf. below, p. 325, note 3.

[5] *Synthèse subjective*, p. 19.

principle of fetishism, which stocks things with anthropomorphically conceived wills.[1] "Inaugurated as the adoration of Humanity, Positive worship is next addressed to the World, and should be completed by including Destiny."[2]

"A trinity which admits of no change" thus directs "our conceptions and our adoration, both always relative, first to the Great Being, then to the Great Fetish and lastly to the Great Milieu".[3] The Great Fetish is the Earth which nourishes us and must be regarded as animated by a blindly but inexhaustibly beneficent will. "Our homage is next paid to the active and benevolent seat whose voluntary though blind concurrence is always indispensable for the supreme existence."[4]

As to the Great Milieu, that is, the Space—to whose regenerated theory[5] is dedicated the first volume (the only one published), or Treatise on Mathematical Philosophy, of the *Subjective Synthesis*—we must conceive it as an animated receptacle, "passive no less than blind, but always benevolent",[6] which kindly receives and preserves, thanks to its "generally fluid character"[7] and its "sympathetic suppleness",[8] not only all the geometrical forms and situations, but "densities, savours, temperatures, scents, colours, sounds, and all the other material attributes",[9] abstractedly separated from the bodies. This "fictitious medium, hitherto turned to account only in mathematics, but henceforward available for all external phenomena", is the "residence" required by the "worship" of the "supreme destiny".[10]

[1] "Nothing can give a better idea of the two extreme regimes [fetishism and positivism] than their inherent tendencies always to give dominion, the one to Wills, the other to laws. . . ." But, on the other hand, "fetishism may be considered as having spontaneously introduced the subjectivity which Positivism has systematically to make paramount in the universal synthesis". (*Ibid.*, p. 6.) It is to this final subjective synthesis that corresponds the "need, both theoretical and practical, which I have characterized in this systematic line: *To complete laws, we need wills.*" (*Ibid.*, p. 25.)

[2] *Ibid.*, p. 18.

[3] *Ibid.*, p. 24.

[4] *Ibid.* This "active and benevolent seat", incidentally, "is not at all limited to the Earth with its twofold liquid envelope", but it "includes also the stars which are really connected with the human planet as objective or subjective adjuncts; and especially the Sun and the Moon, which we must specially honor".

[5] "After having irrevocably regenerated, in this volume, the fundamental science. . . ." *Synthèse subjective*, p. 772.—"Limited to the Great-Milieu, the fundamental science aspires to the Great-Fetish, through the mediation of the heavens and of the twofold terrestrial envelope in order to attain to the Great-Being, when vegetable life followed by animality renders it theoretically accessible." (*Ibid.*, p. 769.)—The "final systematization of mathematical studies", by reaching minds engaged in practical life, will have considerable social efficacy. "But the result of the final regeneration of the mathematical spirit must then consist in having it gradually obtain the most decisive sanction, by reconciling to it the poetical and feminine natures whom its dryness repelled. They can already perceive, in the founder of positivism, the extent to which the most profound influence of the mathematical beginning is becoming normally compatible with the most active impulse of synthetic and sympathetic dispositions which subordinate dogma to worship." (*Ibid.*, p. 771.)

[6] *Ibid.*, p. 24.

[7] *Ibid.*, p. 22.

[8] *Ibid.*, pp. 24–25.

[9] *Ibid.*, p. 22.

[10] *Ibid.*, p. 21.

9. There is something at once quite pitiable and surely affecting in the daily worship paid by Auguste Comte to Clotilde de Vaux: idealization of a frustrated eroticism accompanied by a real purification of feelings and a manifest moral renewal. But in the poetical incorporation of fetishism required by the "definitive regeneration"[1] there is nothing but repugnance to the mind. The primitive man had an authentic belief in myths which, arisen from the collective unconsciousness, came to him, as he saw them, from the bottom of the ages, and from a past more divine than time. But the faithful of the positive religion know perfectly well that the things they worship are "purely fictitious existences, the subjective origin of which must admit of no doubt".[2] The spectacle of the high priest of humanity warming up his sympathetic instincts, and those of his disciples, at the fire of his own laboriously combined fables, and offering his and their hearts to imaginary, deliberately invented beings, is a remarkable indication of the degradation to which the intellect could be exposed in the nineteenth century.[3]

Moreover, the Trinity of the Great Being, the Great Fetish and the Great Milieu do not exhaust the mythopoetical genius of the positive religion. We are offered quite a number of other sympathetic fictions which similarly ape, by depriving them of reality, things which Catholicism venerates, and by which Comte was singularly obsessed. Thus he has his "positivist prayer", which "takes complete possession of the highest domain formerly reserved for

[1] *Synthèse subjective*, p. 43. [2] *Ibid.*, p. 19.

[3] Besides, no matter how honestly these fictions are put forth as such, it appears clear that, by a practically unavoidable effect of our psychological mechanism, the state of mind developed by the positive worship resolves in fact into pure and simple idolatry—an object sincerely adored, Great-Being, Great-Fetish or Great-Milieu, losing by the very fact of this adoration the psychological possibility of being regarded, at the very moment when the mind prostrates itself before it, as a purely fictitious existence. Scorn is all the more inevitable the more the fictions in question are constructed on something "demonstrated" (the Great-Being, for example, on humanity as the object of sociology). Will not Comte present Humanity as "the only true Great-Being" (*Polit. pos.*, I, p. 330)? In contradistinction to this authentic Goddess will he not speak of the chimerical beings whom "religion provisionally made use of" before the coming of positivism (*Catéch. pos.*, p. 58); and of "the *fictitious nature* of provisional religion" in which worship had reference to "*imaginary* beings" (*Polit. pos.*, IV, p. 87; italics ours)? Comte was the first to be caught in the trap; he was an idolater of the most authentic and the most pathologically prostrated sort.

Cf. the accurate remarks of Edward Caird (*La Philosophie sociale et religieuse d'Auguste Comte*, pp. 129–130) quoted by H. de Lubac, *Le drame de l'humanisme athée* (3rd ed., Paris: Spes, 1945), p. 235: Comte feels that "the idea of an indifferent exterior necessity must be a hindrance to the perfect union of submission and love. Hence he calls on poetry to revive the spirit of fetishism and to reanimate the world by the images of benevolent divine agents. Comte thus ends in what someone has called the system of "spiritual book-keeping by double entry", which permits imagination to revive, for practical purposes, the fictions which science has destroyed. Poetry . . . has to make us forget in our worship the antagonism of Nature and Humanity, and to reconcile us to Fate by giving it the semblance of a Providence. It is obvious that poetry is thus made into a kind of deliberate superstition. . . ." (this text does not appear in the English translation of de Lubac's work that we have been citing).—See also Jean Devolvé, "Auguste Comte et la religion," *Revue d'histoire de la philosophie*, 1937.

supernatural grace".[1] He has his guardian angels[2] who are Clotilde his chaste companion, Rosalie Boyer his venerable mother, and Sophie Bliot his worthy servant, whom he had raised to a spiritual daughter. He wants each of his faithful to be assisted by a similar angelic triad. He has his saints who are the benefactors of humanity inscribed in the positivist calendar, and his elect, those canonized by the ninth social sacrament, the *incorporation*.[3] He has his worship of the Virgin-Mother, and this is for him the supreme utopia, because it corresponds, as an "ideal limit",[4] to our paradoxical aspiration to raise woman, insofar as she has a mission to give life to a new member of humanity, above the lust of the sexual instinct, itself nevertheless destined to the perpetuation of life. In other words, and in a more Comtian language, woman's life-giving task, if it were exempted from the "brute passions of man",[5] and from the carnal love between her and a male individual, would become more altruistic and change into a function purely social, "in its origin and its accomplishment" as well as "in its results".[6] (If artificial insemination had been known at Comte's time, he would, doubtless, have greeted it as an irrevocable step in the direction of his utopia; we can imagine the new spiritual power directing by its advice the generalized practice of this method in view of the eugenic improvement of the Great Being.)

10. On Monday, Homer 20, 63, in a letter to his disciple, Dr. Audiffrent,[7] Comte announces that he himself will assist at the inaugural ceremony of the new religious regime at Notre Dame of Paris, "which must become the great Western Temple where the status of Humanity will have for pedestal the altar of God", surrounded by the "sacred wood" in which "will be assembled the tombs of the twenty-four principal great men of the modern West". On

[1] Cf. *Catéchisme posit.*, p. 96.—"To wish with fervor to become more tender, more reverential, or even more courageous, is already to realize, to some degree, the desired improvement; at least by a sincere avowal of our actual imperfection, the first condition of the subsequent improvement." (*Ibid.*)

[2] *Ibid.*, pp. 109 ff.

[3] "Seven years after death, when all the disturbing passions are sufficiently quieted, and yet while the best special documents are still available, a solemn judgment, the germ of which sociocracy borrows from theocracy, irrevocably decides the lot of each. If the priesthood pronounces for incorporation, it presides over the stately transfer of the sanctified remains which, up till then deposited in the civic burial-place, now take their place for ever in the sacred wood that surrounds the temple of Humanity. Every tomb in it is ornamented with a simple inscription, a bust, or a statue, according to the degree of glorification obtained."

But Comte does not forget the rejected ones either. "As to exceptional cases of marked unworthiness, the disgrace is manifested by transporting with propriety the ill-omened burden to the wilderness allotted to the rejected ones, among the executed criminals, the suicides, and the duellists." *Catéchisme positiviste*, pp. 122–123.

[4] *Politique pos.*, IV, pp. 241, 275.

[5] *Catéch. positiv.*, p. 288.

[6] *Politique pos.*, IV, p. 68.

[7] *Lettres d'Auguste Comte à divers*, published by the executors of his testament, Vol. I, Part I, Paris, January 1902, 114th year of the Great Crisis.—On Archimedes 23, 63 (April 22, 1851) he wrote to de Tholouze: "I am sure that before 1860, I shall preach positivism in Notre-Dame, as the only real and complete religion." (*Correspondance inédite*, III, p. 101.)

another day, after another prophetic vision, he described the Pantheon transformed into a Temple of Humanity. After the service, a woman cries out in tears: "Thank thee, adored Master, I will endeavor to imitate thy courage, and shall succeed by nourishing myself on thy example. Thou too hast seen how people were unaware of thy generosity and sacrifices; nevertheless thou remained faithful to thy duty. Auguste Comte, our father, founder of our Holy Church, may thy memory guide, sustain and conserve me, a faithful daughter of Humanity, from this day on until the hour of my death. Amen."[1]

The correspondence with Audiffrent does not lack particularly instructive details. There we see our philosopher organizing with great apostolic zeal the "female proselytism". After congratulating Audiffrent for "his lucky positivist attempts toward the beautiful Marseillaises", and recommending to him a "worthy female propaganda", preferably among the "worthy Catholic types" of the South, he declares on Charlemagne 20, 63: "Having become, for Humanity, a double organ, I feel in advance to be a true brother, and, if necessary, father or son, of every worthy woman."[2]

It is known with what imperturbable gravity Comte fulfilled his pontifical functions, asking for all the decisions of the "supreme organ of Humanity" an "act of faith", and a "holy worship", "stigmatizing" the "unworthy" positivists who were contemning his authority, solemnly defining the "utopias" proposed to the faithful of Humanity, initiating the institution of the priesthood[3] and of the "nine social sacraments",[4] as well as the regulation of the positivist marriage, which carries the "engagement of an eternal widowhood"[5] and the law of a previous "trimester" of "objective continence".

[1] Cf. *Revue Occidentale*, September, 1889, p. 169.—"Often," said Longchampt, "he changed the Parisian Pantheon into the temple of Humanity; he placed there the statues, the portraits and the inscriptions of all those whose memory will be blessed by posterity. On the central altar shone the supreme image, a woman of thirty years holding her son; in front of the altar the holy seat; all around, the saintly widows. Then came the faithful in great numbers, the organ wailed; succeeding an harmonious orchestra; then the deep voice of the kneeling celebrant intoned three times: *Amem te plus quam me*, and each time the choir, supported by the instruments, responded: *nec me nisi propter te*." Quoted in Georges Dumas, *op. cit.*, p. 220.

[2] *Catéch. positiviste*, p. 20: "It is through her ['the angelic interlocutress who, after a single year of objective influence, has been now for more than six years subjectively associated with all my thoughts as well as with all my feelings'] that I have finally become for Humanity a truly twofold medium, as does anyone who has worthily submitted to woman's influence."

[3] "More even than the theological priesthood does the positive priesthood require complete maturity, especially in virtue of its immense encyclopaedic preparation. That is why I have fixed the ordination of the priests of Humanity at the age of forty-two, after the complete termination of the bodily and cerebral development, as also of the first social life." *Catéch. positiv.*, p. 22.—The positivist clergy will renounce all wealth and all inheritance, but will be "maintained by the active class"; and Comte takes care to fix "the yearly stipends appropriate to the different sacerdotal ranks". *Ibid.*, pp. 271–274.

[4] Cf. *Catéch. positiv.*, pp. 116 ff.

[5] "Without such a complement, monogamy becomes illusory, since the new marriage always creates a psychological polygamy, unless the previous wife is forgotten, which can but little comfort the other." *Ibid.*, p. 291.

Let us add that the first positivist marriage was solemnly administered by Comte in June 1848. In the course of the ceremony, "the wedded couple, after a worthy exhortation on the new marriage, have signed, all in tears, the free engagement of the eternal widowhood". On Thursday, November 28, 1850, Auguste Comte conferred, in the presence of about twenty-five positivists of both sexes, "the first social sacrament, the presentation of the young child", the offspring of this marriage. The parents were poor workers. Two or three years later, as Comte explains in his letter of Frederick 8, 64, the unfortunate father, "fallen into a state of senile idiotism, in contradiction with his age of thirty-nine years", had to be delivered to a lunatic asylum. This persevering man finally received, under the presidency of Auguste Comte, "on Saturday, Dante 1, 65, a fully positivist burial in the cemetery of Montparnasse", and the high priest of Humanity proceeded without delay to release his widow, "only twenty-five years old, beautiful and witty", from the ties of eternal widowhood.

II

THE ETHICS OF MESSIANIC POSITIVISM

The supreme Science

11. In the hierarchical organization of sciences established by Comte at the time of his *Cours de philosophie positive*, there are six fundamental sciences: Mathematics, Astronomy, Physics, Chemistry, Biology, Sociology. But in his second career Comte understood that sociology was not the definitive summit. Above it, and distinct from it, must come the seventh, more elevated science—Ethics.[1] This is perfectly coherent, on the one hand, with the general, essentially practical, scope of Comte's philosophy, and on the other, with the principles which had led him to the subjective synthesis. The seventh science supposes all the others, especially sociology. But it could not be treated as long as we remained in the (provisional) perspective of knowledge and mind, and did not turn to the (definitive) perspective of feeling and religion. The reason for this is that moral science, a science which deals with the direction of human actions, is conceivable only from the point of view of the subjective synthesis, and as an instrument of religion. In other words, Ethics is by nature a sacerdotal science.[2] It is *par excellence* the science of the high priest of

[1] "Whether ascending or descending, the encyclopaedic course always represents ethics as the science *par excellence*, since it is at once the most useful and the most complete." *Catéch. positiv.*, p. 175. Cf. *Polit. pos.*, II, pp. 434–438; III, pp. 46–50; IV, p. 233.

[2] "Its spontaneous study belongs to all, in proportion to their natural aptitude and their empirical lights. But *it can be systematized only by the priesthood*, according to its necessary relations with the ensemble of real theories." Thus ethics is "the essential domain of religion, first as science, then even as art". *Catéch. positiv.*, p. 249. (Italics ours.)

Humanity, who uses it to guide people, and who *knows* that the most important thing in human conduct is the improvement of feelings.[1] The encyclopaedic culture of the positive clergy must be crowned by a science which is the science of the heart.

Comte died before he could write the treatise on Ethics which was destined to bring his work to completion. But, even without speaking of the quite summarily drafted sketch he made of it, and which was published by Pierre Laffitte,[2] we find in his other works, notably in *Politique positive*, *Synthèse subjective* and *Catéchisme positiviste*, sufficient and precise enough data to form an idea of Comtian ethics.

Because of Comte's general principles which forbade him to go beyond the phenomena and the relative, this ethics is not, and cannot be, a moral philosophy properly so called. It offers us no systematic and critical reflexion on the principles of human action, or on the meaning and import of moral obligation and conscience, or on the rational validity of the laws with respect to which men feel obliged. Instead of the building which he refused to construct, all we can find is, on the one hand, the foundations which would have supported it, and on the other, suspended, so to say, in the air, the furniture which would have decorated that building, had it existed. The furniture consists of a kind of "ethical psychology",[3] the essentials of which are supplied by the "cerebral table"; entirely busy with practical application, it is destined to supply the casuistics needed by the positive clergy for the government of souls. The foundations interest us more. They are the theoretical views which correspond to the speculative background presupposed by every moral philosophy. In Comte, they can only be concerned with the "encyclopaedic" laws, the contents of which come from the sciences of phenomena. The first theoretical view concerns the order of the world, to the knowledge of which all the sciences contribute. The second deals with the notion of humanity which we owe to sociology. This science already has for its object the moral facts (moral fact and social fact are synonymous for Comte); but it is occupied with establishing the general laws of order (social statics) and of progress (social dynamics)[4] of human societies, rather than with ordering and directing (always from the point of view of the social, and in

[1] ". . . The perfecting of our feelings surpasses, in importance and in difficulty, the immediate improvement of our actions." *Catéch. positiviste*, p. 77.—Cf. *ibid.*, p. 25: speaking of his second Guardian Angel, Comte declares that the remembrance of his mother "will always be an incitement to me to give precedence, more than in my youth, to the constant cultivation of feeling over that of intelligence and even of activity". And p. 224: "Their [feelings'] proper laws can be suitably studied only by ethics, where they acquire the preponderance due to their higher dignity in the sum total of human nature."

[2] Cf. the Appendix to *Catéchisme positiviste*, 3rd ed., pp. 396–397.

[3] Cf. Lévy-Bruhl, *op. cit.*, p. 349.

[4] "You must, my daughter, conceive at the outset this great science as composed of two essential parts: the one static, which constructs the theory of order; the other dynamic, which develops the doctrine of progress." *Catéch. positiv.*, p. 211.

view of the social)[1] the conduct of individuals, which is the proper task of Ethics.[2]

12. The order of the world is revealed to us by science. This is a relative and phenomenal order, the totality of all the verifiable laws or invariable relations between phenomena which science discovers, and the immense network of which does not cease to extend and become more unified.[3] This idea of universal order is the highest encyclopaedic notion. To what degree this idea is an extrapolation with regard to positive science, and how much it really depends on inherited metaphysical preconceptions, particularly those of Descartes, unconsciously accepted, is another question. Comte himself held it to be a purely "positive" notion. And from the positive point of view, we must not submit ourselves to a sort of stoic fate, evincing the inflexible wisdom of a God immanent in the world, but to a fate which is the necessity of the mere course of phenomena, without any reference whatever to a cause, or a why. Moreover, this fate or fatality is modifiable, so that the fundamental duty of resignation is joined by that of effort and active cooperation in progress.[4]

Another essential theoretical presupposition of Ethics—and the most essential of all—is the notion of Humanity which we owe to sociology. Here again we have a notion which Comte holds to be scientific, but which, in reality, bulges with metaphysical preconceptions handed down to our philosopher by his "precursors" (he himself was a more striking example than he thought of the law that the living are governed by the dead). Be this as it may, Humanity for Comte is not only the human species; she is also, and indivisibly, the social human community—a social whole which carries in itself a radical exigency of unity, and irresistibly advances toward it through the vicissitudes of history. This implies that progressive preponderance of sympathetic inclinations over egoistic instincts, the fostering of which is the essential mission of religion

[1] "Although each human function is necessarily performed by an individual medium, its true nature is always social." *Catéch. positiv.*, p. 277.

[2] "Thus you see why, at the top of the encyclopaedic scale, I place *Ethics* or the science of the human individual." *Ibid.*, p. 166.

"Auguste Comte had first made no distinction between Ethics and Sociology. Beginning in 1848, with his *Discours sur l'ensemble du positivisme*, he makes this necessary separation, which he accomplishes definitively in his *Système de politique positive* (1851–1854).

"Sociology studies the structure and the evolution of the collective beings formed by man. Ethics, on the contrary, studies individual man as developed for and by the collective beings: Family, Fatherland, Humanity." Pierre Laffitte, *Appendix* to *Catéchisme positiviste*, 3rd ed., p. 395.

In the synthetic table found on p. 170 of *Catéchisme positiviste* Comte divides the "direct study of the human order" into the study of the collective order, or Sociology properly so-called, and the study of the individual human order, or Ethics.

[3] "The fundamental dogma, then, of the universal religion is the established existence of an immutable order to which all events of every kind are subject. . . . Such an order can only be established, never explained." *Catéch. positiv.*, p. 54.

[4] Cf. *Catéch. positiv.*, p. 57.

(in other words, the fact that "man becomes more and more religious").[1] And Humanity, conceived as a collective whole, is the true human reality; the individual is an abstraction, because he exists, lives, acts, has value and dignity only as a part of this whole. All he is, and all he has, he got from Humanity. Since he lives by her, he must live for her.

But then, one will ask, how do we pass from a theoretical presupposition to a moral conclusion, from discovering the order of the world to a precept to submit ourselves to it, from a sociological theory of Humanity as a whole on which the individuals depend to a precept to dedicate ourselves to her service, and love her more than ourselves? To this question Comte does not give, and cannot give, any philosophical answer (it would be necessary to enter the territory of the *why*). He entrusts man's moral instinct, the spontaneous feeling of the common conscience, with giving the answer in his stead. In fact, he refers to this spontaneous feeling as a factual datum which he uses, but which he does not criticize any more than he criticized that factual datum which is the knowledge of the world obtained by the sciences. I do not mean to say that he erected a philosophy of natural moral feeling into a system;[2] I mean to say that he rested on the natural moral feeling in order to make up for a lack of philosophy. And he is doubtless right in respecting moral knowledge in its pre-philosophical state, latent as it is in the instinct and the spontaneous inclinations of the common conscience.[3] But he is wrong, on the one hand, in paying attention neither to the deeper data which are necessarily implied in the judgments of the common conscience, nor to the heterogeneous elements which they can contain, and which must be sifted; and on the other hand, in not understanding that it is the proper task of philosophy to make the pre-philosophical knowledge in question rationally explicit and critically justified.

13. If the "worthy" female type or the "worthy" proletarian type (not to speak of the "worthy" banker and the "worthy" physician) whom Comte addresses, spontaneously judge that we must gladly submit ourselves to the universal order discovered through the sciences, this is because they obscurely think that this universal order is *good*; and if they think that this order of the world is good, this is because they think, still more obscurely, that it carries an imprint of a certain wisdom, of a certain purpose directed toward the good of the whole. In short, that same moral instinct, of which Comte takes advantage

[1] "Attributing to the best of words the sense normally corresponding to its origin and first meaning, you would not hesitate to congratulate me for having systematically summed up the true philosophy of history in this fundamental aphorism: *Man becomes more and more religious.*" *Synthèse subjective*, Dedication, p. lxv.

[2] Although he claims kinship for himself with the Scottish school, all the while criticizing it.

[3] Cf. *Polit. positive*, I, 9.—"Already," writes L. Lévy-Bruhl, "positive science is a prolongation of political reason. . . . Likewise, systematic morality is a prolongation of spontaneous morality." *Op. cit.*, p. 356.

to excuse himself from philosophizing, implies a natural belief, unformulated and unconscious as it may be, in natural law, which in the logical order is totally repugnant to positive philosophy.

Likewise, the people whom Comte addresses, once persuaded that we have everything from Humanity and live by her, will quite naturally admit, by an instinctive sense of justice, that it is our duty to live for her, and serve her by loving her more than ourselves. Comte himself will note this explicitly when he says that, since "everything in us belongs to Humanity", and "everything comes to us from her", we must "duly feel that we are necessarily destined to her unintermitting service"[1]—thus transferring to the "new Supreme Being" what the theologians teach of God and the creature's obligations toward him. This obligation of everyone toward Humanity is the only relation of justice which finds a place in Comte's thought; though it is nothing more than a spontaneous manifestation, in our philosopher himself, of the instinct of justice which is at work in the common conscience—without ever giving rise in him to the least philosophical elaboration.

Although spontaneous morality has something to say, it remains a fact, for all that, and Comte knows it very well indeed, that nature by itself is not enough, and needs the support of an ideology and a discipline. As concerns ideology, Comte is forbidden by the positivist system to look for any rational justification of our moral obligations; so he replaces it by the fictions of regenerated fetishism, in accordance with the exigencies of the heart. He injects into the world (the Great Fetish and the Great Milieu) benevolent and beneficent wills, and makes of Humanity the Great Being. As a result we shall not only submit ourselves to the order of the world, we shall adore fate; not only shall we understand that "between Man and the World, Humanity must be",[2] but we shall also adore the Great Being and address to it "the admirable wish through which the sublimest of the Mystics foreshadowed in his own way the moral motto of Positivism (Live for others): May I love Thee more than myself, nor love myself save for Thee. *Amem te plus quam me, nec me nisi propter te!*"[3]

But discipline, we must admit, is more important than ideology, because the only problem which interests Comte in ethics is purely practical—to develop and strengthen, against the egoism of the individual, sympathetic feelings and inclinations. And discipline is the business of the priesthood. Without

[1] *Catéch. positiv.*, pp. 277–278.—"The least gifted man feels himself continually *indebted* to Humanity for a host of other treasures. . . . The cleverest and most active man can never *pay back* but a very slight portion of what he *receives*. He continues, as in his childhood, to be fed, protected, developed, etc., by Humanity. . . . To live for others becomes then in each of us the enduring *duty* which results rigorously from this irrecusable fact: to live by others." *Ibid.*, pp. 278–279. (Italics ours.)

[2] "Such a regime is summed up in this systematic line: *Between Man and the World, Humanity must be*." *Synthèse subjective*, p. 35.

[3] *Catéch. positiv.* (Preface to the first edition), 3rd ed., p. 35.—"The sublimest of the Mystics" is the author of the *Imitation*, whom Comte read assiduously.

the power of signs with which worship surrounds and nourishes our lives, and, above all, without the constant pressure of instructions and prescriptions issued by the spiritual authority, there is no assured moral progress for men. One would say that philosophers who, like Hegel, misconstrue or, like Comte, completely reject, the notion of natural law, are forced to ask either from the authority of the State, or from that of a godless positivist clergy, the prime rational incitement toward a right moral life which they can no longer find in human nature as an interior principle present in every man.

Love as Our principle[1]

14. Comte understood much better than the positivists of to-day that Ethics cannot be reduced to the positive sciences, not even to sociology. But according to his principles, Ethics, which is at once a science and an art, and which itself remains, as science, a science of (moral) phenomena, is totally measured by the social (in the progress of which it is supposedly obligatory to cooperate). On the other hand, by the very fact that Ethics cannot be reduced to the sciences, which are the prerogative of the intellect, Ethics can have its principle only in feeling (sympathy, instincts of sociability), that is to say, feeling as an autonomous source springing forth entirely apart from the intellect.

The crucial importance of benevolence, of good, of the sense of human communion, the necessary preponderance of the heart and the primacy of love, the fact that without love the best things can make us only worse, that love is at the beginning and at the end of our moral progress—such ideas (Christian in their origin, but de-christianized and mutilated by Comte) belong to the stock of those few "simple and powerful" ideas, as has been said,[2] which serve as a support to the Comtian follies and explain the prestige of the positivist system in certain well-intentioned minds deprived of critical sense. But in what consists, and what is worth a love whose source is entirely separated from intelligence? It is impossible not to ask the question whether what Comte calls love really deserves the name.

True love passes through the Good. True love—I mean properly or specifically human love, the soul of human morality—is a movement of the power of desire which is rooted in the intellect (in other words, a movement of the will),[3] and thus necessarily presupposes the universal idea of good which is proper to intellectual knowledge, and is beyond the province of simple sense knowledge. True love goes out to an object which, no matter how attractive it might also be to the senses and the instincts, is, insofar as it is an object of

[1] The "mere idea" of the Great Being "suggests at once the sacred formula of Positivism: *Love for principle, Order for basis, and Progress for end*". *Catéch. positiv.*, p. 59.

[2] Cf. H. de Lubac, *The Drama of Atheist Humanism*, pp. 144 ff.

[3] I am referring here to the Aristotelico-Thomistic concept, not to the Kantian conception of will. On the Thomist positions concerning love, cf. L. B. Geiger, *Le problème de l'amour chez Saint Thomas d'Aquin*, Paris: Vrin, 1952; and Jean-Hervé Nicolas, "Amour de soi, amour de Dieu, amour des autres", *Revue Thomiste*, 1956, No. 1.

properly human love, first grasped as good by the intellect. In this sense it must be said that true love passes through intelligence and through the good (the transcendental Good, not necessarily the moral Good). And since it supposes the idea of good, it supposes, by the same token, the idea of the absolute Good, which can remain outside the field of explicit thought, and even outside the field of consciousness, but which is implicitly tied up with the idea of good. Thus man cannot love another being with a genuinely human love without, in fact, having God in his mind, at least in an unconscious manner.

But what is unconsciously in the mind, can, if certain obstacles are removed, one day rise to consciousness. Here is a risk for atheism—and this is, no doubt, the true reason why Marxist atheism so carefully keeps away the idea of love. Comtian atheism, on the contrary, holds to this idea; however, in order to avoid the risk in question, and to be sure that God is eliminated, love is given the same kind of treatment as knowledge was given. As knowledge for Comte deals purely and exclusively with phenomena, in the same way love for him has its origin in the mere instinct. Lest it pass through the Good, it does not go through the intellect. It has its source springing forth entirely apart from intelligence, in the territory of feeling, tendencies, natural inclinations, conceived as the domain of sense and instinct. Atheistic love is a headless love, it is secure only when, even rationalized, it keeps to the level of animality in man. What remains of fraternal love, when it has "irrevocably" been cut away from the love of God by the perfected methods of positivism, are natural inclinations toward benevolence and sociability insofar as they emanate only from instinct.

15. It never occurred to Comte to get exact information on Catholic theology before criticizing it, and the study of what Catholic theology teaches on the radical goodness of human nature—which is perfected, not destroyed, by grace—was sure to be contrary to his "cerebral hygiene". If he indulged in absurdly reproaching Christianity for its so-called denial of the existence in us of disinterested natural inclinations and natural tendencies toward benevolence, goodness, devotedness, this was because he believed, and wanted to believe, that for Christianity nature was purely and simply bad—he was, no doubt, misled in this by the old French Jansenistic rhetoric, and perhaps also by the vocabulary, not theological, but mystical and practical, of the *Imitation*. Be that as it may, the existence of the inclinations in question, and the fact that they are a precious natural preparation for virtues, have always been recognized, and people did not wait for Doctor Gall to become aware of so obvious a datum. Comte nevertheless attaches crucial importance to what he considers the incomparable discovery of Gall.[1] Why? Because he saw in the

[1] On Gall's system, of which Comte retains, with admiration, the principle and the directive idea, but not the detail, cf. *Cours*, III, pp. 626–668; *Polit. pos.*, I, pp. 729–732; *Catéch. positiv.*, p. 229.

phrenological theory the possibility of henceforth reducing the inclinations we just mentioned to the sole domain of nature's instinct and of the superior animality which is that of man[1]—whereas, in reality, these natural inclinations proceed both from the instinct of nature characteristic of the animal realm, and from a spontaneous propensity of reason itself acting beneath the level of conceptual deliberation and free choice, in a way which is natural too, but natural to man as endowed with spiritual powers.

The most obvious result of Gall's "discovery", as re-interpreted and systematized by Comte, is henceforth the drama of moral life that takes place at the level of nature's instinct (reason intervenes, it is true, but from outside). We have, on the one hand, egoistic natural inclinations peculiar, both in man and animal, to individuality; and on the other, sympathetic natural inclinations, present both in animal and man, but more developed in man and showing that he belongs to the Great Being. The whole human problem boils down to making, by means of an appropriate training, the latter predominate over the former which will always be present, but can be surmounted.[2]

But there is something that cannot be surmounted—namely the kind of Manichean division which, despite the supreme "harmony" whose secret Comte boasted to know, is inevitably implied in such a conception of moral life. In fact, no reconciliation is possible (but only a sort of practical arrangement or compromise) between love for oneself, if it is conceived as always and in every case egoistic, and love for others, if it is conceived as repugnant by its very nature to every kind of love for oneself.

In the Catholic system, re-interpreted in his own way, Comte saw the same type of conflict between nature and grace; and he extolled Saint Paul for having recognized in us, in his doctrine on grace, the existence of natural inclinations of benevolence and sympathy.[3] The genius of Gall brought that of Saint Paul to completion: "The imaginary conflict between nature and grace was thenceforth replaced by the real opposition between the posterior mass of the brain, the seat of the personal instincts, and its anterior region, the distinct seat of the organs for the sympathetic impulses and the intellectual faculties."[4]

[1] Their [duty's and happiness'] necessary harmony results directly from the natural existence of benevolent inclinations, which was scientifically demonstrated, in the last century, from a general survey of animals, in which the respective roles of heart and mind can be more easily perceived." *Catéch. positiv.*, p. 279.—We know that according to Auguste Comte the study of mental and moral functions has for principle "*sociological inspiration controlled by zoological appreciation*". (*Polit. pos.*, I, pp. 671, 673.)

[2] Cf. *Catéch. positiv.*, p. 237.

[3] "The great St. Paul, in constructing his general doctrine on the permanent conflict between nature and grace, really sketched, in his own way, the whole moral problem, not merely the practical, but also the theoretical problem. For this valuable fiction was provisionally a compensation for the radical incompatibility of monotheism with the natural existence of the benevolent instincts, which impel all creatures to mutual union instead of devoting themselves separately to their Creator." *Catéch. positiv.*, p. 227.

[4] *Ibid.*, p. 299.—"Such is", Comte adds, "the indestructible basis on which the founder of Positive religion then constructed the systematic theory of the brain and soul, when he had instituted sociology, from which alone could come the requisite inspiration."

16. But let us leave aside this remarkable phrenological exegesis. Two points interest us more. First: although the idea of love for others in the Comtian sense directly relates, as we have seen, only to the instinctive inclinations of benevolence and sympathy, it implies, nevertheless, a requirement for cultivating, developing and strengthening these instinctive inclinations by means of a training by reason, so that they may become a dominant disposition in which conscious reflection takes pleasure. Second: once the preponderance of sympathy over egoism is assured by the holy influences of positive religion and of the positivist clergy, love, which will then prevail over "personal" instincts among men (and is already prevailing over them in the high priest of humanity), will be a love without the slightest trace of any reference whatever to the proper good of the subject, an atheistic "pure love".[1] It is true that the egoistic inclinations are ineradicable and will always be present in us. But to the extent to which they will be satisfied (and to which positive religion itself will take care of satisfying them through subjective immortality and incorporation into the Great Being), this will be only through a necessary concession—legitimate and beneficial, moreover, once altruism wins the game—to the imperfection of our nature and to the inevitable evil of individuality. The inclination to personal good, because it is held to be essentially egoistic, will never be integrated into disinterested love of others, and the latter will never admit the slightest trace of the former, because love for others is supposed to be essentially a repudiation of every kind of love for oneself.

In the reality of things the picture is quite different. In actual fact, disinterested love for others does not truly exist, and cannot truly prevail over egoism, unless it draws to itself, and transforms into itself, the natural love which the existing subject has and must have for himself. I am in no way suggesting that natural self-love should be considered the end to which love for others is directed, as the theoreticians of egoism absurdly believe. But because the one whom I love is another myself, my natural love for myself is the matrix in which a new love, utterly different, takes form, loving another not for my sake, but for his sake, and loving him as myself, that is, as truly and really as I love myself—and, as to quantitative measure, sometimes less than, sometimes as much as, sometimes more than myself. Thus, natural love for oneself is always there, as an ontological support, vitally involved in disinterested love of others, even when this love for others grows to such dimensions that it entirely eclipses natural self-love.

But analyses of this kind, because they go further than phenomena, have no sense for Comte.[2] For him everything is reduced to a duel between pure love located in the anterior lobes of the brain, and pure egoism located in the

[1] "No interested motive any longer stains the purity of our effusions." *Ibid.*, p. 96.

[2] In Comte's eyes, *to love one's neighbor as oneself* stems from "a purely personal calculation". The *as oneself* shocks him; "one thus sanctions egoism instead of repressing it". *Ibid.*, p. 281.

posterior cerebral mass. And when pure love has won, the sensational turn of events—necessary, according to the laws of rationalist dramatics, to make everything end well—causes happiness, which has supposedly nothing to do now with the desire for personal good because it is purely supererogatory, to spring forth from this pure love, which carries it with itself to the blue skies of disinterestedness.[1]

Contrariwise, when a good Christian, as Comte sees him, performs his duty for the love of God—that is, "without any human sympathy"[2]—he does so only in virtue of a personal calculation which is in reality degrading, "from the lure of an infinite reward or from the fear of an eternal punishment".[3] Briefly, Christian charity dissimulates a fundamental egoism modelled on "the absolute egoism of the supreme type";[4] care for salvation, and the idea that we are exiled on earth,[5] impresses on it an indelible "stain of selfishness".[6]

It is indeed remarkable that both Marxist and Comtian atheism endeavor to calumniate charity with similar zeal. But in the case of Marxist atheism, this is done in order to throw out love (confounded with vain sentimentality) from the realm of the historico-social forces; in the case of Comtian atheism, this is done in order to install, as the supreme historico-social force, a love supposedly better than charity. Later on we shall come back to speak of the meaning and import of this difference. As regards Auguste Comte, if that atheistic love which he calls altruism is, in his eyes, essentially superior to "theological love",[7] this is so because he conceives it as a love of others from which is excluded all love for the lover's own being and his proper perfection. No doubt, it does not eliminate "the personal instincts"; even, once they have been subordinated to pure love, it "implicitly sanctions" them, "as necessary conditions of our existence".[8] But in itself, this atheistic love is nothing but a tender adoration of the Great Being which leaves no place in us for any desire for the good of our own person. When it prevails in us, our life is no longer, under any aspect, *for us*, but exclusively *for others*.

Headless love

17. The trouble is that, properly speaking, there are no longer others. True love tends to others because it passes through the intellect, and because the intellect—that is, undiminished intellect, not phenomenalized intellect—tends to being, and grasps not only me, but also the one who is not me, as a being

[1] According to the illusionist psychology of Comte, the good positivist performs his duty out of pure love. But (here is the wonder) into the bargain he is overwhelmed with delights by "that pure and disinterested love" which is "true happiness", and "in which really consists the sovereign good that former philosophers sought so futilely" (*Politique positive*, I, p. 221),—duty and happiness being thus melted with one another (cf. *Catéchisme posit.*, p. 279) in an epicureanism of disinterestedness which is a brilliant lucky find.

[2] *Ibid.*, p. 281.

[3] *Ibid.*, p. 30 (cf. above, chapter XI, p. 309, note 2).

[4] *Polit. positive*, III, p. 447.

[5] *Catéch. posit.*, p. 72.

[6] *Ibid.*, p. 281.

[7] *Ibid.*, p. 281.

[8] *Ibid.*, p. 282; cf. p. 51.

which subsists and has value in itself; the intellect knows others as persons or subjectivities (beings for themselves, ontological depths, absolute entities), that is to say, precisely as others. Therefore, there can be a love or affective union with others which really is a gift of one's life, a death of oneself for the good of others—which is the mark of true love.

But headless love cannot tend to others as such. Others are for it only a point of outlet for an inclination, or an object proposed to action, not a "thou". Here, as in the realm of knowledge, to use the expression of Martin Buber, the "essential relation" has disappeared and given way to the "technical relation", where others are not a "thou", but an "it".[1] In the illusory perspective in which Comte places himself, love does not even tend, as in the animal, to a "thou" blindly grasped by senses. The intellect through which it does not pass, but which cultivates and sustains it, and which is entirely phenomenalized, presents to it in others only qualities or observable features, taken in their relation to the spectator and cut off from any ontological density, cut off from the absolute of the subjectivity.

How, then, would the love in question, in spite of its claim to pure disinterestedness, escape in reality the clutches of the ego (or of the super-ego), the ruses and disguises of egocentrism thriving on the very sublimity and delights of devotedness? It is a love or an affective union to others which really is not at all a gift of self and of one's life, but a complacency and delectation in the sweetness of being good and feeling oneself to be good and beneficent. This sentimental hedonism is the characteristic of false or abortive love.

Thus, there can be a love (an abortive love) without the gift of self. And, inversely, there can be a gift of self without love. This remark adds a complement to our reflections on atheism. For, although the kind of cleavage I just mentioned can arise from any causes, one of them surely is absolute atheism. We saw in the preceding chapter[2] that Marxist atheism demands from man a real gift of his life, a total gift of self to the movement of becoming and to revolution, to what we called the blind god of history. But this gift of self does not involve love: it is, in fact, an immolation of the human self carried along in the dialectical transformation of the world; whereas love is, by essence, union in duality, and necessarily implies that everyone remains himself while giving himself to the other. Contrariwise, Comtian atheism proclaims love to be its principle, but involves only an illusion of the gift of self.

I am well aware of the fact that, when we come to the conduct of individuals, here again, spontaneous restorations effected by nature can baffle the internal logic of the system. Cases can occur in concrete existence, and doubtless they are not rare, where an authentic love of mankind and an authentic love of the oppressed may become grafted, in actual fact, on the Marxist gift of self to the Revolution; similarly, an authentic gift of self may

[1] Cf. above, chapter XI, p. 298.
[2] Cf. chapter X, pp. 233–234.

happen, in actual fact, to be grafted on the sentimental hedonism of positivist love. Do we not know that in the moral behavior of Comte himself a striking progress occurred, as in his second career he strove to be good, and to live only for the love of Clotilde and of Humanity? His saintly colleague restored in him, at least as far as she was concerned, the sense of *thou*. Georges Dumas notes with emotion that Comte "reconciled himself with Arago whom he hated, with his family at Montpellier whom he scarcely loved; he inspired such an affection in Sophie Bliot and her husband that, when he was in difficult straits, these two servants offered him, of their own accord, what they possessed. He was chaste, he was sober, and ended with refusing the least pleasures of the table; he abolished the dessert to mortify himself, and every evening he finished his meal with a piece of dry bread in order to remind himself of the unfortunate who died from hunger. . . . He lived . . . with his eyes fixed on Clotilde, with his soul turned toward her, sharing with her in his daily prayers, in his confessions, experiencing the joy of feeling her familiar figure accompany him everywhere, and applauding himself for having transformed his sexual instincts into 'necessary stimulants of the most eminent affections'."[1] All this is true. The writer could have even added, if he had been a believer, that, after all, no one can know if the very God whom Comte rejected did not profit by the altruistic effusions provoked by Comte's worship of "the new Beatrice"[2] and his worship of Humanity, in order to inject there, secretly, some impulse of true charity, and thus make His entrance again into the philosopher's soul.

18. We do not doubt that, as far as God is concerned, such a fact was possible, by reason of the very humility of divine ways, and also with a view, perhaps, to teasing the logic of theologians. But, looking at it more closely, it seems to us very doubtful that, as far as Comte himself was concerned, and despite his total sincerity, abortive love ever made way in him to authentic love and to a real gift of self. No doubt, as he advanced in years, his moral life became purified, and he went in for goodness. But, at the same time, he became more and more intoxicated with the sublimity of his own enterprise; he grew firmer in his pride, in his dreams of grandeur and in his ambition to attract upon himself the thanksgiving of mankind *in saecula saeculorum*; he shut himself up more and more in the circle of his ego and of the imaginary world in which he took pleasure. And his delight in being good did not succeed in preventing him from preparing a carefully poisoned posthumous weapon against his "unworthy wife".[3]

[1] Georges Dumas, *op. cit.*, p. 218. [2] *Catéch. positiv.*, p. 21.

[3] In a sealed envelope inscribed *Addition secrète au testament d'Auguste Comte*, he revealed "that Mme. Comte, under her maiden name Caroline Massin, had been a prostitute before her marriage", and, with the objectivity peculiar to long resentments, he described the ingratitude and misconduct which had followed. "The executors were to break the seal and make use of this revelation against Mme. Comte if she refused to comply with the last wishes of her husband." George Dumas, *op. cit.*, p. 124.

But what make us most of all suspect the psychological quality of the love which Comte fostered in himself, are the very expressions he used to describe it. He owed to Clotilde, as he put it, his having "experienced the full strength of that feeling which is most fitted to bringing man out from his primal personality, *by making his own satisfaction depend on another*".[1] "Before I became Positivist," he has the Woman say in *Catéchisme positiviste*,[2] "I used to say: '*What pleasures can be greater than those of self-devotion?*' Now I shall be able to defend this holy principle against the sneers of egoists, and perhaps raise in them emotions which will prevent their doubting it." To this the Priest replies: "Those degraded beings, who in the present day aspire only *to live*, would be tempted to give up their brutal egoism had they but once really tasted what you so well call *the pleasures of self-devotion*. . . . Our imperfect nature will indeed always need a real effort to subordinate to sociability that personality of ours which is constantly stimulated by the conditions of our existence. But such a triumph once gained, it tends of itself, not to mention the power of habit, to gain strength and *to grow by virtue of the incomparable charm inherent in sympathetic emotion and sympathetic actions*."[3] All this indicates pretty well the hedonism inhering in altruistic effusions, and the curious affinities between Comte's sentimentality and that of Jean-Jacques Rousseau. We see, by the same token, the true significance of the famous phrase: "we tire of thinking and even of acting; we never tire of loving".[4] The pleasure we feel in loving is so incomparable that it makes any tiredness impossible.

Quaerens me, sedisti lassus. Whoever has gone through the merciless demands, discouragements and agonies of true love for others, knows what tiredness it sometimes requires man to overcome. Comte's idea of love suits only the love of complacency with one's own goodness—abortive love.

19. *True love consummates justice and does not supplant it*. It is so because true love passes through the intellect. On the other hand, love which is only sentimental effusion, disguised seeking for the ego contemplated in the mirror of its own goodness, and complacency with *the pleasure of self-devotion*, is inconvenienced by justice. Justice contends with it, supposedly intervenes only to excuse from loving;[5] this love does not superabound beyond the relations of justice, it suppresses them.

The notion of right and that of justice are banished from Comtian philosophy and the Comtian city. What's the use of defending my rights when I

[1] *Polit. positive*, I, p. vii. [2] *Catéch. positiv.*, p. 279. [3] *Ibid.*, p. 280.

[4] Cf. L. Lévy-Bruhl, *op. cit.*, p. 358; Georges Dumas, *op. cit.*, p. 208.

[5] "The intervention of *right*," said the lady catechumen (and in quite feminine terms), "has almost always appeared to me as designed to dispense with reason and affection. It is fortunately forbidden to women, and they are the better for it. You know my favorite maxim: *More than others, our species needs duties to engender feelings*." *Catéch. positiv.*, p. 298.

live for others, and the others live for me? Man has no rights, he has only duties. "The vain and tempestuous discussion about rights" must give way to the "fertile and salutary appreciation of duties, whether general or special".[1]

"We feel how false as well as immoral is the notion of *Right*", because it always "implies absolute individuality", wrote Comte in *Système de politique positive*.[2] "In the Positive state, where no supernatural claims are admissible, the idea of *Right* will entirely disappear."[3] And in *Catéchisme positiviste*: "The idea of right has to disappear from the political, as the idea of *cause* from the philosophical domain. For both notions refer to wills above discussion.[4] Thus, all rights whatever imply of necessity a supernatural source, for no other can place them above human discussion. . . .[5] Positivism never admits anything but duties, of all to all. For its persistently social point of view cannot tolerate any notion of *right*, constantly based on individualism. . . . Whatever may be our efforts, the longest life well employed will never enable us to pay back but an imperceptible part of what we have received. And yet it would only be after a complete return that we should be justly authorized to require reciprocity for the new services. All human rights then are as absurd as they are immoral. As divine right no longer exists, the notion must pass completely away, as relating solely to the preliminary state, and directly incompatible with the final state, which admits only duties, as a consequence of functions."[6]

Comte had the merit of pushing to the end the logic of positivism and the exclusively social conception of the human being. This conception, even if, as in his case, it admits and exalts love—because love is affective and subjective—irrevocably rejects justice, because justice claims, by its very concept, to be objective and exigible in reason, and thus depends upon truths superior to time. Comte clearly saw that right is nothing if there is no intangible dignity in the individual who possesses it, and if its source is not in a wisdom superior to the world. He was more decisive than any other philosopher in expelling the notion of natural law and denying that human being possesses by nature any right. This makes his memory particularly dear to political schools which are inconvenienced by freedom: they are grateful to him for having explicitly offered to modern times the idea of a social order in which the individual

[1] *Discours sur l'esprit positif* (1944), Paris: Soc. pos. intern., 1914, p. 145.

[2] *Polit. posit.*, I, p. 363; cf. *ibid.*, II, p. 87.

[3] *Ibid.*, I, p. 361.

[4] "Above discussion," that is to say, which admit of no discussion.

[5] In this, Comte is quite right. One of his disciples (Antoine Baumann, *La religion positive*, 1903, 222, quoted by de Lubac, *op. cit.*, p. 156) will likewise say: "If one rules out the hypothesis of a God who is master of the world . . . I cannot see on what reality you can base the notion of a right enabling the individual, as an isolated monad, to set himself up in front of the other beings around him and to say to them: 'There is something intangible in me which I conjure you to respect because its principle is independent of you.'"

[6] *Catéch. positiv.*, pp. 298–300. Cf. *Polit posit.*, I, p. 361: "Each has duties, and towards all; but no one has a right properly speaking."

person, deprived of every title to invoke justice, is charged only with duties and obligations.

20. In Comte's system, the positive clergy has a mission to teach us these duties and obligations. This is an essentially moral mission; and, by the very fact that Comte professes the distinction between the two powers and the primacy of the spiritual power over the temporal power, he also professes the primacy of ethics over politics. Yet, the very ethics in question has only social criteria.

By reason of the distinction between the two powers, it is no longer the State, as Hegel wanted it, that determines and promulgates the objective rule of morality; it is the spiritual power, the atheistic clergy of positivism. For all that, as we observed previously, the final end remains the temporal order and temporal progress, which the clergy is only busy with aiming at from a higher point of view.

The positive clergy take an oath never to aspire after temporal domination[1] and political power. What's the use, moreover, of aspiring after them? Truth to tell, the positive priests already have them *eminently*, because their government of souls, and the religion which they inculcate, have no other final object than to organize the temporal welfare and political life of men according to the rules of positivist wisdom; the duty of political authorities is merely to supervise detailed application of these rules in particular cases.[2] "It is thus that the priesthood", whose function consists in advising (that is, directing souls and controlling feelings and thoughts), "becomes the soul of the true sociocracy."[3] In Comte's thought, the temporal power, charged with commanding, is by essence only an executive agent, the secular arm of the spiritual power.[4] On the one hand, this implies an entire elimination of the democratic principle[5] and of the notion of an authority for self-government possessed by

[1] Cf. *Catéch. positiv.*, p. 271.

[2] Comte promises the positivists "the universal empire" in the following terms: "Take possession of the social world, for it belongs to you, not according to any right, but according to an evident duty, founded on your exclusive capacity to direct it well, whether as speculative counsellors or as active commanders." *Lettres inédites à C. de Blignières*, p. 35 (27 Dante 63).—"Speculative counsellors" designates the spiritual power; "active commanders", the temporal power: both of them have an "evident duty" to direct the world.

[3] *Catéch. positiv.*, p. 305.

[4] "'Spiritual power will be in the hands of the savants and temporal power will be exercised by those in charge of industrial enterprises.' [*Opusc.*, 93]. But naturally the latter would only be the instruments of the former: they were to be a kind of 'overseers of Western affairs' under the direction of the priesthood." H. de Lubac, *op. cit.*, p. 148.

[5] "Any choice of superiors by inferiors is profoundly anarchical." *Catéch. positiv.*, p. 309. —This assertion has a semblance of truth which explains its success in anti-democratic circles. As a matter of fact it is purely sophistical, and would have sense only if it were a question of "superiors" already superior and of "inferiors" already inferior (*as to human quality*) before the choice; whereas in reality it is the choice itself which makes the ones "inferiors" and the others "superiors" (*as to authority*). An intellectual and moral superiority in the subject who will hold authority is certainly eminently desirable; but what constitutes

the people, in which men designated by the people are made participant. And on the other hand, it entails a reduction and a general weakening of the organs and functions of temporal authority to the advantage of a really sovereign spiritual authority. Thus Comte turned the distinction between the two powers into an instrument of perfect atheistic theocracy which he calls sociocracy. Less prudent than Marx, who left to the dialectical movement of history the care of enlightening us on the structures of the new Jerusalem where all will be reconciled, Comte, on the contrary, bestows upon us every precise detail of the final reorganization of the West under the auspices of this sociocracy—it seems that positivist utopia is by nature a blueprinting utopia.

There will be only small countries with "a population of one to three million inhabitants, at the average rate of one hundred and fifty per square mile".[1] "Before the end of the nineteenth century", France will thus "of its own free will be divided into seventeen independent republics, each comprising five of the existing departments."[2] And the Great Western Republic will comprise sixty republics of similarly limited extension which "will have really in common only their spiritual regime".[3] The public regime will wholly and entirely consist "in the due realization of these two maxims: Devotion of the strong to the weak; veneration of the weak for the strong".[4] In virtue of the principle of sociocratic heredity, "the worthy organ of any function whatever" will itself choose his successor, "submitting, however, this designation to his own superior".[5] "All citizens" will be raised to the condition of "social functionaries".[6] "In each separate republic, the government properly so-called, that is to say, the supreme temporal power, will be vested naturally in the three leading bankers, respectively, in charge of the operations of commerce, manufacture and agriculture. It is therefore first of all to these two hundred triumvirs that the Western priesthood, under the direction of the High Priest of Humanity, will have worthily to submit the legitimate claims of an immense proletariat,"[7] to whom, incidentally, the priests will have proved "the thorough reality of that admirable maxim of the great Corneille: *On va d'un pas plus ferme à suivre qu'à conduire*—'With firmer step we follow than we lead.' "[8] "The main office of the patriciate" will be "to secure to all the peaceable enjoyment" of "domestic satisfactions, in which our true happiness chiefly lies".[9] A new chivalry, to which "many industrial chiefs, especially

---

the specific object of choice or election is not the designation of the best or the granting of an award for virtue, but the designation of a leader—and, besides, choice or election has more chances than heredity of providing leaders endowed with at least certain superior human capabilities. In religious Orders superiors are elected by those who will thenceforth be their "inferiors", and these Orders have never been regarded as incarnating the anarchical principle.

[1] *Catéch. positiv.*, p. 303. [2] *Ibid.*, p. 304. [3] *Ibid.*, p. 320.
[4] *Ibid.*, p. 304. [5] *Ibid.*, p. 309. [6] *Ibid.*, p. 311.
[7] *Ibid.*, p. 311. [8] *Ibid.*, p. 312. [9] *Ibid.*, p. 312.

amongst the bankers" will be affiliated, "will busy itself, either of its own impulse, or on an appeal from the priesthood, with generous intervention in the more important contests".[1] Finally, there will never arise "a temporal power with a possibility of universal dominion, such as the phantom emperor of the Middle Ages";[2] and "the sixty republics of the regenerated West" will have only a "religious and not political" union among them, so that "the High Priest of Humanity will be, more truly than any mediaeval pope, the only really Western chief".[3] This is obviously the great affair in which Auguste Comte is most interested. The labors of the great precursor, Gregory VII, will thus be worthily brought to consummation.

But what about the poor sinners, the ones unfaithful to humanity: by what means will the priesthood bring them back on the right road? First, no doubt, by means of persuasion, "by acting first on the culprit's heart, then on his intellect".[4] But in case of failure the priesthood must have recourse to other means which depend on the "real coercive power"[5] which is constituted by the judgment of others. Then the priesthood will, in the first place, use "a simple remonstrance in the family, before the relatives and the friends called together for the purpose; then a public censure, proclaimed in the temple of Humanity; lastly, social excommunication, either for a time or for ever", by pronouncing, "in the name of the Great Being, the absolute unworthiness of a false servant, thus rendered incapable of sharing in the duties and benefits of human society".[6] We see that, although the spiritual power "advises" and does not "command", it is far from being disarmed; it can exercise against the nonconformists various sanctions which reach them in the most vulnerable points of their socio-temporal existence and, if necessary, cut them off from human communion.[7]

The Comtian city is not submitted to a totalitarianism properly so called, but to an omnipotent atheistic clericalism and a spiritual dictatorship of sociocrats, technocrats and psycho-technicians who hold all the resources of our life and our activity under their dominance. Our conduct is exposed there to the "examination of an inflexible priesthood".[8] Under the pretext that it is necessary to "live openly",[9] everyone's existence is entirely socialized. No place of refuge where God might appear behind closed doors. The Great

[1] *Catéch. positiv.*, p. 320. [2] *Ibid.*, p. 320–321. [3] *Ibid.*, p. 321.
[4] Cf. *Ibid.*, p. 266–267. [5] *Ibid.*, pp. 267. [6] *Ibid.*, pp. 267–268.

[7] "Then [after social excommunication] the guilty one, however rich or powerful he may be, will at times, without undergoing any material loss, see himself gradually abandoned by his subordinates, his servants, and even his nearest relatives. Despite his wealth, he might, in extreme cases, be reduced to getting his own food, as no one would be willing to serve him. Though free to leave the country, he will escape the censure of the universal priesthood only by taking refuge with populations not as yet acquainted with the Positive faith, which will ultimately extend over the whole human planet." *Catéch. positiv.*, p. 268.

[8] *Lettres inédites à C. de Blignières*, p. 58.

[9] *Catéch. positiv.*, p. 30.

Being controls the brains and the hearts, its piercing eye is everywhere, it has microphones in all the walls.[1]

21. *The lesson of Auguste Comte.* We see, then, to what final point the positivist principles: *love is our principle* and *live for others,* are leading us. These sacred formulas of positivism are a mystification, because the love they invoke is an abortive love which stops at sentimentality, effusions of nature, pleasure in being good, and which makes justice and right null and void. As Father de Lubac remarks, "Auguste Comte was able to harbour illusions regarding the character of the 'harmony' which he wished to establish. He was steeped in sheer Utopianism. Nevertheless, he illustrated that too-often-neglected truth that charity without justice inevitably turns into oppression and ruins the human agent which it ought to ennoble."[2]

Here Auguste Comte teaches us a lesson worth retaining which touches what is most profound in the problems concerning human morality. No doubt, the first precept of moral law is love; and without love moral law, holy as it may be, has no other effect except to aggravate our misery. And ethics itself tends to a superior regime where love becomes the only regulator of action. But, in all this, the great question is to know which love must be at work. For Saint Paul, this love is the supernatural virtue of charity, which is the greatest of the three theological virtues; whereas for the philosopher who saw in Saint Paul his incomparable predecessor, love means the sympathetic instincts seated in the front portion of the brain.

Already in the natural order we must distinguish between abortive love which is a tyrant and which enslaves, and true love which liberates. As in God the Spirit proceeds from the Word, in the same way in us true Love passes through the Intellect; and because it superabounds beyond justice, it necessarily presupposes justice. Pardon does not destroy justice but consummates it (because to forgive is to give, and if I give to the one who robbed me that which he had taken from me, he no longer owes me anything; thus justice is satisfied without having had to be exercised). But if at the outset there had been no debt which it is the property of pardon thus to remit, there would be pardon no longer.

It is to true love that our moral life aspires; it is true love that moral law prescribes. If abortive love takes its place, the whole moral order flounders.

[1] The founder of positivism did not foresee the microphone, but he knew that the police system must be regarded "as eminently social, the decrease of its role being due only to the indifference for the general interest as a result of the total absence of real convictions". He counted, in this regard, on the services rendered "almost without charge" by "true believers"—who "will feel themselves obliged to provide the priesthood with the personal information without which its influence would be too uncertain". *Lettres à divers,* I, 2, pp. 367–368 (Homer, 1, 69).

[2] H. de Lubac, *op. cit.,* pp. 156–157.

III

A COSMIC-NATURALISTIC AND SOCIAL ETHICS

Ethics and Religion

22. Comte teaches us in yet another way, which this time is rather amusing. It is, in fact, difficult not to appreciate both the funny and the instructive in the double spectacle jointly offered by him and certain of his adversaries.

On the one hand, we have the respectable choir of those theologians and, if not those Christian philosophers (this expression would run the risk of annoying them), at least those Christians who are philosophers, in whose eyes moral philosophy, on penalty of losing its philosophical character, is bound chastely to remain ignorant of any religious or theological data.

On the other hand, we have a philosopher, as atheist as possible, in whose eyes ethics is so strongly bound to religious faith that he feels himself obliged to found at last the true religion—that of the Great Being, the Great Fetish and the Great Milieu—in order to be able rationally to establish moral science and the rules of human conduct.

Value and Finality

23. In characterizing Comtian ethics, we may ask ourselves, in the first place, what part is played in it by value and finality.

To the extent to which Comte, in fact, uses as basic reference, but without philosophical elaboration—we saw this previously[1]—the spontaneous morality at work among men and the pre-philosophical notions of good and evil, of duty, etc., which it involves, to the same extent his entire ethics, as that of the common conscience, is an ethics of value and finality. But if we consider the order of system and conceptualization, finality has in his ethics, as in that of Hegel and Marx, and, in general, in every essentially social ethics, a decisive preponderance over value. In Comte, this is all the more evident because his absolutization of the relative makes the relativity of all values an essential point of doctrine. Just as in the realm of science he confuses the relative state of our knowledge with a so-called relativity of truth itself, so in the realm of morality he confuses the relativity (on account of historical development, conditions of environment, etc.) *of our own mode of knowing* with a so-called relativity of the object known, or of the very value of our acts—briefly, with a so-called relativity of good and evil. Lévy-Bruhl benign but vainly undertakes to reassure our timid minds on this point by promising that, when we shall have recognized that "there are indeed 'moral standards', as well as 'truths', which are provisional and temporary"[2] (such is, he really means, the case with every "moral standard"), ethics will be none the worse for it.

Let us pass, then, to the consideration of finality. For Comte, no doubt,

[1] See above pp. 230–231. [2] L. Lévy-Bruhl, *op. cit.*, pp. 355–356.

the ultimate end is immutably fixed—"the persistent aim of human life" is "the preservation and perfecting of the Great Being whom we must at once" —as the Catholic catechism says of God—"love, know and serve".[1] But by virtue of the variety of historical conditions what is good to-day with regard to such an end, will be bad to-morrow. All depends on the moment in time and on the cultural environment to which we are and must be adjusted. "In all respects, each of us depends entirely on Humanity, especially with regard to our noblest functions, always subordinated to the time and place in which we live, as you are reminded by these fine verses in *Zaïre:*

> 'I had been, by the Ganges, the slave of false gods,
> Christian in Paris, Moslem where I am.'[2]

Further, it seems that Comte—after having imagined in the most vulgar manner the way in which believers think of the relationship of their actions to their ultimate end (my actions have no value in themselves, they are good or bad only insofar as they help me or not to attain Beatitude)—simply transferred this way of thinking into his own perspective. There is no absolute value, but there is a relatively supreme end: namely Humanity and her progress, to which everyone is called to cooperate; and, secondly, with regard to everyone in particular, incorporation into the Great Being. And our actions have a moral value only and exclusively as *means* to this end—a value which changes with the movement of history, since the ultimate end itself is within history. But this does not prevent the absolute, banished from the sphere of knowledge, from returning into that of commandment; for, although all the values of our conduct are irrevocably relativized, the imperative which we obey "by the Ganges" or "in Paris" is unconditioned[3]—this imperative emanates not from the State, as in the case of Hegel, but from the Great Being itself and from the social environment modelling "our noblest functions", as well as from the two powers, spiritual and temporal, the directions of which we must venerate.

And we are free in obeying them—not because the law of the city is interiorized in us by reason and the sense of justice, but because the instincts of sympathy and sociability have definitely gained the upper hand over the egoistic instincts and over personality. "Our young disciples will be accustomed, from childhood, to look on the triumph of sociability over personality as the grand object of man."[4] Each one of us is man only by Humanity;[5] he is truly man only if every claim of the individual person in him fades away when confronted with the exigencies of the social.

[1] *Catéch. positiv.*, p. 165. [2] *Ibid.*, p. 167.

[3] "This necessary subordination" to the "social purpose" is "the only possible basis of really unassailable prescriptions". *Ibid.*, pp. 282–283.

[4] *Catéch. positiv.*, p. 263.

[5] Cf. above, pp. 320–321, and the text of *Synthèse subjective* we have quoted there: "The necessary basis of human order" is "the entire subordination of man to Humanity".

A Cosmic and Naturalistic Ethics

24. If the ethics of Comte has an essentially social character, it has also an essentially cosmic character. In fact, the Great Being which is at the peak of animality, but does not go beyond it through any spiritual and eternal element,[1] is all the more submitted to the world, since it is its noblest manifestation.[2]

The ethics of Comte is cosmic in the sense (and this is a great verity in our eyes) that it restores the ties between the universe of nature and the universe of morality, and sees in the rules of human conduct an eminent case of the laws that govern the universal order. But, going to the opposite extreme of Kantian apriorism, this ethics is cosmic also in another sense (and this is a great error in our eyes): Comtian ethics makes human morality depend on *nothing but the earth*—on the world alone and its order alone (taken, incidentally, as a simple factual existence, without knowable cause or why)—and refuses to see that the rules of human conduct, although an eminent case of the laws governing the order of the universe, transcend this very order. Thus Comtian ethics belongs to the category of what we may call the "cosmic-closed".

The last word of this ethics is submission to the world. "True happiness is above all the result of a worthy submission."[3] "*Between Man and the World, Humanity is needed*. . . . Modifying the World and swaying Man, Humanity transmits to man the main influence of the former whilst perfecting that influence more and more."[4] By this subordination to Humanity, therefore, man is definitively submitted to the domination of the World, a domination which Humanity perfects and reinforces. We have to "ennoble our inevitable resignation by converting it into active submission",[5] which will foster "of itself a sincere social affection".[6] For it is not enough that we are necessarily dominated by the social and the cosmic; we must be dominated voluntarily, offering ourselves, of our own accord, to their verifiable sovereignty—contented mercenaries who think they are free, because the individual person has been defeated in them; servants of Humanity who are, certainly, no longer "slaves of God", but worshippers of the World and "slaves of the elements of the world".[7]

[1] "Humanity being, in fact, but the principal degree of animality", we must consider "each animal species as a more or less abortive Great-Being. . . . For collective existence always constitutes the necessary tendency of the life of relation which characterizes animality." *Catéch. positiv.*, pp. 202–203.—Cf. Lévy-Bruhl, *op. cit.*, pp. 244–246.

[2] Confusing the notion of *being materially conditioned by* with the notion of *being subordinated to*, Comte holds as a fundamental encyclopaedic law that "the noblest phenomena are everywhere subordinated to the lowest". *Catéch. positiv.*, p. 179; *Polit. posit.*, II, p. 274.

[3] *Catéch. positiv.*, p. 280.

[4] *Synthèse subjective*, pp. 35–36.

[5] *Polit. positiv.*, II, p. 42.

[6] *Ibid.*, p. 375.

[7] Saint Paul, *Gal.*, 4, 3.

25. Finally, however much Comte depends on the rationalist and Cartesian tradition, his ethics must be called naturalistic: in this sense that the inclinations, the instincts and feelings, the determinations of nature usurp in Comtian ethics a function which in reality pertains to reason. Not that he would not indicate the importance of reason for human conduct. His failure is in ignoring the nature and the why of this importance, and the essential function, the specifically ethical function, which reason exercises in moral life.

We have here a rather delicate point, which is worth understanding. Just as in the order of knowledge, the function of reason is, in the eyes of positivism, to connect, formulate, integrate, construct and deduce by manipulating signs, but not at all to *see* into things (there is no intelligible object which the intellect would grasp beyond phenomena), in the same way, in the order of action, positivism is ignorant of the specifically ethical function of reason, which is to regulate and to direct our conduct from within by means of normative judgments (it is up to the free will to conform itself to them or not). The only function of reason in moral life which positivism recognizes consists merely in cultivating the instinctive inclinations by appropriate psychological devices: favoring the growth and development of some, the diminution of others. Of course, one of the functions of reason is to influence our conduct in this manner. But this is not its principal and specifically ethical function in the order of human actions: it is a technical or psycho-technical function by which reason orientates moral life only from the outside and indirectly. Briefly, in the positivist perspective, reason is for the moral universe an extrinsically regulating principle; only feelings and instincts are the intrinsically governing principles of human conduct.

Comte is right in observing that in most cases people obey, as a matter of fact, feeling and instinct more than reason. But he is wrong in regarding this factual situation as normal, and in making it the basis of ethics, because he is wrong, in the first place, about the structure and the primary exigencies of human nature. It is important to submit the interior world of instinctive inclinations and feelings to a rational cultivation and development; but it is still more important to strive to live according to reason, and to develop in ourselves moral virtues: this is, doubtless, the surest way finally to improve our inclinations and feelings. It is enough to push a trifle further the Comtian conception on the uniquely technical or psycho-technical function of reason in moral life, and the conclusion will be that the best, if not the only way to raise the moral level of the human species is that afforded by inhibiting or stimulating chemical products (not to speak of brain surgery). Not only will such means be considered advisable in certain pathological cases, but they will one day permit the medical art to play at will with our instincts and inclinations, peace of soul being then assured by tranquilizers. After all, our race will then perhaps be somewhat less tormented; but the government of self will have been delegated to physicians, pharmacists and services of social security and there is little probability that general happiness will gain much thereby.

Another sign of the naturalism inherent in Comte's thought can be found in his very concept of human society. Man is by nature a political animal—for Aristotle, this meant that human nature, because it is rational, prompts man to the act of reason and will from which results life in common in a society properly so-called. In the positivist perspective, it means that life in society necessarily results from instinctive inclinations of nature; in other words, from the instinct of sociability which is more developed in man than in animals; reason is only for perfecting, by a kind of art, that which has been done by instinct. In his reaction against the Rousseauist "contract", Comte plunges into the opposite error. No doubt, he knows well that human society is not a colony of polyps;[1] but he does not know that, however great may be the dispositive or preparatory part which is played by instinctive inclinations and pressures, as well as by external necessities, political society is, in its essence, a work of reason and of virtue.

Between the religion of the Great Being and the Myth of Science

26. We have previously noted[2] that, in the ethical realm, positivism is in a direct reaction against Kantian formalism. With regard to the ethics of Comte himself, or the ethics of Messianic positivism, this reaction against Kant manifests itself by many fundamental characteristics: preponderance of finality over value; relativization of all values; the triple character—essentially social, cosmic and naturalistic—of the ethics in question.

However, if Comtian ethics is wholly incompatible with the Kantian doctrine on the postulates of practical reason, nevertheless it, too, requires—this time as an intrinsic necessity—the assistance of a belief; to constitute itself as ethics and as a power to direct human conduct, it must be hooked up to the religion of humanity, to its worship and dogma, and to its regenerated fetishism. On the other hand, it remains a normative ethics, the principal function of which is to prescribe duties and to regulate human conduct; and in this way it has something in common with traditional ethics, and even, at least for a summary evaluation, with the ethics of Kant.

The reaction against Kant will become complete with the purely scientistic-positivist, or secularized-positivist conception of ethics (or of what remains of ethics). This conception was briefly characterized at the beginning of the preceding chapter; its essential feature is the rejection of all normative morality. We shall have to discuss it, especially in its sociologist form, in the second volume of this work.

What we would like to note here is that positivism, taken generally, by the very fact that for it intelligence and philosophy are enclosed in the realm of

[1] Cf. *Cours*, IV, p. 351; L. Lévy-Bruhl, *op. cit.*, p. 274 and p. 388.
[2] See above, chapter XI, pp. 262–263.

phenomena and can see nothing beyond that realm, is purely and simply incapable of establishing a moral philosophy properly so called. Either Messianic positivism absorbs ethics into religion (atheistic religion worshipping the great Social Whole); or secularized positivism absorbs ethics into science (the sciences of phenomena and, above all, sociology, which are held, on the one hand, to be the only sort of knowledge capable of objective certitude, and on the other hand, are considered the only kind of knowledge required and sufficient for the good state of human affairs, and made in actual fact mythical substitutes for wisdom).

PART THREE

MORAL PHILOSOPHY'S CRISIS OF RE-ORIENTATION

13

PERSON AND LIBERTY

I

THE KIERKEGAARDIAN PROTEST (MEDITATION ON THE SINGULAR)

Coming to terms with self-knowledge

1. In the six preceding chapters we have attempted a critical analysis of the thought of Hegel, Marx and Auguste Comte, which, though certainly not exhaustive, would be at least as comprehensive and thorough as our present research, confined to moral philosophy, required. It was a question of examining three systems whose influence has deeply penetrated the contemporary world, and of taking the measure of three great exponents of modern anthropocentrism whose work has seriously disorganized moral knowledge, not only among philosophers but also in broad sectors of the common conscience. We shall proceed in a different manner in the present chapter and the following one, devoted to what we might call the crisis of re-orientation through which moral philosophy is trying at the present time to rediscover itself by rediscovering, in opposition to Kant, its realist and "cosmic" character, and, in opposition to Hegel, Marx and Comte, the primary truths on which it rests in the recesses of the human person. We shall not undertake an intensive study of Kierkegaard, Sartre, Dewey and Bergson. It will suffice for our purpose to disengage from the testimony of each a certain note, a certain characteristic sign, which will serve as a theme for our reflections.

Søren Kierkegaard was a contemporary of Marx. But it was only at the beginning of the twentieth century that his name began to become famous and his influence to be felt. He was the herald of the crisis of re-orientation of which we just spoke.

Neither a philosopher in the strict sense of the word—although nourished in philosophy—and yet a philosopher in the sense of being a lay thinker; nor a theologian nor a prophet (obsessed by his feeling for the requirements of the Gospel and by his own unworthiness, he hardly dared to profess himself a Christian),[1] and yet a kind of prophet and a knight of the faith, and, at

[1] "Therefore neither do I call myself yet a Christian, I am still far behind." *The Instant,* No. 6, in *Kierkegaard's Attack Upon "Christendom" 1854–1855,* trans. by Walter Lowrie, Princeton: Princeton University Press, 1944, p. 189, note; (Oxford: O.U.P., 1945). Cf. *Concluding Unscientific Postscript,* trans. David Swenson, completed by Walter Lowrie, Princeton: Princeton University Press, 1941, p. 417; (Oxford: O.U.P., 1942).

Cf. Jean Wahl, *Études Kierkegaardiennes,* 2nd ed., Paris: Vrin, 1949, pp. 442–443.

the end of his life, "a witness to the truth" in his passionate revolt against the established church, this *poet of the religious*, as he called himself, is a figure complex and ambiguous enough to occupy generations of interpreters and to justify their disagreements.

Fascinated as Kierkegaard was by Socrates, it is not without reason that from the very beginning his attention was fixed upon Irony. His own situation was intrinsically ironic. A philosopher without a system but a philosopher, as we have just said, in the sense of being a lay thinker, it was necessary for him to be a philosopher of the faith, in opposition to a theology invaded and degraded by rationalism. The non-philosophy of this dandy, armed with the sling of David and pebbles from the torrent, was an authentically Christian philosophy holding its own against the arrogant phantom of Christian philosophy raised up by the Hegelian gnosis. In the most tragically paradoxical form, he inaugurated the Destiny of the Christian philosopher in the historical era in which the Christian philosopher, although he was actually becoming indispensable to culture, appeared as a scandal to the official general staffs of the intellect and was refused all right to exist.

2. For our present purposes, it is the theme of the singular (*enkelte*)[1] which is of most significance for us in Kierkegaard. This theme is obviously related to the theme of subjectivity. Morbidly, no doubt, but with an insight all the keener for that, Kierkegaard's thought was concentrated upon his own suffering subjectivity. And the more he experienced its utter ineffability, the more he nevertheless sought to tell and make manifest something of it; and the more he tried to reveal something of it, the more he felt the duty to respect its impenetrability. Tormented by himself in this way, hiding himself under masks and pseudonyms which were still himself, and at intervals giving a glimpse of his own visage as still another mask, in such a way as to render the masquerade still more puzzling, irony[2] was for him the witness and the cloak of his own secret. And just as in the realm of religion humor was, in his view, the state of mind required for honoring the transcendence of divine things, so in the human realm all that complicated and naïvely tortuous apparatus of irony was the rite necessarily required for in some way revealing the subjectivity without at the same time profaning it.

Truth to tell, was not Kierkegaard in fact too preoccupied with his singularity to be able quite to keep himself from betraying its mystery? And is it not by avoiding mirrors instead of seeking them, and by forgetting oneself in the object, that a man can best respect the integrity of his own inner

[1] Cf. Pierre Mesnard, *Le vrai visage de Kierkegaard*, Paris: Beauchesne, 1948, pp. 421–422.

[2] We are thinking now of irony as Kierkegaard practised it, rather than of the irony of which he spoke in his inaugural Dissertation. There, with youth and an overly brilliant mind to excuse him, he succumbed to an immoderate taste for systematic construction. (Cf. above, Chapter I, pp. 7–8.)

depths, all the while knowing them, but with an inexpressible knowledge? It is here that the disconcerting ambiguity of the Socratic *know thyself* arises.

There is a *know thyself* in which the subject sees himself without the least discursive objectification. His consciousness grasps within him his interior movements and deep inner states by means of a simple gaze which does not conceptualize, *in the manner*, one might say (though the germ of a mental word be there) in which the senses grasp the sensible, without the intermediary of any image or *species expressa.* A simple knowledge of the *quia est*, of existence. No ripple on the surface of the waters—a certain transparency where this absolutely naïve gaze penetrates is the reward for renouncing the analysis of oneself.

And there is another *know thyself* in which the reflexive intelligence strives to seize and explain to itself in some way the inner depths of the subject, through a process, be it obscure and unavowed, of discursive objectification, and by producing interpretative constructions or conceptualizations. An effort to grasp even a little of the inexhaustible, to know in some degree the *quid est* or the "essence" of the subjectivity. It is this kind of *know thyself* which as a general rule it would be better to replace by a *forget thyself.* For in general it has the effect of agitating and troubling the waters into which the gaze would like to plunge—not to speak of the illusions it can produce in poorly integrated psyches, the false elaborations insidiously built up by the super-ego. In only two cases, we believe, does such a *know thyself* really "come off", and then it offers treasures to the nostalgia man has to know himself: I mean in the case of the saints and the great contemplatives, when the grace of an inspired psychological lucidity is given them, and in the case of souls wounded by neurosis or by remorse, when their passion to grasp themselves and their own ill, instead of turning toward illusory construction, develops a morbid psychological lucidity which a fundamental rectitude of moral conscience and of mind sharpens still further and keeps pure.

I think Kierkegaard fell into the latter category (as, on another level and without the religious profundity characteristic of Kierkegaard, did Proust and Kafka). And I note (something which I believe casts a certain light on existentialism) that the irony of the matter is that what made Kierkegaard an existential thinker was precisely the fact that he never contented himself with the first, simply existential *know thyself* through which the singular grasps itself, but was constantly obsessed by the second *know thyself*, in which the soul, with a look not naïve but terrifically intelligent, tries to enter into the secrets of the incommunicable "*essence*" of its singularity. In other words, it was his desperate effort to understand existence and subjectivity by a process of conceptual interpretation which he turned constantly back upon the pure subjective singular but which remained in spite of everything what it is by nature, discursive objectification in search of the *quid est.* Thus it is that in order to propose to the world a philosophy of pure existence and pure subjectivity, Kierkegaard's heirs will be forced, while taking all possible pains to conceal the fact, to have recourse to the very thing they proscribe, to that discursive objectification and that groping towards essence without which the intellect cannot advance: this contradiction is at the heart of existentialism insofar as it is a philosophy. The truth of the matter is that the only one who has a truly existential knowledge is the one who, in order to know himself introspectively,[1] does not think his subjectivity but only attains it in a simple look, innocently receptive, stupidly with no question whatever, as the bull sees a daisy or a poppy in the pasture. But this knowledge is not a philosophy.

Philosophy demands of the philosopher that he lose himself in the object. This does not mean, however, that his singularity and his subjectivity are less involved in his work than those of the existentialist, or, to choose a better term of comparison, the artist or the poet. They are involved in the work not in order to be sought for and revealed but in order to be consumed, and thereby to exalt the impetus of the objective grasp.

Incomprehensible vicissitudes, nights, joys, torments and lacerations in the experience of the self attain exceptional depths with the mystics, but in one form or another they are the lot of every human being: either he benumbs himself in order to escape them by lying to himself, or he enters with courage into simple knowledge of himself. The philosopher goes through this just like any other; and he knows better than the next man, perhaps, from what profound sources in us emanate *acedia*, anguish and despair. *Clear thou me from my hidden faults.* The fault or the infirmity that I see, that has a form and a name—however heavily it weighs upon me, I still have sufficient stature to measure myself against it, through repentance or patience. But the most burning thorn is the hidden evil I bear within myself. If only my body were my own, made from the dust of the earth! But there is no worse nightmare than heredity.

Auguste Comte liked to say that the living are governed by the dead—he did not suspect the far-reaching significance of that terrifying assertion. All of the dead hidden in my heredity weigh in me upon my destiny. Their dreams and their poisons which are fermenting within me are the hidden evil through which I am lost. For in every hereditary line there are particular disequilibriums and disorders which, to the extent to which the determinism of matter is at play, inexorably push the unfortunate survivor toward the abyss. Alone as he is at the extreme point of that accursed ride, there exist in his immortal soul free will and grace as the unique chance of delivering himself and of entering one day into possession of his true name, and of his veritable *self.* Then he will walk in the ways of truth and let the dead bury their dead. But how is it possible that black grief and fear should not sometimes

[1] I am not referring here to poetic knowledge or to the natural mystical experience, which pose quite different problems.

fall upon him, whispering in his ear that whatever he does his dead will get the better of him, tie him to some fate—the vertigo of Icarus or the torpor of Caliban—more crushing than that of the stars? It was thus that, haunted by his father, Kierkegaard saw himself receiving life and damnation from him at the same time. It was thus that in becoming engaged to Regina he doubtless (without quite believing in it[1]) tried to expect from marriage its highest good, through which two human persons are each other's salvation, and in the hard discipline of daily renunciation of which love renders them capable, help each other to break forever the fate to which their ancestors would like to chain them.

The champion of the Singular

3. In the philosophical order there is one very simple but obviously crucial truth that the modern era is indebted to Kierkegaard for having reminded us of, and having made luminously clear. By virtue of the very fact that his introverted thought was wholly centered in his own subjectivity and his own unique singularity, he restored, in opposition to Hegel, that truth that the singular *par excellence*—the point where singularity and subjectivity have their full reality and meaning—is not the so-called concrete universal, but the individual immediately born into existence, the human atom. And this simple awareness was enough to change everything. By this very fact Kierkegaard escaped idealism and recovered the realist perspective natural to the intelligence, but without confusing reality with matter, as did Marx. His realism, exclusively concerned with the human person, is above all a spiritual realism. And he freed himself of the Hegelian dialectic as well, doubtless not completely, but at least in the essentials, and more truly than his existentialist successors were to be capable of doing. His conceptualization remained unfortunately subjected to the dialectical scheme, in particular to the dialectical category of the stages of existence,[2] but this subjective and pathetic dialectic had lost all pretension to being an instrument of knowledge and explanation and became, with him, purely descriptive.

In short, he put ethics back on its feet.[3] And by the same token he

[1] "... to live with her in the peaceful and trusting sense of the word never occurred to me." *The Journals of Søren Kierkegaard*, 1841, ed. and trans. by Alexander Dru, London–New York–Toronto: Oxford University Press, 1951 no. 377, p. 98. "... I had never really thought of being married." *Ibid.*, no. 383, p. 99.

[2] Cf. in particular *Either/Or, A Fragment of Life*, trans. by David F. Swenson and Lillian Marvin Swenson, Princeton: Princeton University Press, 1944, 2 vols. (Oxford: O.U.P., 1945), and *Stages on Life's Way*, trans. by Walter Lowrie, Princeton: Princeton University Press, 1940. On the role of the dialectic in Kierkegaard, see Jean Wahl, *op. cit.*, pp. 140–148, 165–166, 490–492, 546.

[3] "The only reality that exists for an existing individual is his own ethical reality." *Concluding Unscientific Postscript*, p. 280. "... Hegelian philosophy, by failing to define its relation to the existing individual, and by ignoring the ethical, confounds existence." *Ibid.*, p. 275. "The seriousness of sin is its reality in the individual, whether it be thou or I. Speculatively one has to look away from the individual. So it is only frivolously one can

re-established the individual person (no longer exalted to the skies as by Kant, but crying out to God from the bottom of the abyss) in its authentic absolute value, he restored the morality of the conscience, and he banished the Hegelian *Sittlichkeit* and the Emperor of this world.

But it was at the price of a radical irrationalism that all this was accomplished—not that Kierkegaard denied reason (he denied it no more than he denied the world), but he disapproved of it. To put one's faith in the objectively rational was pure vanity of soul and idolatrous worldliness, and lost man in the shams of generality.[1] In order to recover the true singular (that of the human atom) and its unique ethical and religious value, Kierkegaard turned his back on the universe of demonstration and objective certitudes, on the universe proper to reason. It was from a delving into the singular itself, in its own incommunicable subjectivity—"subjectivity is truth"[2]—that he expected the discovery of the absolute.

I am quite aware that at first there was an exaggerated and greatly oversimplified idea of Kierkegaard's irrationalism; to-day, by way of reaction, some of his best interpreters[3] endeavor to extenuate this irrationalism by

---

talk speculatively about sin." *The Sickness unto Death*, in *Fear and Trembling and The Sickness unto Death*, trans. Walter Lowrie, New York: Doubleday Anchor Books, 1955, p. 251.

[1] Cf. Jean Wahl, *Etudes Kierkegaardiennes*, pp. 175 ff. Not only is it impossible for reason to prove the existence of God, but "to prove the existence of someone who is there is a joke. To prove the existence of a God who is there is a joke and an impiety." *Ibid.*, p. 181.

"Now how are the sciences to help? Simply not at all, in no way whatsoever. They reduce everything to calm and objective observation—with the result that freedom is an inexplicable something. . . ."

"In that way man is left juggling with a phantom: freedom of choice—with the question whether he does or does not possess it, etc. And it even becomes scientific. He does not notice that he has thus suffered the loss of his freedom." *The Journals*, 1850, no. 1051, pp. 371–372.

[2] Kierkegaard was certainly neither an idealist nor a subjectivist! For him the real is not in the notion, but in extra-mental existence, and truth is independent of man. (Cf. Th. Haecker, *La notion de la verité chez Sören Kierkegaard*, trans. J. Chuzeville, in *Essais sur Kierkegaard, Pétrarque, Goethe*, Courrier des Iles, no. 4, Paris: Desclée De Brouwer, 1934, pp. 9–83.) In this sense, if we want to speak in these terms, there is in spite of everything—and in spite of himself—a certain "objectivity" for him. The fact remains, however, that in his eyes not only is it nothing to know without the passion by which the subject seizes truth and makes it really or existentially his own, but to turn away from the object and turn oneself toward the subjectivity is the only way—uncertain and anguished—of arriving, always at the price of risk and anxiety, at the truth and at the absolute.

The most decisive critique of Kierkegaard was formulated by Erik Peterson, when he wrote: "Subjectivity is truth—this statement, which applies only to Christ, is applied by him to every man; this is a deification of the self and of immanence." *Was ist Theologie*, pp. 9–12. (Quoted by Jean Wahl, *op. cit.*, p. 445.)

[3] I am thinking, for example, of Cornelio Fabro ("Foi et raison dans l'oeuvre de Kierkegaard," *Rev. des sc. Phil. et théol.*, 32 (1948), 169–206; Introduction to Italian translation: Kierkegaard, *Diario*, I, Brescia: Morcelliana, 1948), of Walter Lowrie, of James Collins. But how are we to leave out of account the quite opposite interpretation, founded on a profound spiritual connaturality, of a Chestov or a Fondane? It was near the end of his life that the attention of Chestov was directed to Kierkegaard, in the course of a conversa-

insisting on the traditional rationality which in fact appears in many of his views, and which sometimes seems to draw this Lutheran in a Catholic direction, even to ally his thought more or less with that of St. Thomas Aquinas. There is a misunderstanding here, in our opinion. One must not forget the cleavage which, for a thinker like Kierkegaard, precisely because he is an authentic existentialist (an "existential existentialist", not an "academic existentialist"),[1] separates one from another the *real movement of thought* and what I shall call the *ideological discourse.*[2]

In the ideological discourse, Kierkegaard will be as rational, even as "Aristotelian", as "Thomist", as you like. For after all, when one is employing rational discourse one might as well use it properly. But in the eyes of Kierkegaard this ideological discourse, this rational discourse *is of no importance.* Not that it is false, it is true on its level—but not on the level that matters, on the level of the absolute, of the truth that grips my vitals and on which I risk my life, my eternal destiny. In other words, the ideological discourse, with all its truths, is relativized, in the sense that while it is valid in general it is unconditionally valid only in general, but for no one in particular.

But when it comes, contrariwise, to the real movement of thought, by which I go to the absolute and am saved in it, this movement, for Kierkegaard, requires first of all a rupture with the world of ideological discourse; it leaves this world behind it, in order to immerse itself in the subjective singularity,

---

tion with Karl Barth. He read him passionately then, and recognized himself in him, and he was certainly a competent expert in the matter of irrationalism. Cf. Chestov, *Kierkegaard et la philosophie existentielle*, Paris: V. Vrin, 1936.

On this question of interpretation, the work of Pierre Mesnard preserves, in our opinion, a judicious mean.

In connection with the problems under discussion here—morality and faith in relation to the Singular—we believe more than ever that it is in *Fear and Trembling* that one must look for the essential thought of Kierkegaard. This work, which he held to be his masterpiece, corresponds in an absolutely characteristic manner to his personal experience. It is just because he reveals himself in these pages that he hides himself under the pseudonym of Johannes de Silentio. It would in any case be absurd to write such things if one did not believe in them deeply. James Collins (*The Mind of Kierkegaard*, Chicago: Regnery, 1953, pp. 66–67) is right to point out that the use made by Sartre of the Kierkegaardian suspension of morality is contrary to the authentic thought of Kierkegaard. Kierkegaard himself took care to rule out any such interpretation. The fact remains that he regarded the Singular, in its "absolute relation with the absolute", as obeying a singular law which placed it above the general and could command it "to do that which morality forbade". If my remarks in *Existence and the Existent* "on the need to interiorize the natural law and appropriate it as the principle of one's individual conduct come close to the solution at which Kierkegaard ultimately aimed" (James Collins, *op. cit.*, p. 280, note 23), the fact remains that he did not arrive at this solution, and that he was kept from arriving at it by the idea he formed of the passage from the stage of morality to the stage of faith.

[1] Cf. our book *Existence and the Existent*, New York: Pantheon, 1948, pp. 123–127.

[2] An analogous distinction must be made in the case of the idealist philosopher, this time between two kinds of discourse, the discourse of daily life (in which he speaks of things like everyone else) and ideological discourse (the discourse proper to his philosophy).

in whose depths the existential adhesion to the true is accomplished, in the blood as well as in the mind.

Here we have definitely left the world of objects. Instead of our objectifying ourselves intentionally in the real, it is the real which subjectifies itself existentially in us. The impulse or the passion by which the subjectivity gives itself over to what is[1] replaces the specification of the intelligence by the object; and what counts is the mode or quality of this impulse or passion, *how* it approaches the real and suffers it.[2] That is why, where the supreme reality is concerned, the transcendence of God is only respected and faithfully recognized, if insecurity and doubt, the fear of not really having the faith[3]—a kind of Hegelian "labor of the negative"—cause the certitude *par excellence* to groan, that absolute certitude from which the whole subjectivity is suspended (as if it were necessary that the very adhesion of faith should incarnate in its own interior laceration the two modes, cataphatic and apophatic, in which God offers Himself to our knowledge).

It is in passing from one incommunicable experience to another, each with its own burden of revelation of being, that the real movement of thought proceeds. Passing through the experience of anguish, of sin, of despair, at the end it casts the dismembered subjectivity into the incommensurable—the singular finds itself alone before the God of faith. But this faith, which is existential adherence at its height, stripped of every kind of objectivity[4] (because there is no infallible Church, no human-divine Subject to propose the content thereof), can only be for Kierkegaard (still fundamentally Lutheran in this respect) a supreme act of rupture with reason, a leap into the absurd—the absurd being confused with the *stultitia Gentibus*, the scandal of the eternal enclosed within time, of God dead and resurrected.[5] We may add that the process of deepening the subjectivity which leads to this supreme

[1] "... subjectivity is essentially passion, and in its maximum an infinite, personal, passionate interest in one's eternal happiness." *Concluding Unscientific Postscript*, p. 33. On faith as "the highest passion to which man can attain", cf. Pierre Mesnard, *op. cit.*, pp. 344–345.

[2] Jean Wahl, *op. cit.*, pp. 276–277.

[3] Cf. *ibid.*, pp. 299–301. "In *Fear and Trembling* ... Kierkegaard only considers the faith of Abraham in connection with the test of the sacrifice of Isaac. He says nothing of the faith which adheres to the universal divine truths: as if the latter did not exist for him, or were to be identified with the former. ... It is true that in relation to the universally proposed divine truths, however firm its adherence, faith involves an incompleteness, a certain *inquisitio*, as St. Thomas says (*De veritate*, 14, 1) which is like an uneasiness of the intelligence; but which, except in great spiritual trials, does not have the character of anguish in the sense Kierkegaard means." Raïssa Maritain, *Histoire d'Abraham*, Paris: Desclée De Brouwer, 1947, p. 47.

[4] "Faith is: that the self in being itself and in willing to be itself is grounded transparently in God." *The Sickness unto Death*, trans. W. Lowrie, *op. cit.*, p. 213.

[5] The Christian must "give up his reason". *Concluding Unscientific Postscript*, p. 337. "The Socratic inwardness in existing is an analogue to faith; only that the inwardness of faith, corresponding as it does, not to the repulsion of the Socratic ignorance, but to the repulsion exerted by the absurd, is infinitely more profound." *Ibid.*, p. 184. Cf. *ibid.*, pp. 338, 413, 449.

act of rupture, though it is absolutely valid for the singular person in the depths of whom it occurs, is really valid only for that singular person, and is in itself entirely lacking in rational necessity. For every other singular person it remains, in the last analysis, arbitrary and ambiguous. For everything depends on what, in fact, *already is* the singular subjectivity of this one or that one. It is because Kierkegaard is a Christian that at the end of his existential dialectic he finds himself face to face with God; an atheist, at the end of his existential dialectic, will find himself face to face with the void.

4. One would try in vain to find in the singularity of the subject a criterion of knowledge and the ways of establishing communicable certitudes. Even in the case of infused faith, where in the solitude of the mystery of grace that pure and sublime Singular which is the primary Truth itself touches the heart of the created singular and infuses into it the *lumen fidei*, there is an object—a truth shouted from the roof-tops and offered to all souls—proposed to the intelligence by the ministry of a visible mystical Body. The fact remains, however, and Kierkegaard saw this with admirable clarity, that it is the singular which performs the act of existing, the singular which performs the act of knowing and the act of believing, the singular which in the midst of singular circumstances performs the act of free choice and moral judgment, the singular which is healthy or vicious in its love, which ends up in slavery or autonomy, which is saved or lost forever, and which by its actions and nihilations in its relation to God and to creatures helps to fashion the destinies of the world. And it is a singular Son of Man, at a singular instant of time, and on a singular cross, who saved the world.

Kierkegaard was the champion of the singular, of the unicity and incommunicability which characterize every individual person. But the word "singular" is an uneasy word. It has two meanings. And it was Kierkegaard's destiny to be the champion of the singular not only in the sense in which the singular is the *individual*, but also in the sense in which the singular is the *exceptional*, in which a singular man is a strange and suspect man, who is not like others, a "character", a buffoon, a misfit (*atopotatos*), like Socrates, according to Plato, and Kierkegaard does not fail to note this.[1] With all this, Kierkegaard could try as he would to find an alibi in the concept of the "justified exception"[2]—he knew quite well that an adjective does not suffice to tame the exceptional.[3]

[1] Cf. Plato, *Phaedrus*, 230c; *Republic*, 475d.—Kierkegaard, *The Point of View, etc.*, trans. Walter Lowrie, London, etc.: Oxford University Press, 1939, p. 61.

[2] Cf. "Observations about marriage" in *Stages on Life's Way*, trans. by Walter Lowrie, pp. 171 ff.

[3] "He who has learned that to exist as the individual is the most terrible thing of all will not be fearful of saying that it is great. . . ." *Fear and Trembling*, trans. W. Lowrie, *op. cit.*, p. 85.

In line with one type of exceptional singularity, the person is exceptional who bears within him a secret evil, a hidden sore, a "thorn in the flesh", which makes of him a kind of outcast from the human community. The paradoxes and elegances of Kierkegaard concealed a tragic singularity—his father's pact with the Enemy [i.e., the Devil], his own misery, the solitary despair he bore within him from adolescence, the bruising of the sensuality by the imaginary (aided by the music of Mozart),[1] and, finally, impotence.[2]

He hoped to escape through the love of Regina; he tried to behave like others, to marry. He had to give it up. "Had I had faith I should have remained with Regina."[3] The breaking off of his engagement threw him back upon his wounded singularity. Guilty? Not guilty?[4] He would have made Regina unhappy by marrying her. Yes, that is true. But it was in order to cure himself that he began to make himself loved; he played upon her as upon an instrument, a simple means. And when he suddenly realized that it was a human person, an imperishable soul who was caught in the trap and wounded for the rest of her life, it was too late. The trap had closed on him as well. He had sinned towards her? And in the way he tortured her in order to free her of him, in the way he blackened himself, and in all that obscure strategy to recover his solitude and his freedom, who could distinguish the pure from the impure? God the Saviour! Towards Him alone could he turn in his mortal doubt. The God who had made him singular would take pity on his wounded singularity.

Kierkegaard was aligned against the *general*, in a state of constant protest against it. This is not to say that he denies the world of ethics and the value of the general law; he knows this law is good, and that what is asked of man is to interiorize it through conscience and thus to make his singularity coincide with the general:[5] here we have the rational Kierkegaard, the Kierkegaard of the ideological discourse, who, just as he did in his eloquent apology for marriage[6] (whatever his real feelings in this connection),[7] gives the wisdom

[1] *Either/Or*, Vol. I, p. 104.

[2] Cf. Mesnard, *op. cit.*, p. 278.

[3] *The Journals*, May 17, 1843, no. 444, p. 121.

[4] As we know, that is the title of one of the writings of Kierkegaard: *Guilty? Not Guilty?* This kind of imaginary confession occurs in *Stages on Life's Way*.

[5] "This shows that the individual is at once the universal and the particular. Duty is the universal which is required of me; so if I am not the universal, I am unable to perform duty. On the other hand, my duty is the particular, something for me alone, and yet it is duty and hence the universal. Here personality is displayed in its highest validity. It is not lawless, neither does it make laws for itself; for the definition of duty holds good, but personality reveals itself as the unity of the universal and the particular." *Either/Or*, Vol. II, pp. 220–221.

[6] Discourse of the Assessor, in *Either/Or*.

[7] In the bottom of his heart, he disapproved of marriage, as becomes evident at the time of *The Instant*: "There is no doubt," says Mesnard (*op. cit.*, pp. 404–405), "that the condemnation of 'Christian' marriage had its profound source in shame for the informal union contracted by his father and consummated well in advance of its benediction by the priest. One understands better in this perspective our author's severe judgment on the procreation

of the universal order its due. Though he certainly does not present a doctrinally articulated moral philosophy, still he always maintained his spontaneous adherence to the injunctions of the natural law and the Decalogue. He knows it would be absurd to try to justify his singularity by making of it a norm in its turn; and in his very opposition to the general there was never any question of his scorning the precepts and making a hero of the criminal.

His problem is entirely different, and much more subtle. It is the problem of the singular decision, in a singular situation, by which a man elects not to do as others do, to be an exception. He will defy and offend the *general conduct*, and commit an act which appears to everyone to be a fault—not in defiance of precept but (given his obscure appreciation of the particular case, in which different precepts and opposing duties are in conflict) at the risk perhaps of being guilty in committing this act, which he does not wish to be a fault but which perhaps is one, and which is all the more likely to be one because what is at the bottom of the singularity of his case is an affliction he bears within him, a thorn in his flesh.

Involved in this humanly irremediable doubt there is probably the kind of exaggerated feeling of guilt peculiar to Lutheranism, in whose eyes every trace of egoism or of concupiscence, even though involuntary or not consented to, is a sin, so that for a human act to be exempt from blame it would require an angelically pure psychological context. But more than this, it seems that for Kierkegaard a certain confusion came to exist between defying the general conduct and offending the general law, not marrying like everybody else and breaking a universal commandment: are not *ethics* and *marriage* two convertible terms for him?[1] In any case, the result of the situation we have described is that the exceptional singular, condemned by the human community, the possibly guilty one who has risked everything for what he believed to be a good, has no refuge but God. He is nearer to God than ever.[2] His secret evil, his hidden sore, his thorn in the flesh become a sign of a relation with God which is itself exceptional and privileged, of a vocation to sacrifice. Did not Kierkegaard finally sacrifice himself to the bourgeois

---

of children: 'From the Christian point of view it is the height of egoism that, because a man and a woman have not been able to control themselves, another being should be introduced into this valley of tears' (*L'Instant*, p. 112)."

[1] Also in his defense of marriage Kierkegaard holds that marriage is *forbidden* to all by ethics. That is one of the reasons why the assessor condemns mysticism. "Now since in my opinion . . . it is the duty of every man to marry, . . . you will easily see that I must have an aversion to all mysticism." *Either/Or*, Vol. II, p. 205.

Cf. *ibid.*, p. 254: "The ethical teaches him that this relationship [marriage] is the absolute. For the relationship is the ordinary and universal."

[2] There is good reason for Régis Jolivet (*Introduction à Kierkegaard*, pp. 154–158) to insist on the importance of the notion of "the individual before God" for Kierkegaard. "Only when the self as this definite individual is conscious of existing before God, only then is it the infinite self. . . ." *The Sickness unto Death*, trans. W. Lowrie, *op. cit.*, p. 211.

happiness of Regina, now married to her former preceptor Frederick Schlegel, was he not a victim offered in sacrifice *for the happy ones*,[1] for those who are at home with the general, who are and who act like everyone else! Certainly he does not deny ethics, does not revolt against it. In passing beyond marriage, he passed beyond ethics.

Ethics and supra-Ethics

5. I have spoken of wounded singularity, of the singularity of affliction. There is another kind of singularity-by-exception, namely singularity by election. And, as we have just seen, the former demands nothing better than to be transmuted into the latter by some means.

The purest type of this singularity by election is the religious hero, the person chosen by God as a unique witness, and who receives from God an absolutely individual, unique command. The example *par excellence* and above all others is Abraham, the father of believers, to whom in the terror of an incomprehensible revelation the order was given to put Isaac to death, and to make an exception, in regard to his own unique son, to the *thou shalt not kill* which conscience, even before it was formulated in the revealed Law, recognized as a universal precept. Here is supreme defiance of the general law, here is the singular command which prescribes for one man what is forbidden to all others, and which Abraham obeys, because he is the hero of the faith. He prepares to execute the order of homicide, he lifts the knife against his son.[2]

Thus for Kierkegaard we leave behind us, without abolishing it certainly but transcending it, the world of ethics, which is the world "of the measurable",[3] and we cross the threshold of the world of faith. If there is, as he puts it, "a teleological suspension of the moral",[4] it is because at a certain moment—the instant we pass the threshold and enter the presence of sovereign Freedom, our ultimate End in person—everything else is necessarily

[1] "If no one has had compassion upon me, what wonder that compassion has fled like me out among the graves, where I sit comforted as one who sacrifices his life to save others, as one who voluntarily chooses banishment to save others", Kierkegaard makes the leper say in *Guilty? Not Guilty?* (5 February at midnight), in *Stages on Life's Way*, p. 221.

Speaking of the poet who loves religion like an unhappy lover, he writes: "His collision is essentially this: is he the elect, is the thorn in the flesh the expression for the fact that he is to be employed as the extraordinary, is it before God quite as it should be with respect to the extraordinary figure he has become? or is the thorn in the flesh the experience he must humble himself under in order to attain the universal human?" *The Sickness unto Death*, trans. W. Lowrie, *op. cit.*, p. 209.

[2] On the deeper meaning of these things and on the sanctity of Abraham, see the study by Raïssa Maritain, *Histoire d'Abraham* (Paris: Desclée De Brouwer, 1947); English translation in *The Bridge*, Vol. I, ed. by John M. Oesterreicher, New York: Pantheon Books, 1955, 23–52.

[3] "The domain of ethics and the domain of the measurable." Jean Wahl, *op. cit.*, p. 588. The author cites in this connection A. Gilg, *S. Kierkegaard*, 1926, p. 140.

[4] "The story of Abraham contains therefore a teleological suspension of the ethical. As the individual he became higher than the universal." *Fear and Trembling*, trans. W. Lowrie, *op. cit.*, p. 77.

eclipsed. Then "the ethical is reduced to a position of relativity"[1] and itself "constitutes temptation".[2] For really from this moment on there is only one absolute rule and obligation, that which deals with one's direct connection with the ultimate End itself,[3] and which directs the singular to go to the bottom of the abyss of singularity in obeying in every instance the singular command of faith.[4]

If ethics (now become supra-ethics) is restored, it is only in virtue of this singular commandment, which has replaced the general, even when it causes to be performed (but through the obedience of faith, not in conformity with the rational universal) the same action which the general law and general conduct on their subordinate level present as obligatory. But the case of the exceptional and scandalous commandment, of the sacrificial commandment,

[1] *Fear and Trembling*, trans. W. Lowrie, *op. cit.*, p. 80.

[2] *Ibid.*, p. 124. "Whoever has had inwardness enough to lay hold of the ethical with infinite passion, and to understand the eternal validity of duty and the universal, for him there can neither in heaven or on earth or in hell be found so fearful a plight, as when he faces a collision where the ethical becomes the temptation." *Concluding Unscientific Postscript*, p. 231.

[3] "The paradox of faith is this, that the individual is higher than the universal, that the individual (to recall a dogmatic distinction now rather seldom heard) determines his relation to the universal by his relation to the absolute, not his relation to the absolute by his relation to the universal. The paradox can also be expressed by saying that there is an absolute duty toward God; for in this relationship of duty the individual as an individual stands related absolutely to the absolute." *Fear and Trembling*, trans. W. Lowrie, *op. cit.*, p. 80.

[4] "The paradox is that he [Abraham] as the Individual put himself in an absolute relation to the absolute." *Ibid.*, p. 72.

"Either there is . . . the paradox that the individual as the individual . . . stands in an absolute relation to the absolute/or . . . Abraham is lost." *Ibid.*, p. 91.

"For if the ethical (i.e. the moral) is the highest thing, and if nothing incommensurable remains in man in any other way but as the evil (i.e. the particular which has to be expressed in the universal), then one needs no other categories besides those which the Greeks possessed or which by consistent thinking can be derived from them. . . . Faith is precisely this paradox, that the individual as the particular is higher than the universal, is justified over against it, is not subordinate but superior—yet in such a way, be it observed, that it is the particular individual who, after he has been subordinated as the particular to the universal, now through the universal becomes the individual who as the particular is superior to the universal, for the fact that the individual as the particular stands in an absolute relation to the absolute." *Ibid.*, pp. 65–66.

Then "interiority can no longer be expressed externally, as morality demands. The religious man is as necessarily enclosed within himself as the criminal and the hypocrite. He hides himself, but it is because he has within him something better which he hides; such is the man of the Gospel, who hides his face when he prays." Jean Wahl, *op. cit.*, p. 193.

Cf. Pierre Mesnard, *op. cit.*, p. 344: "The man who truly has faith can experience only that reflection which consists of constant meditation on the nourishing rapport which unites him with his master. He no longer has any duty except an absolute duty toward God: to realize himself fully as an individual with the help of faith."

Is not God himself the "rule of the individual", as Martin Thust said (*Sören Kierkegaard, des Dichter des Religiosen*, Munich, 1931)? "He is the original, absolute exception, the absolute *other* who justifies all exceptions. He is, as the story of Job demonstrates, the one for whom the ethical categories are absolutely suspended." Jean Wahl, *op. cit.*, p. 189. (Poor Job, the exhortations of his friends were not enough—he still had to suffer the exegeses of the philosophers.)

still remains possible,[1] as Kierkegaard himself experienced it at the time of his articles in *The Instant* (*Ojeblikett*), when he was hurled into the struggle against false Christendom as a *witness of the truth*, an "individual in opposition to the others".[2]

For we know perfectly well that "In every generation that man is a rarity who exercises such a power over himself that he can *will* what is not pleasant to him, that he can hold fast *that* truth which does not please him, hold that it is the truth although it does not please him, hold that it is the truth precisely because it does not please him, and then nevertheless, in spite of the fact that it does not please him, can commit himself to it."[3] The fact is that at the time when he wrote such lines Kierkegaard had these inflammatory traits: "So superior is God; so far He is from making it difficult, so infinitely easy it is to deceive Him, that He Himself even offers a prize to him who does it, rewards him with everything earthly."[4]—"The difference between a genius and a Christian is that a genius is nature's extraordinary, no man being able to make himself a genius, whereas a Christian is freedom's extraordinary, or, more properly freedom's ordinary, for though it is found extraordinarily seldom, it is what everyone ought to be."[5]—"What is the Christianity of the New Testament? It is the suffering truth."[6]—"To become a Christian in the New Testament sense is such a radical change that, humanly speaking, one must say that it is the heaviest trial to a family that one of its members becomes a Christian."[7] In a note written three years before, he had said: "It is a matter of being transformed from a natural man into a spirit, and this road passes through dying to oneself, which is extremely painful. . . . So God, in his infinite love, has mercy on you . . . because he loves you! He so aggravates the suffering that he makes you pass through death."[8]

If we return now to our own ethical considerations, we can see that Kierkegaard puts morality on its guard, not only against Hegel but also against Kant. Not, to be sure, in virtue of some positivist, empiricist or naturalist claim, but in virtue of the claims of the moral and religious conscience itself, his desperate insistence on the importance of the singular struck a mortal blow against Kantian formalism.

In the Kantian doctrine of the categorical imperative, I am not only required to obey a general or universal law, but *I* as singular annihilate myself

[1] "The absolute duty may cause one to do what ethics would forbid." *Fear and Trembling*, trans. W. Lowrie, *op. cit.*, p. 84.

[2] *The Instant*, No. 5, in *Kierkegaard's Attack Upon Christendom*, p. 167.

[3] *Ibid.*, no. 4, p. 151.

[4] *Ibid.*, no. 8, p. 256.

[5] *Ibid.*, no. 5, p. 159.

[6] *Ibid.*, no. 9, p. 268.

[7] *Ibid.*, no. 7, p. 221.

[8] Cf. the collection of religious texts taken from the *Papers* of Kierkegaard and published under the title of *Christ* by P. H. Tisseau (Bazoges-en-Pareds, 1940), p. 196 (Mesnard, pp. 375–376).

ethically before the generality or universality of the law.[1] For morality no longer consists in the conformity of my act to a reason *itself measured by things*—first of all by the ends of human nature and its normality of functioning, then by particular circumstances and the personal context in which, in a case which is always unique of its kind, I must myself judge of the application of the law. On the contrary, it is a rationality *emptied of the real*, it is pure generality or logical universality itself, empty generality, in other words the abstract possibility of universalizing the maxim of my action, which constitutes all the force of the moral commandment. In addition, it is uniquely through reverence for the general law that I must be motivated; and if, according to the Kantian theory of autonomy, the noumenal *I* is the author of the law which the empirical *I* obeys, this noumenal *I* is itself universal, being the supra-temporal general will.

Kantian ethics empties the singular of itself, reduces it to making of itself a pure abstract point or derealized logical subject in face of the abstract universal which is the law. Hegelian ethics will give the singular back to itself only insofar as the singular will voluntarily obey the State, and identify itself with the concrete universal in which it is reunited with its own being and substance, and which is the universal will of the Spirit objectified in the State. It is against these two kinds of ethics that the Kierkegaardian singularity cries vengeance.

In regard to ethics itself, the picture is different. If, for Kierkegaard, it is necessary at a certain moment—the moment of passing, or leaping, to a superior order of life—that morality be "suspended", this does not in any way imply that ethics is ever to be abolished, for ethics exists wherever there is choice or will; "the ethical, which teaches us to venture everything for nothing, to risk everything, and therefore also to renounce the flattery of the world-historical in order to become as nothing". But it is just this historical nothing, this nothing in the world which an individual constituted in his autonomous conscience is, which terminates in eternity: "for only in the ethical is your eternal consciousness".[2] No, ethics is not abolished, but

[1] Cf. *Fear and Trembling*, trans. W. Lowrie, *op. cit.*, pp. 64–65. "The ethical as such is the universal, and as the universal it applies to everyone, which may be expressed from another point of view by saying that it applies every instant. It reposes immanently in itself, it has nothing without itself which is its *telos*. . . . Conceived immediately as physical and psychical, the particular individual is the individual who has his *telos* in the universal, and his ethical task is to express himself constantly in it, to abolish his particularity in order to become the universal. . . . Whenever the individual after he has entered the universal feels an impulse to assert himself as the particular, he is in temptation (*Anfechtung*), and he can labor himself out of this only by penitently abandoning himself as the particular in the universal."

Ibid., p. 79: "In the ethical way of regarding life it is therefore the task of the individual to divest himself of the inward determinants and express them in an outward way."

These passages, we believe, relate directly to the morality of Kant, but through it to morality as such, whose concept never ceased to exist for Kierkegaard, under the sign of Kant, just as the concept of speculative reason remained for him under the sign of Hegel.

[2] *Concluding Unscientific Postscript*, pp. 133–136.

when man reaches the true depth where God awaits him, ethics is transmuted or transfigured: so that after having burst through the ceiling of Ethics,[1] the singular finds up above it a new ethics,[2] or rather a supra-ethics, and a new universe of values and norms, those of faith.

6. This problem of a "supra-ethics" is one of the great problems which Christianity, by introducing the notion of an order of supernatural virtues and supernatural gifts, obliges moral philosophy to consider. This is not the moment for us to attack it. What we should prefer now is to try to place the protest of Kierkegaard as a witness of the singular in a proper perspective. In this endeavor we shall take as our point of departure not the ethics of Kant or that of Hegel, but rather the conception of morality which we find in force on the most superficial and most *inexistential*, the most exteriorized level of ordinary moral life, a conception which Kierkegaard did not fail to excoriate frequently. On the level of which we are speaking the moral law means to act as everyone else does. The singular has a clear conscience and feels secure because he does not exist for himself and has no moral experience properly so called; he conforms in a single and identical motion to the general conduct and to an abstract law exterior to him.

Then let us turn our attention toward wounded singularity, of which other examples than that of Kierkegaard easily come to mind. Let it be, for example, a case just the opposite of Kierkegaard's, and one in which the "thorn in the flesh" is of another sort, the case of a homosexual who, dreaming of an ideal communion, decides, after serious moral deliberation, to marry an innocent girl whom he does not inform of his disorder; he loves her, he hopes to be cured through her; in fact, he ruins her life. Guilty? Not guilty? Or let us think of the case of a man whose fiancée has declared that she will marry him only on trial; she repeated this declaration on the day of their marriage; but he has no other proof of this refusal to contract an indissoluble union, no juridically valid proof. She leaves him. Confident that

[1] *Ibid.*, p. 367. "The knight of faith renounces the universal in order to become the individual. . . . He who believes that it is easy enough to be the individual can always be sure that he is not a knight of faith, for vagabonds and roving geniuses are not men of faith. The knight of faith knows, on the other hand, that it is glorious to belong to the universal. He knows that it is beautiful and salutary to be the individual who translates himself into the universal, who edits as it were a pure and elegant edition of himself, as free from errors as possible and which everyone can read" . . . finding his joy "in the security of the universal. He knows that it is beautiful to be born as the individual who has the universal as his home, his friendly abiding-place, which at once welcomes him with open arms when he would tarry in it. But he knows also that higher than this there winds a solitary path, narrow and steep; he knows that it is terrible to be born outside the universal, to walk without meeting a single traveller. He knows very well where he is and how he is related to man. Humanly speaking, he is crazy and cannot make himself intelligible to anyone. And yet it is the mildest expression, to say that he is crazy. If he is not supposed to be that, then he is a hypocrite, and the higher he climbs on this path, the more dreadful a hypocrite he is." *Fear and Trembling*, trans. W. Lowrie, *op. cit.*, p. 86.

[2] Cf. Mesnard, *op. cit.*, pp. 321–322; and Régis Jolivet, *op. cit.*, p. 151.

in the invisible reality of inward intentions this marriage was not a true marriage, and although his moral code forbids divorce and in the eyes of those who believe in the same code he is deemed to have chosen scandal and adultery, he marries another woman, who, for her part, desires to be united with him forever, and in whom he sees his true and unique wife. Guilty? Not guilty? Or yet again, take an ambitious man whom a dictator has showered with honors, and to whom he confides one day that in order to reinvigorate the country he has decided to order his scientists to annihilate by means of a virus those whose coefficient of physical resistance is below normal. Our man knows that if he speaks out no one will believe him; in addition, although his master seems to be quite firm in his resolution, who can say that it is not just a passing whim which will be forgotten to-morrow? Yet he elects to assassinate him. Guilty? Not guilty?

The men whose cases I have just been imagining find themselves involved in a moral experience in which there can no longer be any question of acting like everyone else, and in which the singular person is in the toils of laws whose generality affords no solution to his problem—by the same stroke they find themselves alone (consciously or not), facing another singular person with whom they try their destiny, and who is the Author of the law himself.

Now let us consider the singularity of election. Abraham will always remain the most notable example. But the Bible offers us other examples: did not Hosea receive and execute the order to take unto himself a prostitute and to have children by her?[1] Thomas Aquinas, who interprets this passage quite literally, teaches that this order did not command Hosea to commit fornication, any more than the order Abraham received commanded him to perform an act falling under the moral definition of homicide, because it is God who consigned Isaac to death, as He consigns all men, innocent or guilty, and because in joining Gomer to Hosea He made of her really his wife.[2] Well, it is relevant for us to consider cases in which the exceptional is less scandalously divine, cases exceptional but less extraordinary, whether on the level of the supernatural and holy missions (like Joan of Arc's refusing to the very end to wear women's clothes), or on the level of secular and purely human vocations (like an artist exposing his wife and children to want for the good of his work). In such cases the man departs more than ever from the wholly socialized ethics of doing like everyone else, he is more than ever face to face with God. But he has not left the sphere of ethics (or perhaps supra-ethics) with its universal norms, to enter into the sphere of singular commandment.[3] For in

[1] *Hosea*, 1: 2. [2] *Sum. theol.*, I–II, 94, 5 *ad* 2.

[3] For Kierkegaard, on the contrary, Abraham "overstepped the ethical entirely. . . . For *I should very much like to know how one would bring Abraham's act into relation with the universal, and whether it is possible to discover any connection whatever between what Abraham did and the universal . . . except the fact that he transgressed it.*" *Fear and Trembling*, trans. W. Lowrie, *op. cit.*, pp. 69–70. (Our italics.)

What Kierkegaard does not see is that, as we noted in our *Existence and the Existent*

his exceptional conduct itself there is still a universal norm which comes to be applied—superseding every other obligation—given the absolutely singular context in which the decision takes place.

Whether singularity of election or wounded singularity, what singularity-as-exception forces us to understand is that it is itself only an extreme case of the ethical life in all its extension, in which it is always up to the conscience and the prudence of the singular to carry out the right practical decision, the decision in which the general laws covering the case in question are incarnated and individualized. What we are compelled to understand is that the fact of being face to face with God is at the heart of all moral life and of every authentically moral decision, that the more the moral life and moral experience deepen and become genuine, the more they are interiorized and spiritualized, and by the same token liberated from servile conformity to the socially customary. Finally, we are forced to recognize—here again in opposition to Kierkegaard—that the interiorization of the universal law by the intelligence, the conscience, and the virtues of the individual, and by his love, is not only a truth pertaining to what we have called above the ideological discourse—separated, contrary to the nature of things, from the real movement of thought—and a valid theme for the man installed in the security of the general; it is the existential truth, and the central theme which commands the ethical life in its entirety, and there especially where man is more exposed to the insecurity of the singular because he is entering into those recesses of choice and engagement, which no knowledge of the general can sound, under the eyes of God alone.

II

SARTRIAN EXISTENTIALISM (FREEDOM, THOU REMAINEST, OR THE COURAGE OF DESPAIR)

Descartes and the sailors

1. While at sea in a little boat which he had engaged for himself to go from Emden to West-Frisia, Descartes discovered that he was dealing "with some sailors who were most crude and uncouth. . . . It was not long before he recognized that they were scoundrels, but—after all—they were the masters of the boat. . . . They found him to be in a very tranquil mood, very

---

(p. 67), "Abraham, stricken to the heart by the personal command of God and the contradiction by which he was torn, Abraham still had a universal law, the first of all laws: Thou shalt worship God, the Incomprehensible, and shalt obey Him. Abraham knew obscurely, not out of treatises on moral theology but by the instinct of the Holy Ghost, that the killing of his child was exempt from the law forbidding homicide, because it was commanded by the Master of life."

patient; and judging from the gentleness of his appearance and the courtesy which he showed them that this was an inexperienced man, they decided that they could easily take his life. They did not hesitate to deliberate in his presence, since they did not believe he knew any language other than the one in which he conversed with his servant; and they resolved to overwhelm him, throw him overboard, and take his effects.

"Descartes, seeing that this was quite in earnest, suddenly got up, changed his bearing, drew his sword with an unexpected haughtiness, spoke to them in their language in a tone which gripped them, and threatened to run them through if they dared to insult him. . . . The boldness . . . which he showed on this occasion had a marvellous effect on the spirit of these wretches. . . ."[1]

Nausea

2. The sketch which I propose to trace concerns Sartrian existentialism as I see it. What interpretation of a movement of thought where the individual drama and the author's subjectivity are as decisive as his ideas could be put forth as certain? Although all I know of Sartre's personal history is what critics have published about him—very little to tell the truth—my free interpretation seems to me probable and well-founded, but it remains conjectural. In presenting it explicitly as such, I show more respect for Sartre than he has shown for Baudelaire, in the work where he used him as a guinea pig to test the themes of his own philosophy, not without at the same time satisfying a kind of curious resentment.[2] Insofar as it will be a question, not of the ideas of Sartre, but of his experiences and of his personal history, I will prefer then to present, not Sartre himself, but a fictional personage, a more or less distant cousin of the hero of *Nausea*, but, in contrast to him, a philosopher, whom I will call Eleutherius.

I imagine that Eleutherius began like many young Frenchmen of his generation. Good and inoffensive, but not wishing to seem so, with a bourgeois formation and a Cartesian tradition, he repudiated, in a crisis of adolescence which his gifts and his extremely refined intellectual sensibility only rendered more acute, his class and the "stuffed ideology" which it

[1] *Vie de Monsieur Descartes*, by Adrien Baillet, Paris: Ed. de la Table Ronde, 1946, pp. 47–48.

[2] In a brief note of Pierre Reverdy on Baudelaire I find more truth than in all the analyses of Sartre. "I believe," writes Reverdy, "that the best definition of greatness is the power to surmount one's own weaknesses. The man whose acts and works show him exempt from weaknesses does not give proof particularly of greatness—but of strength. Hugo is a fabulous Hercules. Baudelaire is great because one feels him to be weak and he shows himself so; but he is Baudelaire and it is his having known, in part at least, how to surmount his immense weakness, which permitted him all the same to be Baudelaire, what he is for us through his work, what counts after all and despite all, what qualifies the poet. From so many weaknesses surmounted has emerged, above the man, this work, which does not give the impression of genial force which emerges from the work of Hugo, but of a more profound, a keener touch—at once much closer to and much more beyond us." (Pierre Reverdy, *En Vrac*, Monaco: éd. du Rocher, 1956, p. 164.)

uses to justify itself. And he rejected as lies not only the social values invoked by the bourgeoisie, but also all the metaphysical and moral values which seemed to him to be tied to those social values as their guarantee, and above all God, held as the supreme guarantee of all the false authorities.

In an epoch in which everything is turning upside down, and in which the best minds see the individual, in his solitude and distress, obliged to recreate all his norms of conduct against a herd-conformism and to assume absolute responsibilities without any support other than himself, while unmasking the fakery of the ready-made judgments with which the world reassures itself, this Cartesian in revolt against the rationalism of his fathers joins in the brilliant and flourishing enterprise of lucid denudation in which the conformism of our time comes to a peak in the non-conformists; and he conducts this undertaking, for his own part, in the perspective of a total atheism still foreign to any profound spiritual experience, but held as one of the duties of the revolutionary attitude.

There is nothing exceptional in all this, except the superior intelligence of Eleutherius. Because of it he will go farther than many others. In a world from which God and every metaphysical certitude have been cast out, there is no longer for man any objectively valid reason for living and acting. Nothing, nothing and nothing. The more I attach myself to some hope, the more I am caught in the lie. Doubtless at least I can *see*; but what one sees gives nausea. Take away the imposture, there remains the void. Life is completely unjustified.

3. It is notable that the obsessing, sometimes terrifying, feeling of the absurdity of things, and of the radical *non-justification* of being, is bound up in Sartre with the idea of *contingency* or of "gratuity" (this shows to what degree his background was rationalist; existentialism is an inverted rationalism, despairing of the Hegelian saying, all-that-which-is-real-is-rational). "The essential is contingency. I mean that by definition existence is not necessity. To exist is *to be there*, simply; the existents appear, they let themselves be *encountered*, but one can never *deduce* them. . . . Contingency is not a false semblance, an appearance which can be dissipated; it is the absolute—and consequently the perfect gratuity. Everything is gratuitous, this garden, this city, and myself. When it happens that one takes account of it, it twists your heart and everything begins to float, like the other evening . . .: that is Nausea."[1]

[1] Jean Paul Sartre, *La nausée*, Paris: Gallimard, 1938, p. 167.—In the same passage Sartre speaks of the "people" who "have tried to surmount this contingency by inventing a being that would be necessary and cause of itself". These people, at least if it is a question of Aristotle and of Thomas Aquinas, never thought on this account that contingency was "a false semblance, an appearance which can be dissipated"—on the contrary, contingency was for them something most real and entirely impossible to dissipate. Therein lies, doubtless, the fundamental mistake of existentialism, which cannot speak of the great meta-

Eleutherius is thus seized by the nausea of the contingent, of the *irrational and meaningless*, "in the middle of Things, the unnameables". It is at this instant that, in his very vertigo, the original intuition which will always remain at the center of his thought forces itself upon him. "Then, I was just now in the public Garden. The root of the chestnut-tree sank down into the earth, just beneath my bench. I forgot that it was a root. The words were gone and, with them, the meaning of things, their modes of use, the fragile marks which men have traced on their surface. . . . And then I had this illumination.

"It took my breath away. Never, before these last few days, did I have a presentiment of what 'to exist' meant. I was like the others. . . . Like them I said 'the sea *is* green; that white point, way up there, *is* a gull', but I did not perceive that it existed, that the gull was a 'gull-existing'; ordinarily existence conceals itself. It is there, around us, in us, it is *ourselves*, one cannot say two words without speaking of it, and in the end it is untouched.[1] When I believed that I was thinking it, I must assume that I was thinking nothing; my head was empty, or with barely a word in it, the word 'being'. Or I was thinking then—how can I put it?—I was thinking *belonging*, I said to myself that the sea belonged to the class of green objects or that green was one of the qualities of the sea. Even when I was looking at things, I was a hundred miles from dreaming that they existed: they struck me as so much ornamentation. I took them in my hands, they served as instruments for me, I foresaw their resistances. But all this took place on the surface. If someone had asked me what existence was, I would have answered in good faith that it was nothing, barely an empty form which came to be added to things from outside, without changing anything in their nature. And then, behold, all at once, it was there, it was as clear as day: existence had suddenly come to light. It had lost its inoffensive air of an abstract category: it was the very stuff of things, this root was moulded in existence. Or rather, the root, the garden trellis, the bench, the thin grass of the lawn, all that had disappeared; the diversity of things,

---

physicians without calumniating them. The fact remains that if one denies the existence of God, *Ipsum Esse per se subsistens* (it is Descartes who said "cause of itself", the expression is meaningless), then contingency is not only real and irreducible—it is necessary to make it "the absolute", and to posit at the same time the absurdity of being. Sartrian Nausea is a true demonstration through the absurd of the existence of God. As Father Garrigou-Lagrange wrote in 1918: "It is necessary to choose: God or radical absurdity." (*Dieu, son existence et sa nature*, Paris: Beauchesne, p. 342.)—[All translations of Sartre are made directly from the French; no reference will be made to existing English translations.]

[1] For those who are interested in the history of ideas, and in the fact that the same idea can be put into relief—with altogether different connotations—at nearly the same time in very different schools of thought, may I be permitted to refer the reader to my book *Sept leçons sur l'être* (notably pp. 51–57 and 96–99). This book, taken from a course given at the *Institut Catholique* of Paris in 1932–1933, appeared (Paris, Téqui) in 1934. (English trans., *A Preface to Metaphysics*, New York: Sheed and Ward, 1940; London: Sheed and Ward, 1939). *La Nausée* appeared in 1938.

their individuality, was only an appearance, a gloss. This gloss had melted; there remained monstrous and soft masses in confusion—naked with a dreadful and obscene nudity."[1]

I have cited this page at length, because of its importance, and because it describes in excellent terms—just before "crushing the point", as Pascal said, and pushing it to a delirium of the mind—a primordial intellectual experience. A strangely ambivalent intuition of being, authentic and authentically metaphysical in its basis, and turning immediately to the monstrous, to the intolerable, in disgust even more than in fear, under the lamp of atheism.

Being and Nothingness

4. Then comes another crucial moment in the intellectual history of Eleutherius: the moment of systematization or philosophical crystallization. However the case may be with things and the ontological nausea which they provoke, it is not enough to vomit; it is necessary to think, and to think in a coherent and articulate manner. It is necessary to reflect. To conceptualize his intuition of being and to think the world, Sartre, as a very knowledgeable young intellectual, will have recourse, while making an original use of it adapted to his own purpose, to the best and most modern of what our epoch has produced in the way of ideological equipment: Husserl, Kierkegaard, Heidegger.

Was there in this pompous philosophical elaboration an element of humor, as if, hidden in the wrinkle of an imperceptible smile, the idea of playing at making a system "to see what would happen" had had some part in the adventure? Let us admit that considering the result, such a conjecture does not seem in any way valid. It is difficult not to regard *Being and Nothingness* as a formidable triumph of the "spirit of seriousness" in the domain of speculative thought.

Sartre may have had, and we think he did, a metaphysical intuition (immediately spoiled); but he is not for all that a metaphysician. (Besides, he holds metaphysics to be out-of-date, and thinks he has something better.) Like many French philosophers, he is above all a moralist. The severe judgment passed on him by Heidegger is explained by the fact that Heidegger himself is a metaphysician.

The idea of establishing an ontology by the phenomenological method, and of discussing being while setting metaphysics aside, was from the beginning doomed to illusion. From the single fact that phenomenology puts the extra-mental real in parentheses, it excludes all ontology—Husserl himself tended toward a kind of idealism closer to Berkeley than to Hegel. Can one pass beyond phenomenology by plunging into an existential metaphysics of subjectivity? In any case, this is not what Sartre has attempted. Remaining

[1] *La nausée*, pp. 162–163.

within phenomenology, he claims to attain being there, the "being of the phenomenon" as he says. There we have the original and irremediable equivocation; for if it is a question of *that which is* beyond the phenomenon and independently of the mind, then we are beyond phenomenology and in a full metaphysical ontology; if on the contrary it is a question of *that which* the phenomenon *is as phenomenon*, then we are in phenomenology, but entirely outside of ontology; and if it is a question of *that which* the phenomenon *is as being-in-itself*, then we are simply in the absurd. We must agree with Jean Wahl when he refuses any authentically ontological value to the "fundamental concepts on which *Being and Nothingness* seems founded",[1] and with Benjamin Fondane when he criticizes the philosophy of Sartre for being an abortive hybrid of academic rationalism and truly existential thought.[2]

The Sartrian ontology does not seek metaphysical knowledge. It proposes only to *describe*, and in no way to *explain*; this is tantamount to saying that it does not at all propose to *know*. This ontology which does not know is, by definition, arbitrary. It is not on being that it balances itself, but on the presuppositions and purposes of the thought which constructs it. In order that the so-called description in which it consists can take place, certain principles of orientation are needed, but ones that depend on the options of the philosopher. What principles? On the one hand, the double postulate that God does not exist, and that in making itself its own absolute, human freedom recovers its proper good from God; on the other hand, the intentions of a certain psychology on the analyses of which the ontology in question will model itself, and for which lucidity (the great concern being not to be naïve) consists above all in unmasking and laying waste everything in which and by which man seeks to reassure himself: the human mind will truly affirm itself only in unveiling the deception of all that pretends to make it adhere to a good.

Let us say at once that to readers who look here for an ontology properly so-called, a philosophy thus elaborated would have every chance of appearing as a mere logomachy, from the very fact that the language employed by it will refer to being only in passing through disguised or disavowed significations of the psychological order. It will have an ontological bearing and value but a really and surreptitiously psychological sense. So it is that, taking up again the famous Hegelian notion (which has a meaning psychologically and with respect to the contradictions and nostalgias of the human heart, but which has no meaning ontologically speaking) of man who *is not what he is and is what he is not*, existentialist phenomenology will give to it, as did Hegel himself, an ontological signification, and will cheerfully outdo the language of Hegelian metaphysics, by speaking of a being which consists in nihilating or in bringing lack to the core of that which is—or of a choice which precedes

[1] Jean Wahl, "Essai sur le néant d'un problème", *Deucalion*, I, 1946, p. 71.

[2] Benjamin Fondane, "Le lundi existentiel et le dimanche de l'histoire", in *L'Existence*, Paris: Gallimard, 1945, pp. 25–53.

every essence, of a freedom which is not of man but the very being of man, that is to say, his nothingness of being, etc. All this nevertheless will become almost thinkable once it is understood that one is in reality in a pseudo-ontological or *improperly ontological* perspective. And at the same stroke one will understand how a philosopher—above all a post-Hegelian philosopher—can employ a remarkably brilliant intelligence to create on more than seven hundred pages words which, while holding together in virtue of the copula *is*, live in the delights of the contradictory and nevertheless convey a kind of meaning. . . .

5. It is known that in Sartrian "ontology", the opposition, classical in post-Cartesian philosophy, between the matter-object (*res extensa*) and the thought-subject (*res cogitans*) gives way to the opposition between the *in-itself* which is only *res* and the *for-itself* which is not a thing at all, and in regard to which the principle of identity is invalid.[1] Being is divided between an in-itself which is the amorphous and undifferentiated world of the one everywhere identical with itself, of the petrified positivity of things and of their absurd being-there,[2] of "facticity"[3]—of nausea—and a for-itself which is nothing else but consciousness and freedom (human consciousness and freedom—man alone in the world is free), and which, setting itself apart from things and "outside of being",[4] recoiling from them, must be defined as an

[1] Cf. *L'être et le néant* (Paris: Gallimard, 1943), p. 98. The principle of identity defines the in-itself. "Far from being a universally universal axiom", it "is only a synthetic principle enjoying a simply regional universality". Cf. *ibid.*, p. 33 and p. 116.

[2] "Just now, I had the experience of the absolute: the absolute or the absurd. . . . The world of explanations and of reasons is not that of existence. A circle is not absurd, it is explained very well by the rotation of a line-segment around one of its extremities. But also, a circle does not exist. This root, on the contrary, existed in the measure that I was not able to explain it." *La nausée*, Paris: Gallimard, 1938, p. 165.

On the opacity, the total and totally neutral positivity of the in-itself, cf. *L'être et le néant*, pp. 33–34.

[3] "Facticity, that is to say the irremediable contingency of our 'being-there', of our existence without end and without reason." J.-P. Sartre, "Un nouveau mystique", in *Situations*, I, Paris: Gallimard, 1947, p. 154.

"Thus the for-itself is sustained by a perpetual contingency, which it recaptures for its benefit and assimilates without ever being able to suppress it. This perpetually evanescent contingency of the in-itself which haunts the for-itself and attaches it to the being-in-itself without ever letting itself be seized, is what we will call the *facticity* of the for-itself. It is this facticity which permits one to say that it *is*, that it *exists*, although we may never be able to *realize* it and although we always grasp it through the for-itself." *L'être et le néant*, p. 125.

Facticity is thus the proper condition of the in-itself according as it affects and lives off the for-itself itself.

[4] *L'être et le néant*, p. 61. The author adds: "For it [the human-reality], to put a particular existent out of circuit is to put itself out of circuit in relation to this existent. In this case it escapes it, it is out of reach, the existent cannot act on it, it has withdrawn *beyond a nothingness*. Descartes, after the Stoics, gave a name to this possibility for the human-reality of secreting a nothingness which isolates it: it is *freedom*.

"Human freedom precedes the essence of man and renders it possible; the essence of the human being is in suspense in his freedom. What we call freedom is therefore impossible to distinguish from the *being* of the 'human reality'." *Ibid.*

unconditioned power of nihilation, "a being by which nothingness comes to things"[1] (the power and fecundity of the negative, as Hegel said).

It is by a separation, a *not* which was not found in the amorphous magma of things, and which it introduces there, that consciousness differentiates them, gives them a meaning, a form, which makes of them a world. It is through the not that things take on a meaning. Consciousness is a decompression of being.[2]

And freedom itself is conceived in terms of nothingness. Man is free, and is man, only through his power of nihilation, of "secreting a nothingness which isolates him",[3] of absenting himself from being-there, of causing himself to be lacking, and thus to be in need of something other than what is. Let it not be said that freedom crowns the plenitude of being! Where there is plenitude there is no freedom. Nothing is more foreign to Sartre than the idea that freedom is rooted in reason and consists in the mastery of the will over the reasons which determine it. For him, on the contrary, freedom is a Nihilating which hollows itself out by its very self and at the same stroke makes arise in consciousness a *project*, a polarization of the whole movement of being and of desire toward an end—and which precedes essence and reason. For my essence is what I have chosen to be, and the very validity for me of this or that line of reasons for acting depends on this choice: pure choice, "absurd", in this sense—and in this sense only, says Sartre—"that it is that through which all the foundations and all the reasons come to being, that through which the very notion of the absurd receives a sense. It is absurd as being beyond all reasons."[4]

Thus, far from dominating its act and its object through superabundance of being, freedom is a perpetual escape, a nihilation of being and of its universal contingency, through which I perpetually choose, and without any other reason than my choice itself, to make myself lack, to want this or that, and firstly my last ends: choice (choice-in-the-world—and revocable, whence my fragility) of myself by myself, the fundamental or global project *which I am* ("the necessity of perpetually choosing myself is but one with the pursued-pursuing which I am"),[5] and in which are to be integrated my particular projects concerning the realization of such or such particular ends in the world.[6] If man were a plenum, if he were without any lack, like the

[1] *L'être et le néant*, p. 58.—Later (p. 61), the author describes human freedom (which is the very being of man) as that through which nothingness comes to the world.

[2] Cf. *L'être et le néant*, p. 116.

[3] Cf. above, p. 376, note 4.

[4] *L'être et le néant*, p. 559.

[5] *Ibid.*, p. 560.—This fundamental project "sets for its end a certain type of relation to the being which the for-itself wishes to entertain" (*ibid.*, p. 559), and it constitutes the very being of man, the being which man gives himself and chooses for himself. Cf. *ibid.*, p. 61: "Man is not at all a being *first* who would be free *then*, but there is no difference between the being of man and his 'being-free'."

[6] *Ibid.*, p. 560.

God of traditional theology, he could not be free.[1] In a general way, it is to the *Not*, to the power of escaping from being in making nothingness come "to the very womb of being, like a worm",[2] that the privileges of the spirit and of its creativity have passed.

6. Thus then since there are men, men in whom the for-itself forces its way up, it is consciousness itself which, in introducing voids into the obscene contingency and undifferentiation of the in-itself, in tapping with nothingness the formless being of things, gives a sense and a figure to that which faces consciousness. It is freedom itself which, in withdrawing from being in order to project its choices into it, makes values arise in the mass of fundamental meaninglessness in the midst of which freedom acts, and makes of this mass a world. It is "the unique source of value, and the nothingness through which the *world* exists".[3] In this sense one can say that all the immense structure of given conditions, pressures, resistances and historic obstacles before which freedom finds itself has been the work of freedom itself.[4] The fact remains that my freedom can exercise itself only in confronting these obstacles; in other words it can exercise itself only in a given ensemble, as unique and singular as myself, of circumstances and conditions in which is posed the practical problem which my choice will resolve, and which will receive their meaning from this choice, in short in a given *situation*. Thus "there is freedom only *in situation* and there is situation only through freedom. Human-reality everywhere encounters resistances and obstacles which it has not created; but these resistances and obstacles have meaning only in and through the free

[1] "It is because the human-reality *is not enough* that it is free. . . . Man is free because he is not himself but presence to himself. The being which is what it is cannot be free. Freedom is precisely the nothingness which *has been* in the heart of man and which constrains the human-reality to *make itself*, instead of *being*. . . . For the human-reality, to be is *to choose itself*: nothing comes to it from outside, nor from within either, which it can *receive* or *accept*. It is entirely abandoned, without any help of any kind, to the insupportable necessity of making its being even to the last detail. Thus freedom is not *a* being: it is the being of man, that is to say, his nothingness of being. If one first conceived man as a plenum, it would be absurd to seek in him, afterward, moments or psychic regions in which he would be free: you might as well seek the void in a container which has first been filled up to the brim. Man cannot be now free and now slave: he is entirely free or he is not." *Ibid.*, p. 516.

It is curious to remark that, in the reality of things, there is one case, and one alone, where freedom thus consists in nihilating: when it voluntarily defaults and turns the eyes from the norm, thus introducing evil into the choice. Cf. my *St. Thomas and the Problem of Evil*, Milwaukee: Marquette University Press, 1942, and chapter IV of my *Existence and the Existent*, New York: Pantheon, 1948.

[2] "Nothingness can nihilate itself only on the foundation of being; if nothingness can be given, it is neither before nor after being, nor, in a general manner, outside of being; but it is in the very womb of being, in its heart, like a worm." *L'être et le néant*, p. 57.

[3] "It is then that freedom will become aware of itself and discover itself in anguish as the unique source of value, and the nothingness through which the world exists." *Ibid.*, p. 722.

[4] Cf. *ibid.*, pp. 614–615. Freedom is infinite, not in the sense that it has no limits, but in the sense "that it never encounters them. The only limits which freedom runs against at each instant are those which it imposes on itself."

choice which the human-reality *is*".[1] And conversely this free choice which the human-reality is takes place only in the midst of the resistances and obstacles which the situation includes. In this the *in-itself* which the freedom of the *for-itself* has itself structured, from which it has made a world, takes a kind of revenge on this freedom, by conditioning its exercise.

But there is something infinitely more serious, and which gives to the Sartrian ontology its meaningful import. It is not the exterior obstacle which threatens freedom; it is its own constitutive infirmity, its own internal poverty: through this it is doomed to defeat. Here the being-there of things truly has its revenge.

For if I withdraw from being and nihilate it, it is in the last analysis in order to aspire with my whole being, that is to say with my whole lack, to an absolute identification between consciousness or freedom and effectuated existence or being-there, in other words between the *for-itself* and the *in-itself* —absolute identification which characterizes the divine aseity or self-sufficiency, if only God existed. "Human reality is pure effort to become God"[2] and every desire is an expression of this effort. But God does not exist and cannot exist, and an abysmal cleavage will always separate the in-itself from the for-itself which is Nihilation to surmount contingency.

One can see the consequences of the assertion: "my freedom is choice of being God and all my acts, all my projects, express this choice and reflect it in thousands of ways; for there is an infinity of ways of being and ways of having".[3] This is to say at the same stroke that my freedom, and all my choices, and all my projects not only tend to the impossible but are vitiated and corroded by the lie, the illusion acquiesced in, and bad faith. For they act *as if* all that they wish to attain and all that through them I happen to attain and possess were, be it inchoatively, the realization of this *being God*, of this *in-itself-for-itself* which is "beyond all contingency and all existence"[4]—the term in which I claim to install myself once I hold some would-be good, and which I employ all imaginable ruses to guarantee and to stabilize, and to invest with a so-called value-in-itself independent of freedom, which is the unique source of every value.

And so if it is true that by his projects man gives himself a meaning and an essence—no sooner, however, does he realize and supposedly grasp what he has freely projected, than he makes himself a thing and non-free to that very extent, and is caught in the toils of the facticity of the in-itself and of the being-there. And how would he admit to himself that he allowed himself to be

[1] *L'être et le néant*, pp. 569–570.

[2] "Man . . . *is* not at all: he is what he is not and he is not what he is, he is the nihilation of the contingent In-itself in so far as the self of this nihilation is its flight ahead toward the In-itself cause of itself. Human reality is pure effort to become God, without there being any given substratum of this effort, without there being *anything* which thus strives. Desire expresses this effort." *Ibid.*, p. 664.

[3] *Ibid.*, p. 689.

[4] *Ibid.*, p. 664.

thus ensnared and lost by freely betraying his freedom? He is wholly responsible[1] and he does not want to know it. So also the "sincerity" to which a Gide, for example, pretended, and through which I would wish to accept myself as a flower opens its corolla—as if I were only a thing—that so-called coincidence with oneself incompatible by definition with the recoil "outside of being" essential to the for-itself—is only a trap, and a more insidious form of the bad faith "ontologically" inherent in a consciousness which conceals from itself its own freedom in order to escape anguish[2] and which achieves its own freedom only by betraying it.[3] Bad faith, the flight into a being which I am not and which would give me some kind of reason for being, is, according to the phrase of an authorized commentator on Sartre, the very mode of existence of consciousness.[4]

The man of Sartrian existentialism is thus more fundamentally corrupted, more rotten, than the Jansenist man. For original sin has become the very fact of being born, of participating in the being-there of things.[5] All the attainments of man are changed into accursed viscidity, into that "obscene and insipid existence, which" he "is given for nothing".[6] There remains, it is true, what he does attain. He is always running, from failure to failure, after what he does not attain—like the ass that runs after a carrot which dangles before its eyes from a pole attached to the shaft of the cart[7]; and thus only does man remain, in spite of all, free, and a man. He is a useless passion. His death is as vain as his entry into being. "Only musical airs bear proudly their own death in themselves as an internal necessity; yet they do not exist. Every existent is born without reason, endures through weakness, and dies by encounter."[8]

[1] Cf. *L'être et le néant*, pp. 639–642.

[2] Cf. *ibid.*, pp. 111, 329–330, 433–439, 478–481, 537.

[3] "Bad faith . . . is the immediate and permanent menace of every project of the human being, . . . consciousness hides in its being a permanent risk of bad faith. And the origin of this risk is that consciousness, at once and in its being, is what it is not and is not what it is." *Ibid.*, p. 111.

"Whence it is doubtless necessary to conclude—as Sartre himself invited us to do—that 'bad faith', in the ontological sense of 'non-coincidence of self with self', is an evil of consciousness, its very mode of existence, but that it is important not to attribute to it in any way, on this basis, a positive moral signification. Like all the concepts which define the human, this one is ambiguous: man exists in bad faith, but he can, starting from there, realize himself according to bad faith or render himself authentic." Francis Jeanson, *Le problème moral et la pensée de Sartre*, Paris: Ed. du Myrte, 1947, pp. 223–224.

[4] Cf. Francis Jeanson, cited in the preceding note.

[5] "My original fall," writes Sartre, "is the existence of the other." (*L'être et le néant*, p. 321);—but it is at the same time my own *Dasein*.

[6] J.-P. Sartre, *Les mouches*, *Théâtre*, Paris: Gallimard, 1947, p. 102.

[7] Cf. *L'etre et le néant*, p. 253. "We run toward ourselves," adds the author, "and we are, by that fact, the being which cannot rejoin itself."

[8] *La nausée*, p. 170.—Did not Jean-Jacques say: "Only what is not is beautiful"? This detestable phrase enunciates a first postulate of atheistic existentialism. "The real is never beautiful," wrote Sartre in his first book (*L'imaginaire*, Paris: Gallimard, 1940, p. 245).

As Mr. Jeanson has justly noted,[1] *Being and Nothingness* is essentially a statement of failure, the description of the defeat to which man and freedom are irremediably doomed in the conflict which sets them at grips with the world of the unjustifiable, the world of things and of facticity. There is absolutely no hope for man and freedom ever to find in any reality or realization, in anything that is, a true good or a true achievement.

The valuating Decision

7. The ontology of Eleutherius—let us return for an instant to this fictional personage—is fundamentally arbitrary, but it is coherent and articulated. Eleutherius now finds himself caught in the trap of philosophical thought and of conceptualization. Impossible to escape from this picture of reality which, though it expresses only a phenomenological description, is for him an *ersatz* of metaphysics and imposes itself on him with the force of what is held as true. Atheism has now become a primary philosophical position; "Existentialism," Sartre will write,[2] "is nothing other than an effort to draw all the consequences of a coherent atheist position." And in the original atheist perspective henceforth resolutely confirmed, what had first been only a revolt of the subjectivity and a kind of revelation of the *vanity of vanities* has now become a systematic certitude, which reigns implacably over the intellect, of the ontologically irremediable defeat of the "human-reality".

Well and good! There is no question of dodging this certitude nor of seeking evasions; Eleutherius will not slip away. But he is free to pass beyond, to go farther.

It seems clear that phenomenological ontology has never been conceived by Sartre except as a step in a movement. The moment of ontological description is necessary, but has true interest only by reason of the moral moment, which will come afterwards and to which it is directed.[3]

Here in the genesis of Sartrian existentialism takes place the second profound and decisive experience, which is not an intuition this time but rather a decision, a movement of the will. This act of courage of the spirit is quite in the line of Descartes. In a desperate situation, in the face of a band of murderers, one can still act boldly and draw the sword. All is lost, and we likewise; we are in hell, "hell is others" and hell is to have been born. Well, freedom doomed to defeat and constantly betrayed, freedom my abyss and

[1] Cf. F. Jeanson, *op. cit.*, p. 167: "Defeat is the ontological climate of subjectivity"; p. 294: "Such is our freedom, on the ontological plane: freedom in fact, contingent, irreducible, absurd: simple condemnation of the human-reality to never coinciding with itself, perpetual self-evasion of a being which *cannot* 'be itself'. In this sense, our freedom appears rather like a kind of fatal impotence, which fascinates man in proposing to him a value without value, leads him to an absolute defeat, and makes of him 'a useless passion'." Cf. Simone de Beauvoir, *Pour une morale de l'ambiguïté*, Paris: Gallimard, 1947, p. 17.

[2] J.-P. Sartre, *L'existentialisme est un humanisme*, Paris: Nagel, 1946, p. 94.

[3] Cf. the last pages (720–722) of *L'être et le néant*.

my creative nothingness, freedom, thou remainest. I know that in proposing to myself no matter what good I deceive myself; but the act of freely proposing to myself whatever it may be, expecting nothing from anything, this act is mine, it is me; by cutting off, not my action, but my heart from the world of things, by refusing to fix in it any particle of hope, by making my whole final purpose flow back into the sole exercise and expansion of my freedom, I can brave the ocean of being-there and the nausea of the unnameable. Existentialist ethics in its original drive is the courage of despair.

What is most significant in Sartrian existentialism, and what gives it its proper dignity for the philosophical intelligence, is thus the intention of a moral order or the moral movement through which "the rotten being pulls itself together", the supreme recourse to freedom through which it does not deny but determines to transcend the ontological defeat described in *Being and Nothingness*. How can we characterize this drive in its first springing forth? It is a question of being neither "Lâches" (cowards) who conceal their freedom, nor "Salauds" (skunks),[1] established in the bad faith of a clear conscience and of a self-styled justification; the question (we will return to this point in a moment) is to make oneself *authentic*[2] by a "radical conversion".[3] Although the notion of good and evil has no place in the existentialist philosophical lexicon (in fact it nevertheless uses it on occasion[4]—and who could do without it?), let us say that the question is to escape from evil (which consists in making us things and in ensnaring us in the lie of a ready-made value and of a so-called justified being-there);[5] the question is to make ourselves truly autonomous, which means, in the system, to derive our rule of conduct at each instant only from that very freedom to which we are condemned (". . . this terrible necessity of being free which is my lot . . ."),[6] but which we assume, will, and recreate ourselves through our free choice, by a kind of reduplication of freedom: a singular atheism which cannot keep itself from counterfeiting a sort of perverted Christianity, and in which not

[1] Cf. *L'existentialisme est un humanisme*, pp. 84–85: "Those who will conceal, through the spirit of seriousness or through determinist excuses, their total freedom, I will call 'lâches'; the others who will try to show that their existence was necessary, whereas it is the very contingency of the appearance of man on the earth, I will call 'salauds'."

[2] "If he is indifferent to being of good or bad faith, because bad faith recovers possession of good faith and slips itself in at the very origin of his project, this does not mean that one cannot radically escape from bad faith. But this supposes that the rotten being pulls itself together, which we will call authenticity. . . ." J.-P. Sartre, *L'être et le néant*, p. 111, note.

[3] Cf. *L'être et le néant*, p. 484, note. Cited below, p. 387, note 4.

[4] "We can never choose evil; what we choose is always the good, and nothing can be good for us without being good for all." J.-P. Sartre, *L'existentialisme est un humanisme*, pp. 25–26.—Sartre is not alluding here to any value universal in itself; it is of human solidarity that he is thinking, in virtue of which in choosing for myself I choose for the human race.

[5] "Such is Evil for M. Sartre: This violent desire to be a fixed and immutable thing, to make oneself a social object which exists only in an artificial order." R.-M. Albérès, *Jean-Paul Sartre*, Paris: Editions Universitaires, 1953, p. 93.

[6] *L'être et le néant*, p. 450.

grace but pure freedom wrests us from the perdition into which we are thrown by our birth into the world. There is here, moreover, it seems, an air of kinship with a Kantian morality in which the non-temporal freedom of the pure practical reason would be replaced by the freedom-in-time of the singular subject; and some resemblance also to certain virtualities of the Bergsonian pure becoming, which could have inspired a moral theory but which Bergson himself left aside in his ethics.

8. This primordial moment of recovery of self, or of valuating decision, involves an authentic moral drive, however badly conceptualized it is. The maxim ascribed to William of Orange: "There is no need at all to hope in order to venture, nor to succeed in order to persevere", becomes the axiom in which ethical reality reveals itself.

One can nevertheless ask if the construction of an ethics with this moral drive alone and this recourse to freedom alone is not itself a hopeless enterprise. No one, it is true, can prejudge what the moral treatise of Jean-Paul Sartre will be, if he decides to write it;[1] the thought of a philosopher can always take an unforeseen turn. In the meantime, however, we have the book by Francis Jeanson,[2] to which Sartre has given an explicit *approbatur*, and which, moreover, restricts itself to the affirmation of the moral drive of which we have just spoken; and the book by Simone de Beauvoir,[3] which risks going farther and giving some firmer precisions concerning existentialist morality. These two works, to which can be added certain indications offered in the lecture *L'existentialisme est un humanisme*, permit one to gain a sufficiently clear idea of the question.

No nature or essence is presupposed to freedom such as Sartre conceives it.[4]

[1] Since the time that this chapter was written, Sartre has published *Critique de la raison dialectique*, Tome I, Paris: Gallimard, 1960. In our opinion there is nothing in this voluminous work which would lead us to modify our views on the Ethics of atheistic Existentialism.

Let us remark in passing the note on pp. 285–286 of this book of Sartre's: "The fundamental alienation does not come, as *L'être et le néant* might wrongly lead one to believe, from a prenatal choice: it comes from the univocal relationship of interiority which unites man as practical organism to his environment."

If Sartre, who promises us still more works, continues in the path indicated by *Critique de la raison dialectique*, it seems that he is about to proceed to a "dialectical shift" (in the sense of footnote 4, p. 385 of the present volume) which in no way invalidates our analysis, but which causes his thought to lose an element of originality and depth; and which confirms our remarks (p. 389) on the essential role played in him by concern for politics (the politics of men of letters).

[2] *Le problème moral et la pensée de Sartre.*

[3] *Pour une morale de l'ambiguïté.*

[4] "Human freedom precedes the essence of man and renders it possible, the essence of the human being is in suspense in his freedom." *L'être et le néant*, p. 61.—"Human-reality cannot receive its ends . . . neither from the outside nor from a pretended interior 'nature'. It chooses them and, through this choice itself, confers on them a transcendent existence

This freedom is clearly opposed to all determinism,[1] but it is quite another thing from the free choice of the metaphysicians. For, on the one hand, far from proposing to us an analysis of the free act in its relation to its motives or reasons, Sartre disqualifies the voluntary act and regards voluntary deliberation as always faked;[2] and what he sees above all in freedom is the "initial project" or "choice of self" anterior to every reason and absolutely first,[3] as if the notion of an absolutely first choice (without any end already determined and in relation to which it takes place) was not void of meaning.[4] On the other hand, the Sartrian idea of freedom envelops both freedom of independence and freedom of option, and to tell the truth it is nothing else but the freedom of the God of Descartes transferred to man. Just as for Descartes God caused Himself to be Himself and created eternal truths and moral values at the pleasure of His pure will,[5] so Sartre's man will create, at the pleasure of his freedom, meanings and values, and will cause or choose himself. Descartes had simply "given to God what properly belongs to us".[6]

Nevertheless it is not to deify man in the manner of Hegel that Sartre

---

as the external limit of its projects. From this point of view—and if one well understands that the existence of the *Dasein* precedes and commands its essence—human reality, in and by its very rising up, decides to define its own being through its ends. It is therefore the position of my ultimate ends which characterizes my being and which is identified with the original gushing forth of the freedom which is mine." *Ibid.*, pp. 519–520.

[1] On determinism, it is not Sartre, it is Kierkegaard who has written these admirable lines: "The determinist or the fatalist is in despair, and in despair he has lost his self, because for him everything is necessary. He is like that king who died of hunger because all his food was transformed into gold. *Personality is a synthesis of possibility and necessity.* The condition of its survival is therefore analogous to breathing (respiration) which is an in- and an a-spiration. The self of the determinist cannot breathe, for it is impossible to breathe necessity alone, which taken pure and simple suffocates the human self." *The Sickness Unto Death*, trans. by Walter Lowrie, Princeton: Princeton University Press, 1941, p. 62; Oxford: O.U.P., 1942.

[2] Cf. *L'être et le néant*, pp. 527, 550.

[3] Cf. above, pp. 377–378.

[4] This is what Maurice Merleau-Ponty very justly notes: "Choice supposes a preliminary engagement, and . . . the idea of a first choice is a contradiction." *Phénoménologie de la perception*, Paris: Gallimard, 1945, p. 502.—Indeed, as we wrote in our *Existence and the Existent* (p. 7), one sees substituted here "for the unthinkable notion of a subject without nature the notion of pure action or pure efficiency in the exercise of an option, of pure liberty, in short, itself ambiguous and collapsing from within, for although it seems to appeal to a sovereign free will, it really appeals only to a pure spontaneity, which is inevitably suspected of being merely the sudden explosion of necessities hidden in the depths of that nature which was allegedly exorcised."

[5] Cf. our *Le Songe de Descartes*, Paris: Corrêa, 1932, pp. 212–225; English trans. *The Dream of Descartes*, New York: Philosophical Library, 1944, pp. 142–149; London: Editions Poetry, 1946.

[6] "Two centuries of crisis—crisis of Faith, crisis of Science—will be needed for man to recover that creative freedom which Descartes put in God, and for him finally to grasp this truth, the essential base of humanism: man is the being whose appearance makes a world exist. But we will not reproach Descartes for having given to God what properly belongs to us . . ." J.-P. Sartre, *Descartes*, Geneva-Paris: Les Trois Collines, 1946, p. 51.

confers on man what in the eyes of Descartes necessarily presupposed infinite perfection. On the contrary, he leaves man, more than ever, dust. What he discloses to us is a kind of aseity of nothingness.[1]

The paradox is that if Sartre's man recovers from the God of Descartes this freedom cause-of-itself which "properly belongs" to man, and thus assumes a sort of aseity, it is precisely—if we understand the system well—by bringing, through this very freedom, when he truly assumes it in choosing it itself, nothingness into that "pure effort to become God"[2] which is human-reality. We encounter here the problem with respect to which the need of future elucidations furnished by Sartre himself becomes most keenly felt, the few indications which he has given on the matter being merely anticipatory and furnishing us mostly with question-marks. We have noted above that there is for him a "radical conversion" by which man shakes off bad faith and renders himself *authentic.*[3] How is this possible? According to the conjectures which seem to us the best founded, let us say that in this radical conversion which is the free choice of freedom itself, man evidently does not renounce—this seems excluded by definition—the effort to be God[4] which all his acts express and which *is* human-reality. Rather, by a voluntary nihilation in the second degree he withdraws from this effort itself which he is, and becomes distant from it, frees himself of it—at once through knowledge (the "purifying reflection", no longer "conniving")[5] and through willing: by knowing that such an effort to become God is illusory and the root of the bad faith which inevitably possesses us so long as we have not freely pulled ourselves together—and by refusing to consent to what ties us to the world, and to will, in

[1] ". . . The decision to adopt the moral attitude . . . is based on nothing; it is not founded on any absolute sign, no guarantee justifies it from without. In it resides the radical invention of man by man. And if this invention is human, it is because it proceeds from the nothingness of what *is* not, it is because nothing, absolutely nothing indicates its value in advance, and it is because the freedom from which it proceeds is as free to renounce itself as to conquer itself." Francis Jeanson, *op. cit.*, p. 356.

[2] Cf. *L'être et le néant*, p. 664. Quoted above, p. 379, note 2.

[3] Cf. *L'être et le néant*, p. 111 (cited above, p. 382, note 2) and p. 484 (cited below p. 387, note 4).

[4] Or is it necessary on the contrary (for one never knows what shifts a basically dialectical philosophy is capable of) to think that this radical conversion through which the free agent "pursues a radically different type of being" consists in delivering himself purely and simply from the project of being-God which is given in *L'être et le néant* as "the fundamental structure of the human reality"? M. Sartre alone could tell us. In the meantime, the interpretation which we here propose seems to us, although more complicated, to do more credit to the coherence of the system.

[5] Cf. *L'être et le néant*, p. 670: "This particular type of project which has freedom for its foundation and end would merit a special study. It is in fact radically differentiated from all the others in that it aims at a radically different type of being. It would be necessary to explain in full indeed its relations with the project of being-God which has seemed to us the profound structure of the human reality. But this study cannot be made here: it belongs in fact to an *Ethics* and it supposes that one has first defined the nature and the role of the purifying reflection (our descriptions have up to now aimed only at the 'conniving' reflection)". . . .

everything that we will, anything other, in the last analysis, than our freedom itself.[1]

Then we are farther than ever from an impossible divine *in-itself-for-itself* in which the in-itself and the for-itself would be identified; but we can reconcile the in-itself and the for-itself, or arrive at their "synthetic fusion",[2] by making the in-itself, in the depths of our act of choice, a pure occasion for the freedom of the for-itself.

It is thus, we believe (with all due reservations) that whereas sincerity, which does not imply any recovery of self by self, remains a prisoner of bad faith,[3] on the contrary authenticity, which is this very recovery of rotten being by itself, permits us to "escape radically from bad faith".[4] In ceasing to be rotten being and in ceasing to have the source of bad faith ever active in us? No, to be sure; but rather in nihilating by a reduplication of freedom this source of bad faith which is so to speak natural to us, and this rotten being which we are—in other words, in assuming them into the purity of a supreme movement of freedom in which our choice of being God culminates in a choice of being man and nothing but man, without support or prop, absolutely alone and absolutely forsaken, and creating his values by himself alone, responsible without any referee.

If the interpretation here proposed is, as we hope, itself authentic, it helps us to understand why the *authenticity* of the human subject (be he a criminal or a saint, a homicide, a sadist or a martyr, as far as the acts which he does are concerned) is for Sartrian existentialism the decisive and fundamental value, and indeed the unique criterion of morality.

Existentialist Ethics is a Morality of Ambiguity

9. Existentialist ethics is at once a morality of ambiguity and a morality of situation. It is clear that in the system of Sartre every universal value is rejected. "Nothing is in the intelligible heaven";[5] it is man, that is to say each individual in such or such given circumstances, in such or such a "situation", who by his free choice creates the value of his act. The existentialist school is as radically (although for altogether different reasons) opposed as the positivist school to the notion of natural law.

It is quite true, I note in passing, that in a given situation, where some act (to commit murder, or adultery) appears at once as an act to be done (because I want it) and not to be done (because this would be evil), it is freedom alone which decides: "the act in question is to be done by me", or "it is not to be done by me" (because that is the conduct which in the last analysis I prefer). This is what takes place in fact. Well, the operation to which Sartre proceeds is simply to pass from fact to right. Instead of saying: it is I who freely decide

[1] Cf. below, p. 388.
[2] Cf. *L'être et le néant*, p. 721.
[3] Cf. above, pp. 379–380.
[4] Cf. *L'être et le néant*, p. 111, note. Cited above, p. 282, note 2.
[5] J.-P. Sartre, *L'existentialisme est un humanisme*, p. 23.

what I do (in agreement or disagreement with what I ought), it will be necessary henceforth to say: it is I who freely decide *what I ought*; it will be as good, as morally required, to commit this murder or adultery as not to commit it, since it is in creating this *I ought* by a truly free choice—in which is truly expressed my first choice of my "fundamental project", or of myself—that I thus take my risks. Ambiguity in sense No. 1, the ambiguity (*ad utrumlibet*) of the conduct on which I have to decide by my act of election, has become the ambiguity of the moral value itself or of the *I ought* on which I decide or which I "create" by my free choice.

There is no longer any law, everything is permitted. "If God does not exist, everything is permitted."[1] Everything is permitted to me, on condition that I permit it to myself by assuming deeply enough my responsibilities, through a choice in which I tear myself sufficiently away from myself to assume freely the freedom by which I choose myself. Such is the meaning of what we here call ambiguity No. 1.

"In this sense," a disciple of Sartre writes, "the unique moral recommendation of existentialism, a simple transposition of its description of the human, might be 'to live with the rending of conscience'."[2] So be it as to the rending! a rent conscience is worth more than a falsely assured conscience. It is nevertheless permissible to think that this recommendation does not lead very far in the order of practical discernment; and even that, in excluding from the field of the genuinely moral life the higher peace which the world cannot give, it shamelessly contradicts the moral experience of humanity; neither Francis of Assisi nor Benedict Labre had a rent conscience when they chose poverty.

In the existentialist ethics all the values are therefore relativized—save that which freedom gives to itself when it takes itself for supreme end. Totally suspended to freedom as end,[3] this ethics is an ethics of finality. And it is an ethics of salvation.[4] In saving itself, my freedom saves me, removes me from the hell of facticity and of bad faith.

[1] "Dostoievsky had written 'if God did not exist, everything would be permitted'. There is the point of existentialism. In reality, everything is permitted if God does not exist. . . ." *Ibid.*, p. 36.

[2] F. Jeanson, *op. cit.*, p. 352. "One sees," continues the author, "that it is a question of a balance, always to be invented and always unstable, between action—demanding an engagement followed—and reflection—necessitating the consecration, under the form of distance from self, of this hidden rending which presence to self is."

It is known that for Sartre, by reason of our total abandonment in a world in which no recourse is offered to us, "anguish is the mode of being of freedom as consciousness of being". *L'être et le néant*, p. 66. Cf. *ibid.*, pp. 69–71.

[3] "Freedom throughout each concrete circumstance cannot have any other end than to will itself." J.-P. Sartre, *L'existentialisme est un humanisme*, p. 82. "In setting its ends, freedom must put them in parentheses, confront them at each moment *with this absolute end which it itself* constitutes, and debate in its own name the means which it uses to conquer itself." Simone de Beauvoir *Pour une morale de l'ambiguïté*, p. 187. (Italics ours.)

[4] "These considerations do not exclude the possibility of a morality of deliverance and salvation. But this must be reached at the term of a radical conversion of which we cannot speak here." J.-P. Sartre, *L'être et le néant*, p. 484, note.

10. This salvation is, moreover, in no way an evasion of the world. The world is bad, but it is necessary to throw oneself into it. Freedom, being the power of hollowing out the nothingness in being, can exercise itself only by throwing itself into the being-there, only by putting itself "in situation".

But if freedom can save itself, and save me, it is on condition that it will nothing in the world as a good apart from that very freedom, and involving any objective value or value given in itself. It is on condition that freedom will what it wills only as retracted or reabsorbed into itself, having value only through the choice itself, new, unforeseeable, never fixed, which freedom makes of it at each instant. What matters then the ontological defeat, the falsehood of realization? Freedom knows it, it accepts it.[1] It is the devil's due. In virtue of the "purifying reflection", and no longer "conniving reflection",[2] freedom passes beyond. Then even when it inevitably incurs the stain of ensnarement in things, it keeps itself free and renews its youth by traversing this very stain, it makes its salvation and mine from defeat to defeat.[3]

From this point on, and in relation to freedom, one must no longer say that the world of things and of being-there is absurd; one must say that it is ambiguous. For it has neither meaning nor value, this remains true; but at the same time man, by and in his action, unceasingly gives it meanings and values which depend only on his free choice. That is ambiguity No. 2, ambiguity of the being in the midst of which freedom and moral conduct are exercised, and ambiguity of the existence of man as moral agent.[4]

The very word existence, in this moral perspective, takes on a new signification, proper to the freedom reduplicated in the moral drive, to the freedom chosen, to the freedom which saves.[5] According to this new signification, it is necessary to say that what is simply, does not exist truly. To exist is to set oneself apart from being, to make oneself lack, and this by the choice of freedom; in other words, it is freely to assume freedom, and at the same time to create values and meanings, and therefore to unveil being and to re-establish being, doubtless with the ready-made and the unnameable in which being is inevitably ensnared and in which I am inevitably ensnared, but from which at the same time I deliver myself, in the measure that I keep myself free, free from that very thing which I create. Hence the formula of Sartre

[1] ". . . Then he assumes the defeat. And the action condemned insofar as effort for being recovers its validity insofar as manifestation of existence." Simone de Beauvoir, *Pour une morale de l'ambiguïté*, p. 19.

[2] Cf. *L'être et le néant*, p. 670; and F. Jeanson, *op. cit.*, pp. 295–298.

[3] Cf. Simone de Beauvoir, *Pour une morale de l'ambiguïté*, pp. 43–47.

[4] Cf. *ibid.*, p. 81; p. 180.

[5] ". . . He [man] shamefully regrets not being one of those things which need make no effort to exist, while his existence is for him only the constant exercise of his freedom." R. M. Albérès, *op. cit.*, p. 63.

"His being is lack of being, but there is a manner of being this lack which is precisely existence." Simone de Beauvoir, *op. cit.*, p. 19.

to which Madame de Beauvoir attaches a central importance: "Man makes himself lack, so that there may be being."[1]

Thus, as in the theology of Luther, man is at once irremediably bad and saved.[2] To be morally pure, it would be necessary that he be pure freedom, which is by definition impossible. He is rotten insofar as he is, but in the very midst of facticity, freedom saves him, makes him exist truly. Such is the import of what we have called ambiguity No. 2.

11. Historians have noted[3] that Sartre's personal experience, during the years in which he participated in the effort of the Resistance in occupied France, played a decisive role in the elaboration of his philosophical thought. In fact, it was just at the time that he was becoming aware of the importance of political activity that Sartre, in the movement of supreme recourse to freedom which we have pointed out, also became definitely aware of the primacy of the moral in his own thought, and of the necessity of insisting on his thought's ethical implications. It was in the perspective of politics that *the other* was revealed to him no longer as merely the witness in which subjectivity desperately seeks, and in pure loss, a justification of itself, but as another subjectivity which my own freedom recognizes and respects from the moment that this very freedom has been assumed by me as the foundation of my moral life; it was in politics that Sartre discovered the moral importance of the other. Thus at the same stroke we find brought back into play a certain number of classical moral concepts such as that of the dignity of the human person [4] and his character of end in itself, or the duties which bind us toward the other as individual person and freedom, and toward mankind in which each participates and to which each is responsible. And thus at the same stroke a certain number of criteria of conduct are laid down.

Here appears a new kind of ambiguity, to which the theorists of the morality of ambiguity scarcely seem to want to draw our attention. For from the moment that they elaborate a morality it is indeed necessary for them to deal with the criteria of conduct which I just mentioned. Thus therefore *everything is permitted* since there is no God, everything is permitted but *something is forbidden*[5]—any conduct by which freedom, once it has chosen

[1] Cf. Simone de Beauvoir, *op. cit.*, pp. 17–18, p. 165.

[2] *Ibid.*, p. 185: "It has often been noted: only revolt is pure. Every construction involves the scandal of dictatorship, of violence."—p. 216: "It would be absurd to contract a liberating action under the pretext that it involves crime and tyranny; for without crime and without tyranny the liberation of man would not be possible: one cannot escape this dialectic which goes from freedom to freedom through dictatorship and oppression."

[3] Cf. R. M. Albérès, *op. cit.*, pp. 104–106.

[4] To tell the truth, one wonders what sense the expression "human person" can have in an ethics for which, as M. Jeanson writes, human reality is "perpetual self-evasion of a being which *cannot* 'be itself'." (Cf. above, p. 381, note 1.)

[5] This is strongly accentuated in the book of Mme. de Beauvoir—with that kind of ambiguous rigorism, and that revengeful ardor to prohibit and condemn through which existentialism would like to show that it can handle revolutionary thunder with as much

itself as supreme value, would be betrayed. Ambiguity No. 3, ambiguity of the system itself. The criteria of conduct in question remain, it must be added, large enough so that outside of the domain of what is forbidden, "everything" (that is to say, opposite conducts) is still permitted.

The fact remains that, after having begun with the grand atheist defiance of every law, and after having affirmed the radical opposition between the brute and unformed positivity of the in-itself and the freedom of the for-itself —with its corollary: the bad faith inherent in that for-itself prisoner of the in-itself which is man—one is forced in the end to show a way in which, thanks to the purifying reflection, man will be able to escape from bad faith, and, once he has renounced the illusion of "transcendent" values supposedly inscribed in things, and of foreordained ends, will be able—by an incessant effort of auto-creation in which freedom "will become aware of itself and will discover itself in anguish as the unique source of value"[1]—to make himself authentic and give himself for end "the synthetic fusion of the in-itself with the for-itself".[2] Why, moreover, is the author of *L'existentialisme est un humanisme* so anxious to justify himself before so many "salauds" who believe in objective values, be they Communists or Christians?

Well, all will no doubt end less badly than one might think; and we may hope that one day, through some notional recastings and some dialectical turns, the master or one of his disciples will find himself entrusted with delivering the addresses at the French Academy honoring those who have been awarded prizes for virtue.

12. But it is to the original symbiosis, in existentialist thought, between ethics and politics that I wish to return for a moment. This symbiosis has for its effect a curious exteriorization of ethics, and a transposition of political categories into moral categories. Thus, for example, the notion of engagement—of engagement in political activity and a perpetual taking of sides—which has the air of an imitation of the Marxist *praxis*, is in reality only the expression of a certain moralism. For engaging oneself in political action is synonymous with throwing oneself into the world, and it is in throwing himself into the world that man "makes himself" really "lack so that there may be being".

---

energy as Communism can. "So far from the absence of God authorizing every license, it is on the contrary because man is abandoned on the earth that his acts are definitive, absolute engagements." (Which is pure verbiage, from the moment that man thus engages himself only with respect to a destiny and a world without any other value than that which he himself gives to them, and from the moment that no reason or objective norm obliges him in conscience to direct his free choice in one direction or another.) The author adds (and this time this is quite true, to the extent at least that the notion of fault keeps an authentically ethical sense): "A God can pardon, efface, compensate; but if God does not exist, the faults of men are inexpiable." *Op. cit.*, p. 23. Later we are told of "a true terrestrial damnation" (*ibid.*, p. 49).

[1] J.-P. Sartre, *L'être et le néant*, p. 722.

[2] *Ibid.*, p. 721. See above pp. 385–386.

Thus again, the whole moral effort of man seems finally to identify itself with the revolutionary effort of social and political emancipation,[1] itself conceived in such a way that the Hegelian dialectic of the master and slave, which has become in the hands of one of the most appreciated existentialist authors an astonishingly naïve sentimental cliché, will demand throughout the length of history that the moral man take a stand against the same puppet-show "tyrant" bobbing up at every cross-roads.[2] Here again it was natural that existentialism should encounter Marxism so as at once to compete with it and to cling to it. But in such a competition, the faith of Marxism in the objectivity of the dialectical laws of history and in the primacy of the social over the moral was easily to gain the upper hand over the vain attempt to suspend a revolution of the Marxist type to an ethics of freedom, and to the exigencies of a moral conscience whose compass is no longer allowed any pole.

The exteriorization of ethics into politics which I just mentioned can contribute in a certain measure to explain how a philosophy which seemed worried by the fundamental anguish of being-for-nothing, and, thus, destined to a certain greatness, emerges into a kind of pedantic atheism, resourceful and euphoric.[3] This philosophy even encourages us, with all the seriousness of a prison-doctor who pats a condemned man on the back on his way to the electric chair, to the "joy of existence";[4] and it teaches us to juggle away the reality of death in the manner of Epicurus—"death escaping my projects because it is unrealizable" and being foreign "to the ontological structure of the for-itself".[5]

At least Epicurus had enough wit to propose to us at the same time a

[1] "As soon as a liberation appears possible, not to exploit this possibility is a resignation of freedom, a resignation which implies bad faith and which is a positive fault." Simone de Beauvoir, *op. cit.*, p. 56. "To will existence, to will to unveil the world, to will man free, all this is a single will." *ibid.*, p. 122. Cf. *Ibid.*, pp. 114, 124–125.

[2] Cf. *ibid.*, pp. 117 ff.—There is little philosophy in these pages in which the idea of emancipation and of struggle against oppression, in itself a great and holy idea, is turned into the old story of revolutionary pedantism and seasoned with the trash of confusions and untruths in which a facile journalism delights. On the other hand, let us be grateful to the author for having written: "If in all the oppressed countries, the face of an infant is so moving, it is not that the infant . . . has more right to happiness than the others: it is that he is the living affirmation of human transcendence . . ." *Ibid.*, p. 143.

[3] Cf. our *Existence and the Existent*, p. 9; "No need even to mention Pascal," we remarked there. "In existentialism there is nothing equal to the stature of a Nietzsche. This astounding renunciation of any measure of grandeur is probably the most original and most highly appreciated contribution that existentialism has made to our age."

[4] Simone de Beauvoir, *op. cit.*, p. 189.

[5] After having summarized the pages in which J.-P. Sartre (*L'être et le néant*, pp. 615–638) explains that death "cannot belong to the ontological structure of the for-itself" and that finally "death escaping my projects because it is unrealizable, I myself escape death through my project itself" (*ibid.*, pp. 629, 632), M. Francis Jeanson concludes that the free project proper to human reality "suppresses death by making it, as Epicurus said more or less, the moment of life which we never have to live". (*Le problème moral et la pensée de Sartre*, p. 301.)

morality of pleasure, and, when he made death "the moment of life which we never have to live",[1] he truly believed in the subtle atoms of the soul without practising the phenomenological placing of reality in parentheses.

Briefly, except for the movement of courage from which emanates its first decision to save itself despite all by freedom, Sartrian existentialism is so poor in authentic spiritual experience and in interiority that the great problems and decisive tests on which depend the destiny of the person are mentioned by it only to be quickly juggled away. The moral concern there turns most often to the political one. And, more generally, if conscience, *my* conscience, is there interrogated, it is above all, in actual fact, with respect *to the conduct of the other* (how to judge it, how to act or not to act on it, to combat it or to cooperate with it, etc., given the respect which I owe to the free project of the other).[2]

And a Morality of Situation

13. In the absence of every objectively founded value, and of every precept of a universal moral law—now that there is no longer "anyone to give me orders"[3]—it pertains to each singular subject to create or to invent in each case the values which orient his conduct,[4] in relation to those primordial ends, themselves freely chosen, which are the freedom and the liberation of Man. And to be sure it has elsewhere been affirmed that every voluntary deliberation is faked, and that our particular choices are only reassertions of our fundamental free project (through which we have chosen ourselves antecedently to all reason)—reassertions which are freely adjusted to particular situations. The fact remains nevertheless that the particular choices in question cannot take place without a conscientious examination of the situation, in which, if the mind does not deliberate so as to fasten on such or such a reason which in the very act of choice the freedom of the will has made decisive, at least it sufficiently discusses, debates, grinds and fluidifies the elements of the situation so that the fundamental free project emerges without shackles from its original abyss, under a new form flexibly articulated with the particularities of the situation.[5]

Such a process of elaboration of values and rules of action connected with values is by nature—since there is no moral norm absolutely valid in itself—a

[1] Francis Jeanson, *loc. cit.*

[2] See, for example, *L'existentialisme est un humanisme*, pp. 40–47 (cf. our book *Existence and the Existent*, pp. 59–61; or *Pour une morale de l'ambiguïté*, pp. 188–217).

[3] J.-P. Sartre, *Les mouches*, p. 101.

[4] "If I have suppressed God the father, someone is certainly needed to invent values . . ." J.-P. Sartre, *L'existentialisme est un humanisme*, p. 89.

[5] On the notion of "situation", cf. J.-P. Sartre, *L'être et le néant*, pp. 633 sq.; *Situations*, II, Paris: Gallimard, 1948, pp. 26–27, 312.

One can form an idea of the dialectical process we are speaking of here by letting a reading of *Les Mandarins* illustrate that of *Pour une morale de l'ambiguïté* (in particular pp. 180–217).

dialectical process (in the classical sense of this word). It pertains to opinion and the contingency of opinion, like the process by which, in the Resistance, a clandestine group decided on the path to follow in such or such a given occurrence; deliberation in the current accepted meaning of the word, and although it is refused the characteristics of moral deliberation in the philosophical sense.

Moral judgments in the ethics of the situation thus result from a discussion of points of conscience which lacks every absolute criterion of determination, and in which are examined the aspects according to which certain possible conducts appear more or less appropriate to the end (freedom or liberation) which remains transcendent in regard to them. It is clear that such a discussion or "deliberation" (which to tell the truth is distinguished from "voluntary deliberation" intending to base an act of choice on reason, only insofar as it is a rational conversation preparing a choice which is irrational in its root) can go on to infinity, like every deliberation in which by hypothesis an unconditioned value or norm would never intervene. This is doubtless why the existentialist authors and their friends never stop "arguing about the game", while a self-assured pedantry untiringly sustains their anxious casuistry. If nevertheless the discussion terminates at a certain solution, this will never be anything but an opinion which itself presupposes no objectively certain principle of determination. But such a pure probabilism is clearly untenable; even when it remains in doubt or anguish as to the value of a certain conduct, conscience can decide to act only in virtue of some certitude—either the certitude of a singular and incommunicable view which traverses the doubt without dissipating it, or the certitude of a reflex principle which dominates the doubt from outside. Since the morality of situation excludes all certitude of this kind, it has to replace it by another kind of certitude, the "absurd" certitude of the "fundamental project" which freely gushes up antecedently to all reason, and whose sudden emergence is only expressed and let pass by the solution of pure opinion which we spoke of above.

Finally, since every universal precept is looked upon as a "ready-made rule" and is excluded for this very reason, it is, as we have already seen, up to each man to invent, in terms of the singular situation in which he is placed, the singular value and the singular precept of his singular conduct. But in the absence of every universal precept it is clear that according to the diversity of situations *anything whatever* will be able legitimately (that is to say, without lacking in authenticity or in freedom) to be regarded by one or another as morally required.[1] There we are come back to the "everything is permitted" and to "the unique moral recommendation of living with the rending of conscience" discussed above. What interests us here in these two assertions is the way in which through them the ethics of situation avows, or proclaims,

[1] "One can choose all if this is on the plane of free engagement." J.-P. Sartre, *L'existentialisme est un humanisme*, pp. 88–89.

that there is no ethics at all. What is an ethics, in fact, but a knowledge *directive of human acts*? Now it is essential to the ethics of situation *not* to be directive of action. In this it differs from the "class ethics" of the Marxists, although it can appear, in other respects, as a kind of anarchical plagiarism of it.

That every moral decision concerns an individual "in situation" with respect to concrete singular circumstances, and poses for him a unique problem whose solution he has to discover himself, is a very old truth on which the Thomists unceasingly insist in their theory of *prudentia*, or virtue of practical discernment, which is by no right a science because it has to do with the singular and contingent, and which nevertheless makes judgments possessed of truth and certainty *per conformitatem ad appetitum rectum*. But man has need of the indispensable instrumentality of *prudentia* to apply the universal law and the unconditional precept to particular cases. Without the universal law and the unconditional precept, *prudentia* would drift without ever coming to a term.

The morality of situation ignores *prudentia* as it does the universal law. Curiously enough, it replaces *prudentia* by casuistry, and it asks casuistry (but as an escape-valve through which the "fundamental free project" emerges) to invent the precept itself. In the eyes of this morality the question for Abraham[1] was not to obey the particular precept of God against a universal law. It was to prescribe to himself or not to prescribe to himself the immolation of Isaac, by virtue solely of his first choice of himself, and by showing himself authentically faithful to his fundamental free project after having dialectically gone over the "situation".

The preceding discussion has shown us that existentialist ethics, as it results from the principles enunciated by Sartre and his school, is incapable of going farther than the first act of valuating decision, the original moral drive through which it demands salvation of freedom. It exhausts itself in testing the reality of this drive in the diverse situations which history causes to arise, without arriving at anything other than an endless possibility of casuistic controversy and words. It has a very lively sense of freedom and of responsibility, but one that works in a void.

The fact remains that, in Kierkegaard's wake, Sartrian existentialism has recognized anew this primary datum of moral philosophy: the freedom of the singular-in-the-world, of the individual-in-time, at once against Kant and (above all) against Hegel, Comte and Marx. At the same stroke it has brought out—but without seeing that the point is to apply universal and objectively certain values and norms to singular cases always different one from another—the right feeling of the uniqueness of every authentic moral decision.

[1] Cf. J.-P. Sartre, *L'existentialisme est un humanisme*, pp. 29–31; Simone de Beauvoir, *Pour une morale de l'ambiguïté*, p. 186.

Moreover: in insisting on the importance of the moral *conversions* which Sartre mentions in *Being and Nothingness*,[1] and above all of the conversion (more radical, we are told)[2] on which depends "this particular type of project which has freedom for foundation and end",[3] Sartrian existentialism has drawn attention to a fact which few philosophers have studied, and to that truth well known among theologians[4] that the destiny of each human person depends on a fundamental option or on a *first act of freedom*[5] which he accomplishes apart from the world, and wherein without anything here below on which to base himself he takes charge of himself by a radical choice (which bears in reality on the good in which he makes his ultimate Good consist).

In all this, and despite the basic errors from which it suffers, Sartrian existentialism can contribute to a certain righting of the moral philosophy which the modern world has inherited from Kant and his successors. And its very defeat on the plane of ethics can be, if they understand the reasons, instructive for our contemporaries.

[1] Cf. *L'être et le néant*, p. 555.

[2] F. Jeanson, *op. cit.*, pp. 294–295. See above p. 387, note 4.

[3] *L'être et le néant*, p. 670. Cf. Simone de Beauvoir, *op. cit.*, pp. 20–21.

[4] Cf. Saint Thomas Aquinas, *Sum. theol.*, I–II, 89, 6.

[5] Cf. our essay on "The Immanent Dialectic of the First Act of Freedom", in *The Range of Reason.* This first act of freedom is produced, according to St. Thomas, at the moment when in leaving childhood the child deliberates about himself and opts for or against God as ultimate end of his life. Mme. de Beauvoir writes on her part: "It is adolescence which appears as the moment of moral choice: then freedom reveals itself and it is necessary to decide on one's attitude in the face of it." (*Op. cit.*, p. 58.)

14

CLOSED COSMIC MORALITY AND OPEN COSMIC MORALITY

I

JOHN DEWEY AND THE OBJECTIVITY OF VALUES—THE INCONSISTENCY OF ABSOLUTE NATURALISM

Classification of the principal moral theories posterior to the Kantian System

1. In order to clarify matters I should like to try at the beginning of this chapter to draw up a synoptic table of the principal moral theories, subsequent in the history of ideas to the Kantian revolution and the ethics of the categorical imperative, which in my opinion most deserve our attention. Such a table would present itself in this fashion:

I. Post-Kantian dialectic	*Acosmic (pseudo-cosmic) idealist ethics: Hegel* Based on Metaphysics (Onto-logical idealist). Politico-normative morality. *Cosmic (pseudo-cosmic) realist-materialist ethics: Marx* Based on a dialectic of the Hegelian type (historical materialism). Socio-normative morality.
II. The Anti-Kantian reaction: 1. Positivism	Messianic positivism: *"De-philosophized" cosmic (fetishist) ethics: Auguste Comte.* Based on a sociologically required Myth (from the point of view of the subject—the Religion of Humanity). Socio-normative morality. Secularized positivism: *The "de-philosophic" liquidation of ethics: Sociologism.* Ethics replaced by the science of social facts. Non-normative "morality".

III. The Anti-Kantian reaction: 2. In search of an authentically cosmic ethics	*realist-anti-metaphysical*	Based on a philosophy of nature: *Dewey.* Equivocally normative morality.
	realist-metaphysical (in the broad sense of the word)	Based on a Metaphysics of the Subjectivity inhabited by God, and on Faith: *Kierkegaard.* Religiously normative morality (corresponding to the singularity of the relation between God and the self).
		Based on an atheistic phenomenology of the subjectivity, and on Freedom: *Sartre.* Non-normative morality (unless arbitrarily normative, corresponding to the singularity of the situation, in which each one saves himself or not through his own freedom).
		Based on a Metaphysics of the *Elan Vital*, and on the call of creative love: *Bergson.* Mystically normative morality.

2. What is most significant in the third large category of our table is the effort to rediscover a properly philosophical ethics (unlike the ethics of messianic positivism and the non-ethics of secularized positivism) which would be intrinsically related to a conception of being and of nature, and which, freeing itself from idealism, would take into account the situation of man in the midst of a world which exists independently of our thought, would recognize that the way in which he orders his life depends on what things are, and would refuse to separate the world of freedom from the world of nature.

Here we have a remarkable recovery of the general perspective of philosophical morality, which Kant had distorted.

But the undertaking in question did not go forward without misunderstandings and false starts, because it was still burdened with views that were too partial, with prejudices that became more aggressive the less they were submitted to examination, and, sometimes, with very grave errors. In particular, the notion of cosmic morality, whose fundamental importance we have emphasized, was often proposed in its truncated, and deceptive, form (closed-cosmic or cosmic-with-nothing-beyond-this-world)—this was notably the case with Dewey and with atheistic existentialism—instead of being proposed, as was the case with Kierkegaard and with Bergson for example, in its authentic form (cosmic-open or cosmic-transcosmic). Many philosophers in our century, while re-installing the laws and movement of human morality quite rightly within the laws and movements of nature, have not seen that this morality has its primary foundation in the transcendent principle from which nature is suspended, and that it implies a transcosmic relation between man and this principle. They thought they ought to remain piously faithful to the prejudices negating metaphysical knowledge with which Kantianism, positivism, and materialism had vitiated and debilitated the thought of the preceding century.

3. I shall only mention in passing a kind of morality in which this anti-metaphysical attitude appears in a particularly simplist and futile form. I am thinking of that so-called ethics with scientific pretensions for which the only reality to be considered is biology, and, in biology, the evolution of species conceived in the Darwinian manner.

The evolution of species, as a datum of existence and a frame of historical reference (whatever may be the explanations which science and philosophy can advance to account for the historical datum in question), has become, we should note, a kind of axiom or postulate for the majority of scientists. A similar phenomenon occurred in connection with the Galilean conception of inertia. Such notions are more in the nature of postulates than in the nature of demonstrable conclusions, but once they arise in the mind they offer such a satisfactory way of conceiving of things, and possess such a high degree of simplicity and generality, that, by virtue of their outstanding contribution to economy of thought, they impose themselves almost in the manner of self-evident principles.

It is true that the idea of evolution thus forces itself on the mind only as a purely historical idea, or insofar as it signifies that the species of the biological world derive in fact from more primitive forms and are subject to a process of development and diversification in time. How are we to explain this? It is the business of scientific hypotheses, none of which up to the present has shown itself to be fully satisfactory. This is particularly the case with the Darwinian hypothesis, very much in favor to-day but philosophically untenable, according to which fortuitous change, natural selection and the survival of the fittest account for the history and the formation of the world of organisms.

Yet for the popularizers and for current opinion, evolution as an historical idea is not distinguished from evolution as a scientific theory or scientific hypothesis, and the scientific hypothesis profits unduly from the authority which the idea spontaneously acquires over the mind. Furthermore, a scientific theory is hardly formulated before the thinking world seizes upon it to take advantage of it by extrapolation. It is in this way that Darwinism has influenced every sector of the modern intelligence. In the realm of ethics in particular, not only, as Sidgwick remarks, do all contemporary authors admit —rightly—an evolution of morality and of moral reflexion, but the theory (or rather the opinions, the table-talk, the current assertions) which can be called the "morality of evolution" or "evolutionist morality" is not content to insist upon the historical fact of the progress of moral consciousness in the course of the development of humanity, but pretends to find in evolution, and especially in Darwin's idea of evolution, the criteria of judgment of morality itself.[1] Once this point is reached, we encounter not a few minds who consider themselves very acute, assuring us (especially when it is a matter of acquiring power) that the survival of the fittest, while furnishing us with the key to biological evolution, at the same time instructs us in the inflexibly promulgated law of nature concerning human conduct, and concerning the primordial and ineluctible duty to which human conduct is constrained.

I bring up these excessively impoverished ethical views, by-products of Darwinism for which Darwin himself is not responsible, only because they furnished to a Nietzsche a basis or rather a decor and a pseudo-scientific imagery which he could use as a point of reference in appealing (for quite different reasons in reality) to the will to power as the authentic morality of masters, and condemning as a slave morality the respect of the human person, the sense of love and of pity taught by the Judeo-Christian tradition. On the contrary, our critical examination arrives now at the consideration of an authentically philosophical doctrine, as little Nietzschean as possible, moreover, and quite different from the evolutionist pseudo-morality.

The Naturalism of John Dewey

Hegel again, and again an incomplete rupture

4. "From Absolutism to Experimentalism",[2] it is thus that John Dewey himself characterized his own intellectual history. In his youth, in the period when a philosopher formulates the primary controlling apperceptions through which he becomes conscious of his vocation, he had been a Hegelian, under the influence of W. T. Harris and the "School of St. Louis". At the age of thirty, he was still definitely an idealist, and spoke of nature as a moment in the "self-determination of the mind". In the case of a thinker as fundamentally American as Dewey, this Hegelian fervor was no doubt, as has been remarked,[3] the result of a misunderstanding, if it is true that "Hegel can never be Americanized".[4] The fact remains that the imprint of Hegel on Dewey was

[1] Cf. Henry Sidgwick, *Outline of the History of Ethics*, New York: Macmillan, 1931, p. 290; London: Macmillan, 1931.

[2] The title of one of Dewey's best-known essays, which appeared in 1930.

[3] Cf. Leo R. Ward, "John Dewey in Search of Himself", *The Review of Politics*, Vol. 19 (April, 1957), 205–213. The author has condensed in this brief article a remarkably rich and enlightening analysis which constitutes one of the most penetrating essays published on Dewey.

[4] *Ibid.*, p. 206.

a very deep one, and that in a sense it was never effaced, no matter how violent and persevering his effort to root Hegel out of his flesh, to the point of making the need to go counter to Hegel one of the fundamental criteria employed in his thought.[1]

Dewey's revolt against Hegel was incomparably more forceful and more effective than Marx's had been. While Marx remained in the last analysis an Hegelian, by virtue of the fact that the dialectic conceived in the manner of Hegel remained for him the true knowledge, which gives mastery over things, and the instrument of thought *par excellence*, Dewey totally rejected the Hegelian dialectic. In this respect his effort at emancipation was victorious; and, although at a high price, he rendered an outstanding service to the philosophy of the present century, in particular to American philosophy.

5. Nevertheless we can say of him too that his rupture with Hegel was an ncomplete rupture. For he certainly liberated himself from the Hegelian dialectic, and from Hegelian idealism, and this was the main thing. But he retained from Hegel the nostalgia for monism;[2] the very notion of philosophy remained for him identified with an effort of thought to absorb all things into one, and to eliminate, all the while respecting and maintaining the differences, every species of duality as well as every species of transcendence.

In reality such an operation is only possible at the level of the grand sophistics to which the Hegelian dialectic is the key. In refusing the latter with all the force of his native honesty of mind, Dewey condemned himself to search for monism the more ardently because he would never be able to arrive at it, and to conceal from himself, by pretending to eliminate "structure" in favor of "process",[3] the irreducible conflicts which rendered his thought rich in tensions but also, in spite of all his efforts, intrinsically contradictory and finally inconsistent.

In short, for Dewey as for Marx, although with very different connotations, we might speak of a reversal of Hegelianism. This time, in putting philosophy back on its feet, it is no longer Matter—Matter animated by a dialectical

[1] "The fact that Hegel affirmed form, structure, spirit and God was enough to make Dewey deny, skirt, dodge every one of these. . . . Since Hegel had some kind of God, Dewey would have none. . . ." *Ibid.*, pp. 211, 212.

[2] "Dewey spent his mature life fighting dualism, and the evident tension is a hint that perhaps he had not overcome dualism in himself or his thought. . . . All this time he was trying to leave one absolute monism for another, and it may be that he was torn in two between an unachieved new monism and an unappeased old monism, and was left suffering an unconscious and unwanted dualism of the new and the old." *Ibid.*, p. 208.

We may add that not only monism, but the idea—which was fundamental for him, as explained in the volume which Schilpp devoted to him—that nothing is intelligible except in terms of the Whole or can be understood except one understands everything, was in the case of Dewey a direct inheritance from Hegel.

[3] "He finally said that in his old Hegelian philosophy everything was form and structure, and that in his later development structure came to nearly nothing." *Ibid.*, p. 206. Cf. Dewey, *Experience and Nature*, Chicago–London: Open Court, 1925 and 1929, pp. 71–74.

movement—which replaces and exorcises the Spirit; it is Nature[1]—Nature as the source and object of the perpetual creative reshapings and perpetual re-adjustments of human action. We no longer find ourselves faced with a dialectical materialism, but with an instrumentalist naturalism.

And it is by virtue of this Hegelian monism, reversed and become naturalism—in other words it is insofar as Hegel continues in spite of everything to haunt him—that Dewey remains a philosopher and rises above positivism, and, though he continues to see in science the unique type of knowledge, that he maintains the reality and the value of philosophical knowledge—at the price of serious logical inconsistency, no doubt, with honest awareness of the problem and attempting an original solution to it (practical verification as an extension and equivalent for philosophy of what experimentation is for science).[2] It is by reason of this incomplete rupture with Hegelianism that Dewey gives in his philosophy a pseudo-Hegelian interpretation and flavor to the typically American conviction of the inherent necessity for things to change, to progress; whereas in fact this feeling has absolutely nothing to do with a metaphysics of pure Becoming and derives solely from a moral disposition combining creative energy and detachment.[3]

Toward an absolute naturalism

6. John Dewey's effort can be considered as one of the most significant made by modern philosophical thought toward the achievement of an integral or absolute naturalism. We may add that by virtue of this very fact it was one of the efforts of thought most typically subject to a radical ambiguity.

This radical ambiguity shows itself in a perpetual, and equivocal, alternation between "nature" as the object of the investigations of science (in the modern or empiriological sense of this word)—in this use the word "nature" carries a completely phenomenal connotation—and "Nature" as a philosophical entity, with a value all the more prized by a thinker like Dewey because in his passionate desire to arrive at a total organic unification of the field of knowledge he posited Nature to replace Spirit as an antithesis and antidote of Spirit.

[1] "In the Hegelian years, it was all spirit, and ever after, it was all nature." *Ibid.*, p. 207.

[2] Cf. the remarkable study on the philosophy of Dewey published by John Ratner in his Introduction to pages chosen from Dewey and issued under the title *Intelligence in the Modern World*, New York: Random House, 1939.

[3] "To be is to be in process, in change," he said, notably in the essay of 1930 mentioned above. Victims of a *trompe-l'oeil*, many American readers recognize themselves in this formula, which in itself is quite Hegelian if one sees in it a definition (being consists of changing, of becoming), but which in reality only expresses—in the terms of a defective vocabulary—a truth long since proclaimed by Aristotle, if one sees in it a statement of fact concerning our material world (everything here below changes—the being of the material natures which are the object of "physics" is of itself subject to becoming and to change, *ens mobile*).

The ambiguity in question appears also in another connection, still more instructive for us. Taken in its authentic sense, the notion of nature is an essentially analogical notion, which, given the structure of our intellect, directed first toward exterior realities, is realized for us first and above all in the things which fall within the experience of sense; in other words, it has for us its primary analogue in the nature of material things. But this same notion of nature is encountered also—analogically—in the case of spirits (either of the human spirit or of pure spirits); they have a nature; and even God has a nature. With such an analogical notion of nature one understands that the nature *of material things* is transcended by the immaterial or spiritual natures (in other words by the order called metaphysical in Aristotle's sense, or "super-natural" in the Hindu sense); and that every created or creatable nature is transcended by the divine nature and by grace, which is a participation in it (in other words, by the order called supernatural in the Christian sense).

No philosophy can completely forget or reject the authentic sense of the word "nature". But Dewey's philosophy, by the very fact that it wants to be an absolute naturalism, relegates as far as it can this authentic sense of the word "nature", which relates properly to an abstract notion, to the background in order to adopt another sense which for Dewey is evident, sun-flooded, and glorious, a sense in which the word is univocal and mythical and relates to a concrete whole.

This second sense is required by the monism which every absolute naturalism implies. At this point—and notably in the case of Dewey, by virtue of the denial-reversal of Hegelianism which we have pointed out—we have to do with a Nature essentially posited in place of the Spirit and exclusive of the Spirit, in which *physis* in Aristotle's sense finds itself, by the same token, infinitely enlarged, and confused with being in the whole amplitude of the word. Such a Nature is now the reality, univocally one and mythically substantialized, which embraces and vivifies all things: Nature as excluding any possible beyond (any metaphysical beyond as well as any supernatural beyond), Nature absolutized, in which absolute naturalism has its first postulate and the source of its seductive power, but also its radical weakness. To the extent that it realizes this, it must come back more or less openly, but without ever recognizing its analogical character, to the authentic sense of the word "nature" as referring properly to an abstract notion, the sense which it tried to keep in the shadow.

These considerations explain for us why integral naturalism is condemned always to seek itself in vain. On the one hand, the rejection of the absolute is at the very root of every philosophy which wants to be totally naturalist. On the other hand, it is impossible to be totally naturalist without enclosing universal reality in a giant all-embracing Nature, that is, in an absolutized Nature, and thereby re-introducing the absolute in a surreptitious and contradictory manner. In short, there is no integral naturalism without an absolutized Nature—therefore without a reintegration of the absolute which is incompatible with integral naturalism.

But this is not the point on which I wish to insist at this moment; I would prefer rather to stress another typical theme of Dewey's philosophy, one in connection with which, in spite of his naturalist prejudice, the intellectual honesty of which I spoke above and which from the point of view of our present analyses is of particular importance, is clearly evident. Dewey professed an integral naturalism, and yet he maintained (after his fashion no doubt and with his own limitations and paralogisms) the objectivity of values, notably of moral values.

A purely Experimentalist theory of Value

Common Sense vs. Logical Positivism

7. In the great contemporary debate concerning values and value judgments, Dewey, while decrying "absolutism", ranged himself, on the whole, on the side of philosophical tradition, thus furnishing us a remarkable testimony, however deficient it may be. I am alluding to his rigorous critique of the theses of the *logical positivists*, of Alfred J. Ayer in particular, in his *Theory of Valuation*,[1] for the second volume of the *International Encyclopedia of Unified Science*.

Dewey has in common with logical positivism an energetic anti-metaphysical prejudice. Hence the minute care with which he proceeds, in order to guard himself, while reinstating the objectivity of values, from seeming in the least to admit the abhorred values "in themselves". He was to remain decisively enclosed within the empirical perspective of that which pertains to the always relative findings made by an observer, and his own contribution was to show that within this very perspective the notion of value possessed an authentic objectivity, in other words that value judgments cannot be excluded from the domain of science (of empiriological science)—or rather, from a certain scientific domain, that of the human sciences.

The operation he was to undertake had therefore an extremely limited philosophical significance, and a very depressed angle of vision. But it was to be all the more efficacious as an argument *ad hominem* against logical positivism. In itself, moreover, it amounts to a vigorous protest by common sense, faced with the chimeras of a scientism drunk with abstractions.

[1] Chicago: University of Chicago Press, 1939 (8th Impression, 1955).

The work of Ayer to which Dewey refers is *Language, Truth and Logic*, London: Victor Gollancz, 1936.

It is useful to consider *Theory of Valuation* in connection with other writings of Dewey: *Logical Conditions of a Scientific Treatment of Morality*, Chicago, 1903 (reprinted from *The Decennial Publications of the University of Chicago*, First Series, III, 115–139); *The Quest for Certainty*, New York: Minton Balch, 1929, pp. 260–281; and *Problems of Men*, New York: Philosophical Library, 1946, Part III, "Value and Thought", pp. 211–353.

Dewey begins by conceding—far too quickly in our opinion—that the notion of value has no place in the sciences of nature. (In reality, what zoologist will refrain from speaking of "superior" animals and "inferior" animals, or of the greater or lesser degrees of perfection of organization of the nervous system or the ocular apparatus in the animal series or in a given phylum? What physicist will refrain from calling the law of increase of entropy the "law of the *degradation* of energy"? What scientist will ever exorcise from his thought the idea dear to Auguste Comte that the most complex phenomena are also the "highest" phenomena, and that a virus is "higher" in its structure and properties than a crystal of sodium?) What is true is that on the one hand there is obviously no place in the sciences of nature for any *moral* value, or for any value proper to human conduct, and, on the other hand, that the notion of value in general plays no directly constructive or explanatory role in these sciences. Yet we find it in them, inevitably.

However this may be, it is exclusively in the domain of the sciences that have to do with man and with human conduct that Dewey grants a legitimate role to the notion of value. And in this domain it is true that the notion of value has an indispensable practical role.

Disagreeing with those who maintain that the words designating so-called values have a purely emotional signification and are pure interjections or ejaculations by means of which feelings are expressed, and that therefore there can be no *value judgments*, Dewey remarks in the first place that the theory in question derives from a "mentalist" psychology, depending upon "states of consciousness" considered introspectively, to which he denies any scientific status. The truth is, he maintains, that *feelings* taken as entities separated from the external world and envisaged as simple subjective states, as pure thrills of consciousness, have nothing to do with a sane theory of values. What we must start out with in good behaviorist psychology is the concrete whole, accessible to observation, of a given organic situation, of which a cry, tears, a word of appeal or aversion, form only one of the constitutive elements, tending as such to bring about an observable change in observable conditions of behavior.[1] Then we will see that value and valuation depend on desire and interest (through a reversal deriving from the empirical perspective, it is no longer value which creates or provokes desire but desire which creates or determines value), but we will also see that desire and interest themselves must be considered in the existential context of which they form a part, and in relation to which the tension which they envelop is or is not adapted "to the needs and demands imposed by the situation".[2]

Consequently, "since the situation is open to observation, and since the consequences of effort-behavior as observed determine the adaptation,—the adequacy of a given desire can be stated in propositions. The propositions are capable of empirical test because the connection that exists between a given

[1] *Theory of Valuation*, pp. 9–10. [2] *Ibid.*, p. 17.

desire and the conditions with reference to which it functions are ascertained by means of observations."[1]

By the same token it appears that if Dewey does not fully understand the importance of the object of desire or interest, he nevertheless sets off this importance. "Everything depends upon the objects involved in desires."[2] It is not, then, insofar as it is a "feeling", but insofar as it has a given object that the desire or interest counts, once we take the point of view of the concrete context or the existing situation, to the demands or needs of which the act we propose to accomplish will respond more or less adequately. The neo-positivist thesis according to which all desires or interests, by virtue of the fact that they are "feelings" manifested by some gesture or some exclamation, "stand on the same footing with respect to their function as valuators is contradicted by observation of even the most ordinary of everyday experiences".[3]

8. Thus appears the possibility of propositions or judgments *about valuations*, such as those of an anthropologist, for example, about the defamatory character attributed by primitive peoples to intra-tribal marriage.

These are still not value-judgments in the proper sense of the term. In the latter case, acts of valuation are themselves valuated (we say that a given valuation is *better* than another); and this valuation of acts of valuation can modify the direct acts of valuation which follow, since it involves a rule or "norm" (that is, a condition with which one will have to conform when one undertakes a given sort of activity).[4]

That such value judgments and rules of conduct may be objectively based and justified is quite clear, for example, in the case of the rules of hygiene laid down by the medical profession, or the evaluation made by an engineer of the resistance and other qualities of materials to be used. The appreciation of a given procedure as better or worse, more or less advantageous or harmful, is as experimentally justified, as "scientific", as the simple observations with no value component by which a fact is established.[5]

Now the same thing is true, Dewey adds, for all values, including ethical

[1] *Theory of Valuation*, Further on (p. 18) Dewey declares himself in agreement with logical positivism in regarding "vital impulses" (i.e., "organic biological tendencies") as the source or origin from which all values derive. ("Vital impulses are doubtless conditions *sine qua non* for the existence of desires and interests.") But he energetically maintains that vital impulses (simple facts of experience, "*a*-rational like any existence taken in itself") *are* not "valuations" (one might as well say that "trees are seeds since they spring from seeds"). For Dewey it is the activity of desire or interest which is identified with valuation, and desires or interests imply an ideative factor, concerning ends-in-view and means to be employed. On "native impulses" cf. *Human Nature and Conduct*, New York: Henry Holt, 1922, pp. 89–101.

[2] *Ibid.*, p. 18. [3] *Ibid.*, p. 19. [4] Cf. *ibid.*, pp. 20–21.

[5] "Appraisals of courses of action as better and worse, more or less serviceable, are as experimentally justified as are nonvaluative propositions about impersonal subject matter." *Ibid.*, p. 22.

values, which have to do with the conduct of the human being. A person finding himself in a given situation must always estimate the relation of means to end; and the validity of this estimate falls within the realm of observation, is *experimentally verifiable.*

How can this be? Does not the estimate in question presuppose that one has already recognized a value in the end as such, independent of the means, and in a way which is not that of experimental verification? God forbid! Here Dewey deploys all the resources of his argumentation to buttress the solution he has found, a solution peculiar to himself which permits him at the same time to exorcise the metaphysical phantom of ends having value in themselves, and to satisfy his monistic passion, his desire to reduce all duality to the unity of interaction. In the concrete context in which it must be examined, the end itself, he says, is judged good or desirable only insofar as it involves consideration of the means necessary for its realization; and in this way, since the means become part of the very constitution of the end, the traditional division between ends desirable *in themselves* and means desirable (precisely as means) *for the sake of something else* appears illusory. The object finally evaluated as an end to be attained is determined in its concrete composition by appraisal of existing conditions as means.[1] And again: "Anything taken *as end* is in its own content or constituents a correlation of the energies, personal and extra-personal, which operate as means."[2]

Henceforward it is this indivisible concrete ends-means whole which at the end of the deliberation appears as the object of desire and the repository of value. And it is according as it has or has not been constituted on the basis of real conditions, positive or negative, on which its realization depends that it leads to the satisfaction or frustration of the desire it specifies, and can be objectively, experimentally, "scientifically" verified as possessing a real value or an illusory value, and as an end to be pursued or not to be pursued by a reasonable man.

Value judgments are, then, possible in the ethical realm. It is not that for Dewey they are the job of moral philosophy itself; no, they are the job of men who are *hic et nunc* engaged in action, and who fix their own norms of conduct. On this level they are possible, they can constitute authentic objective judgments, but only because they are experimentally verifiable in the same manner as all the other judgments of the sciences of phenomena. And this can only be because the end itself has been brought down to the level of utility and of means. For it is only "in the case of evaluation of things *as means*" that propositions "having evidential warrant and experimental test are possible".[3]

[1] "Any survey of the experiences in which ends-in-view are formed, and in which earlier impulsive tendencies are shaped through deliberation into a *chosen* desire, reveals that the object finally valued as an end to be reached is determined in its concrete makeup by appraisal of existing conditions as means." *Ibid.*, pp. 25–26. [2] *Ibid.*, p. 29.

[3] *Ibid.*, p. 30. Cf. p. 51: "Value-propositions of the distinctive sort exist whenever things are appraised as to their suitability and serviceability as means."

It is in this definitely empirical and utilitarian perspective that Dewey insists on the distinctively human necessity of a rational recasting of desires, and on the essential role of intelligence in the appraisal of values. Wherever there is an end-in-view, he says,[1] there is not only affective-motor but ideational activity. "Nothing more contrary to common sense can be imagined than the notion that we are incapable of changing our desires and interests" as a result of the lesson of experience, "by means of learning what the consequences of acting upon them are, or, as it is sometimes put, of *indulging* them".[2]

Thus the notion of what is *desirable*, as opposed to what is simply desired, or the notion of what *ought* to be desired or valued, emerges, not as descending "out of the *a priori* blue" or "from a moral Mount Sinai"—nor as depending on a normality of functioning expressed by the natural law (natural law and Sinai provoke the same allergies in Dewey)—but purely as a result of the fact that "experience has shown that hasty action upon uncriticized desire leads to defeat and possibly to catastrophe".[2]

Weaknesses of the theory

9. It is certainly moving to see a philosopher's struggle to break the fetters of his own prejudices in the effort to re-establish certain rudimentary truths rejected by colleagues who are sunk even more deeply than he in the empiricist mire. Alas, try as he may, he does not get very far.

The weaknesses of Dewey's experimentalist theory consist above all in a vain effort to reformulate the notion of ends and means, and in a radical misunderstanding of the *bonum honestum* (the good as right).

In the most general way, what Dewey envisages is a systematic and rigorous reduction of value to the relation between means and end. This is another way of saying that he completely eliminates the perspective of formal causality in favor of that of final causality.

In the first place, as a result of the singular confusion of ideas already mentioned above, he makes the means enter into the very constitution of the end. Everyone knows that if in order to find a treasure it is necessary to pass through a country whose inhabitants are going to cut your throat, you will prefer to renounce the treasure, finding that the game is not worth the risk. Thus the means to be employed could cause you to lose an end *a* (your own life) more precious in value than the end *b* (coming into possession of the treasure) at which you are aiming—and for this reason you give up end *b*. But for Dewey this means (under the pretext of considering only concrete cases in concrete instants) that end *b* itself possesses a certain value only in terms of the means to be employed in attaining it: so that in the concrete situation in which the decision is made (and in which Dewey places himself to argue his

[1] On the notion of end-in-view, cf. also Dewey and Tufts, *Ethics*, rev. ed., New York: Henry Holt, 1932, pp. 197–201.

[2] *Theory of Valuation*, p. 31.

[3] *Ibid.*, p. 32.

point) this end *b* has a negative value (an object *not* to be pursued), in other words is not an end, not a desirable object. This in itself reveals how sophistical such an argument is, which brings the end down to the level of the means and defines the value of an end in terms of the general *serviceability* (relative to the other ends which enter into consideration) of the means by which it can be attained in a given case.

Dewey forgets that, as an end once really wished for, end *b* (the discovery of the treasure), once renounced, remains a desirable object, and the end of a possible wish, so much so that in certain cases (for there are many sorts of treasure) regret at having had to renounce a given end can cause one to suffer for the rest of one's life. He forgets too that for the sake of being the first to reach the top of a mountain, or of making a certain profit, or of satisfying some ambition, man is prepared to risk his life and a great many other goods more precious than the object in question—so true is it that every end (even if in other respects it is a means in relation to other ends) is, insofar as it is an end, endowed with a value *in itself*, because it is a good that fits the subject. Otherwise it would not be possible to understand how a reasonable man can risk his life to explore a new land or to push science forward a step, or how an irrational man can risk his life to win an automobile race or enjoy the pleasures of heroin or opium.

In the second place, Dewey not only holds that the value of the end is to be measured by the value of the means (whereas in a healthy philosophy the contrary is true—the means *as such*, existing only for the sake of the end, derives its value only from the end); he also holds that this very end is an end with respect to the means to be used only because and insofar as it is itself a means to an ulterior end, and so on *ad infinitum*. There is no ultimate end, the notion of an ultimate end being considered a chimera of metaphysicians and churchmen, designed to assure the privileges of certain social groups—and we find ourselves faced with an endless series of means and of ends which are themselves only means. This is what Dewey calls the continuum of ends-means,[1] by reason of which a purely experimentalist evaluation is possible, in which all values are measured from the angle of that which is useful-to-procure-a-result, or according to whether a line of conduct is the means to an end (which is itself a means to something else).

It is quite true, we should note in passing, that all of the particular ends which man can wish for here below are also means to other ends and desired for the sake of other ends, so that in the perspective of time and of particular ends the course or spiral of means and ends runs on to infinity. But at the same time this is only possible because there is in man a natural desire for an end—happiness—which is not particular but universal and which as such is superior to time, and for the sake of which all the rest is willed—a final end, in short. But the notion of happiness as a final end arouses Dewey's suspicion,

[1] Cf. *Theory of Valuation*, pp. 40 ff.

and not without reason: it is a dangerous notion for any anti-metaphysical philosophy because, being in itself highly indeterminate and apt to lean in one direction or another, it inevitably requires a choice by which we place our ultimate end or happiness in one concrete thing or another—in the subsistent Good or in some other thing. Awareness of such a fact is as vexing for an experimentalistic monist as it is for a Hegelian or a positivist, for the other thing in question, whatever it may be, obviously remains so far from being able to satiate our desires completely that (at least to the extent to which speculative judgment and philosophical reflexion are concerned) the alternative really leaves too much chance for God.

But let us return to the theory of John Dewey. It must meet the objection which reproaches the *continuum of ends-means* with involving a *regressus ad infinitum* which renders all choice irrational and arbitrary. The objection is not valid, Dewey answers, and a final end from which the whole chain of ends and means would be suspended is not necessary, because each link in the chain takes form by itself without any need of the succeeding link. It is a question in every case of remedying a state of affairs which involves need, deficit or conflict, and it is uniquely according to whether in the given case they are or are not likely to eliminate the need, deficit or conflict that means are judged valid or invalid, good or bad, without having to search for any further reason.[1]

But we must look further if—in accord with common sense which by reason of the subordination of ends only decides actually to pursue an end if the means employed do not compromise a higher end, and in accord with Dewey's own thesis, which, wrongly interpreting the conduct of common sense, claims to measure the value of the end by the means—we do not want to be satisfied with just any means at all of remedying a loss or satisfying a given desire, in other words, to conduct ourselves like the people in Charles Lamb's *Dissertation on Roast Pig*. (In this story which Dewey delights in telling,[2] some men come upon a house which has burned down, and find the pigs in the pigsty roasted by the flames. They happen to pass their hands over the burned animals and when they lick their fingers they are so pleased with the taste that ever afterwards they apply themselves to building houses with pigstys and setting fire to them, thus supplying the lack in the existential situation with respect to their taste for roast pork.)

If in fact some means likely to attain the end in a given case are not employed, it is because the consequences relative to other ends must be considered; and we then find ourselves involved in "coordinations or organizations of activity" or, more precisely, with a "continuous temporal process of organizing activities"[3]—in other words, to use a term dear to Dewey, with a process of *growth*, which implicates the human being's whole capacity for desire, and which, without Dewey's wishing to recognize it, is nothing

[1] Cf. *Theory of Valuation*, pp. 45–47. [2] *Ibid.*, p. 40. [3] *Ibid.*, p. 49.

but a denatured equivalent or empirical counterfeit of happiness as final end.[1]

In addition, the idea (common to Dewey and to all who want to find in biology the primary origin of every process of evaluation) that a desire only arises in a situation where some uneasiness, loss or conflict affects the "vital impulses" does not stand up under scrutiny. For on the one hand, not every tendency or aspiration natural to the human being is identical with a "vital impulse", and on the other hand every desire as such no doubt tends toward a good that one lacks, but not necessarily toward a good that would not be desired except for some previous uneasiness which the satisfaction of natural tendencies or aspirations, or even more the fulfillment of the *vital impulses*, would have sufficed in the beginning to render immune to lack or to conflict.

10. Concerning the moral value *par excellence*, the *bonum honestum*, all the preceding remarks show that this type of value could not fail to be entirely misunderstood by Dewey. For the *bonum honestum* is precisely a value which, in opposition to values of simple utility, is not appraised or measured as a means to an end, and transcends any order of means.[2]

The *bonum honestum* is the good by reason of which an act emanating from the freedom of man is good *purely and simply*, by the nature or ethical constitution of its object, and not because it serves to attain a goal or bring about a *good state of affairs* (*good* being here a synonym of "advantageous"). This is to say that it derives essentially from formal causality, not from final causality. It is the good as right, in relation to which an act is good or bad *in itself*, and in consequence is prescribed or forbidden in an unconditional way.

Here it would be useful to dissipate a certain number of confusions and misunderstandings. Dewey assures us that every quality and especially every value is "intrinsic" or "inherent" by the simple fact that it really belongs to the thing in question, even though this thing be envisaged only as a means, as his theory of evaluation requires. Strictly speaking, then, the expression "extrinsic value" would involve a contradiction in terms.[3]

[1] "Not perfection as a final goal, but the ever-enduring process of perfecting, maturing, refining, is the aim of living," writes Sidgwick apropos of Dewey (*op. cit.*, p. 327); "growth itself is the only moral end."

[2] This is precisely what Dewey rejects from the outset. For him the fundamental error in morals is to want to found moral judgment on "transcendental conceptions" "which have a significance independent of the course of experience as such", and he holds that the possibility of a "logical control of moral judgments" implies the "continuity of scientific judgment" (which does not leave the realm of empirical relativity) in moral experience as in the experience proper to the sciences of nature (nor does he see that the word "experience" itself has a quite different sense in the two cases). Cf. *Problems of Men*, Part III, esp. p. 244. See also *Ethics*, pp. 364–367.

On the relation of the *bonum honestum* to moral obligation, see the following section, devoted to Bergson, pp. 431–435.

[3] Cf. *Theory of Valuation*, pp. 27–28; *Problems of Men*, Part III, pp. 211–353.

These assertions rest on an equivocation. When we say that a quality or a value is "inherent" or "intrinsic", we do not mean only that it belongs to a certain object, but that it belongs to it *by reason of what that object is* in its proper constitution, not by reason of its relation to something foreign to what it is in itself, notably an end to which it is the means. In this latter case the value of an object can be called extrinsic, for whatever its own qualities may be, as means it has no other goodness than that of the end.

Then it must be noted that the term *bonum honestum* designates not only an *intrinsic* value (like that which belongs to some end taken in itself, like honors, health, pleasure . . .); it designates an intrinsic value which is, further, ethically good or desirable in an unconditional way, or absolutely speaking.

Is this to say that the *bonum honestum* is "out of relation to everything else",[1] an absolute fallen from heaven like a meteorite in virtue of the *a priori* "you ought" of Kant, or of an arbitrary decree issued either by a God conceived as pure will or by makers of moral codes who take His place? It is by putting things in this light that Dewey is able to overwhelm with his avenging blows the "absolutism"[2] that he attributes to all who refuse to believe that good and evil consist in serving either to restore to order or to further unsettle "states of affairs" which a lack or conflict renders disadvantageous.[3]

Here again, unhappily, Dewey's argument and his avenging blows are lost in a disastrous confusion of ideas (for which Kant is doubtless responsible in part). The fact is that to say that what has the value of *bonum honestum*, the just for example, is morally good in an unconditional way, or absolutely speaking, in no sense signifies that the *bonum honestum* is without relation to anything else. For this "absolute" only has meaning *in relation to* the nature or essence of man, and to the practical requirements of his normality of function. It is the relation of conformity or non-conformity with reason which makes the object of the act what it is morally, confers upon it its ethical nature or constitution, renders it good or bad in itself and unconditionally.

Thus the *bonum honestum*, the good in and for itself of the moral order, is certainly an intrinsic value, present in the object to which it belongs by reason of what that object *is* in its own constitution, not by reason of its relation to something foreign to what it is in itself. But it is not for this reason without all relation—it is not without relation to the very thing which gives it its own constitution, and by the same token its unconditional character. It is independent (ab-solute) of any advantage or disadvantage of the individual or the social group, of any condition, of no matter what proviso—"*if* you want to attain a given end"; but it is not independent of human nature and its essential inclinations, nor of practical reason; it is measured by them.

[1] *Theory of Valuation*, p. 28. [2] Cf. *ibid.*, p. 56.

[3] "Ends-in-view are appraised or valued as *good* or *bad* on the ground of their serviceability in the direction of behavior dealing with states of affairs found to be objectionable because of some lack or conflict in them." *Ibid.*, p. 47.

On Naturalist Ethics

11. The great problem to which a philosophy like John Dewey's draws our attention is that of the possibility of an ethics regulated exclusively by the positive sciences or the sciences of phenomena. On this question the positions taken by Auguste Comte and those taken by Dewey seem to be in conflict. Both of them reject (with Kant) any metaphysically based morality, and both (contrary to Kant) are seeking a cosmic morality; and it is upon the rational and objective knowledge furnished by the positive sciences, the sciences of phenomena, that this morality is to rest. But for Comte the sciences as such do not suffice; a reversal of point of view must occur, as a result of which, in the name of feeling, the religious fetishism with which human history began will be restored in a superior form, and will change scientists into priests of humanity in order to entrust to them the conduct of the human being.

For Dewey, on the contrary, it is the sciences of phenomena themselves, from physics and biology to sociology, which must suffice for man to regulate his conduct, once they are sufficiently developed and once they are integrated into an experimentalist philosophy of the same type as themselves, a philosophy designed to unify the field of knowledge and train men to judge according to scientific procedures. Then "the operation of desire in producing the valuations that influence human action" will be "ordered by verifiable propositions regarding matters-of-fact".[1] The void between the world of things and the world of man will be filled; and "science will be manifest as an operating unity . . . when the conclusions of impersonal non-humanistic science are employed in guiding the course of distinctively human behavior", characterized by "desire having ends-in-view, and hence involving valuations";[2] science will be in fact as well as by right "the supreme means of the valid determination of all valuations in all aspects of human and social life".[3]

We see, then, in what sense Dewey condemned "failure to recognize the moral potentialities of physical science".[4] "It is impossible to tell," he added, "the extent of the suffering in the world, avoidable or remediable in itself, which is due to the fact that physical science is considered purely physical."[5]

12. I think that the "moral potentialities" which "physical science" possesses, at least in certain respects, must indeed not be neglected. One can speak with good reason of a moral guidance offered by the medical sciences, the psychological sciences,[6] the social sciences, as they make known to man what value certain acts are possessed of and what rules of conduct are indicated

[1] *Theory of Valuation*, p. 66. [2] *Ibid.* [3] *Ibid.*
[4] *Human Nature and Conduct*, p. 10. [5] *Ibid.*
[6] Cf. the excellent remarks of Dr. Charles Odier on what he calls "moral psychology", *Les deux sources, consciente et inconsciente, de la morale*, Neuchâtel: éd. de la Baconnière, 1943 [2nd ed., 1947], pp. 158 ff.

with respect to the requirements of physical health, or psychological health, or of adjustments in human relations calculated to reduce conflict, distress or despair. The moralist ought to attach a great deal of significance to all of this, for it is perfectly true that certain conditions required for a healthy moral life can be established, and a great deal of pain and error avoided through these moral directions of "physical science". Further, by the very fact that they keep closer to the level of the sensible and do not claim to descend from on high, they more easily capture the attention of the rational animal. Although in this case as in others, as Aristotle pointed out, knowledge is not very effective in producing virtue, it is no small thing for a man to know that if he wants to keep his digestive and nervous systems in good condition he must practise sobriety and control his emotions, even, according to Dr. Carton, abstain from the use of foul language and avoid lying.

The fact remains that the guidance in question involves only a kind of *pre-morality*, and only acquires authentically ethical significance if it is regulated and controlled from a higher level by the aid of criteria concerned with the conscience proper. It is true that such pre-moralities, especially if their psychological and social evaluations are sufficiently elaborate, can in the case of many individuals be grafted into the sense of good and evil and natural law instinctively operating in man and henceforward enjoy in their case a moral status properly so called, by virtue of the kind of misapprehension or natural illusion we have previously alluded to (in connection with Marxist morality and Comtian morality, and with the way they are understood by some of those to whom they are taught).[1] But in themselves, deprived of any fixed point and of any final signpost with regard to the conscience, they are unable to provide man with a testing device consistent and definite enough to permit him to regulate his conduct as a man, or as an agent master of his actions.

For it happens—and this is one of the points on which Dewey remains confused—that the ends of a being deprived of reason are determined by nature, so that to help a grape-vine or a horse or a dog to be a good grape-vine, a good horse, or a good dog, it is enough to know under what conditions it profits or prospers best in its specific development. But to profit or prosper in his specific development is quite another matter for the human being, because it is he who fixes for himself the ends of his actions (in conformity or not with the proper ends of the human essence or nature), and who fixes for himself the supreme good (identical or not with his true ultimate end) toward which he directs his life. And the pre-moralities of which we are speaking, like the sciences on which they depend, are interested neither in the human essence as such nor in the ultimate end of human life, any more than in any unconditional value or norm. With respect to these things all their determinations remain up in the air, and all that a sufficiently comprehensive sociology can

[1] See above, chapter 10, pp. 254–256, and chapter 12, pp. 330–331.

show is that without individuals capable of sacrificing everything for the sake of supra-sociological imperatives, the human species would be in a very bad way.

Separated from superior and authentically ethical criteria whose basis is in the metaphysical order, the moral guidance furnished by the positive sciences remains not only completely relative and conditional, it also remains irremediably fluid and arbitrary. Medicine can recommend sobriety, psychology can recommend humility and even, if need be, religious faith as detergents and lubricants for our human springs; but what answer can they give, if not by virtue of some conscious or unconscious metaphysics or anti-metaphysics, when they ask themselves, for example, whether trial marriage, euthanasia, scientifically controlled abortion, the sterilization of certain categories of a-social individuals, the elimination of aggressive instincts by the surgical or bio-chemical manipulation of the nerve centers, are to be recommended or advised against; when they ask themselves whether, when a desire becomes obsessive, it is or is not more reasonable to yield to it to avoid giving rise to a morbid fixation in the psyche; whether for a nation at war it is a crime or a duty to insure victory by using a weapon which annihilates millions of innocent people; and whether it is a sign of mental maturity or a sign of immaturity and infantile pride to risk one's life and the security of one's family and aggravate the tensions of the social milieu on the pretext of defending an innocent man or refusing to deny the truth?

13. A naturalist ethics is one for which what we have called the moral guidance of the positive sciences, or the pre-moralities emanating from these sciences, constitute morality itself. Given the irremediable indetermination and arbitrariness which, as we have just seen, characterize these pre-moralities when they are isolated from higher criteria, a naturalist ethics will be faced with a choice between two very different positions, one rigorously non-normative, the other normative to some degree, and more or less avowedly.

The rigorously non-normative position gives the upper hand to the pure exigencies of the scientific method and scientific objectivity. It demands that the sciences to which man appeals for the improvement of his conduct enlighten him as completely as possible about the immediate and remote consequences of a given line of action; but it holds that it is not at all the business of these sciences to give the clients who consult them any counsels or prescriptions concerning the conduct of their lives. What is to be done in a given case? Insure my career by marrying the stupid and repulsive daughter of an all-powerful executive, or forego the boon my success might bestow upon my country in order to follow the inclinations of my heart? Or try to settle everything by becoming the husband of the executive's daughter and the lover of the young newspaperwoman I adore? The biologist, the geneticist, the psychiatrist, the expert in the social and political sciences, the expert in human relations furnish me with a complete table of the consequences that each of these three lines of action is likely to entail. After that it is up to me to decide what suits me best, not according to any rationally justified moral principle (since by hypothesis there is no other valid morality than the naturalist morality, and this refers me purely and simply back to the sciences of phenomena), but according to the mental habits my educators and environment have inculcated in me, or the ideas on life that I have gathered by chance from my experience, or the calculation of what best serves the interests that happen by chance to predominate in me, or simply, if I like to follow my impulses, according to my own taste and pleasure. I may make a mistake—time will tell. But all things considered, things will turn out well, if not for me then for my species. For if naturalist morality refrains from guiding me, it is that it has confidence in human nature—a limited confidence, it is true, as far as human nature in me is concerned, but unlimited in respect to human nature in the average man. Naturalist morality thinks it is emancipated from metaphysics, but it remains subject to the metaphysics of natural goodness as Rousseau conceived it.[1]

The normative position, on the contrary (normative to some degree and more or less avowedly), gives the upper hand to the human subject and its need to know how to direct its life. Hence it demands of the positive sciences that they fulfill the function of *guidance*, which they can only do if they are integrated into some coherent system possessing firm principles and a definite ideal. Will the requirement in question be met by any anti-metaphysical philosophy whatever, positivist or experimentalist, which, because it does not know of any order superior to the actual course of the world and of human life in time, abstains from frankly proposing a code of life to man? If naturalism really wants to be in a position to guide human life effectively, will it not have to resolve to be fully normative, and thus (since this is impossible for it inasmuch as plain philosophy) make itself into a "religion" in the full social sense of the word? Auguste Comte's religion had at least the merit of undertaking seriously to deliver us once and for all of metaphysics by putting in its place a fetishism and a set of social sanctions more powerful as a constraining force than any abstract precepts, however well-grounded in the invisible. Alone—because he had greater lucidity and intrepidity in his aberration than all the zealots of "physical science" who succeeded him—Comte alone, the prophet of messianic positivism, went to the necessary logical extreme for a fully naturalist morality. It is understandable that those who would like to see morality constituted in a complete metaphysical void should be embarrassed by their great ancestor, and throw a modest veil over the implacable logic by which he leads us to the ultimate regime of conscious and organized sociolatry.

[1] On Rousseau and natural goodness, cf. our work *Three Reformers*, New York: Scribners, 1937, pp. 93–164; London: Sheed and Ward, 1932.

14. At first glance Dewey seems to have chosen the rigorously non-normative position. In his eyes any moral theory that envisages a system of values and norms of conduct is headed toward absolutism. It is up to each individual to find the norm to be followed in a given situation, moral education as experimentalist philosophy conceives it consisting in learning how to proceed correctly in the analysis of particular situations and the consequences of various possible modes of conduct, and the correctness of the decision remaining hypothetical until the predicted consequences have been compared with the real consequences.[1] Is this not a kind of morality of situation,[2] however different it may be from that of Sartre by virtue of its scientism and the rationality it expects in the decisions of man once he is duly enlightened by science?

But here is exactly the point at which the perspective is reversed and Dewey swerves in reality from the rigorously non-normative position. If one looks at it closely one sees that his morality is, in spite of everything, and unadmittedly, normative, or directive of human acts—not directly and in itself, but through the intermediary of apprenticeship in rational or "scientific" methods of valuation.

Not only was Dewey a moralist and a *meliorist* to his marrow,[3] with a religious passion for the growth of life, the perpetual renewal of ends, the expansion of human nature and of its potentialities, the enrichment of existence in significance and powers[4] (however vague these notions may be, they nevertheless point to supreme values and general directions of conduct proposed by his moral philosophy itself); not only did his insistence on the rationality and maturity of mind to be manifested in our choices have a clearly normative significance; but above all, being like every naturalist philosopher more interested in human nature and the human species than in the human person as such, it was toward the social, and toward reciprocal adjustment between the individual and his environment that his whole moral philosophy

[1] Cf. *Human Nature and Conduct*, p. 11; *Ethics*, pp. 347–349; Sidgwick, *op. cit.*, p. 326.

[2] This very notion of "situation" plays an important role in Dewey's thought. Cf. in particular *Logic: The Theory of Inquiry*, New York: Henry Holt, 1938, chapter IV.

Let us note in passing the sophism common to all moralities of situation. They act as if in affirming (rightly) that "it is not the function of the theory to furnish a substitute for reflective personal choice, but to be an instrument which renders the deliberation more effective and the choice therefore more intelligent" (Dewey, *Ethics*, *loc. cit.*), one affirmed by the same token (which is, however, an entirely different assertion) that moral science cannot propose (or, more exactly, cannot reflexively justify) any universal norm, in other words, that not only the ultimate achievement of the normative determination, or the right application of the law in the given case, but the law itself or the very principle of normative determination, derives from the judgment of the individual and from *personal reflective choice* (which amounts to saying, in Thomistic language, that *prudentia* has not only to apply the laws of conduct with absolute rectitude—something no science or theory can do—but has to create these laws in each particular case). Cf. above, chapter XIII, pp. 392–393.

[3] Cf. Leo R. Ward, article cited, p. 211.

[4] Cf. *Human Nature and Conduct*, pp. 288, 292.

was oriented.[1] And he conceived of freedom itself in terms of interaction between man and his environment, in such a way that "human desire and choice count for something" in the matter.[2] Here it is only a question of "an adjustment to be reached intelligently", and "the problem shifts from within the personality to an engineering issue", in other words, "to the establishment of the arts of education and social guidance".[3] What does this mean if not that in the last analysis it is the philosophy of Dewey—which proposes no rules of conduct, but teaches rules and procedures of investigation to be used in determining the value of various possible modes of conduct in a given situation[4]—which will be the guiding spirit of "the arts of education and social guidance"?

In this sense, and with a view not, certainly, toward a Comtian type of "spiritual power", but toward a democratic society that would be controlled without even being conscious of it by a host of well-indoctrinated educators and social guides, Dewey's naturalist morality, in spite of his horror of despotism, does not open up very reassuring perspectives for the human person.

The truth is that Dewey never decisively ranged himself with either of the two positions—rigorously non-normative or more or less normative—which we delineated above. His own position remained ambivalent. And his morality can be described as an equivocally normative morality.

A good many other ambiguities have been pointed out in Dewey's thought.[5] We have already spoken of the ambiguity in his very notion of nature.[6] He wrote a book on *Human Nature and Conduct*, and in his introduction, attacking a pharisaical morality which is nothing more than a caricature of normative systems of morality and even of the Kantian imperative, he says: "Give a dog a bad name and hang him. Human nature has been the dog of professional moralists and the consequences fit the proverb."[7] As for himself, he refuses to separate morality from human nature, and calls for a morality "based on the study of human nature".[8] So it is that when it is a question of

[1] Cf. *Theory of Valuation*, pp. 63–64. "The separation alleged to exist between the 'world of facts' and the 'Realm of values' will disappear from human beliefs only as valuation-phenomena are seen to have their immediate source in biological modes of behavior and *to owe their concrete content to the influence of cultural conditions.*" (P. 64; italics ours.)

[2] *Human Nature and Conduct*, p. 10. [3] *Ibid.*

[4] Cf. *Theory of Valuation*, pp. 57–58.

[5] Cf. Leo Ward, art. cited. The author gives (p. 212) a table of some of the inconsistencies to be found in Dewey: "Man has a nature; Man has no constant nature.—Man is wholly one with nature; By no means; Man is free.—Man is simply to accept nature and the mores and conventions; Man is not to accept nature and the mores and conventions.—Some ends are given; for example, growth, the full stature of our possibilities; No ends are given.—Some norms are given; no norms are given.—Man has intelligence; Man is of a piece with everything else."

[6] Cf. above, pp. 401–402. [7] *Human Nature and Conduct*, p. 12.

[8] *Ibid.*, p. 12. He is quite right in this, or rather he would be if he had in mind human nature in the proper or ontological sense of the term. But this notion remains irremediably ambiguous for him. What he has immediately in mind, in fact, are simply "realities of human physiology and psychology" (*ibid.*, p. 4), that is, phenomena which as such tell

morality the concept of human nature is valid. But when it is a question of theory of knowledge (in which for Dewey the sciences of phenomena are the type of all knowledge) this same concept is no longer worth anything. There is no nature, there is only process. It is more difficult than one would suppose to be a consistent naturalist.[1] And, as Santayana has shown,[2] Dewey certainly did not succeed.

II

BERGSONIAN MORALITY AND THE PROBLEM OF SUPRA-MORALITY

The Bergsonian themes

Pressure and Aspiration

1. When Bergson writes: "there can be no question of founding morality on the cult of reason",[3] does he wish to say simply that it is not the business of philosophical reason (the reason of the theorists of ethics) to discover or invent, and to make effective on the mind the rules of human conduct, in other words, to found them creatively, by an act of initial establishment, in the manner for example in which the science of naval engineering makes the plans for a ship, directs its construction, and provides for its armament, and by the same token binds the officers and the crew to the set of rules without whose observance the ship could not put out to sea? In that sense Bergson's assertion would be correct.

But this assertion goes much further. For Bergson it does not mean that moral philosophy is a reflexive knowledge, prior to which one must presuppose moral experience and the moral life of humanity, the norms of conduct recognized by it in the course of its long gropings and difficult advances —in such a way that the reason of the philosophers and the theorists of ethics validates indeed and confirms, no doubt, the laws recognized spontaneously by conscience, but does so after the event and reflexively, not by initial establishment, and thus explains, refines and makes precise these laws, and

---

nothing of a nature immutably determined in its specific characteristics. But at the same time, for Dewey as theoretician of human conduct, these same "realities" take on a surreptitiously ontological sense and become the unavowed equivalents of the "human nature" of common sense and healthy philosophy—a structural constant identical in all men.

[1] Cf. D. W. Gotshalk, "The Paradox of Naturalism", *Journal of Philosophy*, vol. 43 (1946), pp. 152–157, and "A Suggestion for Naturalists", *ibid.*, vol. 45 (1948), pp. 5–12. Cited by Leo R. Ward, art. cited, p. 210.

[2] Cf. George Santayana, "Dewey's Naturalistic Metaphysics", *Journal of Philosophy*, December 3, 1925. Reprinted in *The Philosophy of John Dewey*, edited by P. Schilpp, New York: Tudor Co., 1939 and 1951, pp. 245–261; Cambridge: C.U.P., 1951.

[3] *The Two Sources of Morality and Religion.* Translated by R. Ashley Audra and Cloudesley Brereton with the assistance of W. Horsfall Carter, Garden City: Doubleday, 1956, p. 89.

submits them to critical examination, but in no way creates or engenders them.

No; what Bergson means to say is that morality and moral philosophy presuppose, as their constitutive sources, forces which do not depend on reason (either philosophical reason or reason in its natural and spontaneous functioning), but on "life" and "the principle of life":[1] there is on one hand an infra-rational or infra-moral energy, which is essentially of the social order, and on the other hand a supra-rational or supra-moral energy, which is essentially of the mystical order. Our morality, and our diverse, more or less "intellectualistic" systems of moral philosophy are a rationalization in which this infra-rational component and this supra-rational component "intermingle and interpenetrate"[2] and mutually influence each other on the level of concepts and logic, and in which the first component passes to the second "something of its compulsive force", the second communicates to the first "something of its perfume".[3] Thus doubtless each of them loses its proper quality for the philosopher who keeps to the conceptual level; they conserve it however for the acting man, in whom, above and below this level, the living sources and the "two moralities" always exercise their power.

2. It will be necessary then for Bergson, by resorting to a method whose disadvantages he is clearly aware of, but which is imposed on him by the nature of things, to consider pure cases which are ideal limits. "Pure aspiration is an ideal limit, just like obligation unadorned."[4]

"The fundamental theme of *The Two Sources* is the distinction and opposition between that which in moral life proceeds from *pressure* and that which proceeds from *aspiration.* Pressure comes from social formations and from the law of fear to which the individual is subject with regard to the rules of life imposed by the group and intended to assure its preservation, and which seeks only to turn to the routine and ferocious automatism of matter.—Aspiration comes from the call of superior souls who commune with the *élan* of the spirit and who penetrate into the infinitely open world of liberty and love, which transcends psychological and social mechanisms; it comes from *the call of the hero*, and from the propulsive force of the emotion"—Plotinus would have said the "conversion"—which turns the soul toward the very principle of life. "To this law of *pressure* and this law of *aspiration* are linked two quite

[1] Bergson describes them as "forces which are not strictly and exclusively moral" (*Ibid.*, p. 96), although "a substantial half of our morality" is constituted by the first, and "the rest of morality" by the second (*ibid.*, p. 49).

[2] *Ibid.*, p. 85.

[3] "Once again, there is some difficulty in comparing the two moralities because they are no longer to be found in a pure state. The first has handed on to the second something of its compulsive force; the second has diffused over the other something of its perfume. We find ourselves in the presence of a series of steps up or down, according as we range through the dictates of morality from one extreme or from the other . . ." *Ibid.*, p. 51.

[4] *Ibid.*, p. 84.

distinct forms of morality: *closed* morality, which, to put it briefly, is that of social conformism; *open* morality, which is that of saintliness."[1]

Although human society is "composed of free wills" while an organism "is subject to inexorable laws",[2] society imitates as much as it can an organism in which habit would play "the same role as necessity in the works of nature";[3] or rather it imitates as much as it can, with its system of habits which weigh on the will of each, the purely instinctive "societies" of which the ant-hill is the prototype. Immanent in each of its members,[4] society makes us, in the most general case, travel the roads laid out by it without our even noticing; or, when we find ourselves faced with a problem or a temptation which necessitates a personal decision, it brings to bear on us a force which can be called "the totality of obligation",[5] and which is "the concentrated extract, the quintessence of innumerable specific habits of obedience to the countless particular requirements of social life".[6]

In a hive or an ant-hill "each rule is laid down by nature, and is necessary", while in human society "only one thing is natural, the necessity of a rule".[7] "Thus the more, in human society, we delve down to the root of the various obligations to reach obligation in general, the more obligation will tend to become necessity, the nearer it will draw, in its peremptory aspect, to instinct. And yet we should make a great mistake if we tried to ascribe any particular obligation, whatever it might be, to instinct. What we must perpetually recall is that, no one obligation being instinctive, obligation as a whole *would have been* instinct if human societies were not, so to speak, ballasted with variability and intelligence. It is a virtual instinct . . ."[8]

With the call of the hero an entirely different universe reveals itself. Then it is "by turning back for fresh impetus, in the direction whence that impetus came"[9]—in other words, in turning toward the very principle of that life which has produced, at one stage of its evolution, the human race and human society, naturally closed—that the soul communicates intuitively with a reality which transcends evolution itself and its products. "It would be content to feel itself pervaded, though retaining its own personality, by a being immeasurably mightier than itself, just as an iron is pervaded by the fire which makes it glow."[10] And it gives itself "by excess" to society, but to a society "comprising all humanity, loved in the love of the principle underlying it".[11]

[1] Cf. Jacques Maritain, *Bergsonian Philosophy and Thomism*, New York: Philosophical Library, 1956, p. 327.

[2] *The Two Sources of Morality and Religion*, p. 9.

[3] *Ibid.*, p. 10. [4] *Ibid.*, p. 20. [5] *Ibid.*, p. 23.

[6] *Ibid.* Cf. p. 25: "Conceive obligation as weighing on the will like a habit; each obligation dragging behind it the accumulated mass of the others, and utilising thus for the pressure it is exerting the weight of the whole: here you have the totality of obligation for a simple, elementary, moral conscience."

[7] *Ibid.*, p. 28. [8] *Ibid.*, p. 28.

[9] *Ibid.*, p. 212. [10] *Ibid.*, p. 212. Cf. p. 100.

[11] *Ibid.*, p. 212.

The saints, the great mystics are rare. They soar so high that it must be said of each of them that "such a one is in fact more than a man".[1] But in the inner being of most men there is "the whisper of an echo".[2] "They have no need to exhort; their mere existence suffices."[3] Let one of these exceptional personalities rise up, and his experience and his example will awaken in the depths of the human race a nostalgia which will cause it to make a kind of leap forward; our moral life with its system of obligations, social in origin, will be pervaded by a superior element and to that extent transformed. This superior element comes from the second morality,[4] from open morality, which "differs from the first in that it is human instead of being merely social".[5] And if it is human, it is because the soul is liberated there in a supra-intellectual[6] emotion in which it yields to the attraction of the very principle of life, and which is the love of Creative Love. "The truth is that heroism may be the only way to love."[7] It is "from the contact with the generative principle of the human species" that man has felt "he drew the strength to love mankind".[8] We are then drawn by the great discoverers who march ahead of us and who have encountered God, by those great mystics for whom the task "is to effect a radical transformation of humanity by setting an example",[9] and who are "the imitators, and original but incomplete continuators, of what the Christ of the Gospels was completely".[10]

3. What I would like to point out first of all in connection with these Bergsonian themes are two contrasting aspects whose importance seems to me to be considerable. On one hand, Bergson insists on a crucial fact which philosophers ordinarily endeavor to conceal—namely, the fact that moral life, considered in its true concrete reality, is wrapped in a double envelope; the stays of social existence, with the pressures to which it submits us, and the atmosphere of mystic and religious experience, with the desire for that union with God and His love of which the saints are the great witnesses. The morality effectively lived by men, with its rules of conduct which they recognize in conscience and which they apply or reject in practice (rejecting more often than practicing them) does not exist without this double envelope. But on the other hand, from this double envelope, the one infra-moral in itself, the other supra-moral, Bergson makes two halves which constitute morality itself, or two moralities, closed morality and open morality, whose coalescence in the course of historical development supposedly makes up morality in the ordinary meaning of the word.

Such systematization makes the Bergsonian theory open to criticism; we

[1] *The Two Sources of Morality and Religion*, p. 213. [2] *Ibid.*, p. 214.
[3] *Ibid.*, p. 34. Cf. p. 72: "Something has supervened which might never have existed, which would not have existed except for certain circumstances, certain men, perhaps one particular man."
[4] *Ibid.*, p. 35. [5] *Ibid.* [6] Cf. *ibid.*, p. 44. [7] *Ibid.*, p. 53.
[8] *Ibid.*, p. 54. [9] *Ibid.*, p. 239. [10] *Ibid.*, p. 240.

will have to come back to this point. For the moment, what matters to us is to note that in seeing in the constraints exercised by the social quasi-instinct and in the attraction of the great mystics the two halves of morality itself, Bergson apparently proceeded as a pure philosopher, in whose ethical theory the sociological element and the mystical element were absorbed. In reality, however, what he proposed to us is a moral philosophy *not exclusively philosophical*, because not only did it take over data received from sociology and ethnology, reinterpreted by it or elevated to its own level; it also received data and testimony which came from a higher source than philosophy. Bergsonian ethics learns from the mystics; it nourishes its philosophic substance itself with the Sermon on the Mount[1] and the morality of the Gospel. And in this it is profoundly revolutionary with respect to the whole modern rationalist tradition (as also, in another sense, with respect to the Medieval tradition, which in ethical matters was turned entirely toward theology, not philosophy; in fact, if not by right, it was with the schools of pagan antiquity and its sages that for the Middle Ages the notion of moral philosophy was associated; and if medieval thinkers were to retain, and with what care, the teachings of the *Nicomachean Ethics*, it was solely to forge with them an instrument for the use of moral theology).

From the moment that one recognizes that mystical contemplation is a supreme (experiential) wisdom of divine things rooted in faith (as Bergson thought from the time of *The Two Sources*, all the while seeming to underestimate the role of faith); and from the moment that one also recognizes (which Bergson at the time of *The Two Sources* left completely aside) that the analysis of the "proper causes" or "proper reasons" of mystical experience pertains to theology, one must conclude that what Bergson proposes to us in reality, and has introduced for the first time into the field of philosophical knowledge, is—still in an inchoate and merely implicit stage—a moral philosophy *adequately taken*, or which makes its own the data concerning human existence received from a superior knowledge. And in this respect whoever has a correct idea of moral philosophy owes him a special debt of gratitude.

Fortunes of Ambiguity

4. From the very fact that he thought he was concerned with a work of pure philosophy when in reality he was philosophizing under the influx of a higher world than that of reason alone, Bergson could not avoid a kind of ambiguity which, varied as might be its forms, consists fundamentally in enclosing within the same notion things which, when one sets about clarifying and distinguishing them with more precision, appear as belonging to different orders.

In a general way the ambiguities which could thus be pointed out in *The Two Sources* could just as well have turned toward a kind of naturalistic biologism as toward the Christian conception of the world. In fact it is in the

[1] Cf. *The Two Sources of Morality and Religion*, pp. 59–60.

Christian direction that they have turned, and Bergson from the outset saw his friends winding up in an authentically Christian mode of thought when he asked them to "read between the lines" of his book.[1] This is why they appear to us as happy or propitious ambiguities.

After having explained that, if one wishes to understand how society obliges individuals, it is necessary to delve, beneath social accretions, down to life—and if one wishes to understand how the individual can judge society and bring it to greater heights, it is necessary to delve right down to the principle of life[2]—Bergson writes: "Let us then give to the word biology the very broad meaning it should have, and will perhaps have one day, and let us say in conclusion that all morality, be it pressure or aspiration, is in essence biological."[3] There is here, it seems, an attempt to reduce the spiritual to the biological (to the biological rendered itself so transcendent that it is conceived as the creative source of worlds).[4] But if one considers that for Bergson "the principle of life" is Subsistent Love, or the super-abundance in pure act of the purely spiritual, then, quite to the contrary, one finds oneself confounded with an attempt at transfiguration of the biological into the spiritual.

The Bergsonian morality is cosmic in so strong and extreme a sense that ethics seems to be absorbed in metaphysics—in the metaphysics of the vital impetus—and that the unforeseeable, more than human adventures of the heroes of the moral life appear there as the peak of the very evolution which has produced the world of the insects and that of the vertebrates. But no! A radical discontinuity enters in. It is in reascending, beyond the whole impetus of evolution, to its first source, and by communing with the pure spirituality of Creative Love, infinitely superior to the whole universe of nature, that the heroes whose call attracts us elevate and transform little by little the moral life of humanity; so that in short if the whole cosmos is interested in the moral effort of men, it is in the sense noted by Saint Paul: all creation travails and aspires to be transformed, groans in awaiting the revelation of the sons of God.

5. When Bergson speaks of nature, he has in view neither the abstract and essentially analogical notion of οὐσία or of intelligible constituent, nor the notion of that which, in contradistinction to the participation by grace in the Uncreated Himself, is called the natural order. He has in mind the concrete power of the vital impetus (in combat with the relapse of matter and grasped again at each step by matter) whose greatest success was the appearance on

[1] It is known that in his will, dated February 8, 1937, Bergson declared that his reflections had "led him closer and closer to Catholicism, in which I see," he said, "the complete fulfillment of Judaism," and that he would have asked to be baptized had he not "wished to remain among those who tomorrow will be persecuted". In conformity with the request expressed in the will, a Catholic priest came to pray over his mortal remains. Cf. our book *Bergsonian Philosophy and Thomism*, p. 337, footnote 1.

[2] Cf. *The Two Sources*, p. 100. [3] *Ibid.*, p. 101.

[4] Cf. our work previously mentioned, *Bergsonian Philosophy and Thomism*, p. 329.

our globe of the human species and human society. It is then allowable for him to speak—in a completely metaphorical way, as he does not fail to emphasize—of what nature "intends", or of what it "wants". Here we have a kind of metaphorical personification of the Aristotelian *physis*. And when one comes to the human race and human society, what nature "wants" is precisely the maintenance and reinforcement of this hard-won success; in fact, what Bergson ascribes to nature is the behavior of the *homo animalis* or ψυχικός ἄνθρωπος of whom Saint Paul spoke, when he considers man in his concrete state as a simple result of evolution—a concrete state where he is capable by himself alone (or, as a Christian would say, by the forces of nature alone) only of a very imperfect and very limited good.

One understands consequently why Bergson, with a realism whose perspicacity far outdistances the optimistic illusions of the great prophets of naturalism, insists on the extreme limitation of the ethical capacities with which nature has provided the human being. Nature tends toward the closed society and closed morality; and what this society and morality were with primitive man remains the real and active centre, always ready to spread its flames, of the effort and ruses of nature in the very fabric of our civilized societies.[1] It is in the manner of bees in the hive or ants in the ant-hill that nature unifies men among themselves, in drawing the outsider away from their horizon and their heart.[2] If nature does not want war for the sake of war, it at least wants the closed society to be always ready for war against an eventual enemy. "The origin of war is ownership, individual or collective, and since humanity is predestined to ownership by its structure, war is natural."[3] And once war comes, the rules of morality which were respected up to that time yield place quite naturally to the morality of the primitive closed society. "Murder and pillage and perfidy, cheating and lying become not only lawful, but they are actually praiseworthy. The warring nations can say, with Macbeth's witches: 'Fair is foul, and foul is fair.'"[4]

Such is nature's ethics, or the thrust of the vital impetus passing through matter at the human level. (We have already noted that Bergson is not interested in the notion of human nature as a universal essence. This lack—one may note in passing—explains why the idea of natural law is absent from his philosophy; not only with the positivists, but also with their adversaries, one could say that for a century this notion disappeared from the thought of philosophers, while among the jurists the need to return to it was increasingly felt. To-day philosophical thought has started once again to be concerned with it, and it is surely one of the notions that philosophers of the next generation will have to re-examine and make valid again.) But let us end this

[1] "It is for closed, simple societies that the moral structure, original and fundamental in man, is made. I grant that the organic tendencies do not stand out clearly to our consciousness. They constitute, nevertheless, the strongest element of obligation." *The Two Sources of Morality and Religion*, p. 56.

[2] Cf. *ibid.*, p. 286. [3] *Ibid.*, p. 284. [4] *Ibid.*, p. 31.

digression. What we are concerned to note is that for Bergson every moral progress in mankind has taken place under the influence of the second morality, the morality of aspiration, and against the grain of nature. Even when its impetus is insufficient or opposed, dynamic religion is of itself "a leap outside of nature".[1]

A remarkable opposition appears at this point between spirit and nature; and if the source at which the spirit is fed when it goes back to the very principle of life is a beyond-nature at once in the Hindu sense[2] and in the Christian sense,[3] this ambiguity at least leaves the door open for grace, for the supernatural as Christianity understands this word, and it even leans in this direction, since, in the last analysis, it is only by virtue of the Gospel and the Christian mystics that open morality, thanks to its long effort through the centuries, has succeeded in fully revealing itself and setting the world in motion.

Authentic love of Humanity

6. It is by virtue of an emotion analogous to the creative emotion of the poet, but higher and more transforming—and with which the person "becomes one"[4]—that the mystics, says Bergson, stir up in humanity the "irresistible attraction"[5] which draws it beyond nature. He takes care however to insist on the fact that the "open morality" of which he speaks is in no way a "moral philosophy of sentiment".[6]

The "emotion" in question has nothing to do with those "disturbances"[7] and that soft-heartedness of the sensible-organic order, even with those pleasures at feeling one's own goodness,[8] where the self remains always central, and which the words "sentiment" and "sentimental" connote. This emotion tears us away from our ego, decenters us from ourselves, centers us in another. It is essentially spiritual. Bergson knew its name; it is called charity.[9]

Having decided to ignore all theology, he says nothing either of the supernatural order on which such "emotion" depends, or of the faith which is at the root of it, according to the testimony of the great mystics whose experience he has examined. However, not only does he leave his doctrine open to these theological truths, but it is in their direction that the ambiguity here again present in his exposition resolves itself: for on one hand the core of the matter, in his eyes, is indeed participation in that love which is the very essence of God—"the divine love is not a thing of God: it is God Himself";[10]—on the

[1] *The Two Sources of Morality and Religion*, p. 223.

[2] I mean to say superior to material nature but remaining metaphysically natural. Cf. above, in reference to John Dewey, chapter XIV, p. 402.

[3] I mean to say superior to all creatable nature.

[4] *The Two Sources*, p. 252. [5] *Ibid.*, p. 96. [6] Cf. *ibid.*, p. 47.

[7] There are, says Bergson, "two kinds of emotion, the one below intellect, which is mere disturbance following upon a representation, the other above intellect . . .". *Ibid.*, p. 252.

[8] See above chapter 12, pp. 336–339. [9] Cf. *The Two Sources*, p. 36. [10] *Ibid.*, p. 252.

other hand, to say that the love which makes the saints the cooperators of God[1] is a "supra-intellectual" emotion, and that "never before" has the soul which feels it "been so charged with thought",[2] is to admit by the same token that it proceeds, not doubtless from an "idea", but from a veiled communication from the divine reality to the knowing faculty.

Saint Thomas teaches on the one hand that every creature naturally loves God more than itself,[3] and on the other hand that the charity by which we love God as His sons and share in His intimate life is essentially supernatural.[4] In an incomplete and ambiguous fashion made inevitable by his decision to remain on a purely philosophical level even when what he is speaking of goes beyond philosophy at all points, Bergson describes to us the impetus of love which, at the call of the saints, carries humanity beyond the closed society and closed morality in terms whose affinity with this twofold doctrine seems to us undeniable. Our deepest wish is to get out of ourselves in order to unite ourselves with the very source of life, this is the instinct which makes men yearn after any kind of rapture; if such a wish emanates from our nature, it is only in a desire and a love which derive from grace that it assumes authentic form and can truly be fulfilled. . . .

But what matters to us above all in the doctrine of *The Two Sources* is the central theme which insists that it is not at all through a progressive extension of love for the family and the city, or, to speak like Auguste Comte, of "sympathetic inclinations" and "instincts of sociability", that man passes to the love of humanity. No; what nature and our instinct of sociability induce us to love is our closed group, those who are *our people*, excluding the outsider whom we naturally tend to ignore, misunderstand or scorn.[5] In order truly to love humanity one must run upwards against the grain of nature and instinct, one must, by a leap of which spirit alone is capable, and a liberation of which God alone can be the author, be transported and carried away in this sovereign love which has made everything, which is at the very origin of worlds and life, and which opens our hearts to all men, making us love them with the same love with which He first loves them. "The utmost we can say is that family and social feeling may chance to overflow and to operate beyond its natural frontiers, with a kind of luxury value; it will never go very far. The mystic love of humanity is a very different thing. It is not the extension of an instinct, it does not originate in an idea. It is neither of the senses nor of the mind. It is of both, implicitly, and is effectively much more. For such a love lies at the very root of feeling and reason, as of all other things. Coinciding

[1] Cf. *The Two Sources*, p. 234.
[2] *Ibid.*, p. 252.
[3] *Sum. theol.*, I, q. 59, a. 5.
[4] *Ibid.*, I–II, q. 109, a. 3; II–II, q. 23.
[5] Cf. *The Two Sources*, p. 285; and p. 33: "It is primarily as against all other men that we love the men with whom we live. Such is the primitive instinct. . . ." We do not come "to humanity by degrees, through the stages of the family and the nation. We must, in a single bound, be carried far beyond it, and, without having made it our goal, reach it by outstripping it."

with God's love for His handiwork, a love which has been the source of everything, it would yield up, to anyone who knew how to question it, the secret of creation. It is still more metaphysical than moral in its essence. What it wants to do, with God's help, is to complete the creation of the human species and make of humanity what it would have straight away become, had it been able to assume its final shape without the assistance of man himself."[1]

7. In the course of a preceding chapter[2] we found in the sentimental hedonism of the philosopher of altruism—"what pleasures can be greater than those of self-devotion?"—an outstanding example of false love or abortive love. Love of humanity does not play any less central a role in Bergsonian ethics than in the ethics of Auguste Comte; it is the very criterion of the "open morality" and the "open society". But Bergson makes us see in what consists genuine love of humanity; he shows us that authentic love and the authentic gift of self by which we dedicate ourselves to all men pass necessarily through God,[3] and that their true name is that fraternal charity which is but one with the love of God. What constitutes the exceptional historic bearing of Bergson's moral philosophy is the fact that it is a testimony borne at the heart of modern thought, both against the pseudo-Christianity of Hegel and the anti-Christianity of Comte. I don't believe that in writing *The Two Sources* Bergson ever thought of Auguste Comte and the religion of Humanity. Yet he sets against them a singularly significant riposte, a moral philosophy where the impetus toward Christianity and the person of Jesus stands out in place of the aversion which Comte nourished in regard to them, and which shuns substituting the "sympathetic impulsions located in the anterior region of the brain" for the grace of God, as the *Positivist Catechism* wished to do.

[1] *The Two Sources*, pp. 234–235.—Cf. *ibid.*, p. 38.—The Stoics did not have a notion of that kind of love. Hence the infinite distance which, despite certain apparent likenesses, separates the Stoic morality from Christian morality, as Bergson has well illustrated ("The Stoics proclaimed themselves citizens of the world, and added that all men were brothers, having come from the same God. The words were almost the same; but they did not find the same echo, because they were not spoken with the same accent." *Ibid.*, p. 60; "But these dicta were the expression of an ideal, an ideal merely conceived, and very likely conceived as impracticable. There is nothing to show that any of the great Stoics, not even the Stoic who was an emperor, considered the possibility of lowering the barrier between the free man and the slave, between the Roman citizen and the barbarian. Humanity had to wait till Christianity for the ideal of universal brotherhood, with its implications of equality of rights and the sanctity of the person, to become operative. Some may say that it has been rather a slow process; indeed eighteen centuries elapsed before the rights of man were proclaimed by the Puritans in America, soon followed by the men of the French Revolution. It began, nevertheless, with the teachings of the Gospels, and was destined to go on indefinitely; it is one thing for an idea to be merely propounded by sages worthy of admiration, it is very different when the idea is broadcast to the ends of the earth in a message overflowing with love, invoking love in return." *Ibid.*, pp. 77–78.)

[2] See above, chapter 12, pp. 336–339.

[3] Cf. *The Two Sources*, p. 33 (cited above, p. 426, note 5), and p. 233: "For the love which consumes him . . . is the love of God for all men. Through God, in the strength of God, he loves all mankind with a divine love."

While for Auguste Comte the notion of right must disappear, "every human right" being "absurd as well as immoral",[1] it is quite remarkable that Bergson insists with a particular emphasis on justice,[2] that justice which, as we have previously noted, true love consummates and does not supplant. It is no less striking to observe that while Comte becomes intoxicated with the authoritarianism of his sociolatric regime, Bergson holds a democracy where mechanics and mysticism call upon each other to be the temporal hope of mankind.[3] A powerful instinct warned the high priest of humanity to be wary of democratic justice and democratic liberties. Bergson knew that the forward leap by which the idea of justice was extended to humanity in its entirety was due to Christianity;[4]—as he knew that taken in its original inspiration "democracy is evangelical in essence" and that "its motive power is love".[5]

If one thinks of the aspirations of human nature metaphysically considered, and of the demands of natural law, one must say that nothing is more natural than the groping effort by which peoples tend toward democratic achievement. But it is by a motion issuing from a higher source than nature, it is by the inspiration of the Gospel at work in secular consciousness, that this effort has been awakened in human history. And if we remember the concrete and limited sense, more biological than metaphysical, and centered on the collective egotism of the species, in which Bergson understood the word "nature", we realize why he "wanted to show, in the democratic mind, a mighty effort in a direction contrary to that of nature",[6] warning us in this manner that the great historical adventure of democracy would go bankrupt if democracy should deny its spiritual origins and relax in its struggle to dominate the animal instincts.

Moral Obligation

8. In order to preserve whatever is valid in the position of the sociologists and to expose the enormous part which the invasion of the social into the recesses of the individual psyche has in our moral life, the Bergsonian theory of closed morality strikes deeper than sociology and sociologism themselves, for it is not only social structures and social taboos that it takes into consideration; it is, behind them, beneath them, the very impulse of nature or "life" to which the human species and human society owe their existence. "Obligation as a whole" which we sense with a mysterious reverential fear weighing on us in each of the particular obligations to which social rules bind

[1] See above, chapter 12, pp. 339–341. [2] Cf. *The Two Sources*, pp. 69–71.

[3] Cf. *ibid.*, p. 309.

[4] Cf. *ibid.*, pp. 76–77: "The progress which was decisive for the substance of justice, as the era of the prophets had been for its form, consisted in the substitution of a universal republic, embracing all men, for that republic which went no further than the gates of the city, and, within the city, was limited to free men. It is from this that all the rest has followed. . . ."

[5] *Ibid.*, p. 282. [6] *Ibid.*, p. 283.

us derives its power from the vital impetus itself. "The pressure of it, compared to that of other habits, is such that the difference in degree amounts to a difference in kind."[1] Bergson's analysis in the first pages of *The Two Sources*, in particular his analysis of the drive which pushes a criminal to denounce himself,[2] contain, from the point of view we have just indicated, unquestionable truths.

The trouble is that this "obligation" at whose root "there is a social claim",[3] which "binds us to the other members of society" by a link "of the same nature as that which unites the ants in the ant-hill or the cells of an organism",[4] this "force of unvarying direction, which is to the soul what force of gravity is to the body" and "which ensures the cohesion of the group by bending all individual wills to the same end"[5]—"that force is moral obligation",[6] writes Bergson—well, no, all this *is not* moral obligation, all this is only a purely factual force, of the same order as cosmic and organic energies and necessities, which is grafted from the outside on authentic moral obligation and increases its power but at the price of an alien contribution, and sometimes initiates it and sometimes enters into direct conflict with it. Of itself this almost physical constraint so well analyzed by Bergson has nothing to do with moral obligation, by which I am bound in conscience to refuse to do what appears as evil in my own eyes, even though all of society and the whole universe and the whole power of cosmic evolution may bring pressure to bear on me to force me to do it.

9. One must say the same of the quasi-obligation which depends on the "second morality", or open morality. Bergson's presentation, moreover, reveals here, and this was inevitable, a certain embarrassment. On the one hand it is essential to the Bergsonian theory that it oppose obligation to aspiration—the obligation of the closed morality to the aspiration of the open morality. Obligation is characteristic, then, of closed morality. On the other hand, however, one must indeed recognize that the morality of aspiration itself admits of a kind of obligation: not only because the two moralities are in fact intermingled, and the attractions felt under the call of the hero happen to be captured in regulations and formulae which depend on the habits developed by obligation as social pressure; but also and primarily because in the very order of open morality we are aware of a duty not to withdraw ourselves from what love asks of us—and "is there such a thing as a duty which is not compulsory?"[7] Not only, then, "should obligation radiate" "and expand", but even come "to be absorbed into something that transfigures it".[8]

In open morality, in other words, "there is still obligation, if you will"[9] (if

[1] *The Two Sources*, p. 10; cf. *ibid.*, p. 100.
[2] Cf. *ibid.*, pp. 17 ff.
[3] *Ibid.*, p. 23.
[4] *Ibid.*, p. 83.
[5] *Ibid.*, p. 266.
[6] *Ibid.*, pp. 266–267.—Cf. p. 56 (cited above, p. 424, note 1).
[7] *Ibid.*, p. 33.
[8] *Ibid.*
[9] *Ibid.*, p. 55: "In the second [morality], *there is still obligation if you will*, but that obligation is the force of an aspiration or an impetus, of the very impetus which culminated in the

you will, says Bergson, and it is the avowal of his uneasiness). But such an obligation is no longer obligation strictly speaking, the quasi-instinctive necessity of the system of habits required for the cohesion of the group; it is "the force of an aspiration of an impetus, of the very impetus which culminated in the human species" . . . Then "the primitive impetus here comes into play directly".[1]

The fact remains—and this is what is important for us to note—that this improperly called (Bergsonian) obligation, this "obligation, if you will" which belongs to the morality of aspiration, is no more an authentic moral obligation than the properly so-called (Bergsonian) obligation. In a sense it is closer to genuine obligation because it is not a force primarily extrinsic to the soul, the force of the social group penetrating and invading the recesses of the individual psyche; it is from the moment of its origin, although coming from a higher source, interior to the soul which undergoes it. But it too has nothing to do with the typical, essential element of moral obligation as such, I mean the paradox of this bond by which free will is held and which nevertheless is connatural to it and leaves intact all its spontaneity, the paradox of this *unique* constraint which does not result from any force exercising an efficient power on the will. Whether he is placed in the perspective of open morality or in that of closed morality, the philosopher of *The Two Sources* passes by authentic moral obligation.

It is so because "the obligation, if you will" which belongs to open morality remains, too, a purely factual force, which no longer brings pressure on the will but draws it and attracts it, a force which is no longer of the same order as the cosmic and organic energies but of a trans-cosmic order and emanates from creative love, and whose power, no longer one of constraint or coercion, but one of aspiration and attraction, has a transcendent efficacy. "This is no longer," Bergson says, "a more or less attenuated compulsion, it is a more or

---

human species, in social life, in a system of habits which bears a resemblance more or less to instinct: the primitive impetus here comes into play directly, and no longer through the medium of the mechanisms it had set up, and at which it had provisionally halted." In regard to the other obligation—obligation strictly speaking, which has its source in the first morality—Bergson writes, p. 83: "In short, the obligation we find in the depths of our consciousness and which, as the etymology of the word implies, *binds us to the other members of society*, is a link *of the same nature as that which unites the ants in the ant-hill or the cells of an organism*; it would take this form in the eyes of an ant, were she to become endowed with man's intelligence . . . It goes without saying that the matter wrought into this form becomes more and more intellectual and self-consistent as civilization progresses . . ." And he adds, thinking of the "obligation, if you will", of the second morality: "And we have seen also how a certain kind of matter which is intended to be run into a different mould, whose introduction is not due, even indirectly, to the need for social preservation, but *to an aspiration of individual consciousness, adopts this form* ["the form that the link of the ant-hill would take in the eyes of an ant, were she to become endowed with man's intelligence"] by settling down, like the rest of morality, on the intellectual plane." (Italics ours.)

[1] *The Two Sources*, p. 55.

less irresistible attraction", manifested by "a certain stirring up of the soul, which you call emotion".[1] He is right to add: "In both cases you are confronted by forces which are not strictly and exclusively moral."[2] Attraction or compulsion, supra-intellectual emotion or quasi-instinctive constraint, these forces exercise a physical causality on us, they do not bind us morally by virtue of what the conscience sees, they do not at all concern this power that the judgment of conscience has to hold in the purely moral order a will which remains physically free to escape from it.

And on the one hand the pressure exercised within me by the ant-hill to which I belong is indeed a constraint, but it is in no way that entirely immaterial constraint, devoid of the least physical compulsion, which constitutes authentic moral obligation. On the other hand the emotion which lifts me up under a more or less irresistible attraction isn't constraint at all—not even that purely immaterial constraint on the free will, without a shadow of physical compulsion, which constitutes authentic moral obligation; it is not physical obligation and it is not moral obligation, it is not obligation at all (even "obligation, if you will").

10. Obligation-in-conscience is an absolutely primary and absolutely irreducible datum of moral experience. And it is something so simple that philosophical reflection either grasps it right away or misses it completely. When he writes that moral obligation "is in no sense a unique fact, incommensurate with others",[3] Bergson shows that his own reflection has completely missed it.

This accident can be attributed to the diminished idea which Bergson had of intelligence in general and of its role in the moral life in particular, and to the "ontological lack" which has been noticed in his doctrine. When he criticizes what he calls intellectualism and the attempts to give an account of moral obligation in dependence on intelligence,[4] he is often right against the theories of philosophers, but in what concerns the function that the intellect really performs in the matter, the remarkably sharp and subtle analyses and discussions which he offers to us simply overlook the issue.[5]

[1] *The Two Sources*, p. 96. [2] *Ibid.*

[3] "Obligation is in no sense a unique fact, incommensurate with others, looming above them like a mysterious apparition. If a considerable number of philosophers, especially those who follow Kant, have taken this view, it is because they have confused the sense of obligation, a tranquil state akin to inclination, with the violent effort we now and again exert on ourselves to break down a possible obstacle to obligation." *Ibid.*, pp. 20–21.

[4] Cf. *ibid.*, pp. 20–23; 85–95.

[5] Moral obligation for Bergson is only a factual necessity of the social-instinctive order; and all that intelligence has to do with obligation is, after having "thrown instinct out of gear", quickly to "set things to rights" in justifying it. He thinks only of the discursive and reflective functions of intelligence, and from this angle he can say: "an act of reasoning will therefore prove that it is all to the interest of the ant to work for the ant-hill, and in this way the obligation will apparently find a basis. But the truth is . . . that obligation already existed in all its force" (which is true, but not at all in the way that Bergson understands it): "intelligence has merely hindered its own hindrance". *The Two Sources*, p. 94.

"No philosopher," adds Bergson, "can avoid initially postulating this compulsion"

The truth is that moral obligation is actually a unique fact incommensurable with any other, and to be mistaken about this fact is to be mistaken about the ethical order as such. Kant had indeed seen the importance of it, but he treated it as a kind of irruption of the sacred realm into the domain of reason, a fact not only primary but inscrutable and defying analysis, and he constructed on it a doctrine so irritating to the mind that the very concept of obligation has been compromised in the thought of philosophers for more than a century.

In reality the fact of which we are speaking can be analyzed by philosophical thought—in the manner however of primary data, and in dependence on self-evident apperception which the cult of the problematic and of the conceptual constructions to be built risks finding too simple.

Everything in this connection boils down, on the one hand, to the relationship between the intellect and the will and to their mutual envelopment, on the other hand to that original and irreducible object of intellectual intuition, that specifically moral determination of being which is the *bonum honestum*, or the good pure and simple, "substantial", in itself and for itself, of the ethical order.

The *bonum honestum*, the quality of an act ethically good by reason of what it is, or of its relation to what man is, independently of all consideration of advantage or utility, as well as pleasure—independently also of every pressure which could weigh on us, and of every emotion and aspiration which could stir us up—the "good as right" is as remarkably absent from Bergson's ethics as from John Dewey's ethics. It is certainly not that Bergson is ignorant of it, he knows it naturally like every man, and he makes allusions to it here and there, particularly in *The Two Sources* when he writes: "To betray the confidence of an innocent soul opening out to life is one of the most heinous offences for a certain type of conscience, which is apparently lacking in a sense of proportion, precisely because it does not borrow from society its standards, its gauges, its system of measurement."[1] But he allots no place to it in his philosophical elaboration. And it is significant that when he believes he is discussing obligation Bergson employs a purely despotic formula, which fits in fairly well with the Kantian imperative and very well with pure social pressure—"you must because you must"[2]—but never dreams of the formulation: "you must because it is good".

The *bonum honestum* is remarkably absent also from the theories of most

(which means, for Bergson, the physical necessity of obligation as link of the ant-hill or the organism); "but very often he postulates it implicitly, and not in words. We have postulated it and said so." *Ibid.*

[1] *The Two Sources*, p. 17. The text continues: "This type of conscience is not the one that is most often at work. At any rate it is more or less sensitive in different people. *Generally the verdict of conscience is the verdict which would be given by the social self.*" (Italics ours.)

[2] Cf. *ibid.*, pp. 25–26.

modern philosophers. Should we be astonished at this? It is a question here of one of those entirely primary and entirely simple things which mankind's common consciousness grasps by so spontaneous, so ordinary, and so banal an exercise of the intellectual faculty that no one pays any attention to it, and which escape by the same token the investigators given to philosophical reflection, unless they possess the gift of the simple metaphysical gaze. From this point of view the *bonum honestum* is to morality what being is to philosophy. And one can say of it what we said of being: "We must remember that the best way of hiding anything is to make it common, to place it among the most ordinary objects. . . . Nothing is more ordinary than being, if we mean the being of everyday knowledge, nothing more hidden, if we mean the being of metaphysics. Like the great saints of poverty it is hidden in light."[1]

11. Let us understand however that on the one hand the good as right, the *bonum honestum* is the good itself of the moral order—that by which, insofar as we belong to human nature and depend on its normality of functioning, a human act is purely and simply good, and a man purely and simply good.[2] And let us understand on the other hand, according to the axiom so often repeated by Saint Thomas in a sense which is not only moral but absolutely universal, that the will tends by necessity of nature to the good which is presented to it by the intellect, and cannot will evil as evil. At the same time we understand that if, at the level of the practical decision or the "practico-practical judgment", it is entirely possible for me to wish to do evil (moral evil) and to want to be bad (morally bad), because then, freely breaking loose from the moral order, I still tend to a good, but one which is not the moral good, and still want to be "good" or to acquire a certain plenitude of being, but not morally—on the contrary, as long as I remain within the moral perspective itself and keep, on the level of the (speculativo-practical) judgment, viewing my conduct in the sole light of universal moral values and norms, prior to my practical decision, as long as I consider my possible action and my possible behavior with respect to the human value that they have of themselves, leaving out of account the inclinations of my subjectivity in the given situation, in short, *as long as I listen to my conscience*, it is impossible for me to wish to do moral evil and to be morally bad: because, insofar as I

[1] Jacques Maritain, *A Preface to Metaphysics*, New York: Sheed and Ward, 1948, pp. 87–88; London: Sheed and Ward, 1939. (*Sept leçons sur l'être*, Paris: Téqui, s.d., pp. 97–99).

[2] It can happen, be it understood, that we may fool ourselves in regard to the *bonum honestum*, and we might regard as *good in itself* cutting off the hand of thieves, putting to death tribal chiefs when they reach old age, burning widows on the funeral pyre of their late husbands, torturing suspects in order to obtain confessions or information, etc. There is a question (a question of the erroneous conscience) which has nothing to do with what we are discussing here and which concerns the *bonum honestum* considered in general, or in its constitutive notion itself.

keep on this level of thought and actually consider the moral rule, to wish to do moral evil and to be morally bad would be tantamount to wishing to be purely and simply bad and to wishing evil as evil, which is contrary to the very nature of the will. So long as I consider right here and now the law, or listen to my conscience, I feel myself bound by it, prevented from willing what is morally bad.

Such is authentic moral obligation, where the force which binds me is absolutely nothing which exercises any "physical" causality on me whatsoever, pressure or aspiration, constraint of society or attraction of creative love. This force is purely that of intellectual knowledge conditioning the exercise of the will. It relates not to efficient causality nor to final causality, but to formal causality, and it is in passing through the will itself, and in virtue of the very nature of the will that it is necessitating.

Thus appears what is unique, irreducible and incommensurable with any other fact, in the fact of moral obligation; thus the paradox to which we alluded above is resolved, the paradox of that bond by which the free will is held and which nevertheless is connatural to it and leaves all its spontaneity intact. For in the heaven of the soul where intelligence and will contain each other, not only is it connatural to the will to emanate from knowledge and to be formed in the light of the intellect, but it is by itself or by its own nature that the will is obliged or necessitated to will that which is morally good and not to will that which is morally bad as long as the gaze of the intellect is set on the law of human conduct or on the value *in itself* of human conduct. A singular constraint, a constraint unique in its kind, this constraint which the intellect considering the moral universe exercises on the will, and which properly constitutes moral obligation.[1] The will is *obliged*, it is constrained, certainly—and so to speak by a torturing iron hand in what concerns the particular movements, whether of desire and passion, or of pure will itself, which, however hopelessly intense they may be, are forbidden (as long as I consider the exigencies of the moral realm) to express themselves in free decision. But in what concerns its very nature, or the first immanent principle of its activity, the will exercises rather than undergoes this constraint; for the iron hand of which I just spoke is nothing else but the nature itself of the will; it is by its very nature itself that, under the light of what the intellect sees, the will is constrained or obliged. So that, by a unique exception, it is possible, in the case of moral obligation, to speak of a constraint naturally undergone, and which does not impede the volitive faculty from remaining master of its action—constraint which implies no element of physical coercion, but only the vision of what is good or bad—and from which I am free consequently to withdraw myself, no longer on the level of the judgment of conscience but of the parctico-practical judgment or election, on condition that I voluntarily

[1] "Vis obligativa in debito morali ex sola recta ratione ut a coactiva virtute proficiscitur." Cajetan, opusc. *De obligatione et observatione praeceptorum*, q. 2.

detach my gaze from the moral perspective, or to put it another way, that in my act of choice I voluntarily cease to "consider the rule".

Supra-morality and the call of Creative Love
The regime of life of the great mystics and the liberty of the Spirit

12. The preceding discussion about moral obligation has shown us that it is useless to wish to make a morality come forth from the mixture and interpenetration of an infra-morality of the social order and a supra-morality of the mystical order. One might as well hope to establish a metaphysics by combining physics and religion, or wish to fabricate wine by mixing brandy and nectar. From this point of view one can say that the morality of *The Two Sources* keeps all of morality except morality itself. But what it has at least revealed to modern philosophy, and with an undeniable authority, is the importance of what one might call the "supra-morality" in the moral life of mankind.

For Bergson this supra-morality, or "open morality", is one of two heterogeneous components which permeate each other in the general behavior of men. One should rather see there in reality a certain regime of moral life where the best among us enter. Be that as it may, Bergson has admirably seen that supra-morality has its pure prototype in the great Christian mystics; and "outside of the analysis *by proper causes*, which the instruments of theology alone allow us to carry out, by informing philosophers of those realities which are grace, the theological virtues, and the gifts of the Holy Spirit, it is impossible to speak of mystical experience with more depth, and with a more intense far-sighted sympathy than the author of *The Two Sources* has done". We have insisted on this point elsewhere and by quoting him at length.[1]

What Bergson also saw quite clearly is that there is no entirely right moral life without that aspiration (it may be more or less unconscious, and more lived than known) which he held to be awakened in the human race by the call of the heroes and saints and which is aspiration to the perfection of love. To find the highest image of the perfection of love and the one richest in meaning, Bergson was right in turning toward the great mystics become one single spirit and love with Subsistent Love Itself, and causing to overflow to all human beings this love that makes a man ready to give his life for one he loves. At the same time he understood that the liberation to which man aspires from the depths of his being is but one with this supreme love. The great philosophers have all sensed the central importance of the problem of deliverance, or the conquest of the freedom of autonomy; Bergson is one of that small number who have sought the solution elsewhere than in substitutes.

But from that moment on the problem of morality and supra-morality is posed in unavoidable terms. For if it is true that the perfection of evangelic love and the superior freedom experienced by the mystics are the peak of

[1] Cf. our work *Bergsonian Philosophy and Thomism*, pp. 337–343.

moral life, it is also true that this peak surpasses the level at which the realm of morality itself is established. The realm of morality applies to human acts the measures of reason, but evangelic love has its source in an order superior to nature and reason. The realm of morality submits man to a law and to a set of rules which not only bind him in conscience, according to that kind of constraint connatural to the will to which we referred above, but also constrain in the proper sense of the word, curb and chain instincts, passions, ardors of nature spontaneously rebellious to the yoke of reason; but the freedom of the saints has passed beyond all constraint properly so-called, even that of the law. In this they have reappropriated to some degree something of the state of innocence. As a spiritual writer puts it, "Adam and Eve knew that it was evil to disobey God. How else would their fault have been a sin, and have had such terrible consequences? But they knew it without having had the experience of evil, and without being subject to the regime of constraints imposed by the Law on a weak and rebellious nature, *the regime of morality*, as it can be called. Mankind did not live under *the regime* of morality, did not learn morality, did not begin to acquire explicit knowledge of the particular rules of morality, did not begin to acquire the science of good and evil, until the day when it had the experience of evil."[1] Its moral science has been "acquired through the experience of sin".[2] "We have received the legacy of sin and the inclination toward evil from our first forbears, but also we have received the instinct for a knowledge of good better than ours; the memory, darkened as it may be, of a state where the relations between man and the universe, and God, were more just and more real. Here is doubtless the origin of this sentiment, so profound, that the Law must be surmounted, and that it is necessary, at any price, to rediscover the pure sources of love and freedom."[3]

Bergson's error was to call "first morality" a purely social code and a system of purely social pressures which far from pertaining to the authentic order of morality constitute only an infra-morality (which moreover plays an enormous part in human life). But he has touched upon important truths in his doctrine of the "second morality", which is however, truth to tell, a supra-morality through which authentic morality itself is super-elevated and consummated—and transfigured.

13. If he had wanted to gather the testimony not only of the great Christian mystics, but also of the faith itself from which they declare their experience proceeds,[4] and of the theological doctrines through which they give us an idea

[1] Raïssa Maritain, *Histoire d'Abraham ou les premiers âges de la conscience morale*, 2nd ed., Paris: Desclée De Brouwer, 1947, pp. 72–73. An English translation of this essay appeared as "Abraham and the Ascent of Conscience," in *The Bridge*, ed. by J. M. Oesterreicher, New York: Pantheon, 1955, pp. 23–52.

[2] *Ibid.*, p. 74. [3] *Ibid.*, p. 77.

[4] Cf. our work, *The Degrees of Knowledge*, new trans. under supervision of Gerald B. Phelan, New York: Scribners, 1959 (London: Bles, 1959), chapter VIII, "Saint John of the Cross, Practitioner of Contemplation," pp. 310–355.

of their mysterious ways, he would have turned first of all to Saint Paul. In what concerns the problem which occupies us—the problem of supra-morality and the regime of life of those who have entered into the fullness of love—the testimony of Saint Paul (to which we have already referred many times in the course of this work) has in itself, as in the history of ideas, a prime authority. "But if you are led by the Spirit," he writes, "you are not under the Law."[1] "For whoever are led by the Spirit of God, they are the sons of God. Now you have not received a spirit of bondage so as to be again in fear, but you have received a spirit of adoption as sons, by virtue of which we cry, 'Abba! Father!' The Spirit himself gives testimony to our spirit that we are sons of God."[2] "Now the Lord is the Spirit; and where the Spirit of the Lord is, there is freedom."[3]

Thereupon follows the commentary which Saint Thomas has given on these celebrated texts in the *Summa contra Gentiles*, and which not only the theologian, but also the philosopher who treats of human conduct always profits by meditating upon. "We must observe," Saint Thomas says,[4] "that the sons of God are moved by the Spirit of God not as though they were slaves, but as being free. For, since to be free is to be cause of one's own actions, we are said to do freely what we do of ourselves. Now this is what we do willingly: and what we do unwillingly, we do as slaves, not as free persons, either because we act under absolute compulsion, or because compulsion is mixed with voluntary decision, as when a man is willing to do or suffer that which is less opposed to his will, in order to avoid that which is more opposed to it. Well, by the very fact that He infuses in us the love of God, it is in making us act according to the very motion of our will that the Spirit of sanctity inclines us to act. (For it is proper to friendship that the friend be at one with the loved one in the things which the latter wishes.) Hence the sons of God are moved by the Spirit of God to act freely and for love, not slavishly and for fear: *Now you have not received a spirit of bondage so as to be again in fear, but you have received a spirit of adoption as sons, by virtue of which we cry, Abba! Father!*

"Now the will is by its nature directed to that which is truly good: so that when a man, under the influence of passion, of a vice or an evil disposition, turns away from what is truly good, this man, *if we consider the essential direction itself of the will*, acts slavishly, since he allows himself to be inclined against this direction by some extraneous principle. But if we consider the act of the will *as it is here and now inclined toward an apparent good*, this man acts freely when he follows his passion or his corrupted disposition, and he acts slavishly if, his will remaining inclined in this way, he holds back from what he wants by fear of the law which forbids the fulfilment of his desire.

"But here it is that the Spirit of God inclines the will to the true good by love; by love it causes the will entirely to lean, here and now, toward that

[1] *Gal.*, 5: 18.
[2] *Rom.*, 8: 14–16.
[3] *II Cor.*, 3: 17.
[4] *Sum. contra Gent.*, IV, 22.

indeed which is in line with its deepest wish. The Holy Spirit, therefore, removes both that servitude whereby a man, the slave of passion and sin, acts against the natural inclination of his will, and that servitude whereby a man, the slave and not the friend of the law, acts in obedience to the law against the present movement of his will: *Where the Spirit of the Lord is*, says the Apostle Paul, *there is freedom*; and: *If you are led by the Spirit, you are not under the Law.*"

We are here in the presence of a regime of life which is peculiar to those who have crossed the threshold of "perfection"—I mean that perfection of evangelic love where one must always progress and which will never be completed here below. Here again I must use the language of theologians: "Led by the Spirit of God", they live no longer under the regime of morality but under the regime of contemplation and of the gifts of the Spirit; in other words these gifts over which theologians are invited to ponder by a famous text of Isaiah, and which make men docile to divine inspiration, have become the habitual principles of their conduct, henceforth animating and guiding them in such a way that their state of life is characterized thereby. These men are borne by the breath of the Spirit, and "no one knows whence it comes or where it goes; so is everyone who is born of the Spirit".[1] They walk upon the earth as others do and nothing distinguishes them from others externally. But they run, because the wings of an eagle which have invisibly sprouted forth on their shoulders make their steps lighter.[2] Bergson used the word aspiration to designate the most typical characteristic of "open morality". He should have used the word inspiration. If we leave aside all the apparatus of extraordinary phenomena, with which common usage, whether it be a question of poetry or sanctity, has foolishly dressed up this word, we must say that those who attain to the perfection of the moral life are necessarily *inspired* men.

The soul which has passed under the regime of the gifts acts according to higher standards than those of human reason; the *medium virtutis*, the just mean of which Aristotle spoke, has been carried to a higher level than that of the natural virtues.[3] This is why the saints ordinarily surprise us; their style is not the one to which we are accustomed.

It is our reason that (even when we make use of the theological virtues) heads our activity. With them, it is the Spirit of God who heads their activity; their reason commands only in being itself acted upon. The man who lives under the regime of the gifts has been—although freer than ever[4]—dis-

[1] *John*, 3: 8.

[2] Cf. John of Saint Thomas, *The Gifts of the Holy Ghost*, trans. by Dominic Hughes, New York: Sheed and Ward, 1951, p. 30; London: Sheed and Ward, 1950.

[3] Cf., *mutatis mutandis*, our remarks on the acquired moral virtues and the infused moral virtues in *Science and Wisdom*, New York: Scribners, 1954, pp. 210–220; London: Bles, 1940.

[4] "... the Lord requires as the very first step in the way of the Spirit that birth from the Spirit contribute to man's freedom of choice rather than take it away. For there would be a great loss in merit if the Spirit determined the will and worked in it by violence rather than by breathing and actuating its inclinations. For this reason the Apostle wrote that *the*

possessed of himself. He has had to pass through mutations worse than death in order to attain this state of deprivation, the condition of his transformation. But in being dispossessed of himself he has entered into the freedom of autonomy to which we all aspire, from however far it may be. He is no longer under the regime of the law; the law no longer curbs his will. He does what the law prescribes, and incomparably better than those who have not crossed the threshold of the inspired life, but he does it by following the attraction of his love and the very instinct of his will, which has ceased to belong to him, and belongs only to the one he loves. He henceforth does only what he wishes, wishing only what the loved one wishes.

14. The truths which I have just recalled were not discovered and formulated by moral philosophy. They spring from a higher source. They correspond, nevertheless, to an aspiration (a trans-natural aspiration) so deeply rooted in man that many philosophers have undergone its attraction, and have tried to transpose it into purely rational terms,[1] an attempt which, lacking the indispensable data, could only be disappointing. And the fact remains that if moral philosophy is really concerned with concrete human conduct and possesses the least existential and genuinely practical value, it cannot be ignorant of that in which the perfection of moral life precisely consists, and of the supreme point whose attraction is exercised upon the ocean of the human heart, either to raise it up to the heroism of true freedom or to spill its energies in pathetically vain tidal waves.

If moral philosophy attempts to express the truths in question in its own language, it will be led to say, I believe, that if most men (even when they have received gifts superior to nature, but leave them more or less unused) live in fact under the regime of morality—where reason exercises its office as immediate rule of human acts only in imposing constraint on a world of desires, instincts and passions drawn of itself toward forbidden goods—a certain number of men, on the other hand, live under a regime which is not that of morality, and which can be called the regime of supra-morality, where they have

---

spirits of the prophets are under the control of the prophets. This is interpreted by St. Thomas to mean that as far as the use of the power of announcing prophecies is concerned the spirits are subject to the will of the prophet and are not like delirious ravings.

"The gifts of the Holy Ghost, therefore, are given to the soul after the manner of habits, so that in a rational and voluntary way the soul may be moved to those works to which it is directed by the Spirit. Thus, those who are conducted by the Spirit are moved not as slaves but as free men, willingly and voluntarily, since the principles which move them, though derived from the Spirit, are inherent in their very souls. They are impelled to operations which by their character and measure exceed all ordinary human standards." John of Saint Thomas, *op. cit.*, p. 28.

[1] I am thinking for example of the Stoic notion of interior freedom (the sage, even in chains, is the equal of Jupiter), or the Spinozist doctrine of the knowledge of the third genus.

conquered their freedom of autonomy and are delivered from all servitude, even in regard to the moral law and reason. In this sense we can say, adopting the phrase of Pierre Mesnard *à propos* of Kierkegaard, that they have "cracked the ceiling of morality"—not, certainly, to pass beyond the distinction between good and evil, but to do the good without their will being curbed by the law.

Such a regime pertains to an order superior to nature, as, each in his own way, Kierkegaard and Bergson have given witness. Here we must point out that Kierkegaard has shown a good deal more deeply and explicitly than Bergson the properly supernatural character, in the Christian sense of the word, of the regime of life in question, and the essential role that faith plays in it. But what Bergson has pointed out better than Kierkegaard is that the "absolute relation", to speak like Kierkegaard, which then exists, above the whole cosmos, between God and the individual subjectivity—let us say the relation of person to person, in the bosom of that other world which is the world of the Godhead and of participation in the Godhead through grace, between the human self and the Divine Self—is normally established, not in virtue of a singular command received from the Almighty through faith, but in virtue of the communion of love, still more singular, still more unique (and which overflows in charity upon the whole of humanity and the whole created universe) with the Ultimate End which is Subsistent Love, and into the very life of which man has been introduced. In loving all men the saint is more than ever alone with God. As Bergson has put it so well, "any mind that sets out on the mystic way, beyond the city gates, feels more or less distinctly that he is leaving men and gods behind him".[1]

We have noted above that one of Bergson's conspicuous merits in the domain of moral philosophy is to have opposed the abortive love which atheistic altruism offers us with the authentic love for all men—"through God, in the strength of God, he loves all mankind with a divine love"[2]—and to have called it by its true name, which is charity. It is this love of charity which, when it has entered into possession of a soul and assumes there without obstacle its full dimensions, introduces man into the regime of supra-morality. *That* love is not sentimentality, it passes through the intellect and bathes in its light. One of its peculiar signs is that by this very charity with which man loves Him from whom moral law emanates, he also loves moral law itself—the psalms of the Bible are flowing with this love of charity for the divine law. If any false love whatsoever, carried away by an intoxication with mystical quietism, or by an intoxication with pride, or by an intoxication with pity, claims to bring us a freedom of its own making by usurping the place of authentic love, it is not into the regime of supra-morality that it will introduce the human being, but into a regime of self-deception whose destructive power is without limits.

[1] *The Two Sources*, pp. 222–223. [2] *Ibid.*, p. 233.

15. How can we characterize the regime of supra-morality? We will say that the soul has left the level at which comes into being the system of values, norms and prescriptions which are proper to morality and which concern, in the last analysis, all those things which, whatever their intrinsic worth may be, play the part of means in relation to the Ultimate End of human life. The soul is no longer centered in that specifically human world, in that world apart from the Ultimate End, which is the world of morality. It has moved to a higher level, where life with the Ultimate End Itself has begun here and now, the level of mutual relations of love with the ultimate End. Only one thing matters for man from that point on, only one thing gives form to his actions: to do what God, whom he loves, wishes. For all that, it is necessary for him to know in fact what God wishes; he knows it through the moral law, by which God beckons to him, and—in what concerns the manner (more unique than ever) of applying the law in a given particular situation—through the inspiration which guides his natural powers of practical discernment. Kierkegaard was in quest of a perfect individualization in the relationship between God and the subjectivity. Well, it is through love that this perfect individualization is brought about. And on this plane it is a question only of loving, and following what love demands; on this plane the celebrated saying: love and do what you wish, is realized in its fullness.

In the regime of morality the human soul is in contact with God (with God as First Cause) through the intermediary of the law, under which it finds itself. In the regime of supra-morality, the human soul is in direct and immediate contact with God (with God as Friend), and it is no longer under the law but in connivance with it.

Morality is neither supplanted, nor abolished, nor "suspended". It is present in its entirety, but transferred to a level which is not its own. Absorbed in love, not by way of disintegration, but by way of transfiguration, it is there (*formaliter-eminenter*) under a more elevated mode than its own, that of the freedom proper to the regime of supra-morality.

Moral law is observed better than ever, but it is no longer a yoke which constrains the will, it is a message which informs the intelligence how to please Him Whom one loves. It is in riveting his eyes on the hands of the beloved that the friend *does what he wants*—what they want.

Moral obligation is always present, and is exercised with a delicacy more inflexible than ever, but the impalpable force with which what is perceived by the intellect binds the will is no longer only connatural with the essence of the will and with its primordial natural determination; it is connatural also with the love in which the freedom of the will is fulfilled, and the option to which the will commits itself takes shape; the bonds of obligation are now means for the freedom or autonomy of love.

Reason remains the proximate rule of human acts: but it is so no longer insofar as it is mere reason, or even insofar as it is reason enlightened by faith;

it is so insofar as it is reason elevated to the superhuman in its very mode of operation, and carried beyond itself by an inspiration which proceeds from the Spirit of God, and from the experience of divine things. From this very fact its standards, as I have previously pointed out, are no longer the same. Moreover, reason has lost its royal function in regard to the governing of human conduct. It still holds the helm, but it does so in being moved by Another—and a better One (since, as Aristotle says, the principle of reason is better than reason), to whom love, at last freeing us from ourselves, and from every servitude, has freely handed over everything.

Theological and Moral

16. Hence what Bergson called open morality in opposition to closed morality must really be considered as supra-morality consummating or transfiguring, in raising it up to itself, morality strictly speaking. And if one takes this supra-morality in the state of fullness or in the integrity of its dimensions, one sees that it constitutes the regime of life which theology characterizes as connected with mystical ways and the habitual influence of the gifts of the Spirit.

In this perspective it appears that the law performs, as Saint Paul said, a pedagogical function, and little by little educates us to pass on to a stage where the very law becomes connatural to us and we become capable of the "freedom of sons". The rules of morality, as they have taken shape in the course of the development of culture—and with the assistance of the social codes of the tribe, then of the city—of themselves impose on the individual so heavy a yoke that many, as a matter of fact, choose the course of violating them more or less openly and in a greater or lesser degree, and that certain theorists, led astray by the kind of tragic pity to which Luther had submitted, regard these rules, as Freud did, for example, as a nemesis responsible for the torments of mankind.

These theorists do not see that the rules in question, while exacting hard sacrifices from individuals, are the safeguard of the human race, which can live only in a state of culture and has no protection against stagnation and death unless difficult things are constantly required of it, let us say, in extreme terms, unless the impossible is demanded of it, and unless it is drawn, even though by force, toward an ideal superior to the behavior of which the average man is naturally capable.

Let us add that if, in fact, although by right all are called to it, the entrance into the regime of supra-morality remains the privilege of a small number (smaller certainly than it could and should be), in return however the energies and gifts of a superior order whose blooming coincides with the entrance into the regime of supra-morality are already—if human liberty does not resist God—substantially present for us, I mean for the huge mass of the "imperfect", at the very core of morality, in such a way as to diminish the heaviness of the law's yoke, and to make possible what was naturally impossible. For grace is given to everyone who does not refuse it. The main element in the Old Law, Saint Thomas said, consisted of the moral prescriptions and the rites, it did not bring with it the Holy Spirit, by whom charity is diffused in our hearts;[1] while "what matters above all in the law of the new covenant, and that in which all its virtue consists, is the grace of the Holy Spirit which is given by living faith".[2] "The main element in the New Law consists in the spiritual grace infused into hearts", and this is why "it is called the law of love".[3] Let us say, using our own vocabulary, that what the New Law has, by right, opened to mankind is the regime of supra-morality (even though for many, in fact, it may remain in an inchoate and merely nascent state, and be consequently substituted for, concealed and masked by the regime of morality).[4]

17. As we have already noted in a preceding chapter,[5] one of the basic changes introduced by Christianity with respect to the moral systems of antiquity has been to place above the virtues called *moral* the virtues called *theological*, which belong to an order superior to nature and reason, and whose object is the mystery of the Godhead. It is these virtues (accompanied by the gifts of the Holy Spirit, as auxiliary forces) which henceforth have the primacy in the moral life of men. Prudence has lost its supreme rank, love passes above it; charity is the "form" of all the other virtues, and without it man is morally only an invalid. It is by charity, which is superior to nature, that man is called to love efficaciously the Principle of Being above all things.

These are the truths on which, implicitly or explicitly, Bergson has directed the attention of moral philosophy. As we have previously written, "in having the moral appendant to the supra-moral, that is to say the theological, in having the law appendant to love and freedom, Bergson saves morality".[6]

By the same token he makes us see, let me observe in passing, one of the two most basic reasons why there is no true ethics where the existence of the

[1] Cf. *Sum. theol.*, I–II, q. 107, a. 1 and *ad* 2.

[2] *Ibid.*, q. 106, a. 1.

[3] *Ibid.*, q. 107, a. 1, *ad* 2; cf. same article, *ad* 3.

[4] "The New Law makes us enter under a rule which is not the one I have here called the rule of morality, but a rule in which morality, not only safeguarded, but interiorized, deepened and refined, is suspended from the redemptive love of Christ." Raïssa Maritain, *op. cit.*, p. 79.

It is indeed in this way that the *general* rule under which humanity lives today is *rightly* characterized (at least in those places where the Gospel has been preached). But what we are speaking of in the present chapter is the *particular* rule under which such and such an individual was *factually* placed. He who does not have grace lives under the rule of morality (not without summons and solicitations which come to him from on high); he who has grace but remains carnal lives inchoatively under the rule of supra-morality but effectively under the rule of morality; he who has grace and is led by the Spirit lives effectively under the rule of supra-morality.

[5] See above, chapter 5, pp. 79–81.

[6] Cf. *Bergsonian Philosophy and Thomism*, p. 344.

transcendent God is not recognized. This reason is that moral life is firmly established in rectitude only by charity. The other reason is that only the transcendent God who is Subsistent Truth can in the last analysis establish a moral law and moral values which impose themselves on the conscience in an unconditional way—and without which there is no longer anything to guide our conduct, except means justified by the end. The great theories of atheism do not hesitate to make the negation of God the first principle of their moral philosophies. It is strange that philosophers for whom God exists show themselves more faint-hearted, and set to work constructing an ethics without making it essentially depend, as on its first principle, on that Existence in pure act which no philosophy can recognize as it ought without finding itself, by such an acceptance of the mystery of transcendence, totally separated from the world of faint-heartedness of mind.

But let us leave this parenthesis. The fact that the moral order is suspended from the theological order, or, if you prefer another perhaps more accurate formula, that the theological order is at the core of the moral order, is not true only for men who live under the regime of supra-morality, it is true also for all of us, who remain in the clutches of the law's constraint, even when the good news of the Gospel and the life of grace have planted freedom in us. Whence it comes that we yearn for the freedom of the Spirit. It is the theological, it is the love of charity, along with faith and hope, which foments in us the aspiration to pass under the regime of the gifts. It is the same fire which here smolders under the ashes, and there inflames the whole soul.

18. Bergson comes back again and again to the theme that the two moralities, closed morality and open morality, interpenetrate each other. "The general formula of morality accepted today by civilized humanity . . . includes two things, a system of orders dictated by *impersonal* social requirements, and a series of *appeals* made to the conscience of each of us by *persons* who represent the best there is in humanity."[1] On the one hand an obligation originally and basically infra-intellectual; on the other hand, a supra-intellectual emotion. "The two forces, working in different regions of the soul, are projected on to the intermediary plane, which is that of intelligence. They will henceforth be represented by their projections. These intermingle and interpenetrate. The result is a transposition of orders and appeals into terms of pure reason. Justice thus finds itself continually broadened by charity; charity assumes more and more the shape of justice . . ."[2]

I have pointed out above the shortcomings of this theory. What I would like to remark now is that the Bergsonian theme of the interpenetration of the "two moralities" keeps its worth if, from the typically Bergsonian perspective of the relationship between closed morality and open morality, you transfer

[1] *The Two Sources*, p. 84.
[2] *Ibid.*, pp. 84–5.—Cf. *ibid.*, p. 59 (cited above p. 419, note 3).

it into the truer perspective of the relationship between morality and supra-morality. Morality and supra-morality necessarily interpenetrate one another. Why should we be surprised at this if all that has been said in the two preceding sections is true?

That the moral penetrates the supra-moral is true in many senses. Have we not seen that in the whole regime of supra-morality, morality still remains, transfigured no doubt, but safeguarded in its entirety? Is it not clear, moreover, that if the soul of the saints is constantly ready to be moved by divine inspiration, in many cases however it does not act under any particular inspiration given here and now? Their reason then rules their conduct according to its ordinary natural mode, not as elevated to and as carrying a supra-human mode and moved by an instinct which transcends it. They live under the breath of the Spirit, but sometimes the high winds risk blowing the sails away, sometimes, and more often, it is a light breeze which merely helps the work of the oars.

If it is a question now of the multitude of those who are not saints, we must say that the very regime of morality, the regime of the law curbing rebellious hearts, is necessary for them—I mean *under a certain aspect*, or to the extent to which the life of the spirit, supposing they have received it, is not yet fully developed in them (although it already bears witness in them, even though inchoatively and intermittently, to the primacy of the theological).

But there is in addition a completely different way—this time I am speaking of an aberrant phenomenon, and of a betrayal of the spirit—in which it happens that the moral flows back in us upon the supra-moral: one witnesses then an attempt of the regime of morality to submit to itself *purely and simply*, and without any longer taking account of the primacy of the theological, those for whom, as I just observed, this regime remains necessary because they have not yet become fully what they are, but who have nevertheless received in its principle and in its germ the condition of freedom proper to the New Law and to the children of "that Jerusalem which is above".[1] Is it not a natural tendency (all too *natural*) for many Christians to try unconsciously to transform their religion into a mere system of orders and constraints, or into a mere moral system? Then, and by a kind of counterattack of the sociological factor, they look as if they were forgetting grace in order to think only of the law. Thus certain ministers of the Gospel apply themselves less to preaching the Gospel than to a constant reiteration of obligations upheld by the law of fear; and thus in former days Christian crowds milled together around the pillory in order to taste the joys and the spectacle of punishment; and thus the Puritans believed themselves bound, if not to stone, at least to mark with a scarlet letter, in order to separate her from the group and spread in everyone the terror of the law, the one of whom Jesus had said: "He that is without sin among you, let him first cast a stone at her."

[1] Saint Paul, *Gal.*, 4: 26.

19. And that the supra-moral penetrates the moral is equally true, in many senses. Have we not seen that in fact, in the concrete condition in which humanity finds itself, the supra-moral is at the core of the moral? Isn't it prescribed to everyone—even to those who although set free by the New Law keep on living, at least as regards the immense mass of their most frequent acts and problems, under the regime of fear and morality—to tend toward the perfection of human life, that is to say toward the perfection of theological charity, each according to his condition and his potentialities? Doesn't Saint Thomas Aquinas teach, in a text which I cited above, that "what matters above all in the law of the new covenant, and *that in which all its power consists*, is the grace of the Holy Spirit which is given by living faith"?[1] These are the truths which Bergson really affirmed when in reference to the advent of Christianity he said in his own way that "the essence of the new religion was to be the diffusion of mysticism",[2] or again that "in this sense, religion is to mysticism what popularization is to science".[3] Let us not forget either that under the impact of the supra-moral the moral has been rendered and continues to be progressively rendered more refined in its own order, more demanding on the one hand and more comprehensive and compassionate on the other, in short more authentically human, and has descended much deeper into the inner movements and invisible recesses where prior to every exterior act man already commits himself to decisive responsibilities.

A final point should be mentioned: at the very heart of the regime of morality which in fact remains prevalent in the vast human family of those who have never taken and will never take the decisive step, it is necessary that touches of what is peculiar to the regime of supra-morality intervene from time to time in human life, if it is finally to escape failure, and attain in spite of everything to a kind of melodic form or completion which gives it a value superior to time, and to death.

At this point the theologians tell us in their language that the gifts of the Holy Spirit, by which man is made ready to be moved by divine inspiration, are necessary for salvation, and are therefore present in whoever has not refused grace.[4] In his own words the philosopher will say that in the evening of his pilgrimage every man—except the saints perhaps—has, in going over his past, the more or less keen feeling that he has bungled his life; as regards, in particular, what was morally required of him he sees so many gaps and weaknesses in what he has done that the chain of his acts appears, taken as a whole, decidedly beneath the demands of the law. Where, in looking at the tableau of his life, will he find hope, if not in some act perhaps, however small it may be, which was not required by the law but to which a movement of love or compassion carried him, and which, going beyond what is strictly demanded in

[1] *Sum. theol.*, I–II, q. 106, a. 1. (Italics ours.)
[2] *The Two Sources*, p. 238.
[3] *Ibid.*, p. 239. [4] *Sum. theol.*, I–II, q. 68, a. 2.

the manner of the evangelical counsels, may perhaps have been somehow capable of raising things to their proper level?

The supererogatory ways of acting of which I have just spoken depend on a moment when the human soul went beyond the standard of sole reason. Some will hold this moment, as we do, to be a moment of secret inspiration. Others, to whom it seems that then reason has lost control, will regard it as a moment of bewilderment of the mind. As a matter of fact the name is of little importance. What matters is the fact that in such moments the ordinary rules are displaced, and in a manner which responds to the spirit of the Gospel—in order to give assistance to human life and to straighten it out. A trifle then, a certain act of giving, of giving away, of forgiving, made almost without thinking, a little water offered to a poor man, a little suffering accepted through pity, a refusal to demand one's due, the simple fact of being present at the material or moral distress of another, or of listening to his despair, a word said for justice or for truth, any task whatever undertaken and pursued through fidelity to some singular call and with a little fraternal love; or else, on the contrary, an exceptionally great act, the long acceptance of a suffering which revolts nature, or of an intolerable burden carried in order to relieve the needs of an ungrateful person, a sacrifice in which the soul truly immolates what it most treasures; there is no common measure for the different kinds of "bewilderment" in question. It is sufficient that there passes into them the force of a love which has no bounds and which is like the breath of Uncreated Love; a human life has borne fruit.

15

BRIEF REMARKS IN CONCLUSION

The method followed in this book

1. May I be permitted to confess that the composing of this large work has brought the author, in addition, a satisfaction of a subjective order? It was, at a time of life when the soul turns towards higher regions, a way for me to pay my respects to, and thus take leave of, the philosophers—in particular the modern philosophers, whose historical work it was once claimed I purely and simply rejected. I believe on the contrary that I have given due credit to them, and that I have, at least after my early years, shown them the sort of intellectual friendship which is proper among seekers and disputants each attached to his own vision. How better to honor them than by taking their effort seriously; by trying to understand and penetrate their movement of thought; by applying oneself to disengage their central intuitions and intentions, and the advances one owes to them; finally, by criticizing them, where they are in error, without indulgence or caution (what philosopher ever asked for indulgence?) but with more attention doubtless and more true respect than they ordinarily show one another. However, I will not be sorry to shake them off.

But let us leave that. The real purpose of my book has nothing to do with the subjective satisfaction mentioned above. As I indicated in the Preface, what I proposed to do was to employ an historical and critical analysis of sufficient depth as an instrument of exploration of the field of moral philosophy. The unfolding of the ethical theories that can be considered the most significant, the apperceptions from which they have sprung, the errors from which they have suffered, thus enable one to have a better awareness of the problematic proper to moral philosophy. And many essential truths are at the same stroke gathered in along the way, in a manner that is non-systematic but perhaps more stimulating for the mind, because they emerge from the long reflection that is pursued from age to age, with its advances and its failures, and from the successive occasions that it offers for discussion. I think that in a general way such a procedure, turning to account, under a resolutely critical light, a heritage of time-honored labors and disputes, could be carried out with advantage by the disciples of the *philosophia perennis* in the most varied fields.

2. It was, I believe, particularly necessary to have recourse to this historico-critical method in the field of moral philosophy, so as to rediscover in a sufficiently concrete and comprehensive manner its place and function among the

philosophical disciplines, and at the same time to recognize its essential distinction from anthropology, on the one hand, and moral theology, on the other, with both of which it is however closely associated.

In the course of our long study we have thus seen take shape little by little the basic notions that must be regarded as the primary notions of moral philosophy, and with which the various thinkers we have considered have all had to do in some way, sending them back and forth, so to speak, from one to the other, to play with them in different ways. "When you play tennis," Pascal said, "you both play with the same ball, but one places it better."

We have likewise seen take shape the principal problems to which the ethician must apply himself, the first of which has to do with the very nature of moral philosophy, its practical and normative (in a sense not at all Kantian) function, its essentially reflexive character, its dependence with regard to certain great metaphysical truths and its dependence with regard to experience, the relations it maintains with the religious experience of mankind and with the theological data concerning the existential condition of man. We have met on our way many other fundamental problems, in particular the problem of natural law and the problem of the relationship between ethics and supra-ethics.

I shall not undertake to enumerate here all the primary notions and all the basic problems to which I have just alluded. Indeed, our whole second volume, given over to the doctrinal examination of the great problems, must constitute the normal conclusion to the long historico-critical introduction that has been the object of the present volume.

On some possible renewals

3. I should like to propose now some remarks of a quite different order. The first have to do with the great challenges to accepted ideas that took place in the course of the nineteenth century, and from which the coarsest materialist metaphysics or anti-metaphysics at first tried to claim the profit. I am thinking of the three great intellectual shocks that shook the confidence of man in himself, and which in reality could be salutary and powerfully assist moral philosophy if we knew how to understand things as they should be understood, and if modern man, instead of abdicating under humiliation, stood erect again in the two conjoined virtues of humility and magnanimity.

The first great disturbance was produced by Darwinism, with the theory of the animal origin of man. Such a shock can have a double result: a result ruinous for moral life, and which dehumanizes man, if one believes that man is only an evolved monkey; one has then the materialist ethic of the struggle for life.

But the same shock can have a salutary result if one understands things in another way, if one understands that the matter out of which man is made is an animal matter, but an animal matter informed by a spiritual soul, so that there is biological continuity in the sense of the natural sciences between the universe of the animal and the universe of man, but irreducible metaphysical discontinuity. The scientific concept of evolution is then likely to lead us to a better appreciation of the vicissitudes and the progress of human history, and to an ethic more conscious of the material roots of the rational animal, of the depths of the dynamism of the irrational element in him, but also of the deeper depths of the dynamism of the spirit in him that makes his grandeur.

4. A second shock was that of Marxism, with its insistence on the economic substructure of our moral ideas and of our rules of moral behavior. Here again a double result is possible. The result is ruinous for human life if one fancies that all that is not the economic factor is only an epiphenomenal superstructure; one moves then towards a materialist ethic—either towards a materialist ethic suspended from the myth of technocracy organizing human life on the basis of pure productivity; or towards a materialist ethic such as the Marxist ethic, suspended from the myth of revolution and from that of the self-creation of man manifested by the titanic struggle of the working class freeing itself through violence from a condition presumed to be irremediably servile, and by the final coming of a universal communist society.

The result can be salutary if the shock in question forces us to be aware of the interdependence and interaction, interpreted in an Aristotelian sense, of economic factors and moral or spiritual factors. Ethics becomes then more conscious of the concrete situation of man, and of the meeting of structures and conditionings dependent upon material causality with what, in the order of formal causality, constitutes morality. A new field of exploration is opened up for ethics, a field independent in itself of the Marxist theory, which however supplied the impulse for this new problematic.

5. The third shock finally was that of the discoveries of Freud, bringing to light the autonomous life and the swarming activity of the unconscious, and the ruses by which it seeks to take control of human conduct.

The result is ruinous for human life if man is looked upon as a creation of mere infra-rational tendencies, of libido and of the unconscious of instinct, without reason being thought to possess any vitality and energy of its own or to exercise any control other than a purely extrinsic one over the forces in conflict in the determinism of nature, and without one's according any reality to the universe of liberty which is the very universe of morality.

The result is salutary if the shock in question leads us to recognize the immense universe of instincts and tendencies at the point of which reason and liberty work. Then ethics becomes more conscious of the concrete situation (no longer social, but psychological) of man, and of the meeting of the precombined structures and disguises of the unconscious with moral conscience. Thence an ethic more truly human, in this sense that it will know better what is human, and in this sense that it will care with more pity for man and his wounds.

The great problem of the relations between the conscious and the unconscious will be one of its principal concerns. It will be a question of establishing a normal relation between the dreaming and sleeping part of man and the waking part. It can happen that the waking part may exercise no rule, no control, or a pseudo-control only, over the dreaming part. Man is then the plaything of unconscious tendencies, which a banal process of lying rationalization will endeavor only to justify.

It can also happen, on the contrary, that the waking part may mistrust the dreaming part, hold it in contempt, and fear it, to such a degree that it may wish at any price to become conscious of all that takes place in us, to light up forcibly all the innermost recesses and to put conscious reason and deliberate will at the origin of all the movements of the soul. It is to be feared that this second method succeeds mainly in developing neuroses and in bringing about the victory of the disguises and ruses of the unconscious.

In other words, a despotic regime with regard to the unconscious is no better than an anarchic regime. What should be sought is—to use one of Aristotle's words—a *politic* control, that is, a control exercising an authority that would be without violence and based on friendship, taming to the spirit the vital spontaneities, in short, supposing a certain confidence in the sleeping part of man and a progressive purification of it. Such a purification is not brought about by trying to make this unconscious emerge from sleep, but by being at once attentive to this sleep and respectful of it, and by recognizing with an entirely frank and pure glance, without fright and without connivance, all that emerges from this sleeping part.[1]

What would also be required, and first of all, is to recognize the existence in man of another unconscious[2] than the animal unconscious of instinct, desires and images, repressed tendencies and traumatic memories, which asks only to be closed up in itself as an inferno of the soul. This other unconscious is the unconscious or pre-conscious of the spirit, which is not separated from the world of conscious activity and the works of reason, but on the contrary is their living source. It is on the activating motions—when man does not betray them—and the radiance of this spiritual unconscious on the whole soul, that depends above all the long work through which the instinctive spontaneities can be, as I said above, *tamed* to the spirit.

[1] See above the remarks made on the *know thyself* (apropos Kierkegaard), chapter XIII, pp. 355–356.

[2] See my book *Creative Intuition in Art and Poetry*, New York: Pantheon, 1953, pp. 91–92; pocketbook edition, New York: Meridian Books, 1955, p. 67; London: Harvill, 1954.

Man and the Human Condition—a problem preliminary to any moral systematization

6. The considerations that follow do not have to do with doctrines and systems, they bear on human conduct itself and on the most general options with which our attitude in life is linked. These considerations are connected however in an indirect way with the philosophical positions examined in the present work; every great moral system, indeed, is in reality an effort to ask man, in one manner or another and to one degree or another, to go beyond his natural condition in some way. But either these same great philosophical doctrines refuse to acknowledge the effort in question, or else they leave in a wholly implicit state the problem it envelops. To my mind, on the contrary, it is important to disengage the problem explicitly. One sees then that it concerns the moral life of each one of us in such a fundamental way, and involves so profoundly the individual subjectivity, that it depends, to tell the truth, on a sort of metaphysics of conduct which precedes moral theories and systematizations. If one tries to examine it in itself, reducing things to the essential, one is led, it seems to me, to distinguish the four different attitudes I am about to discuss, of which the first two, more or less outlined, in fact, in the lives of certain among us, but impossible to carry through, are too irrational to correspond to any definite doctrine; and of which the last two correspond, one to the thought of India, the other, inchoatively, to the Western philosophical tradition, and, under its perfected and really effective form, to Christian thought.

The fact is, I believe, that in the background of all our moral difficulties there is a fundamental problem which is ineluctably posed for each of us, and which in practice is never fully resolved, except in those who have entered into the ways of perfection: the problem of the relation of man to the human condition, or of his attitude in the face of the human condition.

This condition is that of a spirit united in substance with flesh and engaged in the universe of matter. It is an unhappy condition. In itself it is such a miserable condition that man has always dreamed of a golden age when he was more or less freed of it, and so miserable that on the plane of revelation, the Christian religion teaches that mankind was created, with the grace of Adam, in a superior condition in which it was free of sin, of pain, of servitude and of death, and from which it fell through its own fault. The Judeo-Christian tradition also teaches that after the end of history and in a new world the human condition will be supernaturally transfigured. Those who believe neither in the state of innocence nor in original sin put the golden age at the end of history, not at the beginning, and fancy that man will attain it in the last stage of his terrestrial adventure, through his own liberating effort, thanks to science and to radical social transformations; others, who want no part of consoling illusions, try to escape the spectacle of this planet by surrendering to some powerful passion which distracts them day after day from themselves and from the world, or by the ardor of a despairing pity which in a way appeases their hearts while it corrodes them little by little.

Indeed, the tragic perplexity in which we are placed consists in the fact that we can neither refuse the human condition nor accept it purely and simply. I will explain later on in what sense I understand the expression "to accept *purely and simply* the human condition". As to refusing the human condition, it is clear that it is a question there only of a moral disposition. Such a refusal belongs to the world of dream; but man nourishes himself on dreams, and a dream which has its roots in the depths of the individual psychology of the subject can determine his fundamental attitude in life.

The temptation to refuse the Human Condition

7. It is solely in the perspective of nature that we shall consider things in this and the three following sections. We have just noted that the human condition is an unhappy condition. The state of intermediary species is in general a state little to be envied; and it is in a paradoxically eminent manner that the human species, at once flesh and spirit, is an intermediary species. The heavens tell of the glory of God, but the earth that He has made is dreadful to man. A "vale of tears", yes, and this is not a mere poetic image.

It is not a question here of any sort of Manichaeism. It is quite true that the material universe abounds in wonders and is resplendent with an inexhaustible beauty that makes apparent the mark of the Spirit Who created it; it is quite true that despite the cruelty and voracity which inhabit it the world of nature is penetrated with the goodness and the generosity of being, and embraces finally all things in the imperturbable peace of its great laws, and of its great rational necessities which superbly ignore us; it is quite true that in man himself the world of the senses, whatever bitterness it may harbor, is made first and above all to enchant us with its sweetnesses and its joys; it is quite true that human nature is good in its essence, and that for every living being, but eminently for man, to live is a marvellous gift. And yet, for all that, a spirit whose operations have need of matter surmounts matter only at a formidable price and by running immense risks, and is most often scoffed at by it. The spirit is immortal, and matter imposes the law of death on the body animated by it. Man has more grandeur than the Milky Way; but how easy evil is for him, how inevitable (if one considers the species collectively) it is, in a being in which sense and instinct, and the animal unconscious, ask only to elude or to twist the judgment of the mind. As for suffering, it is already a frightful thing to see an animal suffer, but the suffering of beasts is of small account in comparison with the suffering that pierces a flesh united to spirit, or spirit itself.

8. Thus we can understand that the temptation to refuse the human condition has a greater chance of worming its way into us when man has in one

manner or another become better aware of the natural exigencies of the spirit in him—of that spirit which is his soul, and which reveals itself to him in the highest powers of the soul. Such a temptation does not exist in the primitives. We may believe that in the collective history of mankind it is largely this temptation which, at work in us without our being aware of it, makes the very progress through which civilization advances go side by side with delusions which impair it or degradations which corrupt it.

To refuse—in one's innermost heart—the human condition, is either to dream of leaving our limits and to wish to enjoy a total liberty in which our nature would expand through its own powers; or else to play the pure spirit (what I once called the sin of angelism); or else to curse and try to disown all that presents an obstacle to the life of the intellect, and to live in a state of interior revolt against the fact that one is a man; or else to flee by no matter what frenzy, even if it be in the folly of the flesh, this situation of a reason everywhere at loggerheads with matter which is a permanent challenge to the demands of the spirit in us. It is hardly surprising that those who devote themselves to the life of the intelligence, the poet in particular, and the philosopher, are more or less exposed to this temptation. The ancient sages of Greece succumbed to it when they said that the best thing for man is not to have been born.

In the life of an individual the most frequent occasion for this temptation—which does not justify it for all that—is that the man who endeavors, as Aristotle said, "to live according to the intellect", is more conscious than those who live "according to the human" of everything we said above concerning the misery of the human condition. Often even the man dedicated to meditation forgets that the spirit finds, through the senses, the source of its life in the very matter that torments it; he forgets too that the evils that matter causes are made transitory to a certain extent by matter itself, since it is a root principle of change.

But above all, if he pays attention to the lessons of history and to the long cry of the poor and the abandoned, he understands that naked suffering, horror, anguish without consolation—all this is the true background of the world for us, however generous nature may be, and however admirable the victories won by human generations to make things less hostile to man and the structures of his own life more worthy of him, through the progress of civilization, of art and of knowledge. It may be that for a long while we almost lose sight of this background of the world. But every now and then it reappears to us.

The man who has passed the threshold of the life according to the intellect understands all that is offensive and humiliating—for that spirit in which his specific difference itself and his dignity consist—in the radical contingency linked with matter and the dependence with regard to matter which constitute the metaphysical infirmity of our existence. In the eyes of material nature is a man worth any more than the sound of the brook? To pursue its work there the spirit struggles ceaselessly against the fortuitous and the useless; its very movement depends not only on the absolute values in which it has its proper object, it depends also on chance, on good and bad encounters; it advances from generation to generation enduring a perpetual agony, only to have in the end what it has produced here on earth fall—I mean with regard to men, and unless it is divinely protected—under the law of decay and futility which is the law of matter, and only to have what is immortal in itself be received by our species only at the cost of equivocations and misunderstandings that are perpetuated throughout time.

The fact remains that all that must be accepted. Even when they do not repeat in their own way, and however pitifully, the story of Faust, there is no sadder and more fruitless distress than the distress of men who under the pretext of wanting to live according to the intellect allow themselves to be carried away by the temptation to refuse the human condition. They are vanquished beforehand, and their defeat aggravates their subjection.

The temptation to accept purely and simply the Human Condition

9. Would the solution therefore be to accept *purely and simply* the human condition?—This pure and simple acceptance would be just as costly, and is no less impossible. It would be a betrayal of human nature not to recognize the demands, which are consubstantial to it, of the superhuman in man, and this nature's need of the progressive movement of the spirit, with its torments and its dangers, in other words, its need of perpetually going beyond the presently given moment of our condition on earth. And if we want to go beyond it, it is because to that extent we do not accept it without reserve.

It is fitting moreover to see the whole import of the expressions one uses. To accept the human condition is to accept—with all that life offers of the good and the beautiful and the pure, and with all the grandeurs of the spirit, and with "the call of the hero"—the radical contingency, the failures, the servitudes, the immense part of sorrow and (as regards nature) of inevitable uselessness of our existence, sickness, death, the different kinds of tyranny and hypocrisy which prey on social life, the stench of gangrene and the stench of money, the power of stupidity and of the lie. But if it is a question for a man of accepting *purely and simply* the human condition, why then, after all, in accepting all the evil of suffering that our nature entails, should he not accept at the same stroke all the evil of sin to which it is inclined? He has been made as he is, with the weaknesses of his flesh and the covetousness that is in him, with the longing for pleasure and power and the rage of desires, of that obsessing desire especially which does not come from him but from his species, to which his individual person matters little but which has need of his chromosomes in order to perpetuate itself. All that also is part of the human condition. To accept *purely and simply* (if that were possible) the human condition, means to accept it in its entirety, with the misery of sin as well as with the misery of suffering.

This cannot be, moreover, without a fundamental contradiction and without additional torments. For the social groups—horde or society—and the state of culture without which the human species cannot endure on earth require rules and taboos guaranteed by terrifying sanctions; and it is essential to the human condition that the sense of moral obligation, and of the distinction between good and evil, which exists naturally in the soul of each one of us (and which is in itself contradictory to the acceptance of moral evil as supposedly required by our nature), exert itself at least under the wholly exteriorized form of obedience to tribal prohibitions, and according as good and evil appear only as what is permitted or forbidden by the social group. To accept *purely and simply* the human condition is therefore an intrinsically contradictory moral disposition (although more or less outlined in fact in a great number of human beings)—a disposition to accept not only subjection to Sin as well as subjection to Suffering, but also subjection to the law of Fear, which forbids certain definite faults as infractions of the general conduct and the rules of the closed society.

Supposing that it could be fully carried out, such an acceptance of the human condition would make man live on the edge of animality; it is, as we have noted, as impossible in reality as the refusal of the human condition, because to accept fully subjection to moral evil, in whatever manner one conceives it, is not possible for the human being. What we are calling *pure and simple* acceptance of the human condition is only a limit to which, even in its most primitive representatives, our species has never attained. Indeed, it is in more or less approaching this limit that many among us seem to accept purely and simply the human condition. They accept it *almost* purely and simply. They not only have the code of their gang, their class or their accustomed social group (which implies already, though under a very inferior form, the prohibition of wrongdoing), they have also an outline at least, and often a great deal more than an outline, of authentic moral life, by reason of which they do not love the evil that they do. But even if their conscience has in other respects firm convictions, there are a certain number of domains—notably the domain of sex, and, in certain periods, that of "honor" (duel), and that of war—in which to act without taking account of the moral law seems normal in their eyes: it's the human condition that requires it, they believe that at this point it imposes another code on them. Perhaps however they will repent one day of the actions thus committed in contempt of the moral law (not to speak of many others among us who violate the law only in the pangs of remorse). To do evil and to repent of the evil that one does is the minimum of what the human being is capable of to testify that it is impossible to give in completely to the temptation to accept *purely and simply* the human condition.

The answer to Indian spirituality

10. What is asked of man is neither to accept purely and simply nor to refuse the human condition—it is to transcend it.[1] Here too however two very different ways can be envisaged. It can be a question of transcending the human condition in a manner which implies a certain refusal of it (because in this case it is through his own forces that man has to transcend his condition, he must then engage himself in an effort against the grain of nature); or it can be a question of transcending the human condition while consenting to it (because in this case a "new nature" has been grafted on human nature, and permits man to transcend his condition by going, not against the grain of nature, but higher than nature). The first way corresponds to what we shall call, to be brief, the Hindu-Buddhist solution; the second, to what we shall call the Gospel solution.

By abolishing, by means of a sovereign concentration of the intellect and the will, every particular form and representation, the wisdom of India adheres, through the void, to an absolute which is the Self in its pure metaphysical act of existing—experience conceived as leading at the same stroke either to the Transcendence of Being (Atman) or to total indetermination (nirvâna). All the forms of illusion in the midst of which our life is spent have disappeared, everything is denied and annihilated, there remains only the Self in contact with itself.

It is clear that to attain such an end (not to speak even of the "powers" for which one is supposed to search without pause), is to transcend the human condition by dint of spiritual energy. But it is also clear that it is to transcend it by the means of refusal. The living delivered one gains a sort of interior omnipotence by falling back upon himself and separating himself from everything human; he enters into a solitariness incomparably more profound than the solitude of the hermit, for it is his soul itself which has broken with men and all the miseries of their terrestrial existence. To pass beyond illusion, and to deliver oneself from transmigration, or at least from all the sorrow that it carries with it and perpetuates, is at the same stroke to deliver oneself from the human condition. The refusal of this condition is there but a means of transcending it, it is not an act of revolt against it, a pure and simple refusal. It remains however essential to the spirituality of India. That is why, even when the sage, as in the Buddhism of the Great Vehicle (Mahayana), spreads his pity over men, it is as it were through the condescension of a being who no longer belongs to their species, and whose heart—by the very exigency of

[1] I am not speaking of the Hegelian-Marxist answer to the problem of the human condition. In this perspective it is not a question of transcending the human condition, but of transforming it and finally of deifying it, through the work of history and of man himself. Such a solution rests on a manifestly erroneous philosophical postulate, in which the notion of human nature gives way to that of process of self-creation of man by man.

solitariness in nirvâna—is not wounded by their troubles and does not enter into participation with them.

How can we not see in the implicit refusal of the human condition of which I have just spoken one of the weak points of the spirituality of India? If one considers in itself (independently of the graces which in fact can supervene in a soul of good will) this effort to escape the state in which we are naturally placed by our coming into the world, it manifests, along with an exceptional courage, an exceptional pride of spirit. Moreover such a refusal is in reality doomed, whatever victories it may bring, to a final defeat. Courage and pride are precisely two of the most profound features of the human condition. The Hindu or Buddhist sage quits the human condition only by showing in spite of himself his belonging to it—I mean, by the very negations to which he is led and all the apparatus of exercises and techniques he needs, and by the kind of never-ending *tour de force* by means of which he comes to transcend this condition. And the living delivered one still has to die like the others; he is not delivered from that which is the most tragically human in the human condition.

The Gospel answer

11. What of the Christian or Gospel solution? It takes us beyond pure philosophy and pure reason, and yet, by a strange paradox, it is in it and in the mystery that it proposes to us that an authentically rational attitude toward the human condition becomes possible for man.

I said above that every great moral system is in reality an effort to ask man, in one manner or another and to one degree or another, to go beyond his natural condition in some way. These systems in fact (let us mention here only those which have been examined in the present work) ask man—while he rejects moral evil but accepts the suffering to which the human condition is exposed—to go beyond the human condition: either, as with Plato, Aristotle, the Stoics, Epicurus, Kant, Sartre or Bergson, by attaching himself to a good superior to human life, or to a happiness in which human life is achieved rationally, or to virtue, or to pleasure decanted to the point of indifference, or to duty, or to liberty, or to the sovereign love to which the great mystics call us; or, as with Hegel, Marx, Comte or Dewey, by deifying nature. But even in those cases where the effort to go beyond the human condition is the most authentic, there is no question, except in Bergson (and, in the name of faith, in Kierkegaard) of truly transcending it. And the attempt to go beyond the human condition by the sole means of man remains in the last analysis doomed either to futility or to illusion. It is only with Christianity that the effort to go beyond the human condition comes to real fruition.

It is superfluous to remark that I am not speaking here of the average behavior of the mass of people of Christian denomination. I am speaking of the exigencies of Christianity such as they are proposed to every one—and almost completely realized only in saints.

The question for the Christian is to transcend the human condition but by the grace of God—not, as for the Indian sage, by a supreme concentration on oneself—and in consenting at the same time to this condition, in accepting it, although not purely and simply, without balking; for the Christian accepts it as to all that pertains to the evil of suffering proper to the human condition, not as to what pertains to moral evil and sin. Rupture with the human condition as to sin, acceptance of the human condition as to the radical contingency and as to the suffering as well as to the joys that it entails: that is demanded by reason, but is decidedly possible only by the configuration of grace to Him Who is sanctity itself because He is the Word incarnate. At the same stroke, the acceptance of the human condition ceases to be simple submission to necessity; it becomes active consent, and consent through love.

That in a certain measure every soul inhabited by the gifts of grace, and in a full measure the saint, the one who has entered into what we called in a previous chapter the regime of supra-ethics, transcends the human condition—this is obvious to anyone who holds that grace is a participation in the divine life itself. It is the other aspect of the Gospel solution, the simultaneous acceptance (except as to sin) of the human condition that it is important for us to insist on here.

In the human condition thus transcended and accepted at the same time, everything, to tell the truth, remains the same and everything is transfigured. If grace makes man participate in the divine life and if it superelevates his nature in its own order, nevertheless it is a nature still wounded which is thus superelevated, it is a man still devoured by weakness who shares in eternal life and in God's friendship. The human condition has not changed. It has not changed because the Word of God assumed it such as it was and such as it will remain as long as history endures. In taking upon Himself all the sins of the world, He who was without sin also took upon Himself all the languors of the world, and all the suffering that afflicts the human race, and all the humiliation of its dependence with regard to the contingent and the fortuitous. What matter henceforth the contingency and the metaphysical futility to which our existence is subjected, since the most insignificant of our acts, if it is vivified by charity, has an eternal value, and since the Son of God has accepted to undergo Himself the servitudes of our condition?

During His hidden life He was a poor village workman, and His activity as preacher and miracle-worker took place in an historical milieu which made weigh on Him all its circumstances of time and place and all its hazards. He willed to die as the most unfortunate of men died in His time. His passion was an atrocious condensation of all the agony and abjection attached to the human condition since the Fall.

Consequently, when what I called just now the true background of the world—the world of naked suffering, of horror, of anguish without consolation—reveals itself to the Christian and takes possession of him, this matter of accepting (as to the evil of suffering) the human condition takes on an entirely new sense for him, comes to enter into the redemptive work of the Cross, and to participate in the annihilations of Him Whom he loves.[1] No wonder the saints are desirous of suffering. Suffering, because it is for them a signature of their love, and cooperation in the work of their Beloved, has become for them the most precious of goods here on earth.

There they are, then, the saints, who by an apparent contradition give thanks to God for all the goods He heaps upon them and for all the protections, consolations and joys He dispenses to them, and give thanks to Him at the same time for all the evils and afflictions He sends them. We who are wicked, do we give a stone to our children when they ask us for bread? And yet thanks be to God when He gives us bread, and thanks be to Him when He gives us a stone and worse than a stone. The evil of suffering, while remaining what it is, and while being fully experienced as such, is transvalued now in a superior good, one perfectly invisible besides, unless there appear for an instant some sign of the more than human peace that inhabits the tortured soul.

12. The unbeliever sees here only a ghastly facility that religion allows itself, playing on two boards at the same time. The believer sees here the supreme grandeur of a mystery accessible to faith alone, and which can—in faith—be attained in some fashion and stammered by the intelligence, but which remains in itself as incomprehensible as God Himself.

It is doubtless for the philosopher that this mystery is the most incomprehensible, because the philosopher knows too well that essences do not change, and that in the ordinary course of things, suffering, unless the one that it visits undertakes bravely to surmount it, degrades and humiliates the human being. He would be a fool however if he did not bow before the testimony of the saints. But in his perspective as a philosopher the best he can say is that God's love is as transcendent as His being, which is as no thing is; and that it is more difficult still for the heart of man to apprehend the transcendence of Love subsisting by itself than it is for the human intelligence to apprehend the transcendence of Being subsisting by Itself. "Believe that God loves you *in a way that you cannot imagine*," said Dostoevski.[2]

And here again can the philosopher refrain from asking some questions?

He is astonished by another apparent contradiction in the behavior of the saints. They desire suffering as the most precious of goods here below. After all, that's their affair, or rather an affair between God and them. But what

[1] "Our annihilation is the most powerful means we have of uniting ourselves to Jesus and of doing good to souls," wrote Father de Foucauld. Cf. Jean-Francois Six, *Itinéraire spirituel de Charles de Foucauld*, Paris: Seuil, 1958, p. 364.

[2] Cf. Henri Troyat, *Sainte Russie*, Paris: Grasset, 1956, p. 149.

about the others, those whom they love, and who comprise all men? Do they not desire for them also this most precious of goods here on earth? Yet this is not what they do, they spend their time trying to lessen the suffering of men and to cure them of their wounds. The answer, to the extent that one can catch a glimpse of it, concerns the very structure of the spirit.

In itself suffering is an evil, and will always remain an evil. How then could one wish it for those one loves? The simple knowledge possessed by the Christian (and so frequently recalled to his attention by the commonplaces of pious literature) that suffering unites the soul inhabited by charity to the sacrifice of the Cross, superimposes on suffering, ideally and theoretically, a quality thanks to which this knowledge helps one to accept suffering; it cannot make it be loved or desired, it does not transvalue it. If there is real and practical transvaluation, it can only be in the fire of the actual and absolutely incommunicable love between the self of a man and the divine Self; and that remains a closed secret, valid only for the individual subjectivity. Thus the saints would keep for themselves alone what they consider to be the most precious of goods here on earth. Singular egoists! They want suffering for themselves, they do not want it for others. Jesus wept over the dead Lazarus, and over the sorrow of Martha and Mary.

But the philosopher has still other questions. What strikes him above all in the human condition is not the suffering of the saints, it is the suffering of the mass of men, the suffering they have not willed, the suffering that falls on them like a beast. How could he resign himself to the suffering of men?

He knows that the struggle against suffering is one of the aspects of the effort through which humanity goes forward, and that in this struggle the work of reason and the ferment of the Gospel, the progress of science and the progress of social justice, and the progress of the still so rudimentary knowledge that man has of himself, enable us constantly to gain ground. He is not tempted to adore the Great Being, but he renders thanks to the men—to the innumerable workers known and unknown who throughout the course of an immense history, by dint of inventive genius and sacrifice of self, have applied themselves and will always apply themselves to making the earth more habitable. But the philosopher also knows that as one gains ground in the struggle against suffering, new causes of suffering begin to abound, so that man, despite all his progress, will never have done with suffering just as he will never have done with sickness.[1] Modern man suffers in other ways than the cave man. On the whole, one can wonder whether he suffers less; one can wonder whether all the victories gained in the struggle against suffering do not result in maintaining, by compensating the progress in suffering, a kind of middle level at which life as a whole is almost tolerable. However this may be, there will always remain enough suffering to put the heart and the intelligence in anguish.

[1] Cf. René Dubos, *Mirage of Health*, New York: Harper, 1959.

Thus the answers that the philosopher gives himself in thinking about the suffering of men are valid but insufficient. There is another answer still, one that not only concerns terrestrial history but also and above all eternal life. It was given in the Sermon on the Mount.

If there is in humanity an immense mass of suffering which is not redemptive like that of Christ and His saints, it is in order that it may be redeemed, and that everywhere at least where human liberty does not intrude its refusal, those who have wept in our valleys may be consoled forever.

INDEX OF PROPER NAMES